2008

All States Tax Handbook

Steven A. Zelman, (LL.M., NY, NJ Bar), *Senior Vice President, Content Operations*
Linda Scheffel (LL.M., NY Bar), *Vice President and Publisher*
Virginia Lorenzo (LL.M., CT Bar), *Senior Director, State and Local Editorial*
Rick Bivona, *Director, Production Services/Customer Retention & Renewal*

Jose Curammeng, Jr.
(LL.B.)
Managing Editor

Maribel Fajardo
(LL.M., NY, NJ Bar)
Managing Editor

Sheila Leventhal
(J.D., Ill. Bar)
Managing Editor

Edited by:

Andrew Klutkowski
(J.D., NJ Bar)

Peter Pupke
(J.D., NY Bar)

Contributing editors:

Gina M. Briggs
(LL.M., NY Bar)

Teresa Callahan
(J.D., NJ Bar)

Margaret Eisler
(J.D., NJ Bar)

Rita Eng
(J.D., NY, CT Bar)

Samantha Fong
(LL.M., NY, NJ Bar)

Ann Forster
(M.A., LL.M., NY Bar)

Harry Markowitz
(J.D., NY Bar)

Fidel Mendoza
(LL.B., NJ Bar)

Rebecca Newton-Clarke
(J.D., FL Bar)

Paz Nolasco
(LL.M., NY Bar)

Vidor A. Nosce
(LL.M., NY Bar)

Matthew G. Pickelle
(J.D., NY Bar)

Judy Richardson-Dunkley
(J.D., NY, NJ Bar)

Peter Rosa
(J.D., CT Bar)

Alan Rubin
(A.B.)

Saleem Shareef
(LL.M., NY Bar)

Michael Siegel
(M.A, J.D.)

Steven Wang
(J.D., NY Bar)

Ellen Weiss
(J.D., NY, NJ Bar)

Robert Ziegler
(J.D., NJ Bar)

RIA®

THOMSON
TAX & ACCOUNTING™

HOW THIS HANDBOOK HELPS YOU

This 2008 ALL STATES TAX HANDBOOK can help you get answers quickly to basic tax questions for the 50 states and the District of Columbia. All major taxes imposed by states are charted for easy use.

This handbook covers state taxes through November 6, 2007.

Tax systems in graphic form. For your convenience, state tax systems are presented in graphic format—charts, tables, lists, and calendars—for easy comparisons and to save you initial research time. Key tax facts and special tax rules in all states have been reduced to this format so you can easily put your finger on a tax rule in any state.

Immediate help on key tax facts. Key facts on all state taxes are laid out for fast reference. You can conveniently find important working tax rules. These include basis of tax, rate of tax, filing and payment dates for income, franchise, capital values, sales-use, property, unemployment insurance, estate and gift, gasoline, cigarette, alcoholic beverage taxes, and electronic funds transfers. In addition, this Handbook gives multistate businesses the state formulas for apportioning income for tax purposes—with detailed analysis of receipts, payroll, and property factors.

Specialized charts for all states. The Handbook puts at your fingertips the essential information for making tax-related moves in your state and when you cross state lines. Charts answer these questions: What acts in a state would trigger liability for paying income or franchise tax? What acts would require you to collect sales or use tax? What fees do you have to pay when your corporation qualifies in a state? What are the effects on your contracts if you do business in a state without a license? Which business form suits your operations best—Limited Liability Company? S Corporation? Partnership? Limited Liability Partnership? A single idea in this Handbook may save many times the cost of this book.

Tax benefits. Special state tax benefits are listed. These cover rules on capital gains or losses, income tax credits for businesses, income tax deductions, depreciation methods, claiming federal income tax deduction, deadlines for income tax refunds, exemptions granted to new or expanding industries, and freeport exemptions.

Tax calendars. There are also extensive tax calendars listing payment and reporting dates for various state taxes—quarter-monthly, semi-monthly, monthly, quarterly, semiannual, and annual dates.

CHARTS AND CALENDARS

TABLE OF CONTENTS

CHARTS

Paragraph [¶]

GENERAL CHARTS

INCOME TAXES

ALL STATES TAX CHART

¶210 What taxes are levied. This chart shows the main taxes in each state. An asterisk (''*'') means the tax is imposed.

After you have looked at the chart, refer to the notes that follow. Also, about the columnar headings, keep this in mind:

Capital values-franchise: The taxes listed in this column are those that the states levy for the privilege of being or operating as a general business corporation. Franchise taxes on net income are covered under ''Corporate Income.''

Property taxes: All the states, without exception, levy taxes on real property, either on a state or local level. These are not listed because of their universal nature. However, states taxing tangible personalty are listed since not all of the states tax it.

Intangibles taxes: When the chart does not show that a special low intangible personal property tax rate or a special low valuation is permitted, intangibles theoretically are taxed at the general property tax rates and valuations. However, because of the difficulty of enforcement, not much tax is collected on intangibles in those states.

Admissions and amusements: The state taxes listed under this heading take into account taxes on admission price, and taxes or fees determined by gross receipts or seating capacity. In some instances, the tax is imposed under the state sales tax as we indicate.

Taxes / State	Capital Values Franchise	Corporation Income	Individual Income	Sales	Use	Tangible Personalty	Intangibles	Stock Transfer	Recording Documents
Alabama	*	*	*	*	*	*	*		*
Alaska		*		(27)	(27)	*			
Arizona		*	*	*	*	*			*
Arkansas	*	*	*	*	*	*			*
California		*	*	*	*	*			*
Colorado		*	*	*	*	*			*
Connecticut	*	*	*	*	*	*			*
Delaware	*(28)	*	*	(4)	(4)				*
District of Columbia		*	*(8)	*	*	*			*(35)
Florida		*		*	*	*	*(12)		*(38)
Georgia	*	*	*	*	*	*			*
Hawaii		*	*	*	*				*
Idaho		*	*	*	*	*			
Illinois	*	*	*	*(6)	*				*
Indiana		*	*	*	*	*			
Iowa		*	*	*	*		*(30)		*
Kansas	*	*	*	*	*	*	*(12)		*(17)
Kentucky	*	*	*	*	*	*			*
Louisiana	*	*	*	*	*	*	*(18)		
Maine		*	*	*	*	*			*
Maryland		*	*	*	*	*			*(24)
Mass.	*	*	*	*(3)	*(3)	*			*
Michigan	*(49)	*(7)	*(7)	*	*	*			*
Minnesota		*	*	*	*	*			*
Mississippi	*	*	*	*	*	*	*(20)		
Missouri	*	*	*	*	*	*			
Montana		*	*			*			
Nebraska	*	*	*	*	*	*			*
Nevada				*	*	*	*(20)		*
New Hampshire		*(13)	*(9)	(1)		*			*
New Jersey		*	*	*	*	*			*
New Mexico	*	*	*	*	*	*			
New York	*	*	*	*	*			*(32)	*(2)
North Carolina	*	*	*	*	*	*	(14)		*
North Dakota		*	*	*	*	*(22)	*(20)		
Ohio	*(44)	*(44)	*	*	*	*(45)			*
Oklahoma	*	*	*	*	*	*			*(25)
Oregon		*	*			*			
Pennsylvania	*	*	*	*	*		*(39)		*
Rhode Island	*	*	*	*	*	*	*(11)		*
South Carolina	*	*	*	*	*	*			*
South Dakota		*(23)		*	*	*(19)	*(19)		*
Tennessee	*	*	*(9)	*	*	*	*(20)		*
Texas	*			*	*	*	*(20)		
Utah		*	*	*	*	*			
Vermont		*	*	*(3)	*(3)	*			*
Virginia		*	*	*	*	*			*
Washington				*(21)	(21)	*			*
West Virginia	*	*	*	*	*	*	(5)		*
Wisconsin		*	*	*	*	*			*
Wyoming	*			*	*	*			

Taxes / State	Estate (43)	Gift	Inheri-tance	Motor Fuel	Admis-sions & Amuse-ment	Chain Store	Tobac-co	Miner-als	Timber
Alabama	(43)			*	*(15)	*	*	*	*
Alaska	(43)			*			*	*	*
Arizona	(43)			*	*(15)		*	*	
Arkansas	(43)			*	*(15)		*	*	*
California				*			*	*	*
Colorado	(43)			*			*	*	
Connecticut	*(26)	*(10)	(40)	*	*		*		*
Delaware	(43)			*	*		*		
D.C.	*			*	*(15)		*		
Florida	(43)			*	*(15)		*	*	
Georgia	(43)			*	*(15)		*		
Hawaii	(43)			*	*(15)		*		
Idaho	(43)			*	*(15)		*	*	*
Illinois	*(43)			*	*(46)		*		*
Indiana	(43)		*	*	*(15)		*	*	
Iowa	(43)		*	*	*(15)		*		
Kansas	*(36)		(42)	*	*(15)		*	*	
Kentucky	(43)		*	*	*(15)		*	*	
Louisiana	(43)	*(50)	(37)	*	*(15)	*	*	*	*
Maine	*			*			*	*	
Maryland	*(36)		*	*	*	*	*	*(33)	
Mass.	*(36)			*			*		
Michigan	(43)			*	*(15)		*	*	*
Minnesota	*			*	*(15)		*	*	*
Mississippi	(43)			*	*(15)		*	*	*
Missouri	(43)			*	*(15)		*		*
Montana	(43)			*			*	*	
Nebraska	(48)		*	*	*(15)		*	*	
Nevada	(43)			*	*(31)		*	*	
New Hampshire	(43)		*	*			*		
New Jersey	*		*(16)	*	*(15)		*		
New Mexico	(43)			*	*(15)		*	*	*
New York	*(36)	(34)		*	*(15)		*		*
North Carolina	*(43)	*	(41)	*	*		*		*
North Dakota	(43)			*	*(15)		*	*	
Ohio	*(43)			*			*	*	
Oklahoma	*(43)			*	*(15)		*	*	
Oregon	*			*			*	*	*
Pennsylvania	(43)		*	*			*		
Rhode Island	*(43)			*	*		*		
South Carolina	(43)			*	*(15)		*		
South Dakota	(43)		*	*	*(15)		*	*	
Tennessee	(43)	*	*	*	*		*	*	
Texas	(43)			*	*(15)		*	*	
Utah	(43)			*	*(15)		*	*	
Vermont	*(36)			*	*(15)		*		
Virginia	(47)			*			*		*
Washington	*(36)			*	*(15)		*		*
West Virginia				*	*(15)	*(29)	*	*	*
Wisconsin	*(43)			*	*(15)		*	*	*
Wyoming	(43)			*	*(15)		*	*	

FOOTNOTES to chart ¶210 (corresponding to parenthetical numbers in chart):

(1) N.H.—Meals and rooms tax and telecommunications service tax.
(2) N.Y.—Mortgage tax. Realty transfer tax.
(3) Mass. & Vt.—Sales-use tax plus meals and rooms tax.
(4) Del.—Tax is based on gross receipts (retailing, wholesaling, services and other businesses). Use tax on leasing tangible personalty is also levied.
(5) W.Va.—Tax was phased out over 5-yr. period beginning in 1998.
(6) Ill.—Tax is on retailers, servicemen, and specified professionals—based on gross receipts.
(7) Mich.—"Single Business Tax" applicable to corporations and individuals is repealed for tax years starting after 12-31-2007 and replaced by Business Tax, eff 1-1-2008, consisting of a business income tax and a modified gross receipts tax.
(8) D.C.—Net income tax is imposed on unincorporated business also.
(9) N.H. & Tenn.—Tax is on income from intangibles only.
(10) Conn.—Eff 1-1-2005, gift transfer tax is imposed on total gifts that exceed $2 million..
(11) R.I.—Only credit union deposits are taxed. Tax on bank deposits was repealed eff 1-1-1998.
(12) Intangibles are taxable at lower value or lower rate than other property. In Florida, the annual intangible tax is repealed eff 1-1-2007. The nonrecurring intangible tax on notes, bonds, and certain secured obligations to pay is still in effect.
(13) N.H.—Business profits tax is on corporations, partnerships, individuals and other organizations operated for profit. Business enterprise tax on compensation, interest, and dividends is also imposed.
(14) N.C—Repealed eff for returns due after 1995 for tax yrs. starting after 12-31-1994.
(15) Amusements are taxable under gross income, gross receipts or sales tax laws.
(16) N.J.—Inheritance tax is imposed on persons other than the surviving spouse, domestic partner, civil union partner (for decedents dying on or after 2-19-2007), and direct lineal ascendants or descendants.
(17) Kan.—Mortgages—instruments creating liens.
(18) La.—At the 9-21-1996 election, voters approved an amendment to the La. Constitution exempting from property taxes all incorporeal moveables except public service properties, bank stocks, and credit assessments on premiums written in La. by insurance cos. and loan and finance cos. This amendment was eff 11-5-1996.
(19) S.D.—Tax on personalty was repealed eff. 1-1-1979 except for centrally assessed property.
(20) Miss., Nev., N. D., Tenn., Tex.—Nearly all intangibles are exempt by law.
(21) Wash.—Business & occupation tax is also levied.
(22) N.D.—Nearly all tangible personalty is exempt.
(23) S. D.—Only financial institutions pay tax.
(24) Md.—Rates vary locally. State realty transfer tax is added to document recording tax.
(25) Okla.—Recording tax.
(26) Conn.—Eff 1-1-2005, estate/gift transfer tax applies if taxable estate is more than $2 million.
(27) Alaska—Local sales taxes; no state tax.
(28) Del.—No tax on foreign corporations.
(29) W. Va.—Business franchise registration tax is based on number of locations.
(30) Iowa—Intangibles tax applies only to credit unions and loan agencies.
(31) Nev.—Live entertainment tax, eff 1-1-2004.
(32) N.Y.—100% rebate of stock transfer taxes.
(33) Md.—Taxes are collected in some counties.
(34) N.Y.—Gift tax was repealed eff 1-1-2000.
(35) D.C.—Added tax on transfers of realty.
(36) Generation-skipping transfer tax also is levied. In Washington, applicable only with respect to decedents who died on or before 5-16-2005.
(37) La.—Eff 1-1-2008, no inheritance tax is due for decedents' deaths occuring after 6-30-2004.
(38) Fla.—State imposes a documentary stamp tax on certain types of bonds, notes and deeds.
(39) The constitutionality of the Pa. intangibles tax was upheld in *Annenberg v. Cmwlth.* (Pa, 2000) 757 A2d 338; cert. denied, U.S. Sup. Ct., Dkt. No. 00-343, 10-30-2000. However, the court invalidated the exemption for corporations subject to the Pa. capital stock or franchise tax. Jurisdictions were instructed to provide a retrospective remedy, which may include collecting tax on previously exempt stock.
(40) Conn.—Succession tax was repealed eff for estates of persons dying after 12-31-2004.
(41) N.C.—Inheritance tax was repealed eff for estates of persons dying after 12-31-1998.
(42) Kan.—Succession tax was imposed eff 6-6-2002, but was repealed 5-22-2003 retroactive to 6-6-2002.
(43) ¶273 explains the effect on the states of the reduction and repeal of the federal estate and generation-skipping transfer taxes.
(44) Ohio—Tax is generally being phased out (except for certain financial, insurance, and other entities) and gradually replaced by commercial activities tax (CAT) over 5-yr. period starting 7-1-2005.
(45) Ohio—Tax is being phased out.
(46) Ill.—Admissions taxes are imposed on certain events.
(47) Va.—Estate tax is repealed eff 7-1-2007.
(48) Neb.—Estate tax is repealed for decedents dying on or after 1-1-2007.
(49) Mich.—Eff 1-1-2008, financial institutions are subject to a franchise tax based on net capital.
(50) La.—Gift tax is repealed for gifts made on or after 7-1-2008.

STATE TAX OFFICIALS AND ADMINISTRATION

¶211 Top tax officials and administrative agencies. Lists below show the top officials of the main tax administrative agency and taxes grouped by the administrative agencies that administer them in each state.

TOP TAX OFFICIALS

Alabama—Cynthia Underwood, Acting Commissioner, Department of Revenue, 4112 Gordon Persons Bldg., 50 N. Ripley St., Montgomery, Al 36132-7123. Tele: (334)242-1175.

Alaska—Patrick Galvin, Commissioner, Department of Revenue, 11th Floor, 333 Willoughby Ave., P.O. Box 110420, Juneau, AK 99811-0420. Tele: (907)465-2320.

Arizona—Gale Garriott, Director, Department of Revenue, 1600 W. Monroe St., Phoenix AZ 85007-2650. Tele: (602)716-6090.

Arkansas—Richard Weiss, Director, Department of Finance and Administration, P.O. Box 3278, Little Rock, AR 72203. Tele: (501)682-2242.

California—*Franchise, income taxes:* Franchise Tax Board, P.O. Box 942840, Sacramento, CA 94240-0040; John Chiang, State Controller and FTB Chair. Selvi Stanislaus, Executive Officer. Michael C. Genest, Director of Dept. of Finance. *Other taxes:* Betty Yee, Chair, State Board of Equalization, P.O. Box 942879, Sacramento, CA 94279-0090. Ramon (Ray) J. Hirsig, Executive Director, State Board of Equalization, P.O. Box 942879, Sacramento, CA 94279-0090. *Communications to:* Ramon (Ray) J. Hirsig, Executive Director, P.O. Box 942879, Sacramento CA 94279-0090. Tele: FTB general info. desk—from inside US (800)852-5711; from outside US (916)845-6500. SBE general info. desk (800)400-7115.

Colorado—Roxy Huber, Executive Director, Department of Revenue, State Capitol Annex, 1375 Sherman St., Denver, CO 80261. Tele: (303)866-3091.

Connecticut—Pamela Law, Commissioner, Department of Revenue, Services, 25 Sigourney Street, Hartford, CT 06106. Tele: (860)297-5962.

Delaware—Patrick Carter, Director, Division of Revenue, Carvel State Building, 820 N. French St., Wilmington, DE 19801. Tele: (302)577-8686.

District of Columbia—Ben Lorigo, Deputy Chief Financial Officer, Office of Tax and Revenue, 941 North Capitol St., N.E., 8th Floor, Washington, D.C. 20002. Tele: (202)442-6200.

Florida—James A. Zingale, Executive Director, Department of Revenue, 104 Carlton Building, 5050 West Tennessee St., Tallahassee, FL 32399-0100. Tele: (850)488-5050.

Georgia—Bart L. Graham, Commissioner, Department of Revenue, 1800 Century Center Blvd., N.E., Atlanta, GA 30345-3205. Tele: (404)656-8477.

Hawaii—Kurt Kawafuchi, Director, Department of Taxation, P.O. Box 259, Honolulu, HI 96809-0259. Tele: (808)587-4242.

Idaho—DuWayne D. Hammond, Jr., Chairman, State Tax Commission, P.O. Box 36, 800 Park Blvd., Plaza IV, Boise, ID 83722. Tele: (208)334-7660.

Illinois—Brian Hamer, Director, Department of Revenue, 101 West Jefferson St., Springfield, IL 62702. Tele: (217)782-3336.

Indiana—John Eckart, Commissioner, Department of Revenue, 100 North Senate Ave., Indiana Government Center North, Indianapolis, IN 46204-2253. Tele: (317)233-4018.

Iowa—Mark Schuling, Director, Department of Revenue, Hoover State Office Bldg., East 13th & Walnut, Des Moines, IA 50319. Tele: (515)281-3204.

Kansas—Joan Wagnon, Secretary, Department of Revenue, Robert B. Docking State Office Bldg., 915 SW Harrison St., Topeka, KS 66625-0001. Tele: (785)368-8222.

Kentucky—John May, Commissioner, Department of Revenue, 200 Fair Oaks Lane, Frankfort KY 40620. Tele: (502)564-4581.

Louisiana—Cynthia Bridges, Secretary, Department of Revenue, 617 North Third Street, P.O. Box 201, Baton Rouge, LA 70821. Tele. (225)219-2700.

Maine—Jerome D. Gerard, Acting Executive Director, Revenue Services, 24 State House Station, Augusta, ME 04333-0024. Tele: (207)287-2076.

Maryland—Peter Franchot, Comptroller, Goldstein Treasury Bldg., 80 Calvert St., Annapolis, MD 21401. Tele: (410)260-7980.

Massachusetts—Henry Dormitzer, Commissioner of Revenue, Department of Revenue, 8th Floor, 51 Sleeper St., Boston, MA 02205. Tele: (617)626-2201.

Michigan—Robert J. Kleine, State Treasurer, Department of Treasury, Treasury Bldg., 430 W. Allegan St., Lansing, MI 48922. Tele: (517)373-3223.

Minnesota—Ward Einess, Commissioner, Department of Revenue, 600 North Robert St., St. Paul, MN 55101. Tele: (651)296-3403.

Mississippi—Edward H. Buelow, Jr., Chairman and Commissioner of Revenue, State Tax Commission, 1577 Springridge Road, Raymond, MS 39154-9602. Tele: (601)923-7000.

Missouri—Trish Vincent, Director, Department of Revenue, 301 West High St., Jefferson City, MO 65105-0311. Tele: (573)751-4450.

Montana—Dan Bucks, Director, Department of Revenue, 455 Sam W. Mitchell Bldg., 125 N. Roberts, P.O. Box 5805, Helena, MT 59604-5805. Tele: (406)444-6900.

Nebraska—Douglas Ewald, Tax Commissioner, Department of Revenue, 301 Centennial Mall South, P.O. Box 94818, Lincoln, NE 68509-4818. Tele: (402)471-5729.

Nevada—Dino DiCianno, Executive Director, Department of Taxation, Suite 115, 1550 E. College Parkway, Carson City, NV 89706. Tele: (775)684-2000.

New Hampshire—G. Philip Blatsos, Commissioner, Department of Revenue Administration, 45 Chennell Drive, P.O. Box 457, Concord, NH 03301-0457. Tele: (603)271-1302.

New Jersey—Maureen Adams, Acting Director, Division of Taxation, Office of Information and Publications, P.O. Box 281, Trenton, NJ 08695-0281. Tele: (609)292-6400.

New Mexico—Jan Goodwin, Secretary, Taxation and Revenue Department, P.O. Box 630, 1100 S. St. Francis Drive, Santa Fe, NM 87504-0630. Tele: (505)827-0341.

New York—Barbara G. Billet, Acting Commissioner, Department of Taxation and Finance, W. A. Harriman Campus, Building #9, Albany, NY 12227-0125. Tele: (518)457-2244. Marilyn Kaltenborn, Deputy Commissioner and Director, Taxpayer Services Division. Tele: (518)457-1153.

New York City—Martha E. Stark, Commissioner of Finance, 25 Elm Place, Brooklyn, NY 11201. Tele: (718)935-6000 or (718)935-9500.

North Carolina—Reggie Hinton, Secretary, Department of Revenue, 501 N. Wilmington St., P.O. Box 25000, Raleigh, NC 27640. Tele: (919)733-7211.

North Dakota—Cory Fong, Tax Commissioner, Tax Department, 8th Floor, Capitol Bldg., 600 E. Boulevard Ave., Dept. 127, Bismarck, ND 58505-0599. Tele: (701)328-2770.

Ohio—Richard Levin, Commissioner, Department of Taxation, 22nd Floor, 30 East Broad St., Columbus, OH 43215. Tele: (614)466-2166.

Oklahoma—Thomas Kemp, Jr., Chairman, State Tax Commission, 2501 North Lincoln Blvd., Oklahoma City, OK 73194-0001. Tele: (405)521-3160; (800)522–8165.

Oregon—Elizabeth Harchenko, Director, Department of Revenue, Revenue Bldg., 955 Center St., N.E., Salem, OR 97301-2555. Tele: (503)945-8214.

Pennsylvania—Thomas W. Wolf, Secretary, Department of Revenue, 1133 Strawberry Square, Harrisburg, PA 17128-1100. Tele: (717)787-8201; (717) 787-1064.

Rhode Island—David M. Sullivan, Tax Administrator, Division of Taxation, One Capitol Hill, Providence, RI 02908-5800. Tele: (401)222-3050.

South Carolina—Ray N. Stevens, Director, Department of Revenue, 301 Gervais St., P.O. Box 125, Columbia, SC 29214. Tele: (803)898-5000.

South Dakota—Paul Kinsman, Secretary, Department of Revenue and Regulation, Anderson Bldg., 445 East Capital Ave., Pierre, S.D. 57501-3185. Tele: (605)773-3311.

Tennessee—Reagan Farr, Commissioner, Department of Revenue, Andrew Jackson State Office Bldg., 500 Deaderick St., Nashville, TN 37242. Tele: (615)741-2461.

Texas—Susan Combs, Comptroller of Public Accounts, LBJ State Office Bldg., 111 E. 17 St. St., Austin, TX 78774. Tele: (512)463-4000.

Utah—Rodney Marrelli, Executive Director, State Tax Commission, 210 North 1950 West, Salt Lake City, UT 84134. Tele: (800)662-4335.

Vermont—Tom Pelham, Commissioner, Department of Taxes, Pavilion Office Bldg., 109 State St., P.O. Box 429, Montpelier, VT 05609. Tele: (802)828-2505.

Virginia—Janie Bowen, State Tax Commissioner, Department of Taxation, P.O. Box 1115, Richmond, VA 23218. Tele: (804)367-8031.

Washington—Cindi Holmstrom, Director, Department of Revenue, 415 General Administration Bldg., Washington St. East, Olympia, WA 98504-0090. Tele: (360)753-5574.

West Virginia—Christopher Morris, Commissioner, State Tax Department, P.O. Box 11771, Charleston, West Virginia 25339-1771. Tele: (304)558-0751.

Wisconsin—Roger Ervin, Secretary, Department of Revenue, 2135 Rimrock Road, P.O. Box 8933, Mail Stop 624-A, Madison, WI 53708-8933. Tele: (608)266-6466.

Wyoming—Edmund J. Schmidt, Director, Department of Revenue, Herschler Bldg., 2nd Floor West, 122 W. 25th St., Cheyenne, Wyo. 82002-0110. Tele: (307)777-5287.

ADMINISTRATIVE AGENCIES

Administrative agencies and the taxes that they administer in each state are listed below. Also shown are telephone numbers for general taxpayer assistance. The Attorney General in each state enforces most taxes.

ALABAMA

(334) 242-1170

Department of Revenue. Estate tax, business privilege (franchise) tax, gasoline and motor fuel taxes, nursing home and pharmaceutical taxes, income taxes, license fees, lubricating oils tax, motor carrier mileage tax, motor vehicle registration (with local officers), property taxes (with local officers), public utilities tax (license), sales tax, severance tax, telecommunication service tax, tobacco stamp tax, use tax, and utility gross receipts tax.

Alcoholic Beverage Control Board. Alcoholic beverage licenses and taxes.

Department of Insurance. Insurance companies tax.

Department of Industrial Relations. Unemployment compensation tax.

Public Service Commission. Motor carrier fees, utility inspection fees.

Secretary of State. Corporate organization and qualification fees (with Probate Judge).

Local taxing officials. Document filing tax (conveyances and mortgages), license taxes (with Dept. of Revenue), mineral documentary or transfer tax, motor vehicle registration (with Dept. of Revenue), property taxes (with Dept. of Revenue).

ALASKA

(907) 465-2300

Department of Revenue. Alcoholic beverage tax (with Alcoholic Beverage Control Board), cigarette and tobacco tax, estate tax, fisheries taxes, motor fuel tax, vehicle rental excise tax, electric cooperative tax, telephone cooperative tax, corporate net income tax, mining license (income) tax, oil and gas production taxes, oil and gas properties tax and gaming.

Department of Commerce, Community, and Economic Development. Corporate franchise tax, corporate organization and entrance fees (Division of Banking Securities and Corporations), insurance companies tax (Division of Insurance), license fees.

Department of Labor and Workforce Development. Unemployment insurance tax.

Department of Administration. Motor carrier weight fees, motor vehicle registration taxes (Division of Motor Vehicles).

Local taxing officials. Property taxes, tax on casual sales of motor vehicles, trailers and semitrailers.

ARIZONA

(602) 255-3381

Department of Revenue. Alcoholic beverage tax (with superintendent of liquor licenses and control), cigarette and tobacco tax, commercial scheduled air carriers tax, estate tax, income tax, private car companies tax, motor carrier taxes, public utilities tax, property tax (with local taxing officials), rental occupancy tax, severance tax, tobacco products tax, transaction privilege (sales) tax, use tax, water use tax.

Corporation Commission. Corporate organization and qualification fees, corporation annual registration fee, public utilities fees.

Department of Economic Security. Unemployment insurance tax.

Department of Environmental Quality. Environmental fees.

Department of Insurance. Insurance companies tax (with State Treasurer)

Department of Transportation. Annual aircraft license tax, motor carrier taxes, gasoline and fuel use taxes, motor vehicle registration fees.

State Treasurer. Insurance companies tax (with Director of Insurance).

Superintendent of Liquor Licenses and Control. Alcoholic beverage license fees.

Local taxing officials. Property tax (with Department of Revenue).

ARKANSAS

(501) 682-7751

Revenue Division in the Department of Finance and Administration. Alcoholic beverages tax (with Alcoholic Beverage Control Division), estate tax, gasoline tax, gross receipts tax, income tax, motor vehicle registration fees, realty transfer tax, severance or production tax, tobacco products tax, use tax.

Department of Human Services. Personal care service gross receipts tax.

Department of Labor. Unemployment insurance tax.

Highway and Transportation Department. Carrier taxes.

Insurance Department. Insurance tax

Oil and Gas Commission. Oil and gas conservation tax

Public Service Commission. Utilities taxes

Secretary of State. Corporate organization and qualification fees, corporation franchise tax.

Local taxing officials. General property tax.

CALIFORNIA

Franchise Tax Board (800) 852-5711

State Board of Equalization (800) 400-7115

Franchise Tax Board. Bank and corporate franchise tax, corporate income tax, personal income tax.

State Board of Equalization. Alcoholic beverage taxes, cigarette and tobacco products tax, marine invasion species fee, electric utility surcharge, emergency telephone surcharge, general property tax (with local officials), hazardous waste tax, insurance taxes (jointly with Department of Insurance), integrated waste management fee, lead poisoning prevention fees, motor carrier taxes, fuel taxes, oil spill fees, sales and use taxes, tire recycling fee, timber yield tax, use fuel tax.

Department of Alcoholic Beverage Control. Intoxicating liquor license fees.

Department of Conservation. Oil and gas production tax (payment is to State Treasurer).

Department of Employment Development. Unemployment compensation tax, withholding tax.

Department of Insurance. Insurance companies tax (jointly with State Board of Equalization).

Department of Motor Vehicles. Motor vehicle registration fees.

Department of Toxic Substances Control. Lubricating oil tax.

Secretary of State. Corporate organization and qualification fees.

Local taxing officials. General property tax (with State Board of Equalization).

COLORADO

(303) 866-3091

Department of Revenue. Alcoholic beverages taxes, cigarette and tobacco products taxes, estate tax, gaming tax, gasoline tax, income tax, motor vehicle taxes, property taxes (with Dept. of Local Affairs, Dept. of Property Taxation, and local officials) public utility regulatory fees (with Public Utilities Commission), sales tax, severance tax, use tax.

Oil and Gas Conservation Commission. Oil and gas conservation tax.

Division of Insurance. Insurance company taxes.

Department of Labor and Employment. Unemployment insurance tax.

Division of Property Taxation. Public utilities and property tax assessments.

Public Utilities Commission. Public utility fees and motor carrier taxes (with Dept. of Revenue).

Secretary of State. Corporate organization and qualification fees (with Dept. of Revenue).

Local taxing officials. Aircraft fees, property tax (with Department of Revenue), motor vehicle fees, realty transfer tax.

CONNECTICUT

(860) 297-5962

Department of Revenue Services. Admissions tax, bank excise (income) tax, cigarette tax, corporate business tax (including additional tax an oil companies), estate tax, gift tax, hazardous waste assessment, insurance tax (with Dept. of Insurance), liquor tax (with Dept. of Liquor Control), motor carrier fees, motor carrier road tax, motor fuels tax, nuclear station property tax, personal income tax, public utilities franchise tax, sales tax, succession and transfer taxes (with local officials), use tax, utility taxes.

Department of Insurance. Insurance taxes.

Department of Labor. Unemployment compensation tax.

Department of Liquor Control. Alcoholic beverage tax (with Dept. of Revenue Services).

Department of Motor Vehicles. Motor vehicle registration fees.

Department of Transportation. Aircraft registration fees.

Office of Policy and Management. Property tax (with local officials).

Secretary of State. Annual report fee, Corporate organization and qualification fees, Foreign corporation fee.

Local taxing officials. Property tax, and the hazardous waste disposal facility tax, succession and transfer tax.

DELAWARE

(302) 577-8200 personal

(302) 577-8205 business

Division of Revenue in the Department of Finance. Alcoholic beverage taxes (Alcoholic Beverage Control Commission), cable television services tax, cigarette tax, corporate income taxes, estate tax, gas and electric companies' tax, gross receipts tax, hotel occupancy tax, manufacturer's and merchant's tax, personal income tax, railroad companies' tax, realty transfer tax (with county officials), telegraph and telephone companies' tax, tobacco products tax, use tax on tangible personal property leases.

Office of the State Bank Commissioner within Department of Secretary of State. Franchise (income) tax on banking organizations and building and loan associations.

Department of Insurance. Insurance tax.

Department of Labor. Unemployment insurance tax.

Department of Public Safety. Motor vehicle fees.

Department of Transportation. Motor fuel tax, special fuel tax and motor carriers' fuel purchase tax.

Secretary of State—Division of Corporations. Corporate organization and qualification fees and franchise tax., annual LLP/LLC taxes.

Local taxing officials. Property tax and the realty transfer tax (with Dept. of Finance).

DISTRICT OF COLUMBIA

(202) 727-4829

Office of Tax and Revenue. Alcoholic beverages tax, cigarette tax, deed recordation tax, estate tax, gasoline tax, income tax, property tax, real estate transfer tax, sales tax, toll telecommunication service tax, corporate and unincorporated business franchise tax, use tax, gross receipts tax on utilities.

Alcoholic Beverage Control Board. Alcoholic beverage licenses.

Consumer and Regulatory Affairs Department. Corporate biennial reports, corporate organization fees, limited liability company fees and biennial reports, limited liability partnership fees and biennial reports.

Department of Employment Services. Unemployment compensation tax.

Department of Motor Vehicles. Motor vehicle fees.

Department of Public Works. Solid waste facility reports, recycling fees.

Department of Insurance and Securities Regulation. Insurance gross premiums tax.

FLORIDA

(850) 488-6800

Department of Revenue. Corporate income tax and emergency excise tax, communications services tax, documentary stamp tax, intangible personal property tax, motor and other fuel taxes, property tax (with local officials), sales and use tax, unemployment tax, dry cleaning tax, estate tax, gross receipts tax, insurance premium tax, severance taxes and fees, local discretionary sales surtaxes.

Department of Agriculture and Consumer Services. Gasoline tax (with Dept. of Revenue).

Department of Business and Professional Regulation. Alcoholic beverage tax and the cigarette tax.

Department of Highway Safety and Motor Vehicles. Motor vehicle registration fees, aircraft registration fee, special fuel tax.

Department of Labor and Employment Security. Unemployment compensation tax.

Public Service Commission. Gross receipts tax on water and sewer utilities.

Secretary of State. Filing fees, annual report filing fee.

State Treasurer. Insurance company tax.

Local taxing officials. Property tax and tax on commercial hazardous waste facilities (with Dept. of Revenue).

GEORGIA

(404) 656-8477

State Revenue Commissioner, through the Department of Revenue. Alcoholic beverage tax, bank gross receipts tax, corporate franchise tax, estate tax, gasoline tax, general income tax, general property tax (with local officials), realty transfer tax, sales and use tax, tobacco tax.

Comptroller General and Commissioner of Insurance. Insurance company tax.

Department of Labor. Unemployment insurance tax.

Department of Motor Safety. Motor vehicle registration fee.

Public Service Commission. Motor carrier tax.

Secretary of State. Corporate organization and qualification fees, annual certificate registration fee.

Local taxing officials. Property tax (with State Revenue Commissioner).

HAWAII

(808) 587-4242

Department of Taxation, with district tax collectors. Liquor tax, bank franchise (income) tax, estate tax, fuel tax, general excise (sales) tax, income tax, property tax, realty conveyance tax, rental motor vehicle and tour vehicle surcharge taxes, tobacco products tax, use tax, public service company tax, transit accommodations tax.

Department of Commerce and Consumer Affairs. Corporation filing and annual fees, gross premiums tax.

Department of Labor and Industrial Relations. Unemployment insurance tax.

Public Utilities Commission. Public utilities' regulatory fees.

Local taxing officials. Vehicle registration and weight fees and taxes, property tax.

IDAHO

(800) 972-7660

State Tax Commission in the Department of Revenue and Taxation. Alcoholic beverage tax, cigarette tax, corporate franchise tax, income taxes, estate tax, fuels tax, license tax on electricity, sales and use tax, severance tax, tobacco products tax.

Department of Employment. Unemployment insurance tax.

Department of Insurance. Insurance companies tax.

Public Utilities Commission. Public utility fees, motor carrier fees (with Transportation Department).

Secretary of State. Corporate organization and qualification fees, annual corporate reports.

Transportation Department. Motor vehicle fees (with county assessors), motor carrier fees (with Public Utilities Commission).

Local taxing officials. Forest products tax, property tax (with State Tax Commission), motor vehicle registration fees (with Transportation Department).

ILLINOIS

(217) 782-3336

Department of Revenue. Alcoholic beverage tax (with Liquor Control Commission), cigarette tax, fuel taxes, hotel occupancy tax, income tax, motor fuel tax, public utilities and messages taxes (with commerce commission), property tax (with local officials), realty transfer tax, retailers' occupation (sales) and use taxes, service occupation and service use taxes, telecommunications excise tax.

Attorney General. Estate tax.

Director of Insurance. Gross premiums tax.

Department of Labor. Unemployment insurance tax.

Department of Nuclear Safety. Low-level radioactive waste management tax.

Environmental Protection Agency. Hazardous waste disposal tax.

Liquor Control Commission. Liquor licenses.

Secretary of State. Corporate franchise tax, corporate organization and qualification fees, motor vehicles fees.

Local taxing officials. Estate tax (with Attorney General), property tax (with Department of Revenue).

INDIANA

(317) 233-4018

Department of Revenue. Aircraft license excise tax, alcoholic beverage tax, auto rental excise tax, Capital Improvement Board revenue replacement tax, charity gaming excise tax, cigarette tax, commercial motor vehicle excise tax, controlled substance excise tax, corporate income tax, county adjusted gross income tax (CAGIT), county development income tax (CEDIT), county innkeepers tax, county option income tax (COIT), entertainment facility admissions tax, environmental taxes, estate tax, fiduciary tax, fireworks public safety fee, food and beverage tax, fuel taxes, gasoline tax, generation skipping transfer tax, hazardous waste disposal tax, individual adjusted gross income tax, inheritance tax, inventory tax (fuel), malt beverage tax, marine fuel tax, Marion County admissions tax and supplemental auto rental excise tax, motor carrier fuel tax, motor carrier surcharge tax, motor vehicle excise tax, pari-mutuel admissions tax and wagering tax, petroleum severance tax, public utility (railroad car companies/railroads) tax, riverboat admissions tax and wagering tax, sales and use tax, slot machine wagering tax, special fuel tax, tobacco tax (cigarettes and other tobacco products), utility receipts tax, utility services use tax, Vanderburgh County supplemental auto excise tax, withholding tax.

Department of Workforce Development. Unemployment tax.

Department of Insurance. Insurance tax (premium and fire).

Secretary of State. Corporate organization and qualification fees, annual corporation report.

State Auditor. Pari-mutuel, satellite facility, vessels tonnage taxes.

Department of Local Government Finance. Property tax, railroad car property tax.

Board of Tax Review. Appeals of property tax rates.

Utility Regulatory Commission. Public utility assessment fee.

Local taxing officials. Property tax (with Department of Local Government Finance), public utilities tax (with Board of Tax Commissioners).

IOWA

(515) 281-3204

Department of Revenue. Alcoholic beverage tax (with Dept. of Commerce), chain store tax, cigarette and tobacco tax, estate tax (with local officers), financial institutions franchise tax, gasoline tax, income tax, inheritance—succession tax (with local officials), insurance companies tax (with Dept. of Commerce), realty transfer tax (with local officials), sales and use tax.

Department of Commerce. Alcoholic Beverage Division, with Department of Revenue and Finance, administers and collects the alcoholic beverage tax. Insurance Division administers and collects insurance gross premiums tax, with the Department of Revenue and Finance. State Utilities Board administers and collects the utilities taxes.

Department of Employment Services. Unemployment insurance tax.

State Department of Transportation. Interstate fuel use tax, motor carrier fees, aircraft registration.

State Racing and Gaming Commission. Excursion boat gambling tax and license fees (with State Treasurer).

Secretary of State. Annual report fee, corporate organization and qualification fees, franchise tax.

Local taxing officials. Credit unions tax, estate tax (with Dept. of Revenue and Finance), general property tax, grain handlers tax, inheritance-succession tax (with Dept. of Revenue and Finance), loan agencies tax, motor vehicle fees, public utilities tax (with Dept. of Revenue and Finance), realty transfer tax (with Department of Revenue and Finance).

KANSAS

(785) 368-8222

Department of Revenue. Division of Taxation administers and collects alcoholic beverage tax (with Alcoholic Beverage Control), cigarette tax, estate tax, gasoline tax, income tax, motor fuels tax, sales and use tax, severance tax, tobacco products tax, marijuana and controlled substances tax, bingo tax, privilege tax on financial institutions, tire excise tax, transient guest tax. Division of Property Valuation administers general property tax with local officials.

Department of Human Resources. Unemployment insurance tax.

Insurance Department. Insurance tax.

State Corporation Commission. Gas utility pipeline tax, motor carrier tax, oil and gas conservation tax, oil and gas production tax.

Secretary of State. Corporate franchise tax, organization and qualification fees.

Local taxing officials. Property taxes, mortgage registration tax and motor vehicle registration.

KENTUCKY

(502) 564-4581

Department of Revenue. Admissions tax, alcoholic beverage tax, cigarette tax, coal severance tax, corporation income tax, estate and inheritance taxes, general income tax, hazardous substances assessment, insurance companies' taxes (with Insurance Commissioner), motor fuel tax, motor vehicle use tax (with local officials), natural resource severance tax, oil production tax, private car company tax, public utilities tax, sales and use taxes.

Alcoholic Beverage Control Board. Alcoholic beverage license fees.

Cabinet for Human Resources. Unemployment insurance tax.

Public Protection and Regulation Cabinet. Department of Insurance (with Department of Revenue) administers and collects insurance gross premiums tax.

Secretary of State. Corporate organization and qualification fees.

Transportation Cabinet. Motor carrier fuel use tax and registration, motor vehicle registration (with local taxing officials).

Local taxing officials. Property tax (with Dept. of Property Taxation in Department of Revenue), motor vehicle and vehicle use tax (with Dept. of Transportation).

LOUISIANA

(225) 219-2448

Department of Revenue. Corporation franchise tax, income taxes, miscellaneous taxes, severance taxes, automobile rental tax, sales and use tax, beverage taxes, petroleum product taxes, cigarette and tobacco taxes.

Department of Insurance. Insurance companies tax.

Department of Labor. Unemployment insurance tax.

Department of Public Safety. Motor vehicle registration fees, sales and use tax on motor vehicles and trailers.

Department of Public Service. Motor carrier fees.

Department of State. Corporate organization and qualification fees.

Local taxing officials. Chain store tax, estate tax, property tax, and local sales and use taxes.

MAINE

(207) 287-2076

Revenue Services. Cigarette tax, commercial forestry excise tax, estate tax, income tax, insurance tax, health care provider tax, hospital tax, mining excise tax, railroad companies tax, sales and use tax, tobacco products tax, tree growth tax, property taxes, blueberry tax, fuel taxes, mahogany quahog tax, motor vehicle oil change premium, potato tax.

Bureau of Alcoholic Beverages. Alcoholic beverage tax.

Department of Environmental Protection. Hazardous waste facility fee, oil termination fee.

Department of Labor. Unemployment compensation tax.

Environmental Improvement Commission. Oil terminal facility fee.

Secretary of State. Corporate organization and qualification fees, foreign corporation license fee, motor vehicle registration fee.

Local taxing officials. Motor vehicle excise tax, property taxes, motor home excise tax.

Department of Transportation. Aircraft excise tax.

MARYLAND

(410) 260-7980

Comptroller of the Treasury. Alcoholic beverage taxes, tobacco tax, estate tax (with local register of wills), fuel taxes, income tax, inheritance tax (with local register of wills), sales and use taxes, energy generation tax, emergency telephone system tax, local admission tax.

State Department of Assessments and Taxation. Initial fees and taxes, property taxes (with local officials), public service corporations.

Department of Employment and Training. Unemployment compensation (payroll) tax.

Department of Transportation. Motor vehicle registration fees, motor carriers' tax.

Licensing and Regulation Department. Insurance companies tax.

Local taxing officials. Document recording stamp tax, estate tax (with State Comptroller), inheritance tax (with State Comptroller), realty transfer tax.

MASSACHUSETTS

(617) 887-6367

Department of Revenue. Alcoholic beverage tax (with Alcoholic Control Commission), financial institution excise, cigarette tax, corporation excise (income) tax, estate tax, gasoline tax, general property tax (with local officials), hotel room occupancy tax, insurance tax, motor vehicle excise tax (with local officers), personal income tax, real estate transfer tax, sales and use tax, utilities taxes (with Department of Telecommunications and Cable and Department of Public Utilities).

Alcoholic Beverages Control Commission. Alcoholic beverage licenses.

Registrar of Motor Vehicles. Motor vehicle registration fee.

Secretary of State. Corporate organization and qualification fees.

Local taxing officials. Property tax (with Dept. of Revenue), motor vehicle excise tax on value (with Dept. of Revenue)

MICHIGAN

(517) 373-3200

Department of Treasury. Cigarette tax, fuel taxes, financial institutions franchise tax, gas and oil production privilege tax, insurance premiums tax, lodgings tax, Michigan business tax, personal income tax, sales and use tax, single business tax, utilities property tax, state realty transfer tax, estate and generation-skipping transfer tax, insurance companies (foreign) tax (with Commissioner of Insurance), severance tax. State Tax Commission assists, with local officials, in administering property taxes.

Department of Labor and Economic Growth. Business corporation fees, corporation annual report fee, alcoholic beverage tax, unemployment tax.

Insurance Bureau. Insurance companies tax.

Public Service Commission. Motor carriers fee on cars and trucks.

Secretary of State. Motor vehicle fees.

Local taxing officials. Forest lands tax, lodging taxes, property taxes (including state education tax), realty transfer tax.

MINNESOTA

Corporation franchise tax: (651) 297-7000

Income tax: (651) 296-3781 (Metro Twin Cities) or 1–800–652–9094 (Greater Minnesota)

Sales and use taxes: (651) 296-6181

Partnerships, S corporations, estates, and fiduciaries: (651) 296-3475

Withholding tax: (651) 282-9999 or 1–800–657–3594

Department of Revenue. Alcoholic beverage tax, cigarette tax, estate tax, tax on flight property of airlines, gasoline tax, general property tax (with local officials), hazardous waste generators' tax, health care provider tax, income tax, insurance taxes (with Dept. Commerce) mining occupation (with state treasurer and local officials), motor vehicle excise tax, net proceeds tax on mining companies, petroleum inspection fee, sales and use tax, utilities earnings tax.

Department of Commerce. Insurance taxes (with Dept. Revenue).

Department of Public Safety. Alcoholic beverage licenses, motor vehicle registration fee.

Motor Vehicle Registrar. Sales tax on motor vehicles.

Secretary of State. Corporate organization and qualification fees, corporation annual report fees.

State Director of Lands and Forestry. Auxiliary forest acreage tax, auxiliary forest yield tax.

Local taxing officials. Property tax (with Dept. of Revenue), mortgage registry tax, deed tax, taconite and iron sulfides tax, timber tax.

MISSISSIPPI

(601) 923-7000

State Tax Commission. Alcoholic beverage tax, amusement tax, corporate franchise tax, estate tax, finance company privilege tax, gas and oil severance tax, gasoline, oil excise, compressed gas and lubricating oils taxes, general income tax, gaming taxes and fees, malt tax, motor carrier fees, motor vehicle registration fees, public utilities tax, sales (occupation) tax, timber or timber products tax, cigarette and tobacco taxes, use or compensating taxes.

Secretary of State. Corporate organization and qualification fees.

Employment Security Commission. Unemployment insurance tax.

State Oil and Gas Board. Oil and gas production charge.

Local taxing officials. Property tax, mineral documentary tax, motor carrier fees (with State Tax Commission), motor vehicle registration fees.

MISSOURI

(573) 751-4450

Department of Revenue. Alcoholic beverage tax (with Department of Public Safety), cigarette tax, estate tax, express companies tax, financial institutions tax, forest crop land tax (with Conservation Commission), freight line company tax (with State Tax Commission), fuel use tax, gasoline tax, hazardous waste management fees and taxes, income tax, inheritance tax, insurance companies tax (with Dept. of Insurance), motor vehicle registration fee, sales and use tax, use tax on motor vehicles.

Department of Agriculture. Fuel inspection fee.

Department of Economic Development. Motor carrier tax.

Department of Insurance. Insurance companies tax.

Department of Labor and Industrial. Unemployment compensation tax.

Department of Public Safety. Alcoholic beverage tax.

Secretary of State. Corporate organization, qualification and annual registration fees, corporate franchise tax.

State Tax Commission. Airline companies tax, freight line company tax (with Dept. of Revenue), Property tax (with local officials).

Local taxing officials. Boats and vessels (wharfage) tax, general property tax (with State Tax Commission), merchants' and manufacturers' license tax.

MONTANA

(406) 444-6900

Department of Revenue. Alcoholic beverage taxes, bank share tax, cement tax, cigarette tax, coal severance tax, corporate income license tax, estate tax (with local officials), gasoline tax, general property tax, inheritance tax (with local officials), metalliferous mines tax (with State Treasurer), micaceous minerals tax, mineral mining tax, oil and gas producers tax (with Oil Conservation Board), personal income tax, public utilities tax, tobacco products tax.

Board of Oil and Gas Conservation. Oil and gas producers' tax.

Department of Labor and Industry. Unemployment insurance tax.

Public Service Commission. Motor carrier fees.

Secretary of State. Annual corporation report fee, corporate organization and qualification fees.

State Auditor. Insurance companies tax.

State Treasurer. Metalliferous mines and dealers tax.

Local taxing officials. Estate tax (with Dept. of Revenue), general property tax (with Dept. of Revenue), inheritance tax (with Dept. of Revenue), motor vehicle registration fees and use taxes.

NEBRASKA

(800) 742-7474 or (402) 471-5729

Department of Revenue. Air carriers tax, aircraft fuels tax, bank franchise tax, cigarette tax, corporate income tax, estate tax (with State Treasurer), interstate motor vehicles tax, litter tax, motor fuels tax, nonhighway refunds, oil and gas severance tax, personal income tax, railroad excise tax, uranium severance, sales and use tax, diesel fuel tax, alternative fuel, compressed fuel.

Department of Property Assessment and Taxation. General property tax (with local officials).

Department of Insurance. Insurance companies tax.

Department of Labor. Unemployment insurance tax in the state.

Department of Motor Vehicles. Motor vehicle taxes (with county officials).

Liquor Control Commission. Alcoholic beverage tax.

Public Service Commission. Motor carrier fees on all motor carriers.

Secretary of State. Corporate organization and qualification fee, corporation franchise tax.

Local taxing officials. Property tax, grain brokers tax (with State Board of Equalization), inheritance tax, motor vehicle registration fees.

NEVADA

(775) 684-2000

Tax Commission in the Department of Taxation. Alcoholic beverage tax, bank excise tax, business license fee, cigarette tax, estate tax, gasoline tax, general property tax (with local officials), minerals extraction tax (with local officials), modified business tax, realty transfer tax, sales and use tax, insurance premium tax, short-term lessor fees, tire surcharge fee.

Department of Motor Vehicles and Public Safety. Motor carrier license fees, motor vehicle registration fees, special fuels tax.

Employment Security Division in the Department of Employment, Training, and Rehabilitation. Unemployment insurance in the state.

Public Utilities Commission. Utilities tax.

Gaming Commission. Gambling taxes, live entertainment tax.

Secretary of State. Annual corporation report fees, corporate organization and qualification fees.

Local taxing officials. Property tax (with Tax Commission), mines tax (with Tax Commission), utility taxes.

NEW HAMPSHIRE

(603) 271-2191

Department of Revenue Administration. Bank tax (with local officials), tobacco tax, communications service tax, commuter's income tax, corporate gross profits tax, estate tax, gas and electric company tax, hospital tax, inheritance tax, intangible income tax, meals and rooms tax, property tax, realty transfer tax, refined petroleum products tax.

Department of Employment Security. Unemployment insurance tax, oil spillage in public waters fee.

Department of Environmental Services. Hazardous waste cleanup fund.

Department of Safety. Fuel taxes, oil spillage fee, motor vehicle registration fees.

Department of Transportation. Aircraft fees.

Insurance Department. Insurance tax.

Secretary of State. Annual corporation report fee, domestic corporation franchise tax, corporate organization and qualification fees.

State Liquor Commission. Alcoholic beverage tax.

Local taxing officials. Bank tax (with Dept. of Revenue Administration), property tax.

NEW JERSEY

(609) 292-6400

Division of Taxation in the Department of the Treasury. Alcoholic beverage tax (with Dept. of Law and Public Safety), Atlantic City casino parking fee, Atlantic City luxury tax, Cape May County tourism sales tax, cigarette tax, commercial property transfer tax, corporation business tax, cosmetic medical procedures gross receipts tax, domestic security fee, emergency and 911 system fee, fur clothing retail gross receipts tax and fur clothing use tax, gross income tax, HMO assessment, insurance premiums tax (with Dept. of Insurance), landfill closure and contingency tax, litter control fee, local property tax, luxury and fuel-efficient automobile titling fee, motor fuels tax, motor vehicle tire fee, municipal occupancy fee, nursing home assessment, petroleum products gross receipts tax, public community water system tax, public utility taxes, railroad franchise tax, railroad property tax, realty transfer fee, sales and use tax, solid waste services tax, spill compensation and control tax, state occupancy fee, tobacco products wholesale sales and use tax, transfer inheritance and estate taxes.

Department of Labor and Workforce Development. Unemployment and disability benefit tax.

Department of Insurance. Insurance company tax (with Div. of Taxation).

Department of Law and Public Safety. Alcoholic beverage tax.

Department of Health and Senior Services. Ambulatory care facility assessment and hospital assessment.

Motor Vehicle Commission. Motor vehicle registration fees.

State Treasurer. Corporate annual fee, corporate organization and qualification fees.

State Athletic Control Board. Admissions tax and tax on lease of broadcast rights.

Local taxing officials. Property tax, hazardous waste facilities tax.

NEW MEXICO

(505) 827-0700

Taxation and Revenue Department. Car line companies tax, cigarette tax, compensating tax, estate tax, franchise tax, gasoline tax, general property tax (with local officials), gross receipts taxes, income taxes, interstate telecommunications services tax, liquor excise tax (with Dept. of Alcoholic Beverage Control), mining property tax (with local officials), motor vehicles taxes and fees, natural gas processors tax, oil and gas ad valorem production tax, oil and gas conservation tax, oil and gas emergency school tax, oil and gas product equipment ad valorem tax, oil and gas severance tax, resources excise tax, severance tax, special fuels tax, tobacco products tax.

Department of Alcoholic Beverage Control. Alcoholic beverage permit fees.

Department of Labor. Unemployment compensation tax.

Public Service Commission. Utilities taxes.

State Corporation Commission. Annual corporation report fee, initial fees and taxes, insurance gross premiums tax, pipeline tax.

Local taxing officials. Property tax.

Department of Public Safety. Trip tax on foreign motor carriers.

NEW YORK

(800) 225-5829

Department of Taxation and Finance. Corporation Tax Bureau administers and collects: Corporate organization and qualification fees of foreign corporations, franchise taxes, tax on importation of gas services, utility services tax. Income Tax Bureau administers and collects New York state and New York City (NYC) personal income taxes. Sales Tax Bureau administers and collects New York state, NYC, and most local sales and use taxes. Miscellaneous Tax Bureau administers and collects: State alcoholic beverage tax (with State Liquor Authority), NYC beer and liquor excise tax, state cigarette tax, estate tax, state and most local (excluding NYC) mortgage taxes, fuel tax on carriers, gift tax, highway use tax, lubricating oil tax, motor carrier road tax, state and NYC motor fuel tax, petroleum and other energy business tax.

Department of Labor. Unemployment insurance tax.

Department of Motor Vehicles. Motor vehicle registration fees.

Insurance Department. Insurance taxes (with Corporation Tax Bureau).

Department of Transportation. Oil spill cleanup and removal tax.

Secretary of State. Corporate organization and qualification fees.

State Board of Equalization and Assessment. Property taxes (with local officials).

State Liquor Authority. Alcoholic beverage licenses and taxes (with Miscellaneous Tax Bureau).

Local taxing officials. Mortgage tax, property taxes (with State Board of Equalization and Assessment).

New York City Department of Finance. Department administers New York City general corporation tax, unincorporated business tax, commercial rent tax, commercial motor vehicle tax, utility tax, retail beer, wine, and liquor license tax, hotel room occupancy tax, banking corporation tax, taxicab license transfer tax, cigarette tax, real property transfer tax, mortgage recording tax, real property tax, and related charges: **311 or (212) 504-4115 or (212) 639-9675.**

NORTH CAROLINA

(877) 252-3052

Department of Revenue. Alcoholic beverages tax (with Dept. of Commerce), cigarette tax, corporation income tax, corporation franchise tax, estate tax, freight car line company tax, gasoline tax, personal income tax, gift tax, primary forest product assessment, public utilities tax, recordation tax (with register of deeds), sales and use tax, and insurance company gross premiums tax.

Department of Commerce. Administers credit for business expansion.

Department of Transportation. Motor vehicle registration fees.

Secretary of State. Corporate organization and qualification fees.

State Board of Assessment. Property taxes (with local officials).

Utilities Commission. Motor carrier fees.

Local taxing officials. Property taxes (with State Board of Assessment).

NORTH DAKOTA

(701) 328-2770

Tax Commissioner. Financial institutions income tax (with local officials), cigarette and tobacco products tax, coal conversion plant tax, coal severance tax, estate tax, fuel use tax, gasoline and special fuel tax, general income tax, general property tax (with local officials), grain tax (with local officials), mutual or telecommunications carriers tax (with local officials), oil extraction tax, oil and gas production tax, rural electric cooperatives tax (with local officials), sales and use tax.

Aeronautics Commission. Aircraft registration fees.

Department of Transportation. Motor vehicles registration fees, except truck-mile tax.

Insurance Department. Insurance companies tax.

Job Insurance Division. Unemployment insurance tax.

Public Service Commission. Motor carriers' fees.

Secretary of State. Corporate organization and qualification fees, corporation annual report fee.

State Highway Department. Truck-mile tax.

State Treasurer. Alcoholic beverage tax.

Local taxing officials. Financial institutions income tax (with State Tax Commissioner), property tax (with State Tax Commissioner), mobile home tax, grain tax (with State Tax Commission), telecommunications carriers tax (with State Tax Commissioner), rural electric cooperatives tax (with State Tax Commissioner).

OHIO

Businesses: (888) 405-4039. Individuals: (800) 282-1780.

Department of Taxation. All state taxes, except insurance taxes and motor vehicle license tax. Thus, Department of Taxation administers cigarette and tobacco tax, commercial activity tax (CAT), corporation franchise income tax (with State Treasurer), dealers in intangibles tax, estate tax (with local officials), gasoline tax (with State Treasurer), general property tax (with local officials), horse racing wagering tax, kilowatt-hour tax, natural gas consumption tax, natural gas company excise tax, pass-through entity tax, personal income tax (with State Treasurer), public utilities tax (with State Treasurer), sales and use tax, replacement tire tax, resources severance tax.

Department of Jobs and Family Services. Unemployment insurance tax, training tax credit.

Department of Development. Investment tax grant and other incentives.

Bureau of Motor Vehicles. Motor vehicles tax (with local officials).

Department of Environmental Protection. Hazardous waste fees.

Department of Insurance. Insurance tax (with State Treasurer).

Department of Liquor Control. Alcoholic beverage taxes (with Tax Commissioner) and licenses (with State Treasurer).

Secretary of State. Corporation organization and qualification fees.

Local taxing officials. Property tax (with Dept of Taxation), grain handling tax (with Dept. of Taxation), income tax (with Dept of Taxation), estate tax (with Dept. of Taxation), motor vehicles tax (with Motor Vehicles Bureau).

OKLAHOMA

(405) 521-3160

Tax Commission. Corporate income tax, personal income tax, sales and use tax, estate tax, property tax, franchise tax, fuel taxes, gross production taxes, petroleum excise tax, alcoholic beverages taxes, cigarette and tobacco products taxes, utility taxes, property taxes (with local officials), recordation tax, documentary stamp tax, aircraft excise tax, motor vehicle excise tax.

Alcoholic Beverage Laws Enforcement Commission. Alcoholic beverage taxes and licenses.

Department of Environmental Quality. Harzardous waste fee.

Employment Security Commission. Unemployment insurance tax.

Insurance Department. Insurance companies tax.

Secretary of State. Corporate organization and qualification fees.

Local taxing officials. Property tax (with Tax Commission), real estate recordation tax.

OREGON

(503) 378-4988

Department of Revenue. Corporation excise (income) tax, estate tax, forest products severance tax, general property tax (with local officials), inheritance tax, lubricating oil and grease tax, personal income tax, reforestation tax, timber taxes.

Department of Consumer and Business Services. Insurance companies tax.

Energy Office. Energy tax credits.

Department of Human Resources. Unemployment insurance tax.

Department of Transportation. Fuel use tax, motor fuel taxes, aircraft fuel tax, motor vehicle registration fees.

Liquor Control Commission. Alcoholic beverages tax and licenses.

Public Utility Commission. Motor carrier fees, public utilities tax.

Secretary of State. Corporate organization and qualification fees, corporation annual report and fee.

Local taxing officials. Property tax (with Dept. of Revenue).

PENNSYLVANIA

(717) 787-8201

Department of Revenue. Alcoholic beverages tax (with Liquor Control Board), capital stock tax (domestic corporation), cigarette tax, corporate loans tax, corporate net income tax, estate tax, financial institutions tax, foreign corporations (bonus on charters) tax, foreign corporations franchise tax, gasoline tax, inheritance tax, insurance tax, motor-bus road tax, motor carriers tax, oil company franchise tax, personal income tax, public utilities tax, sales and use tax, stock transfer tax, utility taxes.

Department of Labor and Industry. Unemployment insurance tax.

Liquor Control Board. Alcoholic beverages tax and licenses (with Dept. of Revenue).

Local taxing officials. Property tax, intangibles tax.

RHODE ISLAND

(401) 222-1040

Department of Administration (Division of Taxation). Estate tax, admissions tax, alcoholic beverage tax (with General Treasurer), business corporation tax, cigarette tax and tobacco products tax, corporation franchise tax, gasoline tax, hard-to-dispose materials tax, insurance companies tax (with Insurance Commissioner), personal income tax, public utilities tax, realty transfer tax, sales and use tax.

Department of Business Regulation. Alcoholic beverages licenses, insurance premiums taxes (with Dept. of Administration).

Department of Labor. Employment security tax.

Director of Transportation. Motor vehicle registration fees.

General Treasurer. Alcoholic beverages tax (with Dept. of Administration).

Public Utilities Commission. Utility regulation, common and contract carrier certificates and permits.

Secretary of State. Corporate organization and qualification fees annual corporation report fee.

Local taxing officials. Property tax.

SOUTH CAROLINA

(803) 898-5000

Department of Revenue. Admissions tax, airline tax, alcoholic beverages tax (with Alcoholic Beverage Control Commission), cigarette and tobacco tax, franchise fee, estate tax, income tax, malt extract tax, property tax (with local officers), realty transfer tax, sales and use tax, savings and loan tax, solid waste excise tax, bank tax, bingo license and tax, motor fuel tax, forest renewal tax (with Forestry Commission), low-level radioactive waste tax.

Department of Motor Vehicles. Motor vehicle registration fees.

Department of Insurance. Insurance premium tax.

Employment Security Commission. Unemployment compensation tax.

Secretary of State. Corporate and new entity organization and qualification fees.

Local taxing officials. Realty transfer tax (with Department of Revenue), property tax (with Department of Revenue).

SOUTH DAKOTA

(605) 773-3311

Department of Revenue and Regulation. Alcoholic beverage tax, bank franchise tax, cigarette tax, contractors' excise tax, fuel taxes, gross receipts taxes on telephone companies and rural electric companies, motor vehicle registration and licensing (with county treasurers), inheritance tax, oil and gas severance tax, precious metals severance tax, property tax on carriers, public utilities property tax, retail occupational sales tax, special fuel tax, use tax.

Commerce and Regulations Department. Commercial motor vehicle fees (nonresidents).

Division of Insurance. Insurance gross premiums tax.

Department of Labor. Unemployment insurance tax.

Register of Deeds. Tax on realty transfers.

Secretary of State. Annual corporation report tax, corporate organization and qualification fees, limited liability company fees, limited liability partnership fees.

Local taxing officials. Property tax (with Department of Revenue).

TENNESSEE

(615) 253-0700

Department of Revenue. Alcoholic beverage tax, corporation franchise tax, cigarette and tobacco tax, coal severance tax, corporation excise (income) tax, estate tax, fuel use tax, gasoline tax, gift tax, inheritance tax, retailers' sales and use tax, individual income tax, professional privilege tax, automobile rental surcharge tax, bail bond tax.

Comptroller of the Treasury. Assessments of carriers' and utilities' property on behalf of utilities.

Department of Commerce. Insurance companies tax, business privilege tax (with Dept. Revenue).

Secretary of State. Corporation charter tax, annual corporate filing fees, privilege tax on foreign corporations.

Local taxing officials. Business tax, general property tax (with Public Service Commission), mortgage tax, real estate transfer tax, litigation tax.

TEXAS

(800) 252-5555 or (512) 463-4600

Comptroller of Public Accounts. Alcoholic beverage (mixed beverages tax), carriers tax, cement production tax, amusement tax, boat and boat motor sales tax, coin-operated machine tax, franchise tax, gasoline tax, general property tax (with local officials), hotel occupancy tax, inheritance tax, insurance tax, minerals tax, natural gas tax, oil production tax, oil well servicing tax, petroleum tax, public utilities tax (with Public Service Commission), sales and use taxes, sulphur tax, tobacco products tax.

Alcoholic Beverage Commission. Most alcoholic beverage taxes.

Texas Workforce Commission. Unemployment insurance tax.

Public Service Commission. Utility tax (with Comptroller).

Railroad Commission. Motor carrier taxes.

Secretary of State. Corporate organization and qualification fees.

State Lottery Commission. Bingo taxes and fees.

Commission on Environmental Quality. Solid waste reporting and disposal fees.

Local taxing officials. Property tax (with Comptroller), motor vehicle registration fee (with Texas Dept. of Transportation).

UTAH

(801) 297-2200 or (800) 662-4335

Division of Corporations and Commercial Code. Organization or qualification of corporations and fee payment.

Tax Commission. Alcoholic beverages tax (with Liquor Control Commission), cigarette tax, corporate franchise income tax, corporate gross receipts tax, estate tax, motor fuel and special fuel taxes, general property tax (with local officials), insurance companies tax (with commissioner of insurance), motor vehicle registration, personal income tax, public utilities tax, sales and use tax, severance or production tax.

Division of Workforce Information and Payment Services. Unemployment insurance tax.

Department of Alcoholic Beverage Control. Alcoholic beverages taxes and licenses.

Local taxing officials. Property tax.

VERMONT

(802) 828-2505

Department of Taxes. Alcoholic beverages tax (with Dept. of Liquor Control), cigarette and tobacco tax, corporate income tax, electric energy tax, estate tax, railroad and transportation companies tax, hazardous waste tax, inheritance tax, insurance companies tax, meals and room tax, personal income tax, realty transfer tax, sales and use tax, telephone tax.

Commissioner of Motor Vehicles. Gasoline tax, diesel fuel tax, vehicle purchase and use tax, the motor vehicle registration fees.

Department of Employment and Training. Unemployment compensation tax.

Commissioner of Liquor Control. Alcoholic beverages tax (with Dept. of Taxes).

Division of Property Valuation and Review. Property taxes (with local officials).

Secretary of State. Corporate organization and qualification fee.

Local taxing officials. Property taxes (with Division of Property Valuation and Review).

VIRGINIA

(804) 367-8031 or (804) 367-8037

Department of Taxation. Aircraft sales and use tax, bank franchise tax (with local officials), cigarette tax, corporate income tax, deed and mortgage recording taxes (with local officials), forest products tax, gift tax, inheritance tax, intangibles tax (with local officials), personal income tax (with local officials), pipeline company property tax (except companies with operations and facilities wholly in-state), railway company property tax, sales and use tax, watercraft sales and use tax.

Department of Alcoholic Beverage Control. Alcoholic beverage license taxes, state tax on alcoholic beverages.

Department of Aviation. Aviation license fees.

Department of Motor Vehicles. Motor fuel tax, motor vehicle registration and license fees, motor vehicle sales and use tax, oil company excise tax, special fuel tax.

Employment Commission. Unemployment compensation tax.

State Corporation Commission. Annual corporation registration fee, carriers' road (fuel) tax, corporate organization and qualification fees, insurance premiums tax, motor carrier fees, pipeline company property tax (companies with operations and facilities wholly in-state), public utility taxes (local) (with local officials), public utility taxes (state).

Local taxing officials. Bank share tax (with Department of Taxation), deed and mortgage recording taxes (with Department of Taxation), intangibles tax (with Department of Taxation), personal income tax (with Department of Taxation), property tax, public utility taxes (local) (with State Corporation Commission).

WASHINGTON

(800) 647-7706

Department of Revenue. Business and occupation tax, cigarette tax, estate tax, food fish and shellfish tax, general property tax (with local officials), hazardous waste taxes, estate tax, public utility tax, retail sales tax, use (compensating) tax, stumpage value tax on timber.

Department of Employment Security. Unemployment compensation fund.

Department of Licensing. Aircraft and watercraft tax, cigarette dealer permits, fuel taxes, motor vehicles fees (with local officials).

Department of Social and Health Services. Uranium and thorium milling tax.

Department of Transportation. Motor vehicle carrier fees.

Insurance Commissioner. Insurance companies premiums tax.

Secretary of State. Corporate organization and qualification fees, corporate license tax.

State Liquor Control Board. Alcoholic beverages tax and licenses.

State Treasurer. Insurance companies premiums tax (with Insurance Commission).

Local taxing officials. Admissions tax, general property tax (with Department of Revenue), motor vehicle fees (with Department of Licensing), real estate excise tax.

WEST VIRGINIA

(800) 982-8297 or (304) 558-3333

State Tax Department. Alcoholic beverages tax and licenses, business franchise registration certificate, business and occupation tax on utilities (including electric power producers and gas storage), cigarette and tobacco products tax, corporate license tax, corporate franchise tax, corporate net income tax, general property tax (with local officials), estate tax, hazardous waste tax, motor fuels tax, personal income tax, realty transfer tax, sales and use tax, severance and business privilege taxes, soft drinks tax, health care provider taxes, telecommunications tax, insurance premium tax.

Department of Employment Programs. Unemployment compensation law.

Department of Highways. Motor carrier fees (with Public Service Commission), motor vehicle registration fees.

Public Service Commission. Motor carrier fees (with Dept. of Highways).

Secretary of State. Corporate organization and qualification fees, initial franchise tax, tax on corporations holding land.

Commissioner of Insurance. Insurance companies tax.

Local taxing officials. Business license fees, property tax, property transfer tax.

WISCONSIN

(608) 266-2772

Department of Revenue. Alcoholic beverages tax, cigarette tax, iron ore concentrates tax, estate tax, gasoline tax, general income tax, metalliferous minerals occupation tax, public utilities tax, property tax (with State Treasurer), public utilities tax, realty transfer tax, recycling surcharge, sales and use tax.

Department of Industry, Labor, and Human Relations. Unemployment compensation tax.

Department of Transportation. Motor vehicle fees.

Office of Commissioner of Insurance. Insurance tax.

Public Service Commissioner. Motor carrier fees.

Department of Financial Institutions. Annual corporation report fee, corporate organization and qualification fees.

State Treasurer. Public utilities property tax (with Dept. Revenue).

Local taxing officials. Forest lands tax, general property tax, grain tax, vessels tax, wharfage tax.

WYOMING

(307) 777-7961

Department of Revenue. Cigarette tax, estate tax, mining severance tax, property tax (with local officials), public utilities assessment, sales and use tax, alcoholic beverage licenses and taxes.

Department of Transportation. Gasoline and fuel taxes, highway use tax, motor carrier fees, motor vehicle registration fees (with local officials).

Department of Insurance. Insurance companies tax.

Employment Security Commission. Unemployment security tax.

Oil and Gas Conservation Commission. Oil and gas conservation tax.

Secretary of State. Corporate organization and qualification fees, corporation license tax.

Local Taxing Officials. Property tax (with Department of Revenue), motor carrier fees, motor vehicle registration fees.

CORPORATE ORGANIZATION AND ENTRANCE FEES
INITIAL TAXES

¶211-A Fees payable on corporate organization or qualification. The fees payable to a state on corporate organization or qualification to do business there are charted below. Also shown are annual report requirements. In many states, newly organized domestic corporations and qualifying foreign corporations must pay the state's franchise or capital stock tax when organizing, qualifying, or domesticating—the rates and bases of state franchise taxes are shown at ¶ 240.

STATE	MEASURE AND RATE OF TAX	DUE DATES
ALA.	*Organization fee—domestic:* Filing fee $75.	To Probate Judge and Sec'y State.
	Entrance fee—foreign: Filing fee $175.	To Sec'y State.
	Annual report: For domestic and foreign, $10 fee.	To Sec'y State by 3-15.
ALASKA	*Organization fee—domestic:* $250.	To Dept. Commerce Community & Econ. Dev., Div. of Corporations, Businesses, and Professional Licensing, on incorporation.
	Entrance fee—foreign: Certificate of authority, $350.	To Dept. Commerce Community & Econ. Dev., Div. of Corporations, Businesses, and Professional Licensing, on qualification.
	Biennial report & license fee: $100 for domestic; $200 foreign.	To Dept. Commerce Community & Econ. Div. of Corporations, Businesses, and Professional Licensing, by Jan. 1 biennially.
ARIZ.	*Organization & entrance fees—domestic, $60; foreign,* $175.	To Corp. Comm. on organization or qualification.
	Annual report & registration fee: $45 for domestic and foreign.	To Corp. Comm. by staggered date assigned by the Comm.
ARK.	*Organization fee—domestic:* $50.	To Sec'y State on incorporation.
	Entrance fee—foreign: $300.	To Sec'y State on qualification.
	Franchise tax (¶240).	
CALIF.	*Initial taxes—domestic:* Stock corporations, $100. Annual disclosure statement, $25.	To Sec'y State on incorporation. 1st statement due in 90 days after incorporation; later statements, annually by end of anniversary month in which articles were filed.
	Entrance fees—foreign: Stock corporations, $100. Annual disclosure statement, $25.	To Sec'y State on qualification. Annual statement, by end of anniversary month of qualification.
COLO.	*Organization fees—domestic:* Filing articles of incorporation, $125 (E-filing, $25).	To Sec'y State on incorporation.
	Entrance fees—foreign: Application for certificate of authority, $125.	To Sec'y State on qualification.
	Corporate (annual) report: Domestic and foreign, $100 (E-filing, $10).	Annually to Sec'y State by end of 2d month after Sec'y mails form.

STATE	MEASURE AND RATE OF TAX	DUE DATES
CONN.	*Initial taxes—domestic:* 1¢ authorized share on 1st 10,000 shares; next 90,000, 1/2¢ next 900,000, 1/4¢ over 1,000,000 shares, 1/5¢ min. $150. $50 filing fee.	To Sec'y State and town clerk on incorporation.
	Entrance fee—foreign: $50 filing fee; $225 annual license fee plus $75 annual report fee.	To Sec'y State on qualification.
	Annual report: Domestic & foreign—$75 annual filing fee. For foreign, add $225 annual license fee.	To Sec'y State; due dates set by Regs.
DEL.	*Initial tax—domestic:* Par value—2¢ per $100 of authorized capital stock for 1st $2,000,000; 1¢ per $100 on next $18,000,000; .04¢ per $100 over $20,000,000. No-par: 1¢ per share for 1st 20,000 shares; .05¢ per share on next 1,980,000; .04¢ per share over 2,000,000 shares. Min: $15.	To Sec'y State on incorporation.
	Foreign: $160 state tax or filing fee.	To Sec'y State by 3-1.
	Annual report: Domestic and foreign—$25.	To Sec'y State by 3-1.
D.C.	*Organization fee—domestic:* Authorized shares: 3¢ per share on first 10,000; 2¢ next 40,000; 1¢ over 50,000; min. fee $35. $150 filing fee.	To Corp. Div. of Dept. of Consumer & Regulatory Affairs on organization.
	Entrance fee—foreign: Flat fee of $200.	To Corp. Div. of Dept. of Consumer & Regulatory Affairs on application.
	2-yr.—report domestic & foreign— $750 fee.	To Corp. Div. of Dept. of Consumer & Regulatory Affairs by Apr. 15 every 2nd yr.
FLA.	*Organization & entrance filing fees—domestic $35; foreign* $50.	To Dept. of State on incorporation or qualification.
	Annual report: Domestic and foreign: $61.25.	To Dept. of State by May 1.
GA.	*Organization & entrance fees:* Domestic $100; foreign $225.	To Sec'y State on incorporation or qualification.
	Annual registration. Domestic and foreign, $30.	To Sec'y State by April 1.
HAW.	*Organization fee—domestic:* $100; $75 if filed on-line.	File with, pay to Hawaii Director of Commerce & Consumer Affairs on incorporation.
	Entrance fees—foreign. Flat fee of $100 ($75 if filed on-line) plus $25 for good standing certificate. Also license fee; see below.	File with, pay to Hawaii Directory of Commerce and Consumer Affairs on qualification.
	Annual report—domestic and foreign: $25.	File, pay by Mar. 31, June 30, Sept. 30, or Dec. 31, depending on date of incorporation or registration.
	Annual license fee—foreign: $100.	Obtain license from Dept., before doing business.

STATE	MEASURE AND RATE OF TAX	DUE DATES
IDAHO	*Organization & entrance fees—domestic and foreign:* $100 if form typed, $120 if not typed or if with attachments.	To Sec'y State on incorporation or qualification.
	Annual report: Domestic and foreign—no fee.	To Sec'y State by last day of month of incorporation or qualification.
ILL.	*Initial taxes—domestic:* $150 plus franchise tax (¶240).	To Sec'y State on incorporation.
	Entrance fees—foreign: $150 plus franchise tax (¶240).	To Sec'y State on qualification.
	Annual report: Domestic and foreign, $75 plus franchise tax (¶240).	To Sec'y State (See ¶240).
IND.	*Organization & entrance fees:* $90 for domestic and foreign; $75 if filed electronically.	To Sec'y State on incorporation or qualification.
	Biennial report: Domestic and foreign, $30, $20 if filed electronically.	To Sec'y of State every 2nd yr. in month incorporated or qualified.
IOWA	*Organization fees—domestic:* $50 for certificate of incorporation.	To Sec'y State on incorporation.
	Entrance fees—foreign: Filing certificate of authority, $100.	To Sec'y State on qualification.
	Biennial report: $45.	File-pay Sec'y State by Mar. 31 every 2nd yr. after incorporation or qualification calendar yr.
KAN.	*Initial taxes—domestic:* Application and recording fee: $90.	To Sec'y State on incorporation.
	Entrance fee—foreign: $115 fee. Limited partnership and limited liability partnership (LLP) $165 filing fee; business trust $65.	To Sec'y State on qualification.
	Annual report: See ¶240.	
KY.	*Organization fees—domestic:* Par and no value stock—1¢ per share up to 20,000; 1/2¢ on next 180,000 shares; 1/5¢ per share over 200,000. Min. $10. Plus $40 incorporation fee. Plus $10 recording fee to county court clerk.	To Sec'y State on incorporation.
	Entrance fees—foreign: Filing certificate of authority, $90. Plus $10 recording fee to county court clerk.	To Sec'y State on qualification.
	Annual report: Domestic and foreign, $15.	To Sec'y State by June 30.
LA.	*Initial & entrance fees:* Domestic, $60; foreign, $100.	To Sec'y State at time for filing or recording.
	Annual report: domestic and foreign, $25.	To Sec'y State by anniversary of incorporation or qualification.
ME.	*Organization fee* —$145.	To Sec'y State on organization.
	Entrance fee—foreign: $250.	To Sec'y State on qualification.
	Annual report: Domestic, $85. Foreign, $150.	To Sec'y State on staggered basis as per Sec'y.

STATE	MEASURE AND RATE OF TAX	DUE DATES
MD.	*Organization tax—domestic:* Based on authorized capital stock—1st $100,000, $20; next $900,000, $20 plus $1 per $5,000; next $1 million, $200 plus $10 per $100,000; next $3 million, $300 plus $15 per $500,000; over $5 million, $390 plus $20 per added $1 million. No-par value at $20 per share. Min. tax $20. Add $100 recording fee. Domestic without capital stock, savings and loan assns., credit unions, and cooperative assn. pay $100 fee.	To Dept. Assmts. & Tax on incorporation.
	Entrance fee—foreign: $100 flat qualification fee.	To Dept. Assmts. & Tax. on qualification.
	Annual report: Domestic and foreign, $300.	To Dept. Assmts. & Tax with personalty returns (Apr. 15)
MASS.	*Organization fees—domestic:* On authorized stock—1⁄10% of par value. Min. $200.	To State Sec'y on incorporation
	Entrance fee—foreign: Fee for filing initial certificate with State Sec'y, $300.	To State Sec'y on qualification.
	Annual report: Domestic and foreign $85.	To State Sec'y. by 15th day of 3rd mo. after tax year close.
MICH.	*Organization and admission (franchise) fee—domestic and foreign:* $50 for 1st 60,000 authorized shares; $100 for 60,001-1 million shares; $300 for next 4 million shares; $500 for next 5 million shares; $1,000 for each additional 10 million shares over 10 million. Add $10 filing fee.	To Dept. of Labor and Economic Growth, Bureau of Commercial Services, Corporation Division on incorporation or qualification.
	Annual report: Domestic and foreign. $25.	To Dept. of Labor and Economic Growth, Bureau of Commercial Services, Corporation Division by May 15th annually.
MINN.	*Organization tax—domestic:* $100 flat incorporation fee plus $35 filing fee. *Annual report* due; no fee generally; but if corporate name or address is changed, fee is $35.	Sec'y State on organization. *Annual report* due 12-31.
	Entrance fee—foreign: Initial license (qualification) fee is $150 plus $50 filing fee. *Annual report and license fee, $115.*	Sec'y State on qualification. *Annual report, fee,* due by 12-31.
MISS.	*Organization & entrance fees—domestic and foreign:* Fees for filing incorporation articles, $50; application for certificate of authority; $500.	To Sec'y State on incorporation or qualification.
	Initial annual report: Domestic and foreign, pay franchise tax (¶240).	To Tax Comm. by April 1 of year after incorporation or qualification.
	Later annual reports: Domestic and foreign $25.	To Sec'y State by 60th day after incorporation or qualification anniversary or other date set by Sec'y.

STATE	MEASURE AND RATE OF TAX	DUE DATES
MO.	*Organization tax—domestic:* $50 plus $5 per added $10,000 over $30,000 of capital stock (no par shares valued at $1 each). Add $8 filing fee.	To Sec'y State on organization, remit tax to Dir. Rev.
	Entrance fee—foreign: $150 plus added $5 fee.	To Sec'y State on qualification, remit tax to Dir. Rev.
	Annual registration fee: $40.	To Sec'y State (pay fees to Dir. Rev.) with franchise tax report (¶240) or in 30 days of incorporation date.
MONT.	*Entrance fee-foreign:* $100. Add $20 filing fee.	To Sec'y State on qualification.
	Annual report: Domestic and foreign, $15.	To Sec'y State between Jan. 1 and April 15.
NEB.	*Organization fee–domestic and domesticated:* Authorized capital stock: $10,000 or less, $60; $10,001–25,000, $100; $25,001–50,000, $150; $50,001–75,000, $225; $75,001–100,000, $300; over $100,000, $300 plus $3 per $1,000 over $100,000. Add $5-per-page recording fee.	To Sec'y State on organization.
	Entrance fees—foreign: $130; plus $5-per-page recording fee.	To Sec'y State on qualification.
NEV.	*Organization fee—domestic:* Based on authorized capital stock: up to– $75,000, $75; $200,000, $175; $500,000, $275; $1,000,000, $375; $375 plus $275 per $500,000 over $1,000,000. $35,000 max. fee.	To Sec'y State on incorporation.
	Entrance fee—foreign: Same as for domestic.	To Secy. State at time of filing qualifying papers.
	Annual report: Domestic and foreign, $125 initial fee; for each annual list filed thereafter: up to– $75,000, $125; $200,000, $175; $500,000, $275; $1,000,000, $375; $375 plus $275 per $500,000 over $1,000,000. Max. annual fee, $11,000.	To Sec'y State by last day of month in which incorporation or qualification anniversary occurs.
N.H.	*Organization fee—domestic:* $35 filing fee. Added $50 to file registration statement.	To Sec'y State on incorporation.
	Entrance fee—foreign: $35 filing fee. Added $50 to file registration statement.	To Sec'y State on qualification.
	Annual report: Domestic-foreign, $100.	To Sec'y State between Jan. 1 and Apr. 1.
N.J.	*Organization fee—domestic:* $125.	To State Treasurer on incorporation.
	Entrance fee—foreign: $125.	To State Treasurer on qualification.
	Annual report: domestic and foreign, $50.	To State Treasurer within 30 days before or after date State Treasurer chooses for each corp.

STATE	MEASURE AND RATE OF TAX	DUE DATES
N.M.	*Organization & entrance fees—domestic and foreign:* $1 for every 1,000 shares of total capital stock authorized; min. $100 for domestic, $200 for foreign; $1,000 max. No par stock valued at $10 per share.	To Corp. Comm. on incorporation or qualification.
	Biennial report: Domestic and foreign, $25.	To Corp. Comm, in 30 days after issuance of certificate of incorporation or authority; later, every other yr. by 15th of 3rd month after tax yr end.
N.Y.	*Organization tax—domestic:* Tax at 1/20% on par value of shares and 5¢ on each no-par share. Min. $10.	To Sec'y State on incorporation.
	Incorporation fee—domestic: $125. *Entrance fee—foreign:* $225.	To Sec'y State at time of incorporation. To Sec'y State at time of qualification.
	License fee—foreign: Capital stock employed in state 1/20% of par value and 5¢ per share on no-par stock. Min. $10.	To Dept. Tax & Fin. by 2 1/2 months after tax year.
	Maintenance fee—foreign: $300 generally.	To Dept. Tax. & Fin. by 2 1/2 months after tax yr.
	Biennial report—domestic and foreign, $9.	To Sec'y State every 2 yrs. during anniversary month of incorporation or qualification.
N.C.	*Initial taxes—domestic:* $125.	To Sec'y State on incorporation.
	Entrance fee—foreign: $250.	To Sec'y State on qualification.
	Annual report—domestic and foreign: $25 (paper filing); $18 (electronic filing).	To Sec'y of Revenue if in paper form and to Sec'y of State if in electronic form by 15th day of 3rd month after close of corporation's fiscal year.
N.D.	Filing fee: $90.	To Sec'y State on incorporation.
	Certificate of authority: $135.	To Sec'y State on qualification.
	Annual report: Domestic-foreign, $25.	To Sec'y State by Aug. 1 for domestic; May 15 for foreign.
OHIO	*Organization fee—domestic:* Based on shares authorized (par or no-par): up to 1,000 shares, 10¢ per share; next 9,000, 5¢; next 40,000, 2¢; next 50,000, 1¢; next 400,000, 1/2¢; over 500,000 shares, 1/4¢ a share (plus $3,850). Min. $125. Max. $100,000.	To Sec'y State on organization.
	Entrance fee—foreign: $125 filing fee.	To Sec'y State on qualification.
	Annual report—domestic: Report-pay income tax (¶222).	To Sec'y State by March 31.
OKLA.	*Organization fee—domestic:* 0.1% of authorized capital stock. Min. $50.	To Sec'y State on incorporation.
	Foreign—entrance fees: fee is 0.1% of maximum capital invested in-state during current fiscal year. Min. $300.	To Sec'y State on qualification.
ORE.	*Filing fee—domestic:* $50.	To Sec'y on incorporation.
	Entrance fee—foreign: $440.	To Sec'y State on qualification.
	Annual report—domestic corps. $30; foreign, $220.	To Sec'y State by anniversary of incorporation or qualification.

STATE	MEASURE AND RATE OF TAX	DUE DATES
PA.	*Initial fees:* Certificate of incorporation, $100; certificate of authority, $180.	To Sec'y Cmwlth. on organization or qualification.
R.I.	*Organization & entrance fees—domestic and foreign:* If fewer than 75 million shares are authoized, $160 flat fee; 75 million or more authorized shares, 0.2¢ per share. Plus filing fee—domestic, $70; foreign, $150.	To Sec'y State on incorporation or qualification.
	Annual report: Domestic-foreign, $50.	To Sec'y State by March 1.
S.C.	Organization fee—domestic: $100.	To Sec'y State on incorporation.
	Entrance fee—foreign: Certificate of authority, $100.	To Sec'y State on qualification.
S.D.	*Organization fee—domestic:* $125.	To Sec'y State on incorporation.
	Entrance fee—foreign: Certificate of authority, $550.	To Sec'y State on qualification.
	Annual report: Domestic-foreign, $30.	To Sec'y State before 1st day of 2nd mo. after anniversary month of incorporation or qualification.
TENN.	*Organization fee—domestic:* $100 filing fee.	To Sec'y State on incorporation.
	Entrance fee—foreign: $600 filing fee.	To Sec'y State on qualification.
	Annual report: Domestic and foreign, $20 filing fee.	To Sec'y State by 1st day of 4th mo. after fiscal yr.
TEX.	*Organization fee—domestic:* Certificate of formation, $300.	To Sec'y State on incorporation.
	Entrance fee—foreign: Registration to transact business in state, $750.	To Sec'y State on qualification.
	Annual public information report: No fee.	To Comptr. Pub. Accts. with franchise tax return (¶240).
UTAH	*Organization & entrance fees—domestic and foreign:* $52.	To Div. of Corps & Commercial Code on incorporation or qualification.
	Annual report: Domestic and foreign, $12.	To Div. of Corps & Commercial Code by end of 2nd month mailed by Div.
VT.	*Organization fee—domestic:* $75.	To Sec'y State on incorporation.
	Entrance fee—foreign: $100.	To Sec'y State on qualification.
	Annual report: foreign, $150; domestic, $25.	
VA.	*Entrance fees—domestic & foreign:* Authorized shares one million or less, $50 per 25,000 shares; if over one million, $2,500. Add $25 filing fee.	To Sec'y State on incorporation. To Sec'y on qualification.
	Annual registration fees: Domestic and foreign corporations doing business in Va. pay: Up to 5,000 authorized shares, $100; over 5,000, $30 per 5,000 shares or fraction; max., $1,700.	To State Corp. Commr. by day before anniversary of incorporation or qualification.
	Annual report: No fee.	To State Corp. Commr. by day before anniversary of incorporation or qualification.

STATE	MEASURE AND RATE OF TAX	DUE DATES
WASH.	*Organization & entrance fees—domestic & foreign:* $175.	To Sec'y State on incorporation or qualification.
	Annual report: Domestic and foreign, $50 annual license fee.	To Sec'y State by expiration date of domestic corp. license; for foreign corp., by 7-1 or annual expiration date established by Sec'y.
W.VA.	*Initial & entrance fees* —domestic $50 (foreign $100) filing fee plus license tax. (¶240).	To Sec'y State on incorporation or qualification.
	Business activity report: Domestic and foreign (no filing fee).	To Commr. Rev. by 4-15 (15th of 4th mo.)
	Business registration tax: $30 for 2-yr. period.	To Commr. Rev. by 7-1 every other yr.
WIS.	*Organization fee—domestic:* 1¢ per share, with $90 minimum and $10,000 maximum.	To Sec'y State.
	Entrance fee—foreign: $100, plus $3 per $1,000 of capital over $60,000 expected to be employed in-state.	To Sec'y State.
	Annual report: Domestic, $25. Foreign, $50, plus $3 per $1,000 of excess capital.	D—To Sec'y State by end of calendar quarter in which anniversary of 1st filing occurs. F—By 3-31.
WYO.	*Organization fee—domestic:* $100.	To Sec'y State upon organization.
	Entrance fee foreign: $100.	To Sec'y State on qualification.
	Annual reports: Pay license tax (¶240).	To Sec'y State by 1st day of registration month.

DOING BUSINESS PENALTIES

¶212 Penalties. Foreign corporations or their agents are liable for the penalties listed on this chart if operating in a state without authority to do business in that state. Some states make officers and directors personally liable for the penalties. Amounts shown are maximum amounts unless otherwise noted.

STATE	CORPORATION Col. A	DIRECTORS, OFFICERS Col. B	AGENTS Col. C	EFFECT ON CONTRACTS Col. D
Alabama	...	....	....	(14)
Alaska	$10,000 (13,22)	....	....	Valid(4)
Arizona	$1,000 (7)	....	....	Valid(4)
Arkansas	$5,000 (35)	....	....	Valid(4)
California	$250 (10,17,37,38)	....	$600(23)	Valid(4)
Colorado	$5,000 (7,10)	$1,000	$1,000	Valid(4)
Connecticut	$165 (10,17,20)	....	....	Valid(4)
Delaware	$500 (1,17)	....	$500(1)	Valid(4,18)
District of Columbia	$500 (7)	....	....	Valid(4)
Florida	$1,000 (6,13,17)	....	....	Valid(4)
Georgia	$500	....	....	Valid(4)
Hawaii	.... (7)	....	....	Valid(4)
Idaho	.... (17)	....	....	Valid(4)
Illinois	.... (17,25)	....	....	Valid(4)
Indiana	up to $10,000	....	....	Valid(4)
Iowa	$1,000 (7)	....		Valid(4)
Kansas	.... (17,10)	....	....	Valid(4,18)
Kentucky	.... (3,4)			Valid(4)
Louisiana	$1,000 (17)	....	....	Valid(4)
Maine	.... (9)	....	....	Valid(4)
Maryland	$200	$1,000(23)	$1,000(23)	Valid(4)
Massachusetts	$500 (13)	....	....	Valid(28)
Michigan	.... (2,17)	....	....	Valid(4)
Minnesota	$1,000 (12)	....	....	Valid(4)
Mississippi	.... (5)	....	....	Valid(4)
Missouri	$1,000 (29)	....	....	Valid(18,28)
Montana	.... (7,26)	....	....	Valid(4)
Nebraska	.... (33)	....	....	Valid(4)
Nevada	$500 (29)	....	....	(19)
New Hampshire	.... (7)	....	....	Valid(4)
New Jersey	up to $1,000 (32,10)	....	....	Valid(4)
New Mexico	$200 (1,17)	....	....	Valid(4)
New York	.... (17,10)	....	....	Valid(4)
North Carolina	.... (16,22)	....	....	Valid(4)
North Dakota	.... (7,34)	.... (34)	.... (34)	Valid(4)
Ohio	$10,000 (17,10)	(23)	....	Valid(28)
Oklahoma	$500 (1,10,15)	....	$500(1)	Valid(4,18)
Oregon	.... (7)	....	....	Valid(4)
Pennsylvania	.... (24)	....	....	Valid(36)
Rhode Island	.... (17,10)	....	....	Valid(4)
South Carolina	$1,000 (5)	....	....	Valid(4)
South Dakota	.... (7)	....	....	Valid(4)
Tennessee	.... (8)	....	....	Valid(4)
Texas	.... (11)	....	....	Valid(4)
Utah	.... (17,31)	$1,000	$1,000	Valid(4)

STATE	CORPORATION Col. A	DIRECTORS, OFFICERS Col. B	AGENTS Col. C	EFFECT ON CONTRACTS Col. D
Vermont	$1,000 (6,7,10,39)	. . . .	. . . .	Valid(4)
Virginia	. . . .	$5,000	$5,000	Valid(4)
Washington	. . . . (7)	. . . .	. . . .	Valid(4)
West Virginia	. . . . (17)	. . . .	. . . .	Valid(4)
Wisconsin	$5,000 (27)	. . . .	. . . .	Valid(4)
Wyoming	$5,000 (30)	. . . .	. . . .	Valid(4)

FOOTNOTES to chart ¶212 (corresponding to number in parentheses in chart):

(1) For each offense.
(2) Penalty of $100–$1,000 per calendar month (for up to 5 prior yrs.) of transacting business without certificate of authority. Max. penalty is $10,000.
(3) Liable for $2 per day of violation, not to exceed $500.
(4) Cannot institute suit on intrastate business until compliance, but can defend.
(5) Penalty $10 for each day of noncompliance, not to exceed $1,000 per year.
(6) Penalty $500-$1,000 per yr.
(7) Liable for all fees during noncompliance, plus penalty.
(8) Treble all fees, taxes, plus penalties and accrued interest for nonpayment.
(9) $500 penalty for each year transacting business without authority.
(10) Attorney General can restrain unqualified corporation from doing business.
(11) Civil penalty equal to all fees and taxes imposed if the entity had registered when first required, plus penalties and interest. Late filing fee can also be imposed equal to registration amount for each year of delinquency if business is transacted in the state for more than 90 days.
(12) Plus $100 for each month of noncompliance.
(13) Each year or part of year of noncompliance.
(14) Except for certain federally-insured mortagages, contracts are voidable. Cannot maintain a proceeding in the state. Estopped from defending action on grounds that contract was made in violation of the law.
(15) Penalty $200-$500.
(16) Penalty of $10 per day, not to exceed $1,000.
(17) Liable for all applicable fees, taxes, and penalties during noncompliance.
(18) Prohibition does not apply to successors to corporation's interest.
(19) Cannot sue, maintain, or defend any action in any court.
(20) Penalty $165 per month or part of month.
(21) $100-$1,000 per month of noncompliance ($10,000 max.) over preceding 5 years.
(22) Liable for all fees and corporation taxes, plus penalties and accrued interest for nonpayment.
(23) Guilty of misdemeanor.
(24) Title to real estate derived through unqualified corporation is good.
(25) $200 plus $5 for each month or fraction thereof of violation, *or* 10% of the unpaid filing fee, license fee, and franchise taxes, whichever is greater.
(26) The penalty is $5 per day of violation, not to exceed $1,000.
(27) Liable for all fees and charges plus a penalty of 50% of the fees that would have to be paid up to a maximum of $5,000.
(28) Cannot maintain any action on contracts.
(29) Amount listed is minimum penalty; no maximum penalty restriction.
(30) Liable for all fees and license taxes during noncompliance plus 18% interest.
(31) Penalty $100 for each day of noncompliance, not to exceed $5,000 per year.
(32) Penalty up to $1,000 per yr. for up to 5 yrs.
(33) Penalty of $500 per day, not to exceed $10,000 per year.
(34) Penalty up to $5,000; plus director, officer or agent penalty up to $1,000.
(35) Penalty $100–$5,000.
(36) Cannot maintain any action or proceeding in any state court; but may defend.
(37) Misdemeanor punishable by $500–$1,000.
(38) Liable for $20 per day of violation.
(39) Penalty of $50 per day not to exceed $1,000 per yr.

MULTISTATE TAX COMMISSION MEMBERSHIP AND PROJECT OR PROGRAM PARTICIPATION

¶213 Multistate Tax Commission membership and project or program participation. The Multistate Tax Commission (MTC) is an organization of state governments that works with taxpayers to equitably and efficiently administer tax laws that apply to multistate and multinational enterprises. Created by an interstate compact—the Multistate Tax Compact—the MTC encourages tax practices that reduce administrative costs for taxpayers and state governments, develops and recommends uniform laws and regulations that promote proper state taxation of multistate and multinational enterprises, encourages business compliance with state tax laws through education, negotiation, and enforcement, and protects state fiscal authority in Congress and the courts. State membership in the MTC and participation in MTC projects or programs is charted below.

States can join or participate in the MTC as Compact, Sovereignty, or Associate/Project Members. Compact Member states adopt the Multistate Tax Compact, govern the MTC's activities pursuant to the Compact's expressed purposes, and participate in a wide range of MTC projects and programs. Sovereignty Member states join in shaping and supporting the MTC's efforts to preserve state taxing authority and improve multistate tax policy and administration and regularly participate in the MTC's activities. Associate Member states participate in MTC meetings and activities and otherwise consult and cooperate with the MTC and its other member states or, as Project Member states, participate in MTC projects or programs.

States can participate in the MTC's Joint Audit Program for corporate income tax and/or sales and use tax. Under this program, the MTC conducts a joint audit of a business's tax status and liabilities on behalf of participating states simultaneously.

States also can participate in the MTC's National Nexus Program, which provides a centralized business taxpayer registration information service, a liability resolution program, and information sharing among participating states. This program's central database allows participating states to exchange audit information on the potential nexus-creating activities of businesses involved in interstate commerce. The program's voluntary disclosure process allows taxpayers seeking to come into compliance with state tax laws to do so on a multistate basis. Program staff negotiates with taxpayers and prepares draft settlement agreements for acceptance or modification by participating states. Audit follow-up is available to deal with businesses identified as non-complying.

	Membership	Participation in MTC Projects and Programs		
		Joint Audit Program Participation		
	Type of MTC Member	Corporate Income Tax	Sales & Use Tax	National Nexus Program Participant
Alabama	Compact	Yes	Yes	Yes
Alaska	Compact	Yes	No	No
Arizona	Associate/ Project	No	No	Yes
Arkansas	Compact	Yes	Yes	Yes
California	Compact	No	No	Yes

	Membership	Participation in MTC Projects and Programs		
		Joint Audit Program Participation		
	Type of MTC Member	Corporate Income Tax	Sales & Use Tax	National Nexus Program Participant
Colorado	Compact	Yes	Yes	Yes
Connecticut	Associate/ Project	No	No	Yes
Delaware	Non-member	No	No	No
District of Colombia	Compact	Yes	Yes	Yes
Florida	Associate/ Project	No	No	Yes
Georgia	Sovereignty	No	Yes	Yes
Hawaii	Compact	Yes	Yes	Yes
Idaho	Compact	Yes	Yes	Yes
Illinois	Associate/ Project	Yes	Yes	No
Indiana	Associate/ Project	No	No	No
Iowa	Associate/ Project	No	No	Yes
Kansas	Compact	Yes	Yes	Yes
Kentucky	Sovereignty	Yes	Yes	Yes
Louisiana	Sovereignty	No	Yes	Yes
Maine	Associate/ Project	No	No	No
Maryland	Sovereignty	Yes	Yes	Yes
Massachusetts	Associate/ Project	No	No	Yes
Michigan	Compact	Yes	Yes	Yes
Minnesota	Compact	Yes	Yes	Yes
Mississippi	Associate/ Project	No	No	No
Missouri	Compact	Yes	No	Yes
Montana	Compact	Yes	No	Yes
Nebraska	Associate/ Project	Yes	No	Yes
Nevada	Non-member	No	No	No
New Hampshire	Associate/ Project	No	No	Yes

	Membership	Participation in MTC Projects and Programs		
		Joint Audit Program Participation		
	Type of MTC Member	Corporate Income Tax	Sales & Use Tax	National Nexus Program Participant
New Jersey	Sovereignty	Yes	Yes	Yes
New Mexico	Compact	Yes	No	Yes
New York	Associate/ Project	No	No	No
North Carolina	Associate/ Project	No	No	Yes
North Dakota	Compact	Yes	Yes	Yes
Ohio	Associate/ Project	No	No	Yes
Oklahoma	Associate/ Project	Yes	No	Yes
Oregon	Compact	Yes	No	Yes
Pennsylvania	Associate/ Project	No	No	No
Rhode Island	Associate/ Project	No	No	Yes
South Carolina	Associate/ Project	No	No	Yes
South Dakota	Compact	No	No	Yes
Tennessee	Associate/ Project	No	No	Yes
Texas	Compact	No	No	Yes
Utah	Compact	Yes	Yes	Yes
Vermont	Associate/ Project	No	No	Yes
Virginia	Non-member	No	No	No
Washington	Compact	No	Yes	Yes
West Virginia	Sovereignty	Yes	No	Yes
Wisconsin	Associate/ Project	Yes	Yes	Yes
Wyoming	Sovereignty	No	No	Yes

CORPORATE INCOME TAXES—NATURE, BASIS

¶220 Nature and basis of income taxes. The nature and basis of the taxes charted below will considerably influence how far each state will go in taxing a multistate corporation. The U.S. Supreme Court held in its *Complete Auto* decision [*430 US 274*] that privilege (indirect) or "doing business" taxes can be levied on interstate companies so long as the tax is nondiscriminatory and properly apportioned. The states' action is limited only by Fed law (P.L. 86-272) granting narrow protection to interstate order-taking. This chart includes direct income taxes and privilege (indirect or "doing business") taxes imposed by Conn., Fla., Ill., Mich., N.Y., Ohio, and Tenn.

Controlling features: There are four broad classifications that states use to corral interstate income. These are as follows:

States with double-barrelled taxes: States imposing both a privilege tax (to reach all income of qualified domestic and foreign corporations) and a direct income tax (specifically designed to reach the in-state income of interstate corporations) include Calif., Idaho, Mont., Ore., Pa., Utah, and Wis. The DC tax is, in effect, a double-barrelled tax (but see note 13). (The chart is limited to direct income tax provisions of these states' statutes.)

Engaged in interstate commerce: Some states have specific provisions that specifically provide that corporations engaged in interstate commerce are taxable. These states are included in the last column of the chart.

Income from property in-state: Statutes that claim income from property with an instate situs are usually effective even as to companies not active in ordinary business operations in the state. For example, income from patents, copyrights, licenses to use or royalties, would ostensibly be taxable even though the corporate owner had no other contact with the state. This can be effective even as to contracts executed out-of-state and payments made from outside the state.

Income from in-state business: This is a broad classification. However, by interpretation a tax limited to "business" could be less far-reaching than statutes not so restricted (for instance, pure investment income, and income not produced by direct labor employed in the taxing state). But state courts must decide this.

➡ **INCOME FROM SOURCES IN-STATE→** This is probably the broadest classification of all. Theoretically, *any* type of income derived from within the borders of a particular state could be gathered in under this type of clause. Mail or phone order income would conceivably be within its grasp (though no other contact between state and corporation exists) if the line had not been drawn on 9-14-1959 by the Fed law barring such taxation.

"Doing business": This is perhaps the narrowest of the classifications (see notes to chart). State net income tax imposed solely on corporations "doing business" in state tends to restrict reach of tax to solidly emplaced commercial activities.

STATE	CORPORATIONS TAXED ON THESE TYPES OF INCOME Income from in-state property	Income from in-state business	Income from in-state sources (1)	Income from doing business in-state	SPECIFICALLY APPLIED TO CORPORATIONS ENGAGED IN INTERSTATE COMMERCE
Alabama	X(3)		X	X	
Alaska	X(3)	X	X(6)	X	X
Arizona	X	X	X(6,7)	X	X
Arkansas	X(10)	X(10)		X(10)	X
California	X(3,15)	X	X(6,7)	X	X
Colorado		X	X(2,6)	X	X
Connecticut	X	X	X	X	
Delaware(11)	X(3)	X		X	
District of Columbia			X(6,13)	X	(13)
Florida			X	X	X
Georgia	X(4)	X	X		X
Hawaii	X(4)	X	X(6)		
Idaho			X(6)	X	X
Illinois			X(17)		
Indiana		X(2)	X(6)	X(2)	
Iowa		X(12)		X	
Kansas	X	X	X	X	
Kentucky	X(3,15)	X	X(6)		
Louisiana			X(8)		
Maine	X(19)	X(19)	X(19)		
Maryland	X	X			
Massachusetts	X	X		X	
Michigan				X(21)	
Minnesota	X	X	X		
Mississippi	X			X	
Missouri			X		
Montana	X(3)	X	X(20)		X
Nebraska			X		
New Hampshire	X	X	X		
New Jersey	X	X	X	X	X
New Mexico	X(3)	X	X(14)		
New York	X(3)			X	
North Carolina		X	X(6)	X	
North Dakota				X(9,10)	
Ohio	X(3)	X	X	X	X
Oklahoma		X	X(6)	X	X
Oregon	X	X	X	X	X
Pennsylvania	X	X	X	X	X
Rhode Island	X	X	X(6)		X
South Carolina	X	X	X(6)	X	X
Tennessee				X(2)	
Utah			X(6,7)		X
Vermont		X(2)	X		X
Virginia		X	X		
West Virginia	X	X	X		X
Wisconsin	X(3)	X(16)			X

FOOTNOTES to chart ¶220:

(1) If an "X" appears in third column (income from in-state sources), then by implication, statute could be broad enough to cover all other income including that in the first two (2) columns. But if an "X" appears in the first two (2) columns, it means that the statute "tags" only the specific types of income.
(2) Limited by statute to corporations "doing" or "carrying on" business in-state.
(3) Property located in-state.
(4) Property owned in-state.
(5) Property sold in-state.
(6) Income derived from in-state sources.
(7) Income attributable to in-state sources.
(8) Income from in-state sources.
(9) No specific indication of source of income in levy clause; probably includes all items in other columns.
(10) Limited to "doing business."
(11) Del.—Special status corporations are treated differently.
(12) Iowa.—Tax Comm. [Dept. Rev.] says tax does not apply as of 4-13-59 to exclusive interstate commerce (but see explanation of Complete Auto decision above).
(13) DC—Law specifically exempts exclusive in-District solicitation of tangible personalty sales to U.S. government.
(14) NM—Income from employment in state.
(15) Property having situs (legal location) in-state.
(16) Wis.—Which consists exclusively of foreign commerce, interstate commerce, or both.
(17) Ill.—Income earned or received in-state.
(18) (Reserved.)
(19) Me.—Entire taxable income of every "taxable corporation."
(20) Mont.—Income from "any activities carried" in-state.
(21) Mich.—Eff 1-1-2008, "Michigan Business Tax" business income tax component on corporate and noncorporate taxpayers applies to income from in-state business activity. MBT modified gross receipts tax component on corporate and noncorporate taxpayers applies to in-state gross receipts. Until 12-31-2007, "Single Business (privilege) Tax" on corporate and noncorporate taxpayers applies to income from in-state business activity.

FEDERAL INCOME TAX RULES USED IN STATES

¶221 **Fed-state conformity.** The chart below shows how the states follow federal income tax policies and rules for their income tax purposes.

STATE	COMPUTATION STARTING POINT Col. A	OFFICIAL POLICY Col. B	MAJOR RESEMBLANCE Col. C	MINOR RESEMBLANCE Col. D
Alabama	X(C)	A	X(I)	
Alaska	X(C)	A		
Arizona	X(1-1-2007)(20)	A		
Arkansas	(25)	A		X
California	X(1-1-2005)(26)	A		
Colorado	X	A		
Connecticut	X(5)	A		
Delaware	X	A		
District of Columbia	X	A	X	
Florida	(C)(1-1-2007)(17)	A(C)		
Georgia	X(1-1-2007)(29)	A		
Hawaii	X(12-31-2006)(16)	A		
Idaho	X(1-1-2007)(21)	A		
Illinois	X	A		
Indiana	X(1-1-2007)(11)	A		
Iowa	X(1-1-2007)(23)	A		
Kansas	X	A		
Kentucky	X(12-31-2006)(19)	A		
Louisiana	X(C)(4)X(I)			
Maine	X(12-31-2006)(24)	A		
Maryland	X	A		
Massachusetts	X(C)	A		
	X(I)(1-1-2005)(6)	A		
Michigan	X(I)(1-1-96)(15)	A		
	(C)(1-1-99)(28)			
Minnesota	X(12-31-2006)(1)	A		
Mississippi		A(I)(27)		X
Missouri	X	A		
Montana	X(2)	A		
Nebraska	X	A		
Nevada	No income tax.			
New Hampshire	X(12-31-2000)(13)	A		
New Jersey	X(C)	A(C)		X(I)
New Mexico	X	A		
New York	X	A		
North Carolina	X(1-1-2007)(9)	A		
North Dakota	X(8,12)	A		
Ohio	X(12-28-2006)	A		
Oklahoma	X	A		
Oregon	X	A		
Pennsylvania	X(C)	A(C)		X(I)
Rhode Island	X	A		
South Carolina	X(12-31-2006)(3)	A		
South Dakota	No broad-based state income tax.			
Tennessee	X(C)(18)	A(C)		
Texas	(1-1-2007)(30)			
Utah	X	A		X(C)
Vermont	(1-1-2006)(2)	A		
Virginia	X(12-31-2006)(14)	A		
Washington	No income taxes.			
West Virginia	X(12-31-2006)(10)	A		
Wisconsin	X(1-1-2007)(7)	A		
Wyoming	No state income taxes.			

FOOTNOTES to chart ¶221 (corresponding to number in parentheses in the chart):

(1) Eff for tax yrs. starting after 12-31-2005 and before 1-1-2007, state adopts IRC as of 12-31-2006; for tax yrs. starting after 12-31-2006, state adopts IRC as of 5-18-2006.
(2) Eff 1-1-2006.
(3) Eff 4-11-2007; was IRC as of 12-31-2005.
(4) Eff for tax yrs. begun after 12-31-86; was official policy.
(5) Corporation business (income tax) adopts IRC in effect on last day of income yr. Individuals follow current IRC.
(6) Eff for tax years starting after 1-1-2005; was 1-1-98.
(7) Eff for tax yrs. starting after 12-31-2006; was IRC as of 1-1-2006.
(8) Based on percentage Fed tax for individuals in N.D. (if short form used).
(9) 7-31-2007; was IRC as of 6-1-2006.
(10) Eff for tax yrs. starting after 12-31-2005; was IRC as of 12-31-2005.
(11) Eff 1-1-2007; was IRC as of 1-1-2006.
(12) Eff for tax years starting after 12-31-88; was IRC as of 12-31-86.
(13) Applies to business profits tax: eff for tax yrs. starting after 1-1-2002; was IRC as of 12-31-98. Business enterprise tax adopts current IRC.
(14) Eff 2-19-2007; certain exemptions apply; was IRC as of 12-31-2005.
(15) Applies to personal income tax: however, taxpayer can elect current IRC.
(16) Eff for tax years starting after 12-31-2006; was IRC as of 12-31-2005.
(17) For Fla. corporate income tax, eff 1-1-2007; was IRC as of 1-1-2006. Fla. has no personal income tax.
(18) Corporation excise (income) tax.
(19) Eff for tax years starting after 12-31-2006; was 12-31-2004.
(20) Eff for tax yrs. starting after 12-31-2006; was IRC as of 1-1-2006.
(21) Eff 1-1-2007; was IRC as of 1-1-2006.
(22) (Reserved.)
(23) Eff for tax yrs. starting after 12-31-2006; was IRC as of 1-1-2006.
(24) Eff for tax ys. starting after 12-31-2005; was IRC as of 12-31-2005.
(25) IRC as of 1-1-99 (except as noted) as to certain items including depreciation, depletion, foreign income exclusion, interest deduction, business expenses; IRC as of 1-1-2007 as to charitable contributions, deductions for handicap access, capitalization and amortization of starting and organizational expenses, losses for related transactions; IRC as of 1-1-2007 as to employee benefit plans and annuities; IRC as of 1-1-2007 for S corporations.
(26) Applies to taxable years starting after 12-31-2004; was IRC as of 1-1-2001.
(27) Miss. adopts Fed itemized deductions for individuals except for certain taxes paid and gaming losses at Miss. establishments.
(28) Applies to Single Business Tax until 12-31-2007; however, taxpayer can elect current IRC. Eff 1-1-2008, Michigan Business Tax adopts IRC as of 1-1-2008, or taxpayer can elect current IRC.
(29) Eff for tax years starting after 12-31-2006; was IRC as of 1-1-2006.
(30) Eff 1-1-2008; was IRC in effect for the federal tax yr. beginning after 1-1-96 and before 1-1-97. This applies to the Texas corporation franchise tax. Texas has no corporation income tax or personal income tax.

SYMBOLS: ''X'' means the state is represented in that column. ''(C)'' means only corporate taxpayers. ''(I)'' means only individuals and other noncorporate taxpayers. Other symbols ''A'', ''B'' and ''L'' are explained under ''B''-''C''.

COLUMN HEADINGS represent: Column A: Computation Starting Point. Most states here use, by statute, specified Fed figure—Fed gross, adjusted gross, net or taxable income—as adopted or ''presumptive'' starting point. (Various adjustments are then made—for example, to exclude Fed bond interest and include state and municipal bond interest.) Some states adopt Fed law on a given date (as shown). The others adopt current Fed law. Alaska adopts specific subtitles of IRC as state law (instead of Fed figures) and in effect ties in with current IRC. **Column B: Official Policy.** ''A'' means state follows Fed law and rulings if not in conflict with state law. ''B'' means state law says Fed law was used as a source and should be guide. ''L'' means state makes limited use of Fed precedents. **Column C: Major Resemblance.** States have major portions of state law modeled on Fed law. **Column D. Minor Resemblance.** States have few important areas modeled on Fed.

➽ **CONSTITUTIONALITY→** State constitutions generally bar delegation of legislative power. But adopting Fed law on given past date isn't delegation. Although automatic conformity to future Fed amendments might be technical delegations, they nevertheless function in many states (Column A). All possible obstacles disappear when automatic conformity is optional with taxpayer, as in the Mich. individual income tax. Whether adopted or disregarded, it can't be attacked in court.

CORPORATION INCOME—RATES, RETURNS, PAYMENTS

¶222 How much and when. This chart gives the state income tax rates on business corporations, due dates for calendar year corporations, and to whom paid. Filing extensions are explained at ¶ 238.

➳ **WARNING**→ Payment by electronic funds transfer may be required. See ¶ 279.

Col. A RATES and MINIMUM TAX	Col. B RETURN & PAY DATES (1)	Col. C TO WHOM
ALA. 6.5% (37)	Mar. 15	Dept. Rev.
ALASKA 1%, 1st $10,000; 2% next $10,000; 3% next $10,000; 4% next $10,000; 5% next $10,000; 6% next $10,000; 7% next $10,000; 8% next $10,000; 9% next $10,000; 9.4% over $90,000 (11,37)	Mar. 15 (46)	Dept. Rev.
ARIZ. 6.968%. Min. $50.	Apr. 15	Dept. Rev.
ARK. 1% 1st $3,000; 2% 2nd $3,000; 3% next $5,000; 5% next $14,000; 6% next $75,000; 6.5% over $100,000 (25)	Mar. 15	Dir. Fin. & Adm.
CALIF. 8.84%. (3,37)	Mar. 15 (3)	Franch. Tax Bd.
COLO. 4.63% (37)	Apr. 15	Dept. Rev.
CONN. 7.5% (17,30)	Apr. 1 (30)	Commr. Rev. Serv.
DEL. 8.7% (5)	Apr. 1	Div. Rev.
D.C. 9.975%. Min. $100 (37,45)	Mar. 15	Office of Tax & Rev.
FLA. 5.5% (41)	Apr. 1 (4)	Dept. Rev.
GA. 6%	Mar. 15	Commr. Rev.
HAW. 4.4% 1st $25,000; 5.4% next $75,000; 6.4% over $100,000 (24,37,43)	Apr. 20	Tax. Dist. or Dept. Tax.
IDAHO 7.6% (22,37)	Apr. 15	State Tax Comm.
ILL. 4.8% (35)	Mar. 15	Dept. Rev.
IND. 8.5% (10)	Apr. 15	Dept. Rev.
IOWA 6% 1st $25,000; 8% next $75,000; 10% next $150,000; 12% over $250,000 (38)	Apr. 30	Dept. Rev.
***KAN.** 4% + 3.35% surtax on over $50,000 (37)	Apr. 15	Dept. Rev.
***KY.** 4% on 1st $50,000; 5% on next $50,000; 6% over $100,000 (14)	Apr. 15	Dept. Rev.
LA. 4% 1st $25,000; 5% 2nd $25,000; 6% next $50,000; 7% next $100,000; 8% over $200,000	Apr. 15	Dept. Rev.
ME. 3.5% on 1st $25,000; 7.93%, next $50,000; 8.33%, next $175,000; 8.93% over $250,000 (12)	Mar. 15	Rev. Services
MD. 7%	Mar. 15	State Comptr.
MASS. *Excise:* $2.60 per $1,000 on tangible values or net worth + 9.5% (incl. 14% surtax) of net income; $456 min. (29)	Mar. 15	Commr. Rev.
***MICH.** 1.9% (13,37)	Apr. 30	Dept. Treas.
MINN. 9.8% (37,40)	Mar. 15	Commr. Rev.
MISS. 3% 1st $5,000; 4% next $5,000; 5% over $10,000	Mar. 15	Tax Comm.
***MO.** 6.25% (37)	Apr. 15	Dir. Rev.
MONT. 6.75%. Min. $50. (2,9,37)	May 15	Dept. Rev.
NEB. 5.58% 1st $50,000; 7.81% over $50,000	Mar. 15	Dept. Rev.

Col. A RATES and MINIMUM TAX	Col. B RETURN & PAY DATES (1)	Col. C TO WHOM
NEV. No broad based income tax.		
N.H. 8.5% (6)	Mar. 15 (26)	Dept. Rev. Admn.
N.J. 9% (15,17,34,36)	Apr. 15	Div. Tax.
N.M. 4.8% on 1st $500,000; 6.4% on 2nd $500,000; 7.6% on over $1 million (37)	Mar. 15	Tax & Rev. Dept.
***N.Y.** 7.1% (23)	Mar. 15	Dept. Tax. & Fin.
N.C. 6.9%	Apr. 15 (7)	Dept. Rev.
N.D. 2.6% on 1st $3,000; 4.1%, next $5,000; 5.6%, next $12,000; 6.4%, next $10,000; 7%, over $30,000 (37,44)	Apr. 15	Tax Commr.
***OHIO.** 5.1% on 1st $50,000 plus 8.5% on over $50,000, see (19). Min. $50. (19).	Mar. 31	State Treas. (8)
OKLA. 6% (20)	March 15	Tax Comm.
***ORE.** 6.6%. Min. $10 (37,43)	Apr. 15	Dept. Rev.
***PA.** 9.99% (16,17)	Apr. 15	Dept. Rev.
R.I. 9%. Min. $500	Mar. 15	Tax Admr.
S.C. 5%	Mar. 15	Dept. Rev.
S.D. No broad based income tax.		
TENN. 6.5%	Apr. 15	Dept. Rev.
TEXAS. No broad based income tax. See chart at ¶240 for Texas franchise tax.		
UTAH. 5%. Min. $100 (37)	Apr. 15 (39)	Tax Comm.
VT. 6% on 1st $10,000; 7% on next $15,000; 8.75% next $225,000; 8.9% over $250,000 (21)	Mar. 15	Commr. Taxes
VA. 6% (18)	Apr. 15	Dept. Tax
WASH. No broad based income tax.		
W.VA. 8.75% (9% for tax yrs. starting pre-1-1-2007)	Mar. 15	Dept. Rev.
WIS. 7.9% (43)	Mar. 15	Dept. Rev.
WYO. No broad based income tax.		

FOOTNOTES to chart ¶222 (corresponding to parenthetical numbers in chart):

* Local taxes may also be imposed on corporate income.

(1) Fiscal year returns due on corresponding months for calendar returns.

(2) *Mont.*—7% rate if electing water's edge.

(3) *Calif.*—Min. tax is $800 (no min. tax for 1st tax yr. for corps. incorporated or qualified in Calif. after 12-31-99). S corps. pay 1.5%. Alternative min. tax (not S corps.) is 6.65%.

(4) *Fla.*—Returns due 1st of 4th mo. after tax yr. close (4-1) or 15 days after due date (without extensions) for filing Fed return.

(5) *Del.* —$5,000 minimum tax for Headquarters Management Corporations (HMCs).

(6) *N.H.*—Business profits tax on corporations, limited liability companies, partnerships, individuals, orgs. with gross business income over $50,000: 8.5%. Business enterprise tax is imposed on business enterprises (corporations, limited liability companies, partnerships, individuals, orgs.) at rate of 0.75% on gross business receipts over $150,000 or enterprise value tax base over $75,000.

(7) *N.C.*—April 15 eff for tax yrs. starting after 12-31-2007; March 15 eff for tax yrs. starting before 1-1-2008.

(8) *Ohio*—Remit payment to Tax Commissioner, made payable to State Treasurer.

(9) No minimum for direct income tax.

(10) *Ind.*—Utility receipts tax is 1.4% of taxable gross receipts.

(11) *Alaska.*—Personal holding cos., 12.6%; capital gains alternative tax, 4.5%. Alternative minimum tax, 18% of Fed tax rate. Accumulated earnings tax: 4.95%, 6.93% on over $100,000.

(12) *Me.*—Unitary business group applies above rates to first $250,000 and rates apportioned equally among taxable corps. Min. tax is 5.4% of Maine alternative minimum taxable income over regular income tax.

FOOTNOTES to chart ¶222 (corresponding to parenthetical numbers in chart): (continued)

(13) *Mich.*—Until 12-31-2007, Single business tax imposed on corporations, individuals, partnerships, and unincorporated businesses, estates and trusts with business activity in-state. Rate through 2007 is 1.9%. *Alternate tax* at 2% of adjusted business income can be elected by business grossing max. $10 million and electing small business credit. Added insurance company surcharge: 1.26 times regular tax liability. Eff 1-1-2008, Michigan Business Tax imposes tax of 4.95% on business income and 0.8% on gross receipts. Alternative tax at 1.8% of adjusted business income can be elected by business grossing max. $19 million and electing small business credit.

(14) *Ky.*—For tax yrs. starting on or after 1-1-2007, a limited liability entity (LLE) tax is imposed on corporations in addition to the corporate income tax. Minimum tax remains $175.

(15) *N.J.*—Corporation business tax, 9%. Corporation business tax is 7.5% for corps. with entire net income of $100,000 or less, but at least $50,000; tax is 6.5% for corps. with entire net income of $50,000 or less. Additional 4% surtax on corporation businesss tax liability is imposed for tax periods ending after 6-30-2006 but before 7-1-2009.

(16) *Pa.*—Tax rate is 4% on agricultural co-ops.

(17) Added tax on oil cos.: Conn.—5% tax on oil cos.' gross earnings pre-7-1-2005; 5.8% eff 7-1-2005—6-30-2006; 6.3% eff 7-1-2006—6-30-2007; 7% eff 7-1-2007—6-30-2008; 7.5% eff 7-1-2008—6-30-2013; 8.1% eff 7-1-2013. N.J.—2.75% tax on petroleum products gross receipts. Pa.—Added 19.2¢ per gal. of liquid fuel.

(18) *Va.*—0.5% minimum tax on telecommunications cos. Minimum tax on electric suppliers is 1.45% of their gross receipts minus the state's portion of the electric utility consumption tax billed to consumers.

(19) *Ohio.*—For tax years before 2007: Basis B rate is shown. If higher, tax calculated at Basis A applies—4 mills times portion of stock value. Max. tax, $150,000. *Litter tax:* 1st Tier—corps. pay added 0.11% tax and 0.22% on over $50,000 taxable income and 0.14 mills on net worth; max. tax, $5,000. 2nd Tier—Mfrs. or sellers of litter stream products (5% of total sale or such sales in-state over $10 million by mfrs.) pay added tax at 0.22% on over $50,000 taxable income or 0.14 mills on net worth, if greater; max., $5,000. *Minimum* tax, $50. But minimum tax is $1,000 for corporation with tax year gross receipts of at least $5 million or having at least 300 employees worldwide. *Tax phase-out:* Tax is generally being phased out, so that 4/5 of applicable tax generally applies for tax year 2006, 3/5 for 2007, 2/5 for 2008, 1/5 for 2009, and tax is zero for 2010 and later (replaced by commercial activities tax (CAT) which gradually phases in over 5-year period starting 7-1-2005). Tax on *financial institutions* (which is not being phased out) is 13 mills of net worth (Basis A); min. tax, $50 (or $1,000, as discussed above). Qualifying holding companies and specified technology companies compute tax only on income basis B.

(20) *Okla.*—Foreign corps. (per IRC) are also taxed at 6% rate.

(21) *Vt.* —Rates shown are for 2006. Min. tax generally, $250; small farm corp., $75. Rates eff for tax yrs. starting on or after 1-1-2007: 6% on 1st $10,000; 7% on next $15,000; 8.5% over $25,000.

(22) *Idaho.*—Min. $20. Added $10 per return showing gross income.

(23) *N.Y.*—7.1% of entire net income for tax yrs. starting after 2006; 7.5%, before 2007. Other minimums: (a) 1.5% of apportioned minimum taxable income; for tax yrs. starting after 2006; 2.5%, before 2007; (b) 1.78 mills on value of apportioned business and investment capital; (c) fixed dollar min. tax of $100 through $1,500 depending on payroll. Special rules apply for small businesses and S corporations. *Added tax:* 0.9 mills per $1 subsidiary capital. *Added surcharge* in Metropolitan Transit District for tax yrs. ending pre-12-31-2009: % needed to keep surcharge at 17% of pre-7-1-98 tax.

(24) *Haw.*—Capital gains alternative tax, 4%.

(25) In ACW, Inc. v. Weiss (Ark. 1997) 947 SW2d 770, the Ark. Supreme Court interpreted Ark. law to mean that the flat 6.5% rate applied to the net income in excess of $100,000, not to the entire net income if taxable income exceeded $100,000.

(26) *N.H.*—15th of 4th mo. for businesses not filing U.S. corporation returns.

(27) (Reserved.)

(28) 3-month deferment allowed for 1/2 tax due after credits and estimates.

(29) *Mass.*—S corps are exempt if receipts under $6 million; if more they pay 3%, or 4.5% tax on net income if total receipts $9 million or more.

(30) *Conn.*—Plus tax equal to amount by which 3.1 mill per $1 of corporate excess exceeds tax above. Min. tax $250. Max. generally $1 million. Added tax (up to $250,000) is imposed on filers of combined returns. S corps., limited liability companies, and limited liability partnerships are subject to a $250 business entity tax.

(31-33) (Reserved.)

(34) *N.J.*—S corp. rate on S corp. with net income over $100,000 on income allocated to NJ is 1.33% through 6-30-2006, 0.67% in 7-1-2006–6-30-2007, 0% for tax yrs. starting after 6-30-2007, on that part not Fed taxed and 9% on that part Fed taxed. Tax on S corp. with net income of $100,000 or less is 0% on that part not Fed taxed and 9% on that part Fed taxed.

(35) *Ill.*—Added personalty replacement tax: 2.5% on corporations; 1.5% on S corporations, partnerships and trusts.

(36) *N.J.*—If NJ gross recipts are less than $100,000, min. tax is $500; if gross receipts $100,000—$249,999, min. tax is $750; if gross receipts $250,000—$499,999, min. tax is $1,000; if gross receipts $500,000—$999,999, min. tax is $1,500; gross receipts $1 million or more, min. tax is $2,000. For affiliated or controlled group with payroll over $5 million, min. tax is $2,000. For RICs and REITs, min. tax is $500.

(37) Multistate Tax Compact member. State rates set under Compact provision requiring optional tax for small taxpayer (only in-state activity sales, not over $100,000 annually, and not owning or renting property in-state). Ala. 1/4% Colo. 1/2% Haw. 1/2%; Idaho 1%; Mont. 1/2%; N.M. 3/4%; N.D. 6/10% on 1st $20,000, 8/10% on $20,001–$55,000, 1% on $55,001–$100,000; Ore. 1/4% (1/8% if return on sales under 5%); 1/2% option repealed in Utah eff 1-1-94. No rates set in other compact states: Alaska, Ark., Calif., D.C., Kan., Mich., Minn., and Mo.

FOOTNOTES to chart ¶222 (corresponding to parenthetical numbers in chart): (continued)

(38) *Iowa*—Alternative min. tax is 7.2%, which is 60% of the max. 12% rate.

(39) *Utah*—Gross receipts tax: last day of July and January.

(40) *Minn.*—Alternative min. tax is excess of 5.8% of Minn. alternative taxable income over regular tax liability. *Additional minimum tax:* If sum of property, payrolls, and receipts is under $500,000, no tax; $500,000–$999,999, $100; $1 million–$4.999 million, $300; $5 million–$9.999 million, $1,000; $10 million–$19.999 million, $2,000; $20 million or more, $5,000 fee.

(41) *Fla.*—3.3% for taxpayers using alternative min. tax for federal purposes. Added 2.2% emergency excise tax on specified Fed ACRS writeoffs (for assets placed in service in 1981–1986).

(42) (Reserved.)

(43) Tax on S corps.' built-in gains imposed at regular rate unless otherwise shown—Haw. (6.4%), Ore., Wis. *Wis.* imposes surcharge to fund recycling at rate of 3% for corporations (0.2% for tax-option corporations) with at least $4 million in gross receipts; min. surcharge, $25; max., $9,800.

(44) *N.D.*—Corporations using the water's edge filing method must pay an additional 3.5% tax. For tax yrs. starting after 12-31-2006, tax rate is 6.5% on taxable income over $30,000.

(45) *D.C.*—6% rate applies to qualified high technology companies.

(46) *Alaska*—Return is due April 15, payment is due March 15.

CORPORATION INCOME ALTERNATIVE MINIMUM TAX

¶222.5 Alternative minimum tax. This chart shows the states that impose an alternative minimum tax (AMT) on corporations' preference items, the rates levied, and the taxable basis.

➽ **WARNING→** Many taxing states use Fed alternative minimum taxable income as basis or computation starting point. States that adopt current IRC have adopted current Fed law changes (¶ 221).

STATE	AMT Imposed?
Alabama	No
Alaska	Yes, at 18% of Fed alternative minimum tax.
Arizona	No
Arkansas	No
California	Yes, at 6.65% of modified Fed alternative minimum taxable income.
Colorado	No
Connecticut	Yes, at $250.
Delaware	No
District of Columbia	No
Florida	Yes, at 3.3% of modified Fed alternative minimum taxable income.
Georgia	No
Hawaii	No
Idaho	No
Illinois	No
Indiana	No
Iowa	Yes, at 7.2% of Iowa alternative minimum taxable income.
Kansas	No
Kentucky	Yes, LLE tax incorporates the $175 minimum tax (3).
Louisiana	No
Maine	Yes, on excess of 5.4% of Maine alternative minimum taxable income over regular tax.
Maryland	No
Massachusetts	No
Michigan	No
Minnesota	Yes, on excess of 5.8% of Minnesota alternative minimum taxable income over regular tax.
Mississippi	No
Missouri	No
Montana	No
Nebraska	No
Nevada	No broad based income tax.
New Hampshire	No
New Jersey	Yes, at graduated rates for gross profits or gross receipts (1).
New Mexico	No
New York	Yes, at 1.5% of N.Y. minimum taxable income base or fixed dollar minimum tax (4).
North Carolina	No
North Dakota	No
Ohio	No
Oklahoma	No
Oregon	No
Pennsylvania	No
Rhode Island	No
South Carolina	No
South Dakota	No broad-based state income tax.
Tennessee	No
Texas	No broad-based income tax.
Utah	No

STATE	AMT Imposed?
Vermont	No
Virginia	No (2)
Washington	No broad-based income tax.
West Virginia	No
Wisconsin	No
Wyoming	No broad-based income tax.

NOTES to chart ¶222.5 (corresponding to numbers in parentheses in the chart):

(1) *N.J.* —Taxpayer elects between using gross profits method or gross receipts method, using same method for next four periods. Using gross profits method, the taxpayer is not assessed on the first $1 million of gross profits. Assessment rate rises from .0025 times the gross profits in excess of $1 million times 1.11111 to .008 times the gross profits of more than $37.5 million. Under gross receipts, taxpayer is not assessed on the first $2 million of gross receipts. Assessment rate rises from .00125 times the gross receipts in excess of $2 million times 1.11111 to .004 times the gross receipts in excess of $75 million. Alternative minimum assessment is capped at $5 million per privilege period.

(2) *Va.* —Telecommunications companies pay a minimum tax at the rate of 0.5% of gross receipts if the 6% income tax is less than the minimum tax.

(3) *Ky.* —Eff for tax yrs. starting on or after 1-1-2007, a limited liability entity (LLE) tax is imposed on corporations in addition to the income tax. The LLE tax replaces the alternative minimum tax and incorporates the $175 minimum tax.

(4) *N.Y.* —For tax yrs. beginning after 2006, the rate is 1.5%. For tax yrs. beginning before 2007, the rate is 2.5%.

CORPORATION INCOME—CONSOLIDATED RETURNS

¶222-A Consolidated return elections and requirements. This chart shows whether or not a state allows corporations to elect to file consolidated returns. It also indicates if there are any state restrictions on or requirements for consolidated filing.

State	Consolidated Returns Generally Allowed?	Restrictions, Requirements
Alabama	Yes	Allowed for members of affiliated group filing or required to file federal consolidated return who are subject to Alabama tax.
Alaska	Yes	Allowed if all corporations joining in are in unitary business and are eligible to file federal consolidated return. Required if federal consolidated return filed and all corps. joining in are in unitary business.
Arizona	Yes	Allowed for federal consolidated return filers. Can be required. Election to file consolidated return is binding for the future unless revenue department consents to change.
Arkansas	Yes	Allowed for members of federally defined affiliated group that have Ark. income.
California	No	Only allowed for specified railroad-related companies. Can be required. Combined reporting allowed or can be required.
Colorado	Yes	Allowed for federally defined affiliated group if all consent.
Connecticut	No	But combined reports allowed or required.
Delaware	No	
District of Columbia	Yes	Corporations in affiliated group can elect to file consolidated return if they have gross income from D.C. sources.
Florida	Yes	Allowed if parent and all members of affiliated group that filed federal consolidated return consent; can be required.
Georgia	No	Must file separately unless Dept. Rev. approves or requests.
Hawaii	Yes	Allowed for Haw. corporations with Haw. taxable income, as allowed for federal, if each affiliate consents.
Idaho	No	But combined reporting required by members of certain unitary businesses.
Illinois	No	But combined reporting required by members of unitary business.
Indiana	Yes	Allowed for federally defined affiliated group if all affiliates consent and have income or loss from Ind. activities.
Iowa	Yes	Allowed for members of affiliated group that file federal consolidated return and are subject to Iowa tax.
Kansas	Yes	Required for affiliated corporations that file consolidated federal return and derive all their income from Kan. sources, others allowed or can be required.
Kentucky	Yes	Consolidated return required for affiliated group, eff for tax years starting on or after 1-1-2005.
Louisiana	No	Consolidated statements can be required.
Maine	Yes	Allowed for members of affiliated group engaged in unitary business.
Maryland	No	
Massachusetts	No	But combined reporting allowed for federal consolidated return filers.

State	Consolidated Returns Generally Allowed?	Restrictions, Requirements
Michigan	Yes	Until 12-31-2007, Single Business Tax consolidated or combined returns are allowed or can be required of an affiliated group of U.S. corporations. Eff 1-1-2008, Michigan Business Tax requires unitary business group to file combined return that includes each U.S. person, other than a foreign operating entity, that is included in the group.
Minnesota	No	But combined reporting is required for unitary corporations with Minn. nexus (with exceptions).
Mississippi	No	But combined reporting may be allowed or required.
Missouri	Yes	Allowed for affiliated group that files federal consolidated return.
Montana	Yes	Allowed for affiliated corps. if 80% of all classes of stock are owned by the affiliated group members and the group is involved in a unitary business. Dept. Rev. approval generally is required.
Nebraska	No	But combined reporting is required for unitary corps.
Nevada	No corporation income tax.	
New Hampshire	No	Combined reporting can be required for businesses conducting unitary business.
New Jersey	No	Required for casinos. Can be required for affiliated groups and controlled groups. Air carriers can elect to file.
New Mexico	Yes	Allowed. Can change to consolidated returns without permission. Can change from consolidated returns under limited circumstances if Dept. Rev. approves or IRC allows.
New York	No	But combined reporting is required if there are substantial intercorporate transactions between affiliated entities.
North Carolina	No	Can be required.
North Dakota	Yes	Required for corps. filing federal consolidated return and operating entirely in N.D. Allowed if compute liability using combined reporting method and Tax Commr. approves.
Ohio	No	But combined reporting allowed or can be required.
Oklahoma	Yes	Allowed for affiliated corporations with part of their income from Okla. sources and filing federal consolidated return; required if all income from Okla.
Oregon	No	Required for affiliated corporations filing federal consolidated returns.
Pennsylvania	No	
Rhode Island	Yes	Allowed for affiliated corporations if all consent; limited to corporations subject to R.I. tax and with same tax yr.
South Carolina	Yes	Allowed but requires separate computation of net income and loss for each consolidated entity.
South Dakota	No broad-based corporation income tax. Can be required for corps. subject to financial entity income tax.	
Tennessee	No	But combined reporting can be required or allowed.
Texas	No broad-based corporation income tax. Eff 1-1-2008, combined reporting is required for franchise tax. Before 1-1-2008, no consolidated or combined reporting is allowed for franchise tax.	

State	Consolidated Returns Generally Allowed?	Restrictions, Requirements
Utah	No	But combined reporting is allowed or can be required.
Vermont	Yes	Allowed if federal consolidated return filed and corps. have Vt. nexus and received any income allocated or apportioned to Vt.
Virginia	Yes	Allowed if one corporation owns 80% of voting stock of another or if at least 80% of voting stock of two or more corps. is owned by same interest. Can be required.
Washington	No corporation income tax.	
West Virginia	Yes	Allowed or can be required.
Wisconsin	No	Consolidated statements can be required.
Wyoming	No corporation income tax.	

STATE TAXATION OF FSCs AND DISCs

¶222-B Income tax treatment of FSCs and DISCs. The chart below shows the state income tax treatment of Foreign Sales Corporations (FSCs) and Domestic International Sales Corporations (DISCs). After 1984, the system of tax deferral for Non-Interest Charge DISCs was terminated as part of the 1984 federal Tax Reform Act introducing FSCs. Under federal law in effect up until the FSC Repeal Act, U.S. exporters could obtain a tax advantage under FSC provisions designed to encourage U.S. exports. A portion of foreign trade income was exempt from federal taxes if the FSC satisfied certain foreign presence, foreign management, and foreign economic processes tests. After 1984, a corporation could obtain tax advantages relating to exports either as a FSC (or Small FSC) or as a Small Interest Charge DISC. Former DISCs or new corporations desiring to be treated as DISCs could elect to operate under a modified DISC system (Interest Charge DISCs) similar to the pre-1985 DISC rules with modifications.

»→ **Federal FSC provisions repealed**→ The federal Foreign Sales Corporation Repeal And Extraterritorial Exclusion Act (FSC Repeal Act; P.L. 106-519), enacted November 15, 2000, repealed the FSC provisions in the IRC for transactions occurring after September 30, 2000, subject to transition rules, and excluded extraterritorial income (ETI) from federal taxable gross income. The Act also provided that no corporation could elect to be a FSC after September 30, 2000. Furthermore, if a FSC has no foreign trade income for five consecutive tax years starting after December 31, 2001, it ceases being treated as a FSC for tax years beginning after that period.

The federal American Jobs Creation Act of 2004 (P.L. 108-357), enacted October 22, 2004, repealed the ETI system of tax benefits, subject to transition rules and grandfather provisions for certain contracts.

STATE	PRE-1985 DISC	FSC
Alabama	No provision	No provision
Alaska	Follows Fed. treatment	Taxed as any other corporation
Arizona	Fed. treatment not recognized	No provision
Arkansas	Fed. treatment not recognized	Taxed as any other corporation
California	Fed. treatment not recognized	Taxed as any other corporation
Colorado	No provision	Follows Fed. treatment
Connecticut	Exempt	No provision
Delaware	Follows Fed. treatment	Follows Fed. treatment
District of Columbia	No information	No information
Florida	Follows Fed. treatment	No provision
Georgia	Follows Fed. treatment	No provision
Hawaii	Fed. treatment not recognized	No provision, treated as ordinary corporations
Idaho	Fed. treatment not recognized	Fed. treatment not recognized
Illinois	Follows Fed. treatment	Follows Fed. treatment
Indiana	Follows Fed. treatment	Follows Fed. treatment
Iowa	Follows Fed. treatment	Follows Fed. treatment
Kansas	Follows Fed. treatment	Follows Fed. treatment
Kentucky	Fed. treatment not recognized	Fed. treatment not recognized

STATE	PRE-1985 DISC	FSC
Louisiana	Fed. treatment not recognized	Taxed as any other corporation
Maine	Follows Fed. treatment	No provision
Maryland	Fed. treatment not recognized	Taxed as any other corporation
Massachusetts	Fed. treatment not recognized	Taxed as any other corporation incorporated outside U.S.
Michigan	Fed. treatment not recognized	Fed. treatment not recognized
Minnesota	Fed. treatment not recognized	Taxed as any other corporation
Mississippi	Fed. treatment not recognized	Taxed as any other corporation
Missouri	Follows Fed. treatment	No provision
Montana	Follows Fed. treatment	No provision
Nebraska	Follows Fed. treatment	No provision
New Hampshire	Taxed as any other corporation.	No information
New Jersey	Fed. treatment not recognized	Taxed as any other corporation
New Mexico	Follows Fed. treatment	Follows Fed. treatment
New York	Follows Fed. treatment	Fed. treatment not recognized
North Carolina	Fed. treatment not recognized	Taxed as any other corporation
North Dakota	Fed. treatment not recognized	Taxed as any other corporation
Ohio	Fed. treatment not recognized	Taxed as any other corporation
Oklahoma	Follows Fed. treatment	Follows Fed. treatment
Oregon	Fed. treatment not recognized	Income included in U.S. corporation
Pennsylvania	Fed. treatment not recognized	Taxed as any other corporation
Rhode Island	Follows Fed. treatment	Follows Fed. treatment
South Carolina	Taxed as any other corporation	Follows Fed. treatment
Tennessee	Fed. treatment not recognized	No provision
Texas	No provision	Taxed as any other corporation
Utah	Follows Fed. treatment	Taxed as any other corporation incorporated outside the U.S.
Vermont	No provision.	Follows Fed treatment.
Virginia	Follows Fed. treatment	Income exempt.
West Virginia	Follows Fed. treatment	No provision
Wisconsin	Fed. treatment not recognized	Taxed as any other corporation

STATE TAXATION OF S CORPORATIONS

¶222-C Income tax treatment of S corporations. Most states follow the federal treatment of S corporations: they're not taxed as a separate entity and their income is taxed to their shareholders. However, the states have set requirements that must be satisfied before this partnership-type treatment can be given to S corporations, arising from constitutional considerations applicable to states' power to tax multistate income and shareholders' income. So, before choosing S Corporation status, a taxpayer should be aware of the state tax consequences of an election.

This chart sets out the tax treatment of S Corporations in each state. The chart shows whether a state will hold an S corporation taxable or exempt (''exempt'' listings include states taxing only federally taxable income such as certain capital gains, excess net passive income, and certain built-in gains); whether a separate state election is needed to adopt S corporation status; and whether additional restrictions or conditions are placed on S corporations by the state.

State	Tax Treatment	Election	Restrictions and Conditions
Alabama	Exempt	Federal	Nonresidents shareholder must file consent to report-pay Ala. tax or S corporation must pay tax at highest personal income tax rate (¶228) on their share.
Alaska	Exempt	Federal	Corporation must file information return.
Arizona	Exempt	Federal	Nonresident shareholders must pay tax on distributive shares of income or loss earned by the S corporation in Arizona.
Arkansas	Exempt	State	Nonresident shareholders must pay state tax.
California	Taxable	Federal	Nonresident shareholders must pay state tax. Corps. taxed at special lower rate.
Colorado	Exempt	Federal	Shareholders pay normal personal income tax rate on their share (¶228).
Connecticut	Taxable	—	Corporate level tax was phased out before 2001, but S corps. are subject to a $250 business entity tax.
Delaware	Exempt	Federal	Withhold tax at highest personal income tax rate (¶228) on nonresident shareholders' shares.
District of Columbia	Taxable	—	Resident shareholders not subject to state tax to extent income taxed to S Corp.; nonresidents are not taxable.
Florida	Exempt	Federal	Corporation taxable on income taxable federally.
Georgia	Exempt	Federal	File consent form for nonresident shareholders; failure to do so negates Ga. recognition of election.
Hawaii	Exempt	Federal	Corporation taxed on federally-taxable income at highest corporation income tax rate (¶222). File consent agreements for nonresident shareholders or pay tax at highest personal income tax rate on their share (¶228).
Idaho	Exempt	Federal	Corporation taxed on certain capital gains. Corporation taxed on compensation, dividends, and other income not reported by nonresident shareholders.
Illinois	Exempt	Federal	Corporation subject to state replacement income tax at special lower rate.
Indiana	Exempt	Federal	Corporation taxed on certain capital gains. Nonresident shareholders must pay state tax, corporation to withhold tax on such payments.
Iowa	Exempt	Federal	Nonresident shareholders must pay state tax. Resident shareholders in "value added" corporation can apportion income if corporation derives income from outside Iowa.
Kansas	Exempt	Federal	Nonresident shareholders must pay state tax.

State	Tax Treatment	Election	Restrictions and Conditions
Kentucky	Exempt	Federal	Subject to limited liability entity (LLE) tax for tax yrs starting on or after 1-1-2007.
Louisiana	Taxable	—	Corporation excludes net income in proportion to La. residents' (filing state returns) ownership of the corp.'s shares of capital stock.
Maine	Exempt	Federal	Taxable under certain conditions.
Maryland	Exempt	Federal	Corporation must file information return, and withhold tax at highest personal income tax rate (¶228) plus lowest county income tax rate on distributive or pro rata share of income allocable to nonresident shareholders that are not pass-through entities. Composite return for nonresident shareholders may be required.
Massachusetts	Exempt	Federal	Corporation with less than $6 million in total receipts is exempt; corp. with $6 million or more in assets is taxed at special lower rate (¶222).
Michigan	Taxable	—	Both single business tax (repealed eff 12-31-2007) and Mich. business tax (eff 1-1-2008) apply to S corporations.
Minnesota	Exempt	Federal	Corporation taxed on built-in gains, capital gains, and excess passive income. It must withhold tax on distributions to nonresident shareholders. It must pay minimum tax (¶222).
Mississippi	Exempt	Federal	Corporation must pay tax for nonresident shareholders on their share of income unless they agree to pay it. Composite returns for nonresident shareholders may be required.
Missouri	Exempt	Federal	Nonresident shareholders must pay state tax. Corporation must withhold tax at highest personal income tax rate (¶228) on pro rata share of nonresident shareholder who has Mo. assignable Fed adjusted gross income of at least $1,200 from the corp.
Montana	Exempt	Federal	Corporation must file copy of Fed election.
Nebraska	Exempt	Federal	Nonresident shareholders must pay state tax or corp. must remit tax on their distributive share.
Nevada	—	—	Nevada has no state income tax.
New Hampshire	Taxable	—	Distributed earnings must be reported as dividends by resident shareholders subject to interest and dividends tax.
New Jersey	Taxable	State	Non-N.J. S corp. is taxed at full corp. rate (¶222). N.J. S corp. is taxed at lower rate; corp. must withhold tax at highest personal income tax rate (¶228) on shares of shareholders not consenting to report, pay. S corps. are not entitled to use AMT (¶222.5).
New Mexico	Exempt	Federal	Corporation taxed on certain capital gains and certain passive income. Corporation electing to be taxed as an S corp. for Fed income tax purposes must file a N.M. income and information return if it is registered to do business in N.M., does business in, into, or from N.M., or derives income from property or employment in N.M. Corporation must withhold and pay income tax for nonresident shareholders who have not filed an agreement to report and pay.
New York	Taxable	State	Pay applicable filed-dollar minimum tax. (¶222). Nonresident shareholder must pay state tax.
North Carolina	Exempt	Federal	Corporation exempt from state tax if electing IRC §1362(a). Corp. must file information return and nonresident shareholder's agreement to pay N.C. tax (or withhold-remit tax on nonresident shareholder's pro rata share).
North Dakota	Exempt	Federal	Corporation can file composite return and pay tax due for nonresident individual shareholders.
Ohio	Exempt	Federal	File Fed election. Nonresident shareholders must pay state tax. S corporation must pay 5% withholding tax if at least one qualifying investor is an individual.

State	Tax Treatment	Election	Restrictions and Conditions
Oklahoma	Exempt	Federal	S corporation is taxed on nonresident shareholders' income unless the corporation files with its return an agreement by the nonresident shareholders to file an Oklahoma income tax return.
Oregon	Exempt	Federal	Corporation taxed on income taxable federally, including built-in gains.
Pennsylvania	Exempt	Federal	Corporation must file information return, and withhold tax on income allocable to nonresident shareholders.
Rhode Island	Exempt	Federal	S corporations must withhold income tax at highest R.I. withholding rate provided for individuals (¶228) or 9% for corporations on members share of income.
South Carolina	Exempt	Federal	Corporation taxed on certain built-in gains and passive income. Nonresident shareholders pay state tax; corp. must withhold tax for them at 5% unless they consent to report-pay.
South Dakota	—	—	S.D. has no state income tax.
Tennessee	Taxable	—	—
Texas	—	—	Texas has no state income tax. S corps. are subject to franchise tax.
Utah	Exempt	Federal	Corporation must pay corporate tax rate or withhold tax at partnership composite return rate on nonresident shareholders' share of income from Utah.
Vermont	Taxable	Federal	Corporation is liable for income taxes imposed on nonresident shareholder. Corporation must declare and pay estimated tax on S corp. income of nonresident shareholders; $250 min. tax applies. Tax Commr. can allow S corporation to file composite returns and make composite payments.
Virginia	Exempt	Federal	Owners of S corps. are liable only in separate or individual capacities.
Washington	—	—	Wash. has no state income tax.
West Virginia	Exempt	Federal	Corporation must file information return; withhold tax on taxable income allocable to nonresidents.
Wisconsin	Exempt	Federal	Corporation taxed on certain built-in gains and liable for recycling surcharge. Nonresident shareholders must pay state tax; corporation must withhold tax from nonresident distributions in excess of $1,000.
Wyoming	—	—	Wyoming has no state income tax.

LIMITED LIABILITY COMPANIES—STATE TAXATION

¶222-D Income tax treatment of limited liability companies. All of the states recognize limited liability companies (LLCs), business entities which combine the limited liability characteristic of a corporation with the income tax benefits of a partnership.

The chart below shows how the states treat LLCs for income tax purposes. ''D'' means domestic LLCs; those formed under the laws of the particular state. ''F'' means foreign LLCs; those formed under the laws of another state or jurisdiction.

Most states follow the federal income tax treatment of LLCs. Some states have enacted statutes clearly saying that LLCs are treated either as partnerships or corporations.

IRC §7701(a)(2) defines a ''partnership'' to include a syndicate, group, pool, joint venture, or other unincorporated organization, through or by means of which any business, financial operation, or venture is carried on, and which is not a trust, estate, or corporation. IRC §7701(a)(3) defines a ''corporation'' to include associations, joint-stock companies, and insurance companies. Federal regulations implement these statutory provisions.

Federal ''check-the-box'' entity classification regulations: The Internal Revenue Service issued revised regulations, eff. 1-1-1997, for determining the classification of businesses as either partnerships or corporations for federal tax purposes. These regulations—26 CFR Reg. §301.7701-1 *et seq.*—replaced the ''preponderance of characteristics'' rules for classifying business entities with a simpler system that generally allows eligible entities to either take no action and be covered by the default classification or actually file a classification election. The revised rules have been dubbed the ''check-the-box'' regulations due to the simplified federal form developed for the election.

Under revised Reg. §301.7701-3, separate business entities that are not automatically classified as corporations under Reg. §301.7701-2 are eligible for the default or election rules. ''Business entity'' here means an entity that is not a trust or otherwise subject to special treatment under the Internal Revenue Code. Whether an entity is treated as separate from its owners for federal tax purposes is a matter of federal tax law and does not depend on whether it is recognized as separate under state law.

These entities are automatically classified as corporations:

- a business entity organized under a federal, state, or federally recognized Indian tribe statute that describes or refers to it as a corporation, body corporate, or body politic;
- an association;
- a business entity organized under a state statute describing or referring to it as a joint-stock company or joint stock association; an insurance company;
- a state-chartered business entity conducting banking activities if any of its deposits are insured under specified federal statutes;
- a business entity wholly owned by a state or political subdivision;
- a business entity treated as a corporation under some other IRC provision;
- certain business entities formed under the laws of a foreign country or U.S. territory which do not meet specified requirements for grandfathering out entities in existence on 5-8-1996 or do not meet other requirements.

The default rule applies to eligible entities which do not file an election. An entity's default classification continues until it elects to change its classification and files an election form. The default rule classifies an eligible domestic entity coming into existence after 12-31-1996 as a partnership if it has at least two members, but disregards it as an entity separate from its owner if it has a single owner. A ''domestic entity'' is one created or organized in the U.S. or under the law of the U.S., any of the 50 states, or the District of Columbia. A ''foreign entity'' is one that is not domestic. The default rule classifies an eligible foreign entity coming into existence after 12-31-1996 as a partnership if it has two or more members and at least one of them have unlimited liability, classifies it as an association subject to taxation as a corporation if all members have limited liability, and disregards it as an entity separate from its owner if it has a single owner that has unlimited liability. (However, many states allow single member LLCs (SMLLCs) to be classified as partnerships.)

The default classification for an eligible entity that was in existence before 1-1-1997 generally is the same as the last classification which the entity claimed under the "preponderance of characteristics" rules in effect on 12-31-1996. But if an eligible entity with a single owner claimed to be a partnership under those rules, the entity is disregarded as separate from its owner. A foreign eligible entity is treated as being in existence before 1-1-1997 only if its classification was "relevant"—that is, it affected the liability of any person for federal tax or information purposes—at any time during the sixty months before 1-1-1997. If a foreign eligible entity's classification is relevant before 1-1-1997, but no federal tax or information return is filed or it does not indicate the entity's classification, its classification for the period before 1-1-1997 is determined under the rules in effect on 12-31-1996.

Instead of having the default classification apply, eligible entities can select another classification, or they can change a classification previously selected, by filing an election with the IRS. An eligible entity with at least two members can elect to be classified as either an association subject to taxation as a corporation or a partnership. An eligible entity with a single owner can elect to be classified as an association taxable as a corporation or to be disregarded as an entity separate from its owner. An eligible entity with a single owner cannot elect to be classified as a partnership.

The federal regulations that were in effect before 1-1-1997 classified unincorporated entities as associations taxable as corporations for federal income tax purposes if they had a preponderance of these corporate characteristics: continuity of life, free transferability of interests, centralized management, and limited liability. Partnership status was accorded to entities lacking that preponderance. Those regulations, together with numerous federal revenue rulings and revenue procedures issued from 1988 through 1996 which are rendered obsolete eff. 1-1-1997, offered guidance in determining when an unincorporated entity had those characteristics.

STATE	LAW AUTHORIZES LLC FORMATION?	STATE INCOME TAX TREATMENT (1)
Alabama	Yes	D (Domestic) & F (Foreign)—Follow Fed.
Alaska	Yes	D & F—for corporation income tax, treated as corporation if so treated for Fed; state has no personal income tax. If an LLC is treated as a partnership for Fed purposes and it has corporate member(s), it must file an information return.
Arizona	Yes	D & F—follow Fed.
Arkansas	Yes	D & F—follow Fed.
California	Yes	D & F—follow Fed.
Colorado	Yes	D & F—follow Fed.
Connecticut	Yes	D & F—follow Fed. LLCs treated as partnerships are generally subject to a $250 business entity tax.
Delaware	Yes	D & F—treated as partnership except as otherwise treated for Fed.
District of Columbia	Yes	D & F—treated as partnership except as otherwise treated for Fed.
Florida	Yes	D & F—for corporation income tax, follow Fed; state has no personal income tax.
Georgia	Yes	D & F—treated as partnership except as otherwise treated for Fed.
Hawaii	Yes	D & F—follow Fed.
Idaho	Yes	D & F—follow Fed.
Illinois	Yes	D & F—follow Fed.
Indiana	Yes	D & F—follow Fed.
Iowa	Yes	D & F—follow Fed.

STATE	LAW AUTHORIZES LLC FORMATION?	STATE INCOME TAX TREATMENT (1)
Kansas	Yes	D & F—treated as partnership except as otherwise treated for Fed.
Kentucky	Yes	D & F—subject to corporate income tax for tax years starting on or after 1-1-2005 and before 1-1-2007. Eff 1-1-2007, subject to limited liability entity (LLE) tax.
Louisiana	Yes	D & F—follow Fed.
Maine	Yes	D & F—treated as partnership except as otherwise treated for Fed.
Maryland	Yes	D & F—follow Fed.
Massachusetts	Yes	D & F—follow Fed.
Michigan	Yes	D & F—follow Fed.
Minnesota	Yes	D & F—follow Fed.
Mississippi	Yes	D & F—follow Fed.
Missouri	Yes	D & F—follow Fed.
Montana	Yes	D & F—follow Fed.
Nebraska	Yes	D & F—follow Fed.
Nevada	Yes	State has no income tax.
New Hampshire	Yes	D & F—follow Fed.
New Jersey	Yes	D & F—treated as partnership except as otherwise treated for Fed.
New Mexico	Yes	D & F—follow Fed.
New York	Yes	D & F—follow Fed.
North Carolina	Yes	D & F—follow Fed.
North Dakota	Yes	D & F—follow Fed.
Ohio	Yes	D & F—follow Fed.
Oklahoma	Yes	D & F—follow Fed.
Oregon	Yes	D & F—follow Fed.
Pennsylvania	Yes	D & F—follow Fed.
Rhode Island	Yes	D & F—follow Fed.
South Carolina	Yes	D & F—follow Fed.
South Dakota	Yes	State has no income tax.
Tennessee	Yes	D & F—subject to Tennessee franchise/excise tax unless a specific exemption under Tennessee law applies.
Texas	Yes	State has no income tax. (LLCs are subject to corporation franchise tax.)
Utah	Yes	D & F—follow Fed.
Vermont	Yes	D & F—follow Fed.
Virginia	Yes	D & F—follow Fed.
Washington	Yes	State has no income tax.
West Virginia	Yes	D & F—follow Fed.
Wisconsin	Yes	D & F—follow Fed.
Wyoming	Yes	State has no income tax.

NOTES to chart ¶222-D (corresponding to numbers in parentheses in the chart):

(1) Many states that follow Fed income tax treatment of LLCs diverge from the Fed entity classification scheme by allowing single member LLCs (SMLLCs) to be classified as partnerships.

INCOME APPORTIONMENT ELEMENTS

¶223 Multistate operations. This chart shows the factors—property, sales or receipts, payroll, and the other components—states use to fix taxable net income of multistate businesses. Also shown are specific items of income directly allocated according to state rules, rather than apportioned.

➳ **WHAT TO DO→** Use this chart to find areas where profits are highest and taxes lowest. Then check ¶ 224—¶ 226-A on how to achieve tax saving by location and placement of sales headquarters, inventory, and other property, and assignment of personnel.

	FACTORS OF APPORTIONMENT FRACTIONS				ITEMS SEPARATELY ALLOCATED	SEPARATE ACCOUNTING ALLOWED?
STATE Col. A	Property Col. B	Receipts Col. C	Payroll Col. D	Others Col. E (27)	Col. F (43)	Col. G (68)
ALA.(6,9)	Yes	Yes	Yes	(32,33)	(44-48)	Yes(68)
ALASKA(6,9)	Yes	Yes	Yes	(32)	(44-48)	Yes
ARIZ.(6)	Yes	Yes(15)	Yes		(44-48)	Yes
ARK.(6,9)	Yes	Yes(15)	Yes	(30,32)	(44-48)	Yes
CALIF.(6,9)	Yes	Yes(15)	Yes	(30)	(44-48)	Yes
COLO.(6,9)	Yes	Yes	No		(63)	Yes
CONN.	Yes	Yes(15,16)	Yes	(30,32)	Yes	
DEL.	Yes	Yes	Yes	(33)	(44-46,48,52,55)	Yes(68)
D.C.(6,9)	Yes	Yes	Yes	(30,32)	(44-48)	Yes(68)
FLA.(4)	Yes(12)	Yes(14)	Yes(24)	(30,32)	(44-48)	Yes
GA.(10)	Yes(10)	Yes(10)	Yes(10)	(30-32)	(45,48,50)	Yes
HAW.(6,9)	Yes	Yes	Yes	(32)	(44-48,73)	Yes
IDAHO(6,9)	Yes	Yes(15)	Yes	(30)	(44-48)	Yes(68)
ILL.	No	Yes	No	(30,32)	(44-48)	Yes
IND.(6,11)	Yes(77)	Yes(21)	Yes(77)		(44-48)	Yes
IOWA	No	Yes	No	(29,32)	(44-48)	Yes
KAN.(6,9)	Yes	Yes	Yes	(30,32, 42)	(44-48)	Yes
KY.(6)	Yes	Yes(15)	Yes	(32)	(44-46,48)	Yes
LA.	Yes	Yes(17)	Yes	(30,32)	(44-48,54)	Yes(68)
ME.(5,8)	No	Yes	No	(32)	(66)	Yes
MD.	Yes	Yes(15)	Yes	(71)		Yes(69)
MASS.	Yes	Yes(15)	Yes		(47)	Yes
MICH.(2,9)	No(22)	Yes(22)	No(22)	(30,32,39)	(62)	Yes
MINN.(9)	Yes(3)	Yes(3)	Yes(3)	(74)	(70)	Yes
MISS.	Yes	Yes(13)	Yes	(31,32)	(44-48)	(75)
MO.(9)	Yes	Yes	Yes	(30,32)	(44-48)	Yes
MONT.(6,8,9)	Yes	Yes	Yes		(44-48)	Yes
NEB.	No	Yes(18)	No	(33)		Yes(68)
N.H.(6)	Yes	Yes(20)	Yes	(33)		No
N.J.	Yes	Yes(15)	Yes		(44-47)	No
N.M.(6,9)	Yes	Yes(15)	Yes	(32,38)	(44-48)	No
N.Y.(10)	No(10)	Yes(10)	No(10)	(34)	(44,47,48)	(67,68)
N.C.	Yes	Yes(15)	Yes	(30,32)	(44-48,50)	Yes(68)
N.D.(6,7,9)	Yes	Yes	Yes	(42)	(44-48)	Yes
OHIO	Yes	Yes(23)	Yes	(32,35)	(64)	Yes(68)
OKLA.(2)	Yes	Yes(53)	Yes	(32)	(44-48)	Yes
ORE.(6,8,9)	Yes	Yes(15)	Yes	(30,32)	(44-48)	Yes
PA.(2)	Yes(19)	Yes(19)	Yes(19)	(40)	(44-48)	Yes
R.I.	Yes	Yes	Yes	(30)	(73)	(67)
S.C.	Yes	Yes(17)	Yes	(36)	(45-48,51, 55,58,59)	Yes
TENN.(2)	Yes	Yes(26)	Yes	(30,32)	(44-48)	Yes
UTAH(6,8,9)	Yes	Yes(76)	Yes		(44-48)	Yes

STATE Col. A	FACTORS OF APPORTIONMENT FRACTIONS Property Col. B	Receipts Col. C	Payroll Col. D	Others Col. E (27)	ITEMS SEPARATELY ALLOCATED Col. F (43)	SEPARATE ACCOUNTING ALLOWED? Col. G (68)
VT.	Yes	Yes(15)	Yes	(33)	(44-46,60)	Yes
VA.(2)	Yes	Yes(15)	Yes	(30-33)	(47)	Yes
W.Va.(7)	Yes	Yes(15)	Yes	(32)	(44-48,65)	Yes
WIS.(4,8)	Yes(12,41)	Yes(14,41)	Yes(24,25,41)	(28-30,32)	(58,61)	Yes

Notes to chart ¶ 223 (corresponding to numbers in parentheses in chart):

(1) Domestic corporations and residents cannot allocate.

(2) Mich.—Until 12-31-2007, Single business tax allocation and apportionment rules are patterned after UDITPA rules. Okla.—Allocation and apportionment provisions are similar to UDITPA provisions. Pa.—Allocation and apportionment formula follows UDITPA formula. Tenn; Va.—Provisions similar to UDITPA have been adopted.

(3) Minn.—11% (9.5% for tax yrs. begun during 2008) of property percentage, 78% (81% for 2008) of sales percentage, and 11% (9.5% for 2008) of payroll percentage. Entire income of unitary business is apportioned. For tax years starting after calendar year 2006, state is phasing in single-factor apportionment formula based solely on sales factor. Sales-factor percentage in formula increases by 3% and property and payroll factors each decrease by 1.5% each year in the period 2007-2013. Sales factor is 100% of formula in 2014 and later.

(4) Disallows equally weighted 3-factor formula.

(5) Me.—Eff for tax yrs. starting on or after 1-1-2007, single factor (sales/receipts) formula applies.

(6) Uniform Div. of Income for Tax Purposes Act (UDITPA) is substantially adopted.

(7) Applies only to corporations.

(8) Only for corporations and nonresident individuals.

(9) State has adopted Multistate Tax Compact (MTC), including 3-factor formula. Taxpayer may elect to allocate by 3-factor formula. However, the equally weighted 3-factor formula cannot be elected in Calif. (see footnote (15) for exception), Mich., Minn., and Ore.

(10) In Ga., single-factor formula based solely on sales/receipts starts to phase in in tax year 2006 and is fully in effect in tax year 2008. In N.Y., phase-in of single-factor receipts formula began in 2006 and is fully effective for tax yrs. beginning in and after 2007.

(11) Foreign corps. don't consider out-US factors (property-sales-payroll).

(12) Factor represents 10% of formula.

(13) Sole factor only for retailing, renting, servicing & merchandising

(14) Factor is 80% of formula.

(15) Sales factor is double-weighted; in VT eff on and after 1-1-2006. In Ida., sales factor is evenly weighted for electric and telephone cos. In NM, eff for tax yrs. starting before 1-1-2011, mfrs, with current yr. tax exceeding past yr's tax, or with sum of current yr. payroll plus property factors exceeding sum of such factors for their 1st tax yr. starting after 12-31-90, can elect double-weighted sales factor. In Calif., taxpayers with over 50% of gross business receipts from S&L activities, banking or financial business activities, or extractive or agricultural business must use equally-weighted 3-factor formula. In Mass., mfg. corps. use 100% of sales factor alone. In Mass., qualified defense corps. can elect 100% sales factor instead of slide-in timetable above. Eff from and after 12-31-2007, but applying retroactively to tax years starting from and after 12-31-2006, Ariz. allows certain corporations to use an alternative formula that further enhances the sales factor and reduces the payroll and property factors of the apportionment formula if they meet certain requirements.

(16) Sole factor for most manufacturers, broadcasters, and other businesses.

(17) In La., for tax years starting on or after 1-1-2006, a single sales-factor formula must be used by taxpayers whose net apportionable income to La. is derived primarily from manufacturing or merchandising; for tax years starting before 1-1-2006, those taxpayers had to use a 3-factor formula in which the sales factor was double-weighted. In S.C., taxpayers whose principal business in S.C. is manufacturing or sales, distribution, or dealership of tangible personalty use double-weighted sales factor.

(18) Sole factor in Neb. for unitary businesses.

(19) In Pa., sales factor is 70%, property factor is 15%, and payroll factor is 15%.

(20) Sales factor is double-weighted (denominator 4).

(21) In Ind., single sales factor method is being phased in: for tax yrs starting after 12-31-2006 and before 1-1-2008, use product of sales factor multiplied by 3 (denominator 5); for tax yrs starting after 12-31-2007 and before 1-1-2009, use product of sales factor multiplied by 4.67 (denominator 6.67); for tax yrs starting after 12-31-2008 and before 1-1-2010, use product of sales factor times 8 (denominator 10); for tax yrs starting after 12-31-2009 and before 1-1-2011, use product of sales factor times 18 (denominator 20); for tax yrs starting after 12-31-2010, use sales factor. For tax yrs starting before 1-1-2007, sales factor was 200% (denominator 4).

(22) Mich.—Until 12-31-2007, single business tax sales factor is 90%, property factor 5%, and payroll factor 5%. Spun-off corps. can elect to calculate sales factor by alternative formula. Denominators for payroll, property, and sales factors for foreign persons include only US payroll, property, and sales. Eff 1-1-2008, Mich. business tax uses single-factor sales only apportionment with no payroll or property factors.

Notes to chart ¶ 223 (corresponding to numbers in parentheses in chart): (continued)

(23) In Ohio, sales factor is 60% of formula, property is 20%, and payroll is 20%.
(24) Factor is 10% of formula.
(25) Payroll factor replaces cost factor.
(26) Tenn.—Sales factor is 200% and denominator is 4.
(27) For state adoption of apportionment regulations for specific industries; like airlines, contractors, railroads, and trucking, see ¶ 226-B.
(28) Manufacturers' costs.
(29) For businesses other than manufacture or sale of tangible personalty, Dir. may make rules.
(30) Special provisions apply to some or all carriers.
(31) Special provisions for construction cos.
(32) Special provisions for specialized businesses (for example, air carriers, utility, oil & gas, insurance, financial and service businesses, telecommunications, etc.).
(33) Such other factors as tax dept. deems applicable.
(34) Investment income and capital; investment income and capital separately treated.
(35) Use net worth (Ohio) allocation if producing greater percentage than average of Col. B, C and D.
(36) Single factor (gross receipts) formula for income other than from mfg., producing, collecting, processing, buying, selling, distributing, or dealing in tangible personalty.
(37) Wages not a separate factor for sellers but part of mfr.'s production cost factor.
(38) Operating expenses.
(39) Special provisions for small in-state sales.
(40) Special provisions for transportation, pipeline, natural gas and water transportation cos.
(41) Transition to single sales factor starts in 2006 and is completed in 2008.
(42) Kan.—Elect 2 factors (property-sales) if payroll factor exceeds average of such factors by 200%.
(43) In the absence of a unitary business relationship, dividends and other passive investment income cannot be apportioned as business income under the U.S. Supreme Court decision in the *Allied Signal* case, (1992) 112 SCt 2251, unless the income arises from an operational function rather than an investment function.
(44) Capital gains (not in La., except in regular course of business); in N.Y., from investment capital; in Pa., "gains."
(45) Rents.
(46) Royalties (in S.C. limited to tangibles).
(47) Dividends (in Mass., & NJ not included in tax base; in N.Y., from investment capital; in Ohio, special rules apply.
(48) Interest (not in La. if from loan business); in N.Y., from investment capital and bank accounts treated as investment capital.
(49) Special rules apply to life insurance cos.
(50) Gain on sale of assets not connected with business.
(51) Income from personal services.
(52) Income from sale of realty. In Del., DC also, gain from of sale of tangible personalty.
(53) Okla.—Sales factor is double weighted for corporations with initial investment or expansion investment cost of at least $200 million.
(54) Income from construction, repairs and similar services.
(55) Gain or loss on realty sale.
(56) Net income of certain manufacturing or processing enterprises.
(57) Farm income.
(58) Gain or loss from intangibles (other than from inventory sales in Wis.).
(59) Investments in subsidiaries, not included in base.
(60) Income from any trade, business, all in-state.
(61) Nonbusiness income or loss from rental and royalties from or sales of tangibles follow property situs; income or gains from intangibles earned by personal holding co. (IRC §1542 as of 12-31-74) are allocated to taxpayer's residence.
(62) Single business tax allows deduction from base: dividends, interest, royalties and certain capital losses.
(63) If electing MTC method, items (43) thru (47) are allocated.
(64) Ohio—Net nonbusiness income allocable.
(65) IRC §(a) and (b) gains from sales of natural resources in-state if nonbusiness income (W.Va.).
(66) All income is apportioned, but see footnote (43) above (Me.).
(67) No specific provision. N.Y.—Combined reporting required for some affiliated entities with substantial intercorporate transactions.
(68) Separate accounting, if allowed, may require official approval.
(69) Denied to unitary businesses.
(70) Income not from trade or business.
(71) Special provisions for manufacturers, carriers, airlines, rental businesses, banks, and movie and TV industry (Md.).
(73) Gain on sale or exchange of an air or water pollution control facility on which amortization has been deducted (Haw.).
(74) Minn.—Banks, athletic teams, investment companies, air carriers, mail order businesses. For tax years starting in calendar year 2007 and later, state is phasing in single-factor apportionment formula for financial institutions based solely on receipts factor. See note (3).

Notes to chart ¶ 223 (corresponding to numbers in parentheses in chart): (continued)

(75) Miss.—Law supporting separate accounting has been repealed. Regulation allowing it has not been revoked.

(76) Utah lets taxpayers elect to use double-weighted sales factors for tax yrs starting on or after 1-1-2006. Once made, election is binding for 5 tax yrs.

(77) In Ind., single sales factor method is being phased in (see note (21)); property and payroll factors are not used for tax yrs starting after 12-31-2010.

RECEIPTS—HOW MEASURED

¶224 Receipts allocation and apportionment. The numerator of a receipts or sales factor is generally the value of business done by a corporation, measured by sales within the state. Chart below lists determinants that states use to make up the receipts numerator. "X" indicates influential elements that make receipts local, not out-of-state.

STATE Col. A (1)	OFFICE WHERE NEGOTI-ATED Col. B	PROPER-TY AT TIME OF ORDER Col. C	RECEIPT OR AC-CEPTANCE OF ORDER Col. D	DELIVERY PLACE Col. E	SHIPMENT ORIGIN Col. F	OTHER Col. G
ALA.				X(15)	X(22,23)	X(30,36)
ALASKA				X	X(22,23)	X(30)
ARIZ.				X	(47)	X(30,36)
ARK.				X(16)	X(22,23)	X(34)
CALIF.				X(12)	X(22,23)	X(30,36)
COLO.(4)				X(17)	X(26)	X(31,42)
CONN.				X		X(29,43)
DEL.				X(12)		X(29)
D.C.				X(15)	X(22,23)	X(30,36)
FLA.				X(15)		X(30,31,36)
GA.				X(12)		
HAW.				X(16)	X(22,23)	X(30,36)
IDAHO				X(16)	X(22,23)	X(30,36)
ILL.				X(16)	X(25)	X(30,36,27)
IND.				X(16)	X(22,23)	X(30,36)
IOWA				X(12,15)		
KAN.				X(16)	X(22,23)	X(30,36)
KY.				X(16)	X(22)	X(30,36)
LA.				X		
ME.				X(16)	X(22,23)	X(30,36,55)
MD.				X(16)		X(45)
MASS.				X(9)		X(10)
MICH.				X(16)	(47)	X(14,30,36,54)
MINN.(4)				X		X(28)
MISS.				X(16,37)	X(22,23,37)	
MO.(4)			X(11)	X	X	X(32)
MONT.				X(16)	X(22,23)	X(30,36)
NEB.(52)				X(16)	X(22,23)	X(30,36)
N.H.				X(16)	X(22,23)	X(30,36)
N.J.				X		X(29,36)
N.M.				X(16)	X(22,23)	X(30,36)
N.Y.				X		X(29,31,40,48-51)
N.C.				X(18)		X(29,33)
N.D.				X(16)	X(22,23)	X(30,36)
OHIO				X(18)		X(5)
OKLA.				X(16)	X(22,23)	
ORE.				X	X(22,23)	X(30,36)
PA.				X		X(30,36)
R.I.				X(20)		X(29,31,46)
S.C.				X(12)		X(30,35,36)

STATE Col. A (1)	OFFICE WHERE NEGOTI-ATED Col. B	PROPER-TY AT TIME OF ORDER Col. C	RECEIPT OR AC-CEPTANCE OF ORDER Col. D	DELIVERY PLACE Col. E	SHIPMENT ORIGIN Col. F	OTHER Col. G
TENN.				X(38)	X(22)	X(30,36)
UTAH	X(6)			X(16)	X(22,23)	X(30,36)
VT.		X(8)	X(8)	X(18)	X	X(29,30,36)
VA.(2)				X(20)	X	X(30,36)
W.VA.				X(16)	X(22,23)	X(30,36)
WIS.	X(6)			X(16)	X(22,23,24)	X(53)

Notes to chart ¶ 224 (corresponding to parenthetical numbers in chart):

(1) For member states of Multistate Tax Compact, see ¶ 223.
(2) Limited to sales connected with US business and if income is Fed taxable.
(3) Not for mfrs. principally in wholesaling. Special rules for financial institutions.
(4) Multistate Tax Compact rules can be elected instead of rules shown. Minn. disallows option.
(5) Ohio—Influential factors: Amount of use in the state and benefit to the buyer; receipts attributable to nonbusiness income are excluded.
(6) Sales through or by in-state offices, agencies or branches and taxpayer not taxed in buyer's state. In Wisc., if goods shipped directly by 3rd party to buyer.
(7) Sales not negotiated or effected by agents or agencies chiefly at, connected with or sent out from business premises out-of-state.
(8) Property in-state on receipt or appropriation to order, or not at taxpayer's out-of-state business place when order received or accepted in-state.
(9) Destination rule; receipt by buyer
(10) Throwback rule: Selling taxpayer is not taxable in state where item is delivered and property is not sold by agent based out of state.
(11) One element of sale.
(12) Deliveries in-state, excluding deliveries for out-shipment. In S.C. except sales to U.S.
(13) Property (except beer, liquor, wine or tobacco products if buyer can sell only in state of domicile) received by buyer at point in-state (dock sales) regardless of FOB point or final destination (excluding deliveries to common carrier or foreign vessel for buyers out-of-state).
(14) In Mich., until 12-31-2007, for sales other than tangible personalty, receipts are attributable to Mich. for single business tax if derived from services performed for in-state planning, designing, or construction activities. Eff 1-1-2008, Mich. business tax sales from performance of services are in Mich. if recipient receives benefit of services in Mich.
(15) Or in-shipments, regardless of F.O.B. point or other sales condition. In Fla. except if made by common or contract carrier.
(16) Deliveries to buyer in-state (other than U.S.) and note (15) applies. In Mich., for both single business tax and Mich. business tax, no exclusion for U.S. and special rules for spun-off corporations.
(17) Note (15) applies and regardless of taxability of corporation in the state or foreign country where goods delivered or shipped. If electing MTC method, note (16) applies.
(18) Deliveries to buyer or designee in-state, excluding deliveries for out-shipments.
(19) Not in-shipments to qualified DISCs.
(20) Not in-shipments to FSCs.
(21) See Col. G entry for state.
(22) If purchaser is U.S. government. But excluded by Ore. if included by another income taxing or apportioning state or country or DC.
(23) If taxpayer is not taxable in purchaser's state. But excluded by Ore. if included by another income taxing or apportioning state or country or DC. Only included in Neb.
(24) Only 50% of tangible personalty sales under "throwback" rule is in numerator.
(25) Footnotes (22) and (23) apply. Out-shipments not local sales if from premises of person independently contracting with seller for printing of newspapers, periodicals or books.
(26) If electing MTC, notes (22) and (23) apply.
(27) Eff for tax yrs. ending on or after 12-31-2008, sales are in Ill. If purchaser is in Ill. or sale is otherwise attributable to Ill. marketplace.
(28) Receipts from leases or rentals of tangible personal property are in Minn. if property is used in Minn. Special rule applies for moving property.
(29) Receipts from sources in-state (in N.Y., receipts must be earned in N.Y.).
(30) For sale of intangibles, allocate in-state if income-producing (earnings-producing, in Tenn.) activity is in-state or footnote (36) applies. In Mich., until 12-31-2007, receipts from sales other than tangible personalty are attributable to Mich. See notes (14) and (54).

Notes to chart ¶ 224 (corresponding to parenthetical numbers in chart): (continued)

(31) Receipts from in-state services and rentals or royalties on property in or used in-state.
(32) All sales or business transacted in state and half transacted in and outside.
(33) Services in-state (in Miss. & N.C., if income-producing activities are in-state).
(34) If income producing activity is instate for nontangibles; if multistate, Ark. share is same formula percentage used in allocating income of year of sale.
(35) Personalty rentals not separately allocated.
(36) For sales other than sales of tangible personalty, state with largest share of costs of performance.
(37) Miss.—Law has been repealed, but regulation has not been revoked.
(38) Delivery to buyer in Tenn., except U.S. government.
(39) For intangibles and services allocate between states in ratio of local-to-local production costs (receipt of service benefits in Minn.).
(40) Sales of closed-circuit or CATV rights to events in-state (employee's performance as entertainers or artists); publishers' receipts from sale of advertising in newspapers or periodicals delivered in state.
(41) Note (38) applies but deliveries in foreign countries and sales to US for resale to foreign govts. are treated as taxable in buyer's state.
(42) Gain from intangibles sale, interest and dividends, if commercial domicile in state.
(43) Net gain from intangibles sale and interest if managed or controlled in state; gain from tangibles located in-state; note (31) also applies.
(44) Sales by or thru DISCs are excluded. Note (39) also applies.
(45) Special rules apply for contracting, intangibles, rentals, and capital gains.
(46) Net income from sale of noninventory, and capital assets, income from sale of securities or financial obligations. Notes (29) & (31) apply except "gross income" from such receipts are used.
(47) In Ariz. and Mich., "throwback rule" is repealed. Eff 1-1-2008, Mich. business tax has no "throwback rule."
(48) Receipts from sale of intangibles included in business capital and held for sale to customers in regular course of business if sale occurs in N.Y. or through taxpayer's N.Y. office.
(49) Receipts from sale of real property held for sale in regular course of business if located in N.Y.
(50) Certain receipts of security and commodity brokers participating in an underwriting syndicate.
(51) Receipts from transportation by omnibus allocable to mileage or time in N.Y.
(52) Neb.—If place of sale cannot be determined, exclude amount from both total Neb. sales and total sales in all jurisdictions.
(53) Wis.—Sales of services are Wisconsin sales if buyers receive the benefit of the services in the state.
(54) Mich.—Eff 1-1-2008, Mich. business tax has specific rules for sales from performance of services, loans secured by realty, interest from loans not secured by realty, gains from sales of loans not secured by realty, credit card receivables, sales of credit card or other receivables, loan servicing fees, and sales of securities and other assets from investment and trading activities. All other receipts not otherwise sourced under MBT must be sourced based on where the benefit to the customer is received or, if where the benefit to the customer is received cannot be determined, to the customer's location.
(55) Me.—Generally, receipts from performance of services are attributed to the state where the services are received. If the purchaser is the federal government or the receipts are otherwise attributable to a state in which taxpayer is not taxable, the receipts are attributable to Maine if a greater proportion of the income-producing activity is performed in Maine than in any other state based on costs of performance. Gross receipts from license, sale or other disposition of patents, copyrights, trademarks or similar items of intangible personal property are attributed to Maine if the property is used in Maine by the licensee or if the taxpayer's commercial domicile is in Maine and the taxpayer is not taxable in the state in which the property is used by the licensee. If the intangible personal property is used by the licensee in more than one state, the income is apportioned to Maine according to the portion of use in Maine, but if the purchaser or licensee is the federal government or the receipts are otherwise attributable to a state in which the taxpayer is not taxable, the receipts are attributable to Maine if a greater proportion of the income-producing activity is performed in Maine than in any other state based on costs of performance. Receipts from sale, lease, rental or other use of real property is sourced to Maine if the real property is located there. Receipts from the lease or rental of tangible personal property are attributed to Maine if the property is located there.

➾ **WHAT TO DO→** Use this chart to channel your selling operations away from high tax areas in favor of states with lower taxes. Because sales receipts are generally sourced to their destination for apportionment purposes, corporations engaged in the manufacturing business and selling in several states can reduce their "home state" tax liability by locating in a state with a weighted sales factor.

PAYROLL—HOW APPORTIONED

¶225 Payroll allocation and apportionment. In allocating and apportioning interstate income, the payroll attributed to a particular state carries as much weight as receipts in most states. In other states, payroll factor is diluted (not as much weight) by being included as one element of total costs of production, operations or business (see Col. C of chart). Broad categories that states use in computing the payroll factor: (1) office location; (2) time spent in-state; and (3) pay earned in-state. Special rules of some states are indicated in last column. Types of employees covered, and kinds of pay to be considered, are at ¶ 226.

➤ **IF "X" APPEARS→** in a particular column for indicated state, the pay of employees must be included in numerator of wage factor. For example, in Alaska include in numerator percentage of employee pay based on time spent in-state.

STATE Col. A (1)	OFFICE LOCATION Col. B	TIME SPENT IN-STATE (11) Col. C	COMPENSATION EARNED IN-STATE Col. D	OTHER Col. E
ALA.	X(10)		X(15,19,20)	
ALASKA	X(10)	X(12)	X(15,19,20)	
ARIZ.	X(10)		X(15,19,20)	X(24)
ARK.	X(10)		X(15,19,20)	
CALIF.	X(10)		X(15,19,20)	X(24)
COLO.(2)	X(10)		X(15,19,20)	
CONN.	X(10)		X(15,19,20)	
DEL.			X(16)	
D.C.	X(10)		X(15,19,20)	
FLA.	X(10)		X(15,19,20)	
GA.	X(10)		X(15,19,20)	
HAW.	X(10)		X(15,19,20)	
IDAHO	X(10)		X(15,19,20)	
IND.(30)	X(10)		X(15,19,20)	
KAN.	X(10)		X(15,19,20)	
KY.	X(10)		X(15,19,20)	
LA.		X	X	X(25)
ME.(28)				
MD.	X(10)		X(10,15,20)	
MASS.	X(10)		X(15,19,20)	
MICH.(29)				
MINN.	X(7)		X(7)	
MISS.(9)	X(10)		X(15,20)	
MO.(2)	X(10)		X(15,19,20)	
MONT.	X(10)		X(15,19,20)	
N.H.	X(10)		X(15,19,20)	
N.J.	X(10)		X(15,19,20)	X(27)
N.M.	X(10)		X(15,19,20)	
N.Y.(28)				
N.C.	X(10)		X(15,19,20)	
N.D.	X(10)		X(15,19,20)	
OHIO	X(10)		X(15,19,20)	X(24)
OKLA.		X(14)	X(22)	X(24)
ORE.	X(10)		X(15,19,20)	

STATE Col. A (1)	OFFICE LOCATION Col. B	TIME SPENT IN-STATE (11) Col. C	COMPENSATION EARNED IN-STATE Col. D	OTHER Col. E
PA.	X(10)		X(15,19,20)	
R.I.				X(26)
S.C.	X(5)		X(19)	
TENN.	X(10)		X(15,19,20)	
UTAH	X(10)		X(15,19,20)	
VT.	X(4,8)	X(13)	X(21)	X(23)
VA.	X(10)		X(15,19,20)	X(26)
W.VA.	X(10)		X(15,19,20)	
WIS.(29)				

Notes to chart ¶ 225 (corresponding to parenthetical numbers in chart):

(1) For member states of Multistate Tax Compact, see ¶ 223.
(2) As member state of Multistate Tax Compact, 3-factor formula (including payroll) may be elected.
(3) Manufacturing and business primarily in research and development allocate according to a special formula.
(4) Vt.—If chief headquarters.
(5) Employees chiefly working at or connected with (or sent out from) business place in state.
(6) If controlling office in state, employee returns to state periodically for business, and employer not taxable in employee's residence state.
(7) Minn.—if either employed in state or identified with (or accountable to) office in state.
(8) Vt.—See Cols. C, D, E if inequitable.
(9) Special rules for financial institutions.
(10) If part performance and controlling base in state, or residence in state.
(11) Applies to those working in and out of state.
(12) Alaska.—Seagoing personnel, use port days. Transportation workers, use working days.
(13) Vt.—If office factor inequitable, for employees paid on time basis.
(14) Okla.—Itinerant employees' (traveling salesmen) expenses on local-to-total time to further enterprise.
(15) If some of the service is performed in state and base of operations or control or individual's residence is in state.
(16) Del.—If employee within state.
(17) (Reserved).
(18) Miss.—Only for manufacturers and noncarrier pipelines.
(19) See Col. B footnote for state.
(20) Also service entirely in-state or having only incidentals out-of-state.
(21) Vt.—If office factor inequitable, see Col. E.
(22) Okla.—Compensation is pay for services to extent related to unitary business, but excludes officers' salaries, wages, other pay and administrative expense.
(23) Vt.—If office factor inequitable: salesmen on commission, on basis of business volume; compensation based on results achieved, on value of in-state services.
(24) Ariz., Calif., Ohio, Okla.—Transportation employees, mileage.
(25) La.—Salesmen, in-state sales.
(26) Connected with in-state activities or transactions.
(27) N.J.—Also if contributions not paid under unemployment compensation law of another state.
(28) Me., N.Y.—Payroll factor is eliminated for 2007 and later tax yrs.
(29) Mich., Wis.—Payroll factor is eliminated for 2008 and later yrs.
(30) Ind.—Payroll factor is eliminated for 2011 and later yrs.

PAYROLL—WHAT PAY IS APPORTIONED

¶226 Employees and compensation. Methods states use to assign payroll to interstate apportionment numerators are at ¶ 225. However, class of employees and type of pay making the payroll factors are also important.

Class of employees: The states use different rules for determining what pay is included in the numerator of the payroll fraction. The pay of "employees" is generally included in the numerator of the fraction. But whether the states consider officers, directors or independent agents within the covered class is shown in Columns B, C, and D.

Type of compensation: Numerators of most state fractions include "pay" or "compensation." Some states spell out in detail what's in the class, while all use catch-all class of "other" pay. Columns E, F, G, and H detail what the states expect you to consider for the payroll percentage.

	CLASS OF EMPLOYEE INCLUDED			TYPE OF COMPENSATION INCLUDED			
STATE Col. A (1)(2)	Officers Col. B	Directors Col. C	Indepen. Agents Col. D	Comm. Col. E	Bonuses Col. F	Board & Lodging Col. G	Other Col. H (24)
ALA.	X			X	X	(22,23)	X(26)
AK.	X		(14)	X	(18)	(22,23)	X(26)
ARIZ.	X			X	X	(23)	X(26)
ARK.	X			X	(19)	(23)	X(26)
CALIF.	X		(14)	X	X	(22)	X(26)
COLO.(3)	X		(14)	X	X	(22)	X(26)
CONN.	X						X(26)
DEL.	(8)				X		X(26)
D.C.	X		(10)	X	X	(22)	X(26)
FLA.	X			X	(19)	(22)	X(12,13,26)
GA.	X		(14)	X		(21)	X(26)
HAW.	X		(14)	X	(17)	(22)	X(26)
IDAHO	X		(14)		(19)	(22)	X(26)
IND.(31)	X		(14)	X	(19)	(22)	X(26)
KAN.	X		(14)	X	(19)	X	X(26)
KY.	X				X	(23)	X(26)
LA.	X				(19)		X(26)
ME.(29)							
MD.	X		(14)	X	X		X(26)
MASS.	(9)			X	(19)	(23)	X(20,26)
MICH.(5)							
MINN.	X						
MISS.				X	X	X	X(26)
MO.(3)	X		(14)	X	(19)	(22)	X(26)
MONT.	X			X	(18)	(23)	X(26)
N.H.	X(9)			X	X	X	X(26)
N.J.	X	(11)		X			X(25,26)
N.M.	X		(11)	X	(19)	(22)	X(26)
N.Y.(29)							
N.C.	(8)		(14)	X	(19)	(22)	X(26)
N.D.	X		(14)	X	(19)	(22)	X(26)
OHIO	X						X(28,30)
OKLA.	(8)			(16)	(16)	(23)	X(27)
ORE.	X		(14)	X	(19)	(22)	X(26)
PA.	(7)						X(26)
R.I.	X		(14)				X(24)
S.C.	(8)	(11)		X	(17)	(23)	X(26)
TENN.	X		(14)	X		X	X(26)
UTAH	X		(14)	X	(18)	X	X(26)
VT.	X			X	(18)		X(26)

STATE Col. A (1)(2)	CLASS OF EMPLOYEE INCLUDED Officers Col. B	Directors Col. C	Indepen. Agents Col. D	TYPE OF COMPENSATION INCLUDED Comm. Col. E	Bonuses Col. F	Board & Lodging Col. G	Other Col. H (24)
VA.	X			X	(19)	(23)	X(26)
W.VA.	(7)		(14)	X	(18)	(22)	X(26)
WIS.(5)							

FOOTNOTES to chart ¶ 226 (correponding to parenthetical numbers in chart):

(1) See column H and footnote (24).
(2) For member states of Multistate Tax Compact, see ¶223.
(3) As member of Multistate Tax Compact, 3-factor formula (including payroll) may be elected.
(4) (Reserved.)
(5) Mich., Wis.—Payroll factor is eliminated for 2008 and later yrs.
(6) For manufacturer-wholesalers & manufacturer-retailers only; pay for general-administrative functions or for nonbusiness-exempt income production is excluded. Special rules for financial institutions.
(7) Compensation paid to officers is subject to withholding and, by analogy, might be held to be allocable compensation.
(8) Pay to general executive officers is specifically excluded.
(9) No express exclusion for officers' salaries.
(10) Compensation only includes remuneration paid to employees.
(11) Specifically excluded. (For N.J., when acting in that capacity; not as employees).
(12) In Fla., compensation for research is excluded.
(13) In Fla., compensation paid to employees of a partnership are included to the extent of the taxpayer's interest in the partnership.
(14) Payments to independent contractors specifically excluded.
(15) Included if tax official OKs.
(16) Itinerant employees' (for example, traveling salesmen) expense.
(17) State withholding specifically covers bonuses so, by analogy, probably considered allocable compensation.
(18) Follows Fed inclusion in gross income.
(19) See Col. H and footnote (24).
(20) Certain amounts paid to employee-leasing companies and temporary services companies.
(21) State income tax may treat board and lodging (subsistence) as taxable compensation, and amounts may be considered allocable compensation.
(22) If "income" under IRC.
(23) See Col. H. and footnote (24).
(24) Catch-all classification, such as "other compensation," might be extended to embrace some of the preceding types of compensation.
(25) N.J.—Includes all compensation reportable to State Div. of Employment Security.
(26) "Compensation" means wages, salaries and any other form of remuneration paid to employees and officers for personal services (not directors' fees).
(27) Compensation is pay for services to extent related to unitary business, but excludes officers' salaries, wages and other pay.
(28) Motor carrier employee pay allocated in ratio of local-to-total mileage.
(29) Me., N.Y.—Payroll factor is eliminated for 2007 and later tax yrs.
(30) Ohio—Exclude remuneration to the extent it relates to nonbusiness income. Other exclusions apply.
(31) Ind.—Payroll factor is eliminated for 2011 and later yrs.

PROPERTY IN APPORTIONMENT NUMERATORS

¶226-A Property is a primary income producer. Generally, income-spreading formulas ''weigh-in'' the property factor at 33⅓% (some at 50%). Some states assign it no weight in allocation, such as Iowa, Mo., and Neb. But a 3-factor formula, which includes the property factor, can be elected; see note (8) for Mo. The chart shows *numerator elements* (values assigned to the taxing state). If an ''X'' appears in a column, that class or type of property is included in the formula.

State (22)	Col. A Owned Realty	Col. B Rented Realty	Col. C Owned Tangible Personalty	Col. D Rented Tangible Personalty	Col. E Goods In Transit	Col. F (7) Migratory Property
ALA.	X	X(2)	X	X(2)	X(23)	X(13)
ALASKA	X	X(2)	X	X(2)	X(23)	X(13)
ARIZ.(4)	X	X(2)	X	X(2,5)	(1)	X(13)
ARK.	X	X(2)	X	X(2)	(31)	(13)
CALIF.	X	X(2)	X	X(2)	X(23)	X(13)
COLO.	X	X(2)	X	X(2)	(1)	(1)
CONN.	X	X(2,17)	X	X(2,17)	(1)	(1)
DEL.(4)	X	X(2)	X	X(2)	(18)	(1)
D.C.	X	X(2)	X	X(2)	(1)	(1)
FLA.(32)	X	X(2)	X	X(2)	X	X
GA.	X	X(2)	X	X	(1)	(1)
HAW.(4)	X	X(2)	X	X(2)	X(18)	X(13)
IDAHO(4)	X	X(2)	X	X(2)	X(23)	X(13)
IND.(4,34)	X	X(2)	X	X(2)	X(23)	X(1)
KAN.	X	X(2)	X	X(2)	X(23)	X(13)
KY.(4,24)	X	X(2)	X	X(2)	(1)	X(13)
LA.(4)	X	(1)	X	(1)	(1,16)	X(14)
ME.(35)						
MD.(4)	X	X(2)	X	X(2)	(23)	(1)
MASS.(25)	X	X(2)	X	X(2)	(18)	(3)
MICH.(33)						
MINN.	X(21)	X(2,21)	X(21)	X(2,21)	(1)	(1)
MISS.(30)	X	X(2)	X	X(2)	X(23)	(1)
MO.(4,8)	X	X(2)	X	X(2)	X(23)	X(13)
MONT.(4)	X	X(2)	X	X(2)	X(23)	X(13)
N.H.	X	X(2)	X	X(2)	(1)	(1)
N.J.	X	X(2)	X	X(2)	X(10,11)	(1)
N.M.(4)	X	X(2)	X	X(2)	X(23)	X(13)
N.Y.(35)						
N.C.(4)	X	X(2,26)	X	X(2)	X(23)	X(13)
N.D.(4)	X	X(2)	X	X(2)	X(23)	X(13)
OHIO(24,29)	X	X(2,20)	X	X(2,20)	(1)	(1)
OKLA.(4)	X	X(2)	X	X(2)	(1)	X(14)
ORE.(4)	X	X(2)	X	X(2)	X(23)	X(13)
PA.(20)	X	X(2)	X	X(2)	(1)	(1)
R.I.	X	X(2)	X	X(2)	(1)	(1)
S.C.(4)	X	X(2)	X	X(2)	(1)	(1)
TENN.	X	X(2)	X	X(2)	(1)	(1)
UTAH(4)	X	X(2)	X	X(2)	X(23)	X(13)
VT.	X	X(2)	X	X(2)	(10-12)	(1)
VA.(5,9)	X	X(2)	X	X(2)	(1)	X(13)
W.VA.(4,28)	X	X(2,28)	X	X(2,28)	(1)	X(13)
WIS.(33)						

Footnotes to chart ¶ 226-A (corresponding to parenthetical numbers in chart):

(1) No specific provision.
(2) 8 times net annual rent.
(3) Mobile property's value is apportioned according to use in Mass. and use everywhere.
(4) If income from property is specifically allocated, nonallocable or exempt, exclude property from numerator.
(5) Property used is included.
(6) Specifically excluded.
(7) Carrier rules for rolling stock listed in absence of general rules.
(8) As member of Multistate Tax Compact, 3-factor formula (including property) may be elected.
(9) Applies to property owned-used or rented-used if connected with US business. Repealed: Exclusion property owned or rented if rentals or royalties specifically allocated.
(10) Goods in transit between out-of-state points included in denominator only.
(11) Goods in transit between in-state points included in numerator and denominator.
(12) Goods in transit between in-state and out-of-state points excluded from numerator and denominator.
(13) In numerator on percentage of time spent basis.
(14) In numerator on percentage of mileage basis.
(15) 3 times net annual rent. If electing MTC method, note (2) applies.
(16) Movable property in US customs-bonded warehouse or foreign trade zones in La. is excluded from factor.
(17) Royalties are excluded.
(18) Treated to be at destination.
(19) Rolling equipment on time spent, mileage or other basis.
(20) Property owned or rented must be used (1) in-state (numerator); (2) everywhere in tax period (demoninator).
(21) Rented and/or used in-state during tax period. U.S. property used is treated as owned by user.
(22) For member states of Multistate Tax Compact, see ¶ 223.
(23) In numerator (destination state).
(24) In-state pollution control facilities are excluded.
(25) "Real and tangible personalty" include leases and their improvements whether in or outside the state.
(26) Subrentals aren't deductible if "business income".
(27) Property for general—administrative functions & transportation equip. are excluded.
(28) Property limited to items reported on Sched. L. Fed 1120 plus realty and tangible personalty leased-used; leasehold improvements included at original cost.
(29) Excluding property used solely for qualified research.
(30) Special rules for financial institutions.
(31) Goods in transit between taxpayer's locations are considered to be at destinations. Goods in transit between buyer and seller included in denominator are included in numerator based on destination.
(32) In Fla., property used in research activities is excluded.
(33) Mich., Wis.—Property factor is eliminated for 2008 and later yrs.
(34) Ind.—Property factor is eliminated for 2011 and later yrs.
(35) Me., N.Y.—Property factor is eliminated for 2007 and later tax yrs.

Ownership and leaseholds. In building up the property fraction, some states concentrate on ownership (Cols. A and C). Others make rental property an integral part of the property fractions (Cols. B and D). Specialized types of property have a part in many property fractions, but it is not uncommon for state rules to ignore or eliminate such items as Columns E and F show.

MTC UDITPA REGS—STATE ADOPTION

¶226-B MTC UDITPA Regs—State Adoption. These charts show the states that have adopted the Multistate Tax Commission regulations on allocation and apportionment of income generally and for certain specialized businesses. The charts also show the states that have adopted the MTC's guidelines on P.L. 86-272—the 1994 version (Phase II) or only the 1993 version (Phase I). State MTC membership and project program participation is explained at ¶ 213.

	ALLOCATION & APPORTIONMENT		AIRLINE		CONTRACTOR	
State	**Formally**	**Informally**	**Formally**	**Informally**	**Formally**	**Informally**
Alabama	Yes		Yes		Yes	
Alaska	Yes		No	No	No	No
Arizona	Yes		No	No	No	No
Arkansas	Partially		No	No	No	No
California	Yes		No	No	Yes	
Colorado	Yes		Yes(1)		Yes	
Connecticut	No	No	No	No	No	No
Delaware	No	No	No	No	No	No
District of Columbia	No	Partially	No	No	No	No
Florida	No	(2)	No	No	No	No
Georgia	No	No	No	No	No	No
Hawaii	Yes		No	No	No	No
Idaho	Yes		Yes		Yes	
Illinois	No	No	No	No	No	
Indiana		Yes	No	No	No	No
Iowa	No	No	No	No	No	No
Kansas	Yes		Yes	No	No	
Kentucky	Yes		No	No	No	No
Louisiana	No	No	No	No	No	No
Maine	Yes(3)		No	No	No	No
Maryland	No	No	No	No	No	No
Massachusetts	No	No	No	No	No	No
Michigan	No	No	No	No	No	No
Minnesota	No		No	No	No	No
Mississippi	No	No	No	No	No	No
Missouri	Yes		Yes		Yes	
Montana	Yes		No	Yes	No	Yes
Nebraska	No		Yes		No	No
New Hampshire	No	No	No	No	No	No
New Jersey	No	No	No	No	No	No
New Mexico	Yes		Yes		Yes	
New York	No	No	No	No	No	No
North Carolina	No	No	No	No	No	No
North Dakota	Yes		Yes		No	No
Ohio	No	No	No	No	No	No
Oklahoma	No	(2)	No	No	No	No
Oregon	Yes		Yes		Yes	
Pennsylvania	(2)	(2)	No	No	No	No
Rhode Island	No	No	No	No	No	No
South Carolina	No	No	No	No	No	No
Tennessee	No	No	No	No	No	No
Utah	Yes		No	No	Yes	
Vermont	No	No	No	No	No	No
Virginia	No	No	No	No	No	No
West Virginia	No	No	No	No	No	No
Wisconsin	(2)	(2)	No	No	No	No

State	RAILROAD Formally	RAILROAD Informally	TRUCKING Formally	TRUCKING Informally	REVISED P.L. 86-272 GUIDELINES Formally	REVISED P.L. 86-272 GUIDELINES Informally
Alabama	Yes		Yes		Phase II(1)	
Alaska	No	No	No	No	No	No
Arizona	No	No	No	No	Phase II(1)	
Arkansas	Partially		No	No	Phase II	
California	Yes		No	Partially	Phase II(1)	
Colorado	Yes		Yes		Phase II	
Connecticut	No	No	No	No	Phase I(1)	
Delaware	No	No	No	No	No	No
District of Columbia	No	No	No	No	Phase I	
Florida	No	No	No	No	Phase I	
Georgia	No	No	No	No	No	No
Hawaii	No	No	No	No	Phase II	
Idaho	Yes		Yes		Phase II	
Illinois	No	No	No	No	Phase I	
Indiana	No	No	No	No	No	No
Iowa	No	No	No	No	No	No
Kansas	No	No	No	No	Phase I(1)	
Kentucky	Yes		No	No	No	No
Louisiana	No	No	No	No	Phase II	
Maine	No	No	No	No	No	Phase II(1)
Maryland	No	No	No	No	No	No
Massachusetts	No	No	No	No	No	No
Michigan	No	No	No	No	No	No
Minnesota	No	No	No	No	No	No
Mississippi	No	No	No	No	No	No
Missouri	Yes		Yes		Phase I	
Montana	No	Yes	No	Yes	Phase II	
Nebraska	No	No	No	No	No	No
New Hampshire	No	No	No	No	No	No
New Jersey	No	No	No	No	Phase II	
New Mexico	Yes		Yes		Phase II	
New York	No	No	No	No	No	No
North Carolina	No	No	No	No	No	No
North Dakota	Partially		Partially		Phase II	
Ohio	No	No	No	No	No	Phase II
Oklahoma	No	No	No	No	No	No
Oregon	Yes		Yes		Phase II(1)	
Pennsylvania	No	No	No	No	No	No
Rhode Island	No	No	No	No	Phase II(1)	
South Carolina	No	No	No	No	No	No
Tennessee	No	No	No	No	Phase I	
Utah	Yes		Yes		Phase II(1)	
Vermont	No	No	No	No	No	No
Virginia	No	No	No	No	No	No
West Virginia	No	No	No	No	No	No
Wisconsin	No	No	No	No	No	No

Footnotes to chart ¶ 226-B:

(1) With exceptions or additions.
(2) No formal adoption, but state's formula is similar to UDITPA; MTC regulations are adopted on a modified basis.
(3) However, Maine adopted a single-factor formula for tax yrs. beginning on or after 1-1-2007.

WAGE AND OTHER WITHHOLDING AND INFORMATION RETURNS

¶227 **Wages and other payments.** Chart below shows what wage withholding and information report states require. Information returns report wages. Information returns on dividends, interest, rents, and royalties are charted at ¶ 227-A. Wage withholding is usually limited to amounts paid employees.

Abbreviations in the table below have the following meaning:

A—Annually
AC—Accelerated
D—Daily
EFT—Electronic funds transfer
EM—Eight-monthly
M—Monthly
MR—Monthly Reconciliation
NBD—Next banking day
ND—Next day
Q—Quarterly
QM—Quarter-monthly
QR—Quarterly Reconciliation
PW—Partial weekly
R—Reconciliation
SA—Semi-annually
SM—Semi-monthly
SW—Semi-weekly
TM—Twice monthly
TP—Transmittal of payment (usually a customized coupon or voucher from a booklet)
TW—Transmittal of forms W-2
W—Weekly

Electronic funds transfer requirements are charted at ¶ 279.

WAGE AND OTHER WITHHOLDING RETURNS

State or City	Individual Form (Wage & Tax Statement)	Summary Form (Employer Returns)	Due Date
Alabama		A-6 (TP)	M
		A-1 (TP)	Q
	A-2 or W-2	A-3 (R)(TW)	Last day of Feb.
Alaska	No withholding	No information returns	
Arizona		A1-WP (TP)	SW
		A1-WP (TP)	M
		A1-QRT	Q
		A1-APR (TW)	Feb. 28
	W-2	A1-R (R)(TW)	Feb. 28
Arkansas		AR-941M (TP)	M
		AR-941A (TP)	A
	W-2	AR-3MAR (R)(TW)	Feb. 28
California (1)			
DE88(TP)	NBD		
		DE 88 (TP)	SW
		DE 88 (TP)	M
		DE 88 (TP)	Q
		DE 6	Q
	W-2	DE 7 (R)	Jan. 31
Colorado (1)		None (EFT)	W
		DR 1094 (TP)	M
		DR 1094 (TP)	Q
	W-2	DR 1093 (R)(TW)	Last day of Feb.
Connecticut		CT-WH (TP)	W
		CT-WH (TP)	M, Q
		CT-941 (R)	Q
	W-2	CT-W3 (R)(TW)	Last day of Feb.

WAGE AND OTHER WITHHOLDING RETURNS
(continued)

State or City	Individual Form (Wage & Tax Statement)	Summary Form (Employer Returns)	Due Date
Delaware		W-1A (TP)	EM
		W-1 (TP)	M
		W-1Q (TP)	Q
	W-2	W-3 (R)(TW)	Feb. 28
District of Columbia		FR-900 (TP)	M
		FR-900A (TP)	A
	W-2	FR-900B (R)	Jan. 31
		W-2T (TW)	Jan. 31
Fla.	No withholding	No information returns	
Georgia (1)		EFT	ND
		EFT	SW
		GA-V (TP)	M or Q
		G-7	Q or M
	W-2	G-1003-(TW)	Feb. 28
Hawaii (1)		EFT	SW
		HW-14	M
		HW-14	Q
		VP-IW (TP)	Q or M
	HW-2 or W-2	HW-3 (R)	Last day of Feb.
Idaho		910 (TP)	SM
		910 (TP)	M
		910 (TP)	Q
		956 (R)	A
	W-2	957-W (TW)	Last day of Feb.
Illinois		IL-501 (TP)	SW
		IL-501 (TP)	M
		IL-941	Q
	W-2	IL-W-3(R)	Feb. 28
Indiana		WH-1 (TP)	M
		WH-1 (TP)	Q
		WH-1 (TP)	SA
		WH-1 (TP)	A
	WH-18 or W-2	WH-3 (R)(TW)	Last day of Feb.
Iowa		eFile	SM
		eFile (TP)	M
		eFile (TP)	Q
	W-2	VSP(R)	Feb. 28
Kansas		KW-5 (TP)	QM
		KW-5 (TP)	SM
		KW-5 (TP)	M
		KW-5 (TP)	Q
		KW-5 (TP)	A
	W-2	KW-3 (R)(TW)	Last day of Feb.
Kentucky		EFT	ND
		K-1 (TP)	TM
		K-1 (TP)	M
		K-1 (TP)	Q
		K-3 (R)	A
	K-2 or W-2	42A806 (TW)	Jan. 31
Louisiana		L-1 (TP)	SM
		L-1 (TP)	M
		L-1 (TP)	Q
		L-1 (TP)	A
	L-2 or W-2	L-3 (R)	Feb. 28

WAGE AND OTHER WITHHOLDING RETURNS (continued)

State or City	Individual Form (Wage & Tax Statement)	Summary Form (Employer Returns)	Due Date
Maine (1)		900-ME (TP)	SW
		941/CNI-ME	Q
	W-2(16)	W-3 ME (R)(TW)	Feb. 28
Maryland (1)		EFT	3rd day after payroll
		MW-506 (TP)	M
		MW-506 (TP)	Q
		MW-506 (TP)	A
	MW-509 or W-2	MW-508 (R)(TW)	Feb. 28
Massachusetts		M-941W (TP)	Weekly
		M-942 (TP)	M
		M-941 (TP)	Q
		M-941D (R)	Q
		M-941A (TP)	A
	W-2	M-3 (TW)	Feb. 28
Michigan		EFT	SW
		Personalized (TP)	M
		Personalized (TP)	Q
	MI-W2 or W-2	165 (R)(TW)	Feb. 28
Minnesota		MW-5 (TP)	SW, M, Q
		(Electronic)	SW
		(Electronic)	M
		(Electronic)	Q
		(Electronic)	A
	W-2	(Electronic)	Feb. 28
Mississippi (1)		89-105 (COUPON)	M
		89-105 (COUPON)	Q
	W-2	89-140 (R)(TW)	Jan. 31
Missouri		MO941P (TP)	QM
		MO-941 (TP)	M
		MO941 (TP)	Q
		MO941 (TP)	A
	W-2	MOW3 (TW)	Last day of Feb.
Montana		MW-1 (TP)	SW
		MW-1 (TP)	M
		MW-1 (TP)	A
		MW3	A
	W-2	MW-3 (R)(TW)	Feb. 28
Nebraska		501 N (TP)	M
		941 N (TP)	Q, A
	W-2	W-3N (R)	Mar. 15
Nevada		No withholding	
New Hampshire		No withholding	
New Jersey		EFT	W
		NJ-500 (TP)	M
		NJ-927 (TP)	Q
	W-2	NJ-W-3 (R)	Feb. 28 or 29
New Mexico		CRS-1 (TP)	M
		CRS-1 (TP)	Q
		CRS-1 (TP)	SA
	W-2	RPD41072 (R)	Last day of Feb.

WAGE AND OTHER WITHHOLDING RETURNS
(continued)

State or City	Individual Form (Wage & Tax Statement)	Summary Form (Employer Returns)	Due Date
New York State	W-2	NYS-1 (TP)	AC
		NYS-45 (TP)(R)	Q
North Carolina (1)		NC-5P (TP)	SW
		NC-5	M, Q
	W-2	NC-3 (R)(TW)	Feb. 28
North Dakota		F-306 (TP)	Q, A
	W-2	F-307 (TW)	Feb. 28
Ohio		EFT	PW
		IT-501 (TP)	M
		IT-501 (TP)	Q
		IT-942 (R)	Q
		IT-941 (R)	Jan. 31
	IT-2 or W-2	IT-3 (TW)	Last day of Feb.
Oklahoma (1)		OW-9 (TP)	SW
		OW-9 (TP)	M
		OW-9 (TP)	Q
	W-2	(R) and (TW) not required	
Oregon		OTC (TP)	NBD, SW or M
		OTC	Q
		OQ	Q
	W-2 (37)	WR (R)	Feb. 28
Pennsylvania		eTides-PA-501(TP)	SM
		eTides-PA-501(TP)	M
		eTides-PA-W-3(TP)	Q
	W-2	eTides REV 1667 (R)(TW)	Jan. 31
Puerto Rico		499-R-1B	Q
		499-R-1A	M
		499-R-1A	SW
		499-R3	Jan. 31
	499 R-2/W-2PR or W-2	(R)(TW) or W-3 (R)(TW)	Jan. 31
Rhode Island (1)		RI-941D	D
		RI-941-QM	QM
		RI-941-M	M
		RI-941Q	Q
		RI-941A	A
	W-2	RI-W-3 (R)(TW)	Feb. 28
South Carolina (1)		EFT	SW
		WH-1601X (TP)	M or Q
		WH-1605 (R)	Q
	W-2	WH-1606 (R)	Last day of Feb.
South Dakota		No withholding	
Tennessee		No withholding	
Texas		No withholding	
Utah		TC-96M (TP)	M
		TC-96Q	Q
	W-2	TC-96Y	A
		TC-96 (R)(TW)	Feb. 28

WAGE AND OTHER WITHHOLDING RETURNS (continued)

State or City	Individual Form (Wage & Tax Statement)	Summary Form (Employer Returns)	Due Date
Vermont (1)		EFT	SW
		WH-431 (TP)	M
		WH-431 (TP)	Q
	W-2	WH-434 (R)(TW)	Feb. 28
Virginia		VA-15 (TP)	SW
		VA-5 (TP)	M
		VA-5 (TP)	Q
		VA-16(R)	Q
	W-2	VA-6 (R)(TW)	Feb. 28
Washington		No withholding	
West Virginia		WV/IT-101	M
		WV/IT-101	Q
		WV/IT-103	A
	IT-102 or W-2	WV/IT-103 (R)(TW)	Feb. 28
Wisconsin		WT-6 (TP)	SM
		WT-6 (TP)	M
		WT-6 (TP)	Q
		WT-7 (TP)	A
	W-2	WT-7 (R)(TW)	Jan. 31
Wyoming		No withholding	

NONWAGE INFORMATION RETURNS FOR PAYMENTS FOR SERVICES OF NONEMPLOYEES

State or City	Minimum Amount Required	Individual Form	Summary Form	Due Date
Alabama	$1,500	99 or Fed-1099-MISC	96 or Fed-1096, A-3 if withholding	Mar. 15, Feb. 28 if withholding
Alaska		No information returns		
Arizona	Any withholding	Fed-1099-MISC		Feb. 28
Arkansas	$2,500	1099-MISC	1096	Feb. 28
California	Over $1,500 to nonresident	592-B	592	Jan. 31
Colorado	Any withholding	1099-MISC	DR 1093	Feb. 28
Connecticut	$600	1099-MISC	CT-1096	Last day of Feb.
Delaware	$600	1099-MISC	W-3	Feb. 28/Mar. 31(online)
District of Columbia	$600	1099-MISC	1096	Feb. 28
Florida		No information returns		
Georgia	Any withholding	1099-MISC	G-1003	Last day of Feb.
Hawaii	$600	1099-MISC	N-196	Feb. 28
Idaho	$600	1099-MISC	96	Last day of Feb.
Illinois		If requested		
Indiana	Any withholding from nonresident	WH-18	W-3	Feb. 28
Iowa	$600	1099-MISC	e-file	Feb. 28
Kansas	$600	1099-MISC	electronic	Last day of Feb.

NONWAGE INFORMATION RETURNS FOR PAYMENTS FOR SERVICES OF NONEMPLOYEES (continued)

State or City	Minimum Amount Required	Individual Form	Summary Form	Due Date
Kentucky	Any withholding	1099-MISC	1096	Feb. 28
Louisiana		If requested		
Maine	Any withholding	1099-MISC		Quarterly
Maryland	$600	1099-MISC	MW 508	Feb. 28
Massachusetts	$600	1099-MISC	1096	Feb. 28
Michigan		If requested by Treas. Dept.		
Minnesota	$600	1099-MISC		Feb. 28
Mississippi	$600	1099	89-140	March 15
Missouri	$1,200	MO-99 1099-MISC	MO-96	Feb. 28
Montana	$600	1099-MISC	1096	Feb. 28
Nebraska	Any withholding	1099-MISC	W-3N	Mar. 15
Nevada		No Information Returns		
New Hampshire		No Information Returns		
New Jersey	Any amount	1099-MISC	NJ-W-3-UNC	Last day of Feb.
New Mexico		Not generally required		
New York State		No Information Returns		
North Carolina	$1,500	1099-MISC	NC-3	Feb. 28
North Dakota	$600	1099-MISC	307	Feb. 28
Ohio		No Information Returns		
Oklahoma	$750	500 or 1099-MISC	501 or 1096	Feb. 27
Oregon		Filing with IRS satisfies state		
Pennsylvania		Not generally required		
Puerto Rico	$500	480.6A	480.5	Feb. 28
Rhode Island	Any state withholding	1099-MISC	1096	Feb. 28
South Carolina	Any state withholding	1099-MISC	1096	Feb. 28
South Dakota		No Information Returns		
Tennessee		No Information Returns		
Texas		No Information Returns		
Utah	Any withholding	1099-MISC	TC-96R	Feb. 28
Vermont	Any services in-state by nonresident	1099-MISC	WH-434	Feb. 28
Virginia	Any withholding	1099-MISC	VA-6	Feb. 28
Washington		No Information Returns		
West Virginia	Any withholding	1099-MISC		Feb. 28
Wisconsin	$600	1099-MISC	WT-7	Feb. 28
Wyoming		No Information Returns		

FOOTNOTES to ¶ 227

(1) Withholding required on nonresident's sale of realty in-state (*Calif., Colo., Ga., Haw., Me., Md., Miss., Okla., R.I., S.C., Vt.*); in *N.C.* information return required from buyer on such sales. Withholding required on nonwage payments to nonresident aliens (*Okla.*), to nonresidents (*Calif., S.C.*), to undocumented workers (Ga.).

NONWAGE INFORMATION RETURNS

¶227-A Interest, dividends, rents-royalties and other payments. Below is a chart giving you a condensed picture of what information reports states expect. Information returns usually report dividends, interest, rents, royalties, and other determinable income payments (Fed 1099 series). The chart shows threshold amounts, the point at which your duty to report becomes a positive obligation, and annual filing dates. Threshold amounts for wages appear at ¶ 227.

Note: States not listed either do not impose personal income taxes or returns are not required. In some states special filing rules apply. Consult state tax officials for instructions.

STATE	DIVIDENDS	INTEREST	RENT-ROYAL	OTHER	RETURNS
ALA.	$1,500	$1,500(4)	$1,500	$1,500	Mar. 15
ALASKA	—Information Returns Not required—				
ARIZ.	—Same as Fed amounts—				
ARK.	(20)	(20)	$2,500(20)	$2,500(20)	Feb. 28
CALIF.	$10	$10	$600(21)	$600	Feb. 28
COLO.			(18)		Feb. 28
CONN.			$600(21)	$600(22)	Feb. 28
DEL.	—Information Return required, if Del. address—				
D.C.	$10	$10	$600	$600	Feb. 28
GA. (11)	$1,500	$1,500	$1,500	$1,500	Apr. 15
HAW.	$10	$10	$600	$600	Feb. 28
IDA.	$10	$10	$600	$600	Last day of Feb.
ILL. (17)	—Information Return Not Generally Required—				
IND. (2)	—Information Return Not Generally Required—				
IOWA	—Same as Fed amounts—				Last day of Feb.
KAN.	—Same as Fed amounts—				Last day of Feb. (9)
KY.	—Information Return Not Required—				
LA.	(15)	(15)	(15)	(15)	
ME.	$10	$10		$600	Feb. 28
MD.	(5)	(5)	(5)		
MASS.	$10(10)	$10(10)	$600(10)		Feb. 28
MICH.	—Only required on notice and demand of Treasury Department(23)—				
MINN.	—Only required on notice and demand of Revenue Commissioner—				
MISS.	$600	$600	$600	$600(16)	Mar. 15
MO.	$100	$100	$1200	$1200	Feb. 28
MONT.	$10	$10	$600	$600	Apr. 15
NEB.	—Information Returns Not Required—				
N.H.	—Information Return Not Required—				

STATE	DIVIDENDS	INTEREST	RENT-ROYAL	OTHER	RETURNS
N.J.	$1000	$1000	$1000	$1000	Feb. 15
N.M.	—Information Return Not Required—				
N.Y.	—Information Returns Not Generally Required—			(7)	Feb. 15
N.C.	(5)	(5)	(5)	(5)	Feb. 28
N.D.	(12)	(12)	(10)	(10)	Feb. 28
OHIO	—Information Return Not Required—				
OKLA.	(6)	(6)	$750(6)	$750(13)	Feb. 28
ORE.	—Same as Fed amounts—				
PA.	$10(25)	(26)	(26)	(26)	Feb. 28
R.I.	$100	$100	$100	$100	Feb. 28
S.C.	$200	$200	$1,200	$500(19)	Mar. 15
S.D.	—Information Returns Not Required—				
TENN.	—Information Return Not Required—				
TEX.	—Information Returns Not Required—				
UTAH	—Information Return Not Required—				
VT.	—Information Return Not Generally Required—				
VA.	—Information Return Generally Not Required (24)—				
WASH.	—Information Return Not Required—				
W.VA.				(8)	Feb. 28
WIS.	Not required	Not required	$600	$100	Mar. 15
WYO.	—Information Return Not Required—				

FOOTNOTES to chart ¶ 227-A (corresponding to numbers in parentheses):

(1) $100, patronage dividends, rebates or refunds. Annuities and profit sharing, $1000; foreign items, $1500.
(2) Ind.—Information returns that do not report withholding of Indiana adjusted gross or county income tax generally are not required to be submitted to the Department of Revenue. Certain forms must be kept for the statutory time period and made available on request.
(3) State law allows revenue commissioner discretion to adopt regulations requiring informational returns for these payments.
(4) Other than interest coupons payable to bearer.
(5) Not required if Fed Form 1099 filed.
(6) Okla.—Report can be required regardless of amount. $100 for corporations on interest and dividend payments; $10 for royalties.
(7) N.Y.—Information return required for annuities if tax is withheld; no threshold.
(8) Pensions and annuities.
(9) Copies of Fed returns required.
(10) Returns are required on same basis as for Fed income tax.
(11) $1,500 total payment to any one payee.
(12) Use Fed Form 1099. In N.D., file only if state income tax is withheld.
(13) Premiums, annuities, oil and gas bonuses, annuities, gambling winnings.
(14) Taxable annuities.
(15) Law sets amount at $1000. However, returns are required only on request of tax officials.
(16) Premiums, annuities and pensions.
(17) Ill.—Copies of Fed returns or other records of specified payments must be kept available for review. Partnerships, S corporations, and trusts required to withhold tax must report and remit withholdings by their return due date for the tax yr.
(18) Colo.—Persons required to file federal Form 1099 must file copy of the form with the Dept. of Taxes.
(19) Prizes and winnings.

FOOTNOTES to chart ¶ 227-A (corresponding to numbers in parentheses): (continued)

(20) Ark.—Returns may be required, regardless of the amount, for interest on bonds, mortgages, deeds of trusts, or other similar obligations of corporations, and dividends paid by corporations. Returns are not required for the payment of interest not subject to Ark. tax. The general dollar threshold for filing, if there is no Ark. income tax withheld, is $2500. If Ark. tax is withheld, a return is required regardless of the threshold amount.

(21) $10 for royalties.

(22) Conn.—Reporting is required if payment from Conn. Lottery is $600 or more; gambling winning is over $5,000; or pension and annuity distribution, military retirement payment, unemployment compensation to those who request withholding, or non-wage payment to athletes or entertainers is over $1,000.

(23) Mich.—Persons required to file federal Form 1099-MISC must file copy with state and city (if city income tax is imposed) by Jan. 31 or date required to file by IRC, whichever is later.

(24) Va.—Pass-through entities doing business in Va. or having income from Va. sources must file a return by Apr. 15. Eff 7-1-2007, pass-through entities required to withhold tax must furnish to nonresident owners a written statement showing: (1) the amount of their allocable Va. taxable income and whether or not distributed for federal income tax purposes to the such nonresident owners; (2) tax withheld as tax; and (3) any other information required by the Tax Commissioner. A copy of the written statements must be filed with the Va. return filed by the pass-through entity for the taxable yr. to which the distribution relates. The written statement must be furnished to each nonresident owner by the due date of the pass-through entity's return for the tax yr., including extensions of time for filing such return, or a later date allowed by the Commissioner.

(25) Pa.—Reporting is required for dividends or distributions on shares of stock or beneficial interest over $10.

(26) Information return is not required.

PERSONAL INCOME TAXES—RATES, EXEMPTIONS, REPORTS

¶228 **What you pay and when.** The chart below is designed for persons with interests in any state having a personal income tax or an unincorporated business tax. In highly condensed form, the main factors for calculating tax are given, as well as dates for reports and payments.

The first column shows tax rates in a state. **Second column** details personal exemptions and dependency credits for single and spouses; also, for special cases such as blind, seniors, etc. **Third column** shows whether you pay balance all at once or installments. **Fourth column** shows last day for returns without penalty for calendar yr. taxpayers.

Extensions. Filing extensions are explained at ¶ 239.

➺ **WARNING**→ Payment by electronic funds transfer may be required. See ¶ 279.

STATE AND RATE	EXEMPTIONS(1)	HOW PAID	FILING DEADLINE(28)
ALA. 2% 1st $500; 4% next $2,500; 5% over $3,000 (5,76)	S-$1,500; M-$3,000; H-$3,000; D-$300 (30)	Full	4-15 (15th of 4th mo.)
ALASKA No personal income tax.			
ARIZ. 2.59% 1st $10,000; 2.88% next $15,000; 3.36% next $25,000; 4.24% next $100,000; 4.54% on over $150,000 (5,93)	S-$2,100; M-$4,200; H-$4,200; D-$2,300; B-$1,500 A-$2,100 (7)	Full	4-15 (15th of 4th mo.)
ARK. 1st $3,599, 1%; next $3,600, 2.5% (less $53.99); next $3,600, 3.5% (– $125.98); next $7,200, 4.5% (– $233.97); next $12,100, 6% (– $503.96); $30,100 and over, 7% (– $804.95) (5,6,68)	S-$22; M-$44; H-$44; D-$22; B-$22; A-$22 (2,6,26)	Full	4-15 (3-1/2 mo. after close of fiscal yr.)
CALIF. 1% 1st $13,654; 2% next $18,716; 4% next $18,718; 6% next $19,832; 8% next $18,708; 9.3% over $89,628 (6,22,24,54)	S-$94; M-$188; H-$94; D-$294; B-$94; A-$94; (2,6,74)	Full	4-15 (15th of 4th mo.)
COLO. 4.63% (4,5,24,63)	$3,400 per Fed exemption (45)	Full	4-15 (15th of 4th mo.)
CONN. 3% 1st $10,000; 5% on the balance (49,52)	S-$12,750 (55); M-$24,000; H-$19,000; no dependent exemption (99)	Full	4-15 (15th of 4th mo.)

STATE AND RATE	EXEMPTIONS(1)	HOW PAID	FILING DEADLINE(28)
***DEL.** No tax 1st $2,000; 2.2% next $3,000; 3.9% next $5,000; 4.8% next $10,000; 5.2% next $5,000; 5.55% next $35,000; 5.95% over $60,000 (80)	$110 (2,48)	Full	4-30 (30th of 4th mo.)
D.C. 4% 1st $10,000; 6% next $30,000; 8.5% over $40,000 (5,25,98)	S-$1,500; M-$3,000; H-$3,000; D-$1,500; B-$1,500; A-$1,500 (8)	Full	4-15 (15th of 4th mo.)
FLA. No personal income tax.			
GA. 1% 1st $750; 2% next $1,500; 3% next $1,500; 4% next $1,500; 5% next $1,750; 6% over $7,000 (62)	S-$2,700; M-$5,400; D-$3,000	Full	4-15 (15th of 4th mo.)
HAW. 1.4% 1st $4,800; 3.2% next $4,800; 5.5% next $9,600; 6.4% next $9,600; 6.8% next $9,600; 7.2% next $9,600; 7.6% next $24,000 7.9% next $24,000 8,25% over $96,000 (5,24,47)	$1,040 per Fed exemption; A-$1,040; B-$7000 (38)	Full	4-20 (20th of 4th mo.)
IDAHO 1.6% 1st $1,198; 3.6% 1st $1,198; 4.1% next $1,198; 5.1% next $1,199; 6.1% next $1,198; 7.1% next $2,995; 7.4% next $14,977; 7.8% over $23,963. Plus $10 excise (5,6,12,24,54)	$3,400 per Fed exemption (45)	Full	4-15 (15th of 4th mo.)
ILL. 3%(61)	$2,000 per Fed exemption (64); A-$1,000; B-$1,000	Full	4-15 (15th of 4th mo.)
***IND.** 3.4%	S-$1,000; M-$2,000 D-$1,000 (95); B-$1,000 (95); A-$1,000 (95)	Full	4-15 (15th of 4th mo.)
***IOWA** 0.36% 1st $1,343; 0.72% next $1,343; 2.43% next $2,696; 4.5% next $6,715; 6.12% next $8,058; 6.48% next $6,715; 6.8% next $13,430; 7.92% next $20,145; 8.98% over $60,435 (6,84)	S-$40; M-$80; H-$80; D-$40; B-$20; A-$20 (2)	Full	4-30 (30th of 4th mo.)

STATE AND RATE	EXEMPTIONS(1)	HOW PAID	FILING DEADLINE(28)
***KAN.** 3.5% 1st $30,000; 6.25% next $30,000; 6.45% on balance (44)	$2,250 per Fed. exemption	Full	4-15 (15th of 4th mo.)
***KY.** 2% 1st $3,000; 3% next $1,000; 4% next $1,000; 5% next $3,000; 5.8% next $67,000; 6% over $75,000 (5)	S-$20; M-$40; D-$20; A-$40; B-$40; E-$20 (2)	Full	4-15 (15th of 4th mo.)
LA. 2% 1st $12,500; 4% next $12,500; 6% over $25,000 (54,58)	S-$4,500; M-$9,000, H-$9,000; D-$1,000 (27)	Full	5-15 (15th of 5th mo.)
ME. 2% 1st $4,750; 4.5% next $4,700; 7% next $9,500; 8.5% over $18,950 (3,6,54,80)	$2,850 per Fed exemption	Full	4-15 (15th of 4th m)
***MD.** 2% 1st $1,000; 3% 2nd $1,000; 4% 3rd $1,000; 4.75% over $3,000 (5,57)	$2,400 per Fed exemption; A-$1,000; B-$1,000	Full	4-15 (15th of 4th mo.)
MASS. Part A income (interest, dividends) 5.3% (5); Part A income (short-term capital gains) 12% (5); Part B income (wages and trade or business income) 5.3% (5); Part C (long-term capital gains) 5.3%.	S-$4,125; M-$8,250; H-$6,375; D-$1,000; A-$700; B-$2,200 (10,29)	Full	4-15 (15th of 4th mo.)
***MICH.** 4.35% (25,34)	$3,400 per Fed exemption (6,77)	Full	4-15 (15th of 4th mo.)
MINN. 5.35% 1st $31,150; 7.05% next $92,600; 7.85% over $123,750 (6,37,80).	$3,400 per Fed exemption(45)	Full	4-15 (15th of 4th mo.)
MISS. 3% 1st $5,000; 4% next $5,000; 5% over $10,000	S-$6,000; M-$12,000; H-$9,500; D-$1,500; A-$1,500; B-$1,500	Full	4-15 (15th of 4th mo.)
***MO.** 1.5% 1st $1,000; 2% next $1,000; 2.5% next $1,000; 3% next $1,000; 3.5% next $1,000; 4% next $1,000; 4.5% next $1,000; 5% next $1,000; 5.5% next $1,000; 6% over $9,000 (5,80)	S-$2,100; H-$3,500; M-$4,200; D-$1,200; A-$1,000	Full	4-15 (15th of 4th mo.)

STATE AND RATE	EXEMPTIONS(1)	HOW PAID	FILING DEADLINE(28)
MONT. 1st $2,500, 1%; next $1,900, 2% (less $25 tax); next $2,200, 3% (– $69 tax); next $2,400, 4% (– $135 tax); next $2,600, 5% (– $225 tax); next $3,300, 6% (– $341 tax); on over $14,900, 6.9% (– $475 tax) (6,24,51)	S-$2,040; M-$4,080; D-$2,040; B-$2,040; A-$2,040 (6,70)	Full	4-15 (15th of 4th mo.)
NEB. 2.56% 1st $2,400; 3.57% next $15,100; 5.12% next $9,500; 6.84% over $27,000 (41,54)	$111 per Fed exemption (2,6,11)	Full	4-15
NEV. No personal income tax.			
N.H. 5%(13,25)	S-$2,400; M-$4,800; B-$1,200; A-$1,200 (56)	Full	4-15 (15th of 4th mo.)
N.J. 1.4% 1st $20,000; 1.75%, on next $30,000; 2.45% next $20,000; 3.5% next $10,000; 5.525% next $70,000; 6.37% next $350,000; 8.97% over $500,000 (67)	S-$1,000; M-$2,000 (9); A-$1,000 (15); B-$1,000; D-$1,500; E-$1,000 (15)	Full	4-15 (15th of 4th mo.)
N.M. 1.7% 1st $5,500; 3.2% next $5,500; 4.7% next $5,000; 5.3% over $16,000; (5,24,50,54,80)	$3,400 per Fed exemption (31,45)	Full	4-15 (15th of 4th mo.)
***N.Y.** 4% 1st $8,000; 4.5% next $3,000; 5.25% next $2,000; 5.9% next $7,000; 6.85% over $20,000; (79,80)	$1,000 per dependent only	Full	4-15 (15th of 4th mo.)
N.C. 6% on 1st $12,750; 7% on next $47,250; 7.75% next $60,000; 8% over $120,000 (18)	$2,500 per Fed exemption (Fed inflation adjustment is reduced) (87)	Full	4-15 (15th of 4th mo.)
N.D. 2.1% on 1st $31,850; 3.92% next $45,250; 4.34% next $83,750; 5.04% next $188,850; 5.54% on over $349,700 (6,42)	$3,400 per Fed exemption (45)	Full	4-15 (15th of 4th mo.)
***OHIO** 0.649% 1st $5,000; 1.299% next $5,000; 2.598% next $5,000; 3.247% next $5,000; 3.895% next $20,000; 4.546% next $40,000; 5.194% next $20,000; 6.031% next $100,000; 6.555% over $200,000 (23)	S-$1,450; M-$2,900; D-$1,450 (75,83)	Full	4-15 (15th of 4th mo.)

STATE AND RATE	EXEMPTIONS(1)	HOW PAID	FILING DEADLINE(28)
OKLA. 0.5% 1st $1,000; 1% next $1,500; 2% next $1,250; 3% next $1,150; 4% next $2,300; 5% next $1,500; 5.65% over $8,700 (86)	$1,000 per Fed exemption; B-$1,000; A-$1,000 (86)	Full	4-15 (15th of 4th mo.)
***ORE.** 5% 1st $2,850; 7% next $4,300; 9% over $7,150 (5,6,24,54,65)	$165 (2,6,46)	4 Instal. (19)	4-15 (15th of 4th mo.)
***PA.** 3.07%	None (66)	Full	4-15 (15th of 4th mo.)
R.I. 1st $31,850, 3.75%; next $45,250, 7%; next $83,750, 7.75%; next $188,850, 9%; on over $349,700, 9.9% (90)	$3,400 per Fed (45)	Full	4-15
S.C. 1st $2,630, 2.5%; next $2,630, 3% (less $13 tax); next $2,630, 4% (-$66 tax); next $2,630, 5% (-$144); next $2,630, 6% (-$250); on over $13,150, 7% (-$381) (5,6,21)	$3,400 per Fed exemption (45)	Full	4-15 (15th of 4th mo.)
S.D. No personal income tax.			
TENN. 6% on income from stock-bonds(16)	S-$1,250; M-$2,500; A(16)	Full	4-15 (15th of 4th mo.)
TEXAS No personal income tax.			
UTAH 2.3% 1st $1,000; 3.3% next $1,000; 4.2% next $1,000; 5.2% next $1,000; 6% next $1,500; 6.98% on over $5,500 (6,24,59)	75% of Fed exemption amount (33,45)	Full	15th of 4th mo.
VT. 3.6% 1st $31,850; 7.2% next $45,250; 8.5% next $83,750; 9% next $188,950; 9.5% over $349,700 (6,20,43,72)	$3,400 per Fed exemption (45)	Full	4-15 (15th of 4th mo.)
VA. 2% 1st $3000; 3% next $2000; 5% next $12,000; 5.75% over $17,000	S-$900 (69); M-$1,600; B-$800; A-$800	Full	5-1 (15th of 4th mo.)
WASH. No personal income tax.			
W.VA. 3% 1st $10,000; 4% next $15,000; 4.5% next $15,000; 6% next $20,000; 6.5% over $60,000 (5,32)	$2,000 per Fed exemption (32)	Full	4-15 (15th of 4th mo.)

STATE AND RATE	EXEMPTIONS(1)	HOW PAID	FILING DEADLINE(28)
WIS. 4.6% lst $12,680; 6.15% next $12,680; 6.5% next $164,850; 6.75% over $190,210 (6,17)	$700 per Fed exemption (100)	Full	4-15 (15th of 4th mo.)
WYO. No personal income tax.			

FOOTNOTES to chart ¶ 228 (corresponding to parenthetical numbers in chart):

*Local taxes may also be imposed on income, earnings or payrolls.

(1) S-Single; M-Married; H-Head of family or household; T-Taxpayer; D-Dependents (each); B-Blind (additional); A-Age 65 min. (additional); E-Education—student dependent.

(2) Credit against tax.

(3) *Me.*—Rates shown are for 2007 and apply to single and separate return filers. 2007 rates for joint returns: 2% 1st $9,500; 4.5% next $9,450; 7% next $19,000; 8.5% over $37,950. 2007 rates for household heads: 2% 1st $7,150; 4.5% next $7,050; 7% next $14,250; 8.5% over $28,450. Min. tax equal to 27% of adjusted Fed tentative min. tax.

(4) *Colo.*—3.47% alternative min. tax.

(5) Optional tax table may be used.

(6) Indexing used. In Utah, indexing used for tax yrs. starting after 2008.

(7) *Ariz.*—Added $2,300 deduction per person age 65 or older if taxpayer pays for medical care or 1/4 cost of maintaining that person in care institution or home (like nursing, supervisory, or adult foster) and payments exceed $800. Married persons claiming at least one dependent can deduct $6,300 instead of the $4,200 figure. Resident taxpayer can deduct $10,000 (instead of the $2,300 dependent exemption and the added $2,300 senior medical care exemption) per parent or ancestor of a parent age 65 or older who needs help with daily living activities, lives in taxpayer's home for entire tax yr., and has over 1/2 of support and maintenance costs paid by taxpayer.

(8) *D.C.*—Amounts shown are for 2007. Amounts eff 1-1-2008: S-$1,675; M-$3,350; D-$1,675; B-$1,675; A-$1,675. For 2009 and later, amounts are adjusted for inflation.

(9) *N.J.*—Includes domestic partner and civil union partner.

(10) *Mass.*—Applied first against Part B taxable income.

(11) *Neb.*—Personal exemption credit for tax yr. 2007.

(12) *Ida.*—Rates shown are for tax yr. 2006 for single persons and married persons filing separately. Rates for 2006 for married persons, surviving spouses, and household heads: 1.6% on the 1st $2,396; 3.6% on the next $2,396; 4.1% next $2,396; 5.1% next $2,398; 6.1% next $2,396; 7.1% next $5,990; 7.4% next $29,954; 7.8% over $47,926.

(13) Base: interest, dividends.

(14) For taxpayer or dependent.

(15) *N.J.*—$1000 additional exemption for disabled taxpayer or spouse, or taxpayer or spouse age 65 or older.

(16) *Tenn.*—Based on income from stocks and bonds (not deposit certificates). 65 or older exempt if income not over $16,200 if single; $27,000 if married.

(17) *Wis.*—Rates shown are for married filing jointly for 2007. 2007 rates for married filing separately: 4.6% on 1st $6,340; 6.15% next $6,340; 6.5% next $82,420; 6.75% over $95,100. 2007 rates for single persons and heads of households: 4.6% on 1st $9,510; 6.15% next $9,510; 6.5% next $123,630; 6.75% over $142,650.

(18) *N.C.*—Rates shown apply to singles for 2007. Spouses filing jointly and surviving spouses for 2007: 6% 1st $21,250; 7% next $78,750; 7.75% next $100,000; 8% over $200,000. Spouses filing separately for 2007: 6% on 1st $10,625; 7% next $39,375; 7.75% next $50,000; 8% over $100,000. Household heads for 2007: 6% 1st $17,000; 7% next $63,000; 7.75% next $80,000; 8% over $160,000. For 2008, the highest bracket is taxed at 7.75%.

(19) Min. total tax installments: Ore., over $25.

(20) *Vt.*—Rates shown are for single for 2007. 2007 rates for joint filers, civil union joint filers, or qualifying widow(er): 3.6% 1st $53,150; 7.2% next $74,650; 8.5% next $67,350; 9% next $153,950; 9.5% over $349,700. 2007 rates for married (or civil union) filing separately: 3.6% 1st $26,575; 7.2% next $37,675; 8.5% next $33,675; 9% next $76,925; 9.5% over $174,850. 2007 rates for head of household: 3.6% 1st $42,650; 7.2% next $67,450; 8.5% next $68,250; 9% next $171,350; 9.5% over $349,700.

(21) *S.C.*—Rates shown are for 2007.

FOOTNOTES to chart ¶ 228 (corresponding to parenthetical numbers in chart): (continued)

(22) *Calif.*—Rates shown are for tax yr. 2007 and apply to joint filers and surviving spouses with dependents; single and married persons filing separately use same rates but on half of income brackets for joint return filers. For 2007, unmarried household heads pay 1% on 1st $13,662; 2% next $18,708; 4% next $9,358; 6% next $9,915; 8% next $9,357; 9.3% over $61,000. Surcharge of 1% is imposed on taxable income exceeding $1 million. Alternative minimum tax is 7%.

(23) Ohio—Rates shown are for 2007. 2008 rates: 0.618% 1st $5,000; 1.236% next $5,000; 2.473% next $5,000; 3.091% next $5,000; 3.708% next $20,000; 4.327% next $40,000; 4.945% next $20,000; 5.741% next $100,000; 6.24% over $200,000.

(24) Alternative tax for small businesses under the Multistate Tax Compact is at ¶ 222, note (37).

(25) Unincorporated business: *D.C.*—same rates as corporation income tax (see ¶ 222). *Mich.*—see ¶ 222 (Single Business Tax and Mich. Business Tax). *N.H.*—see ¶ 222 (Business Profits Tax and Business Enterprise Tax).

(26) *Ark.*—Amounts shown are for 2006.

(27) *La.*—Amounts shown are combined exemption & standard deduction amounts.

(28) Dates in parentheses indicate filing date after end of fiscal year.

(29) *Mass.*—Amounts shown are for 2007.

(30) *Ala.*—dependent exemption for tax yrs. starting after 12-31-2006: $1,000 if AGI $20,000 or less; $500 if AGI over $20,000 but less than $100,000; $300 if AGI $100,000 or more.

(31) If adopting special needs child, $2,500 exemption ($1,250 for spouses filing separately).

(32) *W.Va.*—Rates for married persons filing separately are same but applied to one-half of above income brackets. Surviving spouse gets added exemption for 2 yrs. after year of spouse's death. $500 if dependent (resident) with zero Fed exemption.

(33) *Utah.*—Add exemption equal to 75% of IRC personal exemption for each handicapped dependent.

(34) Mich.—Rate is 3.9% until 9-30-2007; 4.35% eff. 10-1-2007 to 9-30-2011; 4.25% eff. 10-1-2011 to 9-30-2012; 4.15% eff. 10-1-2012 to 9-30-2013; 4.05% eff. 10-1-2013 to 9-30-2014; 3.95% eff. 10-1-2014 to 9-30-2015; and 3.9% eff. 10-1-2015 and after.

(35-36) (Reserved).

(37) *Minn.*—Rates shown are for tax yr. 2007 and apply to joint filers and surviving spouses. 2007 rates for single persons (figures in parentheses apply to household heads): 5.35% 1st $21,310 ($26,230); 7.05% next $48,680 ($79,180); 7.85% over $69,990 ($105,410). 2007 rates for married filing separately: 5.35% 1st $15,580; 7.05% next $46,300; 7.85% over $61,880. *Added taxes:* 6.4% of alternative min. taxable income over regular tax.

(38) *Haw.*—Blind, deaf or disabled—$7,000, instead of personal exemption.

(39–40) (Reserved.)

(41) *Neb.*—Rates shown are for single persons for 2007 and later. Rates for 2007 and later for spouses filing jointly and surviving spouses: 2.56% 1st $4,800; 3.57% next $30,200; 5.12% next $19,000; 6.84% over $54,000. Rates for 2007 and later for married filing separately: 2.56% 1st $2,400; 3.57% next $15,100; 5.12% next $9.500; 6.84% over $27,000. Rates for 2007 and later for heads of households: 2.56% 1st $4,500; 3.57% next $23,500; 5.12% next $12,000; 6.84% over $40,000. Added tax equal to 29.6% of Fed alternative min. tax and Fed tax on premature or lump sum distributions from qualified retirement plans.

(42) *N.D.*—Rates shown are for singles for 2007. 2007 rates for married filing jointly and surviving spouses: 2.10% on 1st $53,200; 3.92% on next $75,200; 4.34% on next $67,350; 5.04% on next $153,850; 5.54% over $349,700. 2007 rates for married filing separately: 2.10% on 1st $26,600; 3.92% on next $37,650; 4.34% on next $33,675; 5.04% on next $76,925; 5.54% over $174,850. 2007 rates for heads of household: 2.10% on 1st $42,650; 3.92% on next $67,500; 4.34% on next $68,250; 5.04% on next $171,350; 5.54% over $349,700.

(43) *Vt.*—Added 5% tax on resident's interest earned on bank deposits out-of-state if other state taxes Vt. bank deposits but exempts deposits in-state.

(44) *Kan.*—Rates shown apply to joint returns. Rates for all others: 3.5% 1st $15,000; 6.25% next $15,000; 6.45% on balance.

FOOTNOTES to chart ¶ 228 (corresponding to parenthetical numbers in chart): (continued)

(45) Fed. exemption amount, as adjusted for inflation, for 2007 is $3,400. Personal exemption is phased out as follows for 2007: 2/3 of the amount of 2% per $2,500 of adjusted gross income over $234,600 for joint filers and surviving spouses; $195,500 for household heads; $156,400 for single persons; 2/3 of the amount of 2% per $1,250 over $117,300 for spouses filing separately. Fed. exemption amount, as adjusted for inflation, for 2008 is $3,500. Personal exemption is phased out as follows for 2008: 1/3 of the amount of 2% per $2,500 of adjusted gross income over $239,950 for joint filers and surviving spouses; $199,950 for household heads; $159,950 for single persons; 1/3 of the amount of 2% per $1,250 over $119,975 for spouses filing separately.

(46) *Ore.*—Amount shown is for 2007. Added $165 credit for severely disabled taxpayer or handicapped child.

(47) *Haw.*—Rates shown are for joint filers and surviving spouses for 2007. Single and married filing separately pay same rates for corresponding yrs. as for joint filers but on one-half of applicable income bracket amounts. Special rates for household heads. Capital gains alternative tax, 7.25%.

(48) *Del.*—$110 credit per Fed personal exemption, plus extra $110 credit if age 60 or over.

(49) *Conn.*—Rates shown are for single and spouse filing separately. Rates for spouses filing jointly and surviving spouses: 3% 1st $20,000; 5% on the balance. Rates for heads of household: 3% 1st $16,000; 5% on the balance.

(50) *N.M.*—Rates shown are for single persons for 2007. 2007 rates for spouses filing jointly and surviving spouses: 1.7% 1st $8,000; 3.2% next $8,000; 4.7% next $8,000; 5.3% over $24,000. 2007 rates for spouses filing separately: 1.7% 1st $4,000; 3.2% next $4,000; 4.7% next $4,000; 5.3% over $12,000. 2007 rates for heads of households: 1.7% 1st $8,000; 3.2% next $8,000; 4.7% next $8,000; 5.3% over $24,000.

(51) *Mont.*—Rates shown are for 2007.

(52) *Conn.*—Alternative min. tax equals lesser of 19% of adjusted Fed tentative min. tax or 5.5% of adjusted Fed alt. min. taxable income. *General credit:* Taxpayers can get credit ranging from 75% to 1% of taxable income based on income bracket and filing status.

(53) Sales tax credit given on basis of income and exemptions (not blind or age).

(54) Income-splitting allowed: on joint returns tax is twice that due if taxable income cut in half.

(55) *Conn.*—S-$13,000 for 2008 tax yr.

(56) *N.H.*—Added $1,200 for disabled and unable to work (under 65 yrs.).

(57) *Md.*—Added local tax is imposed in all counties and Baltimore City.

(58) Tax is computed according to tax tables.

(59) *Utah.*—Rates shown apply to single and spouse filing separately. Rates for spouses filing jointly and household heads are same as shown except income brackets are doubled. For tax yrs. starting in 2007 and later, taxpayers can use either the tax rate bracket schedules or a flat 5% tax rate subject to limited deductions and credits.

(60) (Reserved).

(61) *Ill.*—Added tax imposed on partnerships, trusts, and S corporations—replacing personalty tax (¶ 222).

(62) *Ga.*—Rates shown are for single persons. Jointly filing spouses and heads of household rates: 1% on the first $1,000; 2% on the next $2,000; 3% next $2,000; 4% next $2,000; 5% next $3,000; 6% on the amount over $10,000. Spouses filing separately pay rate ranging from 1% on 1st $500 to 6% on over $5000 (equal to 1/2 of bracket amounts for jointly filing spouses).

(63) *Colo.*—Rate can be temporarily reduced to 4.5% if state budget meets certain targets.

(64) No personal exemption if Ill. base income exceeds the exemption amount and the person is claimed as dependent on another's Fed return.

(65) *Ore.*—Rates shown are for single and spouse filing separately for tax yr. 2007. 2007 rates for spouses filing jointly, heads of household, and qualifying widows or widowers: 5% 1st $5,700; 7% next $8,600; 9% over $14,300.

(66) Special credits for "low income" taxpayers.

(67) *N.J.*—Rates shown are for joint returns, household heads, and surviving spouses. Rates for single and spouse filing separately: 1.4% 1st $20,000; 1.75% next $15,000; 3.5% next $5,000; 5.525% next $35,000; 6.37% next $425,000; 8.97% over $500,000.

(68) Rates shown are for 2006.

(69) *Va.*—Single exemption: $900 before 1-1-2008; $930 after 12-31-2007.

(70) *Mont.*—Amounts shown are for 2007. Disabled dependent child, $4,080.

(71) (Reserved.)

(72) *Vt.*—Special capital gains tax applies to land transfers: If land held less than 6 years—tax ranges from 80% (if gain is 200% or more and land held less than 4 months) to 5% (if gain less than 100% and land held 5 to 6 years).

FOOTNOTES to chart ¶ 228 (corresponding to parenthetical numbers in chart): (continued)

(73) (Reserved.)

(74) *Calif.*—Amounts shown are for 2007 tax yr. Personal exemption credits are reduced if Fed AGI exceeds certain levels.

(75) *Ohio*—Exemption amounts shown are for 2006, as adjusted for inflation.

(76) *Ala.*—Rates shown apply to single, household head, and married filing separately; rates are the same for married filing jointly except income brackets are doubled.

(77) *Mich.*—Exemption amount shown is for 2007. Plus $2,200 if paraplegic, quadriplegic, hemiplegic, totally disabled, blind, deaf, elderly, or receiving at least 50% adjusted gross as unemployment compensation. $1,500 exemption for person who can be claimed as dependent of another. $1,500 exemption for working dependent with $1,500 adjusted gross (max.). Also can deduct from Fed AGI $600 times number of dependents who are children less than 19 yrs. old on last day of tax yr. Eff. for tax yrs. after 2007, additional $250 for each qualified disabled veteran and their dependents.

(78) (Reserved.)

(79) *N.Y.*—Rates shown apply to single and married filing separately. Rates for household heads: 4% on the first $11,000; 4.5% on the next $4,000; 5.25% next $2,000; 5.9% next $13,000; 6.85% on the amount over $30,000. Rates for joint filers or surviving spouses: 4% on the first $16,000; 4.5% on the next $6,000; 5.25% next $4,000; 5.9% next $14,000; 6.85% on the amount over $40,000. 6% min. tax on IRC §157 tax preference items.

(80) Tax on IRC § 1402(e) lump sum distributions imposed at 25% of Fed tax in Iowa; 13% in Kan.; 15% in Me; 10% in Mo. Special computation for Del., Minn., N.M., and N.Y. taxes.

(81–82) (Reserved.)

(83) *Ohio.*—Tax credit for spouses (jointly)—each with $500 (min.) adjusted gross (not interest, dividends, rents, capital gains): $25,000 (max.) adjusted gross, 20%; $25,001–50,000, 15%; $50,000–75,000, 10%; over $75,000, 5%. Max. credit, $650. Added $20 credit per personal or dependency exemption.

(84) *Iowa.*—Rates shown apply to 2007 tax yr. Alternative min. tax is 6.7%, which is equal to 75% of the max. tax rate.

(85) (Reserved.)

(86) *Okla.*—Rates shown are for 2007 for singles and spouses filing separately. Rates for 2007 for jointly filing spouses, household heads, or surviving spouses: 0.5% on the first $2,000; 1% on the next $3,000; 2% next $2,500; 3% next $2,300; 4% next $2,400; 5% next $2,800; 5.65% on the amount over $15,000. *Nonresident aliens,* 8%. *Added exemption* for elderly, $1,000 if Fed AGI not over $15,000 for single filers, $25,000 for joint return filers, $12,500 for spouses filing separately, and $19,000 for household heads. (Okla.)

(87) *N.C.*—Amount shown applies for 2007 if Fed adjusted gross income is less than these amounts: single, $60,000; joint filers, $100,000; married filing separately, $50,000; household head, $80,000. If Fed adjusted gross is not less than those amounts, exemption is adjusted per formulas.

(88-89) (Reserved.)

(90) *R.I.*—Rates shown apply to single filers for 2007. 2007 rates for married filing jointly and surviving spouses: 1st $53,150, 3.75%; next $75,350, 7%; next $67,350, 7.75%; next $153,850, 9%; on over $349,700, 9.9%. 2007 rates for married filing separately: 1st $26,575, 3.75%; next $37,675, 7%; next $33,675, 7.75%; next $76,925, 9%; on over $174,850, 9.9%. 2007 rates for household heads: 1st $42,650, 3.75%; next $67,450, 7%; next $68,250, 7.75%; next $171,350, 9%; on over $349,700, 9.9%.

(91–92) (Reserved.)

(93) *Ariz.*—Rates shown apply to single and married filing separately for 2007. Rates for 2007 are the same for married filing jointly and household heads except income bracket amounts are doubled.

(94) (Reserved.)

(95) *Ind.*—Added $1,500 per dependent child. Added $500 if aged and filer (or joint filers) earn(s) less than $40,000 annually.

(96-97) (Reserved.)

(98) D. C.—Rates shown are for 2006 and later.

(99) *Conn.*— Exemption for single persons is $12,625 in 2005 and 2006, $12,750 in 2007, $13,000 in 2008, $13,500 in 2009, $14,000 in 2010, $14,500 in 2011, $15,000 in 2012 and later. Exemption amounts are reduced per formulas when adjusted gross income exceeds specified amounts.

(100) In *Wis.*, $700 personal exemption is allowed per Fed exemption and added $250 personal exemption is allowed per taxpayer or spouse age 65 or older.

PERSONAL INCOME—ALTERNATIVE MINIMUM TAX

¶228.5 **Alternative minimum tax.** This chart shows the states that impose an alternative minimum tax (AMT) on personal income taxpayers preference items, the rates levied, and the taxable basis.

➾ **WARNING→** Many taxing states use Fed alternative minimum taxable income as basis or computation starting point. States that adopt current IRC have adopted 2004 Fed law changes (¶ 221), including the higher Fed AMT rates (for example, Connecticut) by piggybacking on the Fed AMT tentative tax.

State	AMT Imposed?
Alabama	No
Alaska	No personal income tax.
Arizona	No
Arkansas	No
California	Yes, at 7% of modified Fed alternative minimum taxable income.
Colorado	Yes, at 3.47% of modified Fed alternative minimum taxable income.
Connecticut	Yes, at the lesser of 19% of adjusted Fed tentative minimum tax or 5.5% of adjusted Fed alternative minimum taxable income.
Delaware	No
District of Columbia	No
Florida	No personal income tax.
Georgia	No
Hawaii	No
Idaho	No
Illinois	No
Indiana	No
Iowa	Yes, at 6.7% of Iowa alternative minimum taxable income.
Kansas	No
Kentucky	No
Louisiana	No
Maine	No, but has a state minimum tax in an amount equal to the excess of tentative minimum tax over regular income tax (2).
Maryland	No
Massachusetts	No
Michigan	No
Minnesota	Yes, at 6.4% of modified Fed alternative minimum taxable income.
Mississippi	No
Missouri	No
Montana	No
Nebraska	Yes, at 29.6% of modified Fed alternative minimum tax.
Nevada	No personal income tax.
New Hampshire	No personal income tax.
New Jersey	No
New Mexico	No
New York	Yes, at 6% of N.Y. minimum taxable income.
North Carolina	No
North Dakota	No
Ohio	No
Oklahoma	No
Oregon	No
Pennsylvania	No
Rhode Island	Yes, at the excess of the tentative minimum tax over the regular tax (1).
South Carolina	No

State	AMT Imposed?
South Dakota	No personal income tax.
Tennessee	No broad-based personal income tax.
Texas	No personal income tax.
Utah	No
Vermont	No
Virginia	No
Washington	No personal income tax.
West Virginia	Yes, at the amount that 25% of Fed alternative minimum tax exceeds regular W.V. tax
Wisconsin	Yes, at 6.5% of adjusted Fed alternative minimum taxable income.
Wyoming	No personal income tax.

FOOTNOTES to chart ¶ 228.5 (corresponding to parenthetical numbers in chart):

(1) *R.I.*— "Tentative minimum tax" is the sum of 6.5% of the taxable excess that does not exceed $175,000 ($87,500 for married filing separately) plus 7% of the taxable excess above $175,000 ($87,500 for married filing separately).

(2) *Me.*— "Tentative minimum tax" is the sum of an amount equal to 7% of the amount of the alternative minimum taxable income up to $175,000, plus an amount equal to 7.6% of the amount over $175,000.

CAPITAL GAINS AND LOSSES

¶228-A State treatment of gains (or losses). This chart shows the income tax consequences of profits and losses from sale or exchange of capital assets by individuals and corporations.

First column: "I" means information applies to individuals only; "C" to corporations only; "IC" to both; "RE" applies to realty gain of individuals and corporations. **Second column:** Whether gains and losses are recognized. **Third column:** Holding period required for special capital gain or loss treatment; if "None," length of holding period does not affect treatment. **Fourth column:** Percentage of gain or loss taken when asset held for at least the period in third column. **Fifth column:** To what extent capital losses are credit against other income. **Sixth column:** Number of years, if any, for which loss carryover-allowed.

STATE		GAIN OR LOSS RECOGNIZED?	HOLDING PERIOD	PERCENT RECOGNIZED	LOSS CREDIT v. OTHER INCOME	YEARS LOSS CARRYOVER
ALA.	I	Yes	1y	100%	$3,000	Unlimited
	C	Yes	1y	100%	None	5 yrs(5)
AK.(1)	C	Yes	None	100%	None	5 yrs(5)
ARIZ.(15)	I	Yes	1y	100%	$3,000	Unlimited
	C	Yes	None	100%	$1,000	Unlimited
ARK.(15)	I	Yes	None	100%	$3,000	Unlimited
	C	Yes	None	100%	None	None
CALIF.(15)	I	Yes	1y(9)	100%(9)	$3,000	Unlimited
	C	Yes	None	100%	All	5 yrs
COLO.(15)	I	Yes	5y	100%(22)	$3,000	5 yrs(25)
	C	Yes	5y	100%(22)	None	5 yrs(25)
CONN.(15)	I	Yes	1y	100%	$3,000	Unlimited
	C	Yes	1y	100%	None	5 yrs
DEL.(15)	I	Yes	1y	100%	$3,000	Unlimited
	C	Yes(2)	1y	100%	None	5 yrs(5)
D.C.	I	Yes	1y	100%	$3,000	Unlimited
	C	Yes	1y	100%	None	5 yrs(5)
FLA.(15)	C	Yes	1y	100%	None	5 yrs(5)
GA.(15)	I	Yes	1y	100%	$3,000	Unlimited
	C	Yes	1y	100%	None	5 yrs(5)
HAW.(15)	I	Yes	1y	100%(4)	$3,000	Unlimited
	C	Yes	1y	100%(4)	None	5 yrs(13)
ID.(15)	I	Yes	1y	40%(10)	$3,000	Unlimited
	C	Yes	1y	100%(10)	None	5 yrs(5)
ILL.	I	Yes	1y	100%	$3,000	Unlimited
	C	Yes	1y	100%	None	5 yrs(5)
IND.(15)	I	Yes	1y	100%	$3,000	Unlimited
	C	Yes	1y	100%	None	5 yrs(5)
IOWA(15)	I	Yes	1y	100%	$3,000	Unlimited
	C	Yes	1y	100%	None	5 yrs(5)
KAN.(15)	I	Yes	1y	100%	$3,000	Unlimited
	C	Yes	1y	100%	None	5 yrs(5)
KY.(15)	I	Yes	1y	100%	$3,000	Unlimited
	C	Yes	1y	100%	None	5 yrs(5)
LA.(15)	I	Yes	1y	100%	$3,000	Unlimited
	C	Yes	None	100%	None	5 yrs(5)
ME.(15)	I	Yes	1y	100%	$3,000	Unlimited
	C	Yes	1y	100%	None	5 yrs(5)
MD.(15)	I	Yes	1y	100%	$3,000	Unlimited
	C	Yes	1y	100%	None	5 yrs
MASS.(15)	I	Yes	(23)	(23)	(23)	(23)
	C	Yes	None	100%	None	None
MICH.(15,16,19)	I	Yes	1y	100%	$3,000	Unlimited
	C	Yes	1y	100%	All(19)	None
MINN.(15)	I	Yes	1y	100%	$3,000	Unlimited
	C	Yes	1y	100%	None	15 yrs

STATE	GAIN OR LOSS RECOGNIZED?		HOLDING PERIOD	PERCENT RECOGNIZED	LOSS CREDIT v. OTHER INCOME	YEARS LOSS CARRYOVER
MISS.	I	Yes	1y	100%	$3,000(24)	5 yrs
	C	Yes	1y	100%	None	5 yrs
MO.(15)	I	Yes	1y	100%	$3,000	Unlimited
	C	Yes	1y	100%	None	5 yrs(5)
MONT.(15,29)	I	Yes	1y	100%(7)	$3,000	Unlimited
	C	Yes	None	100%	None	None
NEB.(1,15)	I	Yes	1y	100%	$3,000	Unlimited
	C	Yes	1y	100%	None	5 yrs
N.H.(15)	I	No				
	C	Yes	1y	100%	None	5 yrs(5)
N.J.(18)	I	Yes	None	100%	None	None
	C	Yes	1y	100%	None	None
N.M.(15)	I	Yes	1y	100%	$3,000	Unlimited
	C	Yes	1y	100%	None	5 yrs(5)
N.Y.(15)	I	Yes	1y	100%	$3,000	Unlimited
	C	Yes	1y	100%	None	5 yrs(5)
N.C.(15)	I	Yes	1y	100%	$3,000	Unlimited
	C	Yes	1y	100%	All	None
N.D.(15,30)	I	Yes	1y	100%	$3,000	Unlimited
	C	Yes	1y	100%	None	5 yrs
OHIO(15)	I	Yes	1y	100%	$3,000	Unlimited
	C	Yes	1y	100%	None	5 yrs(5)
OKLA.(15)	I(17)	Yes	5y	100%	$3,000	Unlimited
	C(17)	Yes	5y	100%	None	5 yrs(5)
ORE.(15)	I	Yes	1y	100%	$3,000	Unlimited
	C	Yes	None	100%	All	5 yrs
PA.(15)	I	Yes	None	100%	None	None
	C	Yes	None	100%	None	5 yrs
R.I.(1,15)	I	Yes	1y(27)	100%(28)	$3,000	Unlimited
	C	Yes	None	100%	None	5 yrs(5)
S.C.(15)	I	Yes	1y	56%(20)	None	Unlimited
	C	Yes	None	100%	None	5 yrs
TENN.(15)	I	No				
	C	Yes	None	100%	All	None
UTAH(15)	I	Yes	1y	100%	$3,000	Unlimited
	C	Yes	1y	100%	None	5 yrs(5)
VT.(1,15)	I	Yes	1y	100%	$3,000	Unlimited
	C	Yes	1y	100%	None	5 yrs(5)
	RE(11)	Yes(11)	5 yrs(11)	100%	None	None
VA.(15)	I	Yes	1y	100%	$3,000	Unlimited
	C	Yes	1y	100%	None	5 yrs(5)
W.VA.(15)	I	Yes	1y	100%	$3,000	Unlimited
	C	Yes	1y	100%	None	5 yrs(5)
WIS.(15)	I	Yes	1y	40%(21)	$3,000	Unlimited
	C	Yes	None	100%	All	None

FOOTNOTES to chart ¶ 228-A (corresponding to parenthetical numbers in chart):

(1) Automatically follows Fed treatment. No deduction for excess of net long-term capital gains over short-term capital losses.

(2) Excludes gains and losses from securities of U.S., its agencies-instrumentalities and of Delaware or its political subdivisions.

(3) Tax applies only to net capital gains; same as Fed tax.

(4) *Haw.*—Corps. pay 4% alternative tax; S corporations pay 6.4% tax on Fed built-in gains. Max. tax rate is 7.25% on capital gains for noncorporate taxpayers.

(5) Follows Fed: corporations get 3-year carryback.

(6) Net capital gains are taxed at special rate.

(7) *Mont.*—Follows Fed except 40% of capital gain from pre-1-1-87 sale is excluded for individuals. No capital gain exclusion for estates and trusts.

(8) If part of overall net economic loss.

(9) Allows credit for yrs. 1987—91 equal to 4.5% of capital gain realized from sale of in-state rental residential or farm property.

FOOTNOTES to chart ¶ 228-A (corresponding to parenthetical numbers in chart): (continued)

(10) *Ida.*—60% net capital gain deduction allowed individuals and S corps. for assets with situs in-state: realty held at least 12 mos.; revenue-producing enterprise; timber, cattle or horses, held 24 mos. (other breeding livestock, 12 mos.) if ½ gross from farming or ranching operations in-state.

(11) On land held for less than 5 years, special tax applies.

(12) (Reserved.)

(13) *Haw.*—Carryover period is 15 yrs. for qualified high technology businesses eff for tax yrs. after 12-31-99.

(14) Credit against taxable interest and dividends; excess against net capital gains.

(15) Follows either current IRC or IRC as of specific date (see ¶ 221). For current Fed rule, see note (1).

(16) Excludes losses on Fed obligations.

(17) *Okla.*—Individuals: 5 years eff for tax years beginning after 12-31-2004; 1 year before then. Corporations: 5 years eff for tax years beginning after 12-31-2005; 1 year before then.

(18) Capital losses are recognized to extent of capital gains. Net capital gains are included in gross income; only recognized to extent of capital gains.

(19) "Single Business Tax" allows deduction of capital losses not deducted federally in year loss occurred; disallows loss carryovers.

(20) *S.C.*—Subtraction allowed for 44% of net capital gains on items held for the period provided in IRC §1222 and related sections. For tax yrs. before 2001, a 44% subtraction was allowed for items held 2 years or more.

(21) *Wis.*—Excluding amounts treated as ordinary income and (eff retro. to tax yrs. starting after 12-31-86) sales of dairy cattle under milk production termination program (allowed 60% Fed capital gains exclusion).

(22) *Colo.*—Subtraction from federal taxable income is allowed for net capital gain on property, stock or ownership interest in a Colo. company, LLC or partnership (50% (min.) of property and payroll assigned to Colo.) acquired after 5-8-94 and held, after 5-31-94, for at least 5 years prior to the date of the transaction from which the capital gain arose (effective for tax years starting after 6-30-95). Subtraction is also allowed (subject to availability and amount of surplus state revenues) for gains on property, stock or ownership interest acquired before 5-9-94 and held for at least 5 years prior to the date of the transaction from which the capital gain arose (effective for tax years starting after 12-31-98); and for gains on property, stock or ownership interest that were held for at least 1 year, but less than 5 years, prior to the date of the transaction from which the capital gain arose (effective for tax years starting after 12-31-2000).

(23) *Mass.*—Class C income covers capital gains and losses during their tax phase-out. Percentages of gain and loss recognized drop according to a table based on length of time held. Rates also drop according to a table. Excess loss is a credit against tax on Class A income. Applicable retroactively to tax years beginning on or after 1-1-96, taxpayers can net short and long-term gains and losses or apply Class B losses arising from a trade or business to Class C gains.

(24) $1,500 for married individuals filing separately.

(25) Follows Fed, but no carryback to an earlier tax yr.

(26) Carryover—Individuals, none; corporations, 3-yr. carryback and 5-yr carryforward.

(27) *R.I.*—All capital assets bought before 1-1-2002 and sold on or before 1-1-2007 will be deemed to have a holding period starting 1-1-2002.

(28) *R.I.*—For tax yr. starting in 2007, the capital gains rate for assets held more than 5 yrs. is 8.33% of the Fed capital gains rate in effect before the enactment of the Fed Economic Growth and Tax Relief Reconciliation Act of 2001. For tax yrs. after 2007, the capital gains rate for assets held more than 5 yrs. is 0%.

(29) *Mont.*—Individual taxpayers are allowed a credit against income tax in an amount equal to 1% of the taxpayer's net capital gains for tax years 2005 and 2006 and 2% of capital gains for tax years beginning after 2006. The capital gains credit cannot exceed the taxpayer's income tax liability.

(30) *N.D.*—A reduction of 30% of the excess of the individual's net long-term capital gain for the tax year over the net short-term capital loss for the year is allowed for taxpayers using the short form (simplified) method. Eff for tax years beginning after 12-31-2004, this adjustment if allowed only to the extent the net long-term capital gain is allocated to N.D.

ITEMIZED PERSONAL INCOME TAX DEDUCTIONS

¶228-A.5 Itemized deductions. Itemized deductions from adjusted gross income can be a big tax saver for the personal income taxpayer.

Most states allow itemized deductions. The chart below shows the states that allow the federal itemized deductions from adjusted gross income (AGI) and the state adjustments to the Fed itemized deductions.

This chart also shows each state's IRC conformity date for itemized deductions. States that conform to the current IRC adopt IRC changes as they are made. States that conform to the IRC as of a specified date adopt the IRC as it exists up to that date, but don't adopt later changes to it.

State	IRC conformity date	Follows federal itemized deductions from AGI?
Alabama	Current IRC if not in conflict with state law.	Yes, but with adjustments for medical expenses, state, local, foreign, and occupational taxes, and other items. Can deduct federal income and other specified federal taxes.
Alaska	No personal income tax.	
Arizona	1-1-2007.	Yes, but with specific deductions for medical expenses, casualty and theft losses, charitable gifts, student expenses, interest, long-term care, state taxes, and college tuition expenses.
Arkansas	Varies, depending on item (see ¶221).	Yes, but with adjustments for medical expenses, state taxes, and charitable gifts.
California	1-1-2005.	Yes, but with adjustments for state and foreign income taxes, federal estate taxes, interest, and other items.
Colorado	Current IRC.	Yes, but with adjustments for state tax.
Connecticut	Current IRC.	No.
Delaware	Current IRC.	Yes, with state modifications.
District of Columbia	Current IRC.	Yes, but with adjustments for state taxes.
Florida	No personal income tax.	
Georgia	1-1-2007.	Yes, but with adjustments for state taxes and expenses connected with exempt income.
Hawaii	12-31-2006.	Yes, but with adjustments for state taxes and other items.
Idaho	1-1-2007.	Yes, but with adjustments for state taxes.
Illinois	Current IRC.	No, (state only allows "above-the-line" deductions).

State	IRC conformity date	Follows federal itemized deductions from AGI?
Indiana	1-1-2007.	No.
Iowa	1-1-2007.	Yes, but with adjustments for state taxes, charitable mileage, and other items. Can deduct federal income tax.
Kansas	Current IRC.	Yes, but with adjustments for state taxes.
Kentucky	12-31-2006.	Yes, but with adjustments for state taxes, charitable contributions, and other items.
Louisiana	Current IRC.	Deduction is that portion of federal itemized deductions exceeding the federal standard deduction amount. Can deduct federal income tax.
Maine	12-31-2006.	Yes, but with adjustments for state taxes and other items.
Maryland	Current IRC.	Yes, but with adjustments for state taxes and for contribution of a conservation easement for which a credit is claimed.
Massachusetts	1-1-2005.	No.
Michigan	1-1-96, but taxpayer can elect current IRC.	No.
Minnesota	12-31-2006.	Yes, but with adjustment for state tax.
Mississippi	Current IRC.	Yes, but with adjustment for state tax and, gaming losses from Miss. licensed gaming establishments and gaming taxes collected by such establishments.
Missouri	Current IRC.	Yes, but with adjustment for state taxes and cultural contributions. Can deduct federal income taxes (limited deduction) and other specified federal taxes.
Montana	Current IRC.	Yes, but with adjustments for state tax, insurance expenses, contributions, and other items. Can deduct federal income tax.
Nebraska	Current IRC.	Yes, but with adjustments for state tax.
Nevada	No personal income tax.	
New Hampshire	No broad-based personal income tax.	

State	IRC conformity date	Follows federal itemized deductions from AGI?
New Jersey	No IRC conformity.	No, but nonreimbursed medical expenses exceeding 2% of gross income can be deducted, as well as alimony and support maintenance payments, taxes paid or rent constituting tax paid on homesteads, qualified conservation contributions, and expenses for neighborhood and business child care.
New Mexico	Current IRC.	Yes.
New York	Current IRC.	Yes, but with adjustments for state taxes, foreign income taxes, interest, and other items. Taxpayers can itemize for N.Y. purposes only if they itemize on their federal returns.
North Carolina	1-1-2007.	Yes, but with adjustments for state taxes.
North Dakota	Current IRC.	Yes, but with adjustments for state taxes and medical expenses. Limited deduction is allowed for federal income tax.
Ohio	12-28-2006.	No, but state adjustments allowed for some items.
Oklahoma	Current IRC.	Yes. Limited deduction is allowed for federal income tax.
Oregon	Current IRC.	Yes, but with adjustments for state tax, medical expenses, and other items. Limited deduction allowed for federal income tax.
Pennsylvania	No IRC confirmity.	No, but unreimbursed employee business expenses and employee educational expenses can be deducted.
Rhode Island	Current IRC.	Yes.
South Carolina	12-31-2006.	Yes, but with adjustments for state tax and other items.
South Dakota	No personal income tax.	
Tennessee	No broad-based personal income tax.	
Texas	No personal income tax.	
Utah	Current IRC.	Yes, but with adjustments for state taxes. Limited deduction allowed for federal income tax.
Vermont	1-1-2006.	Yes.
Virginia	12-31-2006.	Yes, but with adjustments for state taxes and other items.

State	IRC conformity date	Follows federal itemized deductions from AGI?
Washington	No personal income tax.	
West Virginia	12-31-2006.	No.
Wisconsin	1-1-2007.	Credit allowed based on specified federal itemized deductions.
Wyoming	No personal income tax.	

CHECKLISTS OF DEDUCTIONS AND INCOME TAX EXEMPTIONS

¶228-B Overview of income tax deduction and exemption checklists. The series of charts at ¶ 228-C through ¶ 230 contain checklists of various types of income tax deductions and exemptions allowed by the states that impose general income taxes. Only broad aspects of those items are covered. Special situations may occur that modify the provisions expressed in the entries.

EXPLANATION OF CHARTS: Symbols and abbreviations used in the charts at ¶ 228-C through ¶ 230 are as follows: (*) = for individuals only; a = adjusted gross income; g = gross income; n = net income; t = taxable income; I = individuals; C = corporations; CR = tax credit; N = no; Y = yes; ND = no deduction; NP = no provision; NT = no tax.

MISCELLANEOUS LIMITED DEDUCTIONS—PART I

¶228-C Contributions, medical expenses, and standard deduction. This chart covers state income tax deductions for the items listed above the columns. Symbols and abbreviations used in this chart are as follows: (*) = for individuals only; a = adjusted gross income; g = gross income; n = net income; t = taxable income; I = individuals; C = corporations; CR = tax credit; N = no; Y = yes; ND = no deductions; NP = no provisions; NT = no tax.

	CONTRIBUTIONS % Limit		MEDICAL EXPENSE(1,23)		OPTIONAL STANDARD DEDUCTION(1)	
STATE	Ind.	Corp.	allowed	$ Limit	% Limit	$ Limit
ALA.	50%a	10%t	4%a (6)	None	20%a	2,000 (40)
AK.	(2)	10%t	(2)	(2)	(2)	(2)
ARIZ.	50%a	10%t	No limit	None	NP	4,247 (21)
ARK.	50%a	10%t	7.5%a (6,23)	None	NP	2,000 (16)
CALIF.	50%a	10%n	7.5%a (6,23)	None	NP	3,516 (17,18)
COLO.	50%a	10%t	7.5%(6,23)	None	NP	5,350 (43)
CONN.	ND	10%t	ND	ND	ND	(26)
DEL.	50%a	10%t	7.5%a (6,23)	None	NP	3,250 (46)
D.C.	50%a	15%n	7.5%a (23)	None	NP	2,500 (24,51)
FL.(2)	(9)	10%t	(9)	(9)	(9)	(9)
GA.	50%a	10%t	7.5%a (6,23)	None	NP	2,300 (19)
HAW.	50%a	10%t	7.5%a (6,23)	None	NP	1,500 (42)
IDA.	50%a	10%t	7.5%a (6,23)	None	NP	5,350 (14,43)
ILL.	ND	10%t (36)	(7)	(7)	ND	ND
IND.	(28)	(28)	ND	ND	ND	ND
IA.	50%a	10%t	7.5%a (6,23)	None	NP	1,700 (18,30)
KAN.	50%a	10%t	7.5% (6,23)	None	NP	3,000 (49)
KY.	50%a	10%t	7.5%a (6,23)	None	NP	2,050 (18)
LA.	50%a	5%n	7.5%a (6,23)	None	(26)	(26)
ME.	50%a	10%t	7.5%a (6)	None	NP	5,350 (52)
MD.	50%a	10%t	7.5%a (6,23)	None	15%a	2,000 (10)
MA.	ND	10%t	7.5% (6,23)	None	NP	NP
MI.(22)	ND	10%t	ND	ND	ND	ND
MN.	50%a	ND	7.5%a (6,23)	None	NP	5,350 (43)
MS.(37)	50%a	20%n	7.5%a (6,23)	None	NP	2,300 (8)
MO.	50%a	10%t	7.5%a (6,23)	None	NP	5,350 (43)
MONT.	50%a	10%t	7.5%a (6,23)	None	20%	3,810 (18,40)
NEB.	50%a	10%t	7.5%a (6,23)	None	NP	5,350 (43)
N.H.(33)	ND	10%t	ND	ND	ND	ND
N.J.(11)	ND	10%t	2%g(25)	None	ND	ND
N.M.	50%a	10%t	7.5%a (6,23)	None	NP	5,350 (43)
N.Y.(34)	50%a	10%t	7.5%a (6,23)	None	NP	7,500 (44)
N.C.	50%a	5%n (50)	7.5%a (6,23)	None	NP	3,000 (29)
N.D.	50%a	10%t	None	None	NP	5,350 (43)
OH.	ND	10%t	(41)	(41)	ND	NP
OKLA.	50%a	10%t	7.5%a (6,23)	None	NP	2,750 (53)
ORE.	50%a	10%t	7.5%a (6,23)	None	13%	1,840 (47)
PA.(22)	ND	10%t	ND	ND	ND	ND
R.I.	50%a	10%t	7.5%a (6,23)	None	NP	5,350 (43)
S.C.	50%a	10%t	7.5%a (6,23)	None	NP	5,350 (43)

STATE	CONTRIBUTIONS % Limit		MEDICAL EXPENSE(1,23)		OPTIONAL STANDARD DEDUCTION(1)	
	Ind.	Corp.	allowed	$ Limit	% Limit	$ Limit
TENN.(4)	ND	None	ND	ND	ND	ND
UTAH	50%a	10%n	7.5%a (6,23)	None	NP	5,350 (43)
VT.	50%a	10%t	7.5%a (6,23)	None	NP	5,350 (43)
VA.	50%a	10%t	7.5%a (6,23)	None	NP	3,000 (48)
W.VA.	ND	10%t	ND	ND	ND	ND
WIS.(45)	CR	10%t	CR	CR	NP	8,790 (18,45)

NOTES to chart ¶ 228-C (corresponding to parenthetical numbers in chart):

(1) Individual taxpayer unless otherwise shown.
(2) No personal income tax.
(3) Each spouse filing separately may take 10% or $1000 (max.).
(4) Limited personal income tax; no deductions.
(5) Per week.
(6) 1% floor on drugs is eliminated for Fed tax purposes but deduction limited to prescription drugs and insulin.
(7) *Ill.*—Deductions exist relating to Medical Savings Acts.
(8) Joint returns, $4,600. For married filing separately, $2,300. Head of family, $3,400. Single, $2,300.
(9) Not applicable.
(10) Spouses filing jointly, $4,000.
(11) Gross (personal) income tax.
(12) Special top limits if over 65.
(13) Includes hospital or medical insurance premiums.
(14) *Ida.*—Married couples can claim basic Fed joint standard deduction plus Ida. marriage penalty amount plus additional Fed standard deduction for aged or blind, if qualified.
(15) Spouses filing jointly, $100 ($50 if separately); single, $60; household head, $88.
(16) *Ark.*—For joint filers, $2,000 for each spouse.
(17) *Calif.*—As adjusted for inflation for 2007 for single or separate filers. Joint filers and household heads, $7,032.
(18) Standard deduction is indexed (multiplied by inflation factor). Amount shown is for 2007.
(19) *Ga.*—$3,000 joint returns ($1,500 spouses filing separately.) Added $1,300 for age or blind.
(20) Pre-1983 Fed rules apply: includes separate deduction for 1/2 health insurance premiums (max. $150).
(21) *Ariz.*—Amount shown is as indexed for 2006 for single or married filing separately; joint filers or household head, $8,494.
(22) Only business deductions. No itemized deductions allowed.
(23) Follows Fed rule: medical deduction limited to expenses exceeding 7.5% of adjusted gross income and no separate deduction for health insurance premiums. *D.C.*—Individual can deduct up to $500 per yr. for long-term care insurance. *Ark.* lets self-employed deduct 60% of medical insurance costs for themselves, spouses, and dependents. *Del.*—Specific provisions may adjust federal deductions.
(24) One-half if spouse files separate.
(25) Medical expenses include drugs-medicines and amounts paid to medical savings accounts.
(26) Combined amounts for standard deduction and exemptions are at ¶ 228.
(27) (Reserved.)
(28) Tax credit for contributions to in-state colleges and nonprofit educational orgs.
(29) Same as Fed amounts (43) but no inflation adjustments (NC): single $3,000; joint filers and surviving spouses $6,000; spouses filing separately $3,000; household heads $4,400.
(30) Single and spouses filing separately—$1,700 for 2007. Spouses filing jointly, surviving spouses and household heads—$4,200 for 2007. (Iowa).
(31) $2,000 total for spouses.
(32) Any medical expense, uninsured, including medical insurance premiums.
(33) For business profits tax only. No deductions for limited personal income.
(34) In N.Y., itemized deductions are allowed only if claimed on the federal return. Varying percentage of total N.Y. itemized deduction disallowed for higher-income taxpayers.
(35) May elect low-income allowance, if greater.
(36) *Ill.*—Corporations can deduct twice the amount of contributions to designated zone organizations for approved enterprise zones or river edge redevelopment zone projects.
(37) *Miss.*—Most Fed nonbusiness itemized deductions allowed.
(38) Allows Fed political contributions (no modification to Fed taxable income).

NOTES to chart ¶ 228-C (corresponding to parenthetical numbers in chart): (continued)

(39) Uninsured amounts exceeding $2,000.

(40) Double for joint filers. Household heads get double amount in Mont.

(41) *Ohio*—Can deduct amounts paid for medical insurance and long-term care insurance cost; and medical care expenses over 7.5% of Fed AGI..

(42) Spouses filing jointly or surviving spouses get $1,900; household heads $1,650; single $1,500; married filing separately $950 (Haw).

(43) As adjusted for inflation for 2007: $5,350 for single person; $10,700 for joint filers or surviving spouses; $5,350 for married filing separately; $7,850 for household head; added $1,050 for blind or senior married (or surviving spouse); added $1,300 for blind or senior single or head of household; standard deduction for person claimed as another's deduction cannot exceed higher of $850 or sum of $300 plus earned income, up to the regular standard deduction amount for that individual. As adjusted for inflation for 2008: $5,450 for single person; $10,900 for joint filers or surviving spouses; $5,450 for married filing separately; $8,000 for household head; added $1,050 for blind or senior married (or surviving spouse); added $1,350 for blind or senior single or head of household; standard deduction for person claimed as another's deduction cannot exceed higher of $900 or sum of $300 plus earned income, up to the regular standard deduction amount for that individual.

(44) *N.Y.*—Single, $7,500; household head, $10,500; joint returns and surviving spouses, $15,000. *Married filing separately* get one-half of joint filers'. *Dependents* denied Fed standard deduction, $3,000.

(45) *Wis.*—Standard deduction for 2007—for single persons: $8,790 minus 12% of Wis. adjusted gross income over $12,670. For married filing jointly: $15,830 minus 19.778% of Wis. AGI over $17,780. For married filing separately: $7,520 minus 19.778% of Wis. AGI over $8,440. For head of household: $11,350 minus 22.515% of Wis. AGI over $12,670.

(46) *Del.*—Single, $3,250; joint filers, $6,500; married person filing separately, $3,250. Added $2,500 for person who is blind or over age 65.

(47) *Ore.*—For 2005: Single or married filing separately, $1,770; joint filers or qualifying widow(er), $3,545; head of household, $2,855. Added $1,000 if senior or blind ($1,200 if unmarried and not surviving spouse). Dependent, $800, or $250 plus earned income, if greater.

(48) *Va.*—$6,000 for married ($3,000 if filing separately); single, $3,000.

(49) *Kan.*—Single, $3,000; head of household, $4,500; married filing jointly, $6,000. Added $850 deduction if either blind or elderly and either single or household head; added $700 deduction if blind or elderly married person.

(50) *N.C.*—Deduction for contributions to donees outside of N.C. are limited to 5% of net income. Contributions to N.C. donees are fully deductible.

(51) *D.C.*—Eff for 2007, deduction is $2,500 ($1,250 if spouse files separate). Eff for 2008, deduction is $4,000 ($2,000 if spouse files separate). For 2009 and later yrs., standard deduction is adjusted for inflation.

(52) *Me.*—As adjusted for inflation for 2007: $5,350 for single filers; $8,900 for joint filers or surviving spouses; $4,450 for married filing separately; $7,850 for household head; added $1,050 if senior or blind ($1,300 if unmarried and not surviving spouse); for dependent, greater of $850 or earned income plus $300 (up to regular standard deduction amount for that individual).

(53) *Okla.*—For 2007: $2,750 for single or married filing separately; $5,500 for joint filers or qualifying widow(er); $4,125 for head of household. For 2008: $3,250 for single or married filing separately; $6,500 for joint filers or qualifying widow(er); $4,875 for household head.

MISCELLANEOUS DEDUCTIONS—PART II

¶228-D Interest, bad debts, obsolescence, depletion, retirement plans, and organizational expenses. This chart covers state income tax deductions for the items listed above the columns. Symbols and abbreviations used in this chart are as follows: (*) = for individuals only; a = adjusted gross income; g = gross income; n = net income; t = taxable income; I = individuals; C = corporations; CR = tax credit; N = no; Y = yes; ND = no deductions; NP = no provisions; NT = no tax.

STATE	INTEREST Paid	INTEREST Accrued	BAD DEBT	OBSOLESCENCE	DEPLETION (11,12)	RETIREMENT PLANS	ORGANIZATIONAL EXPENSES
ALA.	Y	Y	Y	Y	Y(26)	Y	Y
AK.(C)(1)	Y	Y	Y	Y	Y(12,36)	Y	Y
ARIZ.(1)	Y	Y	Y	Y	Y(12)	Y	Y
ARK.	Y	Y	Y	Y	Y(22)	Y	Y
CALIF.(1)	Y	Y	Y	Y	Y(12)	Y	Y
COLO.(1)	Y	Y	Y	Y	Y(12,30)	Y	Y
CT.(C)(1)	Y	Y	Y	Y	Y(12)	Y	Y
DEL.(1)	Y	Y	Y	Y	Y(12,24)	Y	Y
D.C.(2)	Y	Y	Y	Y	Y(34)	Y	Y(7)
FL.(C)(2)	Y	Y(19)	Y	Y	Y(12)	Y	Y
GA.(1)	Y	Y	Y	Y	Y(12)	Y	Y
HAW.(1)	Y	Y	Y	Y	Y(12)	Y	Y
IDA.(1)	Y	Y	Y	Y	Y(12)	Y	Y
ILL.(1,9)	Y	Y	Y	Y	Y(12)	Y	Y
IND.(1,9)	Y	Y	Y	Y	Y(12)	Y	Y
IOWA(1)	Y	Y	Y	Y	Y(12)	Y	Y
KAN.(1)	Y	Y	Y	Y	Y(12)	Y	Y
KY.	Y	Y	Y	Y	Y(12,17)	Y	Y
LA.(1)	Y	Y	Y	Y	Y(18)	Y	Y
ME.(1)	Y	Y	Y	Y	Y(12)	Y	Y
MD.(1)	Y	Y	Y	Y	Y(4,12)	Y(3)	Y
MASS.(I)(1)	Y	Y	Y	Y	Y(12)	Y	Y
(C)(1)	Y	Y	Y	Y	Y(12)	Y	Y
MI.(I)(1,33)	Y	Y	Y	Y	Y(12)	Y	NP
(C)(1,33)	Y	Y	Y	Y	Y(12)	Y	Y
MINN.(1)	Y	Y	Y	Y	Y(16)	Y	Y
MISS.(28)	Y	Y	Y	Y	Y(16)	Y(3)	NP
MO.(1)	Y	Y	Y	Y	Y(12)	Y	Y
MONT.(I)(1)	Y	Y	Y	Y	Y(12)	Y	Y
(C)	Y	Y(7)	Y	Y	Y(12)	Y	Y
NEB.(1)	Y	Y	Y	Y	Y(12)	Y	Y
N.H.(5)	Y	Y	Y	Y	Y(12)	Y	Y
N.J.(1,8,9)	Y	Y	Y	Y	Y(12)	Y	Y
N.M.(1)	Y	Y	Y	Y	Y(12)	Y	Y
N.Y.(1,25)	Y	Y	Y	Y	Y(12,31)	Y	Y
N.C.(1)	Y	Y	Y	Y	Y(12)	Y	Y
N.D.(1)	Y	Y	Y	Y	Y(12)	Y	Y
OHIO(1,9)	Y	Y	Y	Y	Y(12)	Y	N
OKLA.(1)	Y	Y	Y	Y	Y(12,32)	Y	Y
ORE.(1)	Y	Y	Y	Y	Y(23)	Y	Y
PA.(1,9)	Y	Y	Y	Y	Y(12)	Y	Y
R.I.(1)	Y	Y	Y	Y	Y(12)	Y	Y
S.C.(1)	Y	Y	Y	Y	Y(12)	Y	Y

STATE	INTEREST Paid	Accrued	BAD DEBT	OBSO-LES-CENCE	DEPLE-TION (11,12)	RE-TIRE-MENT PLANS	ORGA-NIZA-TIONAL EX-PENSES
TENN.(C)(1,6)	Y	Y	Y	Y	Y(27)	Y	Y
UTAH(1)	Y	Y	Y	Y	Y(12)	Y	Y
VT.(1)	Y	Y	Y	Y	Y(12)	Y	Y
VA.(1)	Y	Y	Y	Y	Y(12)	Y	Y
W.VA.(1,9)	Y	Y	Y	Y	Y(12)	Y	Y
WI.(I)(1,9)	Y(35)	Y(35)	Y	Y	Y(12)	Y	Y
(C)	Y	Y	Y	Y	Y(25)	Y	Y

NOTES to chart ¶ 228-D (corresponding to parenthetical numbers in chart):

(1) State law adopts or accepts Fed provisions.
(2) IRC adopted for individuals in DC; corporations, Fla.
(3) Not Roth IRAs.
(4) Oil percentage depletion allowance disallowed.
(5) For business profits tax only; no deductions for limited personal income.
(6) Limited personal income tax; no deductions.
(7) No specific provision; probable status shown.
(8) Gross (personal) income tax on residents-nonresidents levied on net income from rents, royalties, patents-copyrights, and net business profits (after all costs—expenses per Fed acctg. methods).
(9) For corporations and business persons only; no deductions for personal income tax.
(10) (Reserved.)
(11) State follows these Fed rates (pre-1969): Fed percentage depletion rates based on gross income. *Regardless of deposit situs*—27.5% oil and gas wells; 23% sulfur, uranium; 15% ball clay, bentonite, china clay, some metal mines, rock asphalt, etc.; 10% asbestos, brucite, coal, etc.; 5% brick and tile clay, gravel, etc. *U.S. deposits*—23% anorthosite, asbestos, bauxite, etc.; 23% ores of antimony, bismuth, cobalt, etc.; 15% other metal mines (regardless of situs) if rates above don't apply. State percentages in footnotes (13) to (26) are based on gross income.
(12) *State follows Fed rate:* Fed percentage depletion based on gross income: 22% Oil and gas wells (repealed 1-1-1975 for most taxpayers), sulphur and uranium, and US deposits specified (IRC §613), including molybdenum; 15% US deposits of gold, silver, copper, iron ore and specified oil shale; 14% metal mines (not taxed at 22% or 15% above), rock asphalt, vermiculite, bentonite, and specified clays; 10% brucite, coal, lignite, perlite, sodium chloride, wallastonite and non-US asbestos; 7.5% certain other clays, shale and slate; 5% gravel, pumice, sand, peat, and other shale-clay items; 14% on "all other minerals" not soil, sod, dirt, turf, water or mosses or from sea water or air.
(13) 25% oil and gas wells, 15% metal mines, both up to 50% of net income, no other percentage depletion.
(14) Follows Fed (12) above, except oil-gas and geothermal well, 22% (percentage depletion denied if total exceeds cost).
(15) If nondepreciable otherwise no deduction.
(16) Reasonable allowance. Based on actual cost in Minn. and Miss.
(17) Alternative method for coal (covered by IRC § 1631) depletion: exclude 50% of gross income from coal, if contract expenses aren't claimed.
(18) Follows Fed (1) except may elect oil and gas depletion, 22% of gross income (not over 50% of net income).
(19) *Fla.*—An addback is required for interest excluded for Fed tax purposes, less associated expenses disallowed federally, excluding 60% of amounts included in Fed alternative minimum taxable income, if taxpayer pays Fla. alternative minimum tax.
(20) Use of reserve method held improper by Mont. Sup. Ct.
(21) Deductible in 5 years, 20% (max.) deductible per year.
(22) *Ark.*—Follows Fed, as in effect 1-1-2007, except percentage depletion allowance for oil and gas under IRC §613 is not allowed.
(23) Individuals—follow Fed (12); Corporations—15% of gross income of metal mines up to 50% of net income, reasonable allowance for others.
(24) *Del.*—Addback required for % depletion above cost for individual.

NOTES to chart ¶ 228-D (corresponding to parenthetical numbers in chart): (continued)

(25) Starting 1988, varying percentage of itemized deductions is disallowed, depending on adjusted gross income and filing status. In N.Y., itemized deductions are allowed only if taken on the federal return.

(26) Corporate taxpayers can elect to deduct 12% of gross income for oil-gas wells up to 50% of net income; all others, see (16).

(27) Taxpayers must add back deductions under IRC § 617 to extent deduction when added to like deductions in earlier years exceeds property's costs.

(28) Fed nonbusiness itemized deductions adopted (Miss.)

(29) Fed depletion rules followed but can elect to deduct as depletion (after allocation-apportionment) for mines, oil-gas wells and other natural deposits instate up to 50% of apportioned net income *(S.C.)*.

(30) Special depletion for oil shale.

(31) Reasonable allowance replaces percentage depletion for individuals and unincorporated businesses.

(32) *Okla.*—Oil-gas wells, 22%.

(33) *Mich.*—Until 12-31-2007, "Single Business Tax" requires add-back of interest paid or accrued, and depreciation, amortization or other write-offs (but investment tax credit deduction allowed). Eff 1-1-2008, Mich. Business Tax does not require addback of interest paid or accrued, depreciation, or other write-offs.

(34) Individuals follow Fed rules (note 12)); note (16) provision for corps., unicorp. businesses & partnerships.

(35) Credit based on IRC-deductible interest expense (home-farm loans, employee stock purchase 1986-88 tax year plus up to $1,200 other interest).

(36) *Alaska*–For corporations engaged in oil and gas production, depletion deducted on the percentage depletion basis under IRC §613 must be recomputed and deducted on the cost depletion basis under IRC §612.

MISCELLANEOUS DEDUCTIONS—PART III

¶228-E Net operating losses and specified taxes. This chart covers state income tax deductions for the items listed above the columns. Symbols and abbreviations used in this chart are as follows: (*) = for individuals only; a = adjusted gross income; g = gross income; n = net income; t = taxable income; I = individuals; C = corporations; CR = tax credit; N = no; Y = yes; ND = no deductions; NP = no provisions; NT = no tax.

Extended NOL carryback. The first column in the chart below tells whether or not a state follows the extended net operating loss (NOL) carryback period provided under the Federal Job Creation and Worker Assistance Act of 2002 (P.L. 107-147) for state corporate (C) and individual (I) income taxpayers. States with "Y" in this column follow the federal provision in P.L. 107-147 that extends the general carryback period for NOLs to 5 yrs., from 2 yrs., for NOLs arising in tax yrs. ending in 2001 or 2002. States with "N" do not follow that provision.

	NET OPERATING LOSS (1)						
STATE	EXTENDED CARRYBACK	Carry-back	Carry-over	Nonbusiness (2)	STATE INCOME TAXES (5)	FRANCHISE TAXES	GIFT & DEATH TAXES
AL.(C)	N	N(43)	15y(43)	Y	N	N	N
(I)	N	2y(43)	15y(43)	Y	N	N	Y(52)
AK.(C)(6)	Y	2y(13)	20y(13)	N	N	Y	N
AZ.(I)	Y	2y	20y	Y	Y	Y(22)	N
(C)	N	N	5y	Y	N	Y(22)	N
AR.(C)	N	N	5y(41)	Y	Y	Y	N
(I)	N	N	5y(41)	Y	Y	Y	N
CA.(C)	N	N	10y(57)	Y	N	Y(10)	N
(I)	N	N	10y(57)	Y	N	Y(10)	N
CO.(I)	Y	2y	20y	Y	N	Y(10)	N
(C)	N	N	20y	Y	N	Y(10)	N
CT.(C)	N	N	20y	N	N	N	N
(I)	Y	2y(13)	20y(13)	N	N	N	N
DE.(C)	Y	2y(13,47)	20y(13)	Y	N(26)	Y	N
(I)	Y	2y(13,47)	20y(13)	Y	N(26)	Y	N
D.C.(C)	N	N	20y	Y	N	N(16)	N
(I)	Y	2y	20y	Y	N	N(16)	N
FL.(C)(6)	N	N	20y(31)	Y	N	Y(16)	N
GA.(C)	N	2y	20y	Y	Y(9)	Y(10)	N
(I)	N	2y	20y	Y	Y(9)	Y(10)	N
HI.(C)	N	2y	20y	Y	Y	N	N
(I)	N	2y	20y	Y	Y	N	N
ID.(C)	N	2y(56)	20y	Y	N	N	N
(I)	N	2y(56)	20y	Y	N	N	N
IL.(C)	N	N	12y	N	N(50,51)	N	N
(I)(19)	Y	2y	20y	N	Y(50,51)	N	N
IN.(C)	Y	2y	20y	N	N(51)	Y(22)	N
(I)(19)	Y	2y	20y	N	N(51)	Y(22)	N
IA.(C)	N	2y	20y	Y	N	Y	N
(I)	N	2y	20y	Y	N	Y	N
KAN.(C)	N	N(20)	10y	Y	N	Y(10)	N
(I)	N	N(20)	10y	Y	N	Y(10)	N
KY.(C)	N	N(27)	20y	Y	N	Y	N
(I)	N	2y	20y	Y	N	Y	N
LA.(I)	Y	2y(13)	20y(13)	Y	Y	Y	N
(C)	N	3y	15y	Y	N	N	N
ME.(C)	N	(24)	20y	Y	N	N	N
(I)	N	(24)	20y	Y	N	N	N

STATE	NET OPERATING LOSS (1) EXTENDED CARRY-BACK	Carry-back	Carry-over	Nonbusiness (2)	STATE INCOME TAXES (5)	FRANCHISE TAXES	GIFT & DEATH TAXES
MD.(C)	N	2y	20y	Y	Y	N	N
(I)	N	2y	20y	Y	Y	N	N
MA.(I)	N	N	N	N	N	N	N
(C)	N	N	5y(33)	Y	N	N	N
MI.(I)(19)	Y(14)	2y(55)	20y(55)	N	N(38)	(38)	N
(C)	N(3)	(38)	(38)	N	N	(38)	N
MN.(I)	N	N	15y	Y	N(64)	N(64)	N
(C)	N	N	15y	Y	N(64)	N(64)	N
MS.(I)	N	2y	20y	Y	N	N	N
(C)	N	2y	20y	Y	N	N	N
MO.(I)	N	2y	20y	Y	N	Y	N
(C)	N	2y	20y	Y	N	Y	N
MONT.(I)	Y	2y(13)	20y(13)	Y	N	N	N
(C)	N	3y	7y	Y	N	N	N
NEB.(I)	Y	2y(13)	20y(13)	Y	N	Y	N
(C)	N	N	5y	Y	N	Y	N
N.H.(7)	N	N	10y(36)	N	Y	Y	N
N.J.(I)(12)	N	N	N	N	N	N	N
(C)	N	N	7y(37)	N	N	N(16)	N
N.M.(C)	N	N	5y	Y	Y	Y	N
(I)	N	N	5y	Y	Y	Y	N
N.Y.(I)(40)	Y(71)	2y(28)	20y(28)	Y	N	NP	N
(C)	Y(70,71)	2y(70)	20y(13)	Y	N	N	N
N.C.(C)	N	N	15y(34)	Y	N	Y	N
(I)	Y	2y	20y	Y	N	Y	N
N.D.(C)	Y	2y	20y	Y	N	Y(10)	N
(I)	Y	2y	20y	Y	N	Y(10)	N
OH.(I)	Y	(19)	(19)	N	N	N	N
(C)	N	(23)	20y(23)	Y	Y	Y	N
OK.(C)	Y	2y	20y	N(30)	N	Y(58)	N
(I)	Y	2y	20y	N(30)	Y	Y(58)	N
OR.(C)	N	N	15y	Y	N(49)	Y(10)	N
(I)	Y	2y(13)	20y(13)	Y	N(49)	Y(10)	N
PA.(I)(19)	N	N	N	N	N	N	N
(C)	N	N	20y(48)	Y	N	N	N
R.I. (I)	N	N	20y	Y	Y	Y	N
(C)	N	N	5y	Y	N	N	N
S.C.(C)	N	N	20y	Y	N	Y(10)	N
(I)	N	N	20y	Y	N	Y(10)	N
TN.(I)(11)	N	N	N	N	N	N	N
(C)	N	N	15y(42)	Y	N	N	N
UT.(I)	Y	2y(13)	20y(13)	Y	N	N	N
(C)	Y	3y	15y	Y	N	N	N
VT.(C)	N(65)	N(65)	10y(65)	Y	N	N	N
(I)	Y(13)	2y(13)	20y(13)	Y	N	N	N
VA.(C)	N	2y	20y	Y	N	Y(22)	N
(I)	N	2y	20y	Y	N	Y(22)	N
W.VA.(I)(19)	Y	2y(68)	20y	N	N	N	N
(C)	Y	2y(68)	20y	N	N	N	N
WI.(I)(60)	N	N	15y	N	N	N	N
(C)	N	N	15y	Y	N	N	N

FOOTNOTES to chart ¶ 228-E (corresponding to parenthetical numbers in chart):

(1) Capital gain and loss is at ¶ 228-A.

(2) Incurred in any nonbusiness transaction entered into for profit.

(3) *Mich.*—Until 12-31-2007, for single business tax, all federal NOL carrybacks or carryforwards must be added back when computing tax base. Eff. 1-1-2008, Mich. Business Tax requires add-back of any carryforward or carryover of an NOL to extent deducted for Fed. purposes.

FOOTNOTES to chart ¶ 228-E (corresponding to parenthetical numbers in chart): (continued)

(4) If allowed, limited to gains for wagering.
(5) Deduction for Fed income taxes is at ¶ 230. Resident may get credit for other state's income taxes.
(6) No personal income tax.
(7) Covers business profits tax. No deductions for limited personal income.
(8) Financial institutions back 2 years, forward 8 years.
(9) Out-of-state tax not deductible.
(10) Not deductible if measured by net income or if in lieu of income tax.
(11) Limited personal income tax; no deductions.
(12) Gross (personal) income tax on residents-nonresidents is levied on net rents-royalties and net business profits (after deducting all costs-expenses *except* income taxes).
(13) Follows Fed rules: 20-yr. carryforward. 2-yr. carryback generally; 3-yr. carryback for specified instances; 5-yr. carryback for NOLs arising in 2001 and 2002 and for other specified instances.
(14) *Mich.*—Extended carryback provisions are allowed for taxpayers electing to use IRC currently in effect.
(15) No provision for corporations.
(16) Out-of-state franchise taxes are deductible.
(17) In year sustained or equally over 5 years.
(18) Deductible as nonbusiness itemized deduction.
(19) Only business deductions allowed.
(20) *Kan.*—Net operating farm loss is allowed in some manner as Fed, and can be carried back for 5 yrs. Refunds as a result of a farm NOL carryback are limited to $1,500 per yr. Excess refund amounts can be carried back or forward.
(21) New corporations incurring first-year net operating loss get 1-year carryover if instate permanent investment of realty owned or leased is $100,000 (min.).
(22) Out-of-state franchise taxes not measured by income are deductible.
(23) Corporation franchise tax, Basis B (net income): 20-year carryover.
(24) *Me.*—NOLs for tax yrs. starting or ending in 2001 can be carried back 2 yrs. NOLs for tax yrs. starting after 12-31-2001 cannot be carried back.
(25) (Reserved.)
(26) Residents can deduct foreign taxes; also out-of-state income taxes if credit not taken.
(27) *Ky.*—No carryback for losses incurred for tax yrs. starting on or after 1-1-2005; 2-yr. carryback for losses incurred for tax yrs. starting before 1-1-2005.
(28) Although N.Y. generally follows the 2-yr. carryback and 20-yr. carryforward periods, administrative regulations provide 3-yr. carryback and 15-yr. carryforward periods for certain N.Y. NOLs sustained by nonresidents.
(29) Nonresidents can't carryback losses after 1977 to tax years pre-1-1-78 (Kans.).
(30) *Okla.*—Oklahoma law does not distinguish between "business income" and "nonbusiness income."
(31) Carrybacks (IRC) are treated as carryovers.
(32) (Reserved.)
(33) In the alternative, for its first 5 consecutive tax yrs., a corp. may deduct so much of the NOL as determined by IRC §172 and adjusted for differences between Mass. and Fed. taxable net income, as is represented by NOL carryovers for tax yrs. ending 12-31-75.
(34) 15-yr. carryforward of "Net economic losses"' as defined in law (eff for tax yrs. starting after 12-31-98; was 5-yr.).
(35) Losses from illegal transactions aren't deductible.
(36) Carryover, $1 million max. annually (N.H.).
(37) *N.J.*—15 yrs for certain high-tech corporations.
(38) *Mich.*—Until 12-31-2007, for "Single Business Tax" (SBT) allows 10-yr. carryover of business losses. Deduction of net income taxes (incl. SBT) disallowed; outstate franchise tax probably deductible unless measured by net income. Eff. 1-1-2008, Mich. Business Tax allows subtraction of any available business loss incurred after 12-31-2007 and loss can be carried forward up to 10 yrs. MBT requires add-back of taxes on or measured by net income and the MBT.
(39) (Reserved.)
(40) Taxpayers may take itemized deductions in N.Y. only if they itemized for federal purposes.
(41) 10-year carryover for steel mfrs or operators. 15-year carryover for qualified medical companies.
(42) For tax years ending after 6-30-90, NOL incurred by unitary group member before filing of combined return gets 7-yr carryover.
(43) No carrybacks for corps. 15-Year carryover for NOLs received in a tax year ending after 1984.
(44) Recipients of income with respect of decedents (IRC § 1691) can deduct Ariz. estate tax.
(45) (Reserved.)
(46) (Reserved.)

FOOTNOTES to chart ¶ 228-E (corresponding to parenthetical numbers in chart): (continued)

(47) For corporations NOL deduction carryback limited to $30,000. Amount of carryback disallowance can be carried forward. (Del.)

(48) *Pa.*—For tax yrs. starting after 12-31-2006, greater of: 12.5% of taxable income or $3 million; or the amount of net losses that may be carried over to the tax yr.; or the amount of taxable income. For tax yrs. starting pre-1–1–2007, lesser of: $2 million; or the amount of net losses that may be carried over to the tax yr.; or the amount of taxable income.

(49) Foreign income taxes $3,000 ($1,500 spouses filing separately) max. are deductible if foreign tax credit taken federally.

(50) *Ill.*— No corporation deduction for Ill. Income Tax or Replacement Income Tax. Individuals only add back Ill. income tax deducted on business, farm, or rental schedules.

(51) Resident credit for foreign income taxes paid.

(52) Deduction also allowed for Fed generation-skipping transfer tax (to extent Fed deductible) (Ala.).

(53) (Reserved.)

(54) (Reserved.)

(55) Individual follows current federal rules.

(56) $100,000 max. carryback total.

(57) NOL deduction allowed for yrs. starting after 1999 (except as noted below); 10-yr. carryover of 55% (100% of that part of NOL up to net loss of small business, if under $1 million annual receipts starting 1994) of NOL for 2000-2001 tax yr.; 60%, 2002-2003; 100%, after 2003. 5-yr. carryover for 1987 and pre-2000 tax yr. of 50% NOL, except new business starting after 12-31-93 can carry over for 8 yrs. 100% of that part of NOL up to net loss of new business and 50% of balance attributable to its 1st yr.; 7 yrs., 100% of that part of NOL up to net loss of new business and 50% of balance attributable to its 2nd yr.; 6 yrs., 3rd yr. Qualified business in enterprise zone or program area can also take NOL deduction for yrs. starting in 1991–92. Special 10-yr. carryover is allowed for NOLs attributable to 1987–93 incurred by specified taxpayers in bankruptcy or acquired in transaction qualifying as tax-free reorganization per IRC § 368(a)(1)(G).

(58) *Okla.*—Certain franchise taxes that are measured by income are not deductible for Okla. tax purposes.

(59) (Reserved.)

(60) Credit allowed instead of itemized deductions. Note (19) also applies.

(61–62) (Reserved.)

(63) (Reserved.)

(64) But individuals need not add back to Fed income Minn. taxes on S corps.' built-in gains, capital gains, and passive investment income to extent deducted for Fed AGI.

(65) *Vt.*—Eff 5-9-2006, Vt. allows 10-yr. carryforward from loss yr.; transition rules apply; pre-5-9-2006, Vt. generally followed Fed rules.

(66) (Reserved.)

(67) (Reserved.)

(68) No more than $300,000 of NOL for any tax yr. starting after 12-31-92 can be carried back to any previous tax yr. *(W. Va.)*

(69) *Utah.*— Carryback can't exceed $1 million in Utah taxable income per annual corporation return.

(70) *N.Y.*— IRC § 172 deduction allowed is adjusted to reflect N.Y-specific inclusions and exclusions from entire net income and determined as if taxpayer had elected under IRC § 172 to relinquish entire carryback period with respect to NOL, except with respect to 1st $10,000 of each of such losses, sustained during tax years ending after 6-30-89.

(71) *N.Y.*—New York City also follows the 2002 federal act extension of the carryback period for certain NOLs.

MISCELLANEOUS DEDUCTIONS—PART IV

¶228-F Other miscellaneous deductions. This chart covers state income tax deductions for the items listed above the columns. Symbols and abbreviations used in this chart are as follows: (*) = for individuals only; a = adjusted gross income; g = gross income; n = net income; t = taxable income; I = individuals; C = corporations; CR = tax credit; N = no; Y = yes; ND = no deductions; NP = no provisions; NT = no tax.

STATE	BOND PRE-MIUM AMOR-TIZA-TION (5)	WAR REPA-RA-TIONS	CO-OP (9)	TWO-EARN-ERS	CHILD CARE (24)	ALI-MONY (1,20)	EDU-CATI-ON (1)	HOME USED PART-LY BUSI-NESS (10)
ALA.(I)	N	N	Y	N	N	Y	N	Y
(C)	Y	N	Y	(18)	(18)	(18)	(18)	(18)
AK.(2,4)	Y	(18)	(18)	(18)	(18)	(18)	(18)	(18)
ARIZ.	Y	Y(7)	Y	N	N	Y(20)	Y	Y
ARK.	NP	N	NP	N	CR	Y(20)	Y	Y(17)
CALIF.	Y	Y(7,8)	Y	N	CR	Y(20)	Y	Y(17)
COLO.(4)	Y	N	Y	N	N	Y(20)	Y	Y
CT.(4)	Y	Y(7)	N	N	N	Y(20)	Y	Y(17)
DE.(4)	Y	N	Y	N	CR(1)	Y(20)	Y	Y
D.C.	Y	N	Y	N	CR	Y(20)	Y	Y
FL.(C)(2,4)	Y	(18)	(18)	(18)	(18)	(18)	(18)	(18)
GA.(4)	Y	N	Y	N	N	Y(20)	Y	Y
HI.(4)	Y	N	Y	N	CR	Y(20)	Y	Y
ID.(4)	Y	Y(8)	Y	N	Y	Y(20)	Y	Y
IL.(4)	Y	Y(7)	N	N	CR(30)	Y(20)	Y	Y
IN.(4)	Y(21)	Y(7)	N	N	N	Y(20)	N	N
IA.(4)	Y	Y(8)	Y	N	CR	Y(20)	Y	Y
KS.(4)	Y	N	Y	N	CR	Y(20)	Y	Y
KY.(4)	Y	N	N	N	CR	Y(20)	CR	Y
LA.(14)	Y	N	Y	N	CR	Y(20)	Y	Y
ME.(4)	Y	N	Y	N	CR	Y(20)	Y	Y
MD.(4)	Y	Y(7)	Y	N	Y(28)	Y(20)	Y	Y
MA.(I)(4)	Y(12)	Y(7)	N	N	Y(25)	Y(20)	Y	Y
(C)(4)	Y	N	(18)	(18)	(18)	(18)	(18)	(18)
MI.(4)	Y(21)	Y(7)	N	N	N	Y(20)	N	N
MN.(4)	Y	N	Y	N	CR	Y(20)	Y	Y
MS.(4)	Y	N	Y	N	CR	Y(20)	N	Y
MO.(4)	Y	Y(7)	Y	N	N	Y(20)	Y	Y
MT.(4)	Y	N	Y	N	Y(6)	Y(20)	Y	Y
NE.(4)	Y	N	Y	N	CR	Y(20)	N	Y
N.H.(16)	Y(21)	N	N	N	N	N	N	N
N.J.	Y(21)	Y(7)	N	N	N	Y(20)	N	Y(17)
N.M.(4)	Y	N	Y	N	CR	Y(20)	Y	Y
N.Y.(4,29)	Y	Y(7)	Y	N	CR	Y(20)	Y(3)	Y
N.C.	Y	N	Y	N	CR	Y(20)	Y(22)	Y
N.D.(4)	Y	N	Y	N	N	Y(20)	Y	Y
OH.(4)	Y(21)	N	N	CR	CR	Y(20)	N	N
OK.(4)	Y	N	Y	N	CR	Y(20)	Y	Y
OR.(4)	Y	Y(8)	Y	N	CR	Y(20)	Y	Y
PA.(4)	Y(21)	Y(7)	N	N	N	N	Y(23)	Y(21)
R.I.(4)	Y	N	Y	N	CR	Y(20)	Y	Y
S.C.(4)	Y	N	Y	CR	CR	Y(20)	Y	Y
TN.(4,15)	Y	N	N	N	N	N	N	N

STATE	BOND PREMIUM AMORTIZATION (5)	WAR REPARATIONS	CO-OP (9)	TWO-EARNERS	CHILD CARE (24)	ALIMONY (1,20)	EDUCATION (1)	HOME USED PARTLY BUSINESS (10)
UT.(4)	Y	Y(8)	Y	N	N	Y(20)	Y	Y
VT.(4)	Y	N	Y	N	CR	Y(20)	Y	Y
VA.(4)	Y	Y(7)	Y	N	Y(6)/ CR(6)	Y(20)	Y	Y
W.VA.(4,21)	Y	N	N	N	N	Y(20)	N	N
WI.(I)(4,21)	Y	Y(7)	N	CR	N	Y(20)	N	N
(C)	Y		(18)	(18)	(18)	(18)	(18)	(18)

FOOTNOTES to chart ¶ 228-F (corresponding to parenthetical numbers in chart):

(1) Individual taxpayer.
(2) No personal income tax.
(3) Also deductible: contibutions to higer education fund. Applicable percentage of allowable college tuition expense is also deductible, unless taxpayer opts for alternative credit.
(4) State adopts or accepts Fed provisions.
(5) No premium deduction if bond interest is wholly tax-exempt, and special rules apply if partly exempt—under Fed rules.
(6) Dollar limit on deductions and/or income of parents. Credit for hiring and child-care expenses of welfare recipients.
(7) Deduction applies to qualified reparations made to victims of Nazi persecution. In *Ill.*, also applies to descendants. In *Va.*, applies to spouse, widower, widow, child or stepchild of the victim. In Pa., also applies to damages from Agent Orange exposure and crime victim compensation.
(8) Deduction applies to qualified reparations made to persons of Japanese ancestry who were interned during WWII.
(9) Tenant-stockholder's proportionate share of real estate taxes and interest in a cooperative housing corporation.
(10) Expenses of business owner attributable to such place of business (but *not* fair rental value). Under Fed Tax Reform Act, subject to 2% deduction floor after 1986; deduction limited to business gross income from home office less expenses attributable to that business.
(11) (Reserved.)
(12) Estates & trusts only.
(13) Teachers only while attending summer school or taking special courses required for renewal of contract or employment.
(14) Fed provisions adopted for individuals only.
(15) Limited personal income tax; no deductions.
(16) Applies to business profits tax only. No deductions for limited personal income (investment).
(17) Individual having own business (not as employee).
(18) Not applicable.
(19) To update or keep present levels; to keep present level (not trips abroad or for new skills).
(20) States allow deduction of alimony paid from gross income.
(21) Business deduction only.
(22) IRC rules adopted.
(23) Only if required by law or employer.
(24) Includes dependent care expenses incurred by taxpayer.
(25) Amount exceeding IRC §21 up tp $3,600 for one qualified dependent or $7,200 for 2 or more qualified depenents, or take $2,400 for one qualified dependent or $4,800 for 2 or more qualified dependents.
(26) Expenses allowed as tax credits (limited.)
(27) Follows Fed on exclusion for employer-paid expenses for dependent care.
(28) Add back child care outlays for which qualified employment opportunity credit was granted. Add back expenses of unlicensed child care centers.
(29) *N.Y.*—Varying percentage of total N.Y. itemized deduction is disallowed for higher-income taxpayers. Itemized deductions are allowed only if the taxpayer itemized on the federal return.
(30) *Ill.*—Corporate taxpayers are allowed a credit for a percentage of the cost of providing a child care facility to employees.

DEPRECIATION METHODS

¶229 Fed depreciation rules. The chart below shows the states that follow the Federal ''Modified Accelerated Cost Recovery System'' (MACRS) set by the 1986 Federal Tax Reform Act. It also shows the states that follow the Federal ''Accelerated Cost Recovery System'' (ACRS) that preceded MACRS. The pre-1981 Federal depreciation methods (Col. E) were not obliterated by ACRS and they still apply to property put in service before 1981 and to property not covered by ACRS. ''(C)'' means entry applies to corporations; ''(I)'', to individuals.

➽ **MACRS→** The 1986 Federal Tax Reform Act (TRA) revamped the ACRS system of depreciation introduced by 1981 ERTA. The new system, Modified Accelerated Cost Recovery System (MACRS), which is generally effective for property placed in service after 12-31-1986, retains many of the original ACRS rules. The 3, 5, 10, and 15-year classes are kept and two new classes are introduced (7 and 20-year property). There is no distinction made between new and used property and salvage value continues to be disregarded. Cars and light trucks are shifted from the 3-year to the 5-year class. Office equipment moves from the 5-year class to the 7-year class. Depreciation for property in the 3, 5, 7, and 10-year classes is speeded up from 150% to 200% declining balance. Both residential and nonresidential real property must be depreciated using the straight line method. The recovery period is extended to 27½ years for residential property and to 31½ years for nonresidential property.

➽ **1993 FEDERAL LAW CHANGES→** States that conform to the current IRC or post-1993 IRC (¶ 221) adopt 1993 federal law changes increasing the IRC §179 ceiling on depreciable business assets that can be expensed to $17,500 from $10,000 (eff for property placed in service in tax yrs. starting after 12-31-1992) and increasing the recovery period for depreciation of nonresidential realty to 39 yrs., from 31.5 yrs. (eff generally for property placed in service after 5-12-1993).

➽ **1996 FEDERAL LAW CHANGES→** States that conform to the current IRC or post-1996 IRC (¶ 221) adopt 1996 law changes increasing the IRC §179 ceiling on depreciable assets that can be expensed to $18,000 eff for tax yrs. starting in 1997, $18,500 in 1998, $19,000 in 1999, $20,000 in 2000, $24,000 in 2001 or 2002, and $25,000 for tax yrs. starting after 2002.

➽ **1997 FEDERAL LAW CHANGES→** States that conform to the current IRC or post-8-5-1997 IRC (¶ 221) adopt 1997 law changes which shift qualified rent-to-own consumer durables to the 3-year class from the 5-year class (generally for property placed in service after 8-5-1997).

➽ **30% BONUS DEPRECIATION DEDUCTION→** The second column in the chart tells whether or not a state follows the bonus depreciation deduction provided under the federal Job Creation and Worker Assistance Act of 2002 (P.L. 107-147) for state corporation (C) and individual (I) income taxpayers. The federal 2002 law allows an additional first-year depreciation deduction equal to 30% of the adjusted basis of qualified property acquired after 9-10-2001 and before 9-11-2004 and placed in service after 9-10-2001 and before 2005 (before 2006, for certain property with longer production periods). The 30% bonus depreciation applies retroactively to federal returns for 2001 and later years.

➽ **50% BONUS DEPRECIATION DEDUCTION→** The first column in the chart tells whether or not a state follows the bonus depreciation deduction provided under the federal Jobs and Growth Tax Relief Reconciliation Act of 2003 (P.L. 108-27) for state corporation (C) and individual (I) income taxpayers. The federal 2003 law makes the following changes in the federal depreciation deduction scheme: the 30% bonus first-year depreciation is allowed for qualified property acquired before 2005; an additional first-year bonus depreciation deduction is allowed equal to 50% of the adjusted basis of qualified property acquired after May 5, 2003 and before 2005 (before

2006 for certain property with longer production periods); taxpayers can elect on a class-by-class basis to claim the 30% amount instead of the 50% amount for qualifying property or elect not to claim bonus first-year depreciation at all; and the first-year depreciation limit for qualified passenger automobiles is increased by $7,650, from $4,600, if the passenger automobile is "50-percent bonus depreciation property."

➽ **2004 FEDERAL LAW CHANGES→** States that conform to the current IRC (¶ 221) adopt 2004 federal law provisions that make the following changes: extend the 50% bonus depreciation placed-in-service date for small aircraft by one yr., so that it applies through 2005; extend for an additional two yrs. the increased amounts that a taxpayer may expense under IRC §179 ($100,000 indexed for inflation) and other expensing enhancements, so that they continue through 2007 tax yrs.; treat qualified leasehold improvements and restaurant property placed in service after 10-22-2004 and before 2006 as 15-yr. recovery property depreciated using the straight-line method; and limit IRC §179 expensing for heavy SUVs to $25,000 per yr.

STATE (5) Col. A		FED 50% BONUS DEPRECIATION DEDUCTION	FED 30% BONUS DEPRECIATION DEDUCTION	FED MACRS Col. B.	FED ACRS Col. C	STRAIGHT LINE DEPRECIATION Col. D	FED FAST DEPRECIATION RULES (11) Col. E
ALA.	(C)(6)	Yes	Yes	Yes	Yes	Yes(2)	Yes(2)
	(I)(6)	Yes	Yes	Yes	Yes	Yes(2)	Yes(2)
AK.	(C)(6)	Yes(33)	Yes(33)	Yes(C)	Yes(C)	Yes(C)(1)	Yes(C)(1)
	(I)	State has no personal income tax.					
ARIZ.	(C)(6)	No	No	Yes	Yes	Yes(1)	Yes(1)
	(I)(6)	No	No	Yes	Yes	Yes(1)	Yes(1)
ARK.	(C)(6,31)	No	No	Yes	Yes	Yes(2)	Yes(2)
	(I)(6,31)	No	No	Yes	Yes	Yes(2)	Yes(2)
CALIF.	(C)	No	No	No	No	Yes(2)	Yes(2)
	(I)	No	No	Yes(9)	Yes(9)	Yes(2)	Yes(2)
COLO.	(C)(6)	Yes	Yes	Yes	Yes	Yes(1)	Yes(1)
	(I)(6)	Yes	Yes	Yes	Yes	Yes(1)	Yes(1)
CONN.	(C)(6)	No	No	Yes	Yes(C)	Yes(1)	Yes(C)(1)
	(I)(6)	No(42)	No(42)	Yes	Yes(C)	Yes(1)	Yes(C)(1)
DEL.	(C)(6)	Yes	Yes	Yes	Yes	Yes(1)	Yes(1)
	(I)(6)	Yes	Yes	Yes	Yes	Yes(1)	Yes(1)
D.C.	(C)(6)	No	No	Yes	Yes	Yes(1)	Yes(1)
	(I)(6)	No	No	Yes	Yes	Yes(1)	Yes(1)
FLA.	(C)(6)	Yes	Yes	Yes	Yes(19)	Yes(19)	Yes(19)
	(I)	State has no personal income tax.					
GA.	(C)(6)	No	No	Yes(12)	Yes(12)	Yes(1)	Yes(1)
	(I)(6)	No	No	Yes(12)	Yes(12)	Yes(1)	Yes(1)
HAW.	(C)(6)	No	No	Yes	Yes	Yes(1)	Yes(1)
	(I)(6)	No	No	Yes	Yes	Yes(1)	Yes(1)
ID.	(C)(6)	No	No	Yes	Yes	Yes(1)	Yes(1)
	(I)(6)	No	No	Yes	Yes	Yes(1)	Yes(1)
ILL.	(C)(6)	No	No	Yes	Yes	Yes(1)	Yes(1)
	(I)(6)	No	No	Yes	Yes	Yes(1)	Yes(1)
IND.	(C)(6)	No	No	Yes	Yes	Yes(1)	Yes(1)
	(I)(6)	No	No	Yes	Yes	Yes(1)	Yes(1)
IA.	(C)(6)	Yes	No	Yes	Yes	Yes(1)	Yes(1)
	(I)(6)	Yes	No	Yes	Yes	Yes(1)	Yes(1)
KAN.	(C)(6)	Yes	Yes	Yes	Yes	Yes(1)	Yes(1)
	(I)(6)	Yes	Yes	Yes	Yes	Yes(1)	Yes(1)

STATE (5) Col. A		FED 50% BONUS DEPRECI-ATION DEDUC-TION	FED 30% BONUS DEPRECI-ATION DEDUC-TION	FED MACRS Col. B.	FED ACRS Col. C	STRAIGHT LINE DE-PRECIA-TION Col. D	FED FAST DEPRECI-ATION RULES (11) Col. E
KY.	(C)(6)	No	No	Yes(20)	Yes(20)	Yes(1)	Yes(1)
	(I)(6)	No	No	Yes(20)	Yes(20)	Yes(1)	Yes(1)
LA.	(C)(6)	Yes	Yes	Yes	Yes	Yes(1)	Yes(1)
	(I)(6)	Yes	Yes	Yes	Yes	Yes(1)	Yes(1)
ME.	(C)(6)	No(41)	No(38)	Yes(21)	Yes(21)	Yes(1)	Yes(1)
	(I)(6)	No(41)	No(38)	Yes(21)	Yes(21)	Yes(1)	Yes(1)
MD.	(C)(6)	No	No	Yes	Yes	Yes(1)	Yes(1)
	(I)(6)	No	No	Yes	Yes	Yes(1)	Yes(1)
MA.	(C)(6)	No	No	Yes	Yes(10)	Yes(1)	Yes(1)
	(I)(6)	No	No	Yes	Yes(10)	Yes(1)	Yes(1)
MI.	(C)(3,6)	No(36)	No(36)	No(3)	No(3)	Yes(1)	Yes(1)
	(I)(3,6)	No(36)	Yes(36)	Yes(3)	Yes(3)	Yes(1)	Yes(1)
MN.	(C)(6)	No(34)	No(34)	Yes(17)	Yes(17)	Yes(1)	Yes(1)
	(I)(6)	No(34)	No(34)	Yes(17)	Yes(17)	Yes(1)	Yes(1)
MS.	(C)(6)	No	No	Yes	Yes	Yes(1)	Yes(1)
	(I)(6)	No	No	Yes	Yes	Yes(1)	Yes(1)
MO.	(C)(6)	Yes	No(35)	Yes	Yes	Yes(1)	Yes(1)
	(I)(6)	Yes	No(35)	Yes	Yes	Yes(1)	Yes(1)
MT.	(C)(6)	Yes	Yes	Yes	Yes	Yes(1)	Yes(1)
	(I)(6)	Yes	Yes	Yes	Yes	Yes(1)	Yes(1)
NE.	(C)(6)	No(39)	No(39)	Yes	Yes	Yes(1)	Yes(1)
	(I)(6)	No(39)	No(39)	Yes	Yes	Yes(1)	Yes(1)
N.H.	(C)(6)	No	No	Yes(C)(16)	Yes(C)(16)	Yes(C)(1)	Yes(C)(1)
	(I)	State has a limited personal income tax.					
N.J.	(C)(6,7)	No	No	Yes(7,24)	Yes(24)	Yes	Yes
	(I)(6,7)	No	No	Yes(7,24)	Yes(24)	Yes	Yes
N.M.	(C)(6)	Yes	Yes	Yes	Yes	Yes(1)	Yes(1)
	(I)(6)	Yes	Yes	Yes	Yes	Yes(1)	Yes(1)
N.Y.	(C)(6)	No(28,32)	Yes(28,32)	Yes	Yes(18)	Yes(1,4)	Yes(1,4)
	(I)(6)	No(28)	Yes(28)	Yes	Yes(18)	Yes(1,4)	Yes(1,4)
N.C.	(C)(6)	No	No	Yes	Yes	Yes(1)	Yes(1)
	(I)(6)	No	No	Yes	Yes	Yes(1)	Yes(1)
N.D.	(C)(6)	Yes	Yes	Yes	Yes	Yes(1)	Yes(1)
	(I)(6)	Yes	Yes	Yes	Yes	Yes(1)	Yes(1)
OHIO	(C)(6)	No(8)	No(8)	Yes(15)	Yes(15)	Yes(1)	Yes(1)
	(I)(6)	No(8)	No(8)	Yes(23)	Yes(23)	Yes(1)	Yes(1)
OK.	(C)(6)	Yes	No(37)	Yes	Yes	Yes(1)	Yes(1)
	(I)(6)	Yes	No(37)	Yes	Yes	Yes(1)	Yes(1)
OR.	(C)(6)	Yes	Yes	Yes	Yes(I)(14)	Yes(1)	Yes(1)
	(I)(6)	Yes	Yes	Yes	Yes(I)(14)	Yes(1)	Yes(1)
PA.	(C)(6)	No	No	Yes	Yes(22)	Yes(40)	Yes
	(I)(6)	No	No	Yes	Yes(23)	Yes	Yes
R.I.	(C)(6)	No	No	Yes	Yes	Yes(1)	Yes(1)
	(I)(6)	No	No	Yes	Yes	Yes(1)	Yes(1)
S.C.	(C)	No	No	Yes	Yes	Yes	Yes
	(I)	No	No	Yes	Yes	Yes	Yes
TN.	(C)(6)	No	No	Yes	Yes(C)(26)	Yes(C)(1)	Yes(C)(1)
	(I)	State has a limited personal income tax.					
UT.	(C)(6)	Yes	Yes	Yes	Yes	Yes(2)	Yes(2)
	(I)(6)	Yes	Yes	Yes	Yes	Yes(2)	Yes(2)
VT.	(C)(6)	No	No	Yes	Yes	Yes(1)	Yes(1)
	(I)(6)	Yes	Yes	Yes	Yes	Yes(1)	Yes(1)
VA.	(C)(6)	No	No	Yes	Yes(27)	Yes(1)	Yes(1)
	(I)(6)	No	No	Yes	Yes(27)	Yes(1)	Yes(1)
W.VA.	(C)(6)	Yes	Yes	Yes	Yes	Yes(1)	Yes(1)
	(I)(6)	Yes	Yes	Yes	Yes	Yes(1)	Yes(1)
WIS.	(C)(6)	No	No	Yes	Yes(29)	Yes(1)	Yes(1)
	(I)(6)	No	No	Yes	Yes(29)	Yes(1)	Yes(1)

Footnotes to chart ¶229 (corresponding to parenthetical numbers in chart):

(1) State adopts or accepts pre-1981 Fed provisions.
(2) State law is similar to pre-1981 Fed rules.
(3) Entries apply to individuals only; '86 TRA applicable if electing current IRC. "Single Business Tax" reaching corps.-individuals requires add back of IRC depreciation incl. ACRS (up to 100%) and instead allows investment tax credit.
(4) Depreciation is at twice Fed rates for construction or contract before 1-1-69 for property producing goods by mfg. processing, mining, agriculture, horticulture or commercial fishing; air-water pollution facilities (optional). Disallowed to lessors of tangible personalty. Double depreciation is replaced by investment tax credit.
(5) All states and D.C. allow use of Fed guidelines lives (Rev. Proc. 72-10, 1972-1 SB 721) for depreciating assets.
(6) State adopts Fed rules on Class Life Asset Depreciation Range System (elective).
(7) Gross (personal) income tax on residents-nonresidents reaches net rents and net business profits (after deduction for all costs-expenses per Fed acctg. methods).
(8) Ohio requires an addback of 5/6 of the bonus depreciation deduction taken on the federal return for state tax purposes. 1/5 of that addback amount can be taken as an additional depreciation deduction in each of the following 5 yrs. Requires specified addback for enhanced IRC §179 expensing.
(9) Personal income tax conforms to Fed., except for changes made by 2002 Fed law (P.L. 107-147) (Calif.).
(10) Individuals get ACRS per IRC as of 1-1-88 (Mass.).
(11) Meaning 150%, double declining balance, sum-of-years' digits methods.
(12) Elect method used for state tax purpose or Fed method for tax yr. property placed in service eff. for tax yrs ending after 12-31-86 (Ga.).
(13) Also applies to unincorporated business tax.
(14) Use pre-1981 ERTA depreciation for property placed in service in 1981–1984.
(15) Corps. must add back 25% (20% for 1989; 15% '90; 10% '91; 5% '92; none after 1992) of amount by which Fed taxable income was reduced by ACRS; deduct 20% of pre-1989 addback; deduct 1989-92 addbacks ratably. (Ohio).
(16) Applies to Business Profits Tax on corporations and unincorporated businesses.
(17) For property placed in service after 12-31-87, 100% ACRS deduction allowed.
(18) For property placed in service in tax yrs. starting before 1994, ACRS allowed ¶ 280F on luxury autos for tax yrs ending after 6-18-84 and for recovery property placed in service in-state after 1984.
(19) Pre-ACRS can be elected. Fla. levies tax on excess of ACRS over straight line.
(20) Adopts IRC rules as of 12-31-93; transition rules apply to tax yrs. starting in 1994–1997. For property placed in service—*after 12-31-89, and pre-1-1-94* §168 and 179 rules apply per IRC as of 12-31-89; *pre-1-1-90,* these applied: §167 of 1980 IRC applied to property put in service after 7-31-85. Property placed in service 1-1-81 through 7-31-85, noncorporates use ACRS; corps. with tax yrs. begun after 6-30-84 and pre-7-31-85 divide ACRS by 1.4 or use pre-1981 §167 (Ky.).
(21) Pre-ACRS can be elected. For tax year ending in 1984, these portions of IRC §168 are nondeductible (added back to tax base): 2.5% of deductions for 3-year property; 7.5% for 5-year; 12.5% for 10-year; 20% of deductions for 15-year property; partial deduction allowed in yrs. 1985-1987. Applicable to tax yrs. starting on and after 1-1-2003, federal taxable income or federal adjusted gross income must be increased by an amount equal to the net increase in expensing attributable to the increase in aggregate cost claimed under IRC §179 arising from amendments to the IRC for tax yrs. starting after 12-31-2002. (Me.).
(22) Straight line only allowed for real property (Pa.).
(23) No provision for individuals dealing with ACRS.
(24) IRC rules are adopted for property placed in service after 7-7-93. For property placed in service pre-7-7-93, IRC as of 12-31-80 applies; ACRS deduction (exceeding pre-ACRS allowance) is denied for acctg. periods ending after 1981 except for periods in 1981 and ending in 1982 with respect to property put in service in 1981 (NJ).
(25) Probable status shown.
(26) Not deductible if result of lease characterizations under IRC §1168. (Tenn.).
(27) 30% of ACRS deduction denied for tax yrs begun after 1981 and pre-1-1-88. Subtract 20% of ACRS addback in yr. after a biennium (starting 1982-83) except corps. subtract 10% eff for tax yrs. starting in 1994, and 20% in 1995-97. Individuals subtract ⅔ eff for yrs. starting in 1988 and ⅓ bal. in 1989 (Va.).
(28) For tax yrs. after 2002, for property placed in service on or after 6-1-2003, deduction is limited to deduction allowed under IRC §167 as available to property acquired on 9-10-2001. There is an exception for qualified resurgence zone and qualified New York Liberty Zone property. (N.Y.)
(29) Use IRC as of 12-31-89 or elect IRC in effect for tax yr. for which return is filed. Old state rules apply to property placed in service pre-1987.
(30) IRC rules are adopted for corps. and individuals (eff for tax years starting after 12-31-88; *was* individuals followed IRS practice except §179 expensing) (N.C.).
(31) IRC §167, §168, §179 and §179A expensing is adopted as in effect on 1-1-99 (Ark.).
(32) New York City has generally decoupled from the accelerated depreciation provisions of the 2002 and 2003 federal acts for corporate income tax purposes (N.Y.).

Footnotes to chart ¶229 (corresponding to parenthetical numbers in chart): (continued)

(33) Except for taxpayers engaged in oil and gas production.
(34) Minn. requires 80% of bonus depreciation amount on federal return to be added back to the state return, and allows the taxpayer to subtract the portion of the bonus depreciation that was added back, in equal parts, in the 5 yrs. after the yr. of the addback.
(35) Mo. requires the 30% bonus depreciation deduction relating to property bought between 7-1-2002 and 7-1-2003 to be added back, to the extent the amount deducted exceeds that which would have been deducted under the IRC in effect on 1-1-2002, and subtract the amount that would have been deducted under the IRC in effect for 1-1-2002, to the extent that amount exceeds the amount actually deducted under the IRC as amended.
(36) In Mich., until 12-31-2007, for single business tax, all federal depreciation deductions must be added back to compute tax base. Individual income taxpayers are allowed the bonus depreciation deduction if they elect to use IRC currently in effect. Eff. 1-1-2008, for Mich. Business Tax, federal depreciation deduction is not required to be added back to compute tax base.
(37) Okla. requires taxpayers to add back 80% of the bonus depreciation deduction taken on the federal return for assets placed in service after 9-10-2001 and before 9-11-2004. Taxpayers can subtract 25% of that addback in each of the next 4 tax years.
(38) Applicable to tax yrs. starting on or after 1-1-2002 but before 1-1-2006, federal taxable income or federal adjusted gross income must be increased by an amount equal to the net increase in depreciation attributable to the federal 30% bonus depreciation deduction with respect to property put in service during the tax yr. (Me.).
(39) Neb. requires 85% of amount of bonus depreciation deducted on federal return to be added back on the state return, and allows that amount to be subtracted in later tax yrs.
(40) Pa.—Straight line depreciation only allowed for real property.
(41) Applicable to tax yrs. starting on or after 1-1-2002 but before 1-1-2006, federal taxable income or federal adjusted gross income must be increased by an amount equal to the net increase in depreciation attributable to the federal 50% bonus depreciation deduction with respect to property put in service during the tax yr. (Me.).
(42) To the extent added back in computing adjusted gross income, 25% of the additional federal depreciation allowance in each of the four suceeding tax yrs. can be substracted. (Conn.).

DEDUCTION FOR FEDERAL INCOME TAXES

¶230 Where you can and cannot deduct. One of the most important deductions on a state income tax return is the deduction for federal income taxes. With the federal government taking a big chunk of a corporation's net income and an individual's income, it is obvious that allowance of a deduction for federal taxes has a tremendous effect on the state tax bill. This chart shows which states allow a deduction for federal income taxes.

SYMBOLS appearing in chart entries: Letter *"l"* means deduction is limited.

Letter *"p"* means deduction is for tax paid only. Absence of this letter indicates deduction is allowed on either cash or accrual basis.

Letters *"NT"* mean no state income tax is imposed.

STATE	INDIVIDUALS(1)	CORPORATIONS(1)
ALA.	YES	YES
AK.	NT	NO
ARIZ.	NO	NO
ARK.	NO	NO
CALIF.	NO	NO
COLO.	NO	NO
CONN.	NO	NO
DEL.	NO	NO
D.C.	NO	NO
FLA.	NT	NO
GA.	NO	NO
HAW.	NO	NO
IDAHO	NO	NO
ILL.	NO	NO
IND.	NO	NO
IOWA	YES	YES *l* (7)
KAN.	NO	NO
KY.	NO	NO
LA.	YES	YES
ME.	NO	NO
MD.	NO	NO
MASS.	NO	NO
MICH.	NO	NO
MINN.	NO	NO
MISS.	NO	NO
MO.	YES *l* (3,6)	YES *l* (3,6)
MONT	YES *lp* (10)	NO
NEB.	NO	NO
NEV.	NT	NT
N.H.	NO (8)	NO (2)
N.J.	NO	NO
N.M.	NO	NO
N.Y.	NO	NO
N.C.	NO	NO
N.D.	YES *l* (6,9)	YES *l* (6,9)
OHIO	NO	NO
OKLA.	NO	NO
ORE.	YES *l* (4)	NO
PA.	NO	NO
R.I.	NO	NO
S.C.	NO	NO
S.D.	NT	NT
TENN.	NO (8)	NO
TEX.	NT	NT
UTAH	YES *l* (5)	NO
VT.	NO	NO
VA.	NO	NO
WASH.	NT	NT
W.VA.	NO	NO
WIS.	NO	NO
WYO.	NT	NT

Notes to chart ¶230 (corresponding to parenthetical numbers in chart):

(1) In any state, use of required over-all allocation or apportionment formula may, in effect, limit deduction to tax on in-state income (see also footnote (6) below).
(2) N.H.—For gross profits.
(3) Mo.—Deduction for corporation is limited to 50% of Fed tax. Deduction for individuals filing single returns is limited to $5,000; couples filing jointly, $10,000.
(4) Ore.—For 2006, deduction is limited to $5,000; $2,500 if married filing separately.
(5) Utah.—Deduct one-half of Fed tax paid (after credits).
(6) Specifically limited to Fed tax on income taxed by the state.
(7) Iowa.—Deductible up to 50%.
(8) N.H. and Tenn.—Limited income tax.
(9) N.D.—No deduction if using percentage of Fed tax method (short form filers); for corps. electing water's edge taxing or using cash basis.
(10) Mont.—Deduction for single filers is limited to $5,000; joint filers, $10,000.

REVISION OR REFUND OF STATE INCOME TAXES

¶231 Correcting returns. Taxpayers often discover additional items they should have reported or claimed after their income tax returns are filed. What can be done about it and how much time is there?

Two ways to undo your errors: You can (1) revise the return and apply for a refund, or (2) amend the return. Briefly, you get back overpayments primarily by filing revision or refund applications (the time limits are summarized below), an accompanying amended return is helpful but not usually necessary. Amended returns figure more importantly in putting a stop to delinquent penalties.

EXPLANATION OF CHART: Current general time limits for claiming refunds in the income tax states are charted below. Some laws (as in Minn.) fix alternate periods or time limits—for instance, 2 years after payment or 3½ years after return is due. In those cases, only the longer period is given in the chart. Separate columns are shown for corporations and individuals. Charts at ¶ 295 and ¶ 296 show refund time limits for other taxes. Symbol "d" means days, "y" means years, and star (*) means no tax.

STATE	CORPORATIONS	INDIVIDUALS
ALA.	3y(6)	3y(6)
AK.	3y(6)	*
ARIZ.	4y(5)	4y(5)
ARK.	3y(6)	3y(6)
CALIF.	4y(5)	4y(5)
COLO.	1y(11)	1y(11)
CONN.	3y(4)	3y(4)
DEL.	3y(6)	3y(6)
D.C.	3y(17)	3y(17)
FLA.	3y(1)	*
GA.	3y(16)	3y(16)
HAW.	3y(15)	3y(15)
IDA.	3y(15)	3y(15)
ILL.	3y(6)	3y(6)
IND.	3y(17)	3y(1)
IOWA	3y(5)	3y(5)
KAN.	3y(6)	3y(6)
KY.	4y(17)	4y(17)
LA.	3y(2)	3y(2)
ME.	3y(16)	3y(16)
MD.	3y(20)	3y(20)
MASS.	3y(21)	3y(21)
MICH.	4y(5)	4y(5)
MINN.	3.5y(5)	3.5y(5)
MISS.	3y(5)	3y(5)
MO.	3y(6)	3y(6)
MONT.	3y(5)	3y(6)
NEB.	3y(6)	3y(6)
N.H.	3y(6,12)	3y(6)
N.J.	4y	3y(6)
N.M.	3y(10)	3y(10)
N.Y.	3y(6)	3y(6)
N.C.	3y(5)	3y(5)
N.D.	3y(15,18)	3y(15,18)
OHIO	3y(17)	4y(1)
OKLA.	3y(1)	3y(1)
ORE.	2y(7)	2y(7)
PA.	3y(1)	3y(1)
R.I.	3y(1)	3y(6)
S.C.	3y(20)	3y(20)
TENN.	3y(14)	3y(14)
UTAH	3y(1)	3y(5)
VT.	3y(5)	3y(5)
VA.	3y(9)	3y(9)
W.VA.	3y(5)	3y(5)
WIS.	4y(13)	4y(13)

Footnotes to chart ¶231 (corresponding to parenthetical numbers in chart):

(1) After payment.
(2) From end of year tax was due.
(3) After notice of tax.
(4) After due date of payment.
(5) After due date of return. In N.C., alternatively, within 6 months after paying the tax. In Vt., alternatively, within 6 months after amended Fed return is received with respect to Fed income tax liability or taxable change reported on Fed return, if later.
(6) After return filing. In Ala., Ak., Ark., Mo., Neb., and N.H.: 3y from return date, or 2y from payment, if later. In Ill.: 3 yr. after return filing, or 1 yr. after payment, if later. In N.J., alternatively, within 2 yrs. after paying the tax. In Del., Kan., and R.I., or 2 yrs. after payment, if later. In N.Y., or 2 yrs. after tax paid, if later.
(7) Follows Fed income tax limits.
(8) From 12-31 of year return was due.
(9) *Va.*—Later of 3y. from return due date or 60d from final determination of change or correction in Fed tax liability on which state tax is based.

Footnotes to chart ¶231 (corresponding to parenthetical numbers in chart): (continued)

(10) After end of year payment due.
(11) After filing time expires for Fed refund claim.
(12) For business profits.
(13) After unextended return due date.
(14) From 12-31 of year payment is made.
(15) After return due date or filing, if later.
(16) After return filing or payment, if later.
(17) After return due date or payment, if later.
(18) 6 years if over 25% of taxable income or tax is changed.
(19) (Reserved.)
(20) Within 3 yrs. of return filing or within 2 yrs. of tax payment, if later. Refund based on IRS change must be filed within 180 days from date of IRS change. For Md., if the refund claim is based on IRS change that is more than 3 yrs. from the date the return was filed or more than 2 yrs. from the date the tax was paid, the claim must be filed within 1 yr. of the federal change.
(21) From return due date.

➽ **WARNING**→ (1) If the time limit is measured from the payment or return deadline, the failure to pay or file on time doesn't extend the periods for claiming refunds or applying for revision. (2) Always file separate claims for each taxable year unless a definite local rule permits otherwise. (3) Special rules apply for renegotiation of Fed contracts.

➽ **AFTERTHOUGHTS**→ Have a second or third thought, and file amended returns if you wish, before the last day fixed for filing without penalty. But married people beware: Some of the states will not allow a joint return after one spouse has already filed a separate return when the time is up for that spouse. Also, if a joint return has been filed, spouses usually can't file separately after time has run out for either of them.

➽ **TENTATIVE RETURNS**→ Of course, if a tentative return has been filed and an extension of time has been granted, you must file your ''final'' return before the final deadline.

Amended returns to claim refund or report additional income have been permitted or required in Alabama, Alaska, Arizona, Arkansas, California, Colorado, Connecticut, Delaware, District of Columbia, Florida, Georgia, Hawaii, Idaho, Illinois, Indiana, Iowa, Kansas, Kentucky, Louisiana, Maine, Maryland, Massachusetts, Michigan, Minnesota, Mississippi, Missouri, Montana, Nebraska, New Hampshire, New Jersey, New Mexico, New York, North Carolina, North Dakota, Ohio, Oklahoma, Oregon, Pennsylvania, Rhode Island, South Carolina, Utah, Vermont, Virginia, West Virginia, and Wisconsin. Penalties and interest are payable if the tax is understated or underpaid. Duty to report Fed changes is charted at ¶ 232.

➽ **WHAT TO DO**→ If you discover that you have understated your income or tax, don't be deterred from filing a corrected version as soon as possible, even if the law makes no provision for amended returns. If it's a simple detail, a letter statement will usually do. You have everything to gain and nothing to lose by such action.

FEDERAL INCOME—REPORTING CHANGES

¶232 Duty to report income changes: The chart below shows filing requirements arising from changes in Fed net income, and time limits imposed by states, if any.

Exchange of information between the federal I.R.S. and the states began in 1950 (¶ 235). The checkup can extend from routine inspection to obtaining photostatic copies of tax returns in file. Every taxpayer earning income and paying out deductible amounts has a permanent IRS computer record. The computers give U.S. and state tax authorities prompt, complete access to all tax information.

STATE	CORP.	INDIV.
ALA.	(16)	(16)
AK.	60 d (3,9)	NT
ARIZ.	90 d (6)	90 d (1,6)
ARK.	30 d (20)	30 d (20)
CALIF.	6 m (3,5,6)	6 m (3,5,6)
COLO.	30 d (3,6)	30 d (3,6)
CONN.	90 d (2,6)	90 d (3)
DEL.	90 d (3,6)	90 d (3,6)
D.C.	90 d (3)	90 d (3)
FLA.	60 d (3,22)	NT
GA.	180 d (3)	180 d (3)
HAW.	90 d (8)	90 d (8)
IDA.	(3,7)	(3,7)
ILL.	120 d (3,22)	120 d (3,22)
IND.	120 d	120 d
IOWA	(6)	(6)
KAN.	180 d (14)	180 d (24)
KY.	30 d (18)	30 d (18)
LA.	60 d (3)	60 d (3)
ME.	90 d (6,8)	90 d (6,8)
MD.	90 d (3)	90 d (3)
MASS.	3 m (3)	1 y (3)
MICH.	120 d (15)	120 d (9,15)
MINN.	180 d (15)	180 d (15)
MISS.	30 d (11)	30 d (11)
MO.	90 d (3,6)	90 d (3,6)
MONT.	90 d (2,6)	90 d (2,6)
NEB.	90 d (3,6)	90 d (3,6)
N.H.	6 m (3)	6 m (3)
N.J.	90 d (3,6)	90 d (3,6)
N.M.	90 d (19)	90 d (19)
N.Y.	90 d (3,5,6,17)	90 d (3,6)
N.C.	6 m (2,3)	6 m (2,3)
N.D.	90 d (3,6)	90 d (3,6)
OHIO	1 y (3)	60 d (3)
OKLA.	1 y (1,16)	1 y (1,16)
ORE.	90 d (3,6)	90 d (3,6)
PA.	30 d (2)	30 d (25)
R.I.	60 d (3)	90 d (3,6)
S.C.	180 d (3)	180 d (3)
TENN.	(13)	NP (21)
UTAH	90 d (3,6)	90 d (3,6)
VT.	60 d (2,4,16)	60 d (2,4,16)
VA.	1 y (3,6)	1 y (3,6)
W.VA.	90 d (3,6)	90 d (3,6)
WIS.	90 d (3,6)	90 d (3,6)

Notes to chart ¶ 232 (corresponding to parenthetical numbers in chart): "NT" means no tax; "NP" means no provision; "d" means days; "m" means months; "y" means years.

(1) After change in Fed net income.
(2) After notice of change in Fed net income.
(3) After final determination.
(4) After knowledge of change.
(5) Or as required.
(6) If amended Fed return filed, amended state return required.
(7) Immediately.
(8) After change, correction, adjustment or recomputation is determined or amended return is filed.
(9) After modification, recomputation, or determination or deficiency.
(10) On request.
(11) After agreement to the Fed change.
(12) No specific provision.
(13) Required by regulation to be reported on return.
(14) After IRS adjustments are paid, agreed to, or become final, whichever is earlier.
(15) After final determination by IRS. In Mich., applies to all corporate and non-corporate taxpayers subject to the single business tax and Mich. business tax.

Notes to chart ¶ 232 (corresponding to parenthetical numbers in chart): "NT" means no tax; "NP" means no provision; "d" means days; "m" means months; "y" means years. (continued)

(16) File amended return.
(17) 120 days for taxpayers filing combined reports.
(18) Within 30 days of start of Fed examination; submit copy of final federal determination within 30 days.
(19) After adjustment in computation basis.
(20) After notice and demand for payment by IRS.
(21) Limited income tax is imposed.
(22) Or refund, credit, abatement assessed or paid, if earlier. Ill.: also deficieny, tentative carryback adjustment.
(23) By due date of next return.
(24) Form instructions require adjustments to be reported on return for year adjustment became final.
(25) After discovering error.

➼ **ENFORCEMENT→** Most states have the right to demand supplementary returns once they get notice of an income change. But there's one limitation: resulting assessment would have to be made within time limit fixed by local law (3 to 6 years). Exception—if change is due to fraudulent concealment or omission of taxable income, assessment can generally be made at any time.

➼ **MONEY BACK→** A Fed change can work in your favor, too. If it operates to lower the taxable net income you will usually be in a position to claim a state tax refund (though Fed tax deduction on state return is proportionately decreased). Prompt action should be taken. Sometimes both refund and additional tax are involved. When applying for a refund you don't necessarily have to report added liability unless (1) statute requires report, or (2) state authorities expressly demand report.

➼ **WHAT TO DO→** Coordinate your state and Fed returns. Do them together if possible. Advance your preparation date of state individual and corporation income tax returns normally due in April—do them in February or March. Avoid the innocent discrepancies that can be as expensive as the ones made in bad faith.

INCOME TAXES—ASSESSMENT, COLLECTION

¶233 Going after delinquents. If taxpayers file no returns in states where income is taxable, or omit income from filed returns, what can the taxing states do, and what will they do, about these unfulfilled obligations? The farthest an assessment can go back is the starting date of the tax—or, more accurately, the time when the tax first *could* have been interpreted to reach nonresidents and foreign corporations (see the list following the chart below).

In most states, the running of the statute of limitations on assessment and collection does not begin until a return is filed. The state-by-state details are shown in the chart on the following page. For example, the taxpayer in *Northwestern States Portland Cement Co. [358 US 450]* hadn't filed returns, and the U.S. Supreme Court validated assessments covering 16 years—from 1933, the starting year of the tax, through 1948. A few states have self-imposed limits even if no return was filed. Symbols are explained at the bottom of this page.

Privilege license taxes can now be imposed on foreign corporations doing business exclusively in interstate commerce [*Complete Auto, 430 US 274*]. The U.S. Supreme Court in its *Complete Auto* decision rejected the *Spector rule [340 US 602*] that a state tax on interstate commerce was per se unconstitutional. The chart below gives rules for the privilege income components of the ''double-barrelled'' taxes in California, Montana, New Jersey, Oregon, Pennsylvania, Utah, and Wisconsin and the privilege taxes (''single-barrelled'') in Connecticut, Florida, Massachusetts, Minnesota, New York, Ohio, and Tennessee.

If no return is filed or if a false or fraudulent return is filed with intent to evade tax, there's generally no limit on the time a state can assess and collect.

Court action is the type of collection action treated in the chart. There are many other ways, including issuance of warrants, docketing of assessments as liens, distraint of property, and levy on property.

SYMBOLS: A = Assessment or after finality of assessment. **ACA** = Accrual of cause action. **AP** = Assessment period (time allowed for assessment). **BI** = Base income. **DF** = Discovery of facts, if return was fraudulent or not filed. **DL** = Determination of liability. **ETY** = End of tax year. **Fed** = Follows federal provisions. **GU** = In case of gross understatement of income. **NL** = No limit. **NSP** = Tax law does not mention limits; general principles would apply; this might mean no time limit, in cases involving the state. **PD** = Payment due. **PT** = Privilege tax. **RD** = Date when return was due. **RF** = Date when return was filed. (If return was filed before due date, assessment time limit often runs from due date. Where this small margin actually makes a difference, check wording of statute.) **TD** = Date when tax payment was due. **TP** = Date when tax was paid. **YA** = Year tax accrues. **m** = months after. **y** = years after. **%grO** = If indicated percentage (minimum) of gross income was omitted from return. **%niO** = If indicated percentage (minimum) of net income was omitted from return. **%tiO** = If indicated percentage (minimum) of taxable income was omitted from return. **%iO** = If indicated percentage (minimum) of income omitted from return. **%agO** = If indicated percentage (minimum) of adjusted gross income was omitted from return. **%tfO** = If indicated percentage (minimum) of taxes or fees was omitted from return.

STATE	ASSESSMENT (The fixing and billing by state of tax due from corp. or ind.)		COLLECTION (The institution of proceedings to collect amounts timely assessed.)	
	CORPORATIONS	INDIVIDUALS	CORPORATIONS	INDIVIDUALS
Alabama	3y(RF or RD)	Same	10yA	Same
	6yRF or RD 25%grO	Same		
Alaska	Fed	No Tax	6yA	No Tax
Arizona	4yRF	Same	6yA	Same
	6yRF25%grO	Same		
Arkansas	3yRF	Same	10yA	Same
	6y25%tiO			
California	4yRF	Same	10yDL	Same
	6yRF25%grO	Same		
Colorado	ly(7)	Same	6yA	Same
Conn.	3yRF	3yRF	NSP	NSP
		6yRF25%grO		
Delaware	3yRF	Same	10yA	10yA
District of Columbia	3yRF	Same	10yA	Same
	6yRF25%grO	Same		
Florida	3yRF	No Tax	NSP	No Tax
	3yRF25%grO			
Georgia	3yRF	Same		
	6yRF25%grO	Same	NSP	Same
Hawaii	3yRF or RD(1)	Same	AP	Same
Idaho	3yRF	Same	6yA	Same
Illinois	3yRF	Same	20y(9)	Same
	6yRF25%BI(17)	Same		
Indiana	3yRF	Same	NSP	Same
	6y25%iO	Same		
Iowa	3yRF	Same	NSP	Same
	6yRF25%grO	Same		
Kansas	3y(RF or TP)	Same	AP(5)	Same
	(1)			
Kentucky	4yRF	Same	5yACA	Same
	6yRF25%tiO	6yRF25%niO		
Louisiana	NSP3yETY	Same	3yETY	Same
Maine	3y(RF or RD)(1)	Same	NSP	Same
	6yRF25%grO(15)			
Maryland	3y(RF or RD)(1)	Same	7yA	Same
Massachusetts	3yRF	Same	6yA	Same
	6yRF25%grO	Same		
Michigan	4y(RD or RF)	4y(RD or RF)	NSP	NSP
	2yDF(10)	2yDF		
Minnesota	31/2yRF	Same	5yA	Same
	61/2yRF or RD	Same		
	25%grO(1)			
Mississippi	3y(RF or RD)(1)	Same	NSP	Same
Missouri	3yRF	3yRF	5yACA	Same
	6yRF25%grO	6yRF25%agO		
Montana	3yRF	5yRF	3yRF	NL
Nebraska	3yRF(19)	Same	(4)	Same
	6yRF25%grO			
New Hampshire	3y(TD or TP)	3yRF or RD (11)	NSP	NSP
New Jersey	4yRF	3yRF	10y	6yA
		6yRF25%iO		
New Mexico	3y(2,6)	Same	10yA	Same
	6y(2) 25% tfO	Same		
	7y(2)(13)			
	10y(2)(14)			
New York	3yRF(12)	3yRF	6yA	6yA
	6yRF25%grO	6yRF25%agO(3)		
North Carolina	1yRF or 3yRD(1)	Same	NSP	Same
North Dakota	3yRF(19)	Same	NSP	Same
	6yRF25%tiO	6yRF	Same	
Ohio(16)	3y(RF or RD)(1)	4y(RF or RD)(1)	7y(A) or 4y(A)(20)	7y(A) or 4y(A)(20)

STATE	ASSESSMENT (The fixing and billing by state of tax due from corp. or ind.) CORPORATIONS	INDIVIDUALS	COLLECTION (The institution of proceedings to collect amounts timely assessed.) CORPORATIONS	INDIVIDUALS
Oklahoma	3yRF	Same	3y	Same
Oregon	3yRF 5yRF25%grO	Same	NSP	NSP
Pennsylvania	18mo.RD	3yRF 6yRF25%tfO	NSP	NSP
Rhode Island	3yRF or 3yRD(1) 6yRF25%iO	3yRF Same	NSP	NSP
South Carolina	3yRF or 6yRF20%tfO	Same	10yA	Same
Tennessee	3y(2)	5y(2,18)	6A	Same
Utah	3yRF	3yRF 6yRF25%grO	3yA	NSP
Vermont	3yTD	Same	6yTD	Same
Virginia	3yRF(21)	Same(21)	20yA	Same
West Virginia	3yRD	Same	10yA	Same
Wisconsin	4yRF 6yRD25%niO	Same	NSP	Same

Footnotes to chart ¶ 233 (corresponding to numbers in parentheses in chart):

(1) Whichever is later.
(2) After end of calendar year in which due.
(3) Incl. taxable portion of lump-sum or higher educ. fund distribution & Fed tax preference items.
(4) 3 yrs. from assessment or 10 yrs. from recording tax lien.
(5) Or within 1 yr. after amended return is filed.
(6) *N.M.*—Tax liability.
(7) Plus Fed limits.
(8) Plus anytime in which tax lien is in force.
(9) After filing notice of lien.
(10) *Mich.* Single Business Tax applies to corporate and noncorporate taxpayers.
(11) Tax on residents only.
(12) There is no limitations period if no return is filed, a false or fraudulent return is filed with intent to evade tax, or federal changes are not reported.
(13) For failure to file return.
(14) For false or fraudulent return with intent to evade tax.
(15) *Me.*—6 yrs. if tax liability shown on return is less than 50% of tax liability determined by state tax assessor.
(16) *Ohio*—Doubled for sham transactions; 10 yrs. if no return or report filed but no fraud.
(17) *Ill.*—6 yrs., if failed to include information on reportable transaction.
(18) *Tenn.*—There is no limitation period if no return is filed or a fraudulent return is filed with intent to evade tax.
(19) 3 yr. period is extended to 6 yrs. if understatement of taxable income is in excess of 25%.
(20) Later of 7 yrs. after assessment issued or 4 yrs. after assessment becomes final; transitional rule applies.
(21) Eff 7-1-2007, tax can be assessed within 6 yrs. after return was filed if taxpayer knowingly failed to disclose on return transaction identified by Tax Commissioner as abusive tax avoidance transaction. If return is false or fraudulent, assessment may be made at any time.

How far back? If taxpayers haven't previously reported, the states can't go back farther than the first year in which incomes of nonresidents and foreign corporations were taxed. Those years are listed below. (PT means privilege tax.)

	FIRST TAXABLE YEAR	
STATE	CORPORATE TAX	NONRESIDENTS' INDIVIDUAL TAX
Alabama	1933	1933
Alaska	1949	No Tax
Arizona	1933	1933
Arkansas	1928	1928
California	1937	1935
Colorado	1949	1937
Connecticut	1915PT	1991
Delaware	1957	1949-1950; 1953
District of Columbia	1939	1939
Florida	1972PT	No Tax
Georgia	1929	1929
Hawaii	1901	1901
Idaho	1931	1931
Illinois	1969	1969
Indiana	1963	1963
Iowa	1934	1937
Kansas	1933	1933
Kentucky	1936	1936
Louisiana	1934	1934
Maine	1969	1969
Maryland	1939	1939
Massachusetts	1919PT	1955
Michigan	1967; 1976	1968
Minnesota	1933	1933
Mississippi	1912	1912
Missouri	1917	1917
Montana	1971	1933
Nebraska	1968	1968
New Hampshire	1970	No Tax
New Jersey	1974	1976
New Mexico	1933	1933
New York	1917PT	1919
North Carolina	1921	1921
North Dakota	1919	1919
Ohio	1927	1972
Oklahoma	1931	1915
Oregon	1955	1929
Pennsylvania	1951	1971
Rhode Island	1947	1971
South Carolina	1922	1927
Tennessee	1923PT	No Tax
Utah	1959	1951
Vermont	1966	1947
Virginia	1925	1925
West Virginia	1967	1961
Wisconsin	1911	1911

SOCIAL SECURITY NUMBERS GROUPED BY STATE

¶233-A Social Security numbers grouped by state. This chart may prove helpful in confirming an applicant's previous residence as to a state, also when it is determined that a tax delinquent (''skip'') has returned to his or her home state. Column 1 gives the range of the first three digits of the individual's Social Security number.

Social Sec. No.	State Assigned
001-003	New Hampshire
004-007	Maine
008-009	Vermont
010-034	Massachusetts
035-039	Rhode Island
040-049	Connecticut
050-134	New York
135-158	New Jersey
159-211	Pennsylvania
212-220	Maryland
221-222	Delaware
223-231	Virginia
691-699	
232-236	West Virginia
232	North Carolina
237-246	
681-690	
247-251	South Carolina
654-658	
252-260	Georgia
667-675	
261-267	Florida
589-595	
766-772	
268-302	Ohio
303-317	Indiana
318-361	Illinois
362-386	Michigan
387-399	Wisconsin
400-407	Kentucky
408-415	Tennessee
756-763	
416-424	Alabama
425-428	Mississippi
587-588	
752-755	
429-432	Arkansas
676-679	
433-439	Louisiana
659-665	
440-448	Oklahoma
449-467	Texas
627-645	
468-477	Minnesota
478-485	Iowa
486-500	Missouri

Social Sec. No.	State Assigned
501-502	North Dakota
503-504	South Dakota
505-508	Nebraska
509-515	Kansas
516-517	Montana
518-519	Idaho
520	Wyoming
521-524	Colorado
650-653	
525, 585	New Mexico
648-649	
526-527	Arizona
600-601	
764-765	
528-529	Utah
646-647	
530	Nevada
680	
531-539	Washington
540-544	Oregon
545-573	California
602-626	
574	Alaska
575-576	Hawaii
750-751	
577-579	District of Columbia
580	Virgin Islands
580-584	Puerto Rico
596-599	
586	Guam
586	American Somoa
586	Philippine Islands
700-728	Railroad Board**
729-733	(enumeration at entry)

** 700-728 Issuance of these numbers to railroad employees was discontinued July 1, 1963.

Note: The same area, when shown more than once, means that certain numbers have been transferred from one state to another, or that an area has been divided for use among different geographic locations.

Any number beginning with 000 will *never* be a valid SSN.

STATE TAXATION OF PARTNERSHIPS

¶234-A Income tax treatment of partnerships. Most states follow the federal treatment of business partnerships: They are not taxed as such but are merely treated as tax conduits, with their incomes being taxed to their partners. However, the states are not uniform on their requirements for filing partnership returns. The chart below shows whether a partnership is taxable in a state and whether it must file a state return.

States shown with an asterisk (*) have enacted laws authorizing formation of limited liability partnerships (LLPs). In general, LLPs are governed by traditional partnership rules as modified to provide that, except as otherwise provided in the partnership agreement, partners are not personally liable for the negligence, wrongful acts, or misconduct of the other partners.

State	Tax Treatment	Reporting Requirements
*Alabama	Exempt	File if doing business in-state.
*Alaska	Exempt	Partnerships with corporate partners must file information returns. No tax on personal incomes.
*Arizona	Exempt	File if have gross income allocable to Ariz.
*Arkansas	Exempt	File if have income from sources in state.
*California	Exempt	But limited partnerships pay minimum tax; publicly traded partnerships are taxed as corps. File if doing business or have income from sources in state. No report needed if not doing business or receiving income from sources in-state even if the partnership consists of Calif. residents. Withhold 7% tax on distributions to domestic (non-foreign) nonresident partners; and 9.3% tax (8.84% tax if partner is a general corp.) on distributions to foreign (non-U.S.) partners.
*Colorado	Exempt	Partnerships can choose to file composite returns for their nonresident partners. Partnership can enter into agreement with each partner to file return and be subject to personal jursidiction in Colo. Partnership must either file agreement or pay highest marginal rate times nonresident partner's share of Colo. income. Any amount paid by partnership is considered to be paid by nonresident partner for taxes imposed on that partner for tax period.
*Connecticut	Exempt	File if have income derived from in-state sources. Limited liability partnerships and limited partnerships are subject to a $250 business entity tax for income yr.
*Delaware	Exempt	File if have income from sources in state.
*District of Columbia	Taxable (UBT)	Partnership engaging in trade or business in D.C. or receiving income from D.C. sources must file unincorporated business franchise tax return, if gross income for tax year exceeds $12,000, and it is not exempt (unincorporated business does not include trade, business, or profession that can be incorporated only under law governing professional corporations, or trade or business that by law, custom, or ethics, cannot be incorporated, or in which both of these requirements are met: more than 80% of the gross income is from personal services actually rendered by the members of the partnership, and capital is not a material income-producing factor). Partnerships not filing franchise tax return must file partnership return.
*Florida	Exempt	Corporate partners liable for corporation income tax. Partnerships file information returns if they have corporate partner subject to state tax.

State	Tax Treatment	Reporting Requirements
*Georgia	Exempt	File if individual members or partners are taxable in state. File composite returns for nonresident partners or withhold 4% tax on distributions over $1,000 per yr. per nonresident partner.
*Hawaii	Exempt	No return required from partnership carrying on no business and having no income from sources in-state; but state tax director may require resident partner to file statement.
*Idaho	Exempt	File supplemental return if partnership is transacting business in state.
*Illinois	Taxable	If earning or receiving income in state, report and pay the state replacement income tax; no liability for the regular income tax. Investment partnerships are not subject to the replacement tax.
*Indiana	Exempt	File if doing business or have income from sources in-state, or if have a resident partner. Withhold on payments to nonresident partners. But publicly traded partnership is liable for adjusted gross income tax if treated as a corporation federally.
*Iowa	Exempt	File information return if have business place in state or income from (1) property owned within or (2) business, trade or profession carried on in-state. Director may require or allow filing of composite returns.
*Kansas	Exempt	File return; can elect to file composite returns for nonresident partners. Partnerships electing to be treated as corps. are similarly taxable in Kan.
*Kentucky	Exempt	General partnerships are exempt, but must file copy of Fed return if own property or do business in state; partnership may be required to withhold tax on partner's distribution share. Eff for tax years starting on or after 1-1-2005 and pre-1-1-2007, limited partnerships and limited liability partnerships are subject to corporate income tax. LPs and LLPs must pay limited liability entity tax for tax yrs. starting on or after 1-1-2007.
*Louisiana	Exempt	File if have a member who is not an individual or who is not a resident.
*Maine	Exempt	File if have a partner or income derived from sources in state.
*Maryland	Exempt	Partnerships are taxed at sum of highest personal income tax rate (¶ 228) plus lowest county income tax rate on nonresident partner's share of partnership's nonresident taxable income.
*Massachusetts	Exempt	File if have place of business in state.
*Michigan	Taxable	Partnership is liable for single business tax until 12-31-2007, and eff 1-1-2008 for Mich. business tax. File if apportioned or allocated gross receipts are at least $350,000.
*Minnesota	Minimum fee	File if have gross income assignable to the state. Withhold tax on nonresident partner's distributive share. Composite returns allowed.
*Mississippi	Exempt	Partnerships taxable as corporations under the IRC are also taxed as corporations in Miss. Otherwise, partnership is exempt but is jointly and severably liable for tax of partners who don't pay; not liable if it withholds and remits 5% of partnership gain or profit. File if have income from property owed or business carried on in state.
*Missouri	Exempt	File if have a resident partner or income from sources in state. Partnership must withhold tax at highest personal income tax rate (¶ 228) on pro rata share of nonresident partner who has Mo. assignable Fed adjusted gross income of at least $1,200 from the partnership.

State	Tax Treatment	Reporting Requirements
*Montana	Exempt	File if do business in state.
*Nebraska	Exempt	File if have nonresident partner or income from sources in state.
*Nevada	No income tax.	
*New Hampshire	Taxable	Partnerships pay the business taxes; but partners are exempt from the tax. File BPT return if gross business income exceeds $50,000. File BET return if gross business receipts exceed $100,000 or enterprise value tax base exceeds $50,000.
*New Jersey	Exempt	But partnerships (including limited liability companies and limited partnerships) are required to pay 6.37% tax on nonresident non-corporate partners' share of income apportioned to N.J. and pay 9% tax on nonresident corporate partners' share apportioned to N.J. Qualified investment partnerships and partnerships listed on national stock exchanges are exempt.
*New Mexico	Exempt	Partnerships required to file a Fed partnership return of income must file a N.M. income and information return if they are registered to do business in N.M., do business in, into or from N.M., or derive income from property or employment in N.M. They must withhold and pay income tax for nonresident partners who have not filed an agreement to report and pay.
*New York	Exempt	File if have a resident partner or income derived from NY sources. Filing of combined return for nonresident partners may be allowed.
New York City	Taxable	Report-pay unincorporated business tax.
*North Carolina	Exempt	File information return if have place of business in state. Manager must pay tax on distributive share of nonresident partner.
*North Dakota	Exempt	File if carrying on trade or business in state. Partnerships can file composite return and pay tax due for nonresident individual partners.
*Ohio	Exempt	Partnership may elect to file single return for two or more nonresident partners whose only Ohio income consists of partnership income. Partnership may need to file for and pay pass-through entity tax equivalent to 5% withholding tax if at least one qualifying investor is an individual. The rate for non-individuals is 8.5% or, if corporate income tax phase-out applies, 1.7% in 2008.
*Oklahoma	Exempt	File unless electing not to file under IRC §761. Tax applies to pro rata portion of partnership income allocable to nonresident partners if partnership files a composite return for them.
*Oregon	Exempt	File information return if have a resident partner or income from sources in state.
*Pennsylvania	Exempt	File if have a resident partner or income from sources in state. File copy of Fed Form 1065. Withhold tax on income allocable to nonresident partners.
*Rhode Island	Exempt	Partnerships must withhold income tax at highest R.I. withholding tax rate provided for individuals or 9% for partner's share of partnership's income.
*South Carolina	Exempt	File information return showing partnership's net income and partners' distributive share. Partnership must withhold tax for nonresident partners at 5% rate unless they consent to report-pay.
*South Dakota	No income tax	
*Tennessee	Taxable	Partnerships pay tax on income from stocks, bonds, notes and mortgages.
*Texas	No income tax	

State	Tax Treatment	Reporting Requirements
*Utah	Exempt	File information return if have income derived from sources in state or have resident partner. Can elect to file composite return for individual nonresident partners and pay tax at composite return rate. Partnerships taxable as corporations under the IRC are taxed as corporations for purpose of corporate franchise and income taxes.
*Vermont	Exempt	File if have resident partner or having any income from sources in-state for nonresident. Pay $250 minimum tax and withhold tax for partners at highest Fed marginal tax rate for individuals times Vt. individual income tax rate.
*Virginia	Exempt	Partnership organized in state or having income from sources in state needn't file returns; but Commr. may require filing of copy of Fed returns and schedules.
*Washington	No income tax	
*West Virginia	Exempt	File if partnership is a resident or has a resident partner or income derived from sources in-state. Pay withholding tax equal to 4% of allocable taxable income to nonresident partners who don't consent to report-pay. Or file nonresident composite return and pay 6.5% tax for nonresident partners. File annual business activities report if not paying registration tax or filing income-franchise return.
*Wisconsin	Exempt	File information return and pay temporary cleanup surcharge, but PTPs pay corporate tax if treated as corporation for Fed tax. Withholding is required on distributions over $1,000 to nonresident partners.
*Wyoming	No income tax	

FED-STATE TAX INFORMATION INTER-EXCHANGE

¶235 Coping with inter-government exchange of tax information. Most states permit their tax officials to exchange tax information with the Internal Revenue Service. The states listed below have made tax enforcement agreements with the federal government. Those agreements make it possible to compare federal and state returns or make periodical samplings and spot checks to turn up discrepancies between state and federal figures.

Alabama, Alaska, Arizona, Arkansas, California, Colorado, Connecticut, Delaware, District of Columbia, Florida, Georgia, Hawaii, Idaho, Illinois, Indiana, Iowa, Kansas, Kentucky, Louisiana, Maine, Maryland, Massachusetts, Michigan, Minnesota, Mississippi, Missouri, Montana, Nebraska, New Hampshire, New Jersey, New Mexico, New York, North Carolina, North Dakota, Ohio, Oklahoma, Oregon, Pennsylvania, Rhode Island, South Carolina, South Dakota (tax on financial institutions), Tennessee, Utah, Vermont, Virginia, West Virginia, Wisconsin.

➾ **WHAT TO DO→** Prepare federal and state returns together. Explain discrepancies if not revealed in the reconciliations on the forms. Make sure that your reports agree with all other public reports on file, including nontax reports, or that they are readily reconcilable with them.

CREDITS AGAINST INCOME TAX FOR BUSINESSES

¶236 **Dollar-for-dollar offsets** against income taxes due are allowed by many states to encourage business development and growth. These tax credits are shown below. Tax incentives for pollution control are charted at ¶ 298; alternative energy devices, ¶ 299.

Letter "Y" means "Yes". So if "Y" appears in a particular column for a state—that means that state gives a tax credit for item shown in the column heading. "N" means no credit is given.

STATE Col. A	INVEST-MENTS Col. B	ENTER-PRISE ZONES Col. C(43)	NEW JOBS Col. D	FUEL TAXES Col. E	OTHER CREDITS Col. F
ALA.	Y(106)	Y(66)	Y(66)	N	Y(134)
AK.	Y(4)	N	N	N	Y(153)
ARIZ.	Y(34)	Y(65)	Y(175)	N	Y(175)
ARK.	Y(18)	Y	Y(87)	N	Y(157)
CALIF.	Y(41)	Y(45)	Y(77)	N	Y(144)
COLO.	Y(8)	Y(61)	Y(78,79)	N	Y(129)
CONN.	Y(15)	Y(46)	Y(84)	N	Y(141)
DEL.	Y(21)	Y(110)	Y(78,85)	N	Y(172)
D.C.	N	N	Y(112)	N	Y(121)
FLA.	Y(32)	Y(47)	Y(78)	N	Y(145)
GA.	Y(42)	N	Y(78,92)	N	Y(176)
HAW.	Y(22)	Y(62)	N(78)	Y(116)	Y(128,170)
IDAHO	Y(19)	N	Y(91)	N	Y(124,125,129)
ILL.	Y(27)	Y(49)	Y(88)	N	Y(161)
IND.	Y(20)	Y(48)	Y(93)	Y(188)	Y(129,140,150)
IOWA	Y(16)	Y(75)	Y(80,96)	Y(114,117)	Y(146)
KAN.	Y(23)	Y(50)	Y(23,78,85)	N	Y(131)
KY.	Y(33)	Y(69)	Y(103)	N	Y(156)
LA.	Y(17)	Y(51)	Y(81)	Y(118)	Y(147)
ME.	Y(35)	Y(191)	Y(78,111)	N	Y(132)
MD.	N	Y(52)	Y(164)	N	Y(126)
MASS.	Y(6)	Y(63)	Y(78,94)	N	Y(167,168) (177,180)
MICH.	Y(28)	Y(64)	Y(184)	N	Y(126,129,133)
MINN.	N	N	Y(181)	N	Y(134)
MISS.	Y(24)	N	Y(89)	N	Y(162)
MO.	Y(7,13)	Y(55)	Y(55)	N	Y(129,149)
MONT.	Y(5)	N	Y(81)	N	Y(135)
NEB.	Y(30,100)	Y(73)	Y(82,100)	N	Y(136,192)
N.H.	Y(39)	Y(189)	Y(78,102)	N	Y(137,187)
N.J.	Y(40,151)	Y(60)	N(78,193)	N	Y(151,178)
N.M.	N	Y(74)	Y(185)	N	Y(122)
N.Y.	Y(6)	Y(56)	Y(78,83)	N	Y(138)
N.C.	Y(36)	Y(58)	Y(105)	N	Y(129,179)
N.D.	Y(25)	N	Y(86)	N	Y(129,148)
OH.	Y(31)	Y(57)	Y(78,107)	N	Y(123)
OKLA.	Y(14,37)	Y(71)	Y(90)	N	Y(139)
ORE.	Y(10)	Y(186)	Y(78,104)	N	Y(142)
PA.	Y(26)	Y(190)	Y(98,154)	N	Y(165)
R.I.(2)	Y(6,183)	Y(182)	Y(109)	N	Y(129,160,166)
S.C.	Y(53)	Y(59)	Y(101)	N	Y(143)
TENN.	Y(11)	Y(44)	Y	N	Y(120)
UT.	N	Y(67)	Y(113)	N	Y(174)
VT.(3)	Y(38)	N	N	N	Y(163)

STATE Col. A	INVEST-MENTS Col. B	ENTER-PRISE ZONES Col. C(43)	NEW JOBS Col. D	FUEL TAXES Col. E	OTHER CREDITS Col. F
VA.	Y(12)	Y(72)	Y(78,108)	N	Y(130)
W.VA.	Y(29)	N	Y(95)	N	Y(173)
WIS.	Y(194)	Y(68)	N	N	Y(127,169)

FOOTNOTES to chart ¶ 236 (corresponding to parenthetical numbers in chart):

(1) Fed tax credits are adopted with modifications. *(Alaska.)*

(2) Tax on individuals—but not corporate tax—is based on percentage of Fed tax liability so individuals can also take Fed foreign tax credit and jobs credit. *(R.I.)*

(3) Tax on individuals (not corporate tax) is based on Fed tax liability which is net after allowance of Fed investment credit, Fed foreign tax credit and Fed tax-free convenant bond credit but before allowance of any other Fed business credits (alternative energy device ¶ 299) *(Vt.)*.

(4) (a) Fed investment credit allowed per IRC §46 on 1st $20,000,000 of investment (not for special industrial incentive credit at (b) below);
(b) 25% of eligible costs for specified geophysical work on land and drilling test or exploratory well for oil or gas exploration; 50% of costs if on state-owned land; max credit, $5 million per project, $30 million for all claimants; no credit if incentive credit above is claimed (eff thru 7-1-2007) *(Alaska)*.

(5) Investors in Montana Equity Fund can take credit equal to difference between scheduled returns of invested capital and returns on invested capital. (Mont.).

(6) Credit based on cost of depreciables in-state acquired per IRC §179(d) or leased after 7-1-94: 3% for mfg., farming, fishing or R&D (5% for certified project in economic opportunity area) *(Mass.)*; 5% of 1st $350 million cost of acquisition, construction and reconstruction of "qualified property" (incl. bldgs. and components) less nonqualified nonrecourse financing amount excludable from Fed credit base under IRC §146(c)(8), 4% of balance; or 9% for research-development property if elected *(N.Y.)*; 10% of basis for Fed income tax of tangible personalty, buildings and components, erected or acquired if depreciable property (IRC §167), useful life 4 years (min.), purchased per IRC §179(d), located in RI, and principally for manufacturing, processing or assembling goods *(R.I.)*.

(7) Neighborhood assistance credit—50%–70% of investments; 55% of investment in affordable housing assistance activity (max. credit: $2 million in 1st yr.; added $2 million per credit; 55% of investment in homeless assistance project *(Mo.)* .

(8) 1% of qualifying investment in IRC §38 property, up to max. $1,000 per yr. *(Colo.)*.

(9) Percentage of property tax on newly-acquired engines, machinery, tools & implements for mfg. or refining *(Ohio)*.

(10) 20% of cash investment in certified capitalization of Ore. Capital Corp.; 25% of new investment related to electronic commerce, up to $2 million *(Ore.)*.

(11) Industrial machinery credit—1% *(Tenn.)*.

(12) For tax yrs. beginning before 1-1-2010, credit is allowed in amount equal to 50% of qualified investment in information technology or biotechnology company located in tobacco dependent locality. State deduction allowed for amounts deductible if added Fed investment credit has not been taken *(Va.)*.

(13) $125 to $150 per $100,000 invested in new business facility and if business in enterprise zone credit of 10% of 1st $10,000, 5% next $90,000 and 2% of bal. is allowed. Credit allowed for 50% of contribution to Development Reserve, infrastructure development and export finance funds, or investment of seed capital; 60% of contributions to small businesses, community development corps., or community banks. *(Mo.)*

(14) Okla. Investment credits: credit for 10% of capital costs in qualifying investment; credit for 5% of eligible costs related to investment in commercial space industries; general credit for 1% of cost of investment in qualified property in certain manufacturing facilities or increase in number of jobs at such facilities ($500 per new employee), credit for investments in qualified depreciable property costing $40 million or more (2% of cost of qualified property), and credit for job creation ($1,000 per new employee).

(15) Neighborhood assistance credit—50% of investment in neighborhood programs (job training, crime and fire prevention, community services etc) ($75,000 max.; $250 min.); 50% of investment in nonprofit day care facilities for employee use ($10,000 max.); 60% of investment in energy conservation, employment training for youth and other programs for low income persons; 25% of tax allocable to facility constructed, improved, or renovated; 10% of tax allocable per statutory formula to new mfg. or economic base business facility. 10%–25% of that part of tax allocable per formula to certified new mfg. or economic base business facility. Credit for amount invested thru fund manager in a Conn. insurance business occupying qualified new facility as its home office and employing 25% (min.) of its workers in new jobs; at time of investment, fund must have $30 million asset value (min.) that yr. and 3 investors (min.); take 10% of credit each yr. in yr. 3–6 after investment and 20% each yr. in yr. 7–9. Fixed capital credit for investments in fixed capital assets, 5% of amount invested during income yr. *(Conn.)*

(16) Investment in Iowa Capital Investment Board; seed capital investment credit; venture capital investment credits; Endow Iowa credits. *(Iowa)*.

(17) Specified %s of investment in certified La. capital corporation. 35% of Dedicated Research Investment Fund cash donation, if 1st donation is at least $200,000. 50% of 1st $1 million per year (up to max. of $2 million per business) in certified La. entrepreneurial business (max. $5 million total credits allowed per year) *(La.)*.

FOOTNOTES to chart ¶ 236 (corresponding to parenthetical numbers in chart): (continued)

(18) 10% capital investment credit; 7% manufacturers' investment credit. *(Ark.)*.

(19) 3% of qualified investment, but not to exceed 50% of tax liability. Added credit of 3% of qualified investment in qualfied broadband equipment in Ida., up to max. annual credit of $750,000. *(Ida.)*.

(20) (a) Neighborhood assistance credit—50% of investment or contribution ($25,000 max.) to neighborhood organizations engaging in activities to up-grade neighborhood.
(b) prison investments (per agreement with Dept. of Correction)—equal to lesser of (1) state tax liability; or (2) 50% of investment in qualified property plus 25% of wages paid to inmates or (3) $100,000.
(c) Community revitalization enhancement district credit—25% of qualified investment.
(d) Hoosier business investment credit—30% of qualified investment.
(e) Venture capital investment credit—20% of qualified investment.
(f) Capital investment credit—14% of investment.
(g) Military base investment cost credit—certain % of qualified investment.
(h) Coal gasification technology investment credit—10% of qualified investment for first $500 million invested; 5% of qualified investment over $500 million. *(Ind.)*

(21) For property placed in service in 1997–2006, credit amount is $400 ($650 for qualified facilities in targeted areas) per $100,000 of investment in new facility. Credit is allowed for 50% of qualified investment in qualified neighborhood or community-based organizations; max. credit, $100,000 per business, $500,000 total for all taxpayers per fiscal yr. *(Del.)*

(22) Credit for 35% of investment in yr. made (up to $700,000), 25% in first yr. after investment (up to $500,000), 20% in second yr. (up to $400,000), 10% in third yr. (up to $200,000), and 10% in fourth yr. (up to $200,000) *(Haw.)*. Haw. also has technology infrastructure renovation credit.

(23) 25% of investment in local seed capital pool to fund small business devoted to new product or process. 25% of investments in technology-based venture-capital fund qualify for Kan. venture capital companies credit. Mfg. businesses adding net 2 (min.) jobs and other business (not retail) adding net 5 (min.) jobs get credit of $1,000 per qualified business facility investment of $100,000. Retailers and others adding net 2 (min.), jobs but not claiming above credit, get $100 per qualified business facility investment of $100,000. Max. credit is 50% of tax. Credit is allowed for that part of qualified cash investment in training and education of employees exceeding 2% of total payroll costs; max. credit, $50,000. Credit is allowed for 10% of that part of qualified investment in training-retraining exceeding $50,000, instead of job expansion-investment credit. Credit is allowed for 50% of qualified investment in a capital formation company in Kan. Credits are allowed for tax yrs. starting before 1–1–2011 for certain investments in oil refineries, pipelines, integrated coal or coke gasification nitrogen fertilizer plants, biomass-to-energy plants, or integrated coal gasification power plants. Credits are allowed for tax yrs. starting before 1–1–2012 for certain investments in new renewable electric regeneration facilities or biofuel storage and blending equipment. *(Kan.)*.

(24) Investment in venture capital fund, 30% of investment in cash of not less than $50,000 for corporations and not less than $10,000 for individuals. Credit for total debt service paid under financing agreement with MBFC to finance development projects to induce manufacturing facilities to locate in Miss.; credit cannot exceed the tax on the income from the project (for certain projects, credit is limited to 80% of Miss. taxes due). *(Miss.)*.

(25) 25% of investment in venture capital corp. ($250,000 max) or certified nonprofit development corp. ($2,000 total income tax credit max.). *(ND.)*.

(26) 50% of total investments or 25% of expenditures for qualified investment projects into neighborhood assistance (75% for special program priorities) *(Pa.)*.

(27) 0.5% of property basis if placed in service in Foreign Trade Zone by high impact business and not eligible for enterprise zone credit *(Ill.)*;

(28) Until 12-31-2007, Single Business tax allows credit for 50% of qualified investments in equity interest of minority venture capital co. or MESBIC. Eff 1-1-2008, Mich. Business Tax allows combined compensation/investment tax credit and certain contributions to R&D businesses. For tax yrs. starting after 12-31-2008, taxpayers with a tax voucher for investments in the Michigan Early Stage Venture Capital Fund can use the tax voucher to pay MBT liability. *(Mich.)*

(29) Super credit is replaced by economic opportunity tax credit (applies only to mfrs. information processors, warehouses, goods distributors, and destination-oriented recreation and tourism cos.) based on qualified investment multiplied by new jobs percentage; other credit allowed for investments in facility for producing coal-based liquids used to produce synthetic motor fuel or synthetic special fuel; 15% of qualified investment in an aerospace industrial facility; 50% of the investment in qualified W. Va. capital companies or venture capital; 3% or 10% of eligible RD expenditures; 5% of qualified manufacturing investment. *(W.Va.)*

(30) See Col. D; note 100. *(Neb.)*

(31) Research credits and incentives for new manufacturing machinery and equipment. *(Ohio)*

(32) 5% of eligible capital costs generated by qualifying project, for 1st 20 yrs. of project operation; max. credit: 100% of tax generated by the project for capital investment of at least $100 million; 75%, for investment in $50 million–$99.99 million range. For qualifying project that is a headquarters located in an enterprise zone and Brownfield area, the credit is $15 million or 5% of eligible capital costs for up to 20 yrs. *(Fla.)*

(33) (a) Certified air carrier investing $300 million (min.) in new-expanded facilities-equip. in Ky., can take credit with Dept. Rev. OK for 10% of increase in gross wages paid to qualified employees subject to Ky. income tax as compared to carrier's gross Ky. real wage base, if tax yr. gross wages subject to Ky. income tax are at least $15 million greater than carrier's gross Ky. real wage base; max. credit per carrier: $3 million per yr.; $15 million total; 5-yr. max.
(b) Skills training investment credit, 50% of costs incurred for training program.
(c) Credit for investor contributions to investment funds for development of small business, 40% of cash contribution. *(Ky.)*

FOOTNOTES to chart ¶ 236 (corresponding to parenthetical numbers in chart): (continued)

(34) Credit for cost of constructing qualified environmental technology facility. *(Ariz.)*

(35) 1% of investment credit base—original basis in machy-equip. placed in service for 1st time in Me. in any of past 5 yrs., max. credit lesser of tax or $25,000 plus 75% of tax over $25,000. Up to 40% of seed capital investment. Up to 60% of investment, if located in high unemployment area. Credit is also allowed, for the amount of the investment base, for entities engaged in high technology who buy certain equipment. Up to $3 million credit for qualified shipbuilding facilities. Portion of former Fed investment credit as calculated under IRC §38(b)(1) directly and solely attributed to qualified investment with location in Me. Until 1-1-2009, 25% of expenditures for construction or installation of or improvements to a filling or charging station for providing clean fuels. *(Me.)*.

(36) Credit for investments in business property equal to applicable percentage of excess of eligible investment amount over the applicable percentage—applicable percentages: 7%, area development tier one; 5%, tier two; 3.5%, tier three. Credit for investment in real property equal to 35% of eligible investment amount (repealed for business activities on or after 1-1-2011). *(N.C.)*.

(37) Credit in guarantees OK'd by Okla. Capital Investment Bd. (eff thru 7-1-2015); 20% of investment cost in new qualified recycling facility; 50% of cost of investment in qualified clean-burning motor vehicle fuel property and in qualified electric motor vehicle property (eff. thru 1-1-2009); 30% of investment in Okla. producer-owned agricultural processing cooperatives, ventures, marketing associations. *(Okla.)*.

(38) %, adjusted annually per formula, of investment in housing charity providing affordable housing. *(Vt.)*.

(39) Investment credit allowed for 75% of contribution made to community development finance authority. *(N.H.)*

(40) 4% of corp's investment in qualified machy-equip. used to produce tangible personalty; max. annual credit, $1 million. *(N.J.)*.

(41) 6% of qualified costs of qualified (IRC §1245(a)) mfg., processing, fabricating, recycling, and R&D property (eff if specified state employment conditions are met) *(Calif.)*.

(42) In Tier 1 counties, credit allowed in yr. after qualified acquisition for 5% of cost of qualified manufacturing investment property up to 50% of tax, 8% if property is recycling or pollution control machy-equip. In Tier 2, 3% and 5% respectively. In Tier 3 and Tier 4, 1% and 3%. Optional investment credit available instead. Credit is allowed for 6% of cost of certain investment property for business constructing new manufacturing facility in Ga. that creates new full-time jobs. *(Ga.)*

(43) Businesses located or doing business in enterprise zone (incl high tech zone, economically distressed areas, etc) are allowed credits for investment in zone, creating jobs in zone, or hiring residents in zone etc.

(44) $1,000 per net new employee employed during tax period for min. of 6 months for at least 20 hrs. per week at location in enterprise zone. Max. credit is lesser of $100,000 or 50% of excise tax liability paid for tax yr. *(Tenn.)*

(45) (a) Credit is allowed for qualified employee working in targeted area for 60-month period: 50% of qualified wages in 1st yr; 40%, 2nd yr.; 30%, 3rd; 20%, 4th; 10%, 5th;
(b) 50% of wages of qualified employee working in enterprise zone during 1st yr.; 40%, 30%, 20%, and 10% during 2nd, 3rd, 4th, and 5th years; reduce credit by amount of Fed targeted and Calif. jobs credit;
(c) businesses in enterprise zone or targeted area get credit against tax for sales-use tax paid on qualified machy. and parts. *(Calif.)*

(46) Mfg. facility—50% of tax allocable to business in zone if at least 150 or 30% of employees are full-time and residents in zone *(Conn.)*.

(47) Fla.—Enterprise zone jobs credit: Credit for business located in enterprise zone that demonstrates to Department of Revenue that total number of full-time jobs has increased from the average of the previous 12 months. Credit is based on percentage of actual monthly wages paid in Fla. to each new employee hired when a new job is created. Enterprise zone property tax credit: Credit for additional property tax assessed as result of improvements to property in enterprise zones property acquired to facilitate new business or expansion or rebuilding of business in the zone. (Expires 12-31-2015.) Community contribution credit: Eff through 6-30-2015, credit is allowed for 50% of contributions for projects undertaken by eligible sponsors for the revitalization of enterprise zones to preserve existing historically significant properties within enterprise zones or for the benefit of low-income and moderate-income persons.

(48) (a) Employment expense credit: lesser of 10% × qualified increased employment expenses; or $1,500 × no. of qualified employees employed during tax year;
(b) Zone loan interest credit: 5% × interest received from business in zone;
(c) Up to 30% of investments in interest in businesses in enterprise zone, exact % depends on need for equity financing, type of business, jobs created generally and for zone residents in 1st yr. of ownership, and property investment *(Ind.)*

(49) 0.5% of basis of qualified property placed in service in enterprise zone or River Edge Redevelopment Zone. Similar credit is allowed against replacement income tax. Also, 0.5% of the basis of qualified property placed in service in a River Edge Redevelopment Zone, if taxpayer's base employment increased by 1% or more over the preceding yr. *(Ill.)*.

(50) See Col. B note 23 and Col. D note 85. *(Kan.)*.

(51) The state can enter into contracts with businesses relocating into urban enterprise zones, rural enterprise zones, or economic development zones to provide a tax credit of $2,500 per employee employed in the zone ($5,000 per employee if the job is in the motor vehicle parts, rubber manufacturing, aviation, or aerospace industry or in an urban revitalization zone). *(La.)*

(52) Up to $3,000 per qualified employee who's economically disadvantaged; up to $1,000 to $2,000 of wages paid to others based on requirements met; more in enhanced focus areas *(Md.)*

FOOTNOTES to chart ¶ 236 (corresponding to parenthetical numbers in chart): (continued)

(53) 30% of investment in qualified recycling facilities. Up to $1 million ($8 million total for all claimants) available subject to determination by state agency for users of state port authority facilities who increase base port cargo volume by at least 5%. *(SC).*

(54) Certain percentage of $2,000 ($4,500, in economically distressed county) per new full-time qualified job created before 1-1-2011, based on total number of Tenn. employees; percentage of $5,000 if specified investment requirements are met. Job tax credit for hiring persons with disabilities: applicable to tax periods ending on or after 7-1-2006, credit allowed is equal to $5,000 per net new full-time employee and $2,000 per net new part-time employee with disabilities who is receiving state services directly related to such disabilities. *(Tenn.).*

(55) (a) New or expanded business facility, $400 per new employee (added $400 if new employee resides in zone plus $400 if "hard-core" unemployed); $400 per employee for jobs over 10 in new business or 25 in existing business plus $400 per yr. for each person difficult to employ;
(b) investment, 10% of 1st $10,000; 5% of next $90,000; 2% of bal.;
(c) training expenses, $400 per employee residing in zone or unemployable *(Mo.).*

(56) Economic development zones have become qualified empire zones, and some credits are enhanced and added for qualified empire zone enterprises (QEZEs). Credits include: (1) capital credit of 25% of certain investments and enterprises in empire zones; (2) investment tax credit of 10% of federal income tax basis of depreciable tangible property, subject to restrictions; (3) employment incentive credit (for 3 years after 10% investment credit) of 30% of 10% credit, if 101% number of employees of previous tax year; (4) equivalent wage credit of $3,000 per targeted employee and $1,500 per other employee in empire zone; (5) QEZE real property tax credit equal to product of benefit period factor, employment increase factor, and eligible real property taxes paid or incurred during tax year; and (6) QEZE tax credit reduction equal to the product of benefit period factor, employment increase factor, zone allocation factor, and tax factor (based on larger of tax calculated on entire net income or minimum taxable income). *(N.Y.)*

(57) Benefits include $1,000 for employee training program costs per new employee completing training, $100,000 max.; $1,000 per new eligible temporary employee; $300 for day care per child or dependent of new employees *(Ohio).*

(58) Corporations in Area Development Tier 1 counties get the most benefit; corporations in Area Development Tier 3 counties, the least, per Art. 3J credits. *(N.C.)*

(59) Job development credit: 2% wages $6.95-$9.27/hr.; 3% wages $9.27-$11.58/hr.; 4% wages $11.58-$17.38/hr.; 5% wages $17.38 or more. 1% to 5% of bases of qualified manufacturing and productive equipment property placed in service in economic impact zone. *(S.C.).*

(60) New employed (6 mos. min.) resident of zone—if previously unemployed for 90d (min.) or on welfare, $1,500 credit; others if not employed in taxing municipality immediately before zone work, $500 credit. Similar credit for firms in projects of Urban Dev. Corp. 8% of new investment in zone up to 50% of tax. *(N.J.).*

(61) These enterprise zone credits are available in Colo.: enterprise zone investment credit; new business employment credit; enterprise zone health insurance credit; agricultural processing employees credit; child care credit; credit against tax contributions to enterprise zone administrator; credit for rehabilitation of vacant buildings; credit based on R&D expenditures; and credit for investment in technology infrastructure.

(62) Credit equal to 80% of the tax due on income from business activity in the zone and of unemployment tax paid for enterprise zone employees for 1st yr. to 20% for 7th yr. Targeted jobs credit for employing qualified vocational rehabilitation referrals in the taxpayer's trade or business equal to 20% of the employee's qualified 1st year wages of $6,000 or less *(Haw.).*

(63) 5% of cost of qualifying property bought for business use in economic opportunity area (EOA) *(Mass.).*

(64) SBT (until 12-31-2007) or MBT (eff 1-1-2008) liability (adjusted) times ratio of in zone-to-total Mich. property and payroll for enterprise (SBT only) and renaissance zones (SBT and MBT). *(Mich.).*

(65) 1/4 of taxable wages paid to each qualified employee in 1st yr. worked ($500 max. per net new employee), 1/3 in 2d yr. ($1,000 max.), 1/2 in 3rd yr. ($1,500 max.) *(Ariz.).*

(66) 5-yr credit of varying proportions of taxes due from zone operations is available for businesses if 30% of new permanent employees formerly unemployed at least 90 days before hire. $1,000 (max.) per new employee for expenses of training in new skills. 10% on first $10,000 of new investment in-state, 5% on next $90,000, 2% on rest; also available for improvements to existing facilities if at least 5 new permanent employees hired. Max., $2,500 per new permanent employee hired. *(Ala.).*

(67) Until 6-30-2008; business whose primary activity is within specified SIC codes and at least 51% of employees at its zone facility live in zone, gets $750 per new full-time nonretail job filled for at least 6 months in tax yr. and added $200, or $500, or $750 if job is special category; 10% of 1st $250,000 and 5% of next $1 million of qualifying investment in plant, equipment, or other depreciables; 50% of cash gifts ($100,000 max. credit) to nonprofit in community or economic development; 25% of 1st $200,000 spent on rehabilitating vacant building in zone *(Utah).*

(68) Development zone and enterprise development zone credits: investment credit—2.5% of cost of tangible personalty, or 1.75% of IRC §179 expensed items, for business in zone; jobs credit—amount of Fed targeted jobs credit (40% of 1st $6,000 of 1st-yr. wages paid employee) plus similar portion of 2nd-yr. wages for work in zone, unused credit refunded; location credit—2.5% of cost of acquiring, constructing, rehabilitating, remodeling, or repairing zone realty, 15-yr. carryover (disallowed for property on which investment credit is based); sales tax credit—amount of Wis.-local sales-use tax paid on investment credit property used in zone and materials-supplies used to construct, rehabilitate, repair, or remodel zone realty. *(Wis.).*

FOOTNOTES to chart ¶ 236 (corresponding to parenthetical numbers in chart): (continued)

(69) Statewide enterprise initiative program replaces enterprise zone program. *(Ky.).*

(70) $1,000 per yr. per new full-time employee in designated less developed counties for 5 yrs. starting with yrs. 2–6 after job created *(Ga.).*

(71) Business in enterprise zone is allowed twice job creation credit, note (14). Also, credit of up to 100% of ad valorem tax for new or expanding facility in enterprise zone. *(Okla.)*

(72) Qualified business in enterprise zone is allowed credit for 80% of income tax and 80% of unemployment tax due in 1st yr.; 60% in each of yr. 2 thru 10 *(Va.).*

(73) Microenterprise credit is available for small businesses. Contributions to approved community betterment programs qualify. *(Neb.)*

(74) Owner of qualified business facility (previously-vacant bldg. in N.M. enterprise zone put into service in mfg.-distribution-service industry after fixup) can take credit, for each of up to 3 consecutive yrs., for 50% of cost incurred to restore, rehabilitate, or renovate the facility; max. credit. $50,000 per project per facility; this credit can't be taken for project for which investment or cultural property preservation credit is taken. *(N.M.).*

(75) Quality jobs enterprise zone credit (10% of new investment); eligible housing credit (10% of amount for building or rehabilitating homes in designated enterprise zone); economic development region revolving funds credit (20% of amount contributed). *(Iowa).*

(76) (Reserved.)

(77) 10% of wages paid to prisoners employed per joint venture program with Calif. *(Calif.).*

(78) Wages and amounts not deductible federally as Fed jobs credit taken are deductible for state tax purposes *(Colo.; Del.; Ga.; Hawaii; Kans.; Me.; Mass.; N.H.; N.J.; N.Y.; Ohio; Oreg.; Vt.; Va.). Fla.* has rural job credit, urban high-crime area job credit and enterprise zone jobs credit. *Haw.* allows credit equal to 20% of qualified first-yr. wages of $6,000 or less paid to employee who is a qualified vocational rehabilitation referral.

(79) $500 per new business facility employee; enhanced new business facility employee credit of $200 per new business facility employee working in enhanced rural enterprise zone. Until 12-31-2007, credit of up to $1,200 per new employee hired in aviation development zones. *(Colo.).*

(80) Industrial new jobs; new jobs in enterprise zones; supplemental new jobs withholding credit; targeted jobs withholding tax credit for funding improvements in pilot cities in certain urban renewal areas. *(Iowa).*

(81) $100 per new employee who is resident in-state (max. 50% of tax); $200 if employee is economically disadvantaged or a 1st time drug offender less than 25 yrs. old (max. 50% of tax); $225 if residing in high unemployment area (max. 50% of tax); $150 if rehabilitated felon (max. 50% of tax); $750 per new employee (previously unemployed, or receives specified public payments or participates in specified program) if job exceeds 5% of avg. full-time jobs for last yr.; net benefit rate provided by Dept. of Economic Development multiplied by gross payroll of new direct jobs for tax period as verified by Dept. of Labor for contracts under Quality Jobs Program Act *(La.).* New/expanded industry, 1% of wages if total full-time employment hiked by 30% *(Mont.).*

(82) Wage expense disallowed by Fed targeted jobs credit can't be deducted for state tax *(Neb.).*

(83) Employment incentive credit: For property acquired, built or rebuilt after 12-31-86, 1.5% of state investment credit allowed for 3 yrs. if employees 101% (min.) of previous year's, but less than 102%. 2% if under 103%, 2.5% if at least 103%. Qualified emergency technology company employment credit and Empire Zone employment incentive tax credits are also available. *(N.Y.)*

(84) Apprenticeship training in manufacturing, plastics, plastics-related and construction trades, credit amount varies. Credit for hiring displaced workers, $1,500 per worker. Credit for hiring family assistance recipients, $125 per employee. Eff. for tax yrs. starting on and after 1-1-2006, new jobs creation tax credit (credit amount varies). *(Conn.)*

(85) $400 ($650 in targeted areas) per qualified new employee (min. 5) in new facility (min. $200,000 invested); high paying ($100,000 or more) new jobs (50) with credit based on percentage of withholding (up to 40% credit); additional 10% credit for targeted growth zones and additional 5% credit for former brownfields *(Del.).* Mfg. businesses adding net 2 (min.) jobs and other businesses (not retail) adding net 5 (min.) jobs get credit of $1,500 ($2,500 in nonmetropolitan region) per qualified new employee and $1,000 per qualified business facility investment of $100,000; retailers and others adding net 2 (min.), jobs but not claiming above credit, get $100 per qualified new employee and $100 per qualified business facility investment of $100,000; max. credit is 50% of tax.) *(Kans.).*

(86) 5% of 1st $6,000 of yr. wages paid developmentally disabled or chronically mentally ill employee (max. 50% of tax) *(N.Dak.).*

(87) Business in enterprise zone is allowed credit under various enterprise zone acts. *(Ark).*

(88) $500 per employee in enterprise zone or high impact business in River Edge Redevelopment Zone, Foreign Trade Zone or Sub-zone hired in tax year. *(Ill.)*

(89) Qualified mfrs., distributors, wholesalers, R & D businesses, air carriers, processors, hotels, telecommunication enterprises, and movie studios in Tier 3 areas get $2,000 per new job in yr. 2–6 after job created; Tier 2 areas, $1,000; Tier 1 areas, $500; add $500—$2,000 (up to 50% of tax) per new job for company transferring regional or national headquarters into Miss. or establishing such headquarters in Miss. if at least 35 jobs created; add $1,000 (up to 50% of tax) for new employee in job requiring R&D skills. Credit per new employee who was receiving Aid for Dependent Children is 20%-40% of 1st $5,200 of wages paid to such person (% is keyed to amount of hourly salary above Fed min. wage). *(Miss.)*

(90) Okla. provides "incentive payments" to basic industries that provide qualified employment opportunities, and to "small employers" providing employment opportunities. There is also a credit for providing computer jobs and creating new jobs in connection with investing in qualified property.

(91) $500 ($1,000 if certain salary and benefits requirements are met) per qualified new employee, up to max. credit of 3.25% of net income from business in which the employment ocurred *(Ida.).*

FOOTNOTES to chart ¶ 236 (corresponding to parenthetical numbers in chart): (continued)

(92) $3,500 for business or business headquarters in Tier 1 County and less developed area, $2,500 in Tier 2, $1,250 in Tier 3 and $750 in Tier 4 up to 50% of tax, per new qualified full-time job created in mfg., warehousing and distribution, processing, tourism, telecommunications, and research and development (not in retailing) industry per yr. 2–6 after job created; in Tier 1, credit also allowed to business of any nature for jobs created. Added $500 if in joint development authority. Similar credit for new jobs created in areas designated "less developed." $1,250 for each new job created by business establishing or relocating corporate headquarters in Ga., increased to $5,000 per job if average wage is 200% or more above average county wage. Credit is allowed equal to $5,250 annually per new full-time job created, for 5 yrs. starting with yr. of job creation, for qualified business constructing new manufacturing facility or expanding existing manufacturing facility in Ga. *(Ga.)*

(93) (a) Employer of eligible teacher in qualified position for summer recess gets credit of lesser of $2500 or 50% of compensation paid teacher;
(b) credit for new jobs as agreed to for up to 10 yrs. with Economic Development for Growing Economy Bd. *(Ind.)*

(94) Employers participating in Full Employment Program get credit of $100 per month per eligible participant; for 2005-2009, up to $1,200 per participant, 50% of salary attributable to eligible jobs in biomedical or medical device manufacturing co. *(Mass.)*

(95) $250 for each new job created at a new consumer-ready wood product manufacturing facility in the state. 25% or 30% of wages paid to former military persons. *(W.Va.)*.

(96) Business with agreement with vocational school or community college to create qualified new jobs, 6% of gross wages paid per new job. *(Iowa)*.

(97) $100 per new hiree *(Kans.)*.

(98) New jobs credit—$1,000 per new job (min. 25 new jobs) created. *(Pa.)*

(99) (Reserved.)

(100) 5% of total compensation paid during the yr. that exceeds average compensation paid at the project times the number of base yr. employees; and 10% of investment in the project. $3,000 per new employee in qualified business and $2,750 for each $50,000 in increased investment. *(Neb.)*

(101) $8,000 per new job over 10 in a distressed county, $4,500 per new job in a least developed county, $3,500 in an underdeveloped county, $2,500 in a moderately developed county, $1,500 in a developed county. For employers with 99 or fewer employees who create at least 2 new jobs, but whose gross wages are not at least 120% of the lower of the state's average per capita income, the credit amounts are $4,000 per new job in a distressed county, $2,500 per new job in a least developed county, $1,750 in a underdeveloped county, $1,250 in a moderately developed county, $750 in a developed county. *(S.C.)*

(102) 15% (up to 5% of tax) of compensation paid to eligible employees (eff for tax yrs. starting pre-7-1-97) *(N.H.)*.

(103) Unemployment credit—$100 per hiree if conditions met *(Ky.)*.

(104) First $2,500 of 1st yr. wages paid to eligible student participating in Ore. youth apprenticeship program *(Ore.)*.

(105) Up to $12,500 per new employee in area development tier 1 area, $5,000 in area development tier 2 area, $750 in tier 3 area. *(N.C.)*.

(106) Capital credit equal to lesser of income tax liability generated by project or 5% of capital costs of qualifying project. Similar capital credit allowed for qualifying project related to Alabama State Port Authority infrastructure. *(Ala.)*.

(107) % (specified in agreement with Tax Credit Authority) of new personal income tax revenue for tax yrs. (15-yr. max.) generated by creation of new jobs or retention of jobs. *(Ohio)*.

(108) $1,000 per qualified full-time employee over 100 per facility certified by Dept. Economic Development; max. total credit per taxpayer for all yrs., $1 million; take ⅓ of credit in tax yr. and next 2 yrs. For tax yrs. beginning on or after 1-1-2004, but before 1-1-2006, if facility is located in severely economically distressed area, threshold amount required to qualify for credit is reduced from 100 to 25. However, total amount of credit allowable cannot exceed $100,000. Until 12-31-2011, clean fuel vehicle job creation credit is allowed. *(Va.)*.

(109) $250 per employee for corporations that participate in the bonus program. *(R.I.)*.

(110) Neighborhood assistance credit for impoverished area *(Del.)*.

(111) See column C *(Me.)*.

(112) 50% of wages paid to certified employee during first 24 calendar months of employment by qualified corporation or unincorporated business in economic development zone *(D.C.)*.

(113) 10% of gross wages paid in first 180 days of employment to individual with disability, and 20% of gross wages paid in remaining tax year to individual with a disability (max. $3,000 per year per individual; allowed only for first two years individual is employed by taxpayer) *(Utah)*.

(114) Credit for state taxes on fuel for non-highway commercial use allowed *(Iowa)*.

(115) (Reserved.)

(116) Fuel taxes paid by commercial fishers *(Haw.)*.

(117) Deduction allowed for amounts added under IRC for alcohol fuel credits *(Iowa)*.

(118) Credit for state gasoline, motor fuel, and special fuel taxes paid to run commercial fishing boat *(La.)*.

(119) Commercial lenders' credit for weatherization or alternative device loans; portion of cost of reforestation of unproductive forest lands; gross premiums tax on fire insurers *(Oreg.)*.

(120) 25% (up to $25,000) of cost to build, acquire, or renovate facility to be mainly used for day care for employees' children. Credit for unbudgeted property taxes associated with the low income housing tax credit: 5% of qualified loan or qualified long-term investment; or 3% annually of unpaid principal balance or low-interest loan for life of loan or 15 yrs., whichever is earlier. *(Tenn.)*

FOOTNOTES to chart ¶ 236 (corresponding to parenthetical numbers in chart): (continued)

(121) 50% of workers' compensation insurance premiums attributable to a certified employee during first 24 months of employment that are paid by qualified corporation or unincorporated business in economic development zone *(D.C.)*; amount by which fair market value of space leased to licensed, nonprofit child development center exceeds rent charged to center by qualified corporation or unincorporated business in economic development zone *(D.C.)*. Credit allowed for qualified high technological company for employment relocation costs; wages paid to qualified employees; wages paid to qualified disadvantaged employees; and employee retraining costs*(D.C.)*. Credit allowed for employer-provided homeownership assistance. *(D.C.)* . Credit is allowed for 5 consecutive yrs. for wages of qualified employees hired by CareFirst, not to exceed $1,000 per employee *(D.C.)*. Subject to available funding, nonrefundable credit allowed if employees get paid leave of absence to serve as organ or bone marrow donor *(D.C.)*.

(122) Restoration, rehab or preservation of cultural property, ½ of cost ($25,000 max.) 30% of cost of providing child care services for employees ($30,000 max. credit). Operator of new mfg., processing, or growing business on Native American Indian Tribal land can take credit for up to 50% of lesser of total taxes paid to tribe located in NM or amount of NM corporate income tax liability from new business's activity on tribal land *(N.M.)*.

(123) Generally, narrow-based, special industry credits *(Ohio)* .

(124) 50% of expenses to rehabilitate forest, range, and farm lands, up to $2,000 max per yr. *(Ida.)*

(125) 5% of excess qualified research costs plus 5% basic research amount allowed under IRC §41(c) *(Ida.)*.

(126) Property taxes paid on—gasohol production property *(Fla.)*; realty in poverty areas *(Mass.)*. Until 12-31-2007, credit for tax attributable to high technology in certified central city. Eff 1-1-2008, credit for property taxes on industrial and certain business personalty. *(Mich.)*. Credits are available for hiring and child care expenses of welfare recipients, purchase of Md.-mined coal, rehabilitation of certified heritage structures, and neighborhood and community assistance program contributions, long-term care insurance, employing persons with disabilities, for property taxes on telecommunications and public utility operating real property, wages paid to students under work-based learning programs, for converting agricultural production to nutrient management plan, employer-provided commuter benefits, public service corporation headquarters wages, investment in biotechnology cos. *(Md.)*.

(127) Sales-use taxes on fuel-electricity used in mfg. in-state; farmland preservation credit; up to $1,200 of employment-related day-care expenses for each qualifying individual *(Wis.)*.

(128) 4% of cost of eligible depreciable tangible personalty used in trade-business and placed in service in-state after 1987 *(Hawaii)*.

(129) Contributions to—charities: 25% of wholesale market price or sales price of contributions of crops or livestock, up to max. credit of $1,000 per yr. *(Colo.)*; enterprise zone administrators (25% of contribution; max. credit, $100,000) *(Colo.)*; conservation easement credit of up to $100,000 per donation *(Colo.)*; nonprofit museums or their foundations; public and state libraries and public broadcast system foundations *(Idaho)*; secondary schools or higher educ. (up to 50% in *Ida.*); university-related research parks *(Ida.)*; 50% of contribution to youth and rehabilitation facilities and nonprofit substance abuse centers, up to total credit of lesser of 10% of tax liability or $500 *(Ida.)*; in-state foundations or institutions for higher education (50% of gift, up to lesser of $1,000 or 10% of tax) *(Ind.)*; for SBT and MBT, 50% of contributions to in-state public libraries, colleges, public broadcasting stations, certified community foundations, homeless shelters, food banks, or kitchens (and eff 1-1-2008, educational foundations) (up to max. of 5% of tax or $5,000 if less) *(Mich.)*; 50% of contribution to economic development reserves (Mo.); 50% of gifts to small-business incubator fund or local sponsor *(Mo.)*; nonprofit private schools or colleges in-state (up to 50%) *(N.D.)*; 25% of FMV of NC realty donated for conservation use ($500,000 max.) *(N.C.)*; Homeowners Emergency Mortgage Assistance Fund, 70% of (Pa.) and/or neighborhood assistance programs (job training, crime prevention etc.), 50% of (70% for special programs) (Pa.); education assistance and development—8% of cash in excess of $10,000; 10% (max. $3,000) of wages under juvenile restitution law. *(R.I.)*.

(130) For tax yrs. beginning before 1-1-2010, credit is allowed in amount equal to 50% of amount paid or incurred by taxpayer for eligible research and development activity in tobacco-dependent localities during tax yr. Other credits allowed for recyclable materials processing machinery and equipment, vehicle emissions testing equipment, waste motor oil burning equipment, clean-fuel vehicle and certain refueling property, clean fuel vehicle job creation, coalfield employment enhancement, coal employment and production incentive, donated land for environmental preservation, riparian forest buffer protection for waterways, neighborhood assistance, day care facility investment, agriculture incentives, historic rehabilitation, employee training, low-income housing, rent reduction program, cigarette manufacturing and exporting. *(Va.)*

FOOTNOTES to chart ¶ 236 (corresponding to parenthetical numbers in chart): (continued)

(131) Handicapped accessibility, 50% of costs or $10,000, if less; 25% of cash investment in fund for small business devoted to new product or process; 30% of cost of day care services of facilities-equipment for employees' children ($30,000 max. credit), but 50% of 1st yr. cost of facility ($45,000 max. credit). Certain amounts paid by employers of certain National Guard members for health insurance. 50% of contribution to community service entity; 70%, if in rural community. Credit for 50% of amount spent on qualified alternative-fueled MVs placed in service pre 1-1-2005, up to max. credit of $3,000 for MV with gross vehicle weight under 10,000 lbs; max. $5,000 for heavy duty MV with gross vehicle weight 10,000 to 26,000 lbs; max. $50,000 for MV with gross vehicle weight over 26,000 lbs. 25% of qualified expenditures of at least $5,000 for restoration or preservation of certain historic structures; 30% of qualified expenditures for restoration or preservation of certain non-income producing historic structures. 15% of property tax paid on certain commercial and industrial machinery. 50% of improvement to a qualified swine facility. 25% of property tax levied on qualified business machinery and equipment. 50% of property tax paid on working interest of an oil lease with avg. daily production of 15 bbl. or less when price of oil is $16 per bbl. or less. 100% of amount attributable to the retirement of indebtedness authorized by a single city authority established before 1-1-2002. *(Kan.)*

(132) 30% of seed capital investment (max. taken per tax yr. is 50% of this credit); costs of day care for employees' children equal to lesser of $5,000, 20% of relevant costs, or $100 per full-time enrolled child; costs of long-term care benefits for employees equal to lesser of $5,000, 20% of relevant costs, or $100 per covered employee; research expense credit equal to 5% of excess qualified research expenses plus 7.5% of basic research payments, and a super credit equal to excess qualified research expenses for in-state research over average amount of research expenses for past 3 yrs. increased by 50%. 30% of up to $30,000 for eligible expenditures for child care services. Amount claimed under IRC §47 regarding expenditures for certified historic structures. Starting in 2009, portion of amount contributed to a qualified scholarship organization for need-based scholarships (20% in 2009, 50% after 2009). Starting in 2009, portion of post-secondary loan repayments (15%). 5¢ per gal. of certain biofuel. Until 12-31-2007, credit is allowed for 100% tax otherwise due for a qualified community wind power generator. Eff 3-29-2006, a media production credit is allowed. Until 1-1-2010, credit is allowed for qualified pollution-reducing boilers and furnace systems. Eff 9-20-2007, employers can claim educational opportunity credit for qualified "opportunity program participants". Beginning 1-1-2008 until 1-1-2014, credit for local historic landmark developers in Lockwood Mill Historic Dist. (up to $1 million annually). *(Me.)*

(133) Until 12-31-2007, Single Business Tax credits for—small business with $10 million max. gross receipts and $475,000 max. adjusted business income, greater of (a) 100% minus ratio of adjusted business income over 45% of tax base or (b) amount of tax over 2% of adjusted business income, minus ratio of gross receipts over $9 million to $1 million; unincorporated or Subch. S, 10%-20% of tax. Taxpayers with a preapproval letter for a brownfield project issued after 1999 and before 2008 can claim a credit of up to 10% of the eligible investment (max. credit $30 million), if the project is completed within 5 years after preapproval letter is issued. Credit is allowed for 50% of salary, wages, fringe benefits, and payroll costs paid to apprentice and 100% of classroom instruction costs and expenses (max. credit, $2,000 per apprentice). Credit limit for tool and dye industries is $4,000 per apprentice plus a credit limit of $1,000 per special apprentices. Credit for tax liability attributed to business activity in a renaissance zone. Credit is allowed for 25% of qualified capital expenditures eligible under IRC §47(a)(2) to rehabilitate artificial historic resource under a rehabilitation plan. An investment credit is allowed for tangible non-mobile property used for in-state business activity and physically located in-state, apportioned cost of mobile tangible assets located everywhere, and non-apportioned cost of non-mobile assets acquired out-of-state for in-state business activity. Owners (not individuals, partnerships, or S corp. shareholders) of farmland and related buildings covered by development rights agreements can claim a credit for the amount by which property taxes on the land and structures covered by the agreement exceed 3.5% of the owner's adjusted business income. Credit for $1-per-long-ton of qualified low-grade hematite consumed in an industrial or manufacturing process that is the business activity of the taxpayer. Credit for 6.5% of excess of qualified research expenses paid in yr. relating to eligible taxpayer's pharmaceutical-based business activity in-state over taxpayer's average qualified research expenses of such activity paid in-state in the 3 preceding yrs. Qualified start-up businesses that do not have business income for 2 consecutive tax years can claim a credit for the 2nd of those consecutive years and each mmediately following consecutive tax year in which the taxpayer does not have business income. The credit is equal to the taxpayer's tax liability for the tax year in which the taxpayer has no business income. Credit cannot be claimed for more than a total of 5 years. 50% of the fair market value of an automobile donated to a "Wheels to Work" program. Amount allowable as credit for a tax year cannot exceed $100. Credit is allowed for taxpayer engaged in R&D of a qualified technology equal to 3.9% of compensation for services performed in the qualified facility paid to employees at the facility in the tax yr., if the taxpayer enters into an agreement with the Mich. Economic Growth Authority before 1-1-2007 (max. credit any one taxpayer can claim in a single yr. is $3 million). Eff 1-1-2008, Mich. Business Tax allows credits for: automobile inventory; Brownfield development; certain large grocery stores; historic preservation credit; low-grade hematite; Michigan Speedway; Next Energy business activity; research and development expenses; revenue trigger credit; small business credit; stadium credit; and start-up business credit. *(Mich.)*

FOOTNOTES to chart ¶ 236 (corresponding to parenthetical numbers in chart): (continued)

(134) Job training; alternative min. tax paid; 5% of 1st $2 million of research and experimental costs per formula, 2.5% over $2 million; tax paid to another state; transit passes; starting in 2004, qualified business increasing research activities in a biotechnology and health science industry zone can claim 5% of first $2 million of qualified research expenses over base amount and 2.5% of such expenses over $2 million. Owners of cattle in-state can claim 50% of expenses incurred during the tax yr. to conduct tuberculosis testing on those cattle. *(Minn.)* 20% of cost of approved basic skills education program for employees residing in Ala.; coal producer's credit; tax increment fund payment credit; credit for income generated by project creating industrial or research enterprise for use by approved company. *(Ala.)*

(135) (a) 25% of costs of providing dependent care for employees, $1,575 max. credit.
(b) 10% of contributions to Mont. college endowment fund, $500 max. credit.
(c) Business created as result of loan under MCA §17-6-309(2) and §17-6-316 to build infrastructure (such as water systems, sewer systems, water and sewage treatment facilities, and roads) that allows location or creation of business in Mont., can get credit (up to loan amount) against corporation license (income) tax for portion of fees attributable to use of the infrastructure.
(d) Credit is allowed in the amount of 15% of the cost of storage and blending equipment to be used for blending biodiesel with petroleum diesel fuel; max. credit is $52,500 for special fuel distributor and $7,500 for owner or operator of motor fuel outlet; credit is claimed in tax yr. in which distributor or retailer begins blending biodiesel fuel. *(Mont.)*

(136) Credit for credit union intangibles tax paid, insurance tax and assessments paid, 5% electric cooperatives tax paid; contributions to community betterment programs per Community Development Assistance Act. *(Neb.)*

(137) Credit allowed for gas-electricity utility franchise tax, bank tax & insurance premiums tax *(N.H.)*.

(138) N.Y. offers credits for: minimum tax; special additional mortgage recording tax, agricultural property tax; rehabilitation for historic barns; foreign corp. maint. fee; employing disabled persons; alternative fuels; emerging technology businesses; purchases of automated external defibrillators; green buildings; low-income housing; transportation improvement contributions; industrial or manufacturing business energy taxes; long-term care insurance premiums; film production; security training; commercial production; biofuel production; home heating oil containing biodiesel; handicapped transportation; and rehabilitation of historic properties.

(139) Other Okla. credits include: manufacturers' natural gas; manufacturers' recycling; clean burning motor fuel; renewable energy systems; small wind turbine manufacturing; hazardous waste reduction; coal production incentive; conservation assistance fund; nonstop air transportation provider; child care assistance; health insurance benefits; hepatitus A immunizations; agricultural processing cooperative investment; historic property renovation; and approved tourism projects; certain costs of high speed processing facilities and aircraft manufacturing components.

(140) 15% of cost of industrial recovery site property put in service 20–29 yrs. ago; 20%, 30–39 yrs.; 25% at least 40 yrs. *(Ind.)*.

(141) (a) 20% of amount spent directly on research and experimental costs, exceeding such costs for past tax yr.;
(b) 25% of grant(s) to institution of higher learning in Conn. for technological research and development, exceeding avg. spent for such grants in 3 past tax yrs.
(c) 1% of 1st $50 million of R&D costs, 2% of next $50 million, 4% of next $100 million. 6% of balance max. credit taken per yr. is ⅓ of credit earned that yr.)
(d) 5% of increase of machinery and equip. costs in current yr. over past yr. if company has 251–800 full-time permanent employees; 10% if 250 (max.) full-time permanent employees.
(e) 100% of personal property tax paid on electronic data processing equip. (eff for property appearing on annual grand list).
(f) Computer donation, 50% of value of donation.
(g) Credit for small business guaranty fee paid for SBA financing.
(h) Credit for 50% of value of donation of open space.
(i) Historic rehabilitation credits up to 30% of qualified rehabilitation expenses.
(j) Film production credit, up to 30% of qualified production expenses or costs.
(k) Motion picture infrastructure credit: 10% of investment for projects over $15,000 and less than $150,000; 15% for projects of $150,000 up to $1 million; 20% for projects of $1 million or more.
(l) Digital animation production co. credit: 30% of production expenses/costs over $50,000. (*(Conn.)*

(142) Credit for—Youth Apprentice Sponsorship, First Break, Oregon Capital Corp., scientific equipment, research and development, pollution control, recycling, alternative fuel vehicle filing stations, dependent care, long-term care insurance, bone marrow donors, energy conservation, reforestation, fish habitat and screening, housing rehabilitation, fire insurance premiums, child development, farm worker housing, crop gleaning, claim of right income adjustment *(Ore.)*.

FOOTNOTES to chart ¶ 236 (corresponding to parenthetical numbers in chart): (continued)

(143) 4% of subcontracts with socially and economically disadvantaged small businesses ($50,000 max.). 25% (or $2,500) of cost of conservation tillage equipment etc. 25% ($2,500 max.) of expenditures for water storage and control structures used for soil and water conservation and wildlife management conservation; 30% of investments in qualified recycling facilities. 25% of federal deduction claimed for donation of land or qualified property interest for conservation. Value of land or easements near rivers under the Scenic River Program. 20% of development costs to build or expand corp. headquarters in S.C. and 20% of construction or lease costs for 1st 5 yrs. 50% of 1st $100,000 of capital costs to establish day care program for employees; 50% of payments for child care for employees (max. $3,000 credit per employee); 50% ($10,000 max.) of costs of build or improve infrastructure. 10% of 1st yr. wages ($7,000 max.) per employee terminated as result of closing or realignment of military installation. 10% to 20% ($5,500 max.) per employee formerly receiving Aid to Dependent Families benefits. 1% to 5% of aggregate bases in qualified economic impact zone (county or city within 50 miles of closed Fed military installation or in area adversely impacted) mfg. and productive equip. put in service in zone in tax yr. 5% of qualified research and development expenditures made in-state (up to 50% of tax liability); 33% of investment in a community development corporation or community development financial institution; 20% ($100,000 max.) of investment in a company that develops or produces a qualified motion picture project. 10% of investment ($1 million for all claimants) in production company that produces advertisements. 25% ($5 million max.) of investments in construction conversion or equipment for S.C. motion picture production or post production facility. Milk producer credit of $10,000 for 1st 500,000 pounds of milk sold below production price; $5,000 credit per each additional 500,000 pounds. 20¢ per gallon of biodiesel motor fuel produced mostly from soybean oil and sold for up to 5 yrs. (max. of 3 million gallons); 30¢ per gallon of biodiesel motor fuel produced mostly from non-soybean oil feed stock and sold for up to 5 yrs. (max. of 3 million gallons). 20¢ per gallon of ethanol, corn-based ethanol, or soy-based biodiesel fuel, up to 60 months (max. 25 million gallons); 7.5¢ per gallon of ethanol for new production, up to 36 months (max. 10 million gallons). 25% of cost of constructing or installing property for distributing or dispensing renewable fuel. 25% of cost of constructing and equipping commercial facility for producing renewable fuel. 10% of federal credit for qualified rehabilitation expenditures for certified historic structure. 25% of rehabilitation expenses for site that was sold as a textile manufacturing facility. 10% of rehabilitation expenses for abandoned retail facility site. 100% of contribution to Industrial Partnership Fund (max. of $650,000; total of $2 million for all claimants). 25% of expenditures to develop feedstocks and processes for allulosic ethanol and algae-derived biodiesel (max. of $100,000 for all claimants). 25% of qualified contribution to S.C. Hydrogen Infrastructure Development Fund. 25% of costs of purchasing and installing equipment used to generate energy from fuel consisting of at least 90% biomass resource (max. of $650,000 for all claimants). *(S.C.)*

(144) (a) lesser of 50% or certified amount of farmworker housing construction or rehabilitation costs; banks get additional credit for financing qualified farmworker housing; maximums apply;
(b) 50% of 1st $250 of costs to provide access to disabled persons per IRC §44;
(c) 30% of setting up program or constructing facility in-state for child care primarily for employees, or of contributions to in-state child care info. and referral services, $50,000 max. credit (eff for tax yrs. starting pre-1-1-2007);
(d) 15% of qualified research expenses for business-related research and 24% of basis research expenses for university-based research;
(e) through 2005, 10% of qualified costs of property used in joint strike fighter;
(f) if qualified business, 6% of amount paid or incurred to buy qualified property placed in service in Calif. (eff for income yrs. starting pre-1-1-2001 or longer if specified state employment conditions are met);
(g) if in business or trade in Local Agency Military Base Recovery Area can take credit for 50%—10% of qualified wages of newly hired disadvantaged employees in yr. 1–5 of work, or for sales-use tax paid on qualified property used solely in LAMBRA.
(h) ⅓ of Fed enhanced oil recovery credit;
(i) $15 per ton of rice straw used for other than burning; max total annual credit for all taxpayers is $400,000 (eff for income yrs. starting before 2008);
(j) 50% of cost to transport farm products donated to nonprofit charitable entity;
(k) before 2008, land conservation credit may be allowed—55% of fair market value of qualified contribution made after 1998 under the Natural Preservation Tax Credit Act of 2000 (credit is suspended 2002-05 fiscal years.)
(l) small refiners' credit equal to 5 cents per gallon of ultra-low sulphur diesel fuel (eff for tax yrs. starting pre-1-1-2018). *(Calif.)*

(145) Emergency excise tax community contribution, hazardous waste facility, renewable energy investment and production, AMT, HMO assessment, Rural Jobs and Urban High Crime Area, cleanup of drycleaning solvent, employee childcare assistance, contributions to scholarship funding organizations, and capital investment tax credits. *(Fla.)*

(146) Research activities—6½% of state's apportioned share of qualifying expenditures for research. Business with agreement with vocational school or community college to create qualified new jobs, 10% of new property investment in zone and 6.5% of research increase costs apportioned to Iowa. *(Iowa).*

FOOTNOTES to chart ¶ 236 (corresponding to parenthetical numbers in chart): (continued)

(147) (a) Contributions of sophisticated and technological equipment (computers, etc.) to in-state educational institution, 40% of property's value.
(b) 100% of local property tax paid on mfr.—distributor-retailer inventory.
(c) Cost of basic job skills provided to employees, $250 per participating employee.
(d) Qualified investment in films with certified substantial La. content; specific portion of payroll for La. residents in connection with motion picture production.
(e) 100% of local property tax paid without protest on vessels in Outer Continental Shelf Lands Act waters;
(f) utilities refund credit, if refunds result from denial of rate increase and would result in net loss if deducted in year paid or accrued, credit can be taken to extent that the refunds increased tax.
(g) 70% (up to $250,000 annually) of actual contributions in programs that provide neighborhood assistance, job training, education for individuals, community services or crime prevention in La. and are approved by the commissioner of administration.
(h) qualified rehabilitation costs for historical property.
(i) 25% of bone marrow donor expense paid or incurred during tax year by empolyer to provide program for employees who are potential or who actually become bone marrow donors;
(j) qualified donations made to qualified playgrounds equal to lesser of $1,000 or 50% value of cash, equipment, goods, or services donated. *(La.)*

(148) 8% on 1st $1.5 million of qualified research and experiment costs in-state, 4% on bal. 10% of cost of equip to convert MV to run on alternative fuel; max. per MV up to 10,000 lbs., $200; over 10,000 lbs., $500. *(N.Dak.).*

(149) (a) Business engaged in neighborhood assistance, 70% of investment ($250,000 max.; max exceeded for specified service activity);
(b) 50% of contributions to "qualified fund" (tax credit certificate from Econ. Dev. Dept. is needed) *(Mo.).*

(150) Other *Ind.* credits: $100 per certified computer equip. unit donated to qualified education service center. Eff 1-1-2007, eligible business that completes qualifying project and incurs relocation costs can claim credit of 50% of relocation costs in tax yr. Eff. for tax yrs. after 12/31/2006, 15% of the amount of a qualified investment for manufacturing or assembling alternative fuel vehicles in Ind. Eff. for tax yrs. after 12/31/2008 through 12/31/2010, the lesser of 20% of the amount of expenditures for energy star heating and cooling equipment incurred during tax yr., or $100. *(Ind.).*

(151) Credit, in each of 3 yrs., for 10% of qualified investment in small NJ-based high technology business (max. per yr., $500,000) *(N.J.).*

(152) Research and experimental expenses, 10% of $300,000 if less; technology transfer, 30% of value if transferred to small business; 10% of cost of conservation tillage planter.

(153) All Fed credits are adopted by reference limited to 18%. Education credit is 50% of 1st $100,000 of cash contribution to in-state accredited nonprofit college or university or its foundation, 100% of balance; max credit, $150,000. *(Alaska).*

(154) 100% of tax liability attributable to business activity in Keystone Opportunity Zone (KOZ), KOEZ Zone, or KOIZ Zone; job creation credit of $1,250 per new job in 2004 through 2018. Employment incentive program for hiring person receiving general or temporary assistance to needy families in the last 12 months, or hiring the physically or mentally handicapped: 30% of 1st $9,000 in qualified 1st-yr. wages, 20% of such 2nd-yr. wages, 10% of such 3rd-yr. wages. *(Pa.)*

(155) Construction of (a) multifamily dwellings for handicapped, $550 credit per unit; (b) fuel ethanol distillery, 20% of cost plus 10% of powered by alternate fuel source; (c) peat facility, 20% of costs; (d) photovoltaic equipment facility, 20% of cost; (e) olvine brick facility, 20% of cost; credit allowed for certain real property donations, 25% of fair market value of donated property; for conservation tillage equipment, 25% of cost; for gleaned crop, 10% of market price (N.C.); 50% of contributions to economic development reserves (Mo.); specified entities on contributions to community betterment programs. *(Neb.)*

(156) Credits available include: clean coal initiative credit; Brownfields credit; recycling credits; qualified farming operations; environmental stewardship credit; historic preservation credit. *(Ky.)*

(157) Credits are available for affordable neighborhood housing credit; purchase of qualifying interest in capital development company; biotechnology development and training; capital development; business operating child care facilities; coal mining companies; industrial development corporations; advanced biofuels facilities; economic development; energy technology development; equipment donated to educational institutions; qualified research expenditures; family savings initiatives; geotourism investment; low-income housing; wetlands and riparian zones; public road improvement; rice straw purchases; tourism development; tuition reimbursement; waste reduction or recycling; water resource conservation; workforce training; youth apprenticeship programs and wages paid to employees donating organ for transplant *(Ark.).*

(158) (Reserved.)

(159) 40% of property taxes paid on inventories by mfrs.; corp. providing reduced-rate local telephone service to low-income residents gets credit equal to difference between amount of receipts that would have been collected during tax year at regular rates and amount actually billed; construction *(N.C.)*

(160) Credits are available for hydroelectric power installation, adult education, disabled access for small businesses. *(R.I.)*

FOOTNOTES to chart ¶ 236 (corresponding to parenthetical numbers in chart): (continued)

(161) (a) 5% of IRC §129(d)(7) expenditures by taxpayers primarily engaged in manufacturing, to provide on-site dependent care assistance program.
(b) For tax yrs. ending on or after 12-31-2004, research and development credit is allowed for 6.5% of qualifying expenditures on increasing research activities in Illinois.
(c) Film production services credit until 1-1-2008.
(d) TECH-PREP youth vocational programs credit.
(e) Credit for cost of providing child care facility to employees located in Ill.
(f) Estimated tax payments credit.
(g) Until 12-31-2011, taxpayer who makes donation under Ill. Housing Development Act for development of affordable housing in Ill. is entitled to credit equal to 50% of value of donation.
(h) EDGE tax credits to businesses creating new jobs and making capital investments.
(i) Eff 1-1-2007, credit is allowed for 5% of qualified wages paid to qualified ex-felons.
(j) Eff 1-1-2007, credit is allowed for 5% (up to $600) of gross wages paid to qualified veterans.
(k) Eff 1-1-2007, credit is allowed for certain amounts paid for unreimbursed remediation costs in a River Edge Redevelopment Zone. *(Ill.)*

(162) (a) Credits are available for basic skills training or retraining, child/dependent care;
(b) Credits are available for export charges;
(c) Credits are available for gaming license fees, insurance guaranty assessment, inventory property tax.
(d) Port receiving, handling, and wharfage charges (up to 50% of tax) for using Miss. state or local ports;
(e) Credit equal to gaming license fee paid;
(f) Member issuer of Miss. Life and Health Insurance Guaranty Assn., credit of 20% of association's assessment for each yr. over next 5 yrs.;
(g) Credit equal to finance co. privilege tax;
(h) Financial institution creating or keeping full-time job as result of merger or acquisition, credit ranges from 100% of $1,500 base amount in tax yr. to 20% in 5th yr.
(i) Credit for certain percentage of investments in equipment used in deployment of broadband technologies by telecommunications businesses.
(j) 50% of allowable transaction costs incurred in donating land or interest in land for conservation purposes; max. credit, $10,000.
(k) Credit for 10% of payroll of Miss. residents employed in connection with state-certified motion picture production in Miss.
(l) Brownfield remediation credit. *(Miss.)*

(163) 10% of price of originally issued shares bought pre-1-1-93 in 1st $3 million capitalization from Vt. taxpayers of Vt. Venture Capital Corp. or 50% of tax if less; 8-yr. carryover *(Vt.)*.

(164) Credit for wages paid in specific industries for newly created jobs—lesser of (1) $1,000 times number of qualified employees employed during credit yr. ($1,500 in a revitalization area) or (2) 2.5% (5% in a revitalization area) of wages paid during credit yr. to qualified employees. Max. credit, $1 million per qualified business entity. One Md. credit equal to 100% of eligible project costs for eligible economic development projects in an economically distressed county if a specified number of new jobs are created in specified industries. *(Md.)*

(165) Credit for coal removal and ultraclean fuels; contributions to qualified educational improvement organizations; contributions to the Mortgage Emergency Assistance Fund; credit for providing paid leave for organ donors; neighborhood assistance credit; film production credit; research and development credit; resource enhancement credit; strategic development area credit; waste tire recycling credit. *(Pa.)*

(166) 30% of amount spent for day care (inclu. dependent adult care) services for employees; 30% of amount spent to set up or run day care facility for employees. 10% of cost or other basis for Fed income tax purposes of research and development property acquired, built, or rebuilt after 7-1-94. 5% of excess of qualified research costs after 7-1-94 for tax yr. over base period. 50% of job training expenses for qualifying employees. *(R.I.)*.

(167) 30% of purchase price of co. shuttle vans *(Mass.)*.

(168) Qualifying Fed harbor maintenance tax paid by shippers, exporters, and importers *(Mass.)*.

(169) 5% of costs of IRC §48(g)(2) rehabilitation expenditures for certified structures, credit reduces Wis. adjusted basis. *(Wis.)*

(170) Credit equal to Fed. IRC §41 credit for research activities. Credit for 4% of the qualified expenditures for construction or renovation costs incurred during tax year for each qualified hotel facility located in Haw. Credit for 4% of the cost of depreciable tangible personalty placed in service in the taxpayer's trade or business in Haw. During the tax year and that was subject to the Haw. 4% general excise or use tax. Credit for 30% of the Fed. credit under IRC §42 for qualified low-income housing. Haw. Credit of up to 4% of the production costs for motion picture or TV films (no credit for costs deducted under IRC §179). Credit of up to 7.5% of the actual expenditures for transient accommodations involved in producing motion pictures or TV films. Credit for investing in a qualified ethanol production facility that is in production by 1-1-2017; credit amount ranges from lesser of 30% of the investment or $150,000 for facilities with a nameplate capacity of 500,000–1 million gal. of ethanol annually to a max. of $4.5 million for facilities with a nameplate capacity over 15 million gal. RIC shareholders are allowed credit equal to Haw. Tax on undistributed capital gain required to be included in shareholders' returns under IRC §852(b)(3)(D) if RIC paid Haw. tax on the gain. 10% of value of in-kind contributions for the repair and maintenance of Haw. public schools. Qualified costs to develop facilities for attractions and educational purposes at specified resorts. *(Haw.)*

(171) (Reserved.)

(172) Credits are available for research and development, donation of Del. land to conservation agency, Travelink traffic mitigation, and historic preservation *(Del.)*.

FOOTNOTES to chart ¶ 236 (corresponding to parenthetical numbers in chart): (continued)

(173) 10% of qualified rehabilitative costs for certified historic structures *(W.Va.)*.

(174) (a) 50% of cash contributions ($1,000 max.) to nonprofit rehabilitation sheltered workshop facilities for handicapped operating in-state;
(b) 25% of fair market value of high technology equipment contributed to public education (not more than basis of property);
(c) 25% of cost of residential energy system (incl. installation) completed and placed in service before 1996 in each residential unit in-state owned by business ($1,500 max. total credit);
(d) 10% of cost of commercial energy system (incl. installation) completed and placed in service before 1996 if business buys or funds system and either supplies energy to its commercial units or sells energy produced by this system ($25,000 max. credit per commercial unit;
(e) 1% of gross interest included in state taxable income from securities of U.S. and Utah and its political subdivisions;
(f) amount equal to amount of Fed low-income housing tax credit multiplied by percentage specified in allocation certificate issued by Utah Housing Finance Agency;
(g) 20% of qualified rehabilitation expenditures costing more than $10,000 for residential certified historic building;
(h) low-income housing credit. *(Utah)*.

(175) (a) Research & development costs in-state, $100,000 max. credits in 1st yr., $250,000 2nd yr., $400,000 3rd, $500,000 each yr. after 3rd.
(b) Defense contractor qualified jobs—credit for net increase in jobs under US Defense Dept. contracts or in private commercial jobs due to worker transfers; $2,500 per qualified worker for 1st yr. at job, $2,000 2nd yr., $1,500 3rd, $1,000 4th, $500 5th; no credit if military reuse zone credit below taken for same worker. Defense contractor property taxes—40% of property taxes paid on Class 3 property if more than 900 net new defense-related jobs created, 30% if 601 to 900 jobs, 20% if 301 to 600, 10% if 1 to 300.
(c) Credit for increased jobs in military reuse zone mainly working in mfg., assembling, or fabricating aviation or aerospace products—credit per new job is $500 for 1st yr. at job, $1,000 2nd, $1,500 3rd, $2,000 4th, $2,500 5th; add $500 per worker per yr. 1–5 who's a dislocated military base employee; no credit if credit taken under defense contractor jobs credit above for same worker.
(d) Credit for coal consumed in generating electrical power;
(e) Credit for donation of agricultural preservation district;
(f) Alternative fuel delivery systems, vehicles, and equipment;
(g) Donation of school site;
(h) Energy conservation credit;
(i) Pollution abatement recycling credits. *(Ariz.)*

(176) (a) Lesser of $150 or ⅓ of qualified unreimbursed cost of providing approved basic skills education program per full-time equivalent student employee successfully completing course;
(b) 75% of cost of providing or sponsoring child care for employees, up to 50% of tax; 100% of cost of qualified child care property during yr. 1 of service, then 10% per yr. for 10 yrs.
(c) Lesser of 50% of cost of retraining employee in approved program or $500 per full-time employee.
(d) 10% of excess over base amount of research expenses.
(e) Eligible business increasing exports above threshold amount and qualifying for jobs tax credit can take additional $1,250, up to 50% of tax.
(f) Eligible rapidly growing small business can take credit, for up to 50% of tax, equal to excess over 20% of the percentage growth in the business net taxable income in the current tax yr.
(g) 10% of qualified historic rehabilitation costs.
(h) Motion picture production credit. *(Ga.)*

(177) 10% of excess of qualified research expenses for tax yrs. over base yr. research expenses and 15% of basic research payments after 1-1-91 *(Mass.)*.

(178) 10% of excess of qualified R&D expenses over base amount, plus 10% of basic R&D costs. 10% of commuter transportation expenses paid for employees thru 12-31-2007, up to $141 max. credit per employee for 2007. There are also business relocation grants and business incentive programs that subsidize job costs when at least 25 new jobs are brought into the state; neighborhood and business child care credit in an amount equal to 15% of expenditures and 10% of contributions. Film production credit equal to 20% of taxpayer's qualified film production expenses; credit (50% of cost) for providing equipment used for treatment of effluent for reuse in an industrial process. *(N.J.)*

(179) Amount, per formula, (up to 50% of tax) of cargo owner's wharfage and handling costs to use deepwater ports at Wilmington or Morehead City, N.C. *(N.C.)*.

(180) Taxpayers who are allocated a federal low-income housing tax credit can claim credit with respect to the same qualified project in an amount authorized and allocated by Dept. of Rev. *(Mass.)*

(181) Starting in 2004, qualified business in a job opportunity building, agricultural processing facility, or biotechnology and health science industry zone can claim credit for 7% of : (1) lesser of (a) zone payroll for tax yr., less zone payroll for base yr. or (b) total Minn. Payroll for tax yr., less total Minn. Payroll for base yr; minus (2) $30,000 multiplied by sum of number of full-time equivalent employees that the business employs in the zone for tax yr., minus number of full-time employees In the business employed in the zone in base yr. (not less than zero). Eff for tax yrs. starting during the duration of the zone, equivalent credit available to qualified businesses in an International Economic Development Zone. *(Minn.)*

(182) Enterprise zone credits: Employment credit—50% of total wages and salaries paid to qualified zone employees; max. credit of $2,500 per employee. *(R.I.)*

(183) 25% of state certified production costs incurred directly attributable to activity within R.I. if total production budget is minimum of $300,000 *(R.I.)*.

FOOTNOTES to chart ¶ 236 (corresponding to parenthetical numbers in chart): (continued)

(184) Until 12-31-2007, Single Business Tax allows authorized business to claim amount certified by the Mich. Economic Growth Authority and limited to the payroll (total salaries before reduction for personal exemptions) attributable to employees who perform qualified new jobs multiplied by the appropriate personal income tax rate (¶ 228); no credit is allowed if initial certification is issued after 12-31-2009. Authorized business can claim a credit for the tax liability attributable to authorized business activity (business activity of authorized business certified under the Mich. Economic Growth Authority Act); tax liability is the SBT (after certain other credits are calculated) multiplied by either: (1) for a business locating a facility in-state—numerator is the ratio of the value of facility to all of taxpayer's property in-state plus ratio of taxpayer's payroll attributable to qualified new jobs to all of the taxpayer's Mich. payroll, and the denominator is 2; (2) for a business expanding at an existing site—numerator is ratio of the value of new property added to the site as part of that expansion to all of taxpayer's Mich. property plus ratio of taxpayer's payroll attributable to qualified new jobs to all of the taxpayer's payroll in Mich., and the denominator is 2; no credit allowed if initial certification is issued after 12-31-2009. For tax yrs. starting after 12-31-2003 and before 1-1-2007, a qualified distressed business can claim a credit equal to (1) up to 50% of Mich. unemployment tax paid in the tax year based on qualified new jobs; plus (2) up to 25% of Mich. unemployment tax paid in the tax year based on all jobs other than qualified new jobs. For tax yr. 2005, a credit is allowed for a percentage of compensation paid to employees who perform "created jobs" in manufacturing and high-technology. Credit limited to taxpayers with gross receipts of $10 million or less for tax yr. Eff 1-1-2008, Mich. Business Tax allows combined compensation/investment credit, Next Energy payroll credit, a credit for qualified new jobs or retained jobs under the Michigan Economic Growth Authority Act and, for the 2008, 2009, and 2010 tax yrs., an entrepreneurial credit. *(Mich.)*

(185) Eff for qualified jobs created through 6-30-2005, 6.25% of 1st $16,000 in wages paid for qualifying job in special rural areas. *(N.M.)*.

(186) 62.5% of payroll costs at facility in rural enterprise zone. *(Ore.)*.

(187) Credit against business profits tax for companies paying insurance company premium tax. *(N.H.)*

(188) These credits are allowed for production and sale of biodiesel and blended biodiesel: (1) $1 credit per gallon of biodiesel manufactured in Ind.; (2) two-cent credit per gallon of blended biodiesel produced in Ind. using biodiesel produced in Ind.; and (3) one-cent credit per gallon of blended biodisel sold by Ind. retailers. 12.5-cent credit is allowed per gallon of ethanol produced at qualified facilities. *(Ind.)*

(189) CROP zone credit, determined by adding compensation and interest and multiplying result by current tax rate (0.75%). Credit is only available to taxpayers that have agreement with Commissioner of Resources and Economic Development. *(N.H.)*

(190) Credits are available for qualified activity in areas designated as Keystone Opportunity Zones, Keystone Opportunity Expansion Zones, Keystone Opportunity Improvement Zones/Keystone Innovation Zone. *(Pa.)*

(191) For tax yrs. beginning on or after 1-1-2004, taxpayer that is a qualified PTDZ business is allowed credit in amount of: 100% of tax that would otherwise be due for each of first five tax yrs that taxpayer is required to file return after commencing qualified business activity; and 50% of tax that would otherwise be due for each of tax years beginning with sixth tax yr and ending with 10th tax yr that taxpayer is required to file return after commencing qualified business activity. *(Me.)*

(192) Other Neb. credits: research and development credit; credit for contributions to qualified endowments.

(193) 0.5% credit is allowed for cost of qualified investment in business facility for each 50 jobs created by a large taxpayer and each 5 jobs created by a small taxpayer (% keyed to expected depreciation life) times factor for new jobs created; spread this credit over 5-yr. period, taking 1/5 of it each yr.; max. credit is 10% for large businesses creating 1,000 jobs; for small businesses, credit for every 5 new jobs is 1% (max. is 20%) *(N.J.)*.

(194) Credit allowed for 25% of initial investment with certified fund manager for use in certified business *(Wis.)*.

INDIVIDUAL INCOME TAX CREDITS FOR INDIVIDUAL INCOME TAXES PAID TO OTHER STATES

¶236-A Credits for individual income taxes paid to other states. The chart below shows whether or not a taxing state provides credits to individual income taxpayers for individual income taxes paid to other states and the District of Columbia on income derived from the other jurisdiction which is also subject to the taxing state's tax. The first and second columns of the chart shows whether or not such credits are available to residents and nonresidents of the taxing state. The third column shows whether or not reciprocity is required for nonresidents; that is, whether or not the taxing state allows nonresidents to take a credit for income tax paid to their home state only if the home state allows residents of the taxing state to take a similar credit for income tax paid to the taxing state. The ''comments'' column provides further details or additional requirements.

A taxing state's credit for individual income tax paid to another state generally cannot exceed the ratio of the taxpayer's income derived from the other state to the taxpayer's income taxable in the taxing state or the taxpayer's total income.

The following states also allow credits for income taxes paid to another state's political subdivisions: Connecticut, District of Columbia, Illinois, Kansas, Maine, Missouri, Nebraska, New Jersey, New York.

State	Residents	Nonresidents	Reciprocity Required for Nonresidents?	Comments
Alabama	Yes	No	Not applicable	
Alaska	No individual income tax			
Arizona	Yes	No	Not applicable	No credit is allowed if the other state or country allows AZ residents a credit for AZ income taxes.
Arkansas	Yes	Yes	No	
California	Yes	Yes	No	No credit is allowed if the other state allows CA residents a credit for net income taxes paid to CA. Nonresidents of CA may claim a credit only for net income taxes imposed by and paid to their states of residence and only if such states do not allow their residents a credit for net income taxes paid to CA.
Colorado	Yes	No	Not applicable	
Connecticut	Yes	No	Not applicable	
Delaware	Yes	No	Not applicable	
District of Columbia	Yes	No	Not applicable	
Florida	No individual income tax			
Georgia	Yes	No	Not applicable	

State	Residents	Nonresidents	Reciprocity Required for Nonresidents?	Comments
Hawaii	Yes	No	Not applicable	Credit is allowed if other jurisdiction does not allow taxpayer a credit against the taxes imposed by that jurisdiction for HI income tax or does allow such credit in an amount which has been deducted in computing the amount of the HI credit.
Idaho	Yes	No	Not applicable	
Illinois	Yes	No	Not applicable	Under IL agreements with IA, KY, MI, and WI, wages, salaries, tips, or other employee compensation paid to IL residents working in those states is not subject to IL income tax. Thus, IL residents cannot claim a credit for IA, KY, MI or WI tax paid on such compensation earned in those states. IL residents subject to a tax by a locality in those states can claim a credit for that local tax.
Indiana	Yes	Yes	No	Credit is not allowed to residents for state income taxes paid in states allowing IN residents a nonresident credit. Credit is allowed to nonresidents if the other state allows a similar credit to IN residents.
Iowa	Yes	No	Not applicable	
Kansas	Yes	No	Not applicable	
Kentucky	Yes	No	Not applicable	Under KY agreements with IN, IL, MI, OH, VA, WV, and WI, wage or personal compensation paid to KY residents working in those states is not subject to KY income tax. Thus, KY residents cannot claim a credit for IN, IL, MI, OH, VA, WV, or WI tax paid on such compensation earned in those states.
Louisiana	Yes	No	Not applicable	
Maine	Yes	No	Yes (Residents)	

State	Residents	Nonresidents	Reciprocity Required for Nonresidents?	Comments
Maryland	Yes	No	Not applicable	The credit is not allowed to part-year residents on tax paid to another state during their residency in that state or to a resident (other than a fiduciary) if the laws of the other state allow the resident a credit for state income tax paid to MD. Under MD agreements with DC, PA, VA, and WV, wage or personal compensation paid to MD residents working in those states is not subject to MD income tax. Thus MD residents cannot claim a credit for DC, PA, VA or WV tax paid on compensation earned in those states.
Massachusetts	Yes	No	Not applicable	
Michigan	Yes	Yes (see comments)	(see comments)	Reciprocity is granted nonresidents if MI residents are exempt from paying tax on personal services performed in that state. Under MI agreements with IL, IN, KY, MN, OH and WI, wage or personal compensation paid to MI residents working in those states is not subject to MI tax. Thus, MI residents cannot claim a credit for IL, IN, KY, MN, OH or WI tax paid on such compensation earned in those states.
Minnesota	Yes	Yes (see comments)	(see comments)	Nonresidents are allowed a credit only for the tax paid to the state of the individual's domicile upon the gain on the sale of a partnership interest. Under MN agreements with MI, ND and WI, wage or personal compensation paid to MN residents working in those states is not subject to MN income tax. Thus MN residents cannot claim a credit for MI, ND or WI tax pad on such compensation earned in those states.
Mississippi	Yes	No	Not applicable	
Missouri	Yes	No	Not applicable	

State	Residents	Nonresidents	Reciprocity Required for Nonresidents?	Comments
Montana	Yes	Yes	No	Resident of MT who spends more than half the year in MT but whose domicile is elsewhere and who is taxed on income by the state of domicile, cannot claim the credit from MT unless the state of domicile does not allow a similar credit. Under MT agreement with ND, wage or personal compensation paid to MT residents working in that state is not subject to MT income tax. Thus, MT residents cannot claim a credit for ND tax paid on such compensation earned in ND.
Nebraska	Yes	No	Not applicable	
Nevada	No individual income tax			
New Hampshire	No	Not taxed	Not applicable	
New Jersey	Yes	No	Not applicable	Under a NJ agreement with PA, wage or personal compensation paid to NJ residents working in PA is not subject to PA income tax. Thus, NJ residents cannot claim a credit for PA tax paid on such compensation earned in PA. Note: The agreement does not apply to the wage or income tax imposed by Philadelphia or any other PA municipality. NJ residents can claim a credit for taxes paid to a PA municipality.
New Mexico	Yes	No	Not applicable	
New York	Yes	No	Not applicable	
North Carolina	Yes	No	Not applicable	
North Dakota	Yes	No	Not applicable	Under ND agreements with MN and MT, wage or personal compensation paid to MN or MT residents working in ND is not subject to ND income tax. Thus, ND residents cannot claim a credit for MN or MT tax paid on such compensation earned in ND.

State	Residents	Nonresidents	Reciprocity Required for Nonresidents?	Comments
Ohio	Yes	No	Not applicable	Under Ohio agreements with IN, KY, MI, PA, and WV, wage or personal compensation paid to Ohio residents working in those states is not subject to Ohio income tax. Thus, Ohio residents cannot claim a credit for IN, KY, MI, PA, or WV tax paid on such compensation earned in those states.
Oklahoma	Yes	No	Not applicable	Credit for other state taxes paid by OK residents is limited to taxes paid on compensation for personal services.
Oregon	Yes	Yes	Yes	OR credit is not allowed for taxes paid to a state that allows its residents a credit for income tax paid or payable to OR.
Pennsylvania	Yes	No	Not applicable	Under PA agreements with IN, MD, NJ, OH, VA, and WV, employee compensation paid to PA residents working in those states is not subject to the income taxes of those states. Thus, PA residents cannot claim a credit for those state taxes paid on such compensation earned in those states. However, because the reciprocal agreements do not apply to dual residents, persons who are residents of both PA and one of those states can claim credit for income tax imposed by the other state on employee income.
Rhode Island	Yes	No	Not applicable	
South Carolina	Yes	No	Not applicable	
South Dakota	No individual income tax			
Tennessee	No	Not taxed	Not applicable	
Texas	No individual income tax			
Utah	Yes	No	Not applicable	
Vermont	Yes	No	Not applicable	

State	Residents	Nonresidents	Reciprocity Required for Nonresidents?	Comments
Virginia	Yes	Yes	Yes	If income is from AZ, CA, DC, or OR, claim the credit on that state's income tax return, instead of on the VA return. Under VA agreements with DC, KY, MD PA, and WV, wage or personal compensation paid to VA residents working in those states is not subject to the income taxes of those states. Thus, VA residents cannot claim a credit for those state taxes paid on such compensation earned in those states.
Washington	No individual income tax			
West Virginia	Yes	Yes	Yes	WV credit for residents is not allowed for taxes paid to a state that allows a credit for income tax paid to WV. WV credit for nonresidents is only available to residents of states with which WV has a written agreement, namely, KY, MD, OH, PA, and VA.
Wisconsin	Yes	No	Not applicable	Under WI agreements with IL, IN, KY, MI, and MN, wage or personal compensation paid to WI residents working in those states is not subject to the income taxes of those states. Thus, WI residents cannot claim a credit for those state taxes paid on such compensation earned in those states.
Wyoming	No individual income tax			

TAXATION OF GOVERNMENT OBLIGATIONS

¶237 Taxation of interest from government obligations. The following chart explains the state corporation income and personal income tax treatment of interest from obligations issued by the federal government and the states and their political subdivisions.

Interest from federal obligations. Congress has specifically provided that direct or indirect taxes may not reach federal obligations or interest from them (31 U.S.C. §3124). But this prohibition does not apply to nondiscriminatory franchise taxes and other non-property taxes imposed on corporations instead of franchise taxes. The exemption from state taxation of interest from federal obligations is generally limited to direct obligations of the U.S., such as Treasury bills, bonds, certificates, and Notes, and U.S. Savings Bonds. However, securities issued by the Federal National Mortgage Association (FNMA - Fannie Mae), the Government National Mortgage Association (GNMA - Ginnie Mae), the International Bank for Reconstruction and Redevelopment (World Bank) are not considered to be U.S. obligations because they are neither direct nor certain obligations of the U.S. Accordingly, interest from such securities is taxed by the states. Many states provide detailed examples of taxable and exempt federal securities.

States generally extend this federal exemption to securities issued by U.S. possessions and territories. However, the following states specifically tax such securities: Arizona, Florida, and Oregon. The federal exemption does not apply to securities of the District of Columbia.

In Wisconsin, unless expressly exempted by Wisconsin law, interest on federal obligations is fully taxable and must be added back to federal taxable income for corporate franchise or income tax purposes; however, if the corporation is subject to the income tax, rather than the franchise tax, no addback is required if such interest income is also exempt from income tax under Wisconsin law.

Interest from state obligations. Generally, obligations issued by the taxing state, as well as the political subdivisions of that state, are exempt from the taxing state's income tax. Many states also exempt obligations issued by state or municipal authorities, special districts, etc., of that state. These exemptions are, as a general rule, specifically authorized by statute. However, a number of state corporate taxes do include interest from their own state and local securities in their tax base: Connecticut, Florida, Massachusetts, Minnesota, Montana, New Hampshire (business enterprise tax), New York, Oregon, South Dakota (franchise tax on banking corporations), Tennessee, and Utah.

In Illinois, Iowa, and Oklahoma, interest from state and local obligations, which is tax-exempt for federal income tax purposes, is not exempt from tax unless legislation has been specifically adopted to allow an exemption.

There is no federal constitutional bar preventing a state from taxing the obligations of another state or the instrumentalities or political subdivisions of another state.

STATE	FEDERAL OBLIGATIONS		STATE OBLIGATIONS			
			ISSUED BY TAXING STATE		ISSUED BY OTHER STATES	
	Corporate	Individual	Corporate	Individual	Corporate	Individual
Alabama	Exempt	Exempt	Exempt	Exempt	Taxable	Taxable
Alaska	Exempt	No Tax	Exempt	No Tax	Exempt	No Tax
Arizona	Exempt	Exempt	Exempt	Exempt	Taxable	Taxable
Arkansas	Exempt	Exempt	Exempt	Exempt	Taxable	Taxable
California	Exempt (1)	Exempt	Exempt (1)	Exempt	Taxable	Taxable
Colorado	Exempt	Exempt	Exempt	Exempt	Taxable	Taxable
Connecticut	Taxable	Exempt	Taxable	Exempt	Taxable	Taxable
Delaware	Exempt	Exempt	Exempt	Exempt	Taxable	Taxable
District of Columbia	Exempt	Exempt	Exempt	Exempt	Taxable	Exempt
Florida	Taxable	No Tax	Taxable	No Tax	Taxable	No Tax
Georgia	Exempt	Exempt	Exempt	Exempt	Taxable	Taxable
Hawaii	Exempt	Exempt	Exempt	Exempt	Taxable	Taxable
Idaho	Exempt	Exempt	Exempt	Exempt	Taxable	Taxable
Illinois	Exempt	Exempt	Exempt	Exempt	Taxable	Taxable
Indiana	Exempt	Exempt	Exempt	Exempt	Exempt	Exempt
Iowa	Exempt	Exempt	Exempt	Exempt	Taxable	Taxable
Kansas	Exempt	Exempt	Exempt	Exempt	Taxable	Taxable
Kentucky	Exempt	Exempt	Exempt	Exempt	(15)	(15)
Louisiana	Exempt	Exempt	Exempt	Exempt	Taxable	Taxable
Maine	Exempt	Exempt	Exempt	Exempt	Taxable	Taxable
Maryland	Exempt	Exempt	Exempt	Exempt	Taxable	Taxable
Massachusetts	Taxable	Exempt	Taxable	Exempt	Taxable	Taxable
Michigan	Exempt (2)	Exempt	Exempt (2)	Exempt	Taxable	Taxable
Minnesota	Taxable	Exempt	Taxable	Exempt	Taxable	Taxable
Mississippi	Exempt	Exempt	Exempt	Exempt	Taxable	Taxable
Missouri	Exempt	Exempt	Exempt	Exempt	Taxable	Taxable
Montana	Exempt(13)	Exempt	Taxable	Exempt	Taxable	Taxable
Nebraska	Exempt	Exempt	Exempt	Exempt	Taxable	Taxable
Nevada	No Tax	No Tax	No Tax	No Tax	No Tax	No Tax
New Hampshire	Exempt (3)	Exempt	Exempt (3)	Exempt	Exempt (3)	Taxable
New Jersey	Taxable	Exempt	Taxable	Exempt	Taxable	Taxable (4)
New Mexico	Exempt	Exempt	Exempt	Exempt	Taxable	Taxable
New York	Taxable	Exempt (12)	Taxable	Exempt	Taxable	Taxable (5)
North Carolina	Exempt	Exempt	Exempt	Exempt	Taxable	Taxable
North Dakota	Exempt	Exempt	Exempt	Exempt	Taxable	Taxable
Ohio	Exempt (6)	Exempt (14)	Exempt (6)	Exempt	Exempt	Taxable
Oklahoma	Exempt	Exempt	Exempt	Exempt	Taxable	Taxable
Oregon	Taxable	Exempt	Taxable	Exempt	Taxable	Taxable
Pennsylvania	Exempt	Exempt	Exempt	Exempt	Taxable	Taxable
Rhode Island	Exempt	Exempt	Exempt	Exempt	Taxable	Taxable
South Carolina	Exempt	Exempt	Exempt	Exempt	Taxable	Taxable
South Dakota	No Tax (10)	No Tax	No Tax (10)	No Tax	No Tax (10)	No Tax
Tennessee	Exempt	Exempt	Taxable	Exempt	Taxable	Taxable
Texas	Exempt	No Tax	Exempt	No Tax	Exempt	No Tax
Utah	Taxable (7)	Exempt	Taxable (7)	Taxable (11)	Taxable	Taxable
Vermont	Exempt	Exempt	Exempt	Exempt	Taxable	Taxable
Virginia	Exempt	Exempt	Exempt	Exempt	Taxable (5)	Taxable (5)
Washington	No Tax	No Tax	No Tax	No Tax	No Tax	No Tax
West Virginia	Exempt (8)	Exempt	Exempt (8)	Exempt	Taxable	Taxable (5)
Wisconsin	Exempt (9)	Exempt	Exempt (9)	Exempt	Taxable	Taxable
Wyoming	No Tax	No Tax	No Tax	No Tax	No Tax	No Tax

FOOTNOTES to chart ¶ 237 (corresponding to parenthetical numbers in chart):

(1) *Calif.* —Interest on federal obligations and bonds issued by California or its political subdivisions are exempt from the corporation income tax. Interest received from federal, state, municipal or other bonds is includible in the gross income of taxpayers for purposes of the state franchise tax.

(2) *Mich.* —For Single Business Tax purposes, financial organizations must make the following adjustments for interest income: (1) deduct interest income (to extent included in federal taxable income) derived from U.S. obligations which Mich. cannot tax under federal law, other than nondiscriminatory franchise or nonproperty taxes; and (2) add interest expenses, computed by multiplying total expenses deducted in arriving at federal taxable income and not included in the Mich. SBT tax base by the following fraction: The sum of interest from U.S. obligations that Mich. cannot tax plus interest from Mich. obligations, divided by total interest income. The result cannot exceed interest from U.S. obligations subtracted in arriving from the tax base.

(3) *N.H.* —Chart refers to business profits tax. Under the business enterprise tax, all interest income from U.S. and state and local obligations (including those of N.H.) is taxable.

(4) *N.J.* —Interest from obligations of public corporations created or existing pursuant to an agreement or compact with another state are exempt.

(5) *N.Y., Va., and W. Va.* —Interest income on obligations of another state or of a political subdivision of a state is exempt if created by a compact or agreement to which N.Y., Va., or W. Va. is a party.

(6) *Ohio*—The value of federal, state and local obligations (including those of Ohio) are included when computing the value of issued and outstanding stock on the net worth basis.

(7) *Utah*—Utah allows a nonrefundable tax credit equal to 1% of the gross interest income included in state taxable income from (1) debt instruments issued by the state, its agencies, instrumentalities, or a political subdivision of the state; or (2) stocks, notes or obligations issued or guaranteed by the U.S. government or its agencies or instrumentalities. See also ¶236.

(8) *W.V.* —Taxpayers that own certain tax exempt government obligations and obligations secured by certain residential property located in W.V. can take a special allowance that further reduces federal taxable income.

(9) *Wis.* —Interest on federal obligations is not exempt from the Wis. franchise tax; it is, however, exempt from the corporate income tax.

(10) *S.D.* —South Dakota does not impose a general corporate income or franchise tax. However, for purposes of S.D.'s franchise tax on banks and financial institutions, interest or dividend income from obligations or securities of the U.S., states (including S.D.), or political subdivisions or their authorities that was excluded from federal taxable income must be added back when computing the tax base.

(11) *Utah*—Exemptions are allowed for certain Utah state bonds.

(12) *N.Y.* —Interest from obligations or securities of the U.S. or its instrumentalities should be subtracted from federal AGI when computing N.Y. AGI, to the extent fed. law exempts the interest from state, but not federal, income tax. Certain amts received as dividends from a reg. investment company and derived from obligations of the U.S. should also be subtracted. However, interest from obligations or securities of the U.S. and its instrumentalities must be added back to the extent federal law exempts the interest from federal, but not state, tax.

(13) *Mont.* —Interest on U.S. obligations is taxable under the corporate license tax, but not the corporate income tax.

(14) *Ohio*—Exceptions apply.

(15) *Ky.* —The Ky. Court of Appeals ruled in Davis v. Department of Revenue (Dkt. No. 2004-CA-001940-MR, 1-6-2006; review denied, Ky. Supreme Court, Dkt. No. 2006-SC-105-D, 8-17-2006) that the taxation of income derived from bonds issued outside the state violated the Commerce Clause.

CORPORATION INCOME TAX RETURN FILING EXTENSIONS

¶238 Corporation income tax return filing extensions. Corporate taxpayers who know they cannot file their state income tax returns by the due date (¶ 222) should file for extensions. All of the states offer some type of return filing extension. Many states accept extensions of time to file federal returns as extensions to file their own state returns if specified requirements are met and some even allow more time to file. Extensions to file returns do not extend the time to pay the tax and payment requirements must be met to avoid late payment penalties.

Corporate taxpayers can obtain an automatic 6-month extension to file their federal income tax returns if they file a federal return extension application form and pay the balance of federal tax due by the regular due date.

The following chart shows the general state corporate income tax return extension provisions and indicates whether or not a state accepts or recognizes a federal return filing extension as an extension for filing the final state return.

Separate provisions may apply to certain types of corporations or to special situations, such as natural disasters or terrorist attacks, not covered by this chart.

State	State return filing extension period allowed and application or request requirements	Is a federal return filing extension accepted or recognized as a state extension in lieu of filing a state extension application or request form?
Alabama	6 months, automatic, if state extension request form is filed by regular return due date and tax due paid.	Yes, automatic, for 6 months. Copy of federal extension must be filed with final state return. Only corporations with no tax due or no additional tax due should use automatic extension provided by federal Form 7004.
Alaska	State extension is tied to federal extension.	State does not have its own extension application or request form. Automatic extension is granted to 30 days after federal extended due date. Copy of federal extension must be filed with final state return.
Arizona	6 months, automatic, if state extension application form is filed and at least 90% of tax is paid by regular return due date.	Yes, automatic, for federal extension period, if at least 90% of tax has been paid.
Arkansas	Up to 120 days allowed, if state extension request form is filed by regular due date and good reason is shown. Additional 60 days allowed in extraordinary circumstances.	Yes, automatic, for federal extension period.
California	7 months, automatic and paperless.	No.
Colorado	6 months, automatic and paperless, if 90% of net income tax paid by original due date.	No.

State	State return filing extension period allowed and application or request requirements	Is a federal return filing extension accepted or recognized as a state extension in lieu of filing a state extension application or request form?
Connecticut	6 months, if state extension application form is filed and tax is paid by regular due date and either a federal extension is requested or good cause is shown.	No.
Delaware	6 months, automatic, if state extension request form is filed and tax is paid by regular due date. Additional time is available on written request.	Yes, automatic, for 6 months. Copy of federal extension must be filed with final state return.
District of Columbia	6 months, automatic, if state extension request form is filed and tax is paid by regular due date.	No.
Florida	6 months, if state extension request form is filed and tax is paid by regular due date and either a federal extension is requested or good reason is shown, or 15 days after a federal extension ends (if earlier).	No.
Georgia	6 months, if state extension application form is filed by regular due date and good reason is shown.	Yes, automatic, for up to 6 months. Copy of federal extension must be filed with final state return.
Hawaii	6 months, automatic, if state extension application form is filed and at least 90% of tax is paid by regular due date.	No.
Idaho	6 months, automatic, if at least 80% of current year tax or 100% of past year tax is paid by regular due date.	No.
Illinois	7 months, automatic. Additional 1-month period is allowed beyond federal extension period longer than 6 months.	Yes. State form only for extension longer than 7 months. Copy of such federal extension must be filed with final state return.
Indiana	Federal 6-month extension recognized, plus an additional 30 days; if federal extension not requested or extension is needed in excess of 30 days past the federal extension date, special extension of time to file must be requested before original due date or before current extension of time expires; pay 90% of tax due by original due date.	Yes, automatic, for federal extension period plus an additional 30 days. Copy of federal extension must be filed with final state return.
Iowa	6 months, automatic, if at least 90% of tax is paid by regular due date.	No. No state form required.

State	State return filing extension period allowed and application or request requirements	Is a federal return filing extension accepted or recognized as a state extension in lieu of filing a state extension application or request form?
Kansas	6 months, if at least 90% of current year tax or 100% of prior year tax liability is paid.	Yes, automatic, for federal extension period plus additional month. Copy of federal extension must be filed with final state return.
Kentucky	6 months, automatic, if state extension application form is filed by regular due date.	Yes, automatic, for federal extension period, if copy of federal extension is filed with final state return.
Louisiana	Up to 7 months, automatic, if state extension application form is filed and tax is paid by regular due date.	Yes, automatic, for federal extension period. Copy of federal extension must be filed with final state return.
Maine	7 months, automatic, if state extension application form is filed before regular due date.	Yes, automatic, for federal extension period plus additional 30 days. Copy of federal extension must be filed with final state return.
Maryland	7 months, automatic, if state extension application form is filed and tax is paid by regular due date and good reason is shown.	No.
Massachusetts	6 months, automatic, if state extension application form is filed and at least 50% of tax is paid by regular due date and reason is shown. Additional time is allowed for good cause.	No. A separate request must be filed.
Michigan	180 days, if state extension application form is filed and tax is paid by regular due date. Federal extension period plus 60 days is allowed, if state extension application form and copy of federal extension are filed by regular due date.	No.
Minnesota	7 months, automatic and paperless. 90% of tax must be paid.	No.
Mississippi	6 months, automatic, if state extension application is filed and tax is paid by regular due date.	Tax Commission may recognize a federal return filing extension if no state tax liability exists on the due date of the state return.
Missouri	6 months, if state extension application form is filed and tax is paid by regular due date and either federal extension is attached or good reason is shown. Additional time up to 6 months is allowed if sufficient need is shown.	Yes, automatic, for federal extension period, if state tax has been paid. Copy of federal extension must be filed with final state return.

State	State return filing extension period allowed and application or request requirements	Is a federal return filing extension accepted or recognized as a state extension in lieu of filing a state extension application or request form?
Montana	6 months, automatic and paperless.	No.
Nebraska	7 months, automatic, if state extension application form is filed before regular due date.	Yes, automatic, for federal extension period. Copy of federal extension must be filed with final state return.
Nevada	State has no corporation income tax.	
New Hampshire	7 months, automatic and paperless, if state tax has been paid. If state tax has not been paid, 7 months, automatic, if state extension application form is filed and state tax is paid by regular due date.	No.
New Jersey	6 months, automatic, if state extension application form is filed and tax is paid by regular due date.	No.
New Mexico	Up to 60 days, if state extension application form is filed by regular due date and filing delay is shown to be based on circumstances beyond taxpayer's control. Additional time up to 1 year is allowed if sufficient need is shown.	Yes, automatic, for federal extension period. Copy of federal extension must be filed with final state return.
New York	6 months, automatic, if state extension request form is filed and at least 90% of current year tax or 100% of past year tax is paid by regular due date. Up to two additional 3-month extensions are allowed if good cause is shown.	No.
North Carolina	7 months, automatic, if state extension application form is filed and tax is paid by regular due date.	No.
North Dakota	Reasonable extension period is allowed at Tax Commissioner's discretion, if state extension application form is filed by regular due date and filing delay is shown to be based on circumstances beyond taxpayer's control.	Yes, automatic, for federal extension period, if copy of federal extension is filed with final state return.

State	State return filing extension period allowed and application or request requirements	Is a federal return filing extension accepted or recognized as a state extension in lieu of filing a state extension application or request form?
Ohio	Extension is allowed to May 31, if state extension request is filed and the second ⅓ of the estimated tax is paid by March 31. Additional extension may be allowed to the 15th day of the month after the month to which a federal extension has been granted, if state extension request form is filed and tax is paid by May 31 and copy of federal extension is filed with final state return.	No.
Oklahoma	Up to 7 months allowed for good cause if state extension application form is filed and at least 90% of tax is paid by regular due date. State corporate return extension can exceed federal extension by one month.	Yes, automatic, for federal extension period, if state tax has been paid. Copy of federal extension must be filed with final state return.
Oregon	Up to 6 months allowed, if federal extension form is filed as state extension by writing "For Oregon only" across the top and state tax is paid by regular due date.	Yes, automatic, for federal extension period, if state tax has been paid. Copy of federal extension must be filed with final state return.
Pennsylvania	Up to 60 days, or federal extension period plus additional 30 days, for good cause shown.	No.
Rhode Island	6 months, automatic, if state extension request form is filed and tax is paid by regular due date.	No.
South Carolina	6 months automatic.	Yes, automatic for federal extension period if state tax has been paid. Copy of federal extension must be filed with final state return.
South Dakota	State has no corporation income tax.	
Tennessee	6 months, if state extension application form is filed and at least 90% of tax is paid by regular due date.	Yes, automatic for federal extension period, if state tax has been paid. Copy of federal extension must be filed with state return by extended due date.
Texas	State has no corporation income tax.	
	Texas franchise tax extension of 6 months is allowed, if state extension request form is filed and at least 90% of current year tax or 100% of past year tax is paid by regular due date.	No.

State	State return filing extension period allowed and application or request requirements	Is a federal return filing extension accepted or recognized as a state extension in lieu of filing a state extension application or request form?
Utah	6 months, automatic, if at least 90% of current year tax or 100% of minimum tax due, whichever is greater, or 100% of past year tax is paid by regular due date.	No.
Vermont	Extension is allowed for period at Tax Commissioner's discretion, if state extension application form is filed and tax is paid by regular due date and good reason is shown. Automatic extension for federal extension period plus additional 30 days is allowed, if copy of federal extension is filed with state and state tax is paid by regular due date.	Yes, automatic, for federal extension period plus additional 30 days, if state tax has been paid. Copy of federal extension must be filed with final state return.
Virginia	6 months, or federal extension period plus additional 30 days, if the estimated tax due is paid.	No. State form required.
Washington	State has no corporation income tax.	
West Virginia	Extension can be obtained for reasonable period, if written request is filed with the state before regular due date.	Yes, automatic, for federal extension period. Copy of federal extension must be filed with final state return.
Wisconsin	30 days, if state extension application form is filed by regular due date.	Yes, automatic, for federal extension period plus additional 30 days. Copy of federal extension must be filed with final state return.
Wyoming	State has no corporation income tax.	

INDIVIDUAL INCOME TAX RETURN FILING EXTENSIONS

¶239 **Individual income tax return filing extensions.** Individual taxpayers who know they cannot file their state income tax returns by the due date (¶ 228) should file for extensions. All of the states offer some type of return filing extension. Most states accept extensions of time to file federal returns as extensions to file their own state returns if specified requirements are met and some even allow more time to file. Extensions to file returns do not extend the time to pay tax and payment requirements generally must be met to avoid late payment penalties.

Individual income taxpayers can obtain an automatic 6-month extension of time to file their federal income tax returns if they file a federal return extension application form by the regular due date. Certain taxpayers may be able to use a credit card to get a return filing extension without filing the application form. Extra time may be available for persons who are abroad.

The following chart shows the general state individual income tax return extension provisions and indicates whether or not a state accepts or recognizes a federal return filing extension as an extension for filing the final state return.

Extra time to file federal or state returns, in addition to the provisions covered by this chart, may be available for certain military personnel, persons affected by natural disasters or terrorist attacks, or other specified taxpayers.

State	**State return filing extension period allowed and application or request requirements**	**Is a federal return filing extension accepted or recognized as a state extension in lieu of filing a state extension application or request form?**
Alabama	6 months, if state request form is filed.	No.
Alaska	State has no personal income tax.	
Arizona	4 months, automatic, if state extension application form is filed and at least 90% of tax is paid by regular return due date. Additional 2 months are allowed for good cause.	Yes, automatic, for federal extension period, if at least 90% of tax has been paid.
Arkansas	For tax yrs. starting on and after 1-1-2008, 180 days with no additional extensions.	Yes, automatic, for federal extension period. If the additional federal extension is granted, copy of federal extension not required; tax preparers must check box on state form. request must be filed with final state return.
California	6 months, automatic and paperless. Additional 2 months are allowed if taxpayer is abroad.	No.
Colorado	6 months, automatic and paperless, if at least 90% of net tax is paid by original due date.	No.

State	State return filing extension period allowed and application or request requirements	Is a federal return filing extension accepted or recognized as a state extension in lieu of filing a state extension application or request form?
Connecticut	6 months, automatic, if tax is paid by regular due date and a federal extension is requested. Additional time is allowed if taxpayer is abroad.	No.
Delaware	5 1/2 months, automatic, if state extension request form is filed and tax is paid by regular due date. Additional time is allowed, for federal extension period, if copy of federal extension application is filed with the state by original state extended due date.	No, on-line or paper request is required along with copy of approved federal extension.
District of Columbia	6 months, if state extension request form is filed and tax is paid by regular due date. Automatic extension if total payments exceed estimated liability; extension request form need not be filed. Up to 12 months are allowed if taxpayer is abroad.	No.
Florida	State has no personal income tax.	
Georgia	6 months, if state extension application form is filed by regular due date and good reason is shown.	Yes, automatic, for up to 6 months. Copy of federal extension must be filed with final state return.
Hawaii	4 months, automatic. Additional 2 months are allowed for good cause. Additional time is allowed if taxpayer is abroad and good cause is shown.	No.
Idaho	6 months, automatic, if at least 80% of current year tax or 100% of past year tax is paid by regular due date.	No.
Illinois	6 months, automatic. Additional period is allowed for length of federal extension period longer than 6 months.	Yes. State form only for extension longer than 6 months. Extension is allowed for duration of federal extension period longer than 6 months. Copy of such federal extension must be filed with final state return.
Indiana	60 days, automatic, if at least 90% of tax is paid by regular due date.	Yes, automatic, for federal extension period plus additional 30 days, if at least 90% of state tax is paid by regular due date. Copy of federal extension must be filed with final state return.
Iowa	6 months, automatic, if at least 90% of tax is paid by regular due date.	No. No state form required.

State	State return filing extension period allowed and application or request requirements	Is a federal return filing extension accepted or recognized as a state extension in lieu of filing a state extension application or request form?
Kansas	6 months, if at least 90% of current year tax or 100% of prior year tax liability is paid.	Yes, automatic, for federal extension period. Copy of federal extension must be filed with final state return.
Kentucky	6 months, if state extension application form is filed by regular due date and good reason is shown. Up to 12 months are allowed if taxpayer is abroad.	Yes, automatic, for federal extension period, if copy of federal extension is filed with final state return.
Louisiana	Up to 6 months allowed, if state extension application form is filed and tax is paid by regular due date.	Yes, automatic, for federal extension period. Copy of federal extension must be filed with final state return.
Maine	6 months, automatic. Requests for additional time to file must be submitted in writing before expiration of the 6-month period.	Yes, automatic, for federal extension period. Copy of federal extension must be filed with final state return.
Maryland	6 months, automatic, if state extension application is filed and tax is paid by regular due date. Up to 12 months are allowed if taxpayer is abroad.	Yes, automatic, for federal extension period, if state tax has been paid.
Massachusetts	6 months, automatic, if state extension application form is filed and at least 80% of tax is paid by regular due date.	No. A separate request must be filed.
Michigan	6 months, automatic if state extension is filed and tax is paid by regular due date.	Yes, automatic, for federal extension period, if state tax has been paid. Copy of federal extension must be filed with final state return.
Minnesota	No penalty is imposed for late filing if return is filed by Oct. 15. No form is required.	No.
Mississippi	4 months, automatic, if state extension request is filed and tax is paid by regular due date.	Yes, automatic, for federal extension period, if state tax has been paid.
Missouri	6 months, automatic and paperless, if state tax has been paid. If state tax has not been paid, 6-month extension is allowed if state extension application is filed with payment by regular due date and either federal extension is attached or good cause is shown.	Yes, automatic, for federal extension period. Copy of federal extension must be filed with final state return.

State	State return filing extension period allowed and application or request requirements	Is a federal return filing extension accepted or recognized as a state extension in lieu of filing a state extension application or request form?
Montana	6 months, automatic, if federal extension is granted.	Yes, automatic, for federal extension period, if 100% of current year state tax or at least 90% of past year state tax has been paid. Copy of federal extension must be filed with final state return.
Nebraska	7 months, automatic, if state extension application form is filed before regular due date. Additional time is allowed if taxpayer is abroad.	Yes, automatic, for federal extension period. Copy of federal extension must be filed with final state return.
Nevada	State has no personal income tax.	
New Hampshire	7 months, automatic and paperless, if state tax has been paid. If state tax has not been paid, 7 months, automatic, if state extension application form is filed and state tax is paid by regular due date.	No.
New Jersey	6 months, automatic, if state extension application form is filed and at least 80% of tax is paid by regular due date. Additional time is allowed in exceptional circumstances.	Yes, automatic, for federal extension period, if at least 80% of state tax has been paid. Copy of federal extension must be filed with final state return.
New Mexico	Up to 60 days, if state extension application form is filed by regular due date and filing delay is shown to be based on circumstances beyond taxpayer's control. Additional time up to 1 year is allowed if sufficient need is shown.	Yes, automatic, for federal extension period. Copy of approved federal extension need not be filed with final state return.
New York	6 months, automatic, if state extension application form is filed and state tax is paid by regular due date.	Yes, automatic, for federal extension period, if no state tax is due. Copy of federal extension must be filed with state by regular return due date.
North Carolina	6 months, automatic, if state extension application form is filed by regular due date.	No.
North Dakota	Reasonable extension period is allowed at Tax Commissioner's discretion, if state extension application form is filed by regular due date and filing delay is shown to be based on circumstances beyond taxpayer's control.	Yes, automatic, for federal extension period, if copy of federal extension is filed with final state return.

State	State return filing extension period allowed and application or request requirements	Is a federal return filing extension accepted or recognized as a state extension in lieu of filing a state extension application or request form?
Ohio	6 months, automatic, if federal automatic 6-month extension has been obtained and at least 90% of state tax has been paid by regular due date. Additional time is allowed if obtained federally.	Ohio does not have its own individual income tax extension form. State extension is allowed, automatically, for federal extension period, if at least 90% of state tax is paid by regular due date. Copy of federal extension must be filed with final state return.
Oklahoma	Reasonable extension for filing a return may be granted by Tax Commissioner for good cause pursuant to a written request.	Yes, automatic, for federal extension period, if state tax has been paid. Copy of federal extension must be filed with final state return.
Oregon	Up to 6 months allowed, if federal extension form is filed as state extension by writing "For Oregon only" across the top and state tax is paid by regular due date.	Yes, automatic, for federal extension period, if state tax has been paid. Copy of federal extension need not be filed with state return.
Pennsylvania	Up to 6 months allowed, if state extension application form is filed. Additional time is allowed if taxpayer is abroad.	Yes, automatic, for federal extension period, if state tax has been paid. Copy of federal extension must be filed with final state return.
Rhode Island	6 months, automatic, if state extension request form is filed and tax is paid by regular due date.	Yes, automatic, for federal extension period, if state tax has been paid. Copy of federal extension must be filed with final state return.
South Carolina	6 months, if state extension request form is filed and tax is paid by regular due date and valid reason is shown.	Yes, automatic, for federal extension period, if state tax has been paid. Copy of federal extension must be filed with final state return.
South Dakota	State has no personal income tax.	
Tennessee	6 months, if request for state extension is made in writing by taxpayer and attached to the return filed on or before the extended due date.	Yes, automatic, for federal extension period, if copy of federal extension is filed with the state by extended state return due date.
Texas	State has no personal income tax.	
Utah	6 months, automatic. Tax must be paid by original due date.	No.
Vermont	6 months, automatic, if state extension application form is filed, federal extension form is provided, or letter requesting extension is submitted. Tax must be paid by regular due date.	Yes, automatic, for federal extension period, if copy of federal extension is filed with state before regular state return due date.
Virginia	6 months after the due date.	No. State form required.

State	State return filing extension period allowed and application or request requirements	Is a federal return filing extension accepted or recognized as a state extension in lieu of filing a state extension application or request form?
Washington	State has no personal income tax.	
West Virginia	Up to 6 months, or federal extension period, if state extension application form is filed and tax is paid by regular due date.	Yes, automatic, for federal extension period, if state tax has been paid.
Wisconsin	State extension is based on available federal extension period selected, by filing federal extension form or written statement indicating federal provision chosen with final state return.	Yes, automatic, for federal extension period. Copy of federal extension must be filed with final state return.
Wyoming	State has no personal income tax.	

CAPITAL VALUES TAXES

¶240 What you pay and when. The chart below covers recurrent annual taxes on capital values. It shows the alternate taxes if a choice of bases is required or permitted. If a different fee or base is prescribed for domestic and foreign corporations, these are shown by a ''D'' signifying the rate applies to domestic corporations only, and an ''F'' signifying the rate applies to foreign corporations only. Absence of ''D'' or ''F'' means the statement applies to both. Further explanations of some entries are in the notes following this chart.

➳ **ALLOCATION RULES→** For capital values taxes are at ¶ 241.

➳ **WARNING→** Payment by electronic funds transfer may be required. See ¶ 279.

STATES, BASES AND RATE OF TAX (6)	REPORT DEADLINE (1)	PAYMENT DEADLINE (1)
ALA. $1 per $1,000 of Ala. net worth if taxable income under $200,000; $1.25 per $1,000 if $200,000–$499,999; $1.50 per $1,000 if $500,000–$2,499,999; $1.75 per $1,000 if taxable income at least $2.5 million. Min. tax, $100. Max. tax, $15,000. (8)	3-15 Dept. Rev. (9)	3-15 Dept. Rev. (9)
ALASKA No capital values tax.		
ARIZ. No capital values tax.		
ARK. 0.3% of outstanding capital stock employed in state. Min tax, $150. No par stock, pay $300. (10)	5-1 Sec'y State (2)	5-1 Sec'y State (2)
CALIF. No capital values tax.		
COLO. No capital values tax.		
CONN. Corporate excess (capital stock) tax. $250 min.; $1 million max.	4-1 Dept. Rev.	4-1 Dept. Rev.
DEL. D—Authorized shares to 3000, $35 tax; 3001–5000, $62.50; 5001–10,000, $112.50; $62.50 per added $10,000 (4). Alternative tax—$250 per $1 million assumed "par value capital" (4). Min. $35; max. $165,000. Filing fee $25. F—No capital values tax. For annual report, see ¶ 211-A.	D—3-1 Sec'y State	D—3-1 Sec'y State. If expected tax over $5M, tentative return due. Pay quarterly by 6-1, 9-1, 12-1 and 3-1
D.C. (See chart at ¶ 211-A)		
FLA. No capital values tax.		
GA. Net worth (apportioned for F). To $10,000, $10; $10,000–$25,000, $20; $25,000–40,000, $40; $40,000–$60,000, $60; $60,000–80,000, $75; $80,000–$100,000, $100; $100,000–150,000, $125; $150,000–$200,000, $150; $200,000–300,000, $200; $300,000–500,000, $250; $500,000–750,000, $300; $750,000–1,000,000, $500; Fees cont'd (net worth in millions): $1–2, $750; $2–4, $1,000; $4–6, $1,250;$6–8, $1,500; $8–10, $1,750; $10–12, $2,000; $2500; $14–16, $3000; $16–18, $3500; $18–20, $4000; $20–22, $4500; over $22,000,000, $5000.	3–15 (15th of 3rd mo.) Commr. Rev.	3–15 (15th of 3rd mo.) Commr. Rev.
HAW. No capital values tax.		
IDA. No capital values tax.		
ILL. 0.1% (0.15%, 1st time or added paid-in capital) allocated paid-in capital. Min. $25; max. $2 million plus 0.05% 1st time capital. Filing fee $75.	Sec'y State 60 days before anniversary month of incorp. or issuance of authority, or extended filing month (if so elected)	To Sec'y State. Tax due with report
IND. No capital values tax.		
IOWA No capital values tax.		
KAN. Shareholder's equity: 0.125% if taxable equity attributable to Kan. is $1 million or more (6). Max. tax, $20,000. Annual franchise fee, $55.	15th of 4th mo. Sec'y State	15th of 4th mo. Sec'y State

STATES, BASES AND RATE OF TAX (6)	REPORT DEADLINE (1)	PAYMENT DEADLINE (1)
KY. Investment cos., $2.10 per $1,000 of average net capital. Bank franchise tax, 1.1% of net capital; min $300; capital stock tax on savings & loan associations, $1 per $1,000 paid in capital stock (13)	15th of 4th mo. Dept. Rev.	15th of 4th mo. Dept. Rev.
LA. $1.50 per $1000 on 1st $300,000 of taxable corporation's taxable capital (issued and outstanding capital stock, surplus and undivided profits, and borrowed capital); $3 per $1000 on amounts over $300,000. Min. tax, $10. (12)	15th of 4th mo. Sec'y Rev.	15th of 4th mo. Sec'y Rev.
ME. No capital values tax.		
MD. No capital values tax.		
MASS. (See chart at ¶ 222)		
MICH. No capital values tax. (11)		
MINN. No capital values tax.		
MISS. $2.50 per $1000 assessed value in state realty, tangibles. Capital used, invested, or employed in-state, if larger. Min. $25.	15th of 3rd mo. Tax Comm.	15th of 3rd mo. Tax Comm.
MO. 1/30 of 1% of the value of the outstanding shares and surplus, if they exceed $1 million.	15th of 4th mo. of tax year Dir. Rev. (8).	15th of 4th mo. of tax year Dir. Rev.
MONT. No capital values tax.		
NEB. D—Paid up capital stock: To $10,000; $26; $20,000, $40; $30,000, $60; $40,000, $80; $50,000, $100; $60,000, $120; $70,000, $140; $80,000, $160; $90,000, $180; $100,000, $200; $125,000, $240; $150,000, $280; $175,000, $320; $200,000, $360; $225,000, $400; $250,000, $440; $275,000, $480; $300,000, $520; $325,000, $560; $350,000, $600; $400,000, $666; $450,000, $730; $500,000, $800; $600,000, $910; $700,000, $1,010; $800,000, $1,120; $900,000, $1,230; $1 million, $1,330; $10 million, $1,330 plus $800 per added $1 million over $1 million; $15 million, $12,000; $20 million, $14,660; $25 million, $17,330; $50 million, $20,660; $100 million, $21,330; over $100 million, $23,990. Min. tax $26. F--Property and credits in in-state business; pay double fees for domestic (max. tax $30,000).	4–15 Sec'y State	4–15 Sec'y State
NEV. No capital values tax.		
N.H. None, other than annual report fee, ¶ 211-A.	4–1 Sec'y State	4–1 Sec'y State
N.J. No capital values tax.		
N.M. $50 per tax year or part	15th of 3rd mo. Dept. Rev. & Tax.	15th of 3rd mo. Dept. Rev. & Tax.
N.Y. 1.78 mills per $1 on value of apportioned business and investment capital, up to max. tax of $350,000 for manufacturers and $1 million for others (for alternative tax base for franchise tax, see chart at ¶ 222)	15th of 3rd mo. Dept. Tax. & Fin.	15th of 3rd mo. Dept. Tax. & Fin.
N.C. $1.50 per $1,000 outstanding capital stock, surplus, undivided profit, allocated to state, or assessed value property or investment in in-state tangibles, if greater. Min. tax $35.	15th of 4th mo. Sec'y Rev.	15th of 4th mo. Sec'y Rev.
N.D. No capital values tax.		
OHIO (See chart at ¶ 222)		
OKLA. $1.25 per $1,000 business and investment capital allocated to state Min. $10. Max. $20,000.	8–31(7) Tax Comm.	8–31(7) Tax Comm.
ORE. No capital values tax.		
PA. 3.89 mills per $1 of taxable capital stock value fixed by formula (3).	4–15 (or 30 days after federal return due) Dept. Rev.	4–15 (or 30 days after federal return due) Dept. Rev.
R.I. $2.50 per $10,000 (min. $500) authorized capital stock (5); no-par stock valued $100.	3–15 (2½ mo.) Tax Admr.	15 days after assessment Tax Admr.

STATES, BASES AND RATE OF TAX (6)	REPORT DEADLINE (1)	PAYMENT DEADLINE (1)
S.C. $15, plus $1 per each $1,000 of capital stock plus paid in surplus. Min. fee, $25.	15th of 3rd mo. Dept. Rev.	15th of 3rd mo. Dept. Rev.
S.D. No capital values tax.		
TENN. *Franchise tax:* 25¢ per $100 of net worth. Min. tax, $100.	15th of 4th mo. Commr. Rev.	15th of 4th mo. Commr. Rev.
TEX. *Franchise tax:* Eff for reports due on or after 1-1-2008, 1% of taxable margin; 0.5% of taxable margin for taxable entities primarily engaged in retail or wholesale trade; no tax due if amount of tax computed is less than $1,000 or amount of taxable entity's total revenue from its entire business is less than or equal to $300,000 or the adjusted amount determined under the law per 12-month period on which margin is based. (14)	5–15 Comptr. Pub Accts. 1st plus 2d ones due in 90 days of anniversary of beginning date.	5–15 Comptr. Pub. Accts. 1st plus 2d ones due in 90 days of anniversary of beginning date.
UTAH No capital values tax.		
VT. No capital values tax.		
VA. (See chart at ¶ 211-A)		
WASH. No capital values tax.		
W.VA. *Corporate license:* D–Authorized capital stock. To $5,000, $20; $5,000–$10,000, $30; $10,000–$25,000, $40; $25,000–50,000, $50; $50,000–75,000, $80; $75,000–100,000, $100; $100,000–$125,000, $110; $125,000–150,000, $120; $150,000–175,000, $140; $175,000–200,000, $150; $200,000–1,000,000, $180 plus 20¢ per $1,000 or fraction over $200,000; $1 million to $15 million, $340 plus 15¢ per $1,000 or fraction over $1,000,000; over $15,000,000, $2500. F–Allocated outstanding capital stock at above rates plus 75%. Min. $250. No par value $25.	7–1 Tax Commr.	To Tax Commr. with return.
Business franchise: 0.55% (0.7% for tax yrs. starting pre-1-1-2007) of value of capital. Min. $50.	15th of 3rd mo. Tax Commr.	To Tax Commr. with return.
WIS. (See chart at ¶ 211-A)		
WYO. 0.02¢ per $1 of capital, property, or assets in-state. Min. tax, $50.	1st of registration mo. Sec'y State	1st of registration mo. Sec'y State

NOTES to chart ¶ 240 (corresponding to numbers in parentheses):

(1) Parentheses and relative dates mean days or months after corporation year.
(2) *Ark.*—Report and pay by 5-1 each yr.; 1st report, payment from newly organized or qualifying corp. are due 5-1 of calendar yr. after incorporation or qualification yr.
(3) *Pa.*—Tax rate is 3.89 mills per $1 of taxable capital stock value for tax yr. starting in 2007; 2.89 mills in 2008; 1.89 mills in 2009; 0.89 mills in 2010; no tax is imposed for tax yrs. starting after 12-31-2010.
(4) *Del.*—Or fraction.
(5) *R.I.*—Corporations not engaged in business in R.I. pay $250 on $1 million authorized capital stock plus $12.50 per added $1 million or fraction.
(6) *Kan.*—For tax yr. beginning in 2007, tax rate is 0.125%; in 2008, 0.09375%; in 2009, 0.0625%; in 2010, 0.03125%; after 2010, tax is repealed.
(7) Corporations can choose to file their franchise tax return and pay tax due at same time as their income tax (¶ 222).
(8) *Ala.*—Rates shown are for business privilege tax.
(9) *Ala.*—Returns and payments for corporations are due two and one-half months after the first day of their tax yr. Returns and payments for limited liablitiy entities are due three and one-half months after the first day of their tax yr.
(10) *Ark.*—There is no max. tax; special rates apply to specified corporations.
(11) Until 12-31-2007, Mich. does not impose capital values tax. Eff 1-1-2008, financial institutions are subject to franchise tax equal to 0.235% of the financial institution's net capital after allocation and apportionment. Report and payment is due to Dept. Treas. by last day of fourth month after end of taxpayer's tax year.
(12) *La.*—Tax on borrowed capital is phased out during period 2006—2011. After 2011, borrowed capital is not taxed.
(13) *Ky.*—Corporate license tax ($2.10 per $1,000 of Ky.-apportioned capital used in business) was repealed eff for tax periods ending on or after 12-31-2005.
(14) *Tex.*—For reports due before 1-1-2008, 0.25% of net taxable capital, plus difference between 4.5% of net earned surplus and the tax on net capital; tax under $100 need not be paid.

ALLOCATION FACTORS FOR CAPITAL VALUES TAXES

¶241 Ordinary business corporations. This chart covers the allocation of capital values taxes by ordinary business corporations engaged in the manufacture, sale and distribution of merchandise. It details the factors used by states imposing the capital values taxes listed at ¶ 240.

➽ **NO ALLOCATION→** States that do not allow domestic corporations to allocate are those shown on Column A with a note 1. Some states are not shown on the chart because they levy nominal *flat fees* on all corporations without allocation; for example, N.M.

STATE Col. A (11)	PROPERTY Col. B	BUSINESS OR RECEIPTS Col. C	PAYROLL Col. D
ALA.	Yes	Yes	Yes
ARK.	Yes(13,33)	Yes	Yes
CONN.(2)	Yes(14)	No	No
DEL.	Not applicable	Not applicable	Not applicable
GA.(1)	Yes(13)	Yes(23)	No
ILL.	Yes(13)	Yes(23)	No
KAN.(9,10)	Yes(16)	Yes	Yes
LA.	Yes(13)	Yes(28)	No
MASS.(3)	Yes(15,17,21)	Yes(24,26)	Yes(30)
MICH.(32)	No(32)	Yes(32)	No(32)
MISS.	Yes(16,20)	Yes	No
MO.	Yes(13)	No	No
NEB.(1)	Yes(12)	No	No
N.Y.(5)	Yes(5,16,17)	Yes(5)	Yes(5)
N.C.(9)	Yes(16,17)	Yes(24)	Yes
OKLA.	Yes(13)	Yes(23)	No
PA.(6,8)	Yes	Yes	Yes
R.I.(1)	Yes	Yes	Yes
S.C.(9,34)	Yes(34)	Yes(34)	Yes(34)
TENN.	Yes(22)	Yes(24)	Yes
TEX.	No	Yes(27)	No
W.VA.(1,7)	Yes(18)	No(29)	No(31)
WYO.	Yes(12)	No	No

NOTES to chart ¶ 241 (corresponding to numbers in parentheses in each column of the chart):

(1) No allocation for domestic corporations.
(2) Excise on corporate franchise. Special provisions for air carriers, buses.
(3) There are 3 different procedures, depending on whether taxpayer is
(a) "tangible property corporation",
(b) domestic "intangible property corporation" or
(c) foreign "intangible property corporation".
(4) Special provision for transportation companies.
(5) N.Y.—Tax on capital allocated as follows: investment capital by one-factor formula of intangible property; business capital by single-factor formula based solely on receipts. Also see ¶ 223 to ¶ 226-A.
(6) Special provisions for public utilities and truck, bus, and airline cos.
(7) Entries apply to license tax. For franchise tax, 4-factor formula of property, payroll, and sales (used twice) is used.
(8) Single factor (local-to-total assets) may be elected. Special provisions for holding and regulated investment companies.

NOTES to chart ¶ 241 (corresponding to numbers in parentheses in each column of the chart): (continued)

(9) If allocating for income tax, same formula must be used.
(10) Domestic corporations may allocate.
(11) Special formula may be required or permitted.
(12) Tax based on in-state property; in effect, specific allocation.
(13) All property included.
(14) Business intangibles (except corporate stock) and tangibles (including rentals) at average monthly value.
(15) Sole factor—in effect, specific allocation—for "tangible property corporation".
(16) Tangibles only, including realty.
(17) Rented property included at capitalized value of 8-times annual rent.
(18) See Col. A entries for the state.
(19) Pollution control incentives and effect, if any, on property factor are covered in ¶ 298.
(20) Only property owned.
(21) Only factor in determining property value base; also used in 3-factor formula for net income base.
(22) (16) and (17) apply, but exempt inventory is excluded from the property factor. *(Tenn.)*
(23) Statute labels factor as "business transacted" which apparently includes all income producing activity.
(24) Sales factor is double weighted.
(25) Exclude outshipments if buyer is US.
(26) Used in 3-factor allocation for net income base.
(27) Sale of investments and capital assets included only to extent of net gains. In-state sales include all sales of tangible personalty delivered or shipped to buyer in Tex., regardless of point or origin; or to outshipments if seller not taxed in other states.
(28) La.—Pipeline and air carriers use revenues. Manufacturers use only the net sales and revenue ratio. Special calculations (including audience factors) are used for television, radio, and other broadcasting revenue.
(29) See Col. A entries for the state.
(30) Used in 3-factor allocation for net income base.
(31) See Col. A entries for the state.
(32) Mich.—Eff 1-1-2008, under financial institutions franchise tax, income of taxpayer whose business activities are subject to tax both within and outside Mich. must be apportioned to Mich. by multiplying the tax base by the gross business factor, numerator of which is taxpayer's total gross business in Mich. during tax yr. and denominator of which is taxpayer's total gross business everywhere during tax yr.
(33) Ark.—Single factor (local-to-total assets) can be used. Special provisions for holding companies and foreign corporations.
(34) S.C.—Single factor apportionment based on sales phases in starting in 2007.

➺ **WHAT TO DO**→ Use this chart in corporate planning to spot high-cost or taxfree areas. Business considerations being equal—availability of manufacturing facilities, transportation, power needs, markets—tax considerations can be pivotal in swinging your new operations. In checking for lowest tax cost areas, spot the allocating factors on your planning map. In planning a warehouse, for example, you would avoid places where inventory plays an important part in allocating values. A sales headquarters or office to channel sales would be best placed outside a state that uses receipts or sales or business as a prime allocating element. In settling personnel, by-pass states using payroll to boost their tax. And so on.

SALES-USE TAX RATES, BASES, REPORTS, PAYMENTS

¶250 Rates, basis, and reporting. A comprehensive picture of the sales and use tax rates, and bases on which they are imposed, for all states with general sales or use taxes is presented below. The return and payment dates, and the official to whom the return or payment is made, are also listed. Supplementary or special rates are shown in the notes at the end of this chart. Sales taxes on telecommunication services are charted at ¶ 259.

➳ **MEANING OF A STAR(*)→** In the first column, under the state name, is a starred (*) entry showing whether the primary tax (sales or gross receipts) is a "seller" or "consumer" tax. The designation is important in determining who is primarily liable for the tax for purposes of responsibility and refunds.

➳ **WARNING→** Payment by electronic funds transfer may be required. See ¶ 279.

STATE (1)	RATE OF TAX	BASIS OR MEASURE OF TAX (2)	RETURNS & PAYMENT Last Day Without Penalty	To Whom
Alabama ***Seller (40)**	4%. (10,44).	*Sales:* Gross proceeds. *Use:* Sales price of tangible personalty bought at retail.	Monthly by 20th. (4,76).	Dept. Rev., Montgomery
Alaska ***Seller**	No state tax; but local sales taxes imposed (106).			
Arizona ***Seller (40)**	*Sales:* Retailers, 5.6%; others, 3.125% to 5.5% (10,95). *Use:* 5.6% (10).	*Sales:* Gross proceeds receipts, or gross income. *Use:* Sale price of tangible personalty bought at retail.	Monthly by 20th of mo. after tax accrues (51).	Dept. Rev., Phoenix
Arkansas ***Seller**	6% (10,80).	*Gross receipts:* From sales of tangible personalty and certain services. *Use:* Sale price of tangible personalty or taxable services.	*Gross receipts:* monthly by 20th (4,82). *Use:* monthly by 20th.	Dept. Fin. & Admn., Little Rock
California ***Seller (40)**	7.25% (including uniform 0.75% local tax) (10,46).	*Sales:* Gross receipts. *Use:* Sale price of tangibles.	Last day of month after quarter (37).	State Bd. Equal., Sacramento
Colorado ***Consumer**	2.9% (10).	*Sales:* Purchase price. *Use:* Purchase price of tangibles.	Monthly by 20th (4).	Dept. Rev., Denver
Connecticut ***Consumer**	6% (77).	*Sales:* Gross receipts from sales of goods and certain services. *Use:* Price of tangibles.	Last day of month after month or quarter (6).	Commr. Rev. Services, Hartford
Delaware ***Consumer**	No state or local sales-use tax.; 8% transient lodging tax; 2% on other rental.	Rental charge.	*Lodging:* Monthly by 15th. *Personalty:* Quarterly by last day of Jan., April, July, and Oct.	Dept. Fin., Wilmington.
District of Columbia ***Seller (40)**	5.75% (35).	*Sales:* Gross receipts from sales of goods and certain services. *Use:* Sales price.	Monthly by 20th (61).	Office of Tax & Rev., Wash. D.C.
Florida ***Consumer**	6% (10,36).	*Sales:* Sales price of tangible personalty and certain services. *Use:* Cost price.	Monthly by 20th (55).	Dept. Rev., Tallahasse

STATE (1)	RATE OF TAX	BASIS OR MEASURE OF TAX (2)	RETURNS & PAYMENT Last Day Without Penalty	To Whom
Georgia ***Consumer**	4% (10,83).	*Sales:* Sales price. *Use:* Cost price or fair market value if less.	Monthly by 20th (4,47).	Rev. Commr., Atlanta
Hawaii ***Seller (40)**	4% (10,15). *Use:* 4% (imports for resale, 0.5%). Add 7.25% for transient lodging.	Gross receipts of sale or value of product and services. *Use:* Value of property.	End of month (7,8). Annual return, 20th of 4th mo. after tax year.	Div. Tax. Assr. or Dir. Tax., Honolulu
Idaho ***Consumer**	6%; add 2% for transient lodging. (10).	*Sales:* Total price. *Use:* Value (recent price)	Monthly by 20th (63).	State Tax Comm., Boise
Illinois ***Seller (40)**	*Retailers' occupation (sales) or use:* 6.25% (10,53). *Service occupation or use:* 6.25%. (10,53).	*Retailers' occupation:* Gross receipts. *Use:* Selling price or fair market value. *Service occupation (or use):* Selling price, but not less than cost to serviceman.	20th of month for preceding month (32).	Dept. Rev., Springfield (or Chicago)
Indiana ***Consumer**	*Gross retail (sales) or use:* 6% (10,78).	*Gross retail (sales):* Gross receipts. *Use:* Sale price.	Monthly by 30th (29).	Dept. Rev., Indianapolis
Iowa ***Consumer**	5%; added 5% on MV rental (10, 104).	*Sales:* Sales price. *Use:* Purchase price or installed purchase price.	End of Jan., Apr., July, Oct. (38).	Dept. Rev., Des Moines
Kansas ***Consumer**	5.3% (10, 86).	*Sales:* Gross receipts. *Use:* Purchase price of tangibles.	Monthly by 25th (4,30,71).	Dept. Rev., Topeka
Kentucky ***Seller (40)**	6%.	*Sales:* Gross receipts. *Use:* Sale price of tangibles.	Monthly by 20th (84).	Dept. Rev., Frankfort
Louisiana ***Consumer**	4% generally (10,85).	*Sales:* Gross retail sales, rentals, certain service charges. *Use:* Cost price (39).	Monthly by 20th (4,39).	Sec'y Rev., Baton Rouge
Maine ***Consumer (40)**	5% (9,68).	*Sales:* Gross sales, rental. *Use:* Sales price.	Monthly by 15th (9).	Rev. Services, Augusta
Maryland ***Consumer**	5% (34).	*Sales:* Taxable price of tangible personalty and certain services. *Use:* Same.	Monthly by 20th	Comptr. Treas., Baltimore
Massachusetts ***Consumer (18)**	5% (88).	*Sales:* Gross receipts from sale of goods and certain services. *Use:* Sale price.	Monthly by 20th (49).	Commr. Rev., Boston
Michigan ***Consumer**	6% (72).	*Sales:* Gross proceeds. *Use:* Sales price.	Monthly by 20th (102). Annual return, Feb. 28.	Dept. Treas., Lansing
Minnesota ***Consumer**	6.5% (10,69).	*Sales:* Gross receipts of tangible personalty and services. *Use:* Sales price	Monthly by 20th (57).	Commr. Rev., St. Paul
Mississippi ***Seller (40)**	*Sales:* 7% (10,19). *Use:* 7% (19). *Salesmen's:* 3% retail; 0.125% wholesale.	*Sales:* Gross proceeds. *Use:* Sales price. *Salesmen's:* Gross proceeds.	Monthly by 20th.	Tax Comm., Jackson
Missouri ***Seller (40)**	4.225% (10,100).	Sales: Gross receipts. *Use:* Sales price.	Quarterly by last day of Jan., Apr., July, Oct. (11)	Dir. Rev., Jefferson City

STATE (1)	RATE OF TAX	BASIS OR MEASURE OF TAX (2)	RETURNS & PAYMENT Last Day Without Penalty	To Whom
Montana ***Consumer**	No sales-use tax; 1% public contractors tax; 4% transient lodging tax; local resort tax may be levied (58).	Cost price.	Quarterly by last day of Apr., July, Oct., Jan.	Dept. Rev.
Nebraska ***Consumer**	5.5% (10,93).	*Sales:* Gross receipts. *Use:* Sales price.	Monthly by 25th (4,5).	Tax Commr., Lincoln
Nevada ***Seller**	6.5% incl. uniform local tax (10,99).	*Sales:* Gross receipts. *Use:* Sales price.	Monthly by last day (28).	Dept. Tax., Carson City
New Hampshire ***Consumer**	No sales-use tax; meals-rooms, 8% (105).	*Meals:* Cost price. *Rooms:* Gross rent.	Monthly by 15th.	Dept. Rev., Concord.
New Jersey ***Consumer**	7% (10,66,90).	*Sales:* Gross receipts, service charge (27). *Use:* Price, or service charge (27).	Quarterly (20), 20th of Jan., Apr., July, Oct.	Dir., Div. Tax., Trenton
New Mexico ***Seller (40)**	5% (10,94).	*Sales:* Gross receipts of tangible personalty and services. *Use:* Value.	Monthly by 25th. (92)	Tax & Rev. Dept., Santa Fe
New York ***Consumer**	4% plus up to 4.375% local tax (10,56); NYC total, 8.375% (56).	*Sales:* Gross selling price, service charge. *Use:* Price.	Quarterly by 20th of Mar. June, Sept., Dec. (42).	Dept. Tax. & Fin., Albany
North Carolina ***Consumer**	4.25% (4.5% eff. 10-1-2008) (10,21).	Retail: Net taxable sales or gross receipts. *Compensating use:* Purchase price.	Monthly by 20th (4,64).	Sec'y Rev., Raleigh
North Dakota ***Consumer**	5% (10,81).	*Sales:* Gross receipts. *Use:* Sale price.	Quarterly by last day of Jan., Apr., July, Oct. (74).	Tax Commr., Bismarck
Ohio ***Consumer**	5.5% (10,97).	*Sales:* Price of tangible personalty and certain services. *Use:* Price.	Monthly by 23rd (5).	Tax Commr., Columbus
Oklahoma ***Consumer**	4.5% (10,70).	*Sales:* Gross proceeds. *Use:* Purchase price.	*Sales:* Monthly by 20th (59). *Use:* monthly by 20th.	Tax Comm., Okla. City
Oregon	No state-local tax.			
Pennsylvania ***Consumer**	6% (10,91).	Sales-use: Price of tangible personalty and certain services (3).	Monthly by 20th (13).	Dept. Rev., Harrisburg
Rhode Island ***Consumer**	7% (96).	*Sales:* Gross receipts. *Use:* Sale price.	Monthly by 20th (79).	Tax Adm., Providence
South Carolina ***Seller (40)**	6%; 5% on sales to 85-yr-old (min.); add 7% on transient lodgings (10,73).	*Sales:* Gross proceeds. *Use:* Sale price.	Monthly by 20th (4).	Dept. Rev., Columbia
South Dakota ***Seller (40)**	4% (10,12).	*Sales:* Gross receipts of tangible personalty and many services. *Use:* Purchase price.	Bimonthly by last day after two-month period (89).	Dept. Rev., Pierre
Tennessee ***Seller (40)**	7% (10,33).	*Sales:* sales price. *Use:* Purchase price.	Monthly by 20th (50).	Commr. Rev., Nashville
Texas ***Consumer**	6.25% (10,45).	Sales-use: Sales price, rentals, service charges.	Monthly by 20th (41).	Comptr. Pub. Accts., Austin
Utah ***Consumer**	5.65% (5.75% pre-1-1-2008) inclu. uniform local tax (10,52).	*Sales:* Price paid. *Use:* Same.	Last day of Jan., Apr., July, Oct. (75).	Tax Comm., Salt Lake City

STATE (1)	RATE OF TAX	BASIS OR MEASURE OF TAX (2)	RETURNS & PAYMENT Last Day Without Penalty	To Whom
Vermont ***Consumer**	6% (10,60).	*Sales:* Sales price. *Use:* Purchase price.	Monthly by 25th (87).	Commr. Taxes. Montpelier
Virginia ***Seller (40)**	5% (including 1% local tax) (10,24).	*Sales:* Gross sales (also lease, rental, storage). *Use:* Cost of tangibles.	Monthly by 20th.	Tax Commr., Richmond
Washington ***Consumer**	*Sales-use:* 6.5% (10,62). *Business & Occupation:* 0.138% to 1.5% (67).	Sales-use: Selling price of tangible personalty and services. *B & O:* Value of products, gross proceeds or income.	Monthly by 25th.	Dept. Rev., Olympia.
West Virginia ***Consumer (23)**	*Sales-use:* 6% (10,31). *Business & Occupation:* on utilities only (22).	*Sales:* Monetary consideration for tangible personalty, services. *Use:* Purchase price. *B & O:* Gross Sales Gross proceeds, income.	*Sales-use:* Monthly by 20th (4,54). *B. & O.* Monthly by last day (54).	Dept. Rev., Charleston
Wisconsin ***Seller (40)**	5% (10,43).	*Sales:* Gross receipts. *Use:* Sales price.	Quarterly, last day of Jan., Apr., July, Oct. (25).	Dept. Rev., Madison
Wyoming ***Consumer**	4% (10,48,98).	*Sales:* Sales price or gross rental paid. *Use:* Sales price.	Last day of month (4,14).	Dept. Rev., Cheyenne.

FOOTNOTES to Chart ¶ 250 (corresponding to parenthetical numbers in chart):

(1) Covers statewide sales-use taxes. "Consumer" means state tax was deductible by consumer for Fed income tax purposes as a tax pre-1-1-87; under current Fed. rules, tax is deductible by retailer as expense if collections included in his-her gross income and Fed rule followed by states adopting IRC. See also note (40) for "retailer" taxes.

(2) Use tax usually imposed on property bought for storage, use or consumption in the state. Rentals, see ¶ 253.

(3) Special optional basis for motor vehicle dealers; commercial aircraft operator; and property bought out-of-state by state resident.

(4) Quarterly returns in Jan., Apr., July and Oct. (by 20th unless otherwise shown) allowed if: *Monthly tax*— $100 (max.), *Ark.*; under $200 per mo.during past cal. year, *Ala.*; $100 (max.), *N.C.* (last day of mo.); under $150 in any month in *Wyo.* (last day); $250 or less, W.Va.; under $500, *La.*; under $300, *Colo.*; *S.C.*, $100 (max.); $900-$2,999 in Neb. (25th). *Annual:* not over $3,200, Kan. (25th); under $900, Neb. (25th). Prior Dept. OK may be needed. If *Ark.* monthly tax $25 (max.), *Colo.* monthly tax $15 (max.), annual return by 1-20 allowed. If *Ala.* prior cal. year tax $10 (max.), annual return by 1-20 allowed. In *Ga.,* quarterly returns allowed if tax for 6 consecutive months averages less than $200 per mo.; annual returns allowed if tax for 6 consecutive months averages less than $50 per mo. *W.Va.* annual reconciliation return due 1-30. Annual return by 1-15 if tax for year isn't over $600.

(5) Direct pay permit holders and consumers required to file must file monthly; others, quarterly by 23rd. Permission may be granted to file on some other basis. *Neb.*, direct pay permit holders and consumers must pay monthly by the 25th.

(6) *Conn.* —Quarterly by last of following month if tax for 12-month period ended 9–30 is under $4,000. Annually by 4-15, if under $1,000.

(7) Consolidated returns needed if in two or more like businesses.

(8) Qtrly, by end of Apr., July, Oct., Jan. if yr. tax $4,000 max; semiannually by 7-31 & 1-31 if yr. tax $2,000 max. Dir. Tax. can allow fiscal yr. taxpayers to file by corresponding fiscal yr. dates.

(9) *Me.*—Annually (by 1-15) if less than $50 average annual tax liability; semiannually (by 6-15 and 12-15) if liability is at least $50 but less than $100 per mo.; quarterly (by 3-15, 6-15, 9-15, 12-15) if liability is at least $100 but less than $600 per mo. Use tax not otherwise paid is payable with individual income tax return (¶ 228); can elect to pay at 0.04% of Me. adjusted gross income instead of use tax rate.

(10) Additional local (county, parish, city, town, special district, etc.) taxes ranging from 0.1% to 9% are imposed or authorized in many states including: Ala., Ariz., Ark., Calif., Colo., Fla., Ga., Ida., Ill., Ind., Iowa; Kan., La., Minn., Miss., Mo. Neb., Nev., N.J., N.M., N.Y., N.C., N.D., Ohio, Okla., Pa., S.C., S.D., Tenn., Tex., Utah, Va., Vt., Wash., W.Va., Wis., Wyo. Haw. authorizes 0.5% county tax. Miss. allows certain cities to impose independent limited sales taxes for special purposes.

(11) *Mo.*—If quarterly tax under $45, pay annually by 1-31; tax over $500 for 1st or 2nd calendar quarter month, pay by 20th of next month. Pay sales tax (not use tax) quarter-monthly (by 3rd banking day after 7th, 15th, 22nd and last day of month) if tax is $15,000 or more for each 6 months of past 12 months. If required by Dir. Rev., monthly by last day.

FOOTNOTES to Chart ¶ 250 (corresponding to parenthetical numbers in chart):
(continued)

(12) *S.D.* —Improving realty: 2% on prime contractors; 2% on contractors of utility cos. 4% on receipts from coin-operated amusement devices. 4% on farm machy. Large vessel (min. 12-ft. long) and motor, 3%. MV tire, 25¢ ($1 max. per MV).

(13) If tax for previous 3rd calendar quarter $600 or more, file-pay monthly by 20th. If annual tax is between $75-$600, file quarterly by 4-20, 7-20, 10-20 and 1-20. If annual tax $75 or less, file-pay semi-annually by 2-20 and 8-20.

(14) *Wyo.*—Annual returns can be authorized for non-nexus filers instead of quarterly ones due by last day of month after end of year. Quarterly or annual use tax returns can be authorized if the total use tax due during month is less than $150 on items bought from vendors who do not have place of business in-state.

(15) *Haw.* —Added $3 per day tax per MV rental 6-mo. max (17-passenger max). Added monthly tax per MV use—$15 for 8–25 passenger; $65 for over 25. Wholesalers, 0.5%; manufacturers, producers or blind persons or electricity from non-fossil renewable resources sold to utilities for resale. 0.5%; pineapple canners, sugar processors, 0.5% insurance solicitors, 0.15%. Intermediary sales of services, 0.5%. Tires imported into state, $1 per tire surcharge. Eff. 7-1-2009, 2% on gross sales price of media rights for mixed martial arts event.

(16) (Reserved.)

(17) (Reserved.)

(18) So held by US Sup. Ct. (First Agricultural) and by IRS.

(19) *Miss.* —Retailing generally (incl. computer software sales-services), amusement and entertainment business, wholesaling (beer, alcoholic beverages, 7%; wholesaling food-drinks to vending machine operators, 8%; admissions to publicly owned coliseums and auditoriums, track materials sold to railroads, autos sold by dealers, mobile homes, trucks and truck-tractors, aircraft, self-propelled or specified mounted equip. used in logging, pulpwood-tree farming, certain farm implements, 3%; casual sales of MVs, 5%; MV retail sales of private carriers of passengers and light carrier of property, 5%; MV rental for 30 days (max.), 6% added to regular 7% rate; farm tractors sold to farmers, sales to electric power association for operating generating or distributing system, 1%; machinery-parts, 1.5%; contracting, 3.5%. Sales or construction at moored floating structures (casinos, restaurants, hotels, etc.), 3.5%. Sales of fuel used to produce electric power by cos. mainly in business of producing, generating, or distributing electric power for sale, are tax exempt. Other fuel and electricity sales to manufacturers, custom processors, or public service cos. for industrial, specified farm or domesticated fish, fish products or marine aquaculture products or purposes. 1.5%.

(20) Monthly by 20th if monthly tax exceeds $500.

(21) *N.C.* —General rate 4.75% eff. 10-1-2009. Privilege tax rate is 1% on selected machy. and equipment; supplies for certain businesses. New tires, 2% if bead diameter less than 20 in.; 1% if bead diameter is at least 20 in. Manufactured homes, 2% ($300 max.). Planes and boats, 3% ($1,500 max.). Food, no statewide tax but subject to 2% local tax. Tax is 1.8% (1.4% eff. 7-1-2008; 0.8% eff. 7-1-2009; repealed eff. 7-1-2010) on electricity sold to farmers for farm use or to mfg. industries or plants to run their operations. Tax is 2.83% for commercial laundries or pressing and dry-cleaning businesses to run their machy. MV highway use tax, 3%; $1,000 max. for Class A and B commercial MVs, $1,500 max. on all others. Tax on MV retail value or tax on rental gross receipts is 8% on short-term rentals (under 365 continuous days to the same person) and 3% on long-term rental agreements. $3 advance disposal tax is added to sale of new white goods (refrigerator, washer, range, and similar large appliances).

(22) Rates on utilities range from 1.4% to 4.4%. Electric power, $20.70 per generating unit; gas storage, 5¢ per dekatherms; synthetic fuel from coal, 50¢ per ton. *(W. Va.).*

(23) Gross sales tax is "seller" tax.

(24) *Va.* special rates: food, 1.5%; watercraft, 2% ($2,000 max. tax); MVs, 3%; 3% on MVs mfd. to be run by compressed natural gas, liquefied natural or petroleum gas, hydrogen, or electricity); mobile homes 3%; aircraft, 2%; MV rentals, 4% (plus 6% on daily rental cars). Added $1 per new tire sold. Items sold through vending machine, 6% (5% of wholesale purchase plus 1% local tax). Communications services, 5%.

(25) On Dept. notice: monthly report-pay by last day if quarterly tax over $600.

(26) Report, pay monthly by next 25th (incl. local taxes).

(27) Food-beverages sold thru vending machines are taxed at 70% of retail price.

(28) Qtrly. (1-31, 4-30, 7-31, 10-31) if under $10,000 gross taxable sales per mo. Pay tax on capital goods in mo. installments (with Comm. Econ. Dev.'s OK); $100,000–$349,999 sales price, pay tax in 12 mos.; $350,000–$599,999, 24 mos.; $600,000–$849,999, 36 mos.; $850,000 to under $1 million, 48 mos.; $1 million or more, 60 mos.

(29) Report-pay by 20th if avg. monthly tax for prior yr. over $1000. Less frequent reporting if Dept. Rev. OKs.

(30) Annually by 1-31, if monthly tax not over $5 or annually over $60. In *Kan.*, annually by 1–25 if total tax liability is $80 or less in any calendar yr.

(31) Food and food ingredients for human consumption, 4% of sales price (3% eff 7-1-2008). Motor fuels, 5% of average wholesale price *(W. Va.).*

(32) Annually by 1-20, if monthly average tax $50 or less; quarterly by 20th day following quarter if monthly tax $200 (max.) and if Dept. Rev. allows; quarter-monthly payments by 7th, 15th, 22nd, and last day of current month if average monthly tax $20,000 or more for preceding 4 calendar quarters ($20,000 for past 2 calendar quarters for motor fuel resellers collecting prepaid tax. *(Ill.)*

FOOTNOTES to Chart ¶ 250 (corresponding to parenthetical numbers in chart):
(continued)

(33) *Tenn.* —1% on industrial water sold to manufacturers; 1.5% on energy fuels sold to manufacturers and on electricity and liquefied gas for farmers, and on energy fuels used for nursery-greenhouse crops. Aviation gasoline 4.5%. 3.75% on items sold to common carriers for out-of-state use. Vending machine operator can elect to pay 1.5% receipts tax (2.5% on tobacco item machines) instead of sales tax. $1-per-tire predisposal fee applies to sales of new tires ($1.35-per-tire eff 10-1-2007). Added 3% on retail rental of private passenger MV for up to 31 days. 8.25% on cable TV subscription fees (no tax if fees are less than $15) provided by a cable TV service provider or by provider of wireless cable TV services offered for public consumption. 8.25% on fees for direct-to-home satellite TV services. Interstate communications services, 7.5%; additional local tax of 1.5% also applies to interstate services. 5.5% on food (6% pre-1-1-2008).

(34) *Md.*—Rate applies to 60% of mobile home price in its 1st retail sale. Rate applies to 95.25% of gross receipts from sales through vending or other self-service machines. Rate on passenger car or other class E, F, G, or M MV rented for 180 days or less is 11.5%, imposed at the rate of 23¢ for each exact multiple of $2, prorated for each part of $2 over an exact multiple of $2; for trucks, the tax rate is 8%, imposed at 8¢ on each even dollar plus 2¢ on each 25¢ or fraction over an even dollar. .062¢ per taxable kilowatt hour on electricity not delivered from a utility.

(35) 10% on wine, liquor, beer, food-drink on premises (9% wine, liquor, beer, off premises), prepaid phone cards, rental fleet MV and utility trailer rentals. 14.5%, transient lodging. 12%, MV parking, storage, tobacco products other than cigarettes. Additional 4.25% ballpark and Verizon Center sales taxes on certain transactions. Street vendors make required fixed payments instead of collecting-remitting sales tax. Added $2 per new MV tire. *(D.C.)*

(36) *Fla.* —Special rates: 6.8% on communications services; 10.8% on direct-to-home satellite services. $2 surcharge per day for 1st 30 days of lease-rental of MV for hire, 8-passenger max. Electrical power or energy, 7%. Coin-operated amusement machine charges, 4%. Alcoholic and malt beverages: package store sales (no mixed drinks), 6.35%; package goods (incl mixed drinks), 6.59%. Vendors at carnivals, fairs, etc., and concession stand operators, and vending machine sales of food, beverages, and other tangible personalty divide gross receipts by appropriate county tax rate divisor if impractical to separately state the tax (required for vending machine sales). Motor fuel and special fuel, see ¶ 285. 6% on cost of materials becoming component part of finished asphalt and on transportation costs. Indexed tax on asphalt is 62¢ per ton (37¢ if used in govt. public works project) for 7-1-2007—6-30-2008.

(37) *Calif.* —If estimated tax $17,000 (min.) per month, and if told by SBE in writing, in 1st, 3rd and 4th qtrs. prepay 90% of tax for 1st and 2nd months of each qtr. by 24th day after end of first two monthly periods. In 2nd qtr., 1st prepayment of 90% for 1st monthly period due by 24th day following. Prepay for 2nd monthly period either (1) 90% of liability for 2nd monthly period, plus 90% of liability for first 15 days of 3rd monthly period; or (2) 90% of liability for 2nd monthly period plus 50% of 90% of liability for 2nd monthly period by 24th day of 3rd monthly period. MV fuel distributors-brokers prepay sales tax on fuel monthly by 25th of next mo. at rate SBE sets.

(38) *Iowa* —Quarterly returns must be accompanied by tax deposits for last report period (semimonthly or monthly) shown below. *Sales tax:* If monthly tax over $500 but under $5,000, deposit monthly by 20th of next mo. (not for 3rd mo. of qtr.). If monthly tax over $5,000, deposit tax for 1st and 2nd mo. by 20th of next month. If tax over $2,500 for semimonthly period, pay tax semimonthly by 25th and 10th. (not for last semimonthly period of qtr.). If annual tax is $120 (max.), pay annually by 1-31 with Dept. OK. *Use tax:* over $1500 per month, pay by 20th monthly (not for 3rd month of qtr.). If annual tax $120 (max.), pay annually by 1-31 with Dept approval.

(39) *La.*—For basis: Actual cost or reasonable market value if property is "susceptible to use tax," if less. Tax on manufacturing, farming, and timbering machinery and equipment is phased out in the period 7-1-2004—7-1-2010. State tax is imposed on 46% of retail sales price of new manufactured or mobile homes. Until 1-1-2009, if selling to retailer (not certain dealers to industrial users or contractors, or specified others), collect advanced tax. Exemption from the advance sale requirement is available to dealer with annual sales totaling at least $3 million. Pay tax on leases-rentals in month when payments received.

(40) Retailer can deduct tax for Fed income tax purposes in states following IRC rules. Tax on noncapital item bought in trade or business, is deductible expense for Fed though not separately billed.

(41) If tax under $500 for month or $1,500 for calendar quarter, by 20th after quarter end.

(42) *N.Y.* —Plus monthly reports (using part-quarterly long- or short-form) and payments by 20th of next month if taxable receipts $300,000 or more in any quarter of preceding 4 quarters. Short-form filers report-pay ⅓ of total state-local taxes paid in comparable quarter of prior year, adjusted for local tax changes. Motor fuel distributors with sales of 100,000 or more gal. in any quarter of preceding 4 quarters pay monthly by 20th of next month. Annual report can be filed (by 3-20) if total tax for most recent 6 calendar qtrs. did not exceed $3,000 and total tax for current 12 mos. will not exceed $3,000.

(43) Tax is general sales-use tax on all tangible personalty, unless exempt.

(44) *Ala.* —Vending machine sales: food, coffee & milk, 3%. Rentals, 4% (linens, garments, 2%; MVs. 1.5%). MVs, truck trailers, semitrailers, housetrailers, mobile homes, mobile home set-up materials, casual sales of travel trailers, manufactured homes, and motorboats, 2%. Machy for farming, mining, quarrying, compounding, processing, manufacturing, 1.5%. Contractors (street and highway), 5%. Lodgings, 4% (5% in mountain lakes area). $1 recycling fee on new, used or retread tires.

(45) *Tex.* —MVs: Sales-use, 6.25%; 30-day (max.) rental, 10%; rental over 30 days, 6.25%. Sales of new manufactured homes, 5% of 65% of sales price. Boats and boat motors, 6.25% of total consideration paid. Fireworks, 2% of sales price. Emissions rdeduction plan surcharge on off-road heavy-duty diesel equipment, 2%. Hotel occupancy, 6%—county rates may apply.

FOOTNOTES to Chart ¶ 250 (corresponding to parenthetical numbers in chart): **(continued)**

(46) *Calif.* —7.25% rate is total of 6.25% state rate plus uniform 1% local rate. Added 0.25% – 1.25% transit-traffic taxes where applicable.

(47) Estimate-pay 50% monthly by 20h day of period if mo. state (excl. local) tax for past yr. avg. over $2500 for 3-mo. (min.).

(48) *Wyo.* —4% rate decreases to 3.5% on 7-1 in a yr. in which Governor certifies that statutory funding requirement is met.

(49) *Mass.* —Quarterly (4-20; 7-20; 10-20; next 1-20) if annual tax $101 – $1,200. Monthly by 20th if annual tax is over $1,200. Annually by next 1-20 if annual tax $100 (max.).

(50) *Tenn.* —Qtrly. by 25th if avg. under $200 for 12 consecutive mos. Aviation fuel dealers, qtrly. by 30th.

(51) Payments delinquent if envelope not post-marked 25th or not received before last business day of month. Quarterly payment allowed if estimated yearly tax liability $500 – $1,250; yearly if under $500 annually. If last yr. or estimated current yr. tax $100,000 (min.), prepay ½ of May tax or tax for 1st 15 days of June by 6 – 20. *(Ariz.).*

(52) *Utah.* —Fuel for domestic or residential use, 2%. Added 2.5% tax on motor vehicle rental for up to 30 days. Additional local taxes may apply. State rate on food and food ingredients is 1.75% (2.75% pre-1-1-2008).

(53) *Ill.* —1% reduced rate on specified food for human consumption off-site, drugs, and modifications to make MV useable for disabled person. Gasohol, 6.25% of sales price, 6% of 94% of transient lodging costs. 5% on auto rental use. Tire fee of $2 ($2.50 pre-1-1-2008) per tire sold.

(54) Users-purchasers pay use tax by 4-20, 7-20, 10-20 and 1-20. If monthly B&O tax not over $1,000, report, pay quarterly by 4-30, 7-31, 10-31 and 1-31 (but pay for May by 6-15); annually by 1-31 (upon request) if tax $200 max. annually.

(55) *Fla.* —Quarterly, if tax not over $1,000 for past 4 quarters; semiannually, if tax not over $500 for past 4 quarters.

(56) *N.Y.* Added 5% tax on passenger car rentals. Added 5% on entertainment or info. services received aurally, inclu. 800 and 900 telephone number service. Added 0.375% transit dist. tax in NYC, Dutchess, Nassau, Orange, Putnam, Rockland, Suffolk, and Westchester counties. In New York City (NYC), total state-local tax rate on transient lodging rental is 9% plus added tax ranging from 50¢ to $2 based on daily charge; NYC total state-local tax rate on passengers car rentals is 13.25%.

(57) *Minn.* —Monthly electronic filers report-pay by 20th. Report-pay tax quarterly if tax averages under $500 per month; annually by 2-5 if tax averages under $100 max. per month. Report-pay use tax for calendar yr. by fol. 4-15, if calendar yr. purchases under $18,500 and not required to hold sales tax permit.

(58) *Mont.* —3% on providing lodging for under 30 days and campgrounds (add'l to accommodations tax); 4% on base rental charge for vehicles rented up to 30 days; 3.75% on retail telecommunications services; 1% contractor's license fee on gross receipts from public contracts.

(59) Use tax: semiannually (1-15, 7-15) if tax for one mo. $50 max. If tax liability is $2,500 per mo. or more, report, pay monthly by 20th. *(Okla.)*

(60) *Vt.* —Meals & rooms tax, 9%; alcoholic beverages, 10%. Exempts 40% of receipts from mobile home and modular housing sales. Specified fuels tax—eff thru 6-30-2008, added 0.5% on heating oil and kerosene (non-MV), propane, natural gas, electricity, and coal sales over $10,000 per yr. Motor vehicles, 6%. Short-term rentals of pleasure vehicles: 7%. Telecommunications services, 6%.

(61) If monthly tax under $50, pay annually by Jan. 20.

(62) *Wash.* —Added 5.9% tax on car rental (30-day max.).

(63) *Ida.* —Sellers or persons who owe $600 or less per quarter and have a satisfactory record of timely filing and payment can request permission to flie quarterly or semi-annually instead of monthly. Sellers or persons who have seasonal activities can request permission to file annually. Others may be allowed to file quarterly, semi-annually, or annually.

(64) *N.C.* —Pay tax twice a month if tax more than $10,000 per mo. And file return on a monthly basis by 25th and 10th of following month. Sales-use tax is payable when return is due. Taxpayers who are consistently liable for at least $10,000 a mo. must make monthly prepayments for next month's tax liability. Prepayment must equal at least 65% of any of the following: amount of tax due for current month; amount of tax due for same month in preceding year; or average monthly amount of tax due in preceding calendar year.

(65) Tax rate must be applied to the sale price of item.

(66) Total state plus Atlantic City Luxury Tax rate is 13%; 10% on alcoholic beverages sold by the drink in Atlantic City.

(67) *Wash.* —Leasehold excise tax on rental value of government property leased to private lessees, 12% plus 7% surtax. Sales of spirits and beer in original package taxed at 15% (10% to class H licensees) plus 14% surtax. Added taxes on retail sale of spirits except to Class H licensees: $1.72 per liter, plus 3.4% of selling price, plus 41¢ per liter. Added taxes on retail sale of spirits to Class H licensees: $1.72 per liter, plus 2.3% of selling price, plus 41¢ per liter.

(68) *Me.*—Service provider tax, 5%. Transient lodging, 7%. Car rental (under 1-yr.), 10% (includes certain loaner vehicles). Liquor sold at place licensed for on-site liquor consumption, 7%. 7% on all food prepared by a retailer. Added $1 per new tire.

(69) *Minn.* —9.2% on auto, van, or pickup truck lease or rental (28-day max.). Cigarette sales tax of 6.5% of weighted average retail price is imposed. Liquor gross receipts tax of 2.5% imposed on retail sales in-state of intoxicating liquor and beverages containing intoxicating liquor and 3.2% malt liquor.

(70) *Okla.* —3.25% tax on aircraft, vessels, and MVs. 6% on MV rental up to 90 days. All-terrain vehicles and motorcycles used off-road, 4.5%.

FOOTNOTES to Chart ¶ 250 (corresponding to parenthetical numbers in chart): **(continued)**

(71) *Kan.* —Total tax over $32,000 in any calendar year, file return for first 15 days of each month by the 25th day of that month, balance for that month due with return for such month.

(72) *Mich.* —Electricity, natural gas, and home heating fuel for residential use, 4%. Airport parking in 5 mi. of regional airport, 27%.

(73) *S.C.* —$300 Max. tax on aircraft, MV, motorcycle, boat, light constr. equip., RV, trailer, semitrailer, musical instrument or office equip. sold to religious org. for its exempt purpose; and research and development machy. 10% tax on proceeds from providing "900" or "976" telephone service; 5% surcharge on car rentals (31-day max.). Mfd. homes, 5% tax on 65% of price; max. tax, $300 plus 2% of 65% of price over $6,000; max. if energy standards met, $300 max. tax. 3% on heavy equipment rentals. 5.5% on durable medical equipment and supplies.

(74) *N.D.* —Monthly by last day if tax for prior year $333,000 min, but in odd-numbered yrs. pay May tax by 6-22. If tax drops below $333,000 in a later year, retailer has option of returning to quarterly filing.

(75) *Utah.* —If past yr. state-local tax was $50,000 (min.), report-pay by last day of each month; do so by electronic funds transfer if past yr. state-local tax was $96,000 (min.)

(76) Pay estimated tax if state sales tax averages $1,000 (min) per month in prior calendar year; pay: 66⅔% of (a) tax liability for same calendar month of preceding year or (b) current month's estimated tax, whichever is less.

(77) *Conn.* —Transient lodging, 12%. MV generally, 6%, MV sold to nonresident US military members or their spouses stationed in-state, 4.5%. Added 3% surcharge plus $1 per day tax on MV rental (30-day max.). Modular and prefabricated houses are taxed at 6% of 70% of mfg. price. 3% on sales of media advertising and cooperative direct mail advertising. Added 1.5% surcharge on machinery rental.

(78) *Ind.* —Additional 4% on rentals of passenger cars for under 30 days. Added 25¢ on sale of new or new replacement tire.

(79) *R.I.* —If authorized, report-pay quarterly (1-31, 4-30, 7-31, 10-31) if monthly tax under $200 for 6 consecutive mos. Monthly filers report, pay by 20th. MV rental surcharge report date set annually by Tax Admin. (no later than 2-15).

(80) *Ark.* —Tax on food and food ingredients is 3%. Added 3% tax on liquor, cordials, specialties, wines; added 3% tax on alcoholic beverages for consumption on premises; added 3% tax on beer sold for off-premises consumption; 10% supp. tax on private clubs' mixed drinks, wine or beer, and sales by mixed drink permit holders. Added 2% on tourist attraction admissions, campground fees, condominium or room rentals to transients, and boat-lifejacket-paddle-water ski rentals. Added 1% tax on short-term personalty rental, (not MV, commercial diesel truck, farm machy-equip.). Added 6% tax on short-term rental of licensed motor vehicles. 1.5% tax is imposed on long-term (30-day or longer) rentals of licensed motor vehicles (not specified diesel trucks or farm machy-equip.). Tax on sales of electricity and natural gas to certain manufacturers is 4.375% (3.875% eff 7-1-2008). Waste tire tax of $2 per automobile tire or truck tire plus additional $3 per truck tire. Tax of 6% on vending machine operators in lieu of state and local gross receipts (sales-use) tax.

(81) *N.D.* —New farm machinery, new agricultural irrigation equip., mobile homes, 3%. Alcoholic beverages, 7%. Mfg. machy-equipment for new or expanding plant, no tax. Natural gas, 2%.

(82) *Ark.* —If averaging net sales over $200,000 per month for past cal. yr., pay bimonthly by 12th of accrual month 40% of tax on monthly avg. net sales; 40% by 24th; bal. by 20th of next month.

(83) *Ga.*—Motor fuel for highway use, see ¶ 285. Added $1 per new replacement tire.

(84) *Ky.*—If avg. monthly tax exceeds $10,000, by 25th of month for past 16th—15th period.

(85) *La.*—Intrastate telecommunication services, 3%. Interstate telecommunication services starting or ending in La. and billed to La. address: 2% eff for charges on bills dated up through 3-31-2016; 1% eff 4-1-2016. Added 3% tax eff thru 6-30-2012 on auto rentals (29-day and 8-passenger max.). Food for home consumption and residential use of natural gas, electricity, water, fuel, and gas are exempt from tax. Nonresidential steam and water are taxed at 3.8% thru 6-30-2009, and 1% eff 7-1-2009. Nonresidential electricity and natural gas are taxed at 3.3% thu 6-30-2009, and 1% eff. 7-1-2009. 4% tax eff. through 6-30-2009 and 1% tax eff 7-1-2009 applies to certain "exempt" items.

(86) *Kan.* —10% tax on liquor sold by club, caterer, or drinking establishment. Added 3.5% tax on MV rental up to 28 days. Added 25¢ per new tire sold. No tax on bldg-bridge-highway construction, and utility service needed for mfg., processing, mining, providing services, or irrigating commercial crops.

(87) *Vt.*—Quarterly (4-25, 7-25, 10-25, 1-15) if last calendar yr. tax $501—$2,499; or if 50% of sales for preceding yr. were sales of building materials to contractors for improvement of realty and sales were on credit for a credit period of at least 40 days. Annually, by 1-25, if last calendar yr. tax $500 or less. Meals-rooms tax—Report, pay quarterly by 25th of next month; pay monthly by 25th (23d of Feb.) if past yr. tax over $500. Specified fuels tax—pay quarterly as set by Dept. Tax.

(88) *Mass.* —5.7% on transient lodging.

(89) *S.D.* —If annual tax $1,000 (min.), report-pay monthly by 20th (last day of month if filing electronically). Electronic filers file by 23rd day of month and pay by second to last day of month.

(90) *N.J.* —3.5% on sales by qualified enterprise zone sellers and urban enterprise zone-impacted business district sellers and 6% fur clothing gross receipts tax.

(91) *Pa.*—Add 3% on MV rental over 29 days. Add $2 per day (or part) (29-day-max.) plus 2% per MV rental. Add $1 per new tire.

(92) *N.M.* —If tax averages under $200 per mo. and Dept. Tax & Rev. OK's, report-pay semiannually or quarterly by 25th of fol. mo.

(93) *Neb.* —$1 per ton of commercial fertilizer. Added 1% on transient lodging. Added 4.5% on private passenger MV rental up to 31 days. $1 per tire sold or attached to new MV.

FOOTNOTES to Chart ¶ 250 (corresponding to parenthetical numbers in chart):
(continued)

(94) *N.M.* —Added $2-per-day surcharge on rental of passenger MV (6-passenger max.) by fleet owner (5 MV min.) without driver for up to 6 mos.

(95) *Ariz.* —10.6% on passenger MV (15-passenger max.) rented (180-day max.).

(96) *R.I.* —Added 5% on transient lodging (30-day max.). Added 6% on MV rental (30-day max.). Local 1% tax on meals/beverages sold from eating/drinking establishments. 1% local hotel tax.

(97) *Ohio* — Added $1 per MV tire sold (eff thru 6-30-2011).

(98) *Wyo.* —Added 4% on rental of passenger MV, or U-Drive-It MV, under 30 days.

(99) *Nev.* —2% on transient lodging, 6% on short-term passenger car rental. Live entertainment tax of 10% of admission charge to facility with less than 7,500 seating plus 10% of any amounts paid for food, refreshments and merchandise bought at facility; 5% of admission charge to facility with 7,500 or more seating.

(100) *Mo.*—Tax on food is 1.225% (1% basic rate, plus 0.1% parks and soil and water conservation and 0.125% wildlife conservation taxes).

(101) (Reserved.)

(102) *Mich.*— Electronic funds filers must pay 50% of tax by 20th day of the month and the balance by the last day of the month.

(103) (Reserved.)

(104) *Iowa* —5% tax is imposed on 60% of purchase price of mobile homes and modular homes and on 60% of purchase price or installed purchase price of manufactured housing. Direct permit holders or applicants can ask Dept. of Rev. to make negotiated rate agreements with them.

(105) *N.H.* —8% tax on the gross rental receipts is imposed on MV rentals for a period of 180 days or less.

(106) State imposes vehicle rental tax of 10% of the total fees and costs charged for leasing or renting passenger vehicles and 3% for leasing or renting recreational vehicles. Excise tax of $46 per voyage on passengers traveling on commercial passenger vessels that provide overnight accommodations in Alaska marine waters. (Alaska.)

OUT-OF-STATE SELLERS—DUTY TO COLLECT TAX

¶251 Collection by out-of-state sellers. Retailers who sell tangible personalty for use or consumption within a state must collect the use tax if their selling activities come within the statutory requirements set by the state and those statutory requirements do not run afoul of the federal or state constitutions. Use tax statutes specify when the use tax must be collected. A common approach is to make all retailers "engaged in business" or "doing business" in the state liable for collection of the state's use tax. "Engaged in business," "doing business," or similar terms are regularly defined. The definitions usually include certain elements or activities that may connect the out-of-state retailer with the state and make use tax collection necessary. These elements may be such things as:

Advertising: Ala. Ark. Colo. Conn. Fla. Ill. Iowa Kan. Minn. Mo. Neb. Nev. N.J. N.M. N.Y. N.C. N.D. Okla. Pa. R.I. S.C. S.D. (S.D. only requires seller to name buyer) Tenn. Tex. Utah Vt. Va. Wyo. (but see comment below)

Canvassing: Ala. Ariz. Ark. Calif. Colo. Conn. D.C. Ida. Ind. Iowa Kan. Ky. Md. Mass. Mich. Minn. Miss. Mo. Neb. Nev. N.J. N.M. N.Y. N.C. N.D. Ohio Okla. R.I. S.D. Tenn. Tex. Utah W.Va. Wis. Wyo.

Catalog distribution: Ala. Colo. Conn. Fla. Ill. Kan. La. Minn. Miss. Mo. N.J. N.Y. N.C. N.D. Okla. Pa. R.I. S.C. Tex. Utah Vt. Va. Wyo. (but see comment below)

Consigning: Ark. Ind. Me. Mo. N.J. N.C.

Delivering: Ark. Colo. Conn. D.C. Ga. Ida. Ind. (not common carrier or parcel post) Ky. La. Md. (Miller case holds mere delivery not enough in Md.) Mass. Mich. (not common carrier) Minn. Mo. Nev. N.J. N.M. N.Y. (not common carrier) N.C. Ohio (not common carrier) R.I. S.C. S.D. Tenn. Tex. Utah Vt. Va. W.Va. Wis. (not common carrier) Wyo.

Distribution house or Distributing: Ala. Ark. Calif. Colo. Conn. D.C. Fla. Ga. (not common carrier) Ida. Ill. Ind. Iowa Kan. Ky. La. Me. Md. Mich. Minn. Miss. Mo. Neb. Nev. N.J. N.M. N.Y. N.C. N.D. Ohio Okla. Pa. R.I. S.D. Tenn. Tex. Utah Va. W.Va. Wis. Wyo.

Hawking: Ark. Ind. Mo.

Mail order sales: Ala. Ariz. Calif. Colo. Conn. Fla. Ill. Iowa Kan. Ky. La. Miss. Mo. Neb. Nev. N.Y. N.C. N.D. Okla. S.C. S.D. (seller only required to name buyer) Tenn. Tex. Utah Vt. Va. Wyo. have laws requiring out-of-state sellers by mail order to collect use tax. To the extent that these laws require collection by a mail order seller without a physical presence in the state, they are unenforceable because of the U.S. Supreme Court decision in *Quill v. N.D. (1992) 504 US 298, 112 SCt 1904, 119 LEd2d 91*. In *Quill,* the U.S. Supreme Court held that a mail order seller with economic presence but without physical presence in a taxing state lacks the substantial connection or nexus needed under the Commerce Clause for collection liability. The High Court said that the U.S. Congress has the ultimate power to resolve the issue of the precise use tax collection burdens to be placed on interstate mail order sellers. Congress can decide whether, when, and to what extent the states can burden interstate mail order sellers with a duty to collect use taxes. Congress has yet to act on proposed federal legislation. Texas has language in its laws saying that out-of-state mail order sellers will have to collect its use tax when the U.S. Congress passes federal legislation allowing states to require such collection.

Motor vehicle use: Ark. Iowa (trucker) Kan. (trucker) Minn. (trucker) N.C. (trucker) N.D. (trucker) Okla. (trucker) R.I. (trucker) S.D. (trucker) W.Va. (trucker) Wyo. (trucker).

Peddling: Ala., Ariz. Ark. Conn. D.C. Ida. Ind. Iowa Kan. Ky. Md. Mass. Mich. Miss. Mo. Neb. Nev. N.J. N.Y. N.C. N.D. Ohio Okla. R.I. S.D. Utah W.Va. Wis. Wyo.

Sales or sample room: Ala. Calif. Colo. Conn. D.C. Ida. Ill. Ind. Iowa Kan. Me. Md. Mich. Minn. Miss. Neb. Nev. N.J. N.Y. N.C. Ohio R.I. S.D. Tenn. Utah Vt. Wash. W.Va. Wyo.

Storing: Ala. Calif. Conn. D.C. Fla. Ida. Ind. Ky. Me. Md. Mich. Mo. Neb. Nev. N.J. N.M. N.Y. N.C. Ohio Okla. R.I. S.C. Tenn. Tex. Utah Va. Wash. W.Va. Wis. Wyo.

Warehousing: Ala. Calif. Colo. Conn. D.C. Fla. Ga. Ida. Ill. Ind. Iowa Kan. Ky. La. Me. Md. Mich. Miss. Neb. Nev. N.J. N.C. N.D. N.M. N.Y. Ohio Okla. Pa. R.I. S.C. S.D. Tenn. Tex. Utah Va. Wash. W.Va. Wis. Wyo.

Computer company providing in-state repair services: According to Multistate Tax Commission Bulletin NB 95-1, these states require their use tax to be collected by out-of-state direct marketing computer companies providing warranty repair services to in-state customers: Ala. Ariz. Ark. Colo. Conn. D.C. Fla. Haw. Ida. Kan. Md. Mich. Minn. Mo. Neb. N.J. N.M. N.D. Tex. Utah. and Wash. Calif. asked the MTC to delete its name from this list.

➽ **PROTECTED AREAS→** *Catalog distribution—collection nexus target.* Can states compel foreign mail-order sellers to collect consumer use taxes simply by supplying the local market by mail from across state lines? This would violate the Fed Commerce and Due Process clauses, said the Ala. Supreme Court [*Lane Bryant*]. Distributing catalogs to, and receiving orders from, such customers by mail are exclusively interstate transactions. *Occasional local delivery and non-local advertising* have also been protected by the U.S. Supreme Court [*Miller Bros.*], but courts in states like N.J. have held that occasional local delivery would be enough to support use tax collection requirement.

In 1967, the U.S. Supreme Court handed down a decision of far-reaching importance to companies selling across state lines. It held that a state cannot compel an out-of-state seller to collect its use tax when the seller has only 2 contacts with the state: (1) *It mails in catalogs or flyers and (2) it uses the mail or common carriers to deliver* the ordered goods. [*National Bellas Hess.*] The sharp distinction which these and other decisions have drawn between mail order sellers with retail outlets, solicitors, or property within a State and those who do no more than communicate with customers in the State by mail or common carrier as part of a general interstate business is a valid one and the Court declined to obliterate it. The Supreme Court reiterated this holding in 1992 [*Quill*]. But an out-of-state seller must collect tax if it maintains an office in-state though the office is unrelated to its mail order business [*National Geographic*].

Exploitation of market. If mail order sellers are engaged in any activity other than the protected activity, they are required to collect tax. Many states require mail order sellers to collect use tax if they regularly or systematically exploit the in-state market. But the U.S. Supreme Court *Quill* case has held that a mail-order seller with economic presence but without in-state physical presence lacks substantial nexus needed under the Commerce Clause for collection liability.

Nexus (taxable connection) elements. The chart below summarizes the jurisdictional elements that may require out-of-state sellers to collect tax.

S means sales tax * means use tax				
STATE	AGENT IN STATE (8)	PLACE OF BUSINESS IN STATE (10)	TITLE PASSING IN STATE (18)	OTHER
Ala.	★(4)	★		★(1,11,12,23,25)
Alaska				(9)
Ariz.	★	★		★(2,25,26)
Ark.	★	S	★(3)	★(11,17,36)
Calif.	★	★(3)		★(7,25,26)
Colo.	★	★		★(12,13)
Conn.	★	★(3)	★(3)	S(4,11,12,13,26)
D.C.	★	★		★(3,17)
Fla.	S(5)	S(5)	S	S(5,11,12,25)
Ga.	★	★(3)		★(3,23)
Hawaii	★	★	★	★(4)

S means sales tax * means use tax				
STATE	AGENT IN STATE (8)	PLACE OF BUSINESS IN STATE (10)	TITLE PASSING IN STATE (18)	OTHER
Idaho	★	★		★(20,22,26,38,39)
Ill.	★	★(3,24)		★(11,12,24,25,26)
Ind.	★	★		★(26)
Iowa	★	★		★(14)
Kan.	★	★		★(6,11,12,23,40)
Ky.	★	★		★(19,23,26)
La.	S(5)	S(5)	S(5)	S(5,14,30)
Me.	S	S		★(31)
Md.	★	★		★(16)
Mass.	★(4)	★	★	★(5,17,19,26)
Mich.	★	★	★(3)	★(23,33)

S means sales tax * means use tax

STATE	AGENT IN STATE (8)	PLACE OF BUSINESS IN STATE (10)	TITLE PASSING IN STATE (18)	OTHER
Minn.	★	★		★(6,11,26)
Miss.	★	★		★(13,30)
Mo.	★	★	S	★(11,13,25)
Neb.	★	★(3)		★(4,8,23,25)
Nev.	★	★(3)		★(4,16,19,23,25,26)
N.J.	★	★	★(3)	★(4,5,8,11)
N.M.	★	★		★(8,11,19)
N.Y.	★(3)	★(3,35)	★(3)	★(5,7,12,14,16,34)
N.C.	★	★(3)		★(19)
N.D.	★	★	★	★(11,13,14,17,25)
Ohio	★(3)	★(3)	★(3)	★(7,8,23,28,29,34,37)
Okla.	★	★(3)	★	★(11,13,25)
Pa.	★	★		★(11,12,17)
R.I.	★(3)	★(5)	★(3)	★(6,11,12, 16,19,23,26)
S.C.	★(3)	★(3)		★(1,11,12,25,26)
S.D.	★	★(3)		★(14)
Tenn.	S(5)	S(5)	★(3)	S(5,6,11,12,16,25,32)
Tex.	★	★		★(11,16,19, 23,25,26,27)
Utah	★	★		★(7,20,22,30)
Vt.	S(5)	S(5)		★(11,12,23) (27)
Va.	★(3)	★(3)		★(5,6,7,11,25)
Wash.	★	★		★(20,26)
W.Va.	★	★		★(6,14,16,23)
Wis.	★	★		★(16,19,23)
Wyo.	★	★		★(11,12,16,26)

Notes to chart (corresponding to parenthetical numbers in chart):

(1) Qualification in state.
(2) Delivery through local dealer.
(3) Alternative: sales tax liability also.
(4) If *any* agent or representative involved in taxable sale.
(5) Sales tax embodies use tax features; liability broad.
(6) If seller maintains warehouse or is qualified to do business.
(7) Regular delivery in-state other than by common carrier. In N.Y., 12 deliveries in preceding 4 quarters creates presumption of regular delivery.
(8) Means salesmen and similar representatives.
(9) No state tax imposed; but sales taxes are imposed by localities.
(10) Even though unrelated to selling business.
(11) Advertising in the state (but see comment on "protected areas").
(12) Catalog sales in the state (but see comment on "protected areas").
(13) Mail order sales (but see comment on "protected areas").
(14) Delivery vehicles used in the state.
(15) In-state property, liens on property and choses in action (debts and claims).
(16) Statute requires collection on "deliveries" in the state.
(17) Any activity connected with sale or delivery.
(18) Title passage must be coupled with seller's receiving local benefits and protection on some other activity in-state other than in a "protected area."
(19) Any business activity in-state.
(20) Local stock of goods maintained.
(21) Continuous presence of nonsoliciting employee or making regular (or frequent) deliveries in-state thru employees or agents.
(22) Regular leasing or servicing in-state.
(23) Renting or leasing tangible personalty.
(24) Includes engaging in activities in Ill. that would constitute maintaining place of business in retailer's state of domicile.
(25) Soliciting orders in state by advertising or mail (mail only in Ala.) if regular-systematic plus if deriving benefits (financial-marketing-debt collection); having franchisee-licensee; or in Neb., parent controlling retailers required to collect tax.
(26) Regular-systematic soliciting orders in state through bank, media, service, or facility in state; in Conn., Ill., Ind., and Minn. through media in state; in Ky. also if benefit from agent operating in-state under retailer's name to repair or service items sold by retailer; in Wyo. through media or communication system by 3 or more separate transmittances of ad or ads in any 12-month period in consumer market in state. But Conn. and Wash. revenue departments won't require out-of-state sellers with only "economic presence" in-state to collect use tax.
(27) To extent authorized by Fed law.
(28) Engages in continuing and widespread solicitation of or otherwise purposely directs business activities at in-state residents, and has "substantial nexus" including physical presence of member of affiliated group or is registered-licensed in-state.
(29) Owns, rents, leases, maintains or has the right to use and uses tangible personal or real property that is physically located in-state. Also if registered or licensed to do business in-state.
(30) Regular-systematic soliciting orders in-state by advertising (print, radio, TV) or by mail, telephone, computer data base, or other communication system.
(31) Having "substantial physical presence" in-state that would satisfy Due Process and Commerce Clauses of U.S. Constitution.
(32) Out-of-state vendors with no locations in Tenn. may collect at uniform local rate.
(33) Employee resident or temporarily in-state for 2 days; owning, renting, leasing, using or maintaining in-state office or place of business, including agents, representatives, independent contractors or others acting on out-of-state seller's behalf and used in representing seller; agents, representatives, independent contractors, brokers acting on out-of-state seller's behalf, regularly and systematically present in-state conducting activities to establish or maintain the market for the seller, whether or not residing in-state.
(34) Sales of services performed in-state; repair services performed in-state on property sold to person in-state.
(35) Must also make sales of taxable items or services in-state. Place of business includes maintenance by vendor or its subsidiary in-state of a store, sales room, sample room, showroom, distribution center, warehouse, service center, factory, credit and collection office, administrative office, or research facility. But exemption for fulfillment services by unaffiliated person.
(36) Out-of-state vendors must collect use tax if they have affiliated retailer with in-state sales locations that either sells the same/similar goods or advertises (or promotes) sales to vendors' customers in-state. Affiliation requirement is satisfied if out-of-state vendors hold a substantial ownership interest (directly or through a subsidiary) in the retailer maintaining sales locations in-state, or are owned by the in-state retailer (or by parent or subsidiary). (Ark.)

Notes to chart (corresponding to parenthetical numbers in chart):
(continued)

(37) Out-of-state vendor must collect tax if it has tangible personalty temporarily in-state more than 7 days (need *not* be consecutive), or more than 7 instances of nexus-creating activities, and more than $25,000 in gross sales in-state in the same calendar yr. (Ohio).

(38) Recurring solicitation of purchases from residents of the taxing state or otherwise purposefully directing business activities at residents of the taxing state, and sufficient contact with the taxing state, in accord with the U.S. Constitution to require the seller to collect the taxing state's tax on sales to customers in the taxing state.

(39) Franchisee or licensee operating under seller's name and required to collect taxing state's tax.

(40) Retailer is doing business in Kan. if it has any contact with Kan. that would allow Kan. to require the retailer to collect and remit tax under Fed laws and U.S. Constitution. (Kan.)

SALES-USE TAXES—TAXABILITY OF SPECIFIC TRANSACTIONS—PART I

¶253 Conditional or credit sales, barter, rentals, trade-ins, repossessed property, casual or isolated sales.

	T = taxable E = exempt					
STATE	CONDITIONAL AND CREDIT SALES	BARTER EX-CHANGE	LEASE OR RENTAL (43)	SALE OF TRADE INS OR USED PROPERTY	SALE OF REPOSSESSED PROPERTY	CASUAL OR ISOLATED SALES (63)
Ala.	T	T	T(39,43,46)	T	T(11)	E(20,25)
Ariz.	T(6)	T	T(42,43,47) (48,67,82)	E	T	E(25)
Ark.	T	T	T(43,50,79)	T(16)	T	E(20,25)
Calif.	T(5)	T	T(12,52)	T	T	E(29,28,53) (55,69)
Colo.	T(3,85)	T	E(12,19,43)	T(96)	T	T(11,84)
Conn.	T	T	T(43,46)	T	T	E(20,53,55)
D.C.	T	T	T(43,47)	T(11)	T(11)	E(25,99)
Fla.	T	T	T(12,26,43) (47,54,74)	E(31)	T(98)	E(20,25)
Ga.	T(1)	T	T(43,46,64)	T	T	E(33)
Haw.	T(44)	T	T(43,83)	E(17,37)	T(44)	E(33)
Ida.	T	T	T(43)	T	T	E(18,20,28) (80)
Ill.	T(1)	T(11)	T(19,43,49)	T	T(23)	E
Ind.	T	E(41)	T(43,46)	T(90)	T(11)	E(20)
Iowa	T	T	T(35,43,46,94)	T(11)	T	E(20,65)
Kan.	T(1,4)	T	T(21,25,43)	E(89)	T(71)	E(20,53,55)
Ky.	T(1)	T	T(32,43,47)	T(11)	T	E(28,61)
La.	T	T	T(27,43,50)	T	T	E(20)
Me.	T	T	E(10,12,43) (46,49,101)	T(91)	T	E(20,40,53,100)
Md.	T	T	T(43,51)	T(81)	T(11)	E(36,53)
Mass.	T	T	T(24)	T	T(11)	E(20)
Mich.	T	T	T(24,43,97)	T	T(11)	E(20,25,55)
Minn.	T	T	T(43)	E	T(11)	E(25)
Miss.	T(6)	T	T	T	T(71)	E(20)

STATE	T = taxable E = exempt CONDI-TIONAL AND CREDIT SALES	BARTER EX-CHANGE	LEASE OR RENTAL (43)	SALE OF TRADE INS OR USED PROPER-TY	SALE OF REPOS-SESSED PROPER-TY	CASUAL OR ISO-LATED SALES (63)
Mo.	T(4)	T	T(19,21,24) (43,48,50)	T	T	E(13)
Neb.	T(1)	T	T(43,46,48) (57)	T	T	T(53,65,77)
Nev.	T(5)	T	E(10)	T	T(11)	E(28)
N.J.	T(92)	T	T(43,46)	T(86)	T(11)	E(88)
N.M.	T(2)	T	T(12,49,58)	T(11)	T(11)	E
N.Y.	T	T	T(43,48,49)	T	T	T(20,53,65,77)
N.C.	T(6)	T	T(12,43,47)	T	E(17)	E(25)
N.D.	T(3)	T	T(12,43,46) (50)	T(68)	T	E(25)
Ohio	T(5)	T	T(2,43)	T(11)	T(11)	E(20,62)
Okla.	T	T	T(12,43,50)	T	T	T(11)
Pa.	T	T	T(43)	T	T	E(20)
R.I.	T(11)	T	T(24,43)	T(76)	T(11)	E(20,53,55) (60)
S.C.	T(2)	T	T(12,43,46)	E	T	E
S.D.	T(3)	T	T(43,58,59)	T	T	E(25)
Tenn.	T(5)	T	T(14,29,43) (47)	E	T	E(20,55)
Tex.	T(7,85)	T	T(12,43)	T(102)	T	E(28)
Utah	T	E	T(19,43) (46,103)	T(96)	T	E(20,25)
Vt.	T	T	T(43)	T(11,96)	T	E(20,40)
Va.	T(5)	T	T(42,43)	T	T	E
Wash. (Sales-use)	T(2)	T	T(15,43)	E	T	E(44)
(Bus. & Occup.)	T(3)	T	T	T	T	E
W.Va.	T(3)	T	T	T(11)	T	E
Wis.	T(5)	T	T(15,43,46)	T(11)	T	E(20,25,53) (55)
Wyo.	T(1)	T(75)	T(12,26,43)	T	E(93)	T(78)

FOOTNOTES to chart ¶ 253:

(1) Tax due on payments as received. In Ill, if not using gross sales method; in Ga., Kans., Ky., Neb. if not on accrual method. In Wyo., when title passes at future date.

(2) Seller may pay full tax on sale, or portion on payments as received. In S.C., only on conditional and installment (UCC) sales.

FOOTNOTES to chart ¶ 253: (continued)

(3) On conditional sales extending over 60 days, tax due on payments received.
(4) Tax payable on total price if sale covered by notes or assignable contract or mortgage.
(5) Entirely taxable when sale made.
(6) State may grant application to report on basis of actual receipts.
(7) Retailer may collect and remit full tax on sale, or portion on payments when due.
(8) No specific provision as to manner of payment of tax.
(9) Of like kind unless "boot" received, or property used in lieu of cash.
(10) Taxable if in lieu of sale, or property substantially consumed during lease.
(11) No specific general provision; probable status shown.
(12) Tax measured by rentals paid.
(13) Casual sales exempt: $3,000 (max.) in *Mo.*
(14) Taxable in lump sum at time of execution, or periodically as per contract.
(15) Tax payable on rentals as due.
(16) Exempts value of MV, trailer, semitrailer, house trailer, mobile home, and airplane traded in *(Ark.)*.
(17) Exempt if full tax is paid on total sale price of new article.
(18) Exempt yard sales: 2 sales a year in *Ida.*
(19) Taxable if in lieu of outright sale. In *Colo.*, any right to the continuous possession or use of tangible personalty for 3 yrs. or less under a lease or contract isn't taxed if the lessor paid sales tax when the item was acquired.
(20) Taxable despite being casual sales: *MVs and/or aircraft* in Conn., Fla., Ind., Iowa, La., Me., Mass., Mich., Miss., Neb., R.I. *Aircraft and vessels,* Calif., Ida., Tenn. *MVs, motor boats, trailers and manufactured homes* in Ala. *Boats & vessels* in Conn., Ind., Me. (not to corp. by majority stockholder). *MVs, off-road MVs, mobile homes and commercial coaches* in Calif. *MVs and trailers* in Kan. *Trailers* in Mass., Pa.; *nonresidential trailers*, R.I.; *watercraft and outboard* motors needing title certificate, Ohio; *all purpose MVs, snowmobiles* in Ohio; *mobile homes or housetrailers* in Tenn. *Snowmobiles,* Conn. and Mich.; *aircraft,* Ind. *Boats & snowmobiles* in N.Y. *Aircraft, snowmobiles, motorboats, and vessels over 16 ft. long* in Vt. *Boats, MV's, aircraft & mobile homes* in Fla. *Aircraft, special mobile equip. and livestock trailer,* Me. *Vehicles or vessels* needing registration in Utah. *Aircraft, boats, snowmobiles, all-terrain vehicles, and off-road motorcycles* in Ida. *Off-road MVs, manufactured housing, and watercraft* in Mich. *Aircraft and watercraft* needing titling, licensing, or registration in Ind.; *MVs, trailers, semitrailers, mobile homes or airplanes* in Ark. *MVs, trailers, semi-trailers, motor boats, aircraft* and similar items requiring registration, *Pa.* In some states, applies to MVs and like requiring Fed or state registration.
(21) Exempts rentals of movie film-sound transcripts to theatres. Also exempt in Kan. (refund), machinery leased from municipalities.
(22) If gross receipts from sale of tangible personalty are exempt, the gross receipts from the lease/rental of the property will also be exempt. *(Kan.)*.
(23) Finance company exempt when sells as agent for owner.
(24) Lessor (of MVs in Mo.) may be allowed to base tax on rentals, instead of acquisition cost—in some states if only rental use while held for resale.
(25) But taxable if seller holds himself or herself out as engaged in retail business.
(26) Demurrage charges exempt *(Fla.)*. *Wyo.* exempts demurrage charges on returnable bottles in which certain gaseous products are sold.
(27) *La.*—Exempts planes and equip. leased-rented by commuter airline domiciled in-state. Tax on lease or rental of manufacturing, farming, and timbering machinery and equipment is phased out in the period 7-1-2004—7-1-2010.
(28) More than two retail sales ("taxable sales" in Tex.) in 12-month period loses casual sale exemption.
(29) If rental is a regular business.
(30) Sale of used property other than trade-ins is taxable.
(31) *Fla.*—Trade-ins allowed by dealer are not included in sales price.
(32) Construction contractors pay tax on equipment rentals unless outstate lessor paid Ky. tax.
(33) Retailers' noninventory sales exempt. In Ga. if $500 (max.) in 12 months.
(34) Unless property or purchaser exempt.
(35) Taxed if equipment rentals.
(36) Taxable if $1,000 (min.) or made by auctioneer or other dealer.
(37) Exempt (use tax-exempt in Hawaii) if tax once paid on traded-in property.
(38) Taxable on sales price less credit for trade-in-applies to sales of new, trade-in or used property.
(39) Pollution control devices, nuclear fuel assemblies and intercorporate rentals are exempt. In *Ala.*, rentals of aircraft (including replacement parts, components, systems, sundries and supplies affixed or used on such aircraft and ground support equipment and vehicles used by or for the aircraft or by certified or licensed air carriers with qualifying in-state "hub operations"), film, docks and docking facilities, certain charges by landlord to tenant, certain medical equipment, sale/leasebacks, vessels or RR equipment engaged in interstate/foreign commerce, certain transportation equipment, demurrage charges, and charges to a lessee who leases for subleasing are exempt.
(40) Exempt isolated sale of items not regularly retailed by seller
(41) Like-kind exchange is exempt *(Ind.)*.
(42) Tangible personalty for future use for taxable lease is exempt.

FOOTNOTES to chart ¶ 253: (continued)

(43) Practically every state taxes transient hotel, etc., rentals; also many localities in some states. *Ind.* also taxes cubicle-space used for adult entertainment and rented for under 30 days in hotel, etc. *Conn.* exempts lodging at facility run by nonprofit if rent is exempt from Fed income tax, and campground space. *Wis.* exempts state park camping fees.

(44) Subject to use tax.

(45) Exempt when lessor retains possession.

(46) Certain film or videotape rentals are exempt if to show for fee. Also audio tapes, discs, records *(Ind.; Iowa)*. Rental of video media and equipment is taxable in *Me.* Rental of audio media and equipment and furniture under a rental-purchase agreement is taxable in *Me.*

(47) Exempt: rental of films and recordings to theaters, radio and TV stations. Tenn. also exempts parking privileges sold to students by colleges and tech schools. N.C. also exempts lease-rental of tobacco sheets for handling tobacco in and transporting it to-from warehouse.

(48) Rentals aren't taxable if rented item is exempt on sale.

(49) Tax on short-term renting of MVs. In *Ill.*, for one yr. or less. In *Me.*, includes certain loaner vehicles.

(50) Rentals exempt if tax paid by lessor on purchase, or title transfer. In *Ark.* exemption limited to leases and agreements for 30 days (min). In *Okla.*, exemption limited to 12-month (min.) MV leases.

(51) Rentals of mfg. machy-equip. and agricultural machinery if capitalized and long-term auto rentals are exempt *(Md.)*.

(52) Exempt: motion picture, TV films (not video cassettes videotapes-discs), tapes; linen service; household goods leased with living quarters; tax-paid goods leased same form as acquired (not video cassettes videotapes-discs); mobile transportation equipment; mobile homes (not local property taxed); rent under $20 if lease for one day at grantor's premises.

(53) Transfers in specified business reorganizations or transfers, or between corporation and specified stockholders exempt though items ordinarily taxed as exceptions to casual exemption (see (20) above).

(54) Taxable regardless of prior out-of-state use or out-of-state tax on purchase.

(55) Transfers between specified family members exempt though items ordinarily taxed as exceptions to casual sales exemption (see (20) above). In *NY*, applies only to MVs.

(56) Farm machy. rental use-tax exempt if no buy option (dealer-lessor is sales-taxed).

(57) Intercorporate or inter-family leases of previously sales-taxed items are exempt. In *Ariz.*, between parent and 80% owned sub.

(58) In *S.D.*, mobile home rentals exempt. In *N.M.* manufactured home rentals for 1 mo. (min.) are exempt.

(59) Exempt: vehicles rented for over 28 days (single contract).

(60) Nonexempt if more than five sales in 12-month period.

(61) Exempt if item sold not held or used in activity needing seller's license. First $500 of (a) garage-yard sale of household items, and (b) certain nonprofit organization fund-raising sales are exempt.

(62) Sales from auctioneer's permanent place (defined) of business are taxable.

(63) Footnote (20) exceptions from casual sale exemptions for vehicles, boats, and aircraft apply only in states having no separate general excise tax for registration or titling of such items. Some states exempting casual sales don't carry a footnote (20), yet vehicles and/or boats and aircraft may be taxed under separate general excise tax comparable in most respects to general sales-use tax.

(64) Leases or rentals between persons under common ownership (100%) exempt on previously taxed item (Ga.).

(65) Retailer's bulk sales are exempt *(Iowa; Neb.)*.

(66) Sale of used farm machy.-equipment exempt *(Kan.)*.

(67) Tax also applies to use or occupancy of realty. *Ariz.* exempts realty leased to board horses.

(68) Sales of used mobile homes are exempt if *N.D.* tax paid previously.

(69) Exempt if item sold not held or used in retailing.

(70) Taxable if item previously rented or leased in business.

(71) Generally exempt if repossessed by finance co. or banks.

(72) Exempt if tax paid on previous sale without credit deduction for used or trade in property. Exemption doesn't apply to used autos, used mobile home, used aircraft.

(73) (Reserved.)

(74) Exempt: leases of certain MVs (inclu. taxicabs and related equip. to independent operator) if tax paid on MV purchase *(Fla.)*.

(75) Exempt if between specified corporations or businesses; or in forming or liquidating businesses *(Wyo.)*.

(76) Sale of used textbook is exempt *(R.I.)*.

(77) Transfers of sales-taxed farm machy.-equip. (depreciable capital assets) are exempt *(Neb.)*.

(78) Exempt if made by religious or charitable orgs. *(Wyo.)*.

(79) Rental charges by TV-video-radio service providers are taxable; such charges to them are exempt. Exempts rentals of prescribed adaptive medical equip. Rentals of railroad rolling stock used to transport persons or property in interstate commerce are exempt *(Ark.)*.

(80) Exempts sale by religious org., if proceeds are used solely for its programs, and sale is not in open market in regular competition with for-profits *(Ida.)*.

(81) Exempts value of used component or part ("core value") received from buyers of remanufactured truck parts (air brake system, engine, rear axle carrier or transmission) *(Md.)*.

(82) Exempts realty leased or subleased by a licensed nursing care institution *(Ariz.)* Exempts leases of transportation facilities to private orgs. and tolls collected *(Ariz.)*.

FOOTNOTES to chart ¶ 253: (continued)

(83) Exempts realty leased by labor org. to labor org. or labor org. member service trust fund. Amounts from rental/leasing of certified aircraft or engines used for interstate or interisland air transportation of pasengers or goods is exempt. If property is subleased, a deduction of 87.5% is allowed the lessee who subleases property if the lease and sublease are in writing and any leases or subleases relate to the same realty. *(Haw.)*.

(84) Occasional sales by charities are exempt *(Colo.)*.

(85) Special provisions apply to seller-financed MV sales.

(86) Basis reduced for like kind trade-ins *(N.J.)*.

(87) Rental of furniture under a rental-purchase agreement is taxable. Certain vehicles and aircraft leased by nonresidents and intended to be driven out-of-state are exempt. *(Me.)*

(88) Does not include boats subject to N.J. Boat Act or motor vehicles *(N.J.)*.

(89) Credit allowed in report of gross receipts for amount equal to allowance given for trade in of property.

(90) Like kind exchange is exempt *(Ind.)*.

(91) Trade-in credit allowed for motor vehicles, farm tractors, watercraft, aircraft, livestock trailers, camper trailers, and special mobile equipment *(Me.)*.

(92) At time of sale.

(93) Where the seller has directly or indirectly paid sales or use tax on property *(Wyo.)*.

(94) Aircraft rental for a period over 60 days is exempt *(Iowa)*.

(95) Certain sales at private homes occurring less than 4 days per yr. and having total receipts of $600 or less are exempt *(N.Y.)*.

(96) Less trade-in allowances.

(97) No tax collected on rentals if sale-use tax has been paid by lessor when the property was bought. To make valid election, aircraft lessor must get use tax registration by date set for 1st payment of use tax under lease/rental agreement or 90 days after lessor 1st brings aircraft in-state, whichever earlier. *(Mich.)*.

(98) If dealer repossess tangible personalty that has been sold, dealer may take a credit or obtain a refund for tax paid by the dealer on the unpaid balance due the dealer. If the repossessed personalty is sold, it is taxable *(Fla.)*.

(99) Casual sales at charity auction or fundraiser held by nonprofit teaching hospital not more than 5 times a year are exempt *(D.C.)*.

(100) Casual sales do not include any transaction in which a retailer sells tangible personalty or a taxable servce on behalf of the owner of that property or provider of that service *(Me.)*.

(101) Tax is levied on all casual rentals of living quarters in a hotel, rooming house or tourist or trailer camp. This does not apply to rental of living quarters rented for less than 15 days in calendar year, except a person who owns and offers for rent more than one property in-state during calendar year is liable for collecting sales tax for each unit regardless of the number of days for which it is rented *(Me.)*.

(102) A presumptive value is established for determining the proper amount of motor vehicle sales tax due on private or casual motor vehicle sales transactions.

(103) Certain sale-leaseback transactions exempt *(Utah)*.

SALES-USE TAXES—TAXABILITY OF SPECIFIC TRANSACTIONS—PART II

¶254 Repairs, installation, sales to contractors, manufacturers, or repairers.

	T = taxable E = exempt					
STATE	REPAIR CHARGES	INSTALLATION SERVICE (5)	SALE OF MATERIALS TO CONTRACTORS (7,44)	SALE OF MATERIALS TO MANUFACTURERS, PRODUCERS, PROCESSORS (9)	SALE OF MATERIALS TO REPAIRERS (7)	SALE OF MACHINERY (29) TO CONTRACTORS, MANUFACTURERS, PRODUCERS
Ala.	E(1,2)	E(1)	T	E(15,23)	T(47)	T(30)
Ariz.	E	E	E(60)	E(15,132)	T	E(59)
Ark.	T(88,126)	E(126)	T(6)	E(18,106)	T	T(68,106)
Calif.	E(1,2)	E(1,2)	T(8,10,41)	E(15)	T(27)	T(135)
Colo.	E(1,2)	E(1,2)	T(48)	E(15,23)	T	E(98)
Conn.	T(133)	E(1)	T(50)	E(33,36,39,133)	T(27)	T(133)
D.C.	T	E(1)	T(32)	E(15,23)	E	T(4)
Fla.	T(92)	T	T(6)	E(15,19,106)	E(22)	T(68,106,120)
Ga.	E(1)	E(1)	T(110)	E(15,24)	T	T(68,89,110)
Haw.	T(144)	T	T(16)	T	T(144)	T
Idaho	E(1)	E(1)	T(87)	E(15,91)	T	E(61,84,90)
Ill.	E(1)	E(1)	T(32,136)	E(15,106)	E(8)	T(96)
Ind.	E	E(146)	T(102)	E(15,91,124)	T	E(134)
Iowa	T	E(107)	T(6,103)	E(15,42,79)	E(57)	E
Kan.	T(63)	T(63)	T(35)	E(15,91)	T	T(82,106,119)
Ky.	E(1)	E(1)	T	E(15,56,67,106)	T(116)	T(68,89,95)
La.	T(46)	E(1)	T(6)	E(111)	T(46)	T(97)
Me.	E(1)	E(1)	T(6,102,117,147)	E(19)	T	T(61,94)
Md.	E(1)	E(1)	T(49)	E(15,51)	T(52)	E(72)
Mass.	E(140)	E(140)	T(50)	E(33)	T	E(58,83)
Mich.	E(1,2)	E(1,2)	T(81,141)	E(15,23,80,85,106)	T	T(31,106)
Minn.	E(1)	T	T	E(23,61)	T	E(86,106,143)
Miss.	T(55)	T(55)	T	E(34,106)	T(4)	T(34,106,108)
Mo.	E(1,2)	E(1,2)	T	E(15,19)	T(8,27)	T(28,82)
Neb.	E(2,145)	E(129)	T(35,125)	E(15)	T(125)	T(68)
Nev.	E(1,2)	E(1,2)	T(41)	E(15)	T(27)	T

	T = taxable E = exempt					
STATE	**REPAIR CHARGES**	**INSTALLATION SERVICE** (5)	**SALE OF MATERIALS TO CONTRACTORS** (7,44)	**SALE OF MATERIALS TO MANUFACTURERS, PRODUCERS, PROCESSORS** (9)	**SALE OF MATERIALS TO REPAIRERS** (7)	**SALE OF MACHINERY** (29) **TO CONTRACTORS, MANUFACTURERS, PRODUCERS**
N.J.	T(93,131)	T(63)	T(35)	E(25,106)	E	E(134)
N.M.	T	T	T(53)	E(15,25,132)	T	T
N.Y.	T(45)	T(45)	T(77)	E(45,85)	E(57,77)	E(45)
N.C.	E(1,2)	E(1,2)	T	E(15,115)	E(22)	T(75)
N.D.	E(1)	E(1)	T(8)	E(15)	T(52)	T(130)
Ohio	T(148)	T(40,148)	T(48)	E(21,23)	E	E(21)
Okla.	E	E(1)	T(14,32)	E(127)	T	E(127)
Pa.	T(71)	T(71)	T(78)	E(21,33)	E	E(21)
R.I.	E(1,2)	E(1)	T(8,109)	E(15,91)	T(27)	T(58)
S.C.	E(1,2)	E(2)	T(87)	E(15,23,59)	T(52)	E(59,82)
S.D.	T	T	T	E(15)	E	T(137)
Tenn.	T(73)	T(73)	T(38)	E(19,100)	T(8)	E(100)
Tex.	T(12,123)	T	T(12)	E(15,25,91,122, 123,142)	T(52)	T(106,122)
Utah	T	T(40)	T(43,121)	E(15,113)	E(22)	E(113)
Vt.	T	T	T(78,138)	E(15,99,138)	T(78)	E(11,58,82)
Va.	T(1)	E(1)	T(87)	E(15,106)	E	E(3,106)
Wash. (Sales-use)	T	E(62)	E(15,112)	E	T	T
(Bus. & Occup.)	T	T	T	T	T	T
W. Va. (Sales)	T(128)	T	T	E	E(128)	E(84)
Wis.	T(19)	T(1,76)	T	E(15,91)	T(8)	E(58,74,82)
Wyo.	T(118)	T(1)	T(105)	E(15,23)	E(139)	E

FOOTNOTES to chart ¶ 254:

(1) Exempt when billed separately from materials. *D.C.* taxes installation charges for parts or materials that constitute repair of existing tangible personalty. *Ill.* exempts installation charges when separately contracted for. *Va.* exempts one-half of total charge for maintenance contract that provides both parts and labor. *Wyo.* exempts installation charge when separately stated and installation is to realty.

(2) Books must separately show receipts from sales and from services.

(3) Exemption applies to processor-lessor of laundered textile products *(Va.)*.

(4) No specific provisions: probable status shown.

(5) Charges which are mere incident to sale are usually taxable.

(6) Exempt if purchased for resale by contractor engaged in retail business.

(7) If sale to contractor or repairer is exempt, sale by him or her is taxable, and vice versa.

(8) Exempt if resale or exemption certificate given. In *N.Dak.* use tax applies unless sales or use tax previously paid.

(9) Producing tangible personalty for sale.

FOOTNOTES to chart ¶ 254: (continued)

(10) Fixtures are taxable on sale by contractor, not on sale to him.

(11) *Vt.*—Exempt if machy, for mfg. other machy., parts or supplies for mfg. process.

(12) Exempt if contractor furnishes materials and services under separate contracts. In *Tex.*., repair charges are exempt if repairs of aircraft, commercial ship, motor vehicles.

(13) Except some sales to fulfill contract with state or local government.

(14) Goods for use under local govts., public schools, colleges, contracts or outside U.S. are exempt *(Okla.)*

(15) If becoming an ingredient or component part of property manufactured. In *Ida.*, exemption includes disinfectants used in dairy industry to clean cow udders, pipes, vats, and other milking equip. and plants for farming business. In *Calif.*, exemption for ingredients-components of specified newspapers-periodicals is limited to newspapers-periodicals distributed for free or by-to specified nonprofits. In *Ga.*, exemption phased in for electricity used in manufacturing, if cost exceeds 100% of cost of all materials. In *Mich.* industrial processing exemption includes production or assembly; research or experimental activities; industrial processing-related engineering; inspection, quality control, or testing; planning, scheduling, supervision, or control of production or other exempt activities; design, construction, or maintenance of production or other exempt machinery, equipment, and tooling; remanufacturing; processing of production scrap and waste up to the point it is stored for removal from the plant of origin; recycling of used materials for ultimate sale at retail or reuse; production material handling; and storage of in-process materials.

(16) Goods exempt if consumed in scientific project for U.S. or agency.

(17) Whether or not article manufactured, produced or processed is changed in form.

(18) If becoming integral part of finished product. (Includes aluminum maker's electricity; steel maker's (or wall/floor tile mfr.'s) electricity-natural gas in Ark.) *Ark.* also exempts forms made from plaster, cardboard, fiberglass, natural fibers, synthetic fibers or composites, used to determine physical characteristics of personal property, and destroyed or consumed in mfg.

(19) If becoming part of product, or if used directly or consumed in mfg., processing, etc.

(20) To extent of charges for installing and applying personalty sold.

(21) Exemption for materials and certain equipment used or consumed directly in manufacturing, processing, mining, farming, utilities. In *Ohio*, exemption is limited to primary use in producing product to be sold or product to be used primarily to make sale product; adjuncts, packaging, labels, and certain safety items also exempt.

(22) If attached to or becomes a component part of property repaired or altered. Not applicable in *Fla.* when realty or combination of personalty and realty involved. Tool and equipment sales are taxable in N.C.

(23) Specified fuel used in manufacturing, etc., specifically exempt. *Wyo.* also exempts carbon dioxide and other gases used in tertiary (crude oil) production.

(24) Exempt: Industrial materials, items coated on or impregnated into product in mfg.; agricultural commodities as raw mfg. materials.

(25) Certain chemicals and reagents are exempt. In *N.J.* and *Tex.*, note (106) also applies. *N.J.*, see note (70).

(26) Except where repairer separately bills work and materials to consumer.

(27) When value of materials furnished by repairer is small part of repair charge.

(28) Replacement machinery and equipment used in manufacturing and fabricating as a result of design or product change and machinery and equipment used in new or expanding new manufacturing, mining or fabricating plants are exempt. In *Mo.* includes supplies and materials for machy. installation or construction.

(29) Refers to tools, machinery and equipment not becoming part of product.

(30) Lower rate for machines in mining, compounding, processing, mfg., farming.

(31) Exemption allowed for sale of tools, dies, patterns and machinery used directly in manufacturing process, and for equipment used in pumping and treating crude oil.

(32) Taxable if materials bought by contractor are converted into realty. In *DC* exempt if buyer is *DC* or U.S. or nonprofit. In *Ill.*, also taxable if bought for use or consumption.

(33) If becoming ingredient or component of goods to be sold, or if used or consumed in product to be sold or in farming, fishing, R & D (not in *Conn.*) or furnishing power and utility services.

(34) Preferential rates: 1.5% rate on sales of mfg. machy-equip. 1% rate on farm tractors. Bldg. materials, certain machy.-equip. for cos. qualifying under national-regional headquarters program are exempt. Note (108) also applies. *(Miss.)*

(35) Exempt if for governmental or nonprofit entity with exemption certificate. In *Kan.*, hospitals, schools, govts. (refunds for political subdivs.) and state correctional institutions. In *Neb.*, if contractor appointed as purchasing agent. In *N.J.*, also if to improve certain govt. financed housing projects.

(36) Exemption for fuel, material and tools used in fabricating finished product for sale or to furnish power and public utility services.

(37) Sales to cost-plus-fixed-fee contractors on U.S. projects exempt.

(38) Exempt if sold to U.S. or consumed in church, atomic or certain electrical plants or used in construction-installation of resource recovery facility producing steam or electricity.

(39) Must have life of less than 1 year or be deductible for Fed tax purposes.

(40) Exempt if separately billed, if installations of tangible personalty on realty. Exempt in Ohio if becoming part of realty.

(41) Exempt if for out-of-state construction contract.

(42) Exemption is allowed for sales of argon and similar gases for use in manufacturing process.

(43) Exempt if paid for direct by U.S., religious or charitable organizations and prescribed conditions met; or if tooling, support equip. for aerospace or electronics industry contract with U.S. and title vests in U.S.

FOOTNOTES to chart ¶ 254:
(continued)

(44) Exempt if contract makes contractor government agent and title passes directly from seller to U.S. This rule apparently applies in every jurisdiction.

(45) Exempts sales and servicing of machy. equipment and other items consumed or used for production purposes (including NYC) and maintenance repair for RR rolling stock. Tax credit or refund on items for constructing, expanding or rehabilitating industrial or commercial realty in economic development zone. Installation service is exempt if on tractors, trailers, or semitrailers. Eff. 12-1-2004, exemption also applies to repairs of certain aircraft and vessels.

(46) *La.*—An exemption applies to labor, materials, services, and supplies to repair, renovate, or convert drilling rigs and component-part machinery and equipment used solely for exploration or development of minerals outside La. territorial limits in Outer Continental Shelf waters.

(47) If materials lose identity in repaired products or consumed in repair.

(48) Exempt if for construction or repair of charitable, etc., institutions or in contracts with, U.S. or agency, or state or local government or on out-of-state realty. Also exempt in *Ohio*—bldg. materials and services for out-of-state realty if the other state would exempt those items if sold there.

(49) Unless for: some nonprofit organizations; resale by contractors principally reselling. (*Md.*).

(50) Exempt if contractor in business of selling materials or supplies. In *Mass.*, also if contractor renders service in connection with sale for added price, and also building materials and supplies used in constructing a building owned and used by a tax-exempt entity are also exempt.

(51) Exempt if consumed in 1 year; applies also to assemblers and refiners. Also exempt are items consumed in research and development.

(52) Unless for resale, or repairer sells under contract.

(53) Exempt if component or ingredient of taxable construction project.

(54) Exempt: machy. for new-expanded mfg.; farmer irrigation machy.

(55) Taxed according to class of business.

(56) Exempt property used in production, with useful life under 1 year.

(57) If purchased for resale.

(58) Exempt if used directly (just "used" in *R.I.*) in mfg., processing, refining or production. Includes R&D equip. and tools-supplies to repair-maintain farm equip. in *R.I.* Includes machinery, equipment, and prepress items used in the continuous production flow or process of manufacturing printed material to be sold in *Mass.*

(59) Exempt if used directly in manufacturing, processing, compounding, mining or quarrying. Also, R&D, job printing, metallurgical operations, or egg production in *Ariz.*

(60) If incorporated into project under contract.

(61) Exempt if used directly for production. Note (91) also applies in *Minn.*

(62) Contractor collects tax on transfer to consumer.

(63) Exempt if performed on inventory items; installation in original construction of bldg., construction-repair of bridge or highway. Charges for installation of flooring are taxable.

(64) Contractor purchases on resale certificate and charges tax on transfer to owner.

(65) Exempt if used to manufacture agricultural equipment or used in mining, etc.

(66) When insignificant compared to labor or other service charges.

(67) Special limit on energy-producing fuels.

(68) Machy. for new and expanded industry are exempt. In *Ark.* and *Ga.* if note (61) also applies. In *Fla.* if output upped by 10%, exempt from taxes exceeding $50,000 annually (refund; applies to items used under Fed procurement contracts); new business making purchase before production starts and delivery made in 1 year of purchase. In *Fla.*, mchy. for new business in spaceport activity is exempt. In *Ky.*, doesn't apply to repair-replacement-spare parts nor to replacement machy; machinery delivered out-of-state is exempt. In *Neb.* refund claim is needed. In *Ga.*, machy. bought to upgrade existing machy. in mfg. plant is exempt.

(69) Materials for construction contracts with U.S. are exempt.

(70) Exempt: machy., apparatus or equipment used (direct) in mfg., processing, assembling or refining. Exempt: newspaper production machy. Recycling equip. and cogeneration machy. (incl. bldg. materials.) also exempt in *NJ.*

(71) Exemption applies to charges by construction contractors for repairs or installations to real property. Charges for repairs to clothing or footwear are exempt. *(Pa.)*

(72) Farm vehicles and equipment and mfg. machy. and equipment are exempt.

(73) Applies if goods not becoming fixtures and fee charged for installation. Exempts repair-installation service labor on aircraft engine equip. and main frames, and RR tank car linings and protective coatings. Also exempts repair-installation of industrial machy, and repair of vessels (50-ton min.) used mainly in interstate-foreign commerce. *(Tenn.)*

(74) Exempt if used exclusively and directly by manufacturer.

(75) In N.C., mill machinery, parts and accessories sold to manufacturing industries and plants are exempt from sales-use tax but are subject to a privilege tax of 1% with a maximum tax of $80 per article.

(76) Exempt if price for capital improvements on realty.

(77) Exempt if for exempt entity construction, maintenance, repair or service, if integral component of structure, and if properly documented.

(78) Exempt if in project for state and U.S. govt., or charitable etc. institutions.

FOOTNOTES to chart ¶ 254:
(continued)

(79) Fuel for grain drying, husbandry implements generating electricity and reagents for mfg. are exempt. Newsprint and ink incorporated in newspapers, etc., are taxable. Farm (self-propelled implements or attachments) or industrial machy.-equip. and computers, incl. parts, get tax refund if bought or rented and used in processing. R&D or mfg. processes, meat packing or data processing-storage by insurance-financial cos. or commercial enterprise.

(80) Exempt: office equipment, including data processing equipment, used for an industrial activity; and machinery, equipment, or materials used within a plant site or between plant sites operated by the same person for moving personalty in the process of production. Taxable are: office equipment, including data processing equipment used for nonindustrial processing purposes; office furniture or office supplies; industrial processor's own product or finished good that it uses or consumes for purposes other than industrial processing; personalty used for receiving & storage of materials, supplies, parts, or components purchased by user or consumer; personalty used for receiving or storage of natural resources extracted by user or consumer; MVs; personalty used or consumed for preserving or maintaining finished goods once they first come to rest in finished goods inventory storage; and personalty used in producing computer software originally designed for the purchaser's exclusive use and special needs. *(Mich.)*.

(81) Exempt, if to construct nonprofit housing or hospitals.

(82) Farm machy. is exempt. In *S.C.*, $300 max. tax on R&D machy.

(83) Exempt if used directly in agricultural production, commercial fishing, broadcasting and manufacturing (incl. R&D). Exempt: patterns, molds, dies, tools, sandblasting equipment, machy. and parts for mfg. cast metal products.

(84) *Ida.*—Tangible personalty used exclusively in or to maintain the environment of a clean room is exempt.

(85) Exempt if used for research and development. Exempt if used in research and experimental activities in *Mich.* In *NY*, exemption applies for certain aircraft and vessel repairs.

(86) Exempt: tools, equip. (under 1-yr useful life) for production, research.

(87) Exempts contractor materials for out-of-state realty and no out-of-state tax *(Idaho, SC)*.

(88) Most repair services are taxable; repair services on vessels, barges and towboats of min. 50 tons load displacement are exempt. Also exempt in *Ark.*—repair or maintenance of railroad parts, cars and equipment brought in-state solely and exclusively for the purpose of being repaired, refurbished, modified, or modified; services performed on watches and clocks that are received by mail or common carrier from outside *Ark.* and returned by mail or common carrier or in the repairman's own conveyance to points out-of-state; repair or remanufacture of certain industrial metal rollers or platens which are brought in-state exclusively for repair or remanufacture and then shipped back to state of origin; service of alteration, addition, refinishing, replacement or repair of commercial jet aircraft, components or subcomponents; alteration, addition, refinishing, replacement, or repair of nonmechanical, passive or manually operated components of buildings or other improvements or structures affixed to realty *(Ark.)*.

(89) Farm machy. and equip. are exempt. In *Ga.*, exemption applies to specified items in poultry-egg, milk and livestock production; animal husbandry and tilling soil.

(90) Taxable: hand tools under $100.

(91) Materials consumed in production.

(92) Taxable if any materials furnished. Or if labor furnished in Fla. Exempt: labor charges on repair or maintenance of aircraft with max. take-off weight of more than 15,000 lbs. Exempt are repair and labor charges related to parts and materials incorporated into industrial machinery used in manufacturing. *(Fla.)*.

(93) Exempt if on outstater's goods (not for resale) for use out-of-state.

(94) Exempt: depreciable machy.-equipment for commercial farming or fishing; also machy-equip. for research and development. Also exempt are mchy. and equip. for use in generating radio and TV broadcast signals. *(Me.)*

(95) Exempt: on-farm facilities for grain or soybean storing, drying, processing or handling; note (106) also applies *(Ky.)*.

(96) Sale of machy. and equip. used directly and exclusively in mfg. or assembling personalty for sale, and machy. and equip. used primarily in graphic arts production, is exempt. Farm machy.-equip. exempt. Photo processing machy-equip. exempt. Machy.-equip. for high impact service facility or aircraft maintenance facility in enterprise zone exempt. MV fuel for personal use exempt.

(97) Rubber tired farm tractors, loaders, harvesters, cotton pickers, combines, balers, sprays, spreaders, discs, plows, irrigation wells and equipment, and like items are exempt on first $50,000 per item; note (106) also applies. Tax on manufacturing, farming, and timbering machinery and equipment is phased out in the period 7-1-2004—7-1-2010 *(La.)*

(98) Machines and tools for in-state use are exempt—annual min. purchase $500; note (106) also applies *(Colo)*.

(99) Items for newspaper mfg. are exempt *(Vt.)*; exempt if for free circulation publications *(N.C.)*

(100) Industrial & farm machy. are exempt. Exemption applies to machy. for printing business. Hydraulic fluids, lubricating oils, and greases are exempt industrial machy.

(101) Exempt if new mfg.

(102) Exempt if added to structure-facility of tax-exempts. In *Me.*, also applies to subcontractors.

(103) Refunded if becoming integral part of public project or property for educ. purposes.

(104) Exempt if useful life 6 mos. max. when new and note (61) applies.

(105) Exempt if paid for directly by US. Wyo. and subdivisions.

FOOTNOTES to chart ¶ 254: (continued)

(106) Exemptions or rebates are available for tax on sales to businesses in enterprise zone (Ark., Colo., Fla., Iowa, Kan., Ky.; La.; Mich.; Miss.; NJ; Okla.; Tex.) or border city, job opportunity building, agricultural processing facility, biotechnology and health science industry or international economic development zones *(Minn.)*. In *Va.* all items for businesses in the zone exempt for 5 yrs.; note (59) also applies. In *Ill.*, exempt when for use or consumption in enterprise zone (incl. by aircraft maintenance facilities) or by High Impact Business. *Tex.* also exempts maquiladora enterprises' in-state purchases, for immediate export.

(107) Electrical installation is taxed unless new construction; on bldg. or structure, and separately stated. Broad exemptions apply for other types.

(108) 100% exemption for sales to businesses in Tier 3 areas; 50%, in or Tier 2 areas *(Miss.)*.

(109) Exempt if contract with Fed-state-localities or charitable, religious and educational orgs.

(110) Exempt if furnished by U.S. gov't or *Ga.* locality to contractor for installation, repair or extension of public water, gas, or sewage system of gov't entity.

(111) Exemption includes charges for installing board roads for oil field operators if separately stated. Exemption or partial exemption for raw materials used in printing business. La. also allowed motion picture production cos. claim exemption, until 1-1-2006, for purchases in-state in connection with filming and production of movies or commercials in-state if they spent $250,000 (min.) in-state on filming and producing in 12-month period. Additional exemption was available for qualified production cos. in La., until 1-1-2007.

(112) Exempt if for creating chemical reaction in producing ferro-silicon used in magnesium production.

(113) Exempt if consumed in farming. In *Utah*, also exempts irrigation equipment and supplies used for farm production.

(114) Equipment for commercial farming and agricultural production is exempt.

(115) Exempt if materials for building-repairing commercial poultry or livestock structures. Note (99) also applies *(N.C.)*.

(116) Repair and replacement parts for charter buses are exempt. *(Tenn.)*

(117) Sales to construction contractor/subcontractor of tangible personalty that is to be physically incorporated in and become a permanent part of realty for sale to an exempt organization or government agency is exempt. For service provider tax, this applies to fabrication services. *(Me.)*

(118) Exempt: labor or service charges (incl. transport and travel) to repair, alter, or improve property owned or incorporated in projects under contract to Wyo. or its subdivisions *(Wyo.)*.

(119) Exempt: machy-equip. for mfg., processing, finishing, storing, distributing items in *Kan.* for resale (*Kan*).

(120) Exempt: certain machy-equipment for pollution control *(Fla.)*.

(121) Exempts items incorporated per contract into out-of-state realty, except to the extent other jurisdiction taxes the items and allows credit for Utah tax *(Utah)*.

(122) *Tex.* exempts machy., tools, and equipment used in repair, remodeling, or upkeep of carrier's aircraft, and items permanently affixed or attached to them. *Tex.* also exempts machy-equip. used in film, video, audio record production.

(123) *Tex.* exempts repairs of computer programs not sold by the repairer.

(124) *Ind.* exempts items used in commercial printing.

(125) Contractor or repairperson is taxed as retailer unless electing to be taxed as consumer of items incorporated into realty *(Neb.)*.

(126) Installation charge related to telephone, telecommunications and telegraph services are taxable. Installation of parts incident to alteration, cleanings, replacement or repair of motor vehicles, machinery and certain other items are taxable even if separately stated. Initial installation charges for items affixed to real property (except flooring) also taxable. *(Ark.)*.

(127) *Okla.*—Exemption applied to goods, machinery, and equipment sold to manufacturing for use in manufacturing operation. Machinery sales to contractors are generally taxable.

(128) Exempts repairs and repair, remodeling, or upkeep machy for aircraft or component part operated by certified or licensed carrier or by government *(W.Va.)*.

(129) Installation of tangible personalty by certain telecommunications-related entities is taxable when the sale of property is taxable. Repair, labor, certain lawn care services, and certain agricultural applications are exempt. *(Neb.)*

(130) *N.D.*—Exempts machy-equip. for new or expanding mfg. plant.

(131) *N.J.*—Exempts repair labor for public passenger or carrier school buses.

(132) *Ariz.*—Lets movie cos. claim refund of 50% of tax paid in connection with filming and production of movies in-state if they spent $1 million (min.) in-state on filming-producing in 12-month period and paid expenses with checks drawn on in-state banks. *N.M.*—Allows deduction for receipts from selling-leasing property & services to qualified film production companies.

(133) *Conn.*—Some repairs to residential property (home improvements) are exempt. 50% exemption applies to machy-equip used mainly in mfg. processing, fabricating if for R&D, measuring or testing, or used at any stage from time raw material received to time product ready for delivery-storage, or used mainly to repair-upkeep above machy-equip, or used mainly for metal finishing. Also exempts aircraft mfr. machy-equip. tools, fuel. Also exempts aircraft parts or repairs for certified carrier or factory.

(134) Sales to contractors are generally taxable *(Ind., N.J.)*.

(135) Farming and manufacturing and research equipment of new businesses engaged in line of business described in SIC Manual Code 2000—3999 is exempt from 1st 5.5% portion of state rate *(Calif.)*.

**FOOTNOTES to chart ¶ 254:
(continued)**

(136) *Ill.* exempts sales to contractors for resale. Also exempts bldg. materials sold to contractors for incorporation into nonprofits' or govt. realty, for incorporation into enterprise zone realty, and to High Impact businesses. Certain qualified sales of building materials to be incorporated into realty in a redevelopment project area with an intermodal terminal facility area or a River Edge Redevelopment Zone by remodeling, rehabilitation or new construction is exempt. *(Ill.)*

(137) *S.D.*—Refund/credit allowed for equipment for new or expanded facility to produce, use, or process agricultural commodity, product or by product. Sale of agricultural equip. and industrial production equip. in interstate commerce exempt.

(138) *Vt.*—Exemption applies to building material sold within 3 consecutive calendar yrs., exceeding $1 million in value, and either used solely to build/expand manufacturing facilities or incorporated into a downtown redevelopment project.

(139) *Wyo.*—Exemption applies to purchase of materials, supplies, and fabrication becoming an ingredient of the repair, alteration or improvement of personalty.

(140) *Mass.*—Tax due on any parts or materials furnished in connection with work if value is not inconsequential. Service charges must be stated separately.

(141) Exempt, if to construct church or other religious house of worship.

(142) *Tex.*—Exempt if sold, leased, or rented to, or stored, used or consumed by, a manufacturer: services performed directly on the product being manufactured before its distribution for sale and for the purpose of making the product more marketable; qualified steam production and other power equipment; lubricants, chemicals, chemical compounds, gases, or liquids used or consumed during the actual manufacturing, processing, or fabrication of tangible personalty; and safety apparel or work clothing that is used during the actual manufacturing, processing, or fabrication of tangible personalty for ultimate sale if the manufacturing process would not be possible without the use of the apparel or clothing, and the apparel or clothing is not resold to the employee.

(143) *Minn.*—Capital equipment is exempt. Also exempt are equipment for special construction projects and farm equipment.

(144) *Haw.*—Amounts from the servicing and maintenance of aircraft or from constructing an airport service facility are exempt. Amounts from material parts or tools imported or purchased by a licensed person used for aircraft service work are exempt from use tax.

(145) Motor vehicle painting is taxable *(Neb.)*.

(146) *Ind.*—Separately stated installation charges not taxable.

(147) *Me.*—A reimbursement is allowed for sales-use tax with respect to the sales or use of tangible personalty that is physically incorporated in and becomes a permanent part of realty that is owned by or sold to a qualified Pine Tree Development Zone business and that is used directly and primarily by that business in qualified business activities.

(148) Unless property installed/repaired would be exempt *(Ohio)*.

SALES-USE TAXES—TAXABILITY OF SPECIFIC TRANSACTIONS—PART III

¶255 Sales to nonprofits or governments, withdrawal from stock, wrappers, containers.

STATE	T = taxable E = exempt				
	SALES TO NONPROFIT ORGANIZA-TIONS (1)	SALES TO FED-ERAL GOV-ERNMENT AND ITS AGENCIES (32)	SALES TO STATE, ITS SUBDI-VISIONS & AGENCIES	WITHDRAW-AL FROM OWN STOCK (45)	SALES OF WRAPPERS AND CON-TAINERS
Ala.	T(67)	E	E(37)	T	E(49)
Ariz.	T(34,73)	E(35)	T(65)	T	T(118)
Ark.	T(67)	E	T(43)	T	T(51,71)
Calif.	T(67,74)	E(18,66)	T	T(59)	E(55,69)
Colo.	E	E	E	T(59,70)	T(48)
Conn.	E(1,6)	E	E	T	E(69)
D.C.	E(5)	E	E(77)	T(59)	E(49,50)
Fla.	E	E	E	T	E(49)
Ga.	T(7,28)	E	E	T	E(49)
Haw.	E	E(4)	T	T(3)	T(17)
Idaho	T(14,67)	E	E	T	T(69)
Ill.	E	E	E	E(59)	E(76)
Ind.	E	E	E(27)	T(3)	E(55,81)
Iowa	T(67)	E	E(42,78)	T	E(44)
Kan.	T(28)	E	E(33,39)	T	E(49)
Ky.	E(8)	E	E(27)	T	E(55)
La.	T(67)	E	E(19)	T	E(49,50,52)
Me.	T(67,68)	E(85,92)	E(85)	T(59)	E(41,55,119)
Md.	E	E	E	T(3)	E(50,79)
Mass.	E(8)	E	E	T	E(120)
Mich.	E	E(15)	E(15)	T	E(12,48,49) (50,54)
Minn.	E	E	T(77,112)	T	E(49)
Miss.	E(67)	E(23)	E(15,90)	T	E(41)
Mo.	E	E	E	T	T(48,63)
Neb.	E	E	E	T	E(69,81)
Nev.	E	E	E	T	E(69,81)

STATE	T = taxable E = exempt				
	SALES TO NONPROFIT ORGANIZA-TIONS (1)	SALES TO FED-ERAL GOV-ERNMENT AND ITS AGENCIES (32)	SALES TO STATE, ITS SUBDI-VISIONS & AGENCIES	WITHDRAW-AL FROM OWN STOCK (45)	SALES OF WRAPPERS AND CON-TAINERS
N.J.	E	E(11)	E	T(59)	E(49)
N.M.	E(8)	E(87)	E(38,87)	E(59)	E(49)
N.Y.	E(24)	E(11)	E	E(59)	E(21)
N.C.	T(46)	E	E(46,56,91)	E(59)	E(22)
N.D.	T(40,67)	E	E(77)	T	E
Ohio	E(10)	E	E	T	E(44)
Okla.	T(67)	E	E	T	E(49)
Pa.	E(83)	E(72)	E(72)	T	E(22,49)
R.I.	E	E	E	T	E(69,80)
S.C.	T(73,86)	E(48)	T(73)	T	E(22)
S.D.	T(14,109)	E	E(36,77)	T(59)	E(44)
Tenn.	E	E(23)	E	T	E
Tex.	E	E	E	T	T(111)
Utah	E	E	E(25)	T	E(41,81)
Vt.	E(8)	E	E	T(89)	E(113)
Va.	E(16)	E	E	T(94)	E(93)
Wash. (Sales-use)	T(58,67)	E(29)	T(2,53)	T(59)	E(30)
(Bus. & Occup.)	T(67)	T	T	E	E
W.Va.	E(8)	E(31)	E(31,70,77)	T	E(60)
Wis.	E	E	E	T	E
Wyo.	E(47,84)	E	E	T	E(49,51)

FOOTNOTES to chart ¶ 255:

(1) Refers to sales to charitable, religious, educational, etc., orgs. for use exclusively for charitable, etc., exempt purposes.

(2) Exemption allowed for receipts reimbursed by U.S. for flood control.

(3) No specific provision; probable status shown.

(4) Sales of liquor, tobacco and other tangible personalty by sellers licensed under respective liquor, tobacco and gross income tax laws. Sales to Natl. Banks are taxable.

(5) Buyer must have exemption certificate; vendor must meet record keeping requirements; institution must be located in D.C.; and property or services bought are for use-consumption in operating institution or honoring institution or members.

(6) Sales of food products to nonprofit schools are exempt.

(7) Religious papers for org. benefit are exempt.

(8) Applies only to those orgs. exempt under IRC §501(c)(3) *(Mass.). In Ky., Vt.,* and *W.Va.,* such Fed orgs. are among those exempted.

(9) Restricted to orgs. providing a public benefit.

(10) Exemption also applies to orgs. providing specified services to hospitals and charities; state headquarters of veterans' org.; animal adoption society; community arts center; performing arts; educational TV-radio *(Ohio)*.

(11) Sales to UN are also exempt. In *N.J.* exemption applies to any int'l org. of which U.S. is a member.

FOOTNOTES to chart ¶ 255: (continued)

(12) Taxable if consumer pays separate charge for container.
(13) State purchased textbooks, library books for public schools are exempt.
(14) Exempts sales to nonprofit (and in S.D., religious) educational institutions, and hospitals.
(15) Order must be on prescribed form; paid directly by govt.
(16) *Va.*—Exempt if meets certain criteria.
(17) *Haw.* —Certain amounts received as beverage container deposits are exempt.
(18) Sales to incorporated Fed instrumentalities not wholly owned by U.S. are taxable only when Fed law permits tax. *(Calif.)*
(19) Purchases by La., depts. and agencies, state boards-commissions, school boards, parish and municipalities, parish hospital service and law enforcement dists., public housing authorities, and public libraries are state tax-exempt.
(20) Specifies IRC exempt org. and other such furnishing exempt certificate.
(21) Container with contents for ultimate consumer, exempt; includes permanent labels, name plates for shipping.
(22) Exempt if part of sale, delivery to customer.
(23) If sale made and billed directly to U.S. or agency and paid for directly by U.S.
(24) State approval and exemption certificates required *(N.Y.)*.
(25) Agencies must be performing essential governmental function. Sales of construction materials to state and local government entities are taxable, unless the materials are installed or converted to real property by employees of the public entity. Sales of construction materials to public education institutions taxable unless clearly identified and segregated and installed or converted to realty owned by institution. Eff. 4-30-2007, sales to public transit district including construction materials installed or to be converted to realty are exempt.
(26) Agencies must be owned and controlled by govt.
(27) Sales exempt if used to perform governmental functions.
(28) Sales to nonprofit schools and hospitals are exempt. *Kan.* exempts sales to specified nonprofit organizations. *Ga.* also exempts Fed. tax-exempt organizations providing services to the mentally retarded.
(29) Regulation exempts if govt. agency operates for benefit of public.
(30) Taxable if in litter-producing category.
(31) Sales to govt. and agencies for distribution in public welfare or relief work.
(32) Kern-Limerick (1954) 347 US 110, 74 SCt 403 is paramount Fed law, exempting from use tax and from consumer's sales taxes.
(33) Sales to state, its departments and institutions, for use in governmental capacity.
(34) Exempt: sales to nonprofit hospital, nursing-residential care institutions. Ariz. also exempts food sold to schools (grades K-12), day care centers, facilities for seniors or handicapped, and IRC §501(c)(3)-exempt nonprofits that provide food for free or nominal charge. *Ariz.* exempts items bought by IRC §501(c)(3) (religious, scientific, educational, charitable org.) from parent or affiliate. Ariz. exempts sales to qualifying community health centers and orgs.
(35) Direct sales by in-state manufacturers, assemblers or repairers to U.S. exempt. Sellers for manufacturers etc. making Fed sales pay tax less 50% deduction. Also exempt if items for development of certain Fed research projects *(Ariz.)*.
(36) Proof may be required as to payment of sale with government funds.
(37) Counties and incorporated municipalities.
(38) Agencies not specifically mentioned in law or regulations.
(39) Unless buyer engaged in business subject to sales tax.
(40) Exempts sales to nursing homes. And hospitals in *N.D.*
(41) Non-returnables when sold to manufacturers and wholesalers; and in *Utah* to retailers.
(42) Except sales of goods used to operate municipally owned public utilities.
(43) Exempt items are specified.
(44) Exempt if (a) sold to mfrs., fabricators or processors as raw materials per *S. Dak.* law and used or consumed by mfr.; or (b) sold to retailer using same to hold other taxable personalty. *Iowa* also exempts packaging materials sold for use in agricultural, livestock, or dairy production.
(45) If exempt from sales tax, probably subject to existing use tax. (See (59) below).
(46) Refund of tax on personalty and building material available to certain buyers.
(47) Sales to churches are exempt.
(48) Sales to U.S. are exempt, inclu. charges for transmission of voice or messages. In *Colo.*, exempt if resold or used as ingredient or component part of manufactured or compounded product.
(49) If container is returnable (except food and soft drinks containers), sale is taxable. All returnable containers taxable in *Ala., D.C., Wyo.* In Ala., containers used to deliver baby chicks or eggs, and sausage casings are exempt. Exempt: returnable bottled water containers and cartons, etc. used to transport them *(Okla).*; food or drink containers taxable, but containers used to deliver products to ultimate consumer by manufacturers, processors, farmers, or dairies are exempt *(Pa.);* containers for use in farm enterprise *(N.J.)*.
(50) Taxable if sold to person rendering non-taxable service.
(51) Sales to manufacturers for shipping own product are exempt, including processors & compounders in *Wyo.*
(52) Sales to wholesalers for making single wholesale delivery are taxable.
(53) Sales by one state agency to another are exempt.

FOOTNOTES to chart ¶ 255:
(continued)

(54) Includes sales to wholesalers and others for making deliveries.

(55) Returnable containers sold with contents or resold for filling.

(56) Sales to Dept. Transp. are exempt. *(NC)*.

(57) Sales to persons having no sales tax permit are taxable.

(58) Sales to schools are exempt.

(59) Taxable under use tax.

(60) Containers exempt if returnable and billed separately.

(61) Tax is on retailer so most sales to US are taxed.

(62) If original use substantial, later sale isn't one for resale.

(63) Reusable containers transferred in retail sales are exempt if refundable deposit required; note (64) also applies *(Mo.)*.

(64) Exempt: containers and other disposables furnished free with taxable food, meals or beverages *(Colo., Mo.)*.

(65) State hospitals are exempt.

(66) Nat'l banks are use tax-exempt.

(67) Specified groups exempt.

(68) Except sales to hospitals, medical research centers, schools, churches, monasteries, convents, and local branches of incorporated charities providing free medical supply-equipment loans. In *Me.*, sales to incorporated nonprofit assisted housing programs for elderly and incorporated nonprofit fire depts. and ambulance services; certain sales to incorporated nonprofit snowmobile clubs; and incorporated nonprofit medical clinics providing free care to indigent or uninsured are exempt.

(69) Nonreturnable containers (and returnable dairy product containers in *Conn.*) when sold (or leased in *Calif.*) without contents, returnable (except nonrefillable beverage in *Conn.*) containers when sold with contents, and containers sold (or leased in *Calif.*) with nontaxable contents are exempt.

(70) Sales to Vol. fire dept. and public service districts are exempt.

(71) Items a customer expects to receive as a necessary part of the item purchased are exempt when purchased for resale by a restaurant. Sales of bagging, packaging, and tying materials to in-state cotton gins for their own use and sales of twine for production of tomato crops are exempt.

(72) Building mchy. and equip. sold to contractors and used for gov't. construction contract are exempt. Other items sold to contractor for gov't contract are taxable. *(Pa.)*

(73) Exempts proceeds of sales of textbooks used in schools. In *Ariz.*, exemption applies only to books required by state U or community college.

(74) Exempt if for resale.

(75) (Reserved.)

(76) Exempt if purchased for resale along with contents.

(77) Other states-territories exempt if reciprocal.

(78) Applies to purchases used for public purposes.

(79) Exempt under use tax if purchased by purely public charity.

(80) Returnable and nonreturnable exempt if sold to sellers for filling and sale.

(81) Taxable if sold to final user or consumer.

(82) Exempt if for use by farm or mfrs; also, for shipping household goods outstate.

(83) Building materials, supplies and equipment used in construction, remodeling or repair of organization's realty are taxable. Such items are exempt if used for routine maintenance or repair.

(84) Sales to charities are exempt.

(85) Taxable if title held or taken as finance security *(Me.)*.

(86) Max. state tax on purchase of musical instrument or office equipment by religious organization is $300 per purchase.

(87) Taxable (unless Fed law exempts): nonfissionable metalliferous mineral ore; items for construction or metropolitan redevelopment project; that part of receipts from services reflecting value of personalty used-produced *(N.M.)*.

(88) Exempts if sale of oil drums to nonretailer of such items. Also exempt are sales to persons appointed or contracted by U.S. agencies/instrumentalities if U.S. takes immediate ownership-possession.

(89) But mere withdrawal from storage of tangible personalty by a manufacturer, processor, or assembler is not a taxable use *(Vt.)*.

(90) Title must pass to the government directly *(Miss.)*.

(91) *N.C.* —State agencies are exempt from state and local sales tax on items, but not electricity or telecommunications, bought by the agency for its own use.

(92) Exemption does not apply to corporations organized under Title IV, Part E of the Farm Credit Act of 1971, 12 USC 2211 to 2214. *(Me.)*

(93) Exempt if the items are marketed with the product being sold and become the property of the purchaser. *(Va.)*

(94) Until 7-1-2012, exemption for textbooks withdrawn from inventory at book publishing distribution facilities for free distribution to professors and other individuals who have an educational focus *(Va.)*.

(95—108) (Reserved.)

(109) *S.D.* —Exempts sales of live gamebirds to nonprofits. Exempts sales of tangible personal property and electrical energy, gas, and communication services to nonprofit charity devoted to relief of poor, distressed, or underprivileged.

(110) (Reserved.)

FOOTNOTES to chart ¶ 255:
(continued)

(111) Wrapping, packing, and packaging are taxable; containers are exempt *(Tex.)*.

(112) *Minn.* —Exemptions are limited.

(113) *Vt.* —Exempts returnable and reusable packaging, with life expectancy of up to 3 yrs., used by mfr. or distributor.

(114) (Reserved.)

(115) Exempts food (covered under Fed food stamp program) for homeless or needy sold to nonprofit or sold or donated by nonprofit to another nonprofit. Also exempts sales to charitable, free property tax-exempt hospitals mainly serving children.

(116—117) (Reserved.)

(118) *Ariz.* exempts sale of containers and bottles as sale for resale if buyer is to transfer them with their contents in future sales.

(119) *Me.* —Wrappers and packaging materials sold to: (a) packers or movers: (b) persons for packing goods sold by them or on which they performed certain services.

(120) *Mass.* —Exemption applies to returnable and nonreturnable containers sold without contents, containers sold with exempt contents, returnable containers sold with contents or resold for refilling, and bags in which feed for livestock and poultry is contained. Containers sold to vendors are exempt if exemption certificate is used. Packaging is exempt if used by vendor's customers to transport food or beverages off-premises. Sale of packaging is taxable if used by vendor's customers on vendor's premises.

SALES-USE TAXES—TAXABILITY OF SPECIFIC TRANSACTIONS—PART IV

¶255-A Sales of clothing and footwear. The following chart covers the state sales and use tax treatment of retail sales of clothing and footwear. In addition to retail sales, the chart also covers the taxability of clothing sales on special or custom order, including the situation when a tailor makes clothing from materials provided by the customer. Finally, the chart covers the taxability of charges for altering new clothing. In some instances, alterations are exempt only if separately stated on the bill, and this is indicated in the chart.

Accessories: As a general rule, if clothing is taxable, so are accessories. However, if a state exempts clothing sales, in whole or in part, then the exemption generally does not extend to accessories. Accessories generally include such items as jewelry, handbags, umbrellas, watches, wallets and similar articles. Specific state statutes and administrative pronouncements provide detailed examples of exempt and nonexempt items.

Partial exemptions: A number of states provide a limited exemption for clothing sales, up to a certain amount, and usually per item of clothing. Specific state rules for such sales are noted in the footnotes.

2008 sales tax holidays: A number of states have exempted sales of clothing for a limited period of time. In most cases, these sales tax ''holidays'' are single-time events, running in length from a few days to up to a week. In some instances, the state has enacted an annual sales tax holiday. States currently scheduling tax holidays are: *Alabama* annually exempts sales of articles of clothing with a sales price of $100 or less, per article of clothing during the period first Friday, Saturday, and Sunday in August (August 1–3, 2008). *Connecticut* annually exempts clothing and footwear sales of less than $300 per item during the third Sunday through the next Saturday of August (August 17–23, 2008) (this tax-free week is in lieu of the regular exemption). The *District of Columbia* exempts sales of shoes, clothing, accessory items with a sales price of $100 or less per item during the first Saturday in August through the second Sunday in August and during the fourth Friday in November through the first Sunday in December (August 2–10, 2008 and November 28–December 7, 2008). *Iowa* annually exempts from tax sales of clothing and footwear of less than $100 per article during the first Friday and Saturday of August (August 1–2, 2008). *Louisiana* annually exempts the first $2,500 of certain individual items of tangible personal property (including sales of clothing, footwear and clothing accessories) during the first Friday and Saturday of August (August 1–2, 2008). *Missouri* annually exempts sales of clothing and footwear with a taxable value of $100 or less during the first Friday in August through Sunday of August (August 1–3, 2008). *New Mexico* annually exempts sales of clothing and footwear worth less than $100 each during the first Friday in August and through the following Sunday in August (August 1–3, 2008). *North Carolina* annually exempts sales of clothing, clothing accessories, and footwear of $100 or less per item during the first Friday through Sunday of August (August 1–3, 2008). *Oklahoma* annually exempts sales of clothing and footwear of less than $100 from the first Friday in August through the following Sunday in August (August 1–3, 2008). *South Carolina* annually exempts all clothing and footwear sales, including clothing accessories during the first Friday through Sunday in August (August 1–3, 2008). *Tennessee* annually exempts sales of clothing of $100 or less per item during the first Friday through Sunday of August (August 1–3, 2008). *Texas* annually exempts clothing and footwear sales of less than $100 per article during the third Friday in August through the following Sunday of August (August 15–17, 2008). *Virginia* annually exempts sales of clothing and footwear with a selling price of $100 or less per article during the first Friday, Saturday, and Sunday of August (August 1–3, 2008).

	RETAIL SALES	SPECIAL ORDERS	ALTERATIONS
Alabama	Taxable	Taxable	Exempt (1,7)
Alaska	No Sales Tax	No Sales Tax	No Sales Tax
Arizona	Taxable	Taxable	Exempt (7)
Arkansas	Taxable	Taxable (1)	Exempt (7)
California	Taxable (2)	Taxable (1)	Taxable
Colorado	Taxable	Taxable (1)	Exempt (7)
Connecticut	Exempt if under $50 (3)	Exempt if under $50 (1,3)	Exempt
Delaware	No Sales Tax	No Sales Tax	No Sales Tax
District of Columbia	Taxable	Taxable	Taxable
Florida	Taxable	Taxable	Taxable
Georgia	Taxable	Taxable (1)	Taxable (1)
Hawaii	Taxable	Taxable	Taxable
Idaho	Taxable	Taxable	Taxable
Illinois	Taxable	Taxable	Taxable
Indiana	Taxable	Taxable (1)	Taxable (1)
Iowa	Taxable	Taxable	Taxable
Kansas	Taxable	Taxable (1)	Taxable (1)
Kentucky	Taxable	Taxable	Taxable
Louisiana	Taxable	Taxable	Taxable (1)
Maine	Taxable	Taxable	Taxable
Maryland	Taxable	Taxable	Taxable (1)
Massachusetts	Exempt Up to $175 (4,5)	Exempt Up to $175 (4,5)	Exempt
Michigan	Taxable	Taxable (1)	Exempt
Minnesota	Exempt (5,12)	Exempt (5,12)	Exempt
Mississippi	Taxable	Taxable (1)	Taxable (1)
Missouri	Taxable	Taxable (1)	Taxable (1)
Montana	No Sales Tax	No Sales Tax	No Sales Tax
Nebraska	Taxable	Taxable	Taxable (1)
Nevada	Taxable	Taxable	Exempt (6)
New Hampshire	No Sales Tax	No Sales Tax	No Sales Tax
New Jersey	Exempt (5,11)	Exempt (5,11)	Exempt (5,11)
New Mexico	Taxable	Taxable (1)	Taxable (1)
New York	Exempt Up to $110 (13)	Exempt Up to $110 (13)	Exempt (13)
North Carolina	Taxable	Taxable (1)	Exempt (7)
North Dakota	Taxable	Taxable (1)	Exempt (7)
Ohio	Taxable	Taxable	Taxable
Oklahoma	Taxable	Taxable	Exempt (7)
Oregon	No Sales Tax	No Sales Tax	No Sales Tax
Pennsylvania	Exempt (8)	Exempt (8)	Exempt (8)
Rhode Island	Exempt (5)	Exempt (5)	Exempt
South Carolina	Taxable (9)	Taxable (9)	Exempt (7)
South Dakota	Taxable	Taxable	Taxable
Tennessee	Taxable	Taxable	Taxable (1)
Texas	Taxable	Taxable	Exempt (7)
Utah	Taxable	Taxable	Taxable (1)
Vermont	Exempt (5,14)	Exempt (5,14)	Exempt (1)
Virginia	Taxable	Taxable	Exempt (7)
Washington	Taxable	Taxable	Taxable
West Virginia	Taxable	Taxable	Taxable (1)
Wisconsin	Taxable (10)	Taxable	Taxable (1)
Wyoming	Taxable	Taxable (1)	Taxable

FOOTNOTES to chart ¶ 255-A:

(1) No specific provisions; probable status shown.

(2) *Calif.*—Gross receipts from the sale, storage, use, or other consumption in Calif. of new children's clothing sold to qualifying nonprofit organizations for distribution without charge to elementary school children are exempt.

(3) *Conn.*— If an article of clothing or footwear is sold for more than the $50 exemption limit, tax is computed on the entire purchase price. Articles of clothing or footwear that consist of multiple pieces are treated as one item for purposes of the $50 exemption limit if they are priced as a single item. Multiple-item articles are treated as separate items if each item is priced separately.

(4) Per item.

(5) *Mass., Minn., R.I., Vt.*—Exemption does not apply to special clothing or footwear designed for athletic activity or protective use and is not normally worn except for the athletic or protective use. *N.J.*—Exemption doesn't apply to clothing accessories or equipment, sports or recreation equipment, or certain protective equipment.

(6) *Nev.*—Tax does not apply to materials furnished if the fair retail price of the materials is separately stated.

(7) If charges are separately stated.

(8) *Pa.*—Tax is imposed on accessories, ornamental wear, formal day or evening apparel, formal wear shoes, sports or athletic wear, sports or athletic shoes, and articles made of hides, pelts, or imitation or synthetic fur. If fur (real, imitation, or synthetic) is the most valuable component of an article, the article is taxable only if such fur is worth more than 3 times as much as the next most valuable component material. Also taxable are clergy vestments and choir and altar server clothing. Charges for the service of repairing, altering, mending wearing apparel are exempt. Imprinting or printing of clothing belonging to others is taxable.

(9) *S.C.*—Clothing and other attire required for working in a class 100 or better clean room environment, as defined in Federal Standard 209E, are exempt from tax.

(10) *Wis.*—Cloth diapers are exempt.

(11) *N.J.*—Sales of clothing and accessories made of fur are subject to a 6% fur clothing gross receipts tax.

(12) *Minn.*—Clothing made from fur is exempt from sales tax, but is subject to a 6.5% gross receipts tax.

(13) *New York* — Alterations are exempt if separately stated. In NYC, all clothing and footwear, regardless of cost, is exempt from city sales-use tax eff. 9-1-2007.

(14) *Vt.*—Exemption applies to all clothing and footwear except as noted in footnote (5).

SALES-USE TAXES—BASIS OR MEASURE OF TAX—PART I

¶256 Taxes, transportation charges, interest, trade-ins, discounts.

	T = taxable (included in tax base) E = exempt (excluded from tax base)					
STATE	OTHER TAXES AND LICENSES FEES PAID (1,9)	CREDIT FOR TAX PAID TO OTHER STATE (56)	TRANSPORTATION CHARGES (19)	INTEREST FINANCE AND OTHER CARRYING CHARGES (31)	VALUE OF TRADE-IN PROPERTY (36)	CASH AND TRADE DISCOUNT (40)
Ala.	T	Yes	T(83)	E(22)	T(57)	E(46,117)
Ariz.	T(38,82)	Yes	T(85)	E	E	E(64)
Ark.	T(61)	Yes(67)	T(110)	E(22)	T(115)	E(46)
Calif.	T(4,6,62)	Yes(10)	E(27)	E(35)	T	E(58)
Colo.	T(6)	Yes(10,25,56)	T(3,99)	E(22)	E(51,63)	E(78)
Conn.	T(68)	Yes	T	T(13)	E(34)	E(58)
D.C.	T(6,9,15)	Yes(10)	E(54)	E(22)	T	E(78)
Fla.	T(6)	Yes(25)	T(103)	E(22)	E(118)	E
Ga.	T(6,100)	Yes(67)	T(99)	E	E	E(58)
Haw.	T(6,7,11,14,127)	Yes(10)	T(53,128)	T	T(122)	E(46)
Idaho	T(68)	Yes(10,67)	E(72)	E(22)	E(51)	E(78)
Ill.	T(6,11,130)	Yes(25)	E(66)	E(33)	E(37)	E(44)
Ind.	T(6,17,82,124)	Yes(25,74)	T	E	E(37)	E
Iowa	T(6,79)	Yes(25,56)	E(22,114)	E(22)	E(123)	E(44,64)
Kan.	T(76)	Yes(10,25)	T	E(22)	E	E
Ky.	T(6,11)	Yes(25,67)	T(54)	E(22)	E(37,51)	E(44,46,64)
La.	T(6)	Yes(67)	E(72)	E(102)	E	E(46)
Me.	T(6,79)	Yes(25)	E(22,83)	T	T(21)	E(44)
Md.	T(30)	Yes(25,81)	E(22,132)	E(22)	T	E(78)
Mass.	T(20,24)	Yes(25,67)	E(54)	T	E(57)	E(46)
Mich.	T(11,79)	Yes(10,67)	T(133)	E(22)	T	E(39)
Minn.	T(124)	Yes	T	E(22)	E	E
Miss.	T(6,79,119)	Yes(25)	T	T	E	E(58)
Mo.	T(120)	Yes(25)	T(105)	E(22)	E	E
Neb.	T	Yes(25,67)	T	E	E(51)	E(46)
Nev.	T(6)	Yes(75)	T(55,69)	E(22,35,107)	T(89)	E(44,46)

	T = taxable (included in tax base) E = exempt (excluded from tax base)					
STATE	OTHER TAXES AND LICENSES FEES PAID (1,9)	CREDIT FOR TAX PAID TO OTHER STATE (56)	TRANSPORTATION CHARGES (19)	INTEREST FINANCE AND OTHER CARRYING CHARGES (31)	VALUE OF TRADE-IN PROPERTY (36)	CASH AND TRADE DISCOUNT (40)
N.J.	T(6)	Yes(25,67)	T(134)	E(131)	E(37,51)	E(29)
N.M.	T(38)	Yes(10,25)	T(50)	T(86)	E(37,98)	E(44,46)
N.Y.	T(11,108)	Yes(25,67)	T(129)	E	E(51)	E(78)
N.C.	T(124)	Yes(67)	T	E(22)	T	T(78)
N.D.	T(6,22)	Yes(10,25,67)	T(94)	T(2)	E(51)	E
Ohio	T(38)	Yes(25)	T	E(22)	T(18)	E
Okla.	T(7)	Yes(25)	T(109)	E(22)	T(121)	E(45)
Pa.	T	Yes(67)	T(84)	E	E	E
R.I.	T(124)	Yes(25)	E(54)	E(22)	T(18)	E(46)
S.C.	T(6)	Yes(10,25)	T(54,71)	E(22)	E	E(46)
S.D.	T(7)	Yes(10,25,67)	T	E(112)	E	E(44)
Tenn.	T(6)	Yes(25)	E(59,94)	E(22)	E(37)	E(46)
Tex.	T(6)	Yes(10,25,67)	T	E(22)	E(22)	E(22,46)
Utah	T(91)	Yes(10,25,56)	E(22)	E(13,22)	E	E(44)
Vt.	T(2)	Yes(25,67)	T(133)	T(2)	E	E(78)
Va.	T(6,30)	Yes(25)	E(22)	E(22)	E	E
Wash. (Sales use)	T(17)	Yes(10,25)	T	E(22,35,47)	E(37)	E(44,46)
(B&0)	T(11)	No(13)	T	T	T	E
W.Va.	E	Yes(25)	T	E	E	E(78)
Wis.	T(6,38,79)	Yes(25)	T(54)	E(22)	E	E(65)
Wyo.	T(124)	Yes(116)	E	E(135)	E(52)	E(78)

FOOTNOTES to chart ¶ 256:

(1) Entry shows whether tax included in price to consumer or purchaser is included (T) or deducted (E) from base on which sales tax must be collected. Use tax usually makes no provision for deduction.

(2) No specific provision; law prohibits deduction of any expense.

(3) Before buyer takes title under sales agreement.

(4) Includes Fed-state gasoline excise taxes.

(5) State excise taxes on retail sale of property deductible.

(6) Fed retailers excise tax deductible. But not Fed manufacturers-importers excise tax *(Calif., Fla. and S.C.)*. In *Colo.*, indirect Fed manufacturers excise taxes are taxable, but not direct Fed taxes or Colo. sales-use taxes.

(7) Fed mfr.'s excise deductible on mfr. sales to consumer. In *Haw.*, applies only to special sugar taxes.

(8) (Reserved.)

(9) Deductible taxes usually must be separately billed. Chart doesn't cover taxes excluded from base as item subject to special excise and sales-use tax exempt.

(10) Also, as member of Multistate Tax Compact, tax credit allowed applies first against state use tax, balance against any use tax due a subdivision.

FOOTNOTES to chart ¶ 256:
(continued)

(11) State motor fuels tax deductible. In *Haw., Ind., and Wash.,* Fed. motor fuel tax also deductible. In *Wash.,* fees levied on new replacement tires are also deductible. In *Mich.*, any tax legally imposed on consumers is deductible.

(12) State cigarette tax deductible.

(13) No specific provision; probable status shown. Credits allowed for certain manufacturers and extractors.

(14) State beer tax deductible. *Haw.* liquor tax.

(15) Reimbursement for sales tax is excluded if separately stated. *(D.C.).*

(16) Deductible where discount allowed for prompt payment if so agreed at sale.

(17) Taxes collected as agent excluded.

(18) Trade in for new or used passenger car is exempt. In *R.I.,* also applies to boats. In *Ohio,* trade-in exemption also applies to watercraft, new MVs and outboard motors.

(19) Charges on shipment from retailer to consumer; prior charges ordinarily taxable. This chart does not cover tax on transportation companies as such.

(20) Exclude buyer's sales-use tax reimbursement paid to seller.

(21) Taxable on difference between purchase price of MV, watercraft, aircraft, chain saws, special mobile equip., trailers, and truck campers and sale price of same type property traded in.

(22) If separately stated. *Va.* exempts transportation charges for picking up tangible personalty leased or rented to customers.

(23) If buyer assumes responsibility for charges, regardless of how billed.

(24) Excludes Fed manufacturers' excise levied on motor vehicles by IRC §4061.

(25) Credit for sales or use tax paid other state or *D.C.* is allowed against use tax. But *Va.* credit for MVs applies only if other state allows similar credit (reciprocity). *Miss.* denies credit for MVs, boats, trailers, and all-terrain vehicles. *Vt.* also allows credit against its MV purchase and use tax for tax paid to other states on MVs.

(26) Shipment f.o.b. origin, if separately billed and recorded *(Ind.)*; also shipments f.o.b. destination if "collectible and deductible by buyer from selling price."

(27) If separately stated and (a) reasonable charges (for retailer's facilities) or (b) retailer's cost (for other facilities). If transportation is by retailer's facilities, or sale is for delivered price, exemption covers only transportation after sale to buyer *(Calif.).*

(28) Law specifies discounts for early payment as nondeductible.

(29) *N.J.*—Discounts that represent a price reduction (that is, volume discounts) are deductible; early payment discounts are not deductible.

(30) State-subdivision or Fed excise taxes on consumers deductible. In *Md.*, excise or other taxes not imposed by law directly on buyers are not deductible from the purchase price.

(31) As to practice in absence of specific provision.

(32) Prepaid outgoing freight is deductible unless deliveries in taxpayer's equipment.

(33) Charges must be clearly reflected in books and records.

(34) Exempts vehicle, snowmobile, vessel, farm tractor, and construction equip. or machy. (with own power source) trade-in. *Conn.* also exempts aircraft and core components of certain commercial trucks and trade-ins of all like-kind items intended for resale.

(35) If separate record is kept of such charges.

(36) For taxability of sale of trade-ins or used property, see chart at ¶ 253.

(37) If sale and trade-in sale are of same kind of property.

(38) State-local sales or gross receipts taxes are excluded from definition of gross receipts. Admissions taxes collected by racetracks are taxable *(N.M.). Ariz.* exempts Fed excise taxes on autos, heavy trucks, and use fuel.

(39) Detailed records must be kept.

(40) See also ¶ 253.

(41) Can't be anticipated; credit granted after discount actually allowed.

(42) Not exempt for use tax.

(43) Excludes Federal retailer excise tax on diesel fuel.

(44) If actually taken by buyer.

(45) Discount given after sale is consummated isn't deductible in *Okla.*

(46) Law and/or regulations specifically or generally mention cash discounts only. In *S.D.,* applies to use tax. *La.* exempts vendor-mfr. cash discounts or rebates on new MVs. *Neb.* exempts mfr.-dealer rebates functioning as price discounts on MVs.

(47) Except on rental contracts.

(48) When included in sales price.

(49) Exclusion appears only in use tax.

(50) Transportation by common or contract carrier exempt if paid by buyer to carrier *(N.M.).*

(51) If to be resold in business. In *N.D.,* when property not subject to sales or MV excise tax is taxed as part of consideration of purchase price, purchaser must pay sales tax on full purchase price.

(52) In *Wyo.*, excluded from sale price of new items.

(53) Except where manufactured products are exported or sold on a delivered price.

(54) Exempt if separately stated and transportation occurs after sale. *Wis.* taxes delivery charges. *D.C.* taxes delivery charges separately stated (not of item for resale if *D.C.* resale certificate issued, or of newspapers). Exempt in *R.I.* if property sold is exempt.

(55) Taxable if shipping happens before title passes *(Nev.).*

(56) Credit limit is amount paid other state but not more than local tax would be.

FOOTNOTES to chart ¶ 256:
(continued)

(57) Motor vehicle, trailer or farm machy-equip. trade-in tax basis is difference between price of newly acquired property and credit on the trade-in (also applies to house trailers in Ala.). Also applies to vehicle used parts. In *Ala.* and *Mass.*, deduction allowed for boats and airplanes traded in.
(58) Exemption applies to cash discounts.
(59) If title passes to purchaser at shipping point; separate billing is immaterial.
(60) But cash discounts are included, if cash sale.
(61) Fed manufacturers' excise taxes deductible.
(62) Local sales and use taxes and certain motor vehicles taxes deductible. Also, excluded in *Calif.* are sales taxes imposed by Indian tribes.
(63) Exempts exchanges of MVs, watercraft and aircraft *(Colo.)*.
(64) Trading stamps don't represent cash discounts.
(65) Only cash or term discounts are exempt.
(66) Exempt if not part of sales price and separately agreed on by parties.
(67) Credit allowed if other state allows similar credit (reciprocity). In *La.*, local La. sales-use taxes are credits against local *La.* taxes, as are out-of-state local taxes if the other locality reciprocates.
(68) Excludes any U.S. tax on retail sales, except mfrs.' or importers' excise tax.
(69) Charges for transportation after sales are exempt.
(70) As member of Multistate Tax Compact, credit for outstate taxes paid would be allowed against local use taxes.
(71) In *S.C.*, freight or other transportation charges are taxable if the title passes to the buyer at the destination point. Freight or other transportation charges are exempt if the title to the transported property passes to the buyer at the point of origin.
(72) Transportation provided by seller is exempt if separately identified; note (69) also applies. In *La.*, exemption is also contingent on transportation charge being optional and avoidable if buyer or buyer's carrier or agent picks up the sold item at the seller's location.
(73) Credit against use tax.
(74) Allowed for tax on use of watercraft, aircraft or vehicles required to be titled, registered or licensed by Ind.
(75) *Nev.* cty. sales tax is credit against Nev. cty. use tax.
(76) (Reserved.)
(77) Gasoline tax by Fed licensee *(Wis.*, see note (95)) and state cigarette tax excluded.
(78) Discounts as price adjustments are exempt; not cash discounts for prompt or early payment. In *D.C.* no credit for quantity or trade discount allowed after sale. In *Vt.* cash or term discounts, if not remibursed by a third party, aren't part of sales price. In *Wyo.*, prompt pyt. discount can be deducted when taken and credited against future tax liability.
(79) Excludes Federal tax on Tel & Tel.
(80) Though member of Multistate Tax Compact, no credit allowed against state license tax (no state sales-use or local use tax).
(81) Motor vehicle titling tax extends credit for outstate sales-use taxes paid. *(Md.)*.
(82) Excludes Fed mfrs.' excise on MVs and tires and Fed-state motor fuel taxes.
(83) Excludes transportation by common or contract carrier or U.S. mails. *Ala.* doesn't exclude contract carriers.
(84) Delivery charges made in conjunction with nontaxable transactions (such as purchases for resale) and charges for delivery made and billed by someone other than the vendor are exempt. *(Pa.)*
(85) Excludes "freight-out" if separately stated. In *Ariz.*, cost of direct shipments from mfr. or wholesaler to buyer and collected by seller is also exempt.
(86) Excludes "time price differentials." Also exempt in *N. Mex.*, charges for making or assuming loans or handling loan payments.
(87) Includes 18% emergency liquor tax.
(88) Includes state cigarette tax.
(89) Traded-in farm machinery exempt. In Nev., exempt from local school tax if buying same kind.
(90) Includes Fed and state motor fuel taxes and all cigarette taxes.
(91) Any Fed tax on sales is excluded. In *Utah*, must be separately stated.
(92) Fed excise tax on tires and fishing equip. is deductible whether on retailer, wholesaler or consumer.
(93) Charges "incident to extension of credit" are exempt.
(94) Excluded if f.o.b. origin and seller's delivery facilities not used. In *N.D.* from transportation charges provided by common carrier are exempt if goods' title passes from seller to buyer.
(95) Fed excise taxes included.
(96) Charged for Fed excise tax not deductible from gross selling price.
(97) Deductible if cash discount for timely payment.
(98) *N.M.*—No trade-in allowance for manufactured homes.
(99) Exempt when delivery is made F.O.B. point of origin and freight charges are billed direct to purchaser from carrier.
(100) Excludes state motor fuel tax.
(101) If such services are part of sale valued in money as determined by terms of sale contract; seller must deliver at his own expense.
(102) Exemption for finance charges is limited.

FOOTNOTES to chart ¶ 256:
(continued)

(103) Excluded if f.o.b. origin and paid by buyer. Taxed if billed by seller and papers inadequate to establish point title passed to buyer. Excluded if buyer pays directly to carrier and doesn't deduct from amount due seller. Exempt if delivery charges are paid directly to carrier and seller doesn't deduct the charges from the amount due. Charges also exempt if separately stated and avoidable by the buyer. *(Fla.)*

(104) Fed retailer's excise taxes paid direct to US are deductible; state cigarette tax deductible if retailer not enriched by collecting sales tax on full selling price.

(105) Transportation is exempt if made by persons other than seller; also if title passes to buyer upon delivery to carrier after passage of title to concrete.

(106) Time price additions, interest, finance or handling charges paid by purchasers on installment basis are included.

(107) Only applies to conditional sale or lease contract or other credit sales.

(108) Exclusion applies to Fed taxes on special motor fuel, communication services and taxable transportation. NYC cigarette tax also excluded.

(109) Exempt from use tax when purchaser pays transportation charges directly to carrier. Taxable when transportation charges are included in purchase price in *Okla.* (exempt if separately stated).

(110) Charges billed directly to purchaser by carrier other than seller, exempt *(Ark.)*.

(111) Exempt if on installment accounts.

(112) *S.D.* exempts interest charges and fees or interest for late charges on overdue accounts, no account, and insufficient funds checks.

(113) Personalty taxes on items covered by lease noncancellable for over 1 year, are deductible *(Md.)*.

(114) Transportation charges for supplying electrical energy and for supplying natural gas are taxable.

(115) Core charges for auto parts securing trade-ins are exempt.

(116) *Wyo.* allows credit for other state's sales tax but not use tax.

(117) Volume discounts are deductible.

(118) Exempt if used property traded in.

(119) Tax on non-highway fuels is excluded.

(120) Excluded are Fed excise taxes on retail sales of special fuels, MVs (incl. tires & tubes), petroleum products, lubricating oils, sporting goods, firearms, communications & air transport; state & local sales taxes on Fed excises. *Mo.* sales tax collected is deductible from gross receipts if separately stated to buyer. *Mo.* also exempts deaf relay service fund surcharge on basic phone access line subscribers.

(121) Exempt if trade-in parts (not tires or batteries for MVs, trailer & semitrailer, motorcycle or implements of husbandry) *(Okla.)*.

(122) Trade-in is deductible if price of new item is reported in full as gross income or proceeds. Use tax base for imported autos is landed cost less trade in if old car to local auto dealer. *(Haw.)*.

(123) If trade-in is of type normally sold by retailer and retailer intends to resell it and if such resale is taxable or for remfg. of like item.

(124) Exempt if imposed directly on consumer and separately stated *(Ind., Minn., N.C., R.I., Wyo.)*. In *Ind.*, taxes imposed on seller are included in sales price.

(125) Credit against business allowed for personalty taxes pd. school dist. in Carroll or Gibson county.

(126) Fed excise tax paid on sale of heavy trailer or truck is excluded from taxable gross income by retailer.

(127) Transient accommodations, rental MV and tour vehicle surcharge, nursing facility income tax, if visibly passed on and collected by persons with registration certificates. Also Fed. and state fuel taxes collected by distributors. To the extent any deduction, allocation, or other method to determine tax liability is necessary to comply with the law, taxpayers may offset the amount of sales, gross receipts or use taxes paid on imported property, services or contracting to another state. *(Haw.)*.

(128) Exempts transportation of farm products from one island to another *(Haw.)*.

(129) *N.Y.* exempts cost of delivering promotional materials by U.S. mails.

(130) Cook County liquor tax deductible.

(131) Interest paid by lessor on the purchase price of property intended to be rented is taxed.

(132) Taxable if the transportation service is a taxable service.

(133) Delivery charges don't include charges for delivery of direct mail if charges are separately stated *(Mich.)*. In *Vt.*, separately stated charges for direct mail are excluded.

(134) Whether separately stated or not, delivery charges are included in the sales price and are subject to tax. Previously, delivery charges were included in the sales price, unless separately stated. *(N.J.)*

(135) Separately stated interest, financing, and carrying charges from credit extended on sale are exempt. *(Wyo.)*.

SALES TAXES—BASIS OR MEASURE OF TAX—PART II

¶257 Returned property, bad debts, repossessions.

T = taxable (included in tax base and no credit or refund allowed)
E = exempt (excluded from tax base, or credit or refund allowed)

STATE	REFUNDS FOR RETURNED PROPERTY (1)	BAD DEBTS (17,35)	BALANCE ON REPOSSESSED GOODS (36)
ALA.	E(7)	E(33)	E
ARIZ.	E(2)	E	E
ARK.	E(7)	E	E
CALIF.	E(2,4)	E(20)	E(50)
COLO.	E(2)	E(20)	E(38)
CONN.	E(51)	E(20)	T(49)
D.C.	E(51)	E	T
FLA.	E	E(14)	E
GA.	E	E(10,20)	T
HAW.	E(2)	E(20)	E(3,37)
IDAHO	E(2,4)	E	T
ILL.	E(8,13)	E(15)	E(40)
IND.	E(3)	E(14)	E(3,37)
IOWA	E(2)	E(20)	E(40)
KAN.	E(2)	E(10)	E(40)
KY.	E(2,4)	E(20)	E(39)
LA.	E(2,10)	E(14)	T(37)
ME.	E(2)	E(24)	E(38)
MD.	E(13)	E(43)	E
MASS.	E(51)	E(53)	T(3)
MICH.	E(2,5,12)	E(24)	T
MINN.	E(2)	E	T(52)
MISS.	E(2)	E(26)	E(37)
MO.	E(2,13)	E(20)	T(42)
NEB.	E(2)	E(27)	E
NEV.	E(2,4)	E(24)	T(3)
N.J.	E(6)	E(6,18)	E(6)
N.M.	E(10)	E(24)	E(37)
N.Y.	E	E	T(3,37)

STATE	REFUNDS FOR RETURNED PROPERTY (1)	BAD DEBTS (17,35)	BALANCE ON REPOSSESSED GOODS (36)
	T = taxable (included in tax base and no credit or refund allowed) E = exempt (excluded from tax base, or credit or refund allowed)		
N.C.	E(7)	E(20,54)	T
N.D.	E(2)	E(20)	E(40)
OHIO	E(2,13)	E(25)	T(3,37)
OKLA.	E(2,13)	E(8)	E(8,33)
PA.	E(13,22)	E(41)	T
R.I.	E(32)	E	T
S.C.	E(7,13)	E	E(3)
S.D.	E(8,13)	E(14,23)	E(14,23,45)
TENN.	E	E(14)	E(34)
TEX.	E(2)	E(14)	E(33)
UTAH	E(13,30,33,46)	E(20,30,46)	E(30,33,46)
VT.	E(2)	E	E(38)
VA.	E(2)	E	E
WASH. (sales tax)	E(2,13,16)	E(14)	E(10)
(Business & Occupation tax)	E(2,13,16)	T(10)	E(10)
W. VA.	E(31)	E	T(47)
WIS.	E(2)	E(20)	E(37,50)
WYO.	E(13)	E	T(48)

FOOTNOTES to chart ¶ 257:

(1) Covers deductibility of purchase price refunded to buyer where goods are returned to seller for any reason; doesn't include repossession.
(2) When sale price is refunded either in cash or by credit.
(3) No specific provision; probable status shown.
(4) No exemption if buyer has to buy higher-priced goods to get refund.
(5) No deduction if credit represents trade-in value on another purchase.
(6) Director provides for refund by regulation.
(7) If entire amount paid by buyer is refunded to him.
(8) If seller has paid tax, he may claim credit on subsequent return.
(9) When new article given, tax computed on additional consideration paid.
(10) Refunds deductible if tax previously paid.
(11) (Reserved.)
(12) If returned within reasonable time after date of sale.
(13) Provided tax paid by buyer is refunded to him.
(14) Allowed if charged off for Fed income tax. In *La.*, only refund is available; no deduction is allowed.
(15) When taxpayer reports on gross sales (not gross receipts) basis.
(16) Return of property after guaranty period is presumed an exchange.
(17) When part of purchase price deemed uncollectible, but goods not repossessed.
(18) *N.J.*—Seller allowed a deduction from taxable sales for bad debts, excluding interest.
(19) (Reserved.)
(20) Accounts found worthless and charged off for income or franchise tax purposes.
(21) Amount involved is credited on later return.
(22) Purchaser gets credit or refund for tax on returned goods.
(23) No deduction if taxes have been remitted on cash basis.
(24) Deductible if actually written off books.
(25) Deductible if tax previously paid and debt uncollectible per IRC §166, except repossessed property.

FOOTNOTES to chart ¶ 257:
(continued)

(26) Seller has choice of paying tax on actual collections, or paying at time of sale and later taking credit for uncollectible amounts.
(27) Credit allowed on deduction taken on bad debt, excepting interest.
(28) Allowed only when tax prepaid and uncollectible.
(29) If property returned by buyer in 3 months of purchase.
(30) Seller must establish by records or other means that he has not been reimbursed.
(31) Credit or refund made for goods returned may be deducted from gross proceeds.
(32) When entire amount paid (exclusive of handling charges) by buyer is refunded either in cash or credit, and when property is returned within 120 days from date of delivery.
(33) Credit allowed for tax paid on unrecovered part of price.
(34) If unpaid balance over $500, credit is difference between (a) tax paid on original purchase price and (b) tax owed on purchase price actually paid by purchaser plus tax on 1st $500 of unpaid balance.
(35) In most states exempting bad debts, tax must be paid on amounts collected after debt charged off.
(36) Covers treatment of unpaid purchase price where goods are repossessed: for taxability of sale of repossessed property, see ¶ 253. If seller doesn't pay tax (for example, buyer pays tax on vehicle registration), no credit or refund to repossessor.
(37) See also status and footnotes, if any, in "Bad Debts" column in this chart.
(38) Tax on difference between unpaid balance and value of item at time of repossession is refundable. Not applicable to MVs in Colo., treated as new sale.
(39) If seller advances entire tax, credit allowed for tax on unpaid purchase price.
(40) Credit for unpaid balance if total price already included in taxable receipts.
(41) *Pa.*—For amounts deducted as bad debts under IRC §166 on Fed. returns filed after 2001, vendor can claim refund of the entire amount of tax amount attributable to bad debt written off on vendor's books.
(42) But actual loss deductible as bad debt charge-off.
(43) If account charged off during year, claim refund in 4 years after paying tax.
(44) Tax credit is in ratio of debt uncollectible in tax year to total debt from the transaction.
(45) When conditional sale contract is assigned to finance company, and seller sustains loss on repossession, tax paid is deductible as bad debt.
(46) Credit for tax paid by retailer and not reimbursed to him.
(47) No refund unless merchant refunds full purchase price collected.
(48) Person regularly in business of making loans or supervised financial institution that repossesses MV is exempt from tax for that MV.
(49) Credit is allowed for worthless accounts.
(50) If seller refunds entire amount paid by purchaser and credits him with full price.
(51) When sale price is refunded either in cash or by credit and when property is returned within 90 days from date of purchase.
(52) Pro rata according to payments made and contract price.
(53) *Mass.*—A vendor that has paid tax on a sale for which credit was given to the purchaser and the account is later determined to be worthless can receive reimbursement. An account is deemed worthless if it is written off as uncollectible for federal income tax purposes under IRC §166.
(54) *N.C.*—Separate records must be kept for bad debts representing taxable and nontaxable sales.

SALES-USE TAXES—ADMINISTRATIVE

¶258 License or permit, small sale exemption, passing on and separately stating tax, resale certificate, collection discount.

STATE	LICENSE OR PERMIT REQUIRED (8)	SMALL SALE EXEMPTION (BRACKETS) (35,84)	MUST SELLER PASS TAX ON TO BUYER?	MUST TAX BE SEPARATELY ADVERTISED OR STATED? (45)	RESALE CERTIFICATES REQUIRED (54)	DISCOUNT OR ALLOWANCE FOR COLLECTING TAX? (73)
ALA.	Yes(11); (no fee)	4¢(14)	Yes(37,38)	Yes(22)	No(36,101)	Yes(74)
ARIZ.	Yes; fee $12(2)	No	No(17,38,39)	Yes(17,38)	Yes(101)	Yes; 1%(68)
ARK.	Yes; $50(2,3)	11¢(18)	Yes	No(38,39)	No(101,105)	Yes; 2%(89)
CALIF.	Yes; no fee(2,3)	5¢(14,18)	No	No	Yes(55,62,101)	No
COLO.	Yes; $16(3,59)	17¢(18,25)	Yes(37)	Yes	Yes(101)	Yes; 3.33%
CONN.	Yes; fee $50(3,107)	8¢	Yes(37,38)	No	Yes(62,101)	No
D.C.	Yes; no fee(2,3)	8¢(18)	Yes(38)	Yes	Yes(55,101)	No
FLA.	Yes; fee $5(2,3,85)	9¢	Yes(37,38)	Yes	Yes(55,57)	Yes; 2.5%(96)
GA.	Yes; no fee(2,15)	7¢(18)	Yes(38,39)	No(38,39)	Yes(101)	Yes; 3%(64)
HAW.	Yes; $20(2,3)	No	No(31)	No	No(82)	No
IDA.	Yes; no fee (11)	5¢(25)	Yes(37,38)	Yes	Yes(101)	No
ILL.	Yes; no fee(6,67)	7¢(14)	No(47,53)	No(38,53)	Yes(101)	Yes; 1.75% $5 min. per cal. yr.
IND.	Yes; fee $25(2,3)	8¢(19)	Yes	Yes	Yes(55,57,58)	Yes; 0.83% (110)
IOWA	Yes; no fee(2,3)	8¢	Yes(38)	Yes	Yes(55,101)	No
KAN.	Yes; no fee(2,3)	7¢	Yes(38)	No(39)	Yes(101)	No
KY.	Yes; no fee(2,3)	8¢(25)	Yes(38)	Yes	Yes(101)	Yes; 1.75%(29)
LA.	Yes; no fee(2,3)	5¢(18)	Yes(78)	Yes	Yes(55)	Yes; 1.1%
ME.	Yes; no fee(2,3)	9¢(25)	Yes(38)	No(42)	Yes(55,101,109)	No(72)
MD.	Yes; no fee(2,3)	19¢(20)	Yes(37,38)	Yes(38)	Yes(55,57,62, 99,101)	Yes; 1.2%(92)
MASS.	Yes; no fee(2,66)	9¢(18)	No(38,80)	Yes(38)	Yes(55,62)	No
MICH.	Yes; no fee (3)	No(18)	No(38,43)	No(42)	Yes(16,55,57, 58,62,101)	Yes; 0.75%(83)
MINN.	Yes; no fee(2)	7¢	Yes	Yes	Yes(101)	No
MISS.	Yes; no fee(2)	7¢(18)	Yes(37)	No	No(16)	Yes; 2%(30)

STATE	LICENSE OR PERMIT REQUIRED (8)	SMALL SALE EXEMPTION (BRACKETS) (35,84)	MUST SELLER PASS TAX ON TO BUYER?	MUST TAX BE SEPARATELY ADVERTISED OR STATED? (45)	RESALE CERTIFICATES REQUIRED (54)	DISCOUNT OR ALLOWANCE FOR COLLECTING TAX? (73)
MO.	Yes; no fee	(14,35)	Yes(38)	Yes(37,38)	Yes(101)	Yes; 2%(33)
NEB.	Yes; No fee (2,3)	9¢(14)	Yes	Yes	Yes(101)	Yes; 2.5%(7)
NEV.	Yes; fee $5(2,3)	7¢(18)	Yes(38)	Yes	Yes(49,55,57, 62,101)	Yes; 0.5%
N.J.	Yes; no fee	10¢(25)	Yes	Yes	Yes(101)	No
N.M.	Yes; no fee	No(18)	No	No	Yes(55,101)	No
N.Y.	Yes; no fee(2,3)	(14)	Yes(42)	Yes(38)	Yes(51)	Yes; 3.5%(68)
N.C.	Yes; no fee	(14)	Yes(38)	Yes	No(111)	No
N.D.	Yes; no fee(2,3)	15¢(18,25)	Yes(38)	Yes	Yes(62,101)	Yes; 1.5%(46)
OHIO	Yes; fee $25(3)	No	Yes	No(38)	Yes(55,57)	Yes; 0.75%
OKLA.	Yes; fee $20(3,34)	9¢(14,35)	Yes(37,38)	No	Yes(101)	Yes; 2.25%(100)
PA.	Yes; no fee(11,106)	10¢	Yes(37,38)	Yes(38,39)	Yes	Yes; 1%
R.I.	Yes; fee $10(12)	7¢(18,24)	Yes(38)	No(75)	Yes(49,101)	No
S.C.	Yes; fee $50 (3)	No(18)	No(102)	Yes(26)	Yes(101)	Yes; 3%(4)
S.D.	Yes; no fee(2,3,12)	8¢(14)	Yes	No	Yes(97,101)	No
TENN.	Yes; no fee(2)	10¢	Yes(18,27)	Yes	Yes(101)	Yes; 2%(23)
TEX.	Yes; no fee (11)	7¢	Yes(38,39,47)	Yes(32)	Yes(55,101)	Yes; 0.5%(60)
UTAH	Yes; no fee(2,3)	(14,18,25)	Yes(37)	Yes(52)	Yes(55,97,101)	Yes(95)
VT.	Yes; no fee(2,3)	10¢(104)	Yes(37,38)	Yes	Yes(101)	Yes(21)
VA.	Yes; no fee(2,3)	11¢(18,25)	Yes	Yes(37,38)	Yes	Yes(77)
WASH.	**(Sales-use)** Yes: no fee(2,3,9,10)	7¢(14,19)	No	No	Yes(39,101)	No(69)
	(B&O) Yes; no fee(2,3,9,10)	(1)	No	No(1)	Yes(69)	
W.VA.	**(Consumers)** Yes(59)	(18,27)	Yes(38)	No(1)	Yes	No
WIS.	Yes; fee $20(3)	9¢(18)	(38,41)	Yes(75)	Yes(57,63,101)	Yes; 0.5%(91)
WYO.	Yes; $60(2,3)	No(18)	Yes(38)	Yes(42)	No(108)	No

FOOTNOTES to chart ¶ 258

(1) No specific provision.

(2) License or permit is continuous. In Haw., $5 fee for transient lodging facility with 5 or less units; $15, over 5. In *Ark.*, $50 fee is required.

FOOTNOTES to chart ¶ 258 (continued)

(3) Separate license required for each place of business. In *Iowa*, a vendor is required to get sales tax permits for permanent locations where taxable sales will occur. In *S.D.*, statewide permit can be granted in lieu of obtaining a permit for each place of business.

(4) 3% on amounts under $100; 2% for higher amounts; max. discount $3,000 ($3,100 for taxpayers filing electronically and $10,000 for out-of-staters voluntarily registered and collecting) (S.C.).

(5) Store licensees exempt. mfg.

(6) Sub-certificates of registration for chain stores. In *Ill.*, sub-certificates are required for each added place of business, vending machines, or MV from which sales are made.

(7) 2.5% of 1st $3,000 tax per month *(Neb.)*.

(8) Additional or separate requirements may apply to vending machines, flea markets, yard or tag sales, seasonal or transient sellers, sales events of limited duration, or nonprofit sellers.

(9) Use tax must be separately stated.

(10) Same license covers retail sales and occupational business taxes.

(11) Single license for all places of business. In *Ida.*, if operating under the same business name. In *Pa.*, license for principal place of business.

(12) Nonresident retailer needs certificate of authority to collect use tax; no fee.

(13) $25 fee covers tax on first $20,000 of gross receipts.

(14) Collection brackets vary on basis of combined state-local tax rate.

(15) Permit to import personalty required; no fee.

(16) State-issued resale number or permit must be taken from buyer.

(17) Applies to use tax; net effect similar for transaction (sales) tax.

(18) Retailers pay tax on all receipts, including small sales on which no tax collected.

(19) Small sales to extent noted are deducted from retailers' gross receipts.

(20) Vending machine operators pay 5% tax on 95.25% of the gross receipts.

(21) Amount lawfully collected, under tax bracket schedules, that exceeds amount of tax actually due based on sales *(Vt.)*.

(22) Whenever practical; otherwise retailer must post sign stating charge includes price of item and percentage of tax being collected *(Ala.)*.

(23) Deduct for collection of state tax: 2%, plus 1.15% on over $2,500 per report. *(Tenn.)*.

(24) Retailers with receipts 60% or more from small sales must keep adequate records to exclude these sales from receipts.

(25) Vending machine operators exempt on sales under 10¢ (11¢ or less in Ida., 15¢ or less in Colo. and in N.D.), on food sales over 50% of gross, in Me. In SC and Va., 10¢ or less. 25¢ or less in Ky. and N.J. In Utah, $1.00 on food, candy, etc., vending machine sales if operator reports 150% of costs as goods consumed.

(26) Use tax must be separately stated. No similar restriction for sales tax. *(S.C.)*

(27) 9¢ for sale food or food ingredients *(W.Va.)*.

(28) Applicant who elects to file consolidated return may file single permit application listing all retail locations.

(29) 1.75%, 1st $1,000 tax; 1% over $1,000, if payment timely. Compensation is limited to $1,500 per month. *(Ky.)*.

(30) 2% of tax (not for contracting, cotton ginning, utilities or wholesale tax); not over $50 monthly or $600 annually per store. *(Miss.)*

(31) Out-of-state sellers with any local representation (salesman, agent, etc.) must collect use tax from buyer, unless excused by director.

(32) Or written statement to customer that price includes tax.

(33) Discount denied direct payment permittees.

(34) Added $10 per business place. Permit good for 3 yrs.

(35) Exemptions are usually reduced to amounts listed when local taxes apply.

(36) Seller making retail and wholesale sales must provide sales tax number when buying for resale. Persons without sales tax license must provide exemption certificate. *(Ala.)*

(37) Seller may not absorb tax.

(38) Seller may not advertise or hold out that he or she will absorb tax.

(39) But seller may include tax in selling price.

(40) (Reserved.)

(41) But seller may reimburse himself by adding tax to sale price.

(42) Seller may not advertise that tax isn't considered an element of price.

(43) No unjust enrichment from collection of tax.

(44) Commr. may allow tax prepayment by seller and waive collection from buyer.

(45) In practice, bill or invoice for *completed* sale usually separates tax from price. For advertising absorption, see preceding column and footnotes 37, 38, 42, and 44.

(46) Max. deduction, $85 monthly per business location. *(N.D.)*.

(47) But seller must collect use tax (if payable) from buyer.

(48) Footnotes 55, 58, 62, 63 apply.

(49) Seller has burden of proving sale is nontaxable sale for resale unless seller takes a resale certificate *(Nev., R.I.)*.

(50) Posted notice must state that tax will be added to quoted price, or each posted or advertised price must show tax separately.

(51) Footnotes 55, 57, 58, 62, 63 apply.

FOOTNOTES to chart ¶ 258
(continued)

(52) Seller must add tax as a separate item.

(53) Hotel operator tax may be passed on to customer, if separately billed. Use taxes must be billed separately.

(54) Refers to necessity for seller's getting certificate from buyer as a prerequisite to exemption on sales for resale.

(55) Form or suggested form of certificate is prescribed by regulation or ruling. In *Utah*, use exemption certificate.

(56) Tax not passed on as a tax.

(57) Use of blanket certificate covering continued or grouped sales is authorized. In *Mich.* blanket exemption certificate covers 4-yr. period.

(58) Record of exempt sales for resale must also be kept.

(59) Biennial license. In Colo. $16 plus $50 deposit. In W.Va., $30 fee per business location.

(60) Added discount of 1.25% if estimated tax is prepaid. *(Tex.)*.

(61) Separate list of resales required with monthly report.

(62) Certificate may be taken only from licensed or registered buyers.

(63) Certificate may be taken from out-of-state (or out-city) buyers though unregistered.

(64) 3% of 1st $3,000, 0.5% of rest collected. But 3% of all sales-use tax collected on motor fuel.

(65) *Wyo.* —No fee for prescribed remote vendors.

(66) *Mass.* —Registration certificates can be issued for a period of not less than 3 years.

(67) *Ill.* —Certificate of registration expires 5 yrs. after issuance or last renewal.

(68) Tax Credit: 1%; $10,000 calendar yr. max. *(Ariz.)*. 3.5% of state tax at rate of 4% collected ($150 max. per quarter) *(N.Y.)*.

(69) Footnotes 55, 57, 62, 63 apply.

(70) Footnotes 3, 4, 10 apply.

(71) Footnotes 2, 4, 11 apply.

(72) Sellers keep breakage as collection compensation.

(73) Discount usually depends on timely reports and payment. Timely payment only is required in *La.*

(74) 5% on first $100 of sales, 2% on excess for sales tax. No sellers use tax discount. Maximum $400 per month per retailer regardless of number of retail locations. *(Ala.)*.

(75) Separate listing may be required by regulation. In R.I., labor or service charges subject to tax must be separately stated at buyer's request.

(76) Footnotes 11 and 14 apply.

(77) Deduct these percentages of 1st 3% of tax: 1st $62,500 of monthly taxable sales, 4%; $62.501 — $208,000, 3%; $208,001 and above, 2% *(Va.)*.

(78) Sellers cannot advertise or hold out to the public that they will absorb tax unless they include in the ad that they will remit, on buyer's behalf, any portion of the tax not paid by the buyer, and they give the buyer written evidence that they will be liable for and pay any tax that they relieve the buyer from paying *(La.)*.

(79) Invoice (and seller's copy) must show retailer-buyer's name, address and sales tax acct. number.

(80) Although law requires sellers to collect tax from buyers, it imposes no sanction on vendor who chooses not to charge tax. On purchase of auto from dealer, buyer pays tax directly to Commr. Rev.; on casual sales of autos, purchasers are subject to use tax (paid directly to Commr.).

(81) Certificate of resale where use tax involved.

(82) Certificates only for sales at wholesale.

(83) Collection discount applicable only to 1st 4% of tax due—0.75% of that tax ($20,000 max.) if paid by 12th of month; 0.5% of that tax ($15,000 max.) if paid by 20th; or if greater, tax on $150 of taxable gross proceeds. Collection discount for electronic fund filers applicable only to 1st 4% of tax due—0.5% of that tax if 50% paid by 20th of month and remaining 50% paid by last day of month *(Mich.)*.

(84) Small sale exemptions shown are maximum amounts exempt in highest general total rate bracket. They are either incorporated in law as direct exemption or are allowed by exclusion from bracket schedules.

(85) *Fla.* —Special registration provisions apply to coin-operated amusement machine operators and dry cleaners. Registration fee waived for on-line registration.

(86) Up to $100 tax. 3%; $100–$1,000, 2%; $1,000 or more 1% (max. discount $5,000).

(87) No bracket for retailer's occupation tax; use tax collection brackets vary on basis of combined state-local tax rate.

(88) Vending machine sales taxed on 60% of receipts if tax per sale is under 1¢.

(89) Discount for sales tax, but not for use tax. Max. discount, $1,000 per month per taxpayer (even if multi-location). *(Ark.)*

(90) Regulation requires certain businesses to separate state charges.

(91) *Wis.* —Can deduct greater of 0.5% of taxes or $10 for reporting period, up to amount of taxes payable for reporting period.

(92) 1.2% of 1st $6,000, and 0.9% of rest collected. (Md.).

(93) (Reserved.)

(94) New vendors must prepay $150 (Wyo.).

(95) Monthly filers only: 1.31% of state, 1% of local tax collected; special rule for sellers of food and food ingredients. (Utah).

(96) Retailer's collection discount, 2.5%; on 1st $1,200 of taxes collected (Fla.).

(97) State has no separate resale certificate, but requires exemption certificate to support exemption.

(98) *N.Y.* —State brackets replaced with rounding tax due to nearest penny. No tax collected on sales of personalty producing tax of 5 mills or less.

FOOTNOTES to chart ¶ 258
(continued)

(99) *Md.*—But tax must be collected on sales under $200 if not delivered to buyer's retail location, and buyers can file refund claims.

(100) *Okla.* —Max. discount, $3,300 per reporting period per permit.

(101) State accepts the Multistate Tax Commission multijurisdiction exemption certificate as a resale certificate. *Colo.* doesn't allow use of the certificate for buying taxable services for resale.

(102) *S.C.* —Can't absorb use tax or advertise that use tax be absorbed. No similar restriction on sales tax.

(103) Vendor must collect tax on sales for resale unless they get from buyer a properly executed resale certificate; or proof that the buyer is registered with the Rev. Dept. or in another state and that item is being bought for resale.

(104) *Vt.* —Sales tax calculated either by rounding rule or bracket system.

(105) Seller may accept retail permit number with certification that buyer is engaged in business of reselling *or* resale certificate *(Ark.)*.

(106) License valid for 5 yrs. *(Pa.)*.

(107) Permit valid for 5 yrs. *(Conn.)*.

(108) *Wyo.* —Except when direct pay permit can be used, vendor must get exemption certificate and keep certificate in its records.

(109) *Me.* —Resale certificates are issued to retailers with gross sales of $3,000 or more in the preceding 12 mos.

(110) *Ind.* —0.83% if retailer's tax liability during the state fiscal year ending 6-30 of the immediately preceding calendar year didn't exceed $60,000; 0.6% if over $60,000 up to $600,000, and 0.3% if over $600,000.

(111) *N.C.* —Buyer must provide either Streamlined Sales Tax Agreement Certificate of Exemption or other written evidence adequate to support the conclusion (1) that buyer is either registered with the Dept. Rev. or registered in another jurisdiction for sales and use tax purposes; and (2) that the property is being purchased for resale.

SALES TAXES ON TELECOMMUNICATIONS SERVICES

¶259 Rates and services taxed. Most states and the District of Columbia impose sales or similar excise taxes on telecommunications service transactions. Many of those jurisdictions tax both interstate and intrastate transactions. Some states tax intrastate and local exchange service only, and a few limit the levy to local exchange service. California's tax is a special levy to fund the emergency ''911'' system. Maryland's tax is limited to mobile ''900'' and other specified services. South Carolina taxes local ''900'' and ''976'' services. Added local taxes may be levied.

Mobile Telecommunications Sourcing Act. The Mobile Telecommunications Sourcing Act (P.L. 106-252; 4 U.S.C. §116 *et seq.*), limits the authority to impose taxes, charges, or fees on charges for mobile telecommunications services deemed to be provided by a customer's home service provider to the state and local taxing jurisdictions whose territorial limits encompass the customer's place of primary use, regardless of where the services originate, end, or pass through.

Here is a list of the state sales taxes on telephone calls and other taxable communications:

Statewide	State Tax Rate	Service Taxed
Alabama(1)	6%	Inter- and intrastate; mobile telecommuncations
Alaska	Not taxed	
Arizona	5.6%	Intrastate
Arkansas	6%	Inter- and intrastate
California	0.50% (eff. 11-1-2007 to 10-31-2008; pre-11-1-2007, 0.65%)	Intrastate
Colorado	2.9%	Intrastate
Connecticut	6%	Inter- and intrastate
Delaware	Not taxed	
D.C.(4)	5.75%	Local, "900"-type phone services, and other specified services
Florida(9)	9.17%	Inter- and intrastate
Georgia	4%	Local
Hawaii	4%	Interstate
Idaho	Not taxed	
Illinois	7%	Inter- and intrastate
Indiana	6%	Intrastate
Iowa	5%	Intrastate
Kansas	5%	Inter- and intrastate
Kentucky(15)	6%	Inter- and intrastate
Louisiana	3%(5)	Inter- and intrastate(5)
Maine	5%	Intrastate
Maryland	5%	Mobile telecommunications, "900"-type phone services, and other specified services
Massachusetts	5%	Inter- and intrastate

Statewide	State Tax Rate	Service Taxed
Michigan	6%	Inter- and intrastate; mobile telecommunications, and air-ground radiotelephone services
Minnesota	6.5%	Inter- and intrastate; mobile telecommunications
Mississippi	7%(7)	Inter- and intrastate(7)
Missouri	4.225%	Intrastate
Montana	3.75%	Inter- and Intrastate
Nebraska	5.5%	Intrastate; mobile telecommunications
Nevada	Not taxed	
New Hampshire	7% (13)	Inter- and intrastate
New Jersey	7%	Inter- and intrastate
New Mexico	5%	Intrastate
	4.25%	Interstate
New York	4%(10)	Intrastate
North Carolina	4.25% (4.5% eff. 10-1-2008)	Intrastate
North Dakota	5%	Intrastate
Ohio	5.5%	Inter- and intrastate
Oklahoma	4.5%	Inter- and intrastate(8)
Oregon	Not taxed	
Pennsylvania	6%	Inter- and intrastate
Rhode Island	7%	Inter- and intrastate
South Carolina	6%	Intrastate
	10%	"900" or "976" phone service
South Dakota	4%	Intrastate
Tennessee	7%(11)	Inter- and intrastate
Texas	6.25%	Inter- and intrastate(16)
Utah	5.75%(3)	Intrastate
Vermont	6%	Inter- and intrastate
Virginia(6)	5%	Inter- and intrastate
Washington	6.5%	Inter- and intrastate
West Virginia	Not taxed	
Wisconsin	5%	Inter- and intrastate
Wyoming	4%	Intrastate; intrastate calls using mobile telecommunications services

FOOTNOTES to chart ¶ 259

(1) *Ala.*—4% tax rate on prepaid calling cards or authorization numbers.

(2) *Vt.*—The amount of tax exceeding $10,000 per calendar yr. need not be paid.

(3) *Utah*—Rate shown is total composed of 4.75% state rate plus uniform 1% local rate. Additional local taxes may apply.

(4) *D.C.*—10% (residential customers) or 11% (nonresidential customers) of monthly gross charges on toll and wireless telecommunications. 10% of gross receipts on sale of prepaid telephone calling cards.

(5) *La.*—Intrastate telecommunications are taxed at 3%. Interstate telecommunications are taxed as follows: at 2% until 3-31-2016; 1% eff. 4-1-2016.

(6) *Va.*—Until 1-1-2007, localities could impose a tax on the taxable purchase of local telecommunication service.

(7) *Miss.* —Intrastate and interstate telecommunications are taxed at 7%.

(8) *Okla.* —If sourced to Okla.

FOOTNOTES to chart ¶ 259
(continued)

(9) *Fla.*—Rate shown is total composed of 6.8% sales tax on communications services plus 2.37% gross receipts tax.

(10) *N.Y.*— Additional 5% tax is imposed on furnishing or providing an entertainment or information service through "800" or "900" numbers.

(11) *Tenn.* —Rate shown is for intrastate communications services, and 2.5% local tax for intrastate telecommunications sold to businesses or residences. Rate for interstate communications services is 7.5%. Additional local tax of 1.5% also applies to interstate services sold to residences.

(12) (Reserved.)

(13) *N.H.* —$12 of monthly gross charges for residential customer telephone exchange access is exempt.

(14) (Reserved.)

(15) *Ky.*—Excise tax of 3% is imposed on multichannel video and audio programming services.

(16) *Tex..* —Interstate calls are taxable if they originate from and are billed to a telephone number or a billing or service address in Texas.

SALES TAXES ON COMPUTER SOFTWARE, INTERNET ACCESS, AND INFORMATION SERVICES

¶259-A Computer Software, Internet Access, Information Services The first column of the chart shows the state tax treatment of sales of computer software. The second column shows the state tax treatment of Internet access charges. The third column shows the state tax treatment of the provision of information services. In the third column, the term "not taxed" applies to those states that specifically exempt information services and those states that do not include information services as taxable services.

Internet Tax Freedom Act. On October 31, 2007, President Bush signed the Internet Tax Freedom Act Amendments Act of 2007, P.L. 110-108, which extends until November 1, 2014, the moratorium on taxes on Internet access and multiple and discriminatory taxes on electronic commerce originally enacted by the Internet Tax Freedom Act, P.L. 105-277, §§1101—1104 (10/21/1998), as amended by P.L. 107-75, §2 (11/28/2001) and P.L. 108–435 (The Internet Tax Nondiscrimination Act, 12/03/2004). The moratorium applies to a tax on Internet access, regardless of whether the tax is imposed on a provider of Internet access or a buyer of Internet access, and regardless of the terminology used to describe the tax. Effective November 1, 2007, the term ''Internet access'' includes a home page, electronic mail and instant messaging (including voice- and video-capable electronic mail and instant messaging), video clips, and personal electronic storage capacity, that are provided independently or not packaged with Internet access.

The moratorium does not apply to a tax on Internet access that was generally imposed and actually enforced prior to October 1, 1998, if, before that date: (1) the tax was authorized by statute; and (2) either (a) a provider of Internet access services had a reasonable opportunity to know, by virtue of a rule or other proclamation made by the appropriate administrative agency of the state or political subdivision thereof, that such agency had interpreted and applied such tax to Internet access services; or (b) a state or political subdivision thereof generally collected such tax on charges for Internet access.

The above does not apply to any state that has, more than 24 months prior to November 1, 2007, enacted legislation to repeal the state's taxes on Internet access or issued a rule or other proclamation that the state agency has decided to no longer apply such tax to Internet access.

The grandfather provision generally terminates after November 1, 2014, except that the provision terminates after November 1, 2006, with respect to a state telecommunications service tax that was enacted by state law on or after October 1, 1991, and that applies to Internet access through administrative code or regulation issued on or after December 1, 2002. This provision is applicable only to Wisconsin. In addition, nothing in the Act may be construed to prohibit Texas or a political subdivision of Texas from imposing or collecting the Texas municipal access line fee.

In addition to the grandfather provision applicable to pre-October 1998 taxes, another grandfather clause applies to pre-November 2003 taxes. This provision, designed to protect existing state taxes on digital subscriber line services, does not apply after November 1, 2005.

	Computer Software	Internet Access	Information Services
Alabama	Taxable. Exempt if customized	Exempt	Not taxed
Alaska	No sales tax		
Arizona	Taxable. Exempt for technical services and customized	Exempt	Not taxed
Arkansas	Taxable	Exempt	Not taxed
California	Taxable. Exempt if customized	Exempt	Not taxed
Colorado	Taxable. Exempt if customized	Exempt	Not taxed
Connecticut	Taxable. Exempt if customized	Exempt	Taxable
Delaware	No sales tax		
District of Columbia	Taxable	Exempt	Taxable
Florida	Taxable. Exempt if customized	Exempt	Taxable, unless furnished to TV, radio or news services
Georgia	Taxable. Exempt if customized	Exempt	Not taxed
Hawaii	Taxable	Taxable	Taxable
Idaho	Taxable. Exempt if customized	Exempt	Taxable
Illinois	Taxable. Exempt if customized	Exempt	No provision (service tax applies to items transferred with service)
Indiana	Taxable. Exempt if customized	Exempt	Not taxed
Iowa	Taxable. Exempt if customized	Exempt	Not taxed
Kansas	Taxable. Custom software exempt.	Exempt	Not taxed
Kentucky	Taxable. Exempt if customized	Exempt	Not taxed
Louisiana	Taxable. Exempt if customized	Exempt	Not taxed
Maine	Taxable. Exempt if customized	Exempt	Not taxed
Maryland	Taxable. Custom software services are exempt	Exempt	Not taxed
Massachusetts	Taxable. Exempt if customized	Exempt	Taxable. Exempt if for news media
Michigan	Taxable. Custom software services are exempt	Exempt	Exempt if optional and distinct from rental of property
Minnesota	Taxable. Design and development of custom program exempt	Exempt	Not taxed
Mississippi	Taxable	Exempt	Not taxed

	Computer Software	Internet Access	Information Services
Missouri	Taxable. Exempt if customized	Exempt	Not taxed
Montana	No sales tax		
Nebraska	Taxable	Exempt. Initial set-up of service is taxable if software is provided	No provision. Exemption for certain electronic transmitted information
Nevada	Taxable. Exempt if customized	Exempt	Not taxed
New Hampshire	No sales tax		
New Jersey	Taxable. Exempt if customized. Software delivered electronically is taxable except for sales of software used directly and exclusively in the conduct of the purchaser's business, trade or occupation.	Exempt	Taxable
New Mexico	Taxable. Exempt if customized	Deductible from gross receipts.	Taxable
New York	Taxable. Exempt if customized and sold to a specific purchaser	Exempt	Taxable. Exempt if for news media or for resale
North Carolina	Taxable. Exempt if customized	Exempt	Not taxed
North Dakota	Taxable. Exempt if customized	Taxable	Taxable if sold in same form
Ohio	Taxable. Exempt if customized unless nonapplication software (systems software).	Taxable, if sold for business use	Exempt if true object is receipt of exempt personal or professional service
Oklahoma	Taxable. Exempt if customized	Exempt	Taxable if in tangible personal property form
Oregon	No sales tax		
Pennsylvania	Taxable. Exempt if customized	Exempt	Not taxed
Rhode Island	Taxable. Exempt if customized	Exempt	Not taxed
South Carolina	Taxable. Software delivered electronically isn't taxable.	Exempt	Not taxed
South Dakota	Taxable	Taxable	Taxable
Tennessee	Taxable	Exempt	Not taxed
Texas	Taxable	1st $25 per month is exempt	20% of charge exempt
Utah	Taxable. Exempt if customized	Exempt	Not taxed
Vermont	Taxable. Exempt if customized	Exempt	Not taxed
Virginia	Taxable. Exempt if customized	Exempt	Exempt unless included in sale of tangible personal property

	Computer Software	Internet Access	Information Services
Washington	Taxable. Exempt if customized (sales-use) Taxable (bus. & occ.)	Exempt (sales-use)	Exempt unless included in sale of tangible personal property (sales-use) Taxable (bus. & occ.)
West Virginia	Taxable, unless used in processing data for others, mfg. as components, communication or education	Exempt	Taxable. Sales of primary opinion research services are exempt
Wisconsin	Taxable. Exempt if customized	Taxable	Exempt
Wyoming	Taxable. Exempt if customized	Exempt	Depends on how service is classified

REAL PROPERTY TAX RATES

¶260 Figuring real property tax loads. This chart shows the range of real property tax rates—low and high—per $1,000 of assessed value unless otherwise indicated. If only one rate is shown, it is the rate in current use in the major cities.

The rates shown are composites of many rates applicable locally—city or town rates, county or parish rates, and school district rates. (There may be additional rates applicable locally—special district rates and improvement assessment rates. This chart does not cover those.) The rates represent the range—the lowest and the highest of these composite rates. This chart does not cover personal property taxes.

➾ **TAX LIDS→** Property tax limits are shown in footnotes.

STATE	YEAR	RANGE (in dollars; unless otherwise shown)
ALA.	2006	5.00–40.50 City
		8.50–20.50 County
ALASKA(2)	2006	0.00–20.023 City/Borough
ARIZ.	2006	7.74–18.68
ARK.(2)	2006, payable 2007	38.00-63.30
CALIF.(2,13)	2004–2005	0.05—0.197875
COLO.(2)	2006	39.10–101.35
CONN.(2)	2006–2007	0.38–64.82
DEL.(1,2,14)	2006–2007	16.59–186.40
D.C.(2,10)	2008	Cl. 1 — 8.50
		Cl. 2 — 18.50
		Cl. 3 — 50.00
FLA.(3)	2006	2.30–8.75 City
		6.93–32.65 County
GA.(2)	2007	24.93–50.59 City
		17.80–39.30 County
HAW.(1,2,4)	2006–2007	2.00–14.00 Buildings
		3.50–14.00 Land
IDAHO(2)	2005	5.73–30.68
ILL.(1,2)	2004	37.26–148.55
IND.(2)	2006	1.92–8.25
IOWA(1,3)	2007	29.44–46.70
KAN.(3)	2005	0.69–1.71 County
KY.(9)	2006	1.26–4.18 County
		0.52–8.00 City
LA.(2)	2004	46.5–176.3 (Avg. Millage)
MAINE(2)	2005	8.14-26.65
MD.(2,16)	2007–2008	4.75–11.10 County
MASS.(2,11)	2007	1.87–18.08 Resident
		1.87–33.36 Commercial, Industrial
MICH.(2,15)	2006	14.58–68.17
MINN.(2,17)	2007	52.07–166.82
MISS.(2)	2004–2005	39.30–136.83
MO.(2)	2005	0.0750–1.0000 (Avg. Millage) (City only)
MONT.(2)	2004–2005	2.16–8.91
NEB.(2)	2005	0.02647700–0.63626000 (per $100)
NEV.(2)	2005–2006	21.52–36.60
N.H.(2)	2006	2.64–38.93

STATE	YEAR	RANGE (in dollars; unless otherwise shown)
N.J.(2)	2005	0.47–13.12 Effective tax rates
		0.45–158.88 General tax rates
N.M.(2,8)	2006	14.37–37.26 Resident
		19.99–43.62 Non-Resident
N.Y.(1,2)	2006	4.57–233.67 City
N.C.(2)	2006–2007	3.18–11.10 County
		3.70–8.00 City
N.D.(1,2)	2005	4.1810–5.3498
OHIO	2006	35.90–195.50
OKLA.(2)	2005/2006	58.92–122.26
ORE.(2)	2005–2006	0.0000–11.9152 County
PA.(1,3)	2006	2.13–94.9 County
R.I.(2)	2007–2008	3.17–22.84
S.C.(2)	2005	0.39–1.88 City
		1.96–4.99 County & Sch.
S.D.(1,2)	2003–2004	15.39–32.56 Agr.
		16.13–27.14 Nonagr.
TENN.(2)	2006	0.00–7.47
TEX.(2)	2004	2.58–8.68 City
UTAH(2)	2007	0.000189–0.006319
VT.(2)	2005	193.50–307.50
VA.(2)	2004	City: 5.40–14.50
		Counties: 3.70–11.30
WASH.(2,5)	2004	6.68–15.95
W.VA.(3)	2007	10.66–18.75 Class I
		21.32–37.50 Class II
		42.64–75.50 Class IV
WIS.(2)	2006–2007	Rates: 67.87–108.37
		Gross: 14.63–26.54
		Effective: 13.78–22.89
WYO.(2)	2007	56.20–81.28 (Mills)

FOOTNOTES to chart ¶ 260 (corresponding to parenthetical numbers following state names in chart).

(1) In N.D. and S.D., nearly all tangible personal property is exempt. In other states, tangible personal property is exempt.

(2) In La., Miss., Nev., N.D., R.I., S.D., Tex. and Wyo., nearly all intangible personal property is exempt. In other states, including Alaska, Ariz., Ark., Calif., Colo., Conn., Del., D.C., Ga., Haw., Ida., Ill., Ind., Me., Md., Mass., Mich., Minn., Mo., Mont., Neb., N.H., N.J., N.M., N.Y., N.C., Okla., Ore., S.C., Utah, Vt., Va., Wash. and Wis., intangible personal property is exempt.

(3) Intangible personal property is taxed at lower value or lower rate than other property. In W. Va., the tax on intangible personal property was being phased out over the period 1998–2003. In Fla., the annual intangibles tax is repealed eff. 1-1-2007.

(4) Average of county averages (Haw.).

(5) Aggregate rates can't exceed 1% of value. (Wash.).

(6) (Reserved.)

(7) (Reserved.)

(8) Maximum rates are as follows: county, $11.85 per $1,000 of net taxable value; school districts, max. depends on year and type of property; municipalities, $7.65 per $1,000. (N.M.)

(9) Statutory state rate on realty is 12.4¢ per $100 of value for 2007. Special rates apply to many types of property. (Ky.)

(10) Rates are for 2008 tax year: 10-1-2007—9-30-2008, Cl. 1 is improved residential real property that is used exclusively for nontransient residential dwelling purposes; Cl. 2 is improved commercial property; Cl. 3 is all property that can't be classified as Cl. 1 or Cl. 2 property. (D.C.)

(11) Total taxes assessed on realty and personalty can't, in any year, exceed 2.5% of full and fair cash value, unless voters say otherwise. (Mass.)

(12) (Reserved.)

(13) Maximum amount of any ad valorem tax on realty (except if funding certain voter-approved debt or meeting other specified limited exceptions): 1% of full cash value—county assessors' value as shown on 1975-1976 tax bill or appraised value when bought or newly built after that. But full cash value can reflect year-to-year inflationary rate up to 2%. (Calif.)

FOOTNOTES to chart ¶ 260 (corresponding to parenthetical numbers following state names in chart). **(continued)**

(14) Max. cty, rate in Kent: $0.50 per $100 of assessed value (Del.)

(15) Total taxes that can be imposed on realty and tangible personalty in any year for all purposes can't exceed 15 mills per $1 of assessed value, as finally equalized, unless approved by the voters. This doesn't apply to cities and villages, and to school districts as to repayment of state loans. Property is exempt from millage l evied for local school district or intermediate school district operating purposes, except if for community college purposes. Taxable value of each parcel of property adjusted for additions and losses can't increase each yr. by more than the lesser of 5% or the general price level until ownership is transferred. *(Mich.)*.

(16) Rates shown are used on realty tax bills mailed by local governments after 6-30-2007. *(Md.)*.

(17) Amounts shown are county net tax capcity tax rates. Eff. for taxables payable in 2002 and after, new statewide property tax levy is imposed on commerical and industrial property (except utility electric generating mchy.) *(Minn.)* .

INVENTORY ASSESSMENTS AND RETURNS

¶263 Placing inventories for tax saving. The placement of inventories is not only an annual problem state-to-state, but district-to-district as well. Most states use Dec. 31, Jan. 1, or another specified date as the property assessment and valuation date. Some states may tax on an average basis, either unconditionally or as an option.

The chart below furnishes a quick check as to what states levy property taxes on inventories, the assessment dates or periods, and the report dates. If reports may be filed over a period of time (for example, during the period Feb. 15 to Mar. 15) the chart shows only the last day for filing, since that is the critical date from the taxpayer's standpoint. Similarly, when the due date depends on the assessor's demand, no date is shown (the chart is concerned primarily with action that must be initiated by the taxpayer).

No personal property tax states. Delaware, Hawaii, Illinois, Iowa, New York, Pennsylvania do not have a property or ad valorem tax on tangible personalty, so inventories are not taxable there. North Dakota tax only applies to certain entities required to be assessed by the state board of equalization. South Dakota only taxes centrally assessed personal property (utilities, airlines, express companies, etc.).

No inventory tax states. These states do not levy a property tax on the inventories of merchants and manufacturers held for processing or sale: Alabama, Arizona, California, Colorado, Connecticut, the District of Columbia, Florida, Idaho, Kansas, Maine, Michigan (see note (40)), Minnesota, Missouri, Montana, Nebraska, Nevada, New Hampshire, New Jersey, North Carolina, Oregon, South Carolina, Tennessee, Utah, Virginia, (see note (37)) Washington, Wisconsin, and Wyoming. New Mexico exempts inventories with few exceptions.

STATE	ASSESSMENT DATE	RETURNS DUE	ASSESSMENT RATIOS
Alaska(6)	Jan. 1(2)	(11)	100%
Arkansas	Jan. 1(1)	May 31	20%
Georgia(24)	Jan. 1	Apr. 1(11)	40%
Indiana(14)	Mar. 1(36)	May 15	(21)
Kentucky	Jan. 1	May 15	100%
Louisiana(24)	Jan. 1(20,29)	Apr. 1(15)	15%
Maryland(43)	Jan. 1 (1)	Apr.15	(43)
Massachusetts(7)	Jan. 1	(38)	100%
Michigan(40)	Dec. 31	Feb. 20(9)	50%
Mississippi(42)	Jan. 1(16)	Apr. 1(17)	15%(41)
Ohio(10)	Dec. 31	Apr. 30	12.5%(10)
Oklahoma	Jan. 1(1)	Mar. 15	(8)
Rhode Island(32)	Dec. 31(2)	Mar. 15	10%(22)
Texas(27)	Jan. 1(39)	May 15(9)	100%
Vermont(6)	Apr. 1(28)	Apr. 20(28)	100%
West Virginia	July 1	Oct. 1(9,44)	60%

FOOTNOTES to chart ¶ 263 (corresponding to parenthetical numbers following state names in chart).

(1) Average value over annual period preceding or ending with assessment date.
(2) Value on assessment date, or average of 12 previous months.
(3) When assessed. July 1 to Dec. 15.
(4) To municipal assessor Apr. 1 or 3 months after financial year end; on demand by county assessor.
(5) Corporations file by April 1.
(6) Towns have option to exempt. Exemption doesn't apply to mchy. used in conducting business, but this does not include stock in trade.
(7) Corporate inventories exempt.
(8) Up to 15% of fair cash value.
(9) Dependent on notice, demand or other action by assessor.

FOOTNOTES to chart ¶ 263 (corresponding to parenthetical numbers following state names in chart).
(continued)

(10) In *Ohio,* inventory tax is being phased out over 4 years starting tax year 2005 as follows: assessment rate for inventory is 23% for tax year 2005; 18.75% for 2006; 12.5% for 2007; 6.25% for 2008; and 0% for 2009 and after.

(11) Date varies in taxing districts.

(12) Returns may not be required by local law.

(13) If unjust, assessor may take monthly average of preceding year instead.

(14) Limited 10-year deduction for inventory in maritime dists.

(15) In Orleans Parish, 20 days after receipt of form.

(16) All taxes assessed on stock of goods or merchandise is based on the value of the inventory on Jan. 1 of the tax year or the average monthly inventory during the preceding 12 months from Jan. 1 of each year.

(17) On demand or not later than this date.

(18) All personal property (including merchant's and manufacturer's inventories) is exempt unless it belongs to entities (such as non-railroad public utilities) required to be assessed by the State BEQ, or is subject to a tax imposed in lieu of property taxes, or is a kind or class of property (such as mobile homes or housetrailers) specially taxes.

(19) Covers inventory of business establishements.

(20) In Orleans Parish, assessment date is Aug. 1.

(21) Assessed value is true tax value of property.

(22) Tax on inventory by localities must be phased out over 10-year period starting 7-1-99. Percentage shown is based on 1999 rate. (R.I.)

(23) If on fiscal basis, last day of accounting period.

(24) Local option exemption effective in many counties and municipalities (Ga.). Parish governing bodies can enter into contracts to exempt goods held in inventory by distribution centers from parish, municipal, and special taxes (La.).

(25) If on fiscal basis, by 15th of 4th month after year close.

(26) Localities may set other dates.

(27) Special provisions apply to MV and boat inventories; heavy equipment; and manufactured housing.

(28) If not in business Apr. 1, file inventory 15 days before suspension of business, on average of values during part-year operation.

(29) Assessed value is based on average value during year preceding calendar year in which assessment is made.

(30-31) (Reserved.)

(32) Manufacturer's inventory is exempt but report must be filed.

(33-35) (Reserved.)

(36) Average true cash value during preceding calendar year.

(37) Merchants capital is subject to local tax (Va.).

(38) 10 days after assessor's request (warehousemen) (Mass.).

(39) Can elect preceding Sept. 1 (Tex.).

(40) Inventory is exempt. However, property entitled to IRC deduction for depletion depreciation, or amortization is specifically excluded from definition of inventory.

(41) Assessment ratio for motor vehicles. 30%.

(42) County or city may exempt manufacturers' products that are owned or that are in their possession and are to be shipped or sold to a purchaser other than the final consumer.

(43) Only county taxing inventories is Wicomico, assessment ratio is 35%. Cities may exempt inventories; percentages exempt vary.

(44) By Nov. 1 for noncorporate taxpayers.

INTANGIBLES ASSESSMENT DATES

¶264 Timing assessments. Some states tax intangibles held as of a given day ("assessment day"). Usually this day is January 1, but a few states have a different date (see chart below). Obviously, the less taxable property you hold on assessment day in a taxing jurisdiction, the less tax you will have to pay.

The assessment dates for states taxing intangibles are shown below. Notes to the chart tell whether deposits, stocks or bonds are covered (subject to the qualifications of the particular state's law).

STATE	ASSESSMENT DATE
Alabama	Oct. 1(3)
Florida	(5)
Iowa	Jan. 1(16)
Kansas	(1,2,3,10)
Kentucky	(20)
Louisiana	Jan. 1(11)
Mississippi	Jan. 1(4,8)
Ohio	Dec. 31(6)
Pennsylvania	Jan. 1–15 (2,3,15,18)
Rhode Island	Dec. 31(9)
Tennessee	Jan. 1(13)
Texas	Jan. 1(14)
Wyoming	Mar. 1(19)

FOOTNOTES to chart ¶ 264 (corresponding to numbers in parentheses in the chart):

(1) Taxes money or deposits.
(2) Taxes stocks.
(3) Taxes bonds.
(4) Notes with usurious interest.
(5) Annual intangibles tax is repealed eff. 1-1-2007. Previously, tax was assessed on Jan. 1 and footnotes 2 and 3 applied. However, the repeal does not include: (1) the nonrecurring tax on a note, bond, or other obligation for payment of money that is secured by a mortgage deed or other lien on real property; or (2) the recurring tax on the lease of real property owned by a government and leased to a non-governmental entity when rental payments are due.
(6) Ohio tax only applies to dealers in intangibles.
(7) (Reserved.)
(8) Most intangibles exempt.
(9) Only credit union deposits are taxed.
(10) No assessment date. Intangibles taxed on earnings for income tax year or years ending during last preceding calendar year.
(11) Amendment to La. Constitution exempts all incorporeal movables from property taxation, except public service properties, bank stocks, and credit assessments on premiums written in La. by insurance companies and loan and finance companies.
(12) Retroactive value date set annually. Intangibles taxed on yield, average value, etc. Intangibles of those liable for Single Business Tax are exempt. Alternatively, can use true average method—take monthly balances (except when tax department allows use of balances at end of other periods); divide total of monthly balances by 12 to arrive at true average value. Values of stocks, bonds, mortgages, investments, and gross income actually received or payable on demand, are reported only for period held.
(13) Tax imposed on: stock of loan, investment and cemetery companies; and capital stock of insurance companies. Tax is paid by company. Exemptions apply.
(14) Tax imposed only on: intangibles governed by the insurance code or the finance code.
(15) Exact date is set by appropriate bd. of revision of taxes or county commrs. and specified on returns; if no date set or no date on return, date is Jan. 1.
(16) Taxes legal and special reserves of credit unions and capital employed in state by foreign persons and entities engaged in business as loan agencies.
(17) (Reserved.)
(18) The constitutionality of the Pa. intangibles tax was upheld in Annenberg v. Cmwlth. (Pa. 2000) 757 A2d 338; cert. denied, U.S. Sup. Ct., Dkt. No. 00-343, 10-30-2000. However, the court invalidated the exemption for corporations subject to the Pa. capital stock or franchise tax and instructed jurisdictions to provide backward-looking relief that may include the taxation of previously exempt stock.
(19) Taxes water rights and reservoir rights (Wyo.).
(20) Intangibles tax repealed 1-1-2006. Previously, assessment date was Jan. 1 and footnotes 1 and 3 applied. (Ky.)

FREE PORT STORAGE EXEMPTIONS

¶265 Where stored property is not taxed. Most states allow owners of tangible personal property to store such property within their borders without paying property taxes. Each state has its own rules, but the exemption is frequently restricted to nonresidents and to storage of personal property for shipment outside the state. But some states are more liberal. The chart below lists the states that allow a freeport storage exemption, and the requirements and restrictions that apply. Taxpayers can use this chart as a starting point in inventory assessment tax control. The inventory tax chart is at ¶ 263.

No tax states: Delaware, Hawaii, Illinois, Iowa, New Jersey, New York, and Pennsylvania provide tax-free storage as they do not tax tangible personal property. *Other states:* North Dakota tax only applies to certain entities required to be assessed by the state board of equalization. South Dakota only taxes centrally assessed personal property (utilities, airlines, express companies, etc.). Washington allows partial exemption for each separately assessed stock of merchandise owned or held on January 1, based on experience percentage for preceding year. But, finished plywood, etc. inshipped to be processed for outshipment is exempt during process and 30 days after.

➳ **WATCH OUT**→ Although states listed below may free you from property taxes, their franchise or doing business tax rules may latch on to in-state property establishing nexus for imposition of capital values or income taxes.

STATE	GOODS MUST BE SHIPPED FROM OUT-OF-STATE	TYPE OF STORAGE TO BE USED (1)	ULTIMATE DESTINATION MUST BE (2) OUT-OF-STATE	ONLY ORIGINAL PACKAGES EXEMPT	MUST OWNER FILE EXEMPTION CLAIM OR RETURN? (3)
ALA.(47)	Not limited	W-SA(49)	Out-of-state	No(48)	No.
ARIZ.	Out-of-state	W	Out-of-state	No(4)	Yes(13)
ARK.	Not limited	W-D	Out-of-state	No(39)	No
COLO.(50)	Not limited	Not specified	Out-of-state	No	Yes
CONN.	Not limited	PCW-D(27)	Out-of-state	Yes	No
D.C.	Out-of-state	W	Out-of-state(19)	No	No
FLA.(46)	Out-of-state	Not limited	Out-of-state(46)	No(46)	Yes
GA.(38)	Out-of-state	W	Out-of-state	No(6)	Yes
IDA.	Not limited	W-SA	Out-of-state	No	Yes
IND.(50)	Not limited	W(27)	Out-of-state	No(20)	Yes(14)
KAN.(55)	Not limited	W-SA	Out-of-state	No(5,7)	Yes(26)
KY.(42)	Not limited	PW-DC	Out-of-state(43)	Yes	Yes
LA.	Out-of-state	W-SA-D	Out-of-state	No	Yes(14)
MD.(51)					
MASS.(34)	Out-of-state	LPW(27)	Not limited	Yes	No
MICH.(56)	Not limited	PW-D(27)	Out-of-state	No	Yes(15,16)
MISS.	Not limited	FPW	Out-of-state	No(8)	No(57)
MO.	Out-of-state	W	Out-of-state	No(6)	No
MONT.(41)	Out-of-state	W-SA	Out-of-state	No(6)	Yes(14)
NEV.	Out-of-state	W	Out-of-state	No(5,6)	Yes(13)
N.M.	Out-of-state	W	Out-of-state	No(5)	No
N.C.(11,50)	Foreign country	Not specified	Not limited	No	Yes(44)
OHIO(50)	Out-of-state	W-SA(27)	Out-of-state	No	Yes
OKLA.	Out-of-state	Not specified	Out-of-state(23)	No	Yes
S.C.	Out-of-state	W	Out-of-state	No(4,6)	Yes(13)
TENN.(50)	Out-of-state	W(24)	Out-of-state	No(24)	No(33)
TEX.(35)	Out-of-state	Not specified	Out-of-state	No(21)	Yes(10)
UTAH	Not limited	Not specified	Out-of-state(28)	No(4,5)	Yes(9,14)
VA.(50,52)	Not limited	T	Not limited	No(52)	Yes
WASH.(54)	Out-of-state	Not Specified	Not limited	No(7,8)	Yes
W.VA.	Out-of-state	W	Out-of-state	No(6)	Yes
WYO.	Not limited	W-SA	Out-of-state	No(36)	Yes(37)

FOOTNOTES to chart ¶ 265 (corresponding to numbers in parentheses in chart):

(1) Letter designations mean: W-Warehouse; PCW-Public commercial warehouse; D-Public dock or wharf; DC-Distribution center; PW-Public warehouse; LPW-Licensed public warehouse; CW-Commercial warehouse; FPW-Licensed free port warehouse; BLW-Bonded and licensed warehouse; SA-Storage area; T-marine or airport terminal. Hyphen indicates more than one type of storage qualifies.
(2) Property usually must be labeled as "in transit," in bills of lading, warehouse records or storage reports.
(3) State may require warehouseman to report though owner not required to do so. In "No" states, owners may have to file if requested by local officials.
(4) Law permits "assembling."
(5) Law permits "assembly, manufacturing, processing, or fabricating."
(6) Law permits "disassembling, binding, joining, dividing, cutting, breaking in bulk, relabeling, repackaging." In W.Va., above acts allowed unless they result in a new or different product.
(7) Law permits "labeling, packaging, labeling."
(8) Law permits "breaking in bulk, labeling, relabeling or repackaging." Miss. also allows binding and dividing.
(9) Burden of proof for exemption is on taxpayer.
(10) In Tex., exemption is available for warehouse storing cotton for transportation out-of-state. Claimant must fill one-time exemption claim.
(11) In N.C., inventories of manufacturers, wholesale and retail merchants are exempt; also imports from foreign countries through N.C. seaport terminals and stored there for further shipment for up to 12 months.
(12) Nonresident's property must be in original package.
(13) On official forms; also warehouse certificate showing property "in transit."
(14) On official forms.
(15) Sworn statement with assessor showing Dec. 31 value, out-of-state destination, and warehouse certificate. Owner must be resident or authorized to do business.
(16) Owner, warehouseman or other who had possession reports destination, value, etc.
(17) Sworn statement in official form requires report of value, destination, etc. of goods manufactured or produced in state.
(18) (Reserved.)
(19) Property must be designated as "in transit" on records of warehouse.
(20) Exempt if manufactured in Indiana and not in original package. Must be ready for shipment without additional manufacturing or processing, except for packaging; and owner must show it will be damaged or have its value impaired if it is stored in its original package or final packaging is not practical until receipt of final customer order.
(21) Law permits assembly, storage, manufacturing, processing, fabricating. Exemption applies unless locality levies tax on the property before 4-1-90.
(22) Limited exemption also allowed for goods stored in private warehouse—any building, structure or inclosure—if origin and destination out-of-state.
(23) Exemption only if not in-state over 90 days.
(24) Manufacturer or assembler may inship to plant or warehouse for storage, processing, assembly or repackaging, if for out-of-state nonretail sale.
(25) (Reserved.)
(26) Owner must show at least 30% of previous calendar year's shipments from storage was shipped in interstate commerce to out-of-state point.
(27) No exemption if goods' owner is owner or lessee of public warehouse. In Conn., nonresidents are not subject to tax for property held on public wharf.
(28) Exempts goods for sale or processing in Utah on Jan. 1, outshipped in 12 mos.
(29) Applies only to imports and exports.
(30) In-state goods must be shipped to specific known destination, or brought to warehouse by common carrier.
(31) Exempts goods for sale in interstate commerce if outshipped in 12 mos.
(32) Permits "processing, manufacturing, fabricating, compounding, servicing."
(33) Owner, if required, submits documentary proof to assessor of property's intransit character and final destination.
(34) Applies to nonresidents only.
(35) Exempt only if not in-state over 175 days.
(36) Permits assembly, disassembly, repackaging, processing, fabricating, milling.
(37) Person claiming property to be in transit must do so in form and manner provided by the board. Books and records must be kept in manner that allows assessor to quickly ascertain amount of the property.
(38) Counties and municipalities may give local 12-month exemption for finished goods stored in warehouse, dock or wharf for out-of-state shipment. Exemption may be in increments of 20%, 40%, 60%, 80%, or 100%.
(39) Permits manufacture, process or refining.
(40) Not specified for seaport terminal or outshipment to foreign country.
(41) Not specified for imports.
(42) Exempt from state tax eff. 7-13-2000; previously, lower tax rate applied. Eff. 7-13-2000, an exemption from local property taxes is phased in for in-transit property placed in a warehouse or distribution center for shipment out-of-state. For tax assessments made on 1-1-2000, the tax rate levied by cities, counties, charter counties, urban-counties and schools is 80% of the rate levied on other tangible personalty; 50% for assessments made on 1-1-2001, and completely exempt on and after 1-1-2002.
(43) Personalty is deemed to be held for out-of-state shipment if the owner can reasonably demonstrate that the personalty will be shipped out of the state within the next 6 months.
(44) After 12-month stay.
(45) Exempt if in original form or package.
(46) Allows storage in Fla. for under 181 days. Law permits "breaking in bulk, labeling, packaging, relabeling or repacking." Inventory is tax-exempt.
(47) Exemption only for up to 36 months.

FOOTNOTES to chart ¶ 265 (corresponding to numbers in parentheses in chart): **(continued)**

(48) Law permits property to be "assembled, disassembled, bound, joined, divided, cut, broken in bulk, labeled, relabeled, repackaged, or otherwise processed or fabricated."
(49) Property must be designated "in-transit" on books and records of warehouse or storage area.
(50) Goods in foreign trade zones are exempt.
(51) Counties, municipalities, and Baltimore City can exempt imports (original package) in importers' hands.
(52) Unpackaged import goods taxed on reaching 2nd place of rest or storage after 1st unloading, or after 1st sale or if used in current operations. Also exempt: vessels' cargo containers temporarily in Va. ports.
(53) Law permits binding, dividing, severing.
(54) Partial exemption for stocks of merchandise for resale in same form.
(55) Personalty shipped from out-of-state and stored in licensed warehouse for ultimate out-of-state destination is exempt though interstate movement hasn't been interrupted for more than five years. Goods manufactured in-state are exempt while stored in warehouse or storage area if at least 30% of goods leave Kan.
(56) Exemption doesn't apply to alcoholic beverages.
(57) Warehouses must file reports on inventory on Jan. 1 annually *(Miss.)*.

UNEMPLOYMENT INSURANCE TAXES NUMBER OF EMPLOYEES

¶270 Employment threshold. Employers are taxable (that is, are subject to unemployment insurance laws) when the number of persons they employ equal the number shown in the following chart.

Jurisdiction*	No. of Employees to Make Employer Subject
Alabama	1 for 20 weeks(1,3,6)
Alaska	1 at any time(3,6)
Arizona	1 for 20 weeks(1,3,6)
Arkansas	1 for 10 days(3,6)
California	1 (2,4,6)
Colorado	1 for 20 days(3,4,6)
Connecticut	1 for 20 weeks(1,3,6)
Delaware	1 for 20 weeks(1,3,6)
District of Columbia	1 at any time(3,6)
Florida	1 for 20 weeks(1,3,6)
Georgia	1 for 20 weeks(1,3,6)
Hawaii	1 at any time(3,7)
Idaho	1 for 20 weeks(1,3,6)
Illinois	1 for 20 weeks(1,3,6)
Indiana	1 for 20 weeks(1,3,6)
Iowa	1 for 20 weeks(1,3,6)
Kansas	1 for 20 weeks(1,3,6)
Kentucky	1 for 20 weeks(1,3,6)
Louisiana	1 for 20 weeks(1,3,6)
Maine	1 for 20 weeks(1,3,6)
Maryland	1 at any time(3,6)
Massachusetts	1 for 13 weeks(4,6)
Michigan	1 for 20 weeks(3,4,6)
Minnesota	1 (2,3,6)
Mississippi	1 for 20 weeks(1,3,6)
Missouri	1 for 20 weeks(1,3,6)
Montana	1 (3,4,6)
Nebraska	1 for 20 weeks(1,3,6)
Nevada	1 (3,4,6)
New Hampshire	1 for 20 weeks(1,3)
New Jersey	1 (3,4,6)
New Mexico	1 for 20 weeks(3,4,6)
New York	1 (5,6)
North Carolina	1 for 20 weeks(1,3,6)
North Dakota	1 for 20 weeks(1,3,6)
Ohio	1 for 20 weeks(1,3,8)
Oklahoma	1 for 20 weeks(1,3,6)
Oregon	1 for 18 weeks(3,4,6)
Pennsylvania	1 at any time(3,6)
Puerto Rico	1 at any time(2,3,6)
Rhode Island	1 at any time(3,6)
South Carolina	1 for 20 weeks(1,6)
South Dakota	1 for 20 weeks(1,3,6)
Tennessee	1 for 20 weeks(1,3,6)
Texas	1 for 20 weeks(1,3,6)

Jurisdiction*	No. of Employees to Make Employer Subject
Utah	1 (2,3,6)
Vermont	1 for 20 weeks(1,3,6)
Virginia	1 for 20 weeks(1,3,6)
Washington	1 at any time(3,6)
West Virginia	1 for 20 weeks(1,3,6)
Wisconsin	1 for 20 weeks(1,3,6)
Wyoming	1 (3,4,6)

* All states have adopted provisions extending coverage to the extent required for state law to be certified by U.S. Secy. of Labor.

FOOTNOTES to chart ¶ 270 (corresponding to numbers in parentheses):

(1) One or more employees at any time in each of 20 calendar weeks, or paying wages of $1,500 or more in a calendar quarter, in current or prior calendar year.

(2) One or more employees to which wages were paid within either current or previous calendar year.

(3) Also: employers subject to Fed Unemployment Tax Act.

(4) Employers liable: if payroll in calendar quarter is over $100 in Calif.; $1,500 in Colo. and Mass.; $225 in Nev.; $450 in N.M.; $1,000 in calendar yr. in Mich., Mont., N.J., and Ore. ($225 pre-1-1-2008); $500 in calendar year in Wyo.

(5) Employer liable if payment is made of $300 or more in calendar quarter. (N.Y.)

(6) Employer also liable if it pays wages for domestic service in a private home, local college club, or local chapter of a college fraternity or sorority (private home only in Alaska, N.J., N.Y., Puerto Rico, R.I., and for domestic service in Mich.) of $1,000 in any calendar quarter ($500 in D.C., N.Y.).

(7) Employer also liable if it pays wages for domestic service of $225 to any individual and $1,000 to all individuals in a calendar quarter (Haw.).

(8) Employer also liable if it pays wages for domestic service per quarter of $1,000 in a local college club or local chapter of a college fraternity or sorority; $1,000 per individual in a private home; or $1,500 for two or more individuals in a private home (Ohio).

UNEMPLOYMENT INSURANCE—RATES AND BASES

¶271 Contributions. This chart reflects the current minimum and maximum contribution rates for new and experienced employers; employee contribution rates, where applicable; the taxable wage base; and whether the state accepts voluntary contributions.

Jurisdiction	2007 New Employers	2007 Experienced Employers	2007 Employee Rate	2007 Taxable Wage Base	Voluntary Contributions
Federal	6.2%	6.2%	none	$ 7,000	not applicable
Alabama	2.7%	0.50–6.1%(2)	none	8,000	No
Alaska	(1)	1.0–5.4%	0.5%	30,100	No
Arizona	2%	0.02–5.4%	none	7,000	Yes
Arkansas	3.6%	0.8–10.7%(3)	none	10,000	Yes
California	3.4%	1.5–6.2%(4)	none	7,000	Yes
Colorado	2.52%(1)	0.0–8.92%(5)	none	10,000	Yes
Connecticut	3.1%	1.2–6.1%(6)	none	15,000	No
Delaware	2.3%(1)	0.3–8.2%(7)	none	8,500*	No
District of Columbia	2.7%	1.3–6.6%	none	9,000	No
Florida	2.7%	0.12–5.4%	none	7,000	No
Georgia	2.7%	0.03–5.4%(8)	none	8,500	Yes
Hawaii	1.9%	0.0–5.4%	none	35,300	No
Idaho	1.302%	0.372–5.4%(9)	none	30,200	No
Illinois	3.9%(1)	1.0–8.2%(10)	none	11,500	No
Indiana	2.7%	1.1–5.6%	none	7,000	Yes
Iowa	1%(1)	0.0–8.0%	none	22,000	No
Kansas	(1)	0.0–7.4%	none	8,000	Yes
Kentucky	2.7%(1)	0.5–9.5%	none	8,000	Yes
Louisiana	(1)	0.1–6.2%	none	7,000	Yes
Maine	1.8%	0.54–5.4%	none	12,000	Yes
Maryland	2.4%(1)	0.3–7.5%	none	8,500	No
Massachusetts	2.53%(1)	1.12–10.96%	none	14,000	Yes
Michigan	2.7%(1)	0.6–10.3%	none	9,000	Yes
Minnesota	2.13%(1)	0.4–9.3%(11)	none	24,000	Yes
Mississippi	2.7%	0.7–5.4%	none	7,000	No
Missouri	3.51%(1)	0.0–8.4%(12)	none	11,000	Yes
Montana	(1)	0.13–6.5%(13)	none	22,700	No
Nebraska	1.6%(1)	0.24–5.4%	none	9,000	Yes
Nevada	2.95%	0.25–5.4%(14)	none	24,600*	No
New Hampshire	2.7%(15)	0.1%–6.5%(15)	none	8,000	No
New Jersey(16)	2.8%	0.3–5.4%	0.925%(16)	26,600*	Yes
New Mexico	2.0%	0.03–5.4%	none	18,600	Yes
New York	4.1%	1.1–9.5%(17)	none	8,500	Yes

Jurisdiction	2007 New Employers	2007 Experienced Employers	2007 Employee Rate	2007 Taxable Wage Base	Voluntary Contributions
North Carolina	1.2%	0.0–6.84%(18)	none	17,800	Yes
North Dakota	1.6%(1)	0.34–8.09%	none	21,300	Yes
Ohio	2.7%(1)	0.4–9.0%	none	9,000	Yes
Oklahoma	1.8%	0.2–5.8%(19)	none	13,200	No
Oregon	2.4%	0.9–5.4%	none	29,000	No
Pennsylvania	3.752%(1)	2.008–10.2624%(20)	0.09%	8,000	Yes
Puerto Rico	2.9%	1.4–5.4%(21)	none	7,000	No
Rhode Island	2.41%	1.9–10.0%(22)	none	14,000	No
South Carolina	3.34%	1.24–6.1%(23)	none	7,000	No
South Dakota	1.75%(1)	0.0–9.1%(24)	none	8,500	Yes
Tennessee	2.7%(1)	0.3–10.0%	none	7,000	No
Texas	2.7%(1)	0.29–7.7%(25)	none	9,000	Yes
Utah	(1)	0.3–9.3%(26)	none	25,400	No
Vermont	1.0%(1)	0.8–6.5%	none	8,000	No
Virginia	2.57%(1)	0.17–6.27%(27)	none	8,000	No
Washington	(1)	0.03–6.02%(28)	none	31,400	Yes
West Virginia	2.7%(1)	1.5–8.5%(29)	none	8,000	Yes
Wisconsin	(1)	0.05–9.8%(30)	none	10,500	Yes
Wyoming	(1)	0.47–8.97%	none	18,100	No

FOOTNOTES to chart ¶ 271:

* 2008 Taxable wage base: Delaware, $10,500; Nevada, $25,400; New Jersey, $27,700.

(1) Rates vary by industry.

(2) Alabama—Includes 0.06% special assessment. Doesn't include 0.1% shared cost assessment.

(3) Arkansas—Includes 0.7% stabilization tax and additional assessments for employers with bad experience rating history.

(4) California—Doesn't include 0.1% contribution to employment training fund.

(5) Colorado—Includes surcharge and solvency tax surcharge.

(6) Connecticut—Includes 0.7% fund balance tax rate.

(7) Delaware—Includes 0.2% supplemental assessment rate.

(8) Georgia—Includes 0.08% administrative assessment (not applicable to employers paying the minimum or maximum rate).

(9) Idaho—Includes workforce development tax.

(10) Illinois—Includes a 0.8% fund building rate.

(11) Minnesota—Doesn't include a 0.10% workforce enhancement fee, or the additional assessment tax.

(12) Missouri—Includes percentage increase. Doesn't include surcharge.

(13) Montana—Includes 0.13% administrative fund tax.

(14) Nevada—Doesn't include 0.05% Career Enhancement Program tax, if applicable.

(15) New Hampshire—Positive reserve employers and new employers receive a 1.0% UI tax rate reduction in all four quarters of 2007 due to the size of the state's unemployment trust fund that is not reflected in the above rates.

(16) New Jersey—Includes 0.3825% contribution to the unemployment contribution fund, 0.0425% contribution to the Workforce Development/Supplemental Workforce Funds and 0.5% contribution to the Disability Insurance Fund.

(17) New York—Includes 0.075% re-employment tax and applicable subsidiary tax.

(18) North Carolina—Includes state reserve tax.

(19) Oklahoma—Includes conditional factors tax.

FOOTNOTES to chart ¶ 271:
(continued)

(20) Pennsylvania—Includes 0.4% additional contributions factor and 7.2% surcharge adjustment.
(21) Puerto Rico—Doesn't include the job development tax.
(22) Rhode Island—Includes the 0.21% job development assessment.
(23) South Carolina—Doesn't include the 0.06% contingency fund assessment. Does include a 0.7% adjustment due to the statewide reserve ratio.
(24) South Dakota—Includes applicable investment fee.
(25) Texas—Includes replenishment tax rate of 0.14% and an obligation assessment ratio of 0.24%
(26) Utah—Includes 0.3% social cost.
(27) Virginia—Includes 0.19% pool cost.
(28) Washington—Includes graduated social cost factor and employment administration fund surtax.
(29) West Virginia—Includes a 1% surtax for negative balance employers.
(30) Wisconsin—Includes solvency tax rate.

UNEMPLOYMENT INSURANCE—REPORTS

¶272 When filed. The chart below shows the report dates and periods covered for contributions and wages reports. Notes on following pages add details.

	CONTRIBUTION RETURNS		WAGE REPORTS	
Jurisdiction	Period Covered	Due Date in Month after Period	Period Covered	Due Date in Month after Period
Federal	Year(1)	31st Day	Quarter	Last Day
Alabama	Quarter	Last Day	Quarter	Last Day
Alaska	Quarter(2,3)	Last Day	Quarter(2,3)	Last Day
Arizona	Quarter	Last Day	Quarter	Last Day
Arkansas	Quarter	Last Day	Quarter	Last Day
California	Quarter	Last Day	Quarter	Last Day
Colorado	Quarter	Last Day	Quarter	Last Day
Connecticut	Quarter	Last Day	Quarter	Last Day
Delaware	Quarter	Last Day	Quarter	Last Day
District of Columbia	Quarter	Last Day	Quarter	Last Day
Florida	Quarter(3)	Last Day	Quarter(3)	Last Day
Georgia	Quarter	Last Day	Quarter	Last Day
Hawaii	Quarter	Last Day	Quarter	Last Day
Idaho	Quarter(3)	Last Day	Quarter(3)	Last Day
Illinois	Quarter	Last Day	Quarter	Last Day
Indiana	Quarter	Last Day	Quarter	Last Day
Iowa	Quarter	Last Day	Quarter	Last Day
Kansas	Quarter	Last Day	Quarter	Last Day
Kentucky	Quarter	Last Day	Quarter	Last Day
Louisiana	Quarter(3)	Last Day	Quarter(3)	Last Day
Maine	Quarter	Last Day	Quarter	Last Day
Maryland	Quarter	Last Day	Quarter	Last Day
Massachusetts	Quarter	Last Day	Quarter	Last Day
Michigan	Quarter(2)	25th Day	Quarter	25th Day
Minnesota	Quarter(3)	Last Day	Quarter(3)	Last Day
Mississippi	Quarter	Last Day	Quarter	Last Day
Missouri	Quarter	Last Day	Quarter	Last Day
Montana	Quarter	Last Day	Quarter	Last Day
Nebraska	Quarter(3)	Last Day	Quarter(3)	Last Day
Nevada	Quarter	Last Day	Quarter	Last Day
New Hampshire	Quarter(2)	Last Day	Quarter	Last Day
New Jersey	Quarter(2)	30th Day	Quarter(2)	30th Day
New Mexico	Quarter	Last Day	Quarter	Last Day
New York	Quarter	Last Day	Quarter	Last Day
North Carolina	Quarter(3)	Last Day	Quarter(3)	Last Day
North Dakota	Quarter(3)	Last Day	Quarter(3)	Last Day
Ohio	Quarter	Last Day	Quarter	Last Day
Oklahoma	Quarter	Last Day	Quarter	Last Day
Oregon	Quarter	Last Day	Quarter	Last Day
Pennsylvania	Quarter	Last Day	Quarter	Last Day
Puerto Rico	Quarter	Last Day	Quarter	Last Day
Rhode Island	Quarter(2)	Last Day	Quarter(2)	Last Day
South Carolina	Quarter	Last Day	Quarter	Last Day
South Dakota	Quarter	Last Day	Quarter	Last Day
Tennessee	Quarter	Last Day	Quarter	Last Day
Texas	Quarter(3)	Last Day	Quarter(3)	Last Day
Utah	Quarter(3)	Last Day	Quarter(3)	Last Day
Vermont	Quarter(3)	Last Day	Quarter(3)	Last Day
Virginia	Quarter(2)	Last Day	Quarter(2)	Last Day
Washington	Quarter(3)	Last Day	Quarter(3)	Last Day

	CONTRIBUTION RETURNS		WAGE REPORTS	
Jurisdiction	**Period Covered**	**Due Date in Month after Period**	**Period Covered**	**Due Date in Month after Period**
West Virginia	Quarter	Last Day	Quarter	Last Day
Wisconsin	Quarter(3)	Last Day	Quarter(3)	Last Day
Wyoming	Quarter	Last Day	Quarter	Last Day

FOOTNOTES to chart ¶ 272:

(1) This is federal unemployment tax return; reports and payments are due quarterly.
(2) Some employers may be required to report monthly *(Alaska, Mich., N.H., N.J., R.I., Va.)*.
(3) Electronic fund transfers may be required or allowed. See ¶ 279.

INHERITANCE, ESTATE, AND GIFT TAXES

¶273 **Basis, rates, and reporting.** This chart gives the main features of state inheritance, estate, generation-skipping transfer, and gift taxes. It lists the basis or measure of tax, rates, and return and payment due dates.

➼ **MEANING OF TERMS**→ Unless otherwise shown, state ''estate tax'' is an amount equal to the unused maximum credit that federal law allows for state death taxes. Unless otherwise shown, state ''generation-skipping transfer tax'' is an amount equal to the unused maximum credit that federal law allows for state generation-skipping transfer taxes.

Reduction and repeal of the federal estate and generation-skipping transfer taxes. The Federal Economic Growth and Tax Relief Reconciliation Act of 2001 (EGTRRA) (P.L. 107-16), repeals the federal estate tax and federal generation-skipping transfer (GST) tax for individuals dying after 2009 and gradually reduces the federal estate tax and the federal GST tax for individuals dying after 2001 and before 2010. Starting in 2002 and through 2009, the federal estate tax and GST tax rates are reduced, and the ''exemption equivalent'' of the unified credit and the GST tax exemption amount are increased. Unlimited basis step-up is eliminated after 2009 when the federal estate tax is repealed; heirs instead will generally get a carryover basis with numerous exceptions allowing substantial increases in basis.

EGTRRA reduces the state death tax credit under IRC §2011 by 25% in 2002; 50% in 2003; by 75% in 2004. For decedents dying on or after January 1, 2005, the state death tax credit is repealed and replaced with a deduction. The credit under IRC §2604 against the federal GST tax for GST taxes actually paid to a state for property included in a generation skipping transfer will also be repealed for transfers after 2004. EGTRRA also increases the exemption equivalent of the unified credit against estate tax to $1 million in 2002; $1.5 million in 2004; $2 million in 2006; and $3.5 million in 2009.

Because of Congressional budget reconciliation rules, none of the Act's provisions apply after 2010: effectively, the federal estate tax and the federal GST are repealed only for individuals dying in 2010. Unless there is a later law change, estates of individuals dying after 2010 will be subject to the rules in force before the 2001 Act.

Since EGTRRA repeals the credit for state death taxes, those states that link their estate tax to the amount of the federal credit will see their pickup tax decline and disappear as the federal credit is eliminated. For decedents dying in 2005, there is no pickup estate tax in such states. To make this choice, an automatic update state does not have to take action. Three states—Arkansas, South Carolina, and South Dakota—updated their state law to reflect EGTRRA and have therefore chosen to repeal their estate taxes. Two states, Connecticut and Nebraska, have enacted stand-alone taxes to replace the federal pick-up tax. A number of states have elected to decouple their estate and GST taxes from the federal changes enacted by EGTRRA by adopting a version of the federal estate/GST taxes that predate the effective date of EGTRRA. Finally, some states decoupled from the phase-out of the federal credit for state death taxes, but adopted EGTRRA's higher exemption amounts. The following chart identifies the action taken by the states.

STATE	BASIS AND RATE OF TAX	REPORT—PAYMENT DUE DATES
ALA.	*Inheritance tax:* Not imposed *Estate tax* is not imposed. Due to phase-out of the federal credit (see introductory text), no state estate tax is imposed for decedents dying on or after 1-1-2005. *Generation-skipping transfer tax* is not imposed. Due to phase-out of the federal credit (see introductory text), no state GST tax is imposed for decedents dying on or after 1-1-2005. *Gift tax:* Not imposed.	
ALASKA	*Inheritance tax:* Not imposed. *Estate tax* is not imposed. Due to phase-out of the federal credit (see introductory text), no state estate tax is imposed for decedents dying on or after 1-1-2005. *Generation-skipping transfer tax:* Not imposed. *Gift tax:* Not imposed.	
ARIZ.	*Inheritance tax:* Not imposed. *Estate tax* is not imposed. Due to phase-out of the federal credit (see introductory text), no state estate tax is imposed for decedents dying on or after 1-1-2005. *Generation-skipping transfer tax* is not imposed. Due to phase-out of the federal credit (see introductory text), no state GST tax is imposed for decedents dying on or after 1-1-2005. *Gift tax:* Not imposed.	
ARK.	*Inheritance tax:* Not imposed. *Estate tax* is not imposed. Eff. for decedents dying on or after 1-1-2005, state estate tax is repealed. *Generation-skipping transfer tax:* Not imposed. *Gift tax:* Not imposed.	
CALIF.	*Inheritance tax:* Not imposed. *Estate tax* is not imposed. Due to phase-out of the federal credit (see introductory text), no state estate tax is imposed for decedents dying on or after 1-1-2005. *Generation-skipping transfer tax* is not imposed. Due to phase-out of the federal credit (see introductory text), no state GST tax is imposed for decedents dying on or after 1-1-2005. *Gift tax:* Not imposed.	
COLO.	*Inheritance tax:* Not imposed. *Estate tax* is not imposed. Due to phase-out of the federal credit (see introductory text), no state estate tax is imposed for decedents dying on or after 1-1-2005.	

STATE	BASIS AND RATE OF TAX	REPORT—PAYMENT DUE DATES
	Generation-skipping transfer tax is not imposed. Due to phase-out of the federal credit (see introductory text), no state GST tax is imposed for decedents dying on or after 1-1-2005.	
	Gift tax: Not imposed.	
CONN.	*Inheritance (succession) tax* repealed for estates of decedents dying on or after 1-1-2005.	
	Estate tax is imposed. Applicable to estates of decedents dying on or after 1-1-2005. Imposed if taxable estate is more than $2 million. Rates range from 5.085% for taxable estates over $2 million to 16% for taxable estates over $10.1 million.	Estates over $2 million, report-pay by 9 mos. after death to DRS. Estates of $2 million or less, report to probate court (no tax due).
	Generation-skipping transfer tax is not imposed. Due to phase-out of the federal credit (see introductory text), no state GST tax is imposed for decedents dying on or after 1-1-2005.	
	Gift tax is imposed on Conn. taxable gifts above Fed gift tax threshold made by donor during all calendar years starting on or after 1-1-2005, which exceed $2 million. Rates range from 5.085% of taxable gifts over $2 million to 16% for taxable gifts over $10.1 million.	Report-pay by Apr. 15 after calendar yr. of gift. A return must be filed even if no tax is payable.
DEL.	*Inheritance tax:* Not imposed.	
	Estate tax is not imposed. Due to phase-out of the federal credit (see introductory text), no state estate tax is imposed for decedents dying on or after 1-1-2005.	
	Generation-skipping transfer tax: Not imposed.	
	Gift tax: Not imposed.	
D.C.	*Inheritance tax:* Not imposed.	
	Estate tax is imposed. For decedents dying on or after 12-31-2003, the tax is equal to the federal credit for state death taxes in effect on 1-1-2001, without applying any scheduled increase in the unified credit and the amount of the credit is $345,800. For decedents dying on or after 1-1-2002, the tax is equal to the federal credit for state death taxes in effect on 1-1-2001, without applying any scheduled increase in the unified credit and the amount of the credit is $220,550. For decedents dying after 3-31-87 but before 1-1-2002, the tax is equal to the federal credit for state death taxes as in effect on 1-1-86. Tax is decoupled from federal phase-out and repeal.	Report-pay Office of Tax and Rev. by 10 mos. after death. No return needed if gross estate does not exceed $1 million.
	Generation-skipping transfer tax: Not imposed.	
	Gift tax: Not imposed.	

STATE	BASIS AND RATE OF TAX	REPORT—PAYMENT DUE DATES
FLA.	*Inheritance tax:* Not imposed. *Estate tax* is not imposed. Due to phase-out of the federal credit (see introductory text), no state estate tax is imposed for decedents dying on or after 1-1-2005. *Generation-skipping transfer tax* is not imposed. Due to phase-out of the federal credit (see introductory text), no state GST tax is imposed for decedents dying on or after 1-1-2005. *Gift tax:* Not imposed.	
GA.	*Inheritance tax:* Not imposed. *Estate tax* is not imposed. Due to phase-out of the federal credit (see introductory text), no state estate tax is imposed for decedents dying on or after 1-1-2005. *Generation-skipping transfer tax:* Not imposed. *Gift tax:* Not imposed.	
HAW.	*Inheritance tax:* Not imposed. *Estate tax* is not imposed. Due to phase-out of the federal credit (see introductory text), no state estate tax is imposed for decedents dying on or after 1-1-2005. *Generation-skipping transfer tax* is not imposed. Due to phase-out of the federal credit (see introductory text), no state GST tax is imposed for decedents dying on or after 1-1-2005. *Gift tax:* Not imposed.	
IDA.	*Inheritance tax:* Not imposed. *Estate tax* is not imposed. Due to phase-out of the federal credit (see introductory text), no state estate tax is imposed for decedents dying on or after 1-1-2005. *Generation-skipping transfer tax* is not imposed. Due to phase-out of the federal credit (see introductory text), no state GST tax is imposed for decedents dying on or after 1-1-2005. *Gift tax:* Not imposed.	
ILL.	*Inheritance tax:* Not imposed. *Estate tax* is imposed. For decedents dying on or after 1-1-2003 and before 1-1-2006, tax is equal to amount of the federal credit for death taxes in effect on 12-31-2001 (but allowing the increased applicable exclusion amount through 12-31-2005). For decedents dying after 12-31-2005 and before 1-1-2010, the exclusion amount is $2 million. For decedents dying after 12-31-2009, tax is equal to current federal credit under IRC §2011.	Report to Attny. Gen. and pay (with copy of return) to county treasurer by Fed due date.

STATE	BASIS AND RATE OF TAX	REPORT—PAYMENT DUE DATES
	Generation-skipping transfer tax is not imposed. Due to phase-out of the federal credit (see introductory text), no state GST tax is imposed for decedents dying on or after 1-1-2005. *Gift tax:* Not imposed.	
IND.	*Inheritance tax* is imposed on net taxable value transferred. Rates—Spouse, exempt; Cl. A ($100,000 to child, parent, or another is exempt), tax ranges from 1% on 1st $25,000 to 10% on amount over $1.5 million; Cl. B. ($500 exempt), 7% on 1st $100,000 to 15% on over $1 million; Cl. C ($100 exempt), 10% on 1st $100,000 to 20% on over $1 million. *Estate tax* is not imposed. Due to phase-out of the federal credit (see introductory text), no state estate tax is imposed for decedents dying on or after 1-1-2005. *Generation-skipping transfer tax* is not imposed. Due to phase-out of the federal credit (see introductory text), no state GST tax is imposed for decedents dying on or after 1-1-2005. *Gift tax:* Not imposed.	Report to probate court by 9 mos. after death. Pay to county treasurer for resident, Dept. Rev. for nonresident, by 12 mos. after death.
IOWA	*Inheritance tax* is imposed on taxable property. Rates—Spouse, exempt. Also exempt: parents, grandparents, great-grandparents, other lineal ascendants, children, stepchildren, grandchildren, great-grandchildren, and other lineal descendents. Cl. 2 (under $25,000 estate exempt), from 5% on 1st $12,500 to 10% on over $150,000. Cl. 3 (under $25,000 estate exempt), from 10% on 1st $50,000 to 15% on over $100,000. Cl. 4 (charities and under $25,000 estate exempt), 10%; Cl. 5 (non-charitable entities), 15%. *Estate tax* is not imposed. Due to phase-out of the federal credit (see introductory text), no state estate tax is imposed for decedents dying on or after 1-1-2005. *Generation-skipping transfer tax* is not imposed. Due to phase-out of the federal credit (see introductory text), no state GST tax is imposed for decedents dying on or after 1-1-2005. *Gift tax:* Not imposed.	Report-pay Dir. Rev. & Fin. by 9 mos. after death.

STATE	BASIS AND RATE OF TAX	REPORT—PAYMENT DUE DATES
KAN.	*Inheritance (succession) tax*: Not imposed.	
	Estate tax is imposed. Tax is equal to the federal credit for death taxes as in effect on 12-31-97. Tax is decoupled from federal phase-out and repeal.	Report-pay to Dir. Tax. by Fed due date.
	For decedents dying on or after 1-1-2007 but before 1-1-2010, a stand-alone Kansas estate tax is imposed that no longer follows federal law. Rates for 2007 range from 3% to 10% for taxable estates over $1 million to over $10 million; from 1% to 7% for 2008; and from 0.5% to 3% for 2009. Estates up to $1 million are exempt.	Report-pay to Dir. Tax. within 9 mos. after date of death.
	Generation-skipping transfer tax is imposed. Tax is equal to the federal credit on state generation-skipping taxes as in effect on 12-31-97. Tax is decoupled from federal phase-out and repeal.	Report-pay to Dir. Tax. by Fed due date.
	Gift tax: Not imposed.	
KY.	*Inheritance tax* is imposed on taxable value of share. Rates—Spouse and specified charities, exempt; Cl. A (1st $20,000 to infant child, $5,000 to another exempt; or, if greater: 100% of each beneficiary's interest), tax ranges from 2% on 1st $20,000 to 10% on over $500,000; Cl. B ($1,000 exempt), 4% on 1st $10,000 to 16% on over $200,000; Cl. C ($500 exempt), 6% on 1st $10,000 to 16% on over $60,000.	Report-pay to Dept. Rev. by 18 mos. after death.
	Estate tax is not imposed on decedents dying on or after 1-1-2005.	
	Generation-skipping transfer tax: Not imposed.	
	Gift tax: Not imposed.	
LA.	*Inheritance tax*: Eff. 1-1-2008, no inheritance tax is due for decedents' deaths after 6-30-2004. Until 1-1-2008, for deaths after 6-30-2004, no inheritance tax is due if a judgement of possession is entered or the succession is judicially opened no later than the last day of the ninth month after the decedent's death. Otherwise, inheritance tax applies to taxable value of share at following rates: Spouse and specified charities, exempt; descendants or ancestors ($25,000 exempt), 0.4% tax on 1st $20,000 and 0.6% on rest; collateral relatives ($1,000 exempt), 1% on 1st $20,000 and 1.4% on rest; strangers or nonrelated persons ($500 exempt), 1% on 1st $5,000 and 2% on rest.	Eff 1-1-2008, inheritance tax returns are not required for decedents' deaths after 6-30-2004. Persons who paid inheritance taxes based on decendents' deaths after 6-30-2004 can file a claim for refund of those taxes with Dept. Rev. between 8-1-2008 and 12-31-2009. Until 1-1-2008, for decedents' deaths between 7-1-2004 and 3-31-2007, inheritance tax due must be paid and tax returns must be filed with Dept. Rev. within 9 mos. after decedent's death if tax is due or gross value of decedent's estate is $15,000 or more, unless application is filed with proper court no later than last day of ninth month after decedent's death for judicial opening of succession of decedent's estate, filing of declaration of trust for inter vivos trust, or rendering of judgment of possession.
	Estate tax is not imposed. Due to phase-out of the federal credit (see introductory text), no state estate tax is imposed for decedents dying on or after 1-1-2005.	

STATE	BASIS AND RATE OF TAX	REPORT—PAYMENT DUE DATES
	Generation-skipping transfer tax: Not imposed.	
	Gift tax repealed for gifts made on or after 7-1-2008. For gifts made before 7-1-2008, tax is imposed on taxable value of gift. Single gifts up to the amount of the federal gift tax annual exclusion are exempt annually; $30,000 lifetime exemption. Rates—Spouse, specified charities, Fed. state & local governments are exempt; 1st $15,000, 2%; balance, 3%.	Report-pay to Dept. Rev. & Tax. by Apr. 15 after calendar yr. of gift.
ME.	*Inheritance tax:* Not imposed.	
	Estate tax is imposed. For decedents dying after 12-31-2002, the tax is equal to the federal credit for state death taxes as of 12-31-2002. State does not adopt exemption amount increases under EGTRRA; for 2006-2009, exclusion is $1 million; for 2006-2009, credit is $345,800. Tax is repealed eff. 1-1-2010.	Report-pay to Rev. Services by 9 mos. after death.
	Generation-skipping transfer tax: Not imposed.	
	Gift tax: Not imposed.	
MD.	*Inheritance tax* is imposed on taxable value of property passing from decedent. Rate is 10% on all taxable property (property passing to Cl. A beneficiaries is exempt). Exempt—estate up to $20,000, share up to $150, transfers to specified charities.	Report to Register Wills in 3 mos. after letters of administration granted. Pay State Comptroller at time of accounting for distribution.
	Estate tax is imposed. Tax is equal to the federal credit for state death taxes as in effect before the reduction or repeal of the federal credit. Tax is decoupled from federal phase-out and repeal. The unified credit used for determining the Md. estate tax is limited to $1 million.	Report to Register Wills, pay State Comptroller in 9 mos. after death.
	Generation-skipping transfer tax is not imposed. Due to phase-out of the federal credit (see introductory text), no state GST tax is imposed for decedents dying on or after 1-1-2005.	
	Gift tax: Not imposed.	
MASS.	*Inheritance tax:* Not imposed.	
	Estate tax is imposed. Eff. for decedents dying after 12-31-2002, tax is equal to the federal credit allowed under IRC §2011 as in effect on 12-31-2000. Tax is decoupled from federal phase-out and repeal. State decoupled from exemption amount increases under EGTRRA.	Report-pay Rev. Commr. in 9 mos. after death.
	Generation-skipping transfer tax is imposed. Tax is equal to the federal credit on state generation-skipping taxes as in effect on 12-31-81. Tax is decoupled from federal phase-out and repeal.	Report-pay to Rev. Commr. by Fed due date. Pay Commr.
	Gift tax: Not imposed.	

STATE	BASIS AND RATE OF TAX	REPORT—PAYMENT DUE DATES
MICH.	*Inheritance tax:* Not imposed. *Estate tax* is not imposed. Due to phase-out of the federal credit (see introductory text), no state estate tax is imposed for decedents dying on or after 1-1-2005. *Generation-skipping transfer tax* is not imposed. Due to phase-out of the federal credit (see introductory text), no state GST tax is imposed for decedents dying on or after 1-1-2005. *Gift tax:* Not imposed.	
MINN.	*Inheritance tax:* Not imposed. *Estate tax* is imposed. Tax is equal to the federal credit for death taxes as in effect on 12-31-2000. Tax is decoupled from federal phase-out and repeal. *Generation-skipping transfer tax:* Not imposed. *Gift tax:* Not imposed.	Report-pay to Dept. Rev. in 9 mos. after death.
MISS.	*Inheritance tax:* Not imposed. *Estate tax* is not imposed. Due to phase-out of the federal credit (see introductory text), no state estate tax is imposed for decedents dying on or after 1-1-2005. *Generation-skipping transfer tax:* Not imposed. *Gift tax:* Not imposed.	
MO.	*Inheritance tax:* Not imposed. *Estate tax* is not imposed. Due to phase-out of the federal credit (see introductory text), no state estate tax is imposed for decedents dying on or after 1-1-2005. *Generation-skipping transfer tax* is not imposed. Due to phase-out of the federal credit (see introductory text), no state GST tax is imposed for decedents dying on or after 1-1-2005. *Gift tax:* Not imposed.	
MONT.	*Inheritance tax* was imposed for deaths occurring before 1-1-2001. *Estate tax* is not imposed. Due to phase-out of the federal credit (see introductory text), no state estate tax is imposed for decedents dying on or after 1-1-2005. *Generation-skipping transfer tax* is not imposed. Due to phase-out of the federal credit (see introductory text), no state GST tax is imposed for decedents dying on or after 1-1-2005. *Gift tax:* Not imposed.	

STATE	BASIS AND RATE OF TAX	REPORT—PAYMENT DUE DATES
NEB.	*Inheritance tax* is imposed on taxable value of share. Rates—Spouse and specified charities, exempt; Cl. 1 ($40,000 exempt per share applicable to property passing from a decedent dying on or after 1-1-2008, $10,000 before 1-1-2008), 1% tax; Cl. 2 applicable to all property which passes from a decedent dying on or after 1-1-2008, 1st $15,000, exempt; 13% of the clear market value of the property received over $15,000 (before 1-1-2008, $2,000 exemption, 6% on 1st $60,000 and 9% on rest); Cl. 3, for property passing from a decedent dying on or after 1-1-2008, 1st $10,000 exempt, 18% of the clear market value of the beneficial interests over $10,000 (before 1-1-2008, $500 exemption, and tax ranged from 6% on 1st $5,000 to 18% on over $50,000).	Report, pay county treasurer in 12 mos. after death.
	Estate tax : Repealed eff. 1-1-2007.	Report-pay to Tax Commr. in 12 mos. of death.
	Generation-skipping transfer tax is imposed. The rate is 16%.	Report-pay to Tax Commr. by Fed due date.
	Gift tax: Not imposed.	
NEV.	*Inheritance tax:* Not imposed.	
	Estate tax is not imposed. Due to phase-out of the federal credit (see introductory text), no state estate tax is imposed for decedents dying on or after 1-1-2005.	
	Generation-skipping transfer tax is not imposed. Due to phase-out of the federal credit (see introductory text), no state GST tax is imposed for decedents dying on or after 1-1-2005.	
	Gift tax: Not imposed.	
N.H.	*Inheritance tax* (legacy and succession tax) is not imposed on taxable property transferred. Tax repealed for estates established due to deaths occurring on and after 1-1-2003.	
	Estate tax is not imposed. Due to phase-out of the federal credit (see introductory text), no state estate tax is imposed for decedents dying on or after 1-1-2005.	
	Generation-skipping transfer tax: Not imposed.	
	Gift tax: Not imposed.	

STATE	BASIS AND RATE OF TAX	REPORT—PAYMENT DUE DATES
N.J.	*Inheritance tax* is imposed on taxable transfers. Rates—Spouse, specified charities, and Cl. A, exempt; Cl. C (share under $25,000 exempt) 11% on $25,000 to $1.1 million, 13% on $1.1 million to $1.4 million, 14% on 1.4 million to $1.7 million, 16% on over $1.7 million; Cl. D 15% on 1st $700,000, 16% on rest.	Report-pay Div. Tax. within 8 mos. after death.
	Estate tax is imposed. Tax is equal to the federal credit for death taxes as in effect on 12-31-2001. Tax is decoupled from federal phase-out and repeal.	File copy of Fed return with Div. Tax in 30-days after filing with U.S. Pay within 9 mos. after death.
	Generation-skipping transfer tax: Not imposed.	
	Gift tax: Not imposed.	
N.M.	*Inheritance tax:* Not imposed.	
	Estate tax is not imposed. Due to phase-out of the federal credit (see introductory text), no state estate tax is imposed for decedents dying on or after 1-1-2005.	
	Generation-skipping transfer tax: Not imposed.	
	Gift tax: Not imposed.	
N.Y.	*Inheritance tax:* Not imposed.	
	Estate tax applicable to decedents dying on or after 2-1-2000 is equal to Fed credit for state death taxes as in effect on 7-22-98. Tax is decoupled from federal phase-out and repeal.	Report-pay to Dept. Tax. & Fin. in 9 mos. of death.
	Generation-skipping transfer tax is imposed. Tax is equal to the federal credit on state generation-skipping taxes as in effect on 7-22-98. Tax is decoupled from federal phase-out and repeal.	Report-pay Dept. Tax. and Fin. by Apr. 15 after calendar yr. of transfer.
	Gift tax was repealed eff 1-1-2000.	
N.C.	*Inheritance tax*: Not imposed.	
	Estate tax is imposed. For estates of decedents dying on or after 1-1-2005, tax is equal to amount of state death tax credit that, as of 12-31-2001, would have been allowed under IRC §2011 against the federal taxable estate. Tax may not exceed federal estate tax amount due under IRC. The federal taxable estate and the amount of the federal estate tax due are determined without taking into account deduction for state death taxes allowed under IRC §2058 and the credits allowed under IRC §2011 through IRC §2015. State adopts increases to the exemption equivalent of the unified credit under EGTRRA.	Report-pay to Secy. Rev. by Fed due date.
	Generation-skipping transfer tax is not imposed. Due to phase-out of the federal credit (see introductory text), no state GST tax is imposed for decedents dying on or after 1-1-2005.	

STATE	BASIS AND RATE OF TAX	REPORT—PAYMENT DUE DATES
	Gift tax is imposed on taxable value of net gifts. Rates: spouses and gifts of $5,000 or less per year to any individual are exempt; Cl. A ($100,000 exempt) tax ranges from 1% on the first $10,000 to 12% on over $3 million; Cl. B tax ranges from 4% on the first $5,000 to 16% on over $3 million; and Cl. C tax ranges from 8% on the first $10,000 to 17% on over 2.5 million.	Report-pay Dept. Rev. by Apr. 15 after yr. of gift.
N.D.	*Inheritance tax:* Not imposed. *Estate tax* is not imposed. Due to phase-out of the federal credit (see introductory text), no state estate tax is imposed for decedents dying on or after 1-1-2005. *Generation-skipping transfer tax:* Not imposed. *Gift tax:* Not imposed.	
OHIO	*Inheritance tax:* Not imposed. *Estate tax* is imposed at rate ranging from 2% on 1st $40,000 of taxable estate to 7% on over $500,000. $13,900 credit allowed. Spouse is exempt. *Generation-skipping transfer tax* is not imposed. Due to phase-out of the federal credit (see introductory text), no state GST tax is imposed for decedents dying on or after 1-1-2005. *Gift tax:* Not imposed.	Report-pay probate court by 9 mos. after death.
OKLA.	*Inheritance tax:* Not imposed. *Estate tax* is imposed on taxable value of net estate. Rates—Spouse and specified charities, exempt. Tax ranges from 0.5% on 1st $10,000 to 10% on over $10 million. Prior to 2007, non-lineal heirs were taxed at the following rates: 1% on the 1st $10,000 to 15% on over $1 million. Added tax imposed equal to unused max. credit Fed law allows for state death taxes. Estate tax is repealed eff. 1-1-2010. *Generation-skipping transfer tax:* Not imposed. *Gift tax:* Not imposed.	Report-pay to Tax Comm. in 9 mos. of death.
ORE.	*Estate tax (inheritance tax)* is imposed. For decedents dying on or after 1-1-2003, tax is equal to federal credit for death taxes under IRC §2011 as in effect on 12-31-2000. Ore. return must be filed if estate has gross value of $1 million (unified credit amount is $345,800). *Generation-skipping transfer tax:* Not imposed. *Gift tax:* Not imposed.	Report-pay to Rev. Dept. within 9 mos. of death.

STATE	BASIS AND RATE OF TAX	REPORT—PAYMENT DUE DATES
PA.	*Inheritance tax* is imposed on taxable transfers. Rates—Cl. A ($3,500 family exemption; spouse totally exempt), 4.5% (6% for decedents dying before 7-1-2000); Cl. B, 15%; Cl. C (siblings), 12% for decedents dying after 6-30-2000. Exempt are transfers from a child age 21 or younger to a parent or step-parent. *Estate tax* is not imposed. Due to phase-out of the federal credit (see introductory text), no state estate tax is imposed for decedents dying on or after 1-1-2005. *Generation-skipping transfer tax:* Not imposed. *Gift tax:* Not imposed.	Report-pay county register of wills in 9 mos. of death.
R.I.	*Inheritance tax:* Not imposed. *Estate tax* is imposed. For decedents dying after 12-31-2001, tax is equal to the maximum federal credit for state death taxes allowed under IRC §2011, as in effect on 1-1-2001. Any scheduled increase in the unified credit provided in IRC §2010 in effect on 1-1-2002 or thereafter will not apply. Tax is decoupled from federal phase-out and repeal. *Generation-skipping transfer tax* is not imposed. Due to phase-out of the federal credit (see introductory text), no state GST tax is imposed for decedents dying on or after 1-1-2005. *Gift tax:* Not imposed.	Report-pay to Tax Admin. in 9 mos. after death.
S.C.	*Inheritance tax:* Not imposed. *Estate tax* is not imposed. Due to phase-out of the federal credit (see introductory text), no state estate tax is imposed for decedents dying on or after 1-1-2005. *Generation-skipping transfer tax* is not imposed. Due to phase-out of the federal credit (see introductory text), no state GST tax is imposed for decedents dying on or after 1-1-2005. *Gift tax:* Not imposed.	
S.D.	*Inheritance tax:* Not imposed. *Estate tax* is not imposed. Due to phase-out of the federal credit (see introductory text), no state estate tax is imposed for decedents dying on or after 1-1-2005. *Generation-skipping transfer tax:* Not imposed. *Gift tax:* Not imposed.	

STATE	BASIS AND RATE OF TAX	REPORT—PAYMENT DUE DATES
TENN.	*Inheritance tax* is imposed on taxable value of transferred property. Exemption—Spouse and specified charities, all; others, $1 million ($950,000 for 2005). Rates—Tax ranges from 5.5% on 1st $40,000 to 9.5% on over $440,000.	Report-pay to Dept. Rev. in 9 mos. of death.
	Estate tax is not imposed. Due to phase-out of the federal credit (see introductory text), no state estate tax is imposed for decedents dying on or after 1-1-2005.	
	Generation-skipping transfer tax is not imposed. Due to phase-out of the federal credit (see introductory text), no state GST tax is imposed for decedents dying on or after 1-1-2005.	
	Gift tax is imposed on taxable value of gift. Rates—Spouse and specified charities, exempt; Cl. A ($12,000 exempt, as indexed annually after 1998 for federal gift tax), tax ranges from 5.5% on 1st $40,000 to 9.5% on over $440,000: Cl. B ($5,000 exempt), 6.5% on 1st $50,000 to 16% on over $200,000.	Report-pay to Dept. Rev. by Apr. 15 after yr. of gift.
TEX.	*Inheritance tax:* Not imposed.	
	Estate tax is not imposed. Due to phase-out of the federal credit (see introductory text), no state estate tax is imposed for decedents dying on or after 1-1-2005.	
	Generation-skipping transfer tax is not imposed. Due to phase-out of the federal credit (see introductory text), no state GST tax is imposed for decedents dying on or after 1-1-2005.	
	Gift tax: Not imposed.	
UTAH	*Inheritance tax:* Not imposed.	
	Estate tax is not imposed. Due to phase-out of the federal credit (see introductory text), no state estate tax is imposed for decedents dying on or after 1-1-2005.	Report-pay to State Tax Comm. by Fed. due date.
	Generation-skipping transfer tax: Not imposed.	
	Gift tax: Not imposed.	
VT.	*Inheritance tax:* Not imposed.	
	Estate tax is imposed. Eff. for deaths occurring after 12-31-2001, estate tax is equal to federal credit as in effect on 1-1-2001. Tax is decoupled from federal phase-out and repeal. State adopts exemption amount increases under EGTRRA.	Report to Dept. Taxes by Fed. due date. Pay with return.
	Generation-skipping transfer tax is imposed. Eff. for transfers occurring after 12-31-2001, tax is imposed equal to federal credit in IRC §2604 as in effect on 1-1-2001. Tax is decoupled from federal phase-out and repeal.	Report to Dept. Taxes by Fed. due date. Pay with return.
	Gift tax: Not imposed.	

STATE	BASIS AND RATE OF TAX	REPORT—PAYMENT DUE DATES
VA.	*Inheritance tax:* Not imposed. *Estate tax* is not imposed. Eff. 7-1-2007, the estate tax was repealed. Prior to 7-1-2007, tax was equal to the federal credit for death taxes as in effect on 1-1-78. While tax was decoupled from federal phase-out and repeal, state adopted exemption amount increases under EGTRRA. *Generation-skipping transfer tax* is not imposed. Due to phase-out of the federal credit (see introductory text), no state GST tax is imposed for decedents dying on or after 1-1-2005. *Gift tax:* Not imposed.	Report-pay to Dept. Tax. by Fed. due date.
WASH.	*Inheritance tax:* Not imposed. *Estate tax* is imposed. Stand-alone tax applies to estates of persons dying on or after 5-17-2006 at rates ranging from 10% to 19% of Wash. taxable estate. Estates with a federal taxable estate under $2 million are exempt. Tax is decoupled from federal phase-out and repeal. *Generation-skipping transfer tax* was repealed for decendents dying on or after 5-17-2005. *Gift tax:* Not imposed.	Report-pay to Rev. Dept. within 9 months of death.
W.VA.	*Inheritance tax:* Not imposed. *Estate tax* is not imposed. Due to phase-out of the federal credit (see introductory text), no state estate tax is imposed for decedents dying on or after 1-1-2005. *Generation-skipping transfer tax:* Not imposed. *Gift tax:* Not imposed.	
WIS.	*Inheritance tax:* Not imposed. *Estate tax* is imposed. Eff. for deaths after 12-31-2007, the tax is equal to the federal credit allowed under IRC §2011 as in effect on the date of death. For deaths after 9-30-2002 but before 1-1-2008, the tax is equal to the federal credit for death taxes as in effect on 12-31-2000. Tax is decoupled from federal phase-out and repeal. *Generation-skipping transfer tax:* Not imposed. *Gift tax:* Not imposed.	Report-pay to Rev. Dept. in 9 mos. of date.
WYO.	*Inheritance tax:* Not imposed. *Estate tax* is not imposed. Due to phase-out of the federal credit (see introductory text), no state estate tax is imposed for decedents dying on or after 1-1-2005. *Generation-skipping transfer tax:* Not imposed. *Gift tax:* Not imposed.	

BEER EXCISE TAX RATES

¶274 Beer taxes. This chart lists the state-by-state beer excise tax rates (as rounded off). It also tells whether a state's sales tax (¶ 250) applies to beer. Added local taxes may be levied. The entry "n.a." means not applicable because the state does not have a broad based sales tax. Distilled spirits excise tax rates are charted at ¶ 275; wine tax rates, at ¶ 276.

STATE	EXCISE TAX RATES ($ per gallon)	GENERAL SALES TAXES APPLIED?	OTHER RATES
ALABAMA	$0.53	Yes	$0.52/ gallon added tax
ALASKA	1.07	n.a.	
ARIZONA	0.16	Yes	
ARKANSAS	0.23	Yes	Additional 1% special excise tax eff. 7-1-2007; 14% on on-premise consumption tax
CALIFORNIA	0.20	Yes	
COLORADO	0.08	Yes	
CONNECTICUT	0.20	Yes	20¢ per wine gallon for quantity less than 1/4 barrel.
DELAWARE	0.16	n.a.	
D.C.	0.09	Yes	9% off- and 10% on-premise sales tax
FLORIDA	0.48	Yes	
GEORGIA	0.48	Yes	$10 per 31-gallon container of tap draft beer. 4.5¢ per 12 oz. of malt beverages sold in cans and bottles.
HAWAII	0.93	Yes	draft beer per gal.: 54¢
IDAHO	0.15	Yes	over 4% alcohol, $0.45/ gallon
ILLINOIS	0.185	Yes	$0.16/gallon in Chicago and $0.06/gallon in Cook County
INDIANA	0.115	Yes	
IOWA	0.19	Yes	
KANSAS	0.18	—	$0.18/gal. on beer & cereal malt beverages; $0.20/gal. on all wort or liquid malt; $0.10/gal. on all malt extract. On over 3.2% alcohol, 8% off- and 10% on-premise retail tax; under 3.2% alcohol, 5.3% retail tax.
KENTUCKY	0.08	Yes(1)	11% wholesale tax
LOUISIANA	0.32	Yes	
MAINE	0.35	Yes	7% sales tax for on-premise consumption
MARYLAND	0.09	Yes	
MASSACHUSETTS	0.11	Yes(1)	0.57% on private club sales
MICHIGAN	0.20	Yes	
MINNESOTA	0.15	Yes	under 3.2% alcohol, $0.077/ gallon and 2.5% liquor gross receipts tax(2)
MISSISSIPPI	0.4268	Yes	

STATE	EXCISE TAX RATES ($ per gallon)	GENERAL SALES TAXES APPLIED?	OTHER RATES
MISSOURI	0.06	Yes	
MONTANA	0.14	n.a.	
NEBRASKA	0.31	Yes	
NEVADA	0.16	Yes	
NEW HAMPSHIRE	0.30	Yes(3)	
NEW JERSEY	0.12	Yes	
NEW MEXICO	0.41	Yes	
NEW YORK	0.11	Yes	$0.12/gallon in New York City
NORTH CAROLINA	0.53	Yes	
NORTH DAKOTA	0.16	—	$0.08 in bulk containers. 7% state sales tax
OHIO	0.18	Yes	0.14¢ per oz. for bottles or cans with 12 oz. or less; 0.84¢ per 6 oz. for bottles or cans with over 12 oz.
OKLAHOMA	0.40	Yes	under 3.2% alcohol, $0.36/gallon; 13.5% on-premise tax
OREGON	0.08	n.a.	
PENNSYLVANIA	0.08	Yes	
RHODE ISLAND	0.10	Yes	
SOUTH CAROLINA	0.77	Yes	
SOUTH DAKOTA	0.27	Yes	
TENNESSEE	0.138	Yes	17% wholesale tax and 15% on-premise
TEXAS	0.19	Yes	over 4% alcohol, $0.198/gallon; 14% on-premise and $0.05/drink on airline sales
UTAH	0.4129	Yes	
VERMONT	0.265	Yes(4)	6% to 8% alcohol, $0.55; 10% on-premise sales tax
VIRGINIA	0.26	Yes	
WASHINGTON	0.261	Yes	
WEST VIRGINIA	0.18	Yes	
WISCONSIN	0.06	Yes	
WYOMING	0.02	Yes	

FOOTNOTES to chart ¶ 274 (corresponding to parenthetical numbers in chart):

(1) Sales tax applies to on-premise sales only.

(2) Additional liquor gross receipts tax on sales of intoxicating liquor and beverages containing intoxicating liquor and 3.2% malt liquor imposed at rate of 2.5% *(Minn.)*.

(3) *N.H.* applies 8% meals and lodgings tax.

(4) Prior to 1-1-2007, beer sales were not subject to sales tax *(Vt.)*.

DISTILLED SPIRITS EXCISE TAX RATES

¶275 Distilled spirits taxes. This chart lists the state-by-state distilled spirits excise tax rates (as rounded off). It also tells whether a state's sales tax (¶ 250) applies to distilled spirits. Added local tax may be levied. The entry "n.a." means not applicable because the state does not have a broad based sales tax. Beer excise tax rates are charted at ¶ 274; wine tax rates, at ¶ 276.

STATE	EXCISE TAX RATES ($ per gallon)	GENERAL SALES TAXES APPLIED?	OTHER RATES
ALABAMA	(1)	Yes	
ALASKA	$12.80	n.a.	under 21% alcohol, $2.50/gallon
ARIZONA	3.00	Yes	
ARKANSAS	2.50	Yes	$1.00/gallon under 21% alcohol; $0.50/ gallon under 5% alcohol. $0.25/barrel consumer enforcement tax; $0.20/case 21% alcohol or more; $0.05/case less than 21% alcohol. 14% on-premise consumption tax.
CALIFORNIA	3.30	Yes	over 50% alcohol, $6.60/gallon
COLORADO	2.28	Yes	
CONNECTICUT	4.50	Yes	under 7% alcohol, $2.05/gallon
DELAWARE	3.75	n.a.	25% or less alcohol, $2.50/gallon
DISTRICT OF COLUMBIA	1.50	Yes	9% off- and 10% on-premise sales tax
FLORIDA	6.50	Yes	under 17.259% alcohol, $2.25/gallon; over 55.780% alcohol, $9.53/gallon.
GEORGIA	4.54	Yes	
HAWAII	5.98	Yes	
IDAHO	(1)	Yes	
ILLINOIS	4.50	Yes	over 20% alcohol, $1.845/gallon in Chicago; $2/gallon in Cook County.
INDIANA	2.68	Yes	under 21% alcohol, $0.47/gallon
IOWA	(1)	Yes	
KANSAS	2.50	No	8% off- and 10% on-premise retail tax
KENTUCKY	1.92	Yes(2)	under 6% alcohol, $0.25/gallon; half pint containers, $0.12/half-pint and 11% wholesale tax
LOUISIANA	2.50	Yes	under 6% alcohol, $0.32/gallon
MAINE	1.25(1)	Yes	$1.24/gallon on low alcohol spirits
MARYLAND	1.50	Yes	
MASSACHUSETTS	4.05	Yes(2)	under 15% alcohol, $1.10/gallon; over 50% alcohol, $4.05/proof gallon; 0.57% on private club sales
MICHIGAN	(1)	Yes	
MINNESOTA	5.03	Yes	$0.01/bottle; $0.14/bottle on miniatures and 2.5% liquor gross receipts tax(3)
MISSISSIPPI	2.50(1)	Yes	
MISSOURI	2.00	Yes	
MONTANA	(1)	n.a.	
NEBRASKA	3.75	Yes	
NEVADA	3.60	Yes	under 14% alcohol, $0.70/gallon; under 22% alcohol, $1.30/gallon.
NEW HAMPSHIRE	(1)	n.a.	

STATE	EXCISE TAX RATES ($ per gallon)	GENERAL SALES TAXES APPLIED?	OTHER RATES
NEW JERSEY	4.40	Yes	
NEW MEXICO	6.06	Yes	
NEW YORK	6.44	Yes	under 24% alcohol, $2.54/gallon; under 2% alcohol, $0.0379/gallon; $1.00/ gallon in New York City for over 24% alcohol
NORTH CAROLINA	(1)	Yes	
NORTH DAKOTA	2.50	—	7% state sales tax
OHIO	(1)	Yes	
OKLAHOMA	5.56	Yes	13.5% on-premise tax
OREGON	(1)	n.a.	
PENNSYLVANIA	(1)	Yes	
RHODE ISLAND	3.75	Yes	
SOUTH CAROLINA	1.92	Yes	$5.36/case and 9% surtax for wholesalers; 5% for sales sold by the drink for on-premises consumption.
SOUTH DAKOTA	3.93	Yes	under 14% alcohol, $0.93/gallon. 2% wholesale tax
TENNESSEE	4.40	Yes	15% on-premise.
TEXAS	2.40	Yes	14% on-premise and $0.05/drink on airline sales
UTAH	(4)	Yes	
VERMONT	(1)	No	
VIRGINIA	(1)	Yes	
WASHINGTON	(1)	Yes(2)	
WEST VIRGINIA	(1)	Yes	
WISCONSIN	3.25	Yes	
WYOMING	(1)	Yes	

FOOTNOTES to chart ¶ 275 (corresponding to parenthetical numbers in chart):

(1) The government directly controls the sales of distilled spirits. Revenue is generated from various taxes, fees, and net liquor profits. In *N.C.*, 25% excise tax on price of spiritous liquor. In *Utah*, tax of 13% of retail puchase price.

(2) Sales tax applies to on-premise sales only. In *Wash.*, off-premises retail sales subject to special excise tax in lieu of sales tax.

(3) Additional liquor gross receipts tax on sales of intoxicating liquor and beverages containing intoxicating liquor and 3.2% malt liquor is imposed at rate of 2.5% *(Minn.)*.

(4) Utah—Eff. 7-1-2007, wine and liquor tax repealed. Previously, tax imposed at 13% of retail purchase price.

WINE EXCISE TAX RATES

¶276 Wine taxes. This chart lists the state-by-state wine excise tax rates (as rounded off). It also tells whether a state's sales tax (¶ 250) applies to wine. Added local taxes may be levied. The entry "n.a." means not applicable because the state does not have a broad based sales tax. Distilled spirits excise tax rates are charted at ¶ 275; beer tax rates, at ¶ 274.

STATE	EXCISE TAX RATES ($ per gallon)	GENERAL SALES TAXES APPLIED?	OTHER RATES
ALABAMA	$1.70	Yes	Table wine, up to 14.9% alcohol
ALASKA	2.50	n.a.	$1.07/gallon for cider with 0.5%–7% alcohol by volume.
ARIZONA	0.84	Yes	
ARKANSAS	0.75	Yes	under 5% alcohol, $0.25/gallon. Additional 14% on-premises consumption tax.
CALIFORNIA	0.20	Yes	sparkling wine, $0.30/gallon
COLORADO	0.277	Yes	
CONNECTICUT	0.60	Yes	over 21% alcohol and sparkling wine, $1.50/gallon
DELAWARE	0.97	n.a.	
DISTRICT OF COLUMBIA	0.30	Yes	over 14%, $0.40/gallon; sparkling wine, champagne, artificially carbonated wine, $0.45/ gallon; 9% off- and 10% on-premise sales tax
FLORIDA	2.25	Yes	over 17.259% alcohol, $3.00/gallon; sparkling wine, $3.50/gallon; wine coolers $2.25/gallon; cider with 0.5% to 7% alcohol, $0.89/gallon.
GEORGIA	0.42	Yes	Table wine. Imported table wines, $1.10/ gallon; dessert wines, $1.02/gallon; imported dessert wines, $1.51/gallon.
HAWAII	1.38	Yes	sparkling wine, per gal.: $2.12. Wine coolers per gal.: 85¢.
IDAHO	0.45	Yes	
ILLINOIS	0.73	Yes	Cider 0.5-7% alcohol, $0.185/gallon. In Chicago: $0.246/gallon; over 14% to 20% alcohol, $0.615. In Cook County: $0.16/gallon; over 14% alcohol, $0.30/ gallon.
INDIANA	0.47	Yes	over 21% alcohol, $2.68/gallon
IOWA	1.75	Yes	under 5% alcohol, $0.19/ gallon
KANSAS	0.30	no	over 14% alcohol, $0.75/ gallon; 8% off- and 10% on-premise retail tax.
KENTUCKY	0.50	Yes(2)	11% wholesale
LOUISIANA	0.11	Yes	14% to 24% alcohol, $0.23/ gallon; over 24% alcohol and sparkling wine, $1.59/ gallon
MAINE	0.60	Yes	sparkling wine, $1.24/gallon; 7% sales tax for on-premises consumption
MARYLAND	0.40	Yes	
MASSACHUSETTS	0.55	Yes(2)	sparkling wine, $0.70/gallon;
MICHIGAN	0.51	Yes	over 16% alcohol, $0.76/gallon

STATE	EXCISE TAX RATES ($ per gallon)	GENERAL SALES TAXES APPLIED?	OTHER RATES
MINNESOTA	0.30	Yes	14% to 21% alcohol, $0.95/gallon; under 24% alcohol and sparkling wine, $1.82/gallon; more than 24% alcohol, $3.52/gallon; cider $0.15/gallon; low alcohol dairy $0.08/gallon; $0.01/ bottle (except miniatures) and 2.5% liquor gross receipts tax(3)
MISSISSIPPI	1.00	Yes	champagne and sparkling wine; $0.35/ gallon on other wines.
MISSOURI	0.36	Yes	
MONTANA	1.02	n.a.	Table wine.
NEBRASKA	0.95	Yes	over 14% alcohol, $1.35/gallon
NEVADA	0.70	Yes	14% to 22% alcohol, $1.30/gallon; over 22% alcohol, $3.60/gallon
NEW HAMPSHIRE	(1)	n.a.	
NEW JERSEY	0.70	Yes	Cider containing over 3.2% to 7% alcohol, $0.12/gal.; vermouth and sparkling wine, $0.70/gal.
NEW MEXICO	1.70	Yes	over 14%, $5.678/gallon.
NEW YORK	0.19	Yes	cider (carbonated or natural) over 3.2% alcohol vol., $0.38/gallon
NORTH CAROLINA	0.79	Yes	unfortified; $0.91/gal. fortified
NORTH DAKOTA	0.50	—	over 17% alcohol, $0.60/gallon; sparkling wine, $1.00/gallon; 7% state sales tax
OHIO	0.32	Yes	over 14% alcohol, $1.00/gallon; vermouth, $1.10/gallon; sparkling and carbonated wine and champagne, $1.50/gallon; mixed beverages over 21% alcohol, $1.20/gallon; cider $0.24/gallon.
OKLAHOMA	0.72	Yes	over 14% alcohol, 1.4¢/gallon; sparkling wine, $2.08/gallon; 13.5% on-premise tax
OREGON	0.67	n.a.	over 14% alcohol, $0.77/gallon
PENNSYLVANIA	(1)	Yes	
RHODE ISLAND	0.60	Yes	sparkling wine, $0.75/gallon
SOUTH CAROLINA	0.90	Yes	$0.96/gallon wine sold in less than 1 gallon containers; $0.18/gallon excise tax.
SOUTH DAKOTA	0.93	Yes	under 14% alcohol, $0.93/gallon; over 14% to 20% alcohol, $1.45/gallon; over 21% alcohol and sparkling wine; $2.07/gallon; 2% wholesale tax; cider with 10% or less alcohol, $0.28/ gallon.
TENNESSEE	1.21	Yes	15% on-premise.
TEXAS	0.20	Yes	over 14% alcohol, $0.408/gallon; sparkling wine, $0.516/gallon; 14% on-premise and $0.05/drink on airline sales
UTAH	(4)	Yes	
VERMONT	0.55	No	
VIRGINIA	1.51	Yes	under 4% alcohol, $0.2565/gallon; over 14%, sold through state store
WASHINGTON	0.87	Yes	over 14% alcohol, $1.72/gallon
WEST VIRGINIA	1.00	Yes	over 14% alcohol, sold through state store
WISCONSIN	0.25	Yes	over 14% alcohol, $0.45/gallon
WYOMING	(1)	Yes	

FOOTNOTES to chart ¶ 276 (corresponding to parenthetical numbers in chart):

(1) All wine sales are through state stores. Revenue is generated from various taxes, fees, and net profits. In *Utah*, tax of 13% of retail purchase price.
(2) Sales tax applies to on-premise sales only.
(3) Additional liquor gross receipts tax on sales of intoxicating liquor and beverages containing intoxicating liquor and 3.2% malt liquor imposed at rate of 2.5% *(Minn.)*.
(4) Utah—Eff. 7-1-2007, wine and liquor tax repealed. Previously, tax imposed at 13% of retail purchase price.

ELECTRONIC FUNDS TRANSFER PROGRAMS

¶279 EFT taxes and thresholds. All of the states have a program in place or are studying and planning for the use of electronic funds transfer (EFT) to help collect taxes, especially large amounts due. A survey by the Federation of Tax Administrators finds that all of the states and the District of Columbia are now using EFT or have passed laws authorizing it to collect certain tax payments. The chart below lists the current status of EFT programs state-by-state. Dollar amounts listed are per tax, unless otherwise shown. Some localities also allow or require EFT.

STATE	TAXES AFFECTED	TAXPAYERS AFFECTED
ALABAMA	Individual income tax—withholding only. All other taxes.	Business taxpayers making single tax payments totaling $750 or more. Individual income tax, voluntary.
ALASKA	Insurance taxes.	All taxpayers.
	All other taxes.	All tax payments of $100,000 or more due with a required monthly or quarterly return, and $150,000 or more due with an annual return.
ARIZONA	Withholding, corporate estimated income, motor vehicle and use fuel taxes.	Taxpayers with liability of at least $20,000 per quarter (withholding), or $20,000 per year (corporate estimated income, motor vehicle or use fuel) based on average of previous year. Others, voluntary.
	Transaction privilege (sales) and use, severance, telecommunications service excise, county excise, water use, and jet fuel excise taxes.	Taxpayers with past yr. tax liability of at least $1 million.
ARKANSAS	Withholding, sales/use, privilege, alcoholic beverage excise, tobacco, severance, spirits, soft drink taxes.	Tax liability of $20,000 or greater per month. Registered retailers prepay sales-use tax by EFT if average net sales are over $200,000 a month for the prior calendar year.
	Corporate estimated taxes.	$20,000 or greater per quarter.
	Motor fuel.	All taxpayers.
	Individual income taxes.	Tax liability of $20,000 or greater for calendar year.
CALIFORNIA	Sales & use, bank & corporate income, personal income withholding, disability insurance, fuel, cigarette & tobacco, alcoholic beverage, emergency telephone user's & energy resource surcharges, and insurance taxes.	Bank & corporation income—estimated tax or extension payment of $20,000 or more, or liability of $80,000 or more per tax yr. Others, voluntary.
		Personal income/disability—avg. annual liability of at least $20,000; also applies to payroll reporting agents. Others, voluntary.
		Sales & use, fuel, cigarette & tobacco, alcoholic beverage, emergency telephone user's & energy resources surcharges—avg. liability of at least $10,000 per month. Others, voluntary. Insurance—annual liability of at least $20,000.

STATE	TAXES AFFECTED	TAXPAYERS AFFECTED
COLORADO	Withholding and sales & use taxes.	Taxpayers with over $50,000 annual withholding tax; over $75,000 for sales & use tax in prior calendar year.
	Optional for other taxes.	Other taxpayers have EFT option.
CONNECTICUT	Any tax.	Taxpayers with annual liability of more than $10,000.
DELAWARE	Income tax (optional).	Taxpayers filing quarterly have EFT option.
	Motor and special fuel tax (mandatory).	Taxpayers with over $20,000 monthly liability.
	Withholding tax (mandatory).	Required if taxpayer must deposit federal employment taxes by EFT.
DISTRICT OF COLUMBIA	Withholding, estimated franchise taxes, and sales-use tax.	Required for nonindividual taxpayers if amount due for a period exceeds $25,000. Property owners may pay on-line using an eCheck payment system.
FLORIDA	Sales & use, corporate income, corporate income estimated, franchise tax, motor and aviation fuels, gross receipts, insurance premium, severance, gas & sulphur production, oil & gas production, communications services, emergency excise, pollutants, local option sales taxes, local option fuel tax, solid waste fees, and Dade Lake Belt Mitigation fee.	Taxpayers with prior year liability of $30,000 or more. Unemployment tax from taxpayers with 10 or more employees in any calender quarter in the previous year.
GEORGIA	Sales & use, withholding, motor fuel, & corporate and individual estimated income taxes.	Taxpayers filing return with liability of $5,000 or more for sales-use, and motor fuel distributor taxes may be required by the Commissioner to pay by EFT. Taxpayers filing return with liability of $10,000 or more for corporate and individual estimated payments must pay by EFT. Corporations with quarterly estimated tax payments of $50,000 or more must use EFT. Employers with withholding liability exceeding $50,000 for previous year must use EFT.
HAWAII	Corporate and personal income, general excise (sales) and use, withholding, transient accommodations, rental motor vehicle and vehicle surcharge.	Prior year tax liability of $100,000 or more ($40,000 for withholding taxes). Others can voluntarily participate with prior approval.
IDAHO	Any tax with $100,000 or more paid in one payment.	Payments of $100,000 or more. Voluntary for individuals', trusts' or estates' personal income tax liability.

STATE	TAXES AFFECTED	TAXPAYERS AFFECTED
ILLINOIS	Employer's withholding payments, corporate estimated income and replacement tax, individual estimated income tax, sales-use, electricity excise, gas and electricity providers, telecommunications, alcoholic gallonage, cigarette and tobacco, bingo, and water taxes.	Program is mandatory for taxpayers having annual tax of at least $200,000. Estimated tax threshold is $200,000 quarterly estimated tax payment obligation. Voluntary for lesser amounts or other taxes—no threshold.
INDIANA	Adjusted gross income, and financial institution taxes.	Estimated quarterly tax liability for current yr. or average quarterly tax liability for past yr. exceeding $5,000.
	Sales-use, withholding, and special fuels taxes.	Estimated monthly tax liability for current yr. or average monthly tax liability for past yr. exceeding $5,000.
IOWA	Sales & use, withholding, corporate estimated payments, motor vehicle use, LPG and CNG taxes.	Taxpayers required to file biweekly for sales & use & withholding taxes. Taxpayers with total prior year liability of $80,000 or more in corporate estimated tax.
	Motor vehicle fuel taxes.	Suppliers, restrictive suppliers, importers, & blenders.
KANSAS	Corporate income, financial institution privilege, withholding, sales-use, motor fuel and mineral taxes.	Taxpayers with tax liabilities of at least $100,000. Model 1, Model 2 and Model 3 sellers must remit sales-use taxes electronically. Voluntary for others.
KENTUCKY	Withholding and sales and use taxes.	Taxpayers with avg. payment per period in excess of $25,000.
	Utility gross receipts license, telecommunications, bank franchise and mortor fuel taxes.	Voluntary.
LOUISIANA	Mandatory—Business gasoline, corporate income, franchise, sales-use, and withholding taxes.	Payments in past yr. averaging at least $5,000. EFT is also required if average payment by taxpayer filing more often than monthly exceeds $5,000 per month during past yr. EFT is also required by a company filing withholding taxes, if average total payments exceed $5,000 per month during past yr.
	Optional—all others.	Voluntary, with Department of Revenue approval.
MAINE	Withholding, sales & use, corporate income, cigarette, gasoline, special fuel, unemployment contribution, property, fiduciary, and insurance premium taxes.	Mandatory for taxpayers with withholding tax liability of at least $200,000 for past July 1—June 30 period. Mandatory for other taxpayers with tax liability of at least $400,000 for past yr. Voluntary for others.
MARYLAND	Sales & use, motor fuel, aviation fuel, motor carrier fuel, withholding, and corporate income taxes	Any taxpayer filing a return with liability of $10,000 or more.

STATE	TAXES AFFECTED	TAXPAYERS AFFECTED
MASSACHUSETTS	Withholding, sales, & corporate excise taxes.	Mandatory—Prior year liability of at least $100,000 for corporate excise and $10,000 for sales-use taxes. Voluntary (if approved)—Filers with at least $25,000 annual liability.
	Gasoline taxes.	Mandatory—Prior year liability of at least $100,000. Voluntary (if approved)—Filers with at least $25,000 annual liability.
MICHIGAN	Withholding taxes.	Mandatory—Taxpayers with avg. monthly liability of at least $40,000. Voluntary—All others.
	Sales-use tax.	Taxpayers with prior year tax of at least $720,000.
	Fuels & minerals.	Suppliers, importers.
	Single business taxes.	Voluntary.
MINNESOTA	Sales, withholding, corporate estimated income, MinnesotaCare, & gasoline taxes. Also applies to cigarette and tobacco products tax, distilled spirits and wine tax, gambling tax.	Mandatory for taxpayers generally making $10,000 or larger payments in past year; voluntary for others. Gasoline tax threshold is $0. Threshold for mandatory payment by EFT is $120,000 for distilled spirits and wine, cigarettes and tobacco, and gambling taxes. A taxpayer required to pay one tax by EFT must pay all taxes and fees payable to the Dept. of Revenue by EFT (except individual income tax or estimated tax payments by individuals, trusts or partnerships).
MISSISSIPPI	Gaming, insurance premium, beer excise, tobacco wholesale, timber, and oil & gas severance taxes.	Tax liability of $20,000 or more. State Tax Comm. can require EFT for additional tax types and can require taxpayers to pay by EFT. Others and other taxes—voluntary (if accepted).
MISSOURI	Withholding taxes.	Voluntary.
	Sales-use tax.	Dir. may require sellers that remit on a quarter-monthly basis to remit by EFT.
MONTANA	Any tax where a single tax payment is $500,000 or more. Optional—other withholding, personal income, and motor fuel taxes.	Tax payments of $500,000 or more. Other withholding, personal income, and motor fuel taxpayers have EFT option.
NEBRASKA	Corporate and personal income, withholding, motor fuel excise, and sales & use taxes.	May be required for taxpayers who made payments for a prior year of over $20,000. EFT is required if reporting 100,000 gal. or more of motor fuel per month. Voluntary for others.
NEVADA	Sales-use taxes.	Voluntary.
NEW HAMPSHIRE	Meals & rooms tax, and Medicaid enhancement tax.	Mandatory for all taxpayers.
	Other taxes.	Mandatory for taxpayers with tax liability of at least $100,000 in the past year. Voluntary for others.

STATE	TAXES AFFECTED	TAXPAYERS AFFECTED
NEW JERSEY	All taxes (other than individual gross income, transfer inheritance, and estate taxes).	$10,000 or more prior year liability.
	Gross income tax.	Voluntary subject to Director's approval.
NEW MEXICO	CRS-1 (sales, use & withholding) and oil & gas taxes.	Average monthly combined liability for CRS-1 or oil & gas taxes of $25,000 or more based on previous year or any individual payment of $25,000 or more.
NEW YORK (State, NY City, City of Yonkers)	Income tax withholding.	All taxpayers withholding $35,000 or more semi-annually.
	Sales & use, motor-diesel fuel, and petroleum business taxes.	Prepay by EFT or certified check if tax for the June 1 thru May 31 period immediately before the last one exceeds $5 million for prepaid sales tax on motor or diesel fuel, or for specified motor-diesel fuel taxes and petroleum business taxes, or $500,000 for sales-use taxes, including hotel occupancy taxes. Voluntary (if approved) for others.
	NYC real property taxes.	EFT required for owners with annual liability of $300,000 or more.
NORTH CAROLINA	Withholding, corporate income, personal income, sales-use, utility, franchise, alcoholic beverage, soft drink, tobacco, insurance, and motor fuel (not highway use) taxes.	Mandatory—tax liability of at least $240,000 per year. Also mandatory if required to make federal estimated corporate income tax by EFT. Voluntary allowed per specific requirements.
NORTH DAKOTA	Funding is available. Implementation details need to be worked out.	Voluntary—any tax.
OHIO	Corporation franchise tax.	Required if tax for the second preceding yr. exceeds $50,000.
	Commercial activity tax.	Quarterly taxpayers mandatory; calendar year taxpayers voluntary.
	Sales-use taxes.	Annual liability of at least $75,000.
	Fuel taxes.	Annual liability of at least $600,000.
	Public utility taxes.	Annual liability of at least $50,000.
	Kilowatt-hour, natural gas company excise, and natural gas distribution company (MCF) excise taxes.	Mandatory; various thresholds apply.
	Cigarette tax.	Mandatory for dealers not required to post bond.
	Withholding tax.	Required if actual or required payments for 12-month period ending on the past June 30 exceed $84,000.
	Pass-through entity tax.	Required if tax for the second preceeding yr. exceeds $180,000.

STATE	TAXES AFFECTED	TAXPAYERS AFFECTED
OHIO (continued)	Real property tax prepayments.	Voluntary.
	Above taxes if lower than thresholds shown, or other taxes.	Voluntary.
OKLAHOMA	Gross production, sales-use, tourism, telephone surcharge, waste tire recycling, corporate income, income tax withholding, motor fuel diesel & gasoline, special fuel, motor vehicle prorate & IFTA taxes.	Sales use tax: required if total sales tax in prior fiscal year averaged $2,500 or more per month. Voluntary for others.
OREGON	Withholding and unemployment taxes.	Mandatory if required to deposit Fed taxes by EFT. Voluntary for other employees.
	Estimated corporation income tax	Mandatory if required to make Fed estimated corporation income tax payments by EFT. Voluntary for other corporations.
PENNSYLVANIA	Sales & use, withholding, corporate net income, liquid fuels, motor carrier road, bank shares, mutual thrift, insurance premium, title insurance, capital stock and franchise, public utility realty, public utility gross receipts, oil company franchise, & malt beverage taxes.	$20,000 plus per payment.
RHODE ISLAND	Business, sales & use, utilities, personal income, and withholding taxes.	Tax liability of $10,000 or more per tax return, report, or other document. Voluntary for others if approved.
SOUTH CAROLINA	All taxes—being phased in.	Tax liability of $15,000 or more per tax filing period. Voluntary for others.
SOUTH DAKOTA	Financial institutions income tax, sales-use taxes (incl. municipal), contractors' excise taxes, fuel taxes, severance taxes, property taxes, excise tax on large vessels	Optional—Any taxpayer with tax liability can use EFT.
TENNESSEE	Sales & use, excise, tire, franchise, alcoholic beverage, beer, liquor, gas, gross receipts, and motor fuel taxes.	Taxpayers expecting to average liability of $10,000 or more ($5,000 or more for sales-use tax) per month based on previous year history.
TEXAS	Cigarette tax.	All cigarette tax stamp payments.
	All other taxes and fees.	Taxpayers who paid $10,000 or more during previous fiscal year if the Comptroller reasonably anticipates at least that amount will be paid during current fiscal year.
	Property	If authorized written agreement is made.
UTAH	Withholding & corporate income taxes.	Voluntary—$100,000 threshold.
	Sales tax.	Mandatory for taxpayers remitting $96,000 or more during the previous year.
VERMONT	Estimated corporate income tax.	Can be authorized by Commissioner.
	Withholding.	Taxpayers with payments totalling over $36,000 annually.

STATE	TAXES AFFECTED	TAXPAYERS AFFECTED
VIRGINIA	Withholding, corporation income, and sales-use taxes.	Taxpayers with average monthly liability at least $20,000 in one tax.
	Others and other taxes	Voluntary
WASHINGTON	Combined excise return taxes (sales & use, business occupations, etc).	Taxpayers with combined excise annual liability of $240,000 or more must use EFT. Voluntary for other monthly filers.
WEST VIRGINIA	Withholding, B&O, franchise, tobacco products, sales-use, corporation net imcome, motor fuel, health care provider, personal income, severance, soft drink, solid waste, surface mining, telecommunications, and timber severance taxes.	Taxpayers with $100,000 tax liability.
WISCONSIN	Withholding, corporation and personal income, sales-use, motor vehicle fuel, alternate fuel, aviation fuel, alcoholic beverages and tobacco taxes and petroleum inspection fee.	Mandatory if prior year liability was $40,000 or more ($10,000 or more for sales-use or withholding); voluntary otherwise.
WYOMING	Sales, use, mineral and severance taxes.	Voluntary.

RECORDKEEPING TIME PERIODS

¶280 Protection against arbitrary assessments. Failing to have proper records naturally leaves a taxpayer open to added assessments arbitrarily arrived at by officials. The chart below shows the minimum period that records must be retained for the major taxes in the various states to prevent any unwarranted demands. In determining the period, the statute of limitations controlling assessments was used, unless specific law prescribes a longer period for recordkeeping.

Column headed "Income" covers both ordinary income taxes and corporation franchise taxes based on income. Unless otherwise indicated the period shown applies to both corporation and personal income taxes. "Capital stock" refers to franchise and privilege taxes based on capital values. Column headed "Sales-Use" covers taxes based upon receipts.

➻ **WARNING→** In case of fraud, or if no return has been filed, the periods shown do not apply. In such cases, an assessment can be made at any time.

➻ **PLAY SAFE→** The fact that the minimum time has been reached does not necessarily mean that records should be thrown away. Other factors, such as Fed tax requirements, also must be taken into consideration. If your practice is to microfilm all records for indefinite preservation, that will solve both storage and unforeseen assessment problems. However, even if microfilms are acceptable as evidence under general law, do not throw out the original before the dates in this chart, without a definite ruling.

➻ **MEANING OF SYMBOLS→** Y—Years M—Months NT—No tax NP—No provision *—Time based on minimum assessment period.

STATE	INCOME	CAPITAL STOCK	SALES-USE
ALA.	3Y(11)	3Y(11)	3Y(11)
ALASKA	3Y*(14)	NT	NT(25)
ARIZ.	4Y*(11)	NT	4Y*(15)
ARK.	6Y(4)	6Y(4)	6Y(4)
CALIF.	3Y(3,14)	NT	4Y(17)
COLO.	4Y(9)	NT	3Y
CONN.	3Y*(11,35)	NT(22)	3Y(17)
DEL.	3Y*(4)	NP(10)	3Y*
D.C.	3Y*(4)	NT	3Y*(4)
FLA.	3Y*(11)	NT	3Y*(3)
GA.	3Y(14)	3Y*(3)	3Y
HAW.	3Y(17)	NT	3Y
IDA.	3Y*(11)	NT	3Y*(11)
ILL.	3Y*(4)	7Y*(4,32)	3Y-3½Y (18,19,38) 3Y-3½Y (3,18,20)
IND.	3Y(33)	NT	3Y(33)
IOWA	3Y*(11)	NT	5Y(4)
KAN.	3Y*(14)	NP(10)	3Y(14,31)
KY.	5Y*(4,35)	4Y*(4)	4Y(13,17)
LA.	3Y*(5)	3Y*(5)	3Y*(5)
ME.	3Y(44)	NT	6Y*
MD.	3Y*(11)	NT	4Y(17)
MASS.	3Y(11)	(22)	3Y(11)
MICH.	6Y(1)	NT	4Y*(11)
MINN.	3½Y*(4)	NT	3½Y*(4)
MISS.	3Y*(11)	3Y(11)	3Y(4)
MO.	3Y*(4)	3Y*(4)	3Y
MONT.	3Y(1,14)	NT	NT
NEB.	6Y(41)	NP(10)	3Y*(12,13)
NEV.	NT	NT	4Y(13,16)
N.H.	5Y(2,40)	3Y	3Y
N.J.	5Y(39)	NT	4Y*
N.M.	3Y*	NT	3Y*
N.Y.	3Y*(27)	(22)	3Y*(43)
N.C.	3Y*(11)	(10)	3Y*
N.D.	3Y*(11)	NT	3 1/4 Y
OHIO	4Y	(22)	4Y
OKLA.	3Y*(11)	3Y*(11)	3Y*(11)
ORE.	3Y*(4)	NT	NT
PA.	3Y(2,4) 4Y(1,29)	3Y(4)	3Y(28)
R.I.	3Y*(2,10) 3Y*(1,10)	NP(10)	3Y
S.C.	4Y(2)	3Y(11)	3Y(11)
S.D.	NT	NT	3Y
TENN.	3Y*(10)	NP(10)	3Y(30)
TEX.	NT	7Y*(10)	4Y*(13,18)
UTAH	3Y*(4)	NT	3Y
VT.	3Y*(42)	NT	3Y(17)
VA.	3Y*(4)	NT	3Y
WASH.	NT	NT	5Y
W.VA.	3Y*(9)	(37)	3Y*
WIS.	4Y*(4)	NT	4Y*(34)
WYO.	NT	NP	3Y

FOOTNOTES to chart ¶ 280 (corresponding to numbers in parentheses in the chart):

(1) Personal tax.
(2) Corporation tax.
(3) From due date.
(4) From date return filed.
(5) From Dec. 31 of year tax was due.
(6) Limitation on collection from filing and/or payment date.
(7) After 15th of month following month of proposed assessment, or after return was filed, whichever is later.
(8) From Jan. 1 of year taxes accrued.
(9) From due date of return or payment.
(10) No specific time prescribed, but records should be kept at least as long as for other taxes.
(11) From filing date or due date, whichever is later. For *Ariz.*, 6 yrs. if gross income understated by 25% or more. In *S.C.*, 6 yrs. if gross income understated by 20% or more.
(12) Model 1, 2, 3 sellers may maintain records in accordance with the Streamlined Sales and Use Tax Agreement.
(13) From day record is made.
(14) Till destruction authorized (in Calif., this applies to withholding taxes). Unless Div. Tax. allows earlier disposal (Kan.).
(15) Limit for sales tax assessments is 6 yrs. if receipts are understated by 25% or more.
(16) 8 yrs. if no return filed.
(17) Unless top tax official permits destruction earlier.
(18) Or till destruction authorized.
(19) Sales.
(20) Use.
(21) For proposed assessment only.
(22) Alternate or added tax based on capital or net worth covered under income.
(23) From return due date.
(24) Keep records until taxes prescribe.
(25) State tax repealed 1-1-79 (note 10) applied; but local taxes still collected.
(26) Keep as long as needed in administering tax law.
(27) In NY, personal income and franchise tax records must be kept as long as they may become material in administering the tax.
(28) From Dec. 31 of year covered by records.
(29) From payment date or return due date if later.
(30) From Dec. 31 of year return filed.
(31) Construction contractors keep records of purchases for 5 yrs. if project for US, political subdivision, hospital or school.
(32) Franchise tax.
(33) From date final payment due.
(34) From due date of franchise or income tax return.
(35) Exceptional circumstances may extend period.
(36) Assessment period is 3 yrs. from Dec. 31 of year tax was payable.
(37) Regs can require records to be kept up to 3 yrs.
(38) From date when gross receipts are received.
(39) Personal income tax, 3 yrs.
(40) Or until any litigation of tax is finally determined.
(41) No specific period. Period shown is the period that the State Tax Commission has to make assessments.
(42) From later of due date of payment or date return was filed.
(43) NY sales-use, from date tax is paid in full to Commr.
(44) Certain records may be required to be kept longer (Me.).

RECIPROCAL ENFORCEMENT OF TAXES

¶281 Collection of other state's taxes through comity. Forty-four states and the District of Columbia allow their courts to be used to collect the unpaid taxes of other states. In each case, the right to use the courts of the particular state depends upon reciprocity—that is, the taxing state must extend like courtesy in its courts. It is not necessary to obtain a judgment in the taxing state before filing suit in any of these jurisdictions.

Alabama
Alaska
Arizona
Arkansas
California
Colorado
Connecticut
Delaware
District of Columbia
Florida
Georgia
Hawaii
Idaho
Illinois
Indiana
Iowa
Kansas
Kentucky
Louisiana
Maine
Maryland
Massachusetts
Michigan
Minnesota
Mississippi
Missouri
Nebraska
New Hampshire
New Jersey (income and sales-use taxes only)
New York
North Carolina
North Dakota
Ohio
Oklahoma
Oregon
Pennsylvania
Rhode Island
South Carolina
South Dakota
Tennessee
Texas (sales-use only)
Vermont
Virginia
Washington
West Virginia
Wisconsin

Note: In two states (N.J., and Tex.), the right to sue is limited to specific taxes. Twenty-five states—Ariz., Ark., Calif., Colo., Conn., Ida., Ill., Ind., Iowa, Kan., Ky., La., Mass., Mich., Mo., Neb., N.H., N.J., N.Y., Pa., R.I., Tenn., Vt., Va., and W.Va.—definitely extend the collection privilege to political subdivisions.

Court action: The courts of Nevada and Wyoming have allowed the collection of other state's taxes, although these states do not have reciprocal enforcement statutes.

Federal laws. Under the Full Faith and Credit Clause (U.S. Const., Art. 4, §1) and federal legislation (28 U.S.C. §1738), the courts of every state must give another state's public acts the same full faith and credit that those acts would receive in the courts of their state of origin. However, the courts of one state will not enforce the penal laws of another state, based on comity (*Nelson, Wyo. Sup. Ct. (1967) 429 P2d 324*). Also, the Full Faith and Credit Clause does not compel a state to substitute the statutes of other states for its own statutes dealing with a subject matter about which it is competent to legislate, such as an intentional tort (*Franchise Tax Board of California v. Hyatt (2003) 538 US 488, 123 S Ct 1683, 155 L Ed 2d 702*).

➳ **SUIT IN FEDERAL COURT→** A state cannot prosecute nonfederal claims in the *lower* federal courts. Under the present "diversity of citizenship" provision on federal district court jurisdiction (28 U.S.C. §1332), a state is not a "citizen" of a state (see *Petroleum Exploration, Inc., (1938) 304 US 200, at 217*, and cases cited in footnote 9). However, a state can sue a citizen of another state by filing suit directly in the United States Supreme Court (U.S. Const., Art. 3, §2; 28 U.S.C. §1251(b)(3); Supreme Court Rule 17).

GASOLINE TAX RATES

¶285 Where you can deduct and how much. Motor vehicle gasoline taxes are an important deduction in calculating state and federal income taxes. The total state and federal gasoline tax generally is deductible if you use the vehicle in a business, but not if you use the vehicle for pleasure. The federal income tax deduction is limited to gasoline used in business; the federal rule is adopted in most states (¶ 221). For diesel fuel rates, see footnote (6).

To help figure the deduction, here is a list of per-gallon gasoline taxes:

ALA.	16¢ (4,6,15)
ALASKA	8¢
ARIZ.	18¢
ARK.	21.5¢ (6,15)
CALIF.	18¢ (4)
COLO.	22¢ (6)
CONN.	25¢ (6)
DEL.	23¢ (6)
D.C.	20¢
FLA.	15.3¢ (1,4,6,12)
GA.	7.5¢ (12)
HAWAII(6)	
HAWAII Cty.	25.8¢
HONOLULU Cty.	33.5¢
KAUAI Cty.	30¢
MAUI Cty.	33¢
IDA.	25¢
ILL.	19¢ (1,4,6,16)
IND.	18¢ (6)
IOWA	20.7¢ (6)
KAN.	24¢ (5,6)
KY.	19.6¢ (1,7,14,15)
LA.	20¢ (11,15)
ME.	27.6¢ (6)
MD.	23.5¢ (6)
MASS.	21¢
MICH.	19¢ (3,6,15)
MINN.	20¢
MISS.	18¢ (8,15)
MO.	17¢ (4)
MONT.	27¢ (4,6)
NEB.	27¢ (1)
NEV.	24¢ (4,6)
N.H.	18¢ (15)
N.J.	10.5¢ (6,17)
N.M.	17¢ (4,6)
N.Y.	8¢ (4,6,9,21)
N.Y.C.	1¢ (leaded fuel)
N.C.	29.7¢ (1,15)
N.D.	23¢
OHIO	28¢
OKLA.	16¢ (6,20)
ORE.	24¢ (4)
PA.	12¢ (19)
R.I.	30¢ (1,15)
S.C.	16¢
S.D.	22¢ (4)
TENN.	20¢ (4,6,15)
TEX.	20¢
UTAH	24.5¢
VT.	20¢ (6,18)
VA.	17.5¢ (6)
WASH.	36¢ (2,4)
W.VA.	31.5¢ (12)
WIS.	30.9¢
WYO.	14¢ (10)

FOOTNOTES to chart ¶ 285 (corresponding to parenthetical numbers in chart):

(1) Rate set periodically by tax officials; indexed in Fla.; Ill.; 9% of wholesale price in Ky.; Neb.; includes 7% of wholesale price in N.C., add 0.25¢ inspection fee; 13% of wholesale price in R.I., 26¢ min.

(2) 36¢ eff 7-1-2007—6-30-2008; 37.5¢ eff 7-1-2008 (Wash.)

(3) Motor carrier road tax—15¢ (Mich.).

(4) Local taxes may be imposed.

(5) 24¢ eff thru 6-30-2020; 18¢ eff 7-1-2020 (Kan.)

(6) Diesel fuel rates are same as gasoline rates unless otherwise shown: Ala., 19¢; Ark., 22.5¢; Colo., 20.5¢; Conn., 37¢ (eff. 7-1-2008, diesel rate set annually); Del., 22¢; Fla., 28.5¢; Haw., combined state-county rate—current rates are same as gasoline rate; Ill., 21.5¢ (36.7¢ in 2007 for commercial MVs on in-state highways); Ind., 16¢; Iowa, 22.5¢; Kan., 26¢ (20¢ eff 7-1-2020); Me., 28.8¢; Md., 24.25¢; Mich., 15¢; Mont., 27.75¢; Nev., 27¢; N.J., 13.5¢; N.M., 18¢; N.Y., 8¢; Okla., 13¢; Tenn., 17¢; Vt. distributors: 26¢ (25¢ eff 4-1-2011); Vt. users: 26¢ (25¢ eff 4-1-2011) for MV at least 26,000 lbs. and no tax for MV under 26,000 lbs.; Va., 17.5¢. Add fees or taxes shown at footnote (15).

(7) Special fuels, 16.6¢ (Ky.).

(8) 14.4¢ eff when funding requirements are met (Miss.).

(9) Motor carriers (rates determined quarterly)—composite rate (fuel tax plus sales tax): motor fuel, 22¢; diesel fuel, 22¢. Aggregate rate (fuel tax plus sales tax plus petroleum business tax): motor fuel, 38.6¢ (1-1-2007 thru 9-30-2007); diesel fuel, 36.85¢ (1-1-2007 thru 9-30-2007) (N.Y.).

(10) 13¢ when specified funding requirements are met (Wyo.).

(11) 16¢ when specified state bonds are paid in full (La.).

(12) Includes sales tax at 6% of avg. retail price as set by Dept. Rev., but not lower than 6.9¢ tax per gal. (Fla.). Plus total 4% tax (1% sales tax plus 3% gasoline tax) on retail sales price (Ga.). Includes sales tax at 5% of min. avg. wholesale price as set by Dept. Tax and Rev., currently 11¢ (6.5¢ pre-1-1-2007) tax per gal. (W.Va.).

FOOTNOTES to chart ¶ 285 (corresponding to parenthetical numbers in chart):
(continued)

(13) (Reserved.)
(14) Minimum rate is 15¢ but rate is set quarterly based on 9% of the average wholesale price of motor fuel, plus the supplemental highway motor fuel tax.
(15) Add these environmental fees per gallon: Ark., 0.3¢; Ky., 1.4¢; La., 4/32 of 1¢; Mich. 7/8 of 1¢; Miss., 0.4¢; N.H., 1.5¢; R.I., 1¢; Tenn., 0.4¢. In Ala., add 2¢-per-gal. petroleum products inspection fee on gasoline. In Tenn., add 1¢-per-gal. petroleum products tax. In N.C., add 0.25¢ inspection fee.
(16) 32.9¢ for commercial motor vehicles on in-state highways in 2007 (Ill.).
(17) Add 4¢-per-gal. petroleum products gross receipts tax (N.J.).
(18) Includes 1¢ petroleum cleanup fee which expires 3-31-2011. (Vt.).
(19) Added oil co. franchise tax of 19.2¢ per gal. of liquid fuel; 26.1¢ per gal. of fuel used or sold and delivered by distributors in Pa. (Pa.).
(20) Gasoline and diesel fuel are also subject to a 1¢ per gallon assessment fee in addition to the tax (Okla.).
(21) Additional petroleum test fee of 0.5 mill per gallon is imposed on motor fuel imported, manufactured, or sold in NY by a distributor.

CIGARETTE TAXES—RATES, INCIDENCE, PAYMENT, REPORTS

¶286 Rates, incidence, payment, reporting. The main features of the state taxes on cigarettes are given in the chart below.

RATE PER PACK OF 20	INCIDENCE	PAYMENT METHOD	MONTHLY REPORT REQUIREMENTS (Who, when, and to whom)
ALA. 42.5¢ (5)	Consumer	Stamps	Wholesaler jobber, 20th, Dept. Rev.
ALASKA $2.00 (5)	Seller	Stamps	Licensee, last day, Tax Commr.
ARIZ. $2.00	Seller	Stamps	Distributor, 20th, Dept. Rev.
ARK. 59¢	Seller	Stamps(1)	Distributor, 15th, Dept. Fin. & Adm.
CALIF. 87¢	Consumer	Stamps(2)	Distributor, 25th, State Eq. Bd.
COLO. 84¢	Seller	Stamps	Wholesaler, 10th Dept. Rev.
CONN. $2.00	Consumer	Stamps	Distributor(4), 25th, Commr. Rev. Serv.
DEL. $1.15	Consumer	Stamps	Wholesaler, agent, 20th, Dir. Rev.
D.C. $1.00	Seller	Stamps	Wholesaler, manufacturers, 25th, Office Tax & Rev.
FLA. 33.9¢	Seller	Stamps	Agent, 10th, Tax Dept.
GA. 37¢	Distributor	Stamps	Distributor, 10th, Commr. Rev.
HAW. $1.80 (20)	Seller	Stamps	Wholesaler, retailer, last day, Dept. Tax.
IDA. 57¢	Seller	Stamps	Wholesaler, 20th, Tax Comm.
ILL. 98¢ (5,14)	Seller	Stamps	Distributor(7), 15th, Dept. Rev.
IND. 99.5¢	Consumer	Stamps	Distributor, 15th(8), ABC
IOWA $1.36	Seller	Stamps	Permittees, 10th, Dept. Rev. & Fin.
KAN. 79¢	Seller	Stamps	Wholesaler, 10th, Dir. Tax.
KY. 30¢ (6)	Consumer	Stamps	Wholesaler, 20th, Cabinet Rev.
LA. 36¢ (15)	Seller	Stamps	Dealer, 20th, Sec'y Rev.
ME. $2.00	Consumer	Stamps	Monthly reports not required.
MD. $1.00	Seller	Stamps	Wholesaler, 21st, Comptr.
MASS. $1.51	Consumer	Stamps	Licensee, 20th, Commr. Rev.
MICH. $2.00	Seller	Stamps	Licensee, 20th, Dept. Treas.
MINN. $1.23 (16)	Seller	Stamps	Distributor, 18th, Dept. Rev.
MISS. 18¢	Consumer	Stamps	Wholesaler, 15th, Tax Comm.
MO. 17¢ (5)	Consumer	Stamps	Wholesalers, 20th, Dept. Rev.
MONT. $1.70	Consumer	Stamps	Interstate Carriers, (no fixed dates), Dept. Rev.
NEB. 64¢	Consumer	Stamps	Retailer, wholesaler, 10th, Tax Comm.
NEV. 80¢	Seller	Stamps	Wholesaler, 25th(13), Div. Tax.
N.H. $1.08	Consumer	Stamps	Monthly reports not required.
N.J. $2.575	Consumer	Stamps	Distributor, 20th, Dir. Tax.
N.M. 91¢	Seller	Stamps	Distributor, 25th. Tax. & Rev. Dept.
N.Y. $1.50 (12)	Consumer	Stamps	Agent, 15th, Dept. Tax. & Fin.
N.Y.C. $1.50 (12)	Consumer	Stamps	Agent, 15th, Comm. Fin.
N.C. 35¢	Consumer	Stamps	Distributor, 20th, Sec'y Rev.
N.D. 44¢	Seller	Stamps	Distributor, 15th, Tax Comm.
OHIO $1.25 (5)	Consumer	Stamps	Dealer, 1-31 & 7-31, State Treas.
OKLA. $1.03	Consumer	Stamps	Wholesaler, retailer, 10th, Tax Comm.
ORE. $1.18	Consumer	Stamps	Distributor, 20th (reports; payment, quarterly), Dept. Rev.
PA. $1.35	Consumer	Stamps	Stamping agent-monthly reports.
R.I. $2.46	Consumer	Stamps	Dealer, distributor, 10th, Tax Admr.
S.C. 7¢	Seller	Stamps	Distributor, 20th, Dept. Rev.
S.D. $1.53	Consumer	Stamps	Distributor, wholesaler, 15th, Dept. Rev.
TENN. 60¢	Consumer	Stamps	Distributor, 15th, Dept. Rev.
TEX. $1.41¢	Consumer	Stamps	Distributor, last day, Comptr. Pub. Accts.

RATE PER PACK OF 20	INCIDENCE	PAYMENT METHOD	MONTHLY REPORT REQUIREMENTS (Who, when, and to whom)
UTAH 69.5¢ (19)	Seller	Stamps	Monthly reports not required.
VT. $1.79 (17)	Seller	Stamps	Distributor, wholesaler, 15th. Comm. Taxes
VA. 30¢ (5)	Seller	Stamps	Wholesaler, storer, 10th, Dept. Tax.
WASH. $2.025	Consumer	Stamps	Wholesaler, retailer, 15th, Dept. Rev.
W.VA. 55¢	Consumer	Stamps	Wholesaler, 15th, Tax Dept.
WIS. 1.77¢ (77¢ pre-1-1-2008)(10)	Consumer	Stamps	Mfg. wholesalers, 15th, Dept. Rev.
WYO. 60¢	Seller	Stamps	Wholesaler, 20th, Dept. Rev.

FOOTNOTES to chart ¶286 (corresponding to numbers in parentheses in the chart):

(1) Payment with report for stamps purchased on consignment.
(2) Payment with report for tax not paid by stamp or meter.
(3) City taxes are also in effect in some cities.
(4) Machine dealer and operator with over 5 machines, report on 15th.
(5) Additional city and/or county taxes may be levied.
(6) Added 0.1¢ enforcement and administration fee is imposed per pack of 20 cigarettes (Ky.).
(7) Manufacturer reports on 5th.
(8) Report drop shipment on 15th.
(9) Wholesaler and manufacturers also report.
(10) Wis.—$3.54 per pack of 20 for cigarettes weighing more than 3 lbs. per 1,000 ($1.54 pre-1-1-2008).
(11) (Reserved.)
(12) Rate shown for package of 20 cigarettes. Added 37.5¢ per added 5 cigarettes in pack over 20 cigarettes. NYC cigarette rate (in addition to state rate)—$1.50 per pack of 20.
(13) Metered stamping machine report by 10th.
(14) Cook County has added $2 tax per pack. Chicago has added 68¢ tax per pack.
(15) La.—36¢ eff through 6-30-2012; 32¢ eff. 7-1-2012.
(16) Minn.—Combined rate composed of cigarette tax of 48¢ per pack of 20 plus health impact fee of 75¢ per pack of 20. Additional fee of 35¢ per pack of 20 imposed on cigarettes produced by manufacturers who have not entered a settlement agreement with state.
(17) Vt.—$1.79 through 6-30-2008; $1.99 eff 7-1-2008.
(18) (Reserved.)
(19) Utah—81.5¢ for cigarettes weighing over 3 lbs. per 1,000 cigarettes
(20) Haw.—$1.80 eff. 9-30-2007—9-29-2008; $2.00 eff 9-30-2008—9-29-2009; $2.20 eff. 9-30-2009—9-29-2010; $2.40 eff 9-30-2010—9-29-2011; $2.60 eff. 9-30-2011.

MANUFACTURING—WHAT IS AND WHAT IS NOT

¶290 Classifying businesses as manufacturing or non-manufacturing. For tax purposes, determining whether a particular business activity is manufacturing or non-manufacturing is usually determined by the courts. The manufacturing classification is important in identifying activities entitled to exemption or special treatment in figuring capital values, sales and use, property and corporate excise taxes. The first list below enumerates those activities that are considered to be manufacturing, and the second list identifies activities not considered manufacturing. Items marked with an asterisk (*) have been held to be manufacturing in some states and not manufacturing in other states, or the product involved has been the subject of divergent views based on its use or method of creation.

Manufacturing: The activities listed below have been held to be manufacturing (where product is listed, the making of it is the manufacturing activity).

Acetate of lime
Asphalt floors, roads
Awning, aluminum
Barrels, wood
Bed springs
Boilers
Books and periodicals, printing, binding
Bread and pastry
Brewing malt liquors
Brick manufacturer
Bridges
Building materials
Cabinet making
Cable
Canning*
Castings
Cement
Charcoal
Cloth finishing and dyeing
Coffee brewing, by vending machine
Coke
Concrete mixing
Condiments
Converting or conditioning tangible personalty
Creosoting
Curing and smoking bacon and ham
Dairy products
Doorsteps, slate for
Drain tiles
Drugs
Dyeing and finishing of cotton and woolens
Dyes
Electric fixtures
Electrical machinery
Engines
Feed meal
Fertilizers
Fire brick
Fish cleaning, dressing, brining
Flavoring extract
Furnaces and gas producers, erecting in place
Furniture
Gas, artificial
Gas fixtures
Gas-producers and furnaces
Gasoline products
Generic fungible food products
Glue
Glycerin
Gummed tape
Hide*
Ice, making for sale*
Illuminating oils
Iron
Iron scrap recovery from slag
Jam and jelly canning
Job printing
Lamps
Lard
Leather
Lighting gas
Liverwurst
Lubricating oils
Lumber
Luncheon meats
Machinery, electrical
Machinery need for future production
Margarine
Metal fashioning
Millwork
Monuments, stone
Mulch production
Newspaper publishing*
Oil cloth
Oil refining
Oils
Oleo
Paper cutting, shearing, binding, ruling
Paving mats
Pasteurization*
Peanut butter
Periodicals, printing and binding
Petroleum, crude, refining
Phonographs

Photographs, printing and mounting
Pig iron
Potato chips
Preserving fruit
Publishing
Puddings
Railway cars
Road construction
Roofing, slate
Sandpaper
Sausages
Saw mill making finished product
Sawdust, processing
Scrap iron processing*
Seed separating, grading, cleaning, packing by machine
Sewer pine
Shingles
Shipbuilding
Shoemaking
Slate
Snowmaking
Soap
Soft drinks, mixing*
Steel
Stone processing
Stoves
Tailoring
Tar
Telephone equipment used to create, distribute telephone services*
Tickerscopes
Tiles
Tire recapping and retreading
Tobacco, preparing*
Turntables
Viaducts
Watches, assembling
Wood alcohol

Not manufacturing: The activities listed below have been held to be *not* manufacturing (where product is listed, the making of it is the activity considered).

Artesian wells, drilling
Auto glass processing
Books, printing and binding
Building construction
Canning*
Cleaning solvent making by cleaning company
Cloth processing
Clothing, making
Coal business
Coffee roasting
Cold storage
Compost for mushrooms
Contracting
Construction of houses
Cotton cellulose, treating chemically
Cut stone contracting
Cutting and threading rods
Data transport services
Decaffeinated coffee
Dry dock operation
Electricity, generation of
Embroidering clothing (ready-made)
Engineering
Fabric finishing
Furnace recuperators
Furniture polish making by hotel
Grease
Hair, cleaning and sorting
Hair grading and baling
Heating system installation
Hides*
Homogenization
Honey
Houses, building
Ice, collecting and storing*
Ice, produced for warehouse*
Instant coffee
Laboratory manufacturing
Laundering
Leather cutting
Limestone crushing
Meat packing
Meat processing
Mining*
Molasses processing
Newspaper publishing*
Pasteurization*
Pencils processing, incidental change
Photographic business
Plumbing system installation
Prototypes
Railroad beds
Reinforcing steel products
Scrap metal processing*
Shirts, processing partially
Skin processing
Slaughtering livestock
Soap making by laundry
Soft drink*
Sprinkler installation
Steam power
Stone crushing
Tallow
Tapioca
Test equipment for own use
Tobacco curing*
Warehouse, cold storage
Water distillation and purification*
Well drilling

ESCHEATABLE PROPERTY—UNCLAIMED, ABANDONED

¶291 Threshold period and reporting. The following chart lists states that require holders of property unclaimed or abandoned by others to report and/or to turn the property over to the states.

STATE	PERIOD-PROPERTY COVERED(17)	REPORT-PAY	TO WHOM
***Ala.**	3 yrs. unclaimed (60)	10-31(33)	State Treas.
***Alaska**	3 yrs. unclaimed (13,22)	11-1	Dept. Rev.
***Ariz.**	5 yrs. abandoned (36,68)	10-31(1)	Dept. Rev.
***Ark.**	5 yrs. abandoned (70)	11-1	State Auditor
*** Calif.**	3 yrs. abandoned (36)	10-31(1)	State Comptr.
*** Colo.**	5 yrs. unclaimed (55)		State Treas.
*** Conn.**	3 yrs. abandoned (38)	4-1(3)	State Treas.
Del.	5 yrs. abandoned (7,43)	3-1(4)	Secretary of Finance acting as State Escheator
***D.C.**	3 yrs. unclaimed (5,14)	10-31(1)	Office of Finance & Treasury, Unclaimed Property Unit
***Fla.**	5 yrs. unclaimed (5,32)	5-1	Banking & Fin. Dept.
***Ga.**	5 yrs. abandoned (13)	11-1(1)	Commr. Rev.
***Haw.**	5 yrs. abandoned (5)	10-31(1)	Dir. Fin.
***Ida.**	5 yrs. abandoned (13,48)	11-1	State Tax Comm.
***Ill.**	5 yrs. unclaimed (44,53)	10-31(1)	State Treas.
***Ind.**	5 yrs. unclaimed (16,21,24)	11-1(1,58)	Atty. Gen.
***Iowa**	3 yrs. unclaimed (16,41)	10-31(1)	State Treas.
***Kan.**	5 yrs. unclaimed (13,16,37)	10-31(1)	State Treas.
***Ky.**	3 yrs. abandoned (38,43)	11-1	State Treas.
***La.**	5 yrs. abandoned (45,75)	10-31	State Treas.
***Me.**	3 yrs. abandoned (11,13,63)	10-31(1)	State Treas.
***Md.**	3 yrs. abandoned (38,43)	10-31(1)	State Comptr.
***Mass.**	3 yrs. abandoned	11-1(1,8)	State Treas.
Mich.	5 yrs. abandoned (5,27)	11-1	Dept. Treas.
***Minn.**	3 yrs. abandoned (5,38)	10-31	Dept. Commerce.
***Miss.**	5 yrs. abandoned (16)	10-31	State Treas.
***Mo.**	5 yrs. abandoned (44)	11-1(7)	State Treas.
***Mont.**	5 yrs. abandoned (43)	(6)	Dept. Rev.
Neb.	5 yrs. abandoned (59)	10-31(1)	State Treas.
***Nev.**	3 yrs. abandoned (1,7,16,64)	10-31(7)	State Treas.
***N.H.**	5 yrs. abandoned (13,69,74)	10-31(1)	State Treas.
***N.J.**	3 yrs. abandoned (19)	11-1(1)	State Treas.
***N.M.**	5 yrs. abandoned (16,71)	10-31(1)	Dir. Rev. & Tax.
N.Y.	5 yrs. abandoned (18,16,35)	3-10(12)	State Comptr.
N.C.	5 yrs. abandoned (7,16,39)	10-31(1)	State Treas. or Commr. Ins.
***N.D.**	3 yrs. abandoned (16,45,52)	11-1(7)	Admr. State Abandoned Property
Ohio	3 yrs. unclaimed (2)	10-31(67)	Dir. Commerce
***Okla.**	5 yrs. abandoned (57)	10-31(1)	State Tax Comm.
***Ore.**	5 yrs. abandoned (43,72)	10-31(1)	State Land Div.
***Pa.**	5 yrs. abandoned (65)	4-15	State Treas.
***R.I.**	3 yrs. abandoned (13,29,49)	10-31	Treas. Dept.
***S.C.**	5 yrs. abandoned (66)	11-1	Dept. Rev.
***S.D.**	5 yrs. abandoned (13,40,43)	10-31(1)	State Treas.
***Tenn.**	5 yrs. abandoned (7,43,73)	5-1	State Treas.
Tex.	3 yrs. abandoned (54)	11-1	State Treas.
***Utah**	5 yrs. abandoned (13,47)	4-30	State Treas.
***Vt.**	5 yrs. abandoned (43,62)	4-30	State Treas.
***Va.**	5 yrs. abandoned (5)	10-31(1,33)	State Treas.
***Wash.**	3 yrs. abandoned (37)	10-31(1)	Dept. Rev.
***W.Va.**	5 yrs. abandoned (26)	11-1(1)	State Treas.
***Wis.**	5 yrs. abandoned (13)	11-1	State Treas.
***Wyo.**	5 yrs. abandoned (5,50,51,61)	11-1	State Treas.

FOOTNOTES to chart ¶ 291 (corresponding to parenthetical numbers in chart):

* State substantially adopts Uniform Disposition of Unclaimed Property Act.

(1) Life insurance companies before 5-1. Also in D.C., reports of unclaimed insurance co. demutualization proceeds. In Ill., business associations, utilities, and life insurance corporations. In Me., before 5-1 for amounts owed under life insurance policies, gift obligations and store-valued cards.

(2) Certificates or nonwithdrawable shares of financial organizations 5 yrs; life insurance unclaimed after becoming payable 3 years; instrument representing ownership interest 5 yrs; certified checks or other certified instruments of funds held; 5 yrs. (15 yrs. if payable on demand) Certain capital credits of coops; traveler's checks; 15 yrs. Insolvency distributions, 1 yr. Certain money orders, 5 yrs. Certain business-to-business exceptions.

(3) In 90 days after close of calendar year in which property presumed abandoned.

(4) Banks, 8-1; insurance companies, 5-1; others 3-1.

(5) Wages, 1 year; traveler's checks, 15 yrs.; money orders, 7 yrs.

(6) Insurance companies, banking and financial orgs., and cooperatives, 4-30; others 10-31 every year.

(7) Life insurance unclaimed 7 yrs. (5 yrs. in Tenn, 3 yrs. in Nev., N.C., N.D.); 5-1.

(8) Pay by 6-1.

(9) (Reserved.)

(10) Insurance companies. 6-1.

(11) Life insurance unclaimed, 3 yrs. Money orders, 7 yrs. Refunds held by business assns., 1 yr.; dissolution, 1 yr.

(12) Banks, 8-1; insurance companies, 4-1; utilities, 8-1.

(13) Wages, 1 yr. Traveler's checks, 15 yrs. In Alaska, Ida. and Va., money orders, 7 yrs. In Ida. and S.D., deposits held by utilities, 1 yr.

(14) Intangibles distributable in dissolution of D.C. business assn., banking or financial org., 60 days; intangible held by public corp., authority, or officer of D.C., 1 yr.; gift certificates and credit memos, 5 yrs.; property distributable during ins. co. demutualization, rehabilitation, or reorganization, 2 yrs.; utility deposit or refund, 1 yr.

(15) (Reserved.)

(16) Traveler's checks, 15 yrs; money orders, 7 yrs.

(17) Property is presumed abandoned as of 6-30 preceding filing report in most states. However, property is presumed abandoned as of date prescribed for payment or delivery in Conn., Ga. and Hawaii (stocks and dividends); Ky. and Mass. (preceding 7-1); Minn., life insurance preceding 12-31; Del.; N.Y.; (preceding 12-31); Pa., Wis. (as of 2 preceding yrs.)

(18) Wages, 3 yrs.

(19) Banking or financial organizations, 10 yrs. Traveler's checks, 15 yrs; Money orders, 7 yrs. Deposits held by utility, intangibles held by govt. or distributable in dissolution, 1 yr.

(20) Money orders, 7 yrs.; Minn. utilities, 1 yr.; dividends, 7 yrs.

(21) Banking and financial orgs., business assns., utilities and life insurance cos. not holding abandoned property during reporting yr. must file reports only if requested by Atty. Gen.

(22) Property on consignment or bailment sold after one year; proceeds paid to State Treas. six months after sale.

(23) (Reserved.)

(24) Stock, 3 yrs. after earlier of date the last dividend, stock split or other distribution is unclaimed, or the date of a second mailing of a statement of account was returned as undeliverable.

(25) Pay to State Treas.

(26) Money orders, interest-bearing demand, savings on time deposit, 7 yrs.; traveler's checks, 15 yrs.; tax-deferred compensation accounts, gift certificates, unclaimed life insurance or annuity, 3 yrs.; wages, amounts distributable in dissolution, or by court or government, 1 yr.

(27) Dissolutions/liquidations, 1 yr.; state court and agency refunds, 1 yr.; utility deposits, 1 yr.; stocks or other intangible ownership interests in a business association, 3 yrs.; dividends or other distributions, 7 yrs.; property distributable in course of demutualization of an insurance company, 2 yrs.

(28) Business organizations. Checks, 10 yrs.; financial institutions, traveler's checks and others, 21 yrs.

(29) Family education accounts, 20 yrs.; traveler's checks, 15 yrs.

(30) 3 yrs. For all intangible personal property unless a different time period is shown.

(31) Banking and financial orgs., 5-1 every fifth year. Insurance cos., 5-1 every year.

(32) Property in safe deposit box, 3 yrs.; utility deposit, 1 yr.; equity or debt in business association, 3 yrs.; intangible personalty issued by gov't. or agency or held by court or gov't., 1 yr.; intangible property in dissolution of business association, 6 mos. after date for final distribution; unclaimed amount court-ordered returned by business association, 1 yr.; property distributed in insurance company reorganization, 2 yrs.

(33) Pay in 20 days after filing report. Ala., pay on or before 11-1.

(34) Traveler's checks, 15 yrs.; bank deposits, safe deposit boxes, 5 yrs; property held by public officer/agency, intangibles distributable in voluntary dissolution of business assn. or banking and financial org. 60 days.

(35) Abandonment is 5 years for bank deposits and interest on liquidated mortgages, securities held by foreign corp. not authorized to do business in-state, condemnation awards; yearly for surplus from sale of pledged property (except banks); 5 years for miscellaneous property.

FOOTNOTES to chart ¶ 291 (corresponding to parenthetical numbers in chart):
(continued)

(36) Traveler's checks, 15 yrs.; money orders, 7 yrs.; wages or salaries, 1 yr. Includes all tangible and intangible personal property, including any income after becoming payable or distributable and, in Calif., gift certificate (if with expiration date and given in exchange for money or other thing of value) and insurance co. demutualization distributions.

(37) Govts., utilities, and wages, 1 yr. Property in museums and historical societies, 5 yrs.

(38) Periods vary depending on type of property. Period shown is applicable to many types of property.

(39) Time deposit, 10 yrs.; money or credits owed to a customer due to retail transaction, 3 yrs.; gift certificate or electronic gift card with expiration date, 3 yrs.; property distributable by a business in course of dissolution, 1 yr.; property received by court as proceeds of a class action and not distributed, 1 yr.; property held by a court, 1 yr.; wages, 2 yrs.; utility deposit, 1 yr.; property in an IRA, 3 yrs; debt of a business association, 3 yrs.; stock or other equity interest in a business association, 3 yrs.

(40) Utilities, court-ordered or agency-ordered refund by business assn., intangibles distributable in course of dissolution of business assn., intangibles held for the owner by a court, govt., governmental subdivision or agency or entity, public corporation, public authority or public officer of S.D., 1 yr.; life insurance, endowment or annuity contract, refunds from utility, 4 yrs.

(41) Utility deposit or refund, 1 yr.; business distribution, 1yr.; amount held by court or government agency, 2 yrs.; insurance company demutualization or related reorgnaization, 2yrs.

(42) Traveler's checks, 14 yrs.

(43) Traveler's checks, 15 yrs.

(44) Intangibles in dissolutions, 2 yrs; traveler's checks, 15 yrs.; insurance company demutualization, rehabilitation or related reorganization, 2 yrs. (5 yrs. for mutual insurance company not subject to Mo. Rev. Stat. section 447.510(3)(1)).

(45) Traveler's checks, 15 yrs.; money orders, 7 yrs.; retail customer's money or credits, 3 yrs.; gift certificate, 3 yrs.; insurance amounts, 3 yrs.; (in La., 2 yrs. for property distributable in demutualization, rehabilitation, or related reorganization of insurance company); business dissolution assets, 1 yr.; amount held by court or government agency, 1 yr.; wages or other compensation for personal services, 1 yr. (2 yrs. in N.D.); utility deposit or refund, 1 yr.; IRA or other federal tax-deferred account that became distributable, 3 yrs.; mineral proceeds, 2 yrs (3 yrs. in N.D.).

(46) Retirement and insurance amounts, 5 years; traveler's checks, 15 years; wages, 1 year. (Mich)

(47) Utility deposits, 1 yr.; court or administratively ordered refund, 1 yr.; intangibles distributable in dissolution of business association, 1 yr.; gift certificates or credit memos, mineral proceeds or tangible or intangible property in safe deposit boxes, 5 yrs.

(48) Intangible personal property distributable in course of dissolution of a business association which is unclaimed must be remitted on the date of final distribution.

(49) Bank deposits. 3 yrs.; refund held by, business assns., 6 mos.; property held by police, 6 mos; utility deposits, 1 yr.; property held by courts, 1 yr.; property distributable in course of demutualization of an insurance company, 2 yrs.

(50) Gift certificate or credit memo for over $100, 3 yrs.

(51) Mineral proceeds, 3 yrs.

(52) Utility, 1 yr.; holding in dissolution of business association, 1 yr.; court-ordered refund from business association, 2 yrs.; bank or financial org., 5 yrs.; other uncashed checks for which bank or financial org. isn't directly liable, 2 yrs.

(53) Capital credits or patronage capital retired, returned, refunded, or tendered to member of electric, telephone, or telecommunications co-op, 2 yrs.; intangibles held by court or public entity/officer or political subdivision. 7 yrs.; tangible or intangible personalty held or debts owed by Fed. state, or local government or government subdivision, agency, or officer when owner's last know address in Ill., 7 yrs.; intangibles held by business association, securities depository, government, or other person if no last known address for owner and person originating or issuing intangibles is in Ill., is a political subdivision of the state, or is incorporated, organized, created, or otherwise located in-state. 7 yrs.; intangibles not otherwise covered, 5 yrs.; certain insurance company property, 2 yrs.

(54) Certain securities-related property is 5-yr. property. Wages, 1 yr. if existence and location of owner is unknown to holder and claim has not been asserted. Advertising report must be filed each yr., by Nov. 1, if property is presumed abandoned. Stored value cards issued or activated on or after 9-1-2005: earlier of (a) the card's expiration date; (b) 3rd anniversary of date card issued if card not used after issued, or date card was last used or value added to card; or (c) 1st anniversary of date card was issued if card not used after issued, or date card was last used or value added to card if card's value represents wages.

(55) Travelers checks, 15 yrs.; utility deposits, 1 yr after termination of utility services; business association, 1 yr. after issuance of refund order; holders in dissolution, 1 yr. after distribution date; property held by fiduciaries, 3 yrs.; wages, intangibles held by court, govt. agency, public corp. or authority, 1 yr.; checks, 5 yrs.; money orders 7 yrs.; gift certificates and credit memos, 5 yrs.

(56) Personal property, 2 yrs. after notice published.

FOOTNOTES to chart ¶ 291 (corresponding to parenthetical numbers in chart):
(continued)

(57) Travelers checks, 15 yrs.; checks, 5 yrs.; money orders, 7 yrs.; property held by banks; 5 yrs.; deposits held by utilities, intangible property distributible in dissolution, 1 yr.; property held by courts or public agencies, 1 yr.; credit income, 5 yrs.; unpaid wages, 1 yr.; personal property in safe deposit, 5 yrs.; funds owed under life insurance policy, 5 yrs.; property distributed by insurance reorganization, 2 yrs.; refund held by business, 1 yr.; shares of stock/dividends unmatured or unredeemed debt or matured or redeemed debt, other than a bearer bond or an original discount bond., 3 yrs.

(58) Statute allows 120-day period for publication and additional 25-day period to remit to Attny. Gen.

(59) Retirement funds, 5 yrs.; unpaid wages, 1 yr.; property held in course of dissolution, 2 yrs.; gift certificates, credit memos, deposits and refunds held by utilities, property held by courts, mineral rights and public agencies, 3 yrs.; automatically renewable time deposits, certificates of indebtedness, 5 yrs.; money orders, 7 yrs.; traveler's checks, 15 yrs. In Wyo., sum payable or intangible distributable in dissolution, 6 mos. after final distribution or liquidation; intangibles payable or distributable from classification, litigation, or settlement before judicial admin. agency, 6 mos. after the time for final payment or distribution.

(60) Wages, 3 yrs.; property distributable by business or financial org., class action proceeds, utility deposits or refunds, state (Ala.) checks or warrants, property held by govt. entity or agency, 1 yr.; property distributable in ins. co. demutualization or reorganization, 2 yrs.; money orders, 5 yrs.; traveler's checks, 15 yrs.

(61) Stock and intangibles in business associations, 3 yrs.; utility deposits, 1 yr.; property held by court or public agency, 1 yr.; refund or payments from judicial or administrative proceedings, 6 months after becoming payable.

(62) Tangibles in dissolution, 2 yrs.; money orders, 7 yrs.; checks or other similar instruments, 3 yrs.; stocks, 3 yrs.; savings and other bank accts., 3 yrs.; retail store refunds, 3 yrs.; wages, 1 yr.; utility deposits, 3 yrs.; safe deposit box contents, 5 yrs.

(63) Property in a prearranged funeral or burial plan, 3 yrs. from death of person on whose behalf funds were paid into the plan; proceeds of class action, 1 yr.; utility deposit or refund, 1 yr.; property distributable in the course of a demutualization of an insurance co., 2 yrs.; gift obligations or stored-value cards, 2 yrs. after 12-31 of year in which the obligation occurred or the most recent transaction involving the obligation or card occurred, whichever later; a prefunded bank card, 3 yrs. after 12-31 of year in which the obligation occurred or the most recent activity involving the card occurred, whichever later.

(64) Wages, 1 yr.; bank deposits, 3yrs.; certified checks, 5 yrs.; money orders, 7 yrs.

(65) Gift certificates, 2 yrs. after redemption period (5 yrs. if no redemption period); holders in dissolution, 2 yrs. after distribution date; checks, 5 yrs.; travelers checks, 15 yrs. (Pa.)

(66) Travelers checks, 15 yrs.; stocks and money orders, 7 yrs.; wages, utility deposits, intangibles distributable as a result of a business dissolution, business assoc. refunds, 1 yr.; tax refund checks, 3 mos. (S.C.)

(67) Pay 10% of funds with report; balance must be placed in interest-bearing account to the credit of the Ohio Mortgage Insurance Fund or retained by holder at Director's option.

(68) Property in an IRA account, 3 yrs.; utility deposits, 2 yrs.

(69) Property formerly owned by consumers cooperative associations subject to 3-yr. rule unless another law applies.

(70) Traveler's checks, 15 yrs.; money orders, 7 yrs.; money or credits owed to a customer due to a retail business transaction, 3 yrs.; amounts owed by insurer on life or endowment insurance policy or annuity that has matured or terminated, 3 yrs.; property distributable by business assn. or financial organization in the course of dissolution, 1 yr.; property received by a court as proceeds of a class action, and not distributed under the judgment, 1 yr.; wages or other compensation for personal services, 1 yr.; deposits or refunds owed to utility subscriber, 1 yr.; property in an individual retirement account, defined benefit plan, or other account or plan that is qualified for tax deferral under fed income tax laws, 3 yrs (Ark.).

(71) Gift certificates, 3 yrs.; life insurance policies or annuities, 3 yrs.; property distributable by business assn. or financial institution in dissolution, 1 yr.; property received by a court as proceeds of a class action and not distributed 1 yr.; property held by a court or gov't agency or subdivision, 1 yr.; wages, 1 yr.; utility deposits or refunds, 1 yr.; property in an IRA, defined benefit plan, or similar tax deferred account or plan, 3 yrs. (N.M.).

(72) Money orders, 7 yrs.; utility deposits or refunds, 1 yr.; intangibles of business assns. and banks held in the course of dissolution, 1 yr.; property in safe deposit boxes, 2 yrs.; property held by fiduciaries, 2 yrs.; wages, 3 yrs.; property held by courts or gov't agencies, subdivisions, etc., 2 yrs.; credit memos, 3 yrs.; miscellaneous intangibles, 3 yrs. (Ore).

(73) Money orders, 7 yrs.; property in safe deposit boxes, 2 yrs.; surplus amounts from sale of safe deposit box contents sold for nonpayment, 1 yr.; unclaimed demutualization proceeds, 3 yrs.; undistributed assets and obligations of business assns. and utilities, 2 yrs.; property held by a court or political agency or subdivision, or fed gov't, 1 yr. (Tenn.).

(74) Gift certificates under $100 and store credits are not presumed abandoned. (N.H.)

(75) Stock, stock dividends, and other business interests or distributions, 3 yrs.; property distributable in insurance company reorganizations, 2 yrs.

REFUND TIME LIMITS (I)

¶295 When you must file. Chart below lists refund time limits (notes follow chart). Refund time limits for income taxes are charted at ¶ 231.

EXPLANATION OF CHARTS: Parenthetical numbers ( ) in charts are keyed to notes below each chart. Symbol "d" means days, "m" means months, "y" means years, "NT" means no tax or tax only on very limited group of taxpayers, and "NP" means no specific provision.

Listings in the charts relate to payments made in usual course and as to which there is a reasonable expectation of refund. Some tax laws provide alternate methods and time limits for claiming a refund. In such cases, usually the period after payment is charted and the alternative is noted.

If payment must be protested to claim a refund, this requirement is noted by the parenthetical number 7. Many states permit the claimant to bring a court action for a tax refund *but may require payment under protest first.* "Recovery by suit" (court remedy) is usually available as an alternative to filing claim with a designated state official. *In general, the court remedy uses a shorter time limit for bringing the action than is required in pursuing the administrative remedy.*

TAXES STATE	CAPITAL VALUES FRANCHISE	SALES—USE	REAL PROPERTY	TANGIBLE PERSONALTY	INTANGIBLES
ALA.	3y(97)	3y(97)	2y(1)	2y(1)	2y(1)
AK.	NT	NT(4)	1y(16)	1y(16)	NT
ARIZ.	NT	4y(13); 6m(93)	1y(1); 3y(63)	1y(1)	NT
ARK.	3y(77)	3y(77)	3y(1)	3y(1)	NT
CALIF.	NT	3y(10,74)	4y(1,80)	4y(1,(80)	NT
COLO.	NT	60d(14)	2y(82)	2y(82)	NT
CONN.	(see ¶ 231)	3y(10,74)	3y(16)	6y(1)	NT
DEL.	2y(30)	3(31)	NP(4,7)	NT	NT
D.C.	NT	3y(2,24)	3y(1)	3y(2,24)	NT
FLA.	NT	3y(18)	4y(78)	4y(78)	NT(99)
GA.	3y(1,73)	3y(1)	NP(4,32)	(4,32)	3y(1,33)
HAW.	NT	3y(90,91)	2y(34)	NT	NT
IDA.	NT	3y(48,58)	(35)	(35)	NT
ILL.	3y(1)	3y-3½y(1,19)	5y(66); 30d(5,7)	NT	NT
IND.	NT	3y(43,69)	3y(1)	3y(1)	NT
IOWA	NT	3y(75)	2y(16)	NT	2y(16)
KAN.	3y(6,92)	3y(1)	30d(7,36,68)	30d(7,36,68)	30d(7,36)
KY.	4y(1,62)	4y(1,62)	2y(1,62)	2y(1,62)	NT(56)
LA.	1y(1,19,23)	1y(1,19,23)	1y(1,19,23)	1y(1,19,23)	1y(1,19,23)
ME.	NT	3y(1)	3y(37)	3y(37)	NT
MD.	NT	4y(1)	3y(1)	3y(1)	NT
MASS.	2y	2y(98)	30d(38)	30d(38)	NT
MICH.	(71)	4y(2)	3y(1,51)	3y(1,51)	NT
MINN.	NT	3½y(2)	(4)	(4)	NT
MISS.	3y(1)	3y(5,13,26)	3y(1)	3y(1)	3y(1)
MO.	2y(1)	3y(1)	1y(1)	1y(1)	NT
MONT.	NT	5y(2)	10y(41)	10y(41)	NT
NEB.	NP	3y(10,29,88,89)	2y(1,85)	2y(1,85)	NT
NEV.	NT	37m(1,93)	3y(42)	3y(42)	NT
N.H.	NP(4)	NP(4)	NP(4)	NP(4)	NT
N.J.	(See ¶ 231)	4y(1)	4y(1)	4y	NT
N.M.	NT	3y(76)	60d(94)	60d(94)	NT
N.Y.	(See ¶ 231)	3y(77)	3y(70)	NT	NT
N.C.	3y(86)	3y(86)	5y(96)	5y(96)	NT
N.D.	NT	3y(2,59)	(27)	NT	NP(4)

TAXES STATE	CAPITAL VALUES FRANCHISE	SALES—USE	REAL PROPERTY	TANGIBLE PERSONALTY	INTANGIBLES
OHIO	(See ¶ 231)	4y(1)	1y(7,5)	1y(7,5)	NT
OKLA.	3y(79,80)	3y(79,80)	6m(45)	6m(45)	NT
ORE.	NT	NT	6y(26,5)	6y(26,5)	NT
PA.	3y(15)	3y(1,81)	3y(1)	NT	3y(1)
R.I.	2y(1)	3y(12)	3m(5,7)	3m(5,7)	2y(1)
S.C.	NP(4)	3y(28)	2y(1,87)	2y(1,87)	NT
S.D.	NT	3y(44)	4y(65)	NT	NT
TENN.	3y(53)	3y(53)	3y(53,57,80)	3y(53,57,80)	3y(53,80)
TEX.	4y(16)	4y(16)	3y(1)	3y(1)	3y(1)
UTAH	NT	3y(1)	(5,7)	(5,7)	NT
VT.	NT	3y(84)	(7,5)	(7,5)	NT
VA.	NT	3y(6)	3y(5)	3y(17)	NT
WASH.	NT	4y(1,80)	3y(18,60)	3y(18,60)	NT
W. VA.	3y(31)	3y(31)	3y(31)	3y(31)	NT
WIS.	NT	4y(2)	2y(1,20)	2y(1,20)	NT
WYO.	1y(1)	3y(1,80)	1y(5,61)	1y(5,61)	NT

NOTES to chart at ¶ 295.

(1) After payment.
(2) After return date.
(3) No refund provision.
(4) No specific provision. For general time limits, see ¶ 296.
(5) Recovery by suit.
(6) After due date or filing date.
(7) After protested payment.
(8) After claim accrues.
(9) After return or payment.
(10) After overpaid period.
(11) After overpaid year.
(12) From 15th day after close of month for which overpayment was made, or—for assmt.—6 mos. after payment if later.
(13) After filing return.
(14) After original purchase date.
(15) 3 yrs. after payment if refund for stock value or 6 mos. from notice of assmt., determination or settlement in case of audit.
(16) After tax due date.
(17) From 12-31 of year assessed.
(18) After payment made or due.
(19) Or by suit in 30 days after protested payment.
(20) Cty. Bd. (Milwaukee 3 yrs., Bd. of Review.)
(21) Or 60 days after assmt.
(22) After refund-right accrues.
(23) Or 3 yrs. from 12-31 of yr. tax was due.
(24) Or 3 yrs. after payment, if later.
(25) Recovery by suit in Travis Cty. only.
(26) After assmt.
(27) By 11-1 of year after year when tax becomes delinquent.
(28) After return is timely filed or 2 years of payment date, whichever is later.
(29) Or 6 mos. after final determination or overpayment on determination, if later.
(30) By 3-1 of the 2nd calendar yr. following the close of that calendar yr.
(31) After date return filed or 2 yrs. after payment, if later.
(32) No time limit for Cty. tax. No refund of state tax voluntarily paid.
(33) 30 days after protested payment on long-term realty notes.
(34) After tax year of payment.
(35) Before end of Cty. Comrs.' session.
(36) Apply to BTA within 30 days after notification of results of informal meeting with county appraiser.
(37) From filing or from payment, whichever expires later.
(38) After due date.
(39) Wis.—From due date of franchise or income tax return; 2 yrs. from determination of tax assessed by audit.
(40) Auditor of Public Accts. No fixed time limit if by Cty. Bd. Supvrs.
(41) After due date of 2nd-half taxes.
(42) After local claim arises.
(43) Gross retail tax.
(44) After payment or date return due, whichever earlier.

NOTES to chart at ¶ 295.
(continued)

(45) After final decision on protested payment.
(46) License tax based on gross receipts.
(47) Or 60d after Sec'y State's notice of tax determination.
(48) Refund for worthless accounts is claimed on return for month in which bad debt adjustment is made on taxpayer's books and records.
(49) Sec'y State (legislative action). Or sue after protested payment.
(50) After right to sue accrues.
(51) Sue if clerical or mutual mistake of fact—no protest needed.
(52) File in Santa Fe if valued by Dept., or local district court if locally valued.
(53) From 12-31 of payment year.
(54) File amended return with STC within 3 yrs. of filing date; and/or in 2 yrs. from 12-31 of assmt. year in court.
(55) From last day of tax year for which assmt. made if local levies—apply to court or city court of record. States taxes—in 2 yrs. from 12-31 of yr. assessed.
(56) Tax repealed eff. 1-1-2006. Previously, time limit was 2 yrs. and notes (1) and (62) applied.
(57) If filed with Cty. clerk, 1 yr. Comr. can give refund in 6y after payment if based on court decision.
(58) By 3 yrs. after payment, or by date proceeding is resolved or specified in agreement between taxpayer and Tax Commission, if later.
(59) Or 1 yr. after erroneous payment, if later.
(60) Or pay under protest and sue by 6-30 of year after tax was due.
(61) After illegal assmt., levy or collection.
(62) In cases where a statute is held unconstitutional, application for refund must be made within 2 yrs. from payment date.
(63) From property tax error that resulted in overpayment.
(64) 2 yrs. if payment is invalid; at any time if payment is in excess of proper amount.
(65) After delinquency date for those taxes (11-1).
(66) After payment for incorrect listing: after date right to refund arose for erroneous assessment or overpayment.
(67) See chart ¶ 231.
(68) Or 2 yrs. after clerical error.
(69) After calendar year of payment.
(70) 3 yrs. after final order based on timely assmt. review and involuntary payment.
(71) No capital values tax or franchise tax imposed through 12-31-2007. Eff. 1-1-2008, financial institutions franchise tax is imposed and refund claim time limit is four yrs. from the date set for filing the original return.
(72) To Dept. Tax. Alternative court action, 2 yrs. from 12-31 of year assessed.
(73) Refund suit in 2 yrs. of refund denial.
(74) For assmt., 6 mos. after finality.
(75) State govt. unit, 1 yr. after final settlement.
(76) After 12-31 of year payment due.
(77) 3 yrs. from filing a return or 2 yrs. from payment date, whichever later.
(78) Fla.—After Jan. 1 of tax year for which taxes paid.
(79) After payment if error of fact or computation.
(80) Alternative remedy by court action.
(81) For assmt., 6 mos. after assmt. notice mailed. (Pa.)
(82) 2 yrs. after Jan. 1 of yr. taxes were levied (Colo.).
(83) After overpaid mo. or quarter, or—for assmt.—6 mos. after finality or payment, whichever (of 3) is later.
(84) Sales and use tax and meals and rooms tax—after return date.
(85) Neb.—Treas. of taxing body. For clerical error, in 2 yrs. after payment (Cty. Treas.). For illegal tax, assmt. or penalty, 2 yrs. after final judgment.
(86) After return due date or 2 yrs. after payment date, whichever later (N.C.).
(87) S.C.—2 yrs. after payment for taxes assessed by Dept. Rev.; 2 yrs. after payment for taxes assessed by county assessor (except those based on exempt property); 3 yrs. from filing or 2 yrs. from payment, whichever later, for taxes assessed by county auditor or denial of homestead exemption by county auditor.
(88) 3 yrs. after purchase of depreciable agricultural machinery and equipment bought on or after 1-1-92.
(89) 90 days when amendment of return or change or correction results in reduction of tax or exemption of property.
(90) An extension, by written agreement between taxpayer and tax dept. may be granted.
(91) If an annual return was timely filed or filed within 3 yrs. after the due date, the refund claim must be filed within 3 yrs. after the later of the filing date or the due date; if no annual return was filed or if filed after 3 yrs. from the due date, the refund claim must be filed within 3 yrs. after the later of the time payment was made or the due date.
(92) Must file refund claim.
(93) After full payment of deficiency assessment.
(94) After 1st overpayment is received.

NOTES to chart at ¶ 295.
(continued)

(95) After return filed, assessment paid, or tax paid, whichever is earlier.
(96) After return due date or 6 months after payment date, whichever is later.
(97) Later of 3 yrs. from date return filed or 2 yrs. from payment. 2 yrs. from payment if no return filed.
(98) If no return filed.
(99) Fla.—Annual intangible personal property tax repealed eff. 1-1-2007. Previously, refund time limit was 3 yrs. after the payment was made or due and footnote (8) applied.

REFUND TIME LIMITS (II)

¶296 When you must file. Chart below lists refund time limits (notes follow chart). Also, special extensions may be granted by administrators.

EXPLANATION OF CHARTS: Parenthetical numbers ( ) in charts are keyed to notes below each chart. Symbol ''d'' means days, ''m'' means months, ''y'' means years, ''NT'' means no tax or tax only on very limited group of taxpayers, and ''NP'' means no specific provision.

Listings in the charts relate to payments made in usual course and as to which there is a reasonable expectation of refund. Some tax laws provide alternate methods and time limits for claiming a refund. In such cases, usually the period after payment is charted and the alternative is noted.

If payment must be protested to claim a refund, this requirement is noted by the parenthetical number 7. Many states permit the claimant to bring a court action for a tax refund *but may require payment under protest first.* ''Recovery by suit'' (court remedy) is usually available as an alternative to filing claim with a designated state official. *In general, the court remedy uses a shorter time limit for bringing the action than is required in pursuing the administrative remedy.*

Taxes State	MOTOR FUELS Loss or U.S. Sale(8)	 Non-Highway	 Other(60)	MINERALS SEVERANCE	GENERAL TIME LIMITS
ALA.	(20)	(21)	3y(179)	3y(179)	3y(179)
ALASKA	NP	1y(2)	1y(2)	3y(17,98)	3y(17,98)
ARIZ.	3y(172)	3y(172)	3y(172)	4y	4y
ARK.	1y(10,73)	NP	(71)	(128)	3y(135)
CALIF.	13m(2,68)	13m(2,22,130)	3y(25)	(3,7,79)	NP
COLO.	(73,111)	(111)	NP	3y(1)	1y(99)
CONN.	1y(2,68,174)	1y(2,26)	60d(1,3,27)	(108)	NP
DEL.	(20)	1y(2)	1y(140)	NT	3y(98)
D.C.	3y(1,68,138)	NP	3y(1)	NT	3y(81)
FLA.	3y(1,68,138)	3y(1,91)	3y(1,13)	60d(1,83,141)	3y(1,84)
GA.	6m(2,14,18,73)	18m(2,18,47)	3y(1)	NT	3y(1)
HAW.	(20)	NP	NP	NT	30d(3,7,78,85)
IDA.	(20)	3y(143,148)	3y(142,148)	(6,86,108)	NP
ILL.	2y(1,73,144)	2y(1,144)	3y-3½y(1,128)	NT	NP
IND.	3y	3y	3y(12)	3y(12,87)	3y(1,102)
IOWA	10d(10,73)	4m(2,18,30,120)	1y(1)	NT	NP
KAN.	60d(15,73,137,147)	1y(2,31,148)	3y(149)	3y(89,168)	NP
KY.	NP	90d(18,32,33,90)	NP	(32)	4y(1)
LA.	NP(73)	NP	(175)	1y(1,34,4)	1y(1,34,4)
ME.	90d(125)	1y(2,16)	3y(1,35)	3y(17)	3y(17,98)
MD.	1y(1,115)	1y(1,115)	(178)	(6)	3y(1)
MASS.	(20)	2y(2,122)	NP	3m(109,110)	3y(118)
MICH.	18m(2)	18m(2,100)	18m(1)	4y(1)	4y(166)
MINN.	1y(2)	1y(2)	1y(2)	(6)	3½y(148)
MISS.	3y(136)	3y(2)	3y(19)	(6)	3y(17,94)
MO.	10c(10,28,73)	1y(2,95)	5y(1,5,41)	(108)	2y(1)
MONT.	(138)	36m(2,18,127)	3y(1,40)	NP	5y(1)
NEB.	3y(1,59)	3y(139)	3y(1,29)	NP	3y(96)
NEV.	6m(2,68)	6m(2,44,131)	90d(3,7,152)	3y(153)	1y(5,13,97)
N.H.	(75)	(75)	(75)	NT	2y(104)
N.J.	4y(19,68)	4y(2)	4y(1)	NT	4y(1)
N.M.	6m(72,73)	NP	NP	3y(1,89)	3y(124)
N.Y.	(20)	3y(1,114)	3y(1,114)	NT	3y(17,98)
N.C.	(169)	NP	(169)	NP	3y(49)
N.D.	(20)	6m(90)	(6)	(9)	(20)

Taxes State	MOTOR FUELS Loss or U.S. Sale(8)	Non-Highway	Other(60)	MINERALS SEVERANCE	GENERAL TIME LIMITS
OHIO	30d(15,51,154)	1y(2)	1y(1)	4y(60,87)	1y(1)
OKLA.	3y	3y(23)	(134)	3y(1)	3y(101,4)
ORE.	15m(2,68)	15m(2)	3y(1)	2y(1)	2y(1)
PA.	60d(54,68)	60d(54)	90d(55)	NT	3y(103)
R.I.	240d(2,116)	240d(2)	NP	NT	NP
S.C.	3y(2)	NP	NP	NP	3y(182)
S.D.	15m(2,171)	15m(2)	15m(2,170)	6m(3,7)	3y(140)
TENN.	2y(132)	90d(18,123,129)	(167)	NP	3y(5,12,57)
TEX.	1y(15,70)	1y(70)	NP	NP	4y(92)
UTAH	(20)	(58,139)	3y(1)	3y(1,86)	30d(3,45)
VT.	(20)	(43)	(43)	NT	(3)
VA.	1y(124)	1y(19,61)	1y(1,62)	1y(12,109)	3y(106,156)
WASH.	13m(2,69)	13m(2,18)	3y(1,63)	(108)	4y(1)
W.VA.	3y(64,73)	6m(93)	3y(42)	3y(50)	3y(50)
WIS.	15d(65,73)	12m(2)	NP	NP	NP
WYO.	(20)	(180)	1y(11)	5y(181)	NP

NOTES to Chart at ¶ 296.

(1) After payment. In Colo., applies to oil & gas, conservation tax.
(2) After purchase.
(3) Recovery by suit.
(4) Alternative remedy by court action (uses shorter time limits).
(5) Alternative remedy by court action.
(6) No specific provision.
(7) After protested payment.
(8) Covers loss or destruction; and independently, sales to U.S.
(9) No fixed time limit for administrative remedy.
(10) After discovery.
(11) Claim refund on gasoline or diesel fuel within 1 yr. after purchase on exports if tax has been paid or on sales to University of Wyo., community colleges and public schools. Claim refund within 1 yr. on diesel fuel sold for interstate transportation and used outside Wyo.
(12) After close of calendar year.
(13) After refund right accrues.
(14) Evaporation and/or shrinkage loss.
(15) After loss.
(16) For aircraft 12 mos. from date of purchase.
(17) After filing return.
(18) Refund permit required.
(19) After sale. In Miss., after sale or delivery.
(20) No provision for loss or U.S. sale (credit allowed or sale exempted). Deduction allowed in Utah for motor fuel loss but not special fuel loss. In Ala., discount allowed to cover losses of gasoline or motor fuel; sales of gasoline or motor fuel to U.S. are exempt; seller can deduct sales of gasoline to U.S. covered by certificate of exemption; credit or refund for tax paid on motor fuel sold to U.S.; claim refund within later of 3 yrs. from date return filed or 2 yrs. from payment date, or if timely return not filed, within 2 yrs. from payment date. In Wyo., credit for shrinkage (evaporation) allowed.
(21) In Ala., diesel fuel for off-road agricultural equipment is exempt. End-user gets refund for fuel used in off-road vehicle or equipment; file 3 yrs. from purchase date. Farmers get annual refund of state gasoline tax; file by 3-31.
(22) Or. 3 mos. after export.
(23) Deduction allowed since exempt.
(24) After fiscal yr. end when accrued.
(25) 3 yrs. from date motor vehicle or diesel fuel was purchased, or within 6 months from date invoice for tax was received, if later.
(26) Farm use, by 3-31 for 12-31 fiscal year.
(27) Special fuel use, 3 years after payment and alternate remedy by Ct. action. Out-of-state use, 1 year from quarterly return due date.
(28) Other than distributor.
(29) On gasoline tax (distributors). On fuel use (applies only to special fuel in Nebr.) 1 yr. after payment (users).
(30) By non-licensee.
(31) Need refund permit.
(32) Gasoline and aviation fuel used in farms. Aircraft last day of mo. after use. Motorboats 4 mos. after purchase. Natural resources tax, 4 years after return due or tax paid.
(33) 60 days after credit period expires (on fuel also taxed outstate where used).
(34) Or 3 years from 12-31 of year tax was due, if later.
(35) Other than gasoline. No special provision on gasoline.
(36) Or from date of assessment if assessment rendered.

NOTES to Chart at ¶ 296. (continued)

(37) After final action, ruling, determination, order or receipt of contested tax bill proceed before tribunal. (Other taxes have own rules.)
(38) Aviation, by 4-15 of next year. Outstate use, 30 days after tax paid there.
(39) Aviation, last day of 12 mo. after purchase mo.
(40) Distributors.
(41) On gasoline (distributor); 3 years on special fuels (dealer or user).
(42) From end of mo. when paid.
(43) As determined by Comr.
(44) On exports; 3-month claim period. No refund on recreation watercraft.
(45) After order constituting final agency action is issued.
(46) Action must be started within 3 mos. after payment.
(47) For farm use.
(48) Aircraft use, 60 days after payment without penalty; after that, with penalty.
(49) After filing due date, or 2 yrs. after payment; if later; 1-yr. limit for unconstitutional taxes. (N.C.).
(50) After return due date or 2 years from payment, whichever later. If erroneously collected later of 5 yrs. from return filing or 4 yrs. after payment.
(51) Or after discovery. Evaporation, 120 days after calendar half-yr. (retailer).
(52) For corporate tax.
(53) Or 6 mos. after final assessment.
(54) After close of quarter. (Pa.)
(55) After 6-30 fiscal yr. end. (Pa.)
(56) No refund for aircraft or watercraft.
(57) With Comr. Rev. If filed with City Clk., 1 year. Comr. can give refund in 6 years after pyt. if based on a final court adjudication. Corporate excise taxes 2 yrs. after redetermination by IRS.
(58) By 4-15 following calendar year.
(59) Refund allowed on motor fuel destroyed. No provision on U.S. sale (Neb.).
(60) Illegal, erroneous or excessive payment unless otherwise shown.
(61) Gasoline, including boat use; special fuels and farms.
(62) By any licensee (special fuels).
(63) Carriers, 5 years from date of overpayment.
(64) From end of mo. of loss; evaporation: from end of year.
(65) After loss or destruction. 1 yr. after purchase, for retailer's evaporation.
(66) After year ended 6-30 (farm use).
(67) After receipt by dealer.
(68) For U.S. sales only.
(69) On U.S. sales. On loss by casualty, 30 days after discovery (except by evaporation, shrinkage or unknown cause).
(70) From 1st day of calendar mo. after purchase or use.
(71) Refund determined by return. Once Dir. certifies amount of refund, distributor deducts amount from next payment. Fire departments file annual refund application; permit required. (Ark.)
(72) After 1st purchase of fuel.
(73) For designated losses only. No provision for U.S. sales but credit is allowed or sale is exempted.
(74) After final value determination.
(75) Not later than Fed excise tax filing deadline (N.H.).
(76) After due date (local taxes). For state taxes to Dept. Rev., no fixed time limit (if suing, pay under protest).
(77) Mining, oil, gas companies (see property tax ¶ 295.
(78) 5 yrs. for excess or duplicate payments not made under protest.
(79) Sue State Treas. by 3rd Mon. in Feb. after tax due date (oil, gas production).
(80) Or 3y from license expiration, if later, for occupation or business license.
(81) From return date or payment date, whichever later (not for real property taxes).
(82) Quarterly by retailers with refund permit (evaporation).
(83) Oil, gas production tax or charge.
(84) State Comptroller.
(85) Paid over to a public accountant.
(86) Mining tax.
(87) Severance tax.
(88) 4-15 of following year; 30 days late—25% penalty; over 30 days to 6 mos.—50%penalty; barred after.
(89) Oil production tax or assessment. Oil & gas severance in Mich; oil & gas taxes in N. Mex. In N.M., 3 yr. after final determination of value as to overpayment resulting from Fed, N.M. or court disapproval of increase in value of product subject to oil & gas taxes.
(90) After close of calendar year in which tax fuel was purchased.
(91) For agricultural, aquacultural or commercial fishing purposes (municipal fuel tax).
(92) From tax due date or 6 mos. after jeopardy or deficiency assessment becomes final.
(93) From mo. of purchase or delivery; 12 mos. if used for agriculture.
(94) But for income taxes, up to 6 years in certain cases.
(95) For gasoline. Special fuels in 6 mos.
(96) 3 yrs. from the time return was filed or 2 yrs. from the time tax was paid, whichever later. If the period of assessment of tax was extended by agreement between taxpayer and Tax Commissioner, refund claim must be filed within 6 mos. of the expiration of the extended period. (Neb.)
(97) State claims. Local claims, 3 years.
(98) If later, or if no return filed, 2 years after payment.
(99) After receipt or collection of the money by the state.
(100) Marine fuel, 6 mos. after purchase.

NOTES to Chart at ¶ 296. (continued)

(101) After payment (Tax Comn.) if error; 1 yr. if misinterpretation of law (with exceptions).
(102) Or 3 years after filing.
(103) After payment or settlement if act unconstitutional or erroneously-interpreted.
(104) Refund claim must be made within 2 yrs. of payment or 3 yrs. of tax due date if for tax, penalty, or interest paid as result of assessment or demand for payment. Refund claim must be made in 120 days of tax due date if based on argument that tax or any provision of tax law is unconstitutional under Fed or state constitution. (N.H.).
(105) From 12-31 of year assessed.
(106) Recovery by suit. Administrative remedy available in some cases (Dept. Taxation; State Corp. Comn.); time limits vary. Special provisions for local levies.
(107) Includes timber taxes.
(108) Timber follows general property or own provisions.
(109) Forest products tax.
(110) After notice or date of application, whichever later, for abatement appeal to appellate tax bd.
(111) Within 12 months after date of purchase.
(112) For agricultural and commercial use only.
(113) Excluding non-commercial watercraft.
(114) Or 3 yrs. after tax-paid fuel sold.
(115) No claims after 10-1 if annual claim is filed for 12-mo. period ending 6-30, or for period of under 1 yr., 3 mo. after end of period for which claim is filed.
(116) Purchased for sale outside state or to U.S. govt. (R.I.).
(117) Or from date of delivery; special fuel: 1 yr. from 1st calendar mo. Invoiced or required to be invoiced.
(118) After return due date, within 2 yrs. from assessment or 1 year after payment, if later.
(119) 6 mos. For aviation fuel 6 mos. After sale for fuel use.
(120) Special permit for aviation fuel.
(121) Or after end of month during which export fuel used or tax assessed.
(122) Farm use, by 15th of 4th month. Watercraft fuel, 6 mos. after purchase or invoice.
(123) For auxiliary engines; for agricultural file semiannually 4-15 and 10-15 or annually 4-15.
(124) 3 yrs. if purchased by licensed exporter and transported and delivered to another state for sales or use if the tax applicable in the destination state has been paid.
(125) 90 days after 6-30 and 12-31 by retailers for shrinkage.
(126) Refunds on sales to U.S. armed forces.
(127) Special fuel users, dealers, from date license canceled.
(128) Incorporates sales tax credit-refund provisions.
(129) After 6-30 and 12-31.
(130) For MV off highway use. Use fuel for construction equipment (in project) and agricultural vehicles off highway.
(131) Specified refund on aircraft fuel, claim refund in same way as for vehicle.
(132) From end of any quarterly or annual reporting period (Tenn.).
(133) From 1st day of calendar mo. Of use when fuel consumed outstate.
(134) Credit for taxes paid on fuel purchased and used in vehicles out-of-state. If credit in any calendar quarter exceeds the tax liability, motor or diesel fuel licensee can file claim for refund within 24 months from 1st day of calendar quarter when the gasoline or diesel fuel was used; 1 year from month when special fuel was used by licensed dealer; unlicensed first time users, report taking the credit or refund claim must be filed in 30 days from payment date or credit or refund will not be allowed.
(135) From date filed or 2 yrs. from date tax was paid, whichever later.
(136) After date of loss; 250 gal. min. loss for oil.
(137) Special fuel exempt to U.S. agencies and National Guard of any state.
(138) No provision for loss.
(139) Pre-1-1-2005, there was a credit for motor fuel tax for nonhighway use.
(140) After earlier of return due date or payment.
(141) Solid mineral severance tax—"reclamation" refund filed on annual basis within 60 days after payment for preceding year up to 5 years from payment.
(142) Distributors claim refund for taxes erroneously paid in 3 yrs. after payment.
(143) No refund for fuel for nonhighway use by recreational MV or fishing boat.
(144) 80% refund given for claims filed over 1 yr. after payment but under 2 yrs.
(145) File affidavit in 60 days after notice.
(146) Includes refund for tax on taxicab fuel.
(147) File affidavit in 30 days.
(148) From return due date or date filed, if later.
(149) By special fuel dealer or user.
(150) Refund for fuel for buses used in specified municipal transport. system.
(151) For overpayment file in 5 yrs. after payment.
(152) Special fuel: 12 mos. after payment.
(153) Patented mining claims.
(154) US sales: 80 days from purchase. Shrinkage or evaporation; 60 days after last day of Feb. or 8-31.
(155) From discovery but limited to 4 yrs. from payment.
(156) From assessment.
(157) (Reserved.)
(158) Transporters of tax-paid motor fuel to another state are refunded 11¢ per gallon for the tax paid.
(159) A credit or refund is available if fuel is not resold as a motor fuel or if tax previously paid exceeds tax due on resale. File claim within 1y of date of purchase.
(160) Refund is available when fuel is purchased for nonhighway use in a foreign country.

NOTES to Chart at ¶ 296.
(continued)

(161) Refund for tax-paid purchases of fuel in excess of fuel used on Tenn. Highways by a common carrier.

(162) Fuel tax refund is allowed to anyone, other than a licensed distributor, dealer or user of fuel, who uses motor fuel or special fuel to product denatured alcohol.

(163) Fuel tax refund for five gallons or more of fuel purchased for use in race cars and/or school buses.

(164) Disallowed refund on motor fuel and special fuel tax paid on fuel used in aircraft.

(165) Persons subject to Ohio excise tax imposed on persons liable for the Ohio highway use tax who purchase motor fuel in Ohio for use in another state are allowed a credit or refund on a reciprocal basis equal to the amount of motor fuel tax paid to Ohio.

(166) After filing of original return.

(167) For petroleum products subsequently sold to governmental agencies, on or before the last day of the 2nd mo. following the month in which the exempt sales were made (Tenn.).

(168) 3 yrs. from filing return or 1 yr. after tax assessment, whichever is later.

(169) Governments, nonprofits file quarterly refunds by end of month after calendar quarter close; annual refunds due by 4-15 (after calendar yr. end) for fuels used in other than licensed MVs.

(170) Credit only for tax mistakenly paid.

(171) Sales to U.S. or defense supply center.

(172) 3 yrs. from date of purchase or invoice for licensed sellers; 6 mos. from date of sale for persons who aren't licensed suppliers, interstate users, restricted distributors or use fuel vendors; 3 yrs. from report due date for interstate users; monthly or up to once per week for fuel used to propel light class MVs or use class MVs exempt from the weight fee. (Ariz.)

(173) (Reserved.)

(174) Claim must be made by 3-31 for purchases in past calendar yr.

(175) Special fuels tax—6 mos. after purchase of special fuels by commercial fishermen.

(176) Quarterly claims by last day of month after end of quarter. Monthly claim by 22nd day after end of month, or on application.

(177) In case of audit, 6 months after notice of assessment, determination, or settlement.

(178) Motor carriers file for refund of excess credit within 24 months of end of period when credit was developed. (Md.)

(179) Later of 3 yrs. from date return filed or 2 yrs. from date payment made. 2 yrs. from payment if no return filed. (Ala.)

(180) Credit for farm use (gasoline). Distributors apply by last day of mo. for previous mo. for refund. Undyed diesel fuel for farm use exempt from precentage of tax. Nonhighway operation, 1 yr. after purchase (diesel). (Wyo.)

(181) By end of 5th yr. after calendar yr. which included mo. overpyt. was made. (Wyo.)

(182) After timely return is filed or 2 yrs. after taxes were paid, whichever later. (S.C.)

POLLUTION CONTROL TAX INCENTIVES

¶298 Income, franchise, sales-use, and property tax incentives. Air and water pollution have become national concerns in recent years. As a result, many states offer tax incentives to encourage businesses to help in the clean-up. Together with the Fed deduction (60-month amortization) for pollution control equipment (IRC §169), state tax incentives add up to substantial savings for business. State tax incentives are being offered to offset income, franchise, sales-use and property taxes and take the form of credits, deductions, exemptions or special rates.

How to use this chart: ''D'' shows state has pollution control equipment deduction: ''CR'', a tax credit; ''E'', an exemption or exclusion from tax. *Special situations*, such as special rates or assessment rules are explained in footnotes. Also, many states base income taxes on IRC taxable income. This usually means fast amortization under IRC §169 is picked up automatically.

STATE(11)	INCOME TAXES (27)	CAPITAL VALUES (FRANCHISE) TAXES	SALES-USE TAXES	PROPERTY TAXES
ALABAMA		D	E	E
ALASKA				E(7)
ARIZONA	D; CR(47)		E(56)	
ARKANSAS	CR(41)		E	
CALIFORNIA	D		(34)	
COLORADO	CR(8)			(49)
CONNECTICUT	CR(12,45)	(2)	E(5)	E
DELAWARE	CR(48)			
FLORIDA	CR(59)		E(61)	E(13)
GEORGIA	CR(51)		E	E
HAWAII			E(11)	E(11)
IDAHO	CR(52)		E	E
ILLINOIS	CR(58)		E(64)	(3)
INDIANA			E	E
IOWA			E(39)	E
KANSAS	CR(69)			E(68)
KENTUCKY	(24); CR(43)		E(31)	(31)
LOUISIANA	(27); CR(44)		E	(32)
MAINE	CR(37)		E	E
MARYLAND			E	E(70)
MASSACHUSETTS	D or CR (12,16,65)		(19)	E
MICHIGAN	(26)		E	E(30)
MINNESOTA	D		E	E
MISSISSIPPI	D		D(62); E(53)	
MISSOURI		D(33)	E	(20)
MONTANA				(21,11)
NEBRASKA			E(25)	
NEVADA				E
NEW HAMPSHIRE				E(4)
NEW JERSEY	CR(36)		E(1,36)	E
NEW YORK	CR(42)		E(55)	E(6,7)
NEW YORK CITY				E(6,7)
NORTH CAROLINA	D	D	E(60)	E
NORTH DAKOTA			E(54)	E(66)
OHIO	(24)	E(24,29)	E(29)	E(29)

STATE(11)	INCOME TAXES (27)	CAPITAL VALUES (FRANCHISE) TAXES	SALES-USE TAXES	PROPERTY TAXES
OKLAHOMA(11)	CR(22)		(19)	
OREGON	CR(15,29)			E(15,29)
PENNSYLVANIA	D(38)	E	E(9)	
RHODE ISLAND	D(12) or CR(73)		E	E
SOUTH CAROLINA	CR(63)	CR(63)	E(17)	E
SOUTH DAKOTA				E(67)
TENNESSEE	C(72)	C(72)	E(10); CR(50)	E(28)
TEXAS				E
UTAH	CR(57)		E(71)	
VERMONT				E
VIRGINIA	CR(40)		E	E(35)
WASHINGTON			E or CR(14)	
WEST VIRGINIA	D(12,18)		E(46)	E(28)
WISCONSIN	D		(19)	E
WYOMING				E(23)

FOOTNOTES to chart ¶ 298.

(1) *N.J.*—Zero emission vehicles are exempt.

(2) *Conn.* —Utilities may claim credit against gross earnings taxes.

(3) *Ill.*—Facilities valued on 33.3% of fair cash value of their economic productivity to owners. No tax on personalty.

(4) *N.H.*—Commission certifies percentage of installation exempt to local taxing body, which reduces assessment accordingly.

(5) *Conn.* —Exemption for pollution control and cleanup equipment.

(6) *N.Y.*—Exempts industrial waste treatment and air pollution control facilities to extent of increase in value.

(7) *Alaska, N.Y.:* Localities may exempt pollution control facilities.

(8) *Colo.* —Part of investment credit provisions. Applies to pollution control facilities with useful life of at least 3 yrs. if elect to amortize under Fed 60-month rule. Allows credit for expenses relating to redevelopment of contaminated land and for investments in plastic recycling technologies.

(9) *Pa.*—Exemption based on Regs interpreting manufacturing and utility exemptions.

(10) *Tenn.* —Exempt. Tenn. exemption includes chemicals-supplies used in air-water pollution facilities for pollution control.

(11) Entries apply to all (air-water) pollution control except only air in *Haw.*

(12) *Conn.; Mass.; R.I.; W.Va.* For corporate income tax.

(13) *Fla.* —Assessment limited to market value as salvage. Credit is allowed for new business, restoration of old business, or expansion, including pollution control facilities.

(14) *Wash.* —Original cost exempt from sales-use taxes or credit against sales-use or business & occupation taxes may be elected.

(15) *Ore.* —Cooperative corporations can elect income tax credit or property tax 10-yr. exemption. Credit is allowed for installation of pollution-eliminating production technology or process certified by the Environmental Quality Commission; maximum account of credit is lesser of the taxpayer's tax liability or 10% of costs certified by Commission.

(16) *Mass.* —Deduction or credit may be elected.

(17) *S.C.* —Applies to facility used in mining, quarrying, compounding, processing and manufacturing, installed to comply with U.S. or S.C. order. Exempts specifically designated solid waste disposal collection bags required per locality's disposal plan.

(18) *W.Va.* —Deduction elective instead of Fed depreciation-amortization.

(19) *Mass., Okla., S.D., Wis.* Sales-use tax exempts manufacturers plant equipment. Pollution control machinery in production line or production area may qualify—taxpayers may wish to ask for official rulings on tax status.

(20) *Mo.*—Pollution control tools treated as a separate subclass of personalty and assessed at 25% of true value.

(21) *Mont.* —Air-water pollution control facilities taxed at lower assessed value.

(22) *Okla.* —Up to 20% credit for investment in facilities for recycling, reuse, or destruction of industrial waste. Credit allowed for 50% of cost of qualified clean-burning MV fuel property (equip. to modify MV power from gasoline or diesel fuel to at least 50% compressed or liquified natural gas) or at least 85% methanol. Credit of $5 per ton for purchase and transfer of poultry litter.

FOOTNOTES to chart ¶ 298.
(continued)

(23) *Wyo.* —Includes "land" pollution.
(24) *Ky.; Ohio.* Excluded from property factor of allocation formula.
(25) *Neb.* —Must apply for refund.
(26) *Mich.* —SBT (until 12-31-2007) or Mich. Business Tax (eff. 1-1-2008) investment tax credit rules apply.
(27) In addition to specific provision, many states allow Fed amortization and depreciation specifically or by adopting Fed taxable income.
(28) *Tenn.; W.Va.* Facilities valued at "salvage value."
(29) *Ore.* includes "noise pollution" control.
(30) *Mich.* —Also exempts water conditioning systems used for residential dwellings.
(31) *Ky.*—Subject to state property tax only. Sales tax exemption applies to recycling machy-equip.
(32) *La.*—Limited to new mfg. places; valuation limited to actual cash value at voluntary sale taking into account depreciation and condition.
(33) *Mo.*—Uses market value of assets for franchise tax purposes.
(34) Transfers or leases by *Calif.* Pollution Control Financing Authority of personalty constituting project or pollution control facility are exempt; deduction is allowed for certain machy. used in pollution control.
(35) *Va.*—Exempt from state tax; localities may exempt totally or partially.
(36) *N.J.* —Sales of recycling equipment or effluent treatment or conveyance equipment are exempt. Corporate income tax credit equal to 50% of cost of equipment.
(37) *Me.*—Eff. for tax yrs. starting on or after 1-1-2006 and before 1-1-2010, credit for pollution-reducing boiler or furnace systems. Credit for 25% of expenses incurred or paid to construct or install improvements to filling or charging stations to provide clean fuels for MVs thru 12-31-2008.
(38) *Pa.*—Deduction allowed for pollution control facilities amortized under IRC §169.
(39) *Iowa.* — Sale-use tax exempts industrial machy-equipment, computers and replacement parts mainly used in waste product recycling or reprocessing if depreciable for Fed-state income tax.
(40) *Va.*—Credit to qualified farmers for 25% of cost of certified equip. for more precise pesticide-fertilizer application; max. credit $3,750. Credit for 10% of IRC §179A deduction for clean-fuel or qualified electric MV and specified refueling property, limited to clean-fuel MV principally garaged in Va. or refueling property placed in service in Va. or 10% of cost used to compute IRC §30 credit. Clean fuel vehicle job creation credit; for tax yrs. starting before 1-1-2007, credit for recylable materials processing machinery and equipment; vehicle emissions testing equipment credit; credit for waste motor oil burning equipment.
(41) *Ark.* —Credit for 30% of qualified recycling equip. bought for solid waste recycling business.
(42) *N.Y.* —Credit is allowed for 50% of cost of electric vehicle (up to max. $5,000 credit), 60% of cost of clean-fuel vehicle property (up to max. $5,000 credit), and 50% of cost of clean-fuel refueling property placed in service in tax yrs. starting in 1998—2-28-2005. Investment credit of 5% for the 1st $350 million of the investment credit base; 4% on excess, for certain industrial waste treatment or air pollution facility used in the taxpayer's trade or business. Credit of 10% of the cost or other federal basis for federal income tax purposes of certain industrial waste treatment facilities or air pollution control facilities used in the taxpayer's trade or business located within a designated economic development zone.
(43) *Ky.*—Clean coal incentive credit. Environmental remediation (Brownfields) credit. Environmental stewardship credit. Recycling credits.
(44) *La.*—Conversion of MVs to alternative fuel usage—Credit is 20% of cost of qualified clean-burning MV fuel property or, if MV mfr.-installed, lesser of $1,500 or 20% of 10% of MV's cost.
(45) Eff for tax yrs. starting pre-1-1-2008: (a), corporate income tax credit for 10% of (a) difference between cost of MV run only by clean alternative fuel (natural gas) and similar MV not so run; (b) equip. costs for compressed natural gas filling station; 50% of amount spent to construct or improve filling station to dispense compressed natural gas, liquefied petroleum gas, or liquefied natural gas.
(46) *W.Va.* —Exemption for pollution control costs related to activities involving transportation, communications, transmission, and the manufacturing or producing of natural resources.
(47) *Ariz.* —Credit for construction costs of qualified environmental technology facility—10% of amount spent during tax yr. to construct qualified facility (inclu. land acquisition, improvements, bldg. improvements, machy. & equip.), up to 75% of tax; if this credit is taken, no credit allowed under recycling equip. above for same recycling equip. Credit for 10% of certified cost of correcting release of regulated substance from underground storage tank. Credit for 10% of cost of real or personal property used to control or prevent pollution; max. credit per yr., $500,000; no credit if taking recycling credit above for same equip. Credit for cost of purchasing or converting to alternative fuel vehicle, up to $1,000 per purchase in lieu of deduction. Deduction for amortization of pollution control devices. Deduction for alternative fuel vehicle, and related equipment purchases.

FOOTNOTES to chart ¶ 298.
(continued)

(48) *Del.*—$400 credit ($250 for property placed in service before 1997) per 10% of mfr's waste reduction (50% (min.) over past yr.) in tax yr. 1–4. If 25% of raw materials from recycled items and $200,000 invested in new or expanded Del. facility, mfr. gets $650 credit ($900 in targeted areas) per qualified employee plus $650 ($900 in targeted areas) per $100,000 invested; for property placed in service before 1997, credit was $500 ($750 in targeted areas). Credit for processing materials removed from Del. solid waste stream for resale as raw materials to mfrs. who invest $200,000 (min.) in a qualified facility and employ 5 (min.) qualified employees—$650 credit ($900 in targeted areas) per qualified employee plus $650 ($900 in targeted areas) per $100,000 invested; for property placed in service before 1997, credit was $500 ($750 in targeted areas).

(49) Special valuation for pollution control systems.

(50) *Tenn.* —Auto body shop, 100% of tax paid on equip. needed to comply with emission control standards; dry cleaners, 50%; others per Commr. Rev. pollution control rules, 100%.

(51) *Ga.*—In Tier 1 counties, credit allowed in yr. after qualified acquisition for 8% of cost of qualified investment property up to 50% of tax if property is recycling or pollution control machy-equip. In Tier 2, 5%. In Tier 3 and Tier 4, 3%.

(52) *Ida.* —20% (up to $30,000) of cost to buy qualified machy-equipment used to manufacture products using postconsumer or postindustrial waste.

(53) *Miss.* —Pollution control equipment to manufacturers or custom processors for industrial use are exempt.

(54) *N.D.* exempts recycling machinery and equipment.

(55) *N.Y.* exempts waste treatment equip. used directly and predominantly in manufacturing, assembling, refining, mining, or extracting if it's bought by the manufacturer and used predominantly to actually treat, bury, or store waste materials from the production process, and over 50% of the waste treated, buried, or stored results from the production process. Sales of machinery or equipment used or consumed directly and predominantly in the control, prevention, or abatement of pollution or contaminants from manufacturing or industrial facilities are exempt. Also exempt are receipts from removing waste material from transfer stations or construction and demolition debris processing facilities.

(56) *Ariz.* exempts coal petroleum coke, natural gas, virgin fuel oil, and electricity sold to environmental technology manufacturer, producer, or processor if used to generate or provide on-site power or energy solely for producing, processing, or environmental protection. Also exempt: Machy, equip. and other materials used to construct qualified environmental technology facility.

(57) *Utah* .—Credit, for encouraging development of mfg. businesses using recycled materials, equal to 5% of purchase price of machy. and equipment; up to $50 for items using cleaner burning fuels; clean fuel vehicle tax credit of up to $500 of cost of new motor vehicle, up to $400 of cost of equipment for converting motor vehicles, and up to $500 for cost of converting a special fuel mobile equipment engine.

(58) *Ill.*—Credit for certain amounts paid for unreimbursed eligible remediation costs within River Edge redevelopment zones.

(59) *Fla.* —Credit allowed for: (1) voluntary cleanup of drycleaning solvent at contaminated sites; and (2) certain expenses incurred by hazardous waste facilities.

(60) *N.C.* —Exempt from sales tax but subject to privilege tax.

(61) *Fla.* —Exempts machinery, equipment, facilities, devices, or fixtures used mainly to control or abate pollution or contaminants in mfg., processing, compounding, or producing tangible personalty for sale.

(62) Taxed at preferential rate.

(63) *S.C.* —Corporations can take credit for 30% of investment in qualified recycling facility.

(64) *Ill.* —Low sulfur dioxide emission coal-fueled devices.

(65) *Mass.* —Credit for 25% of net response and removal costs related to oil and hazardous material cleanup. Amount of the credit is 50% for taxpayers who achieve and maintain a permanent solution or remedy operation status.

(66) *N.D.* exempts pollution abatement improvements.

(67) *S.D.* —Property owned by regional recycling and waste management districts are exempt from state and local taxes, except for special assessments.

(68) *Kan.* —Exempt are pollution control devices used at electric generation facilities placed into service after 12-31-2000.

(69) *Kan.* —Credit for 50% of amount spent on qualified alternative-fueled MVs placed in service pre-1-1-2005, up to max. credit of $3,000 for MV with gross vehicle wt. under 10,000 lbs.; max. $5,000 for heavy duty MV with gross vehicle wt. 10,000 lbs to 26,000 lbs. max; max. $50,000 for MV with gross vehicle wt. over 26,000 lbs.

(70) *Md.*—Exempt is 95% of the assessment of certitifed coal pollution control facilities or coal waste disposal power project. Qualified personalty owned by nonprofit marine spill response orgs. are exempt. Exemption for clean-burning refueling equipment or mchy. phased out starting 2002.

FOOTNOTES to chart ¶ 298.
(continued)

(71) *Utah* —Property, materials or services used in constructing, or incorporated in, pollution control facilities are exempt.

(72) *Tenn.* —Credit of 1% of purchase price of industrial machinery.

(73) *R.I.* —Investment tax credit against personal income tax for air or water pollution control facilities.

ENERGY SAVING—TAX BENEFITS

¶299 The energy crisis has spawned numerous state tax benefits. These take the form of credits, deductions, exemptions, refunds, or assessment reduction.

How to use this chart: ''Cr'' means credit. ''D'' means deduction. ''E'' means exemption or exclusion from tax. ''R'' means refund.

Solar energy devices generally applies to installation of solar energy, wind, geothermal or hydrothermal devices. Specifics are covered in the footnotes.

Energy conservation devices: This category covers renewable energy resource systems or cogeneration facilities, conversion of fossil fuel systems to nonfossil fuel systems, insulation, storm windows or storm doors. Specific items are footnoted.

Heating fuels: This deals with various tax breaks given for use of fuels such as coal, wood, gas, oil, and electricity. Footnotes cover specifics.

	INCOME TAX		SALES-USE TAX			PROPERTY TAX	
STATE	Solar Energy Devices	Energy Conserva-tion	Solar Energy Devices	Energy Conser-vation	Heat-ing Fuels	Solar Energy Devices	Energy Conser-vation
Ala.		D(39)			E(45)		
Ak.	Cr(64)	Cr(64)					
Ariz.	Cr(10)	Cr(26)	E(57)				
Ark.							
Calif.	E(50)	D(76); E(50)	E(66)	E(66)		E(67)	
Colo.	Cr(80)	Cr(80)			E(40)		
Conn.	Cr(25)	Cr(25)	E(100)	E(100)	E(24)	E(52)	
Del.							
D.C.					E(89)		
Fla.			E		E(46)		
Ga.							
Haw.	Cr(31)	Cr(31)	(31)	(31)		E(32)	E(32)
Ida.	D(62)	D(62)	R(1)	R(1)			
Ill.						(22)	
Ind.		Cr(88)		Cr(88)		D	D(49)
Ia.	Cr(98)					E	
Kan.	Cr(58)					E(60)	
Ky.	E(102)	E(102);Cr(82)	E(102)	R(101)	E(70)	E(70)	
La.	Cr(65)	Cr(65)			E(8)	E(71)	
Me.		Cr(92)		E(93)	E(71)		
Md.		Cr(16)			E(33)	E(73)	E(73)
Mass.	Cr(11)	D(55); Cr(12)	E(14)		E(14)	E(13)	E(13)
Mich.	Cr(68,77)	Cr(68,77)			E(74)	E(34)	E(34)
Minn.			E(85)	E(85)	E(36)	E	E
Miss.					E(36)		
Mo.					E(36)		
Mont.		Cr(61)				E(61)	E(61)
Neb.							
Nev.					E(27)	E(28)	

STATE	INCOME TAX Solar Energy Devices	INCOME TAX Energy Conservation	SALES-USE TAX Solar Energy Devices	SALES-USE TAX Energy Conservation	SALES-USE TAX Heating Fuels	PROPERTY TAX Solar Energy Devices	PROPERTY TAX Energy Conservation
N.H.						E(43)	E(43)
N.J.			E(15)				
N.M.							
N.Y.	Cr(91)	Cr(42)		E(37)	E(53)	E(69)	E(44)
N.C.	Cr(29)	Cr(29,90)				(86)	
N.D.		Cr(69)				E(18)	
Ohio				E(9)			E(9)
Okla.		Cr(75)					
Ore.		Cr(51)				E	E(56)
Pa.							
R.I.	Cr(83)	Cr(83)	E(87)	E(87)		(81)	
S.C.	Cr(99)	Cr(72)			E(19)		
S.D.						Cr(30)	Cr(38)
Tenn.					E	E(4)	
Tex.					E(103)	E	
Utah	Cr(48)		E(96)		(21)		
Vt.			E(97)		E	E(41)	E(41)
Va.		D(94)		E(78)	E(84)	E(6)	E(6,79)
Wash.			E				E(54)
W.Va.							
Wis.					E(63)	E(69)	
Wyo.			E(7)	E(7)			

FOOTNOTES to chart ¶ 299 (corresponding to numbers in parentheses in the chart):

(1) Ida.—Through 6-30-2011, purchasers of machinery and equipment used directly in generating electricity through fuel cells, low impact hydro, wind, geothermal resources, biomass, cogeneration, solar power, or landfill gas as the principal source of power are allowed a rebate of the tax paid on that machinery and equipment, if the purchaser uses those items to develop a facility capable of generating at least 25 kilowatts of electricity.

(2) Alternative energy equipment.

(3) If sale of energy fuel directly to consumer for residential use.

(4) Applies to both solar, wind and geothermal devices.

(5) *Miss.* —Applies to colleges and universities.

(6) Localities can exempt.

(7) *Wyo.*—Equipment used to generate electricity from renewable resources is exempt from sales-use tax. Expires 6-30-2012.

(8) *La.* exempts butane and propane and other LPGs used or consumed for farm purposes. Certain utilities and fuel and gas for residential use are exempt from tax. Lower tax rates apply to certain utilities for nonresidential use.

(9) *Ohio.* —Exempts transfers of personalty to holder of exempt facility certificate if the personalty is incorporated into the facility (sales-use). Exempts energy or solid waste conversion and thermal efficiency improvement facility (property tax).

(10) *Ariz.* allows 25% credit (in lieu of depreciation) up to $1,000 per yr. per residence of cost of solar energy device in yr. of installation.

(11) Corporations can deduct expenses of solar or wind powered unit.

(12) Credit for renewable energy source property for single family residential property. In Mass., credit is lesser of $1,000 or 15%.

(13) Exempts solar or wind powered system or device, and hydropower facility.

(14) *Mass.* —Exempts solar, wind-powered or heat pump systems for heating or energy for principal residence.

(15) *N.J.* —Sales-use and property tax exemptions apply to solar heating or cooling systems.

FOOTNOTES to chart ¶ 299 (corresponding to numbers in parentheses in the chart):
(continued)

(16) *Md.*—Credit for 15% of the total installed costs of solar water heating property ($2,000 max.) or photovoltaic property ($1,000 max.) placed in service during the taxable year for property; credit cannot be claimed for property placed in service before 7-1-2000 or after 12-31-2004. Credit allowed of 85¢ for each kilowatt hour of electricity taxpayer produces from qualified energy resources at a qualified Maryland facility during the 10-year period starting on the date the facility was originally placed in service and sold by the taxpayer to other than a related person under IRC §45. If the facility produces electricity from a qualified energy resource that is co-fired with coal, the credit is 5¢ per kilowatt hour. Facility must be located in Md., and originally placed in service on or after 1-1-2001 but before 1-1-2005.

(17) *Me.*—Exempts coal, oil, wood for residential use, including first 750 kilowatt hrs. of electricity per month and gas for cooking and heating.

(18) Exempt for 5-yr. period.

(19) *S.C.* —Exempts electricity, natural gas, fuel oil, LP gas, coal or other combustibles for residential heating.

(20) *Utah.* —Credit for 10% (max. $50) of cost of pellet burning, high mass wood stove, or solid fuel burning device certified by Fed EPA, inclu. natural gas or propane free standing fireplaces and inserts (not fireplace logs).

(21) *Utah.* —Special rate for residential gas, electricity, heat, coal, fuel oil or other fuels.

(22) *Ill.* —Solar energy systems receive special alternative valuation.

(23) *Conn.* —Exempts system utilizing cogeneration technology and renewable energy system if sold pre-7-1-91.

(24) Exempts fuel used for heating purposes in residences and certain mfg. facilities.

(25) Credit for investment in energy conservation programs for low incomes.

(26) *Ariz.* —Credit up to $75 per installation of solar hot water heater plumbing stub outs & electric vehicle recharge outlets installed in dwelling units.

(27) *Nev.* —Exempts wood, coal, petroleum and gas for domestic heat.

(28) *Nev.* —Partial abatement for new or expanding facility for generating electricity from renewable energy.

(29) *N.C.* —Credit of 10% of costs for construction of cogenerating power plants. Credit for 35% of cost of investing in renewable energy property. Credit of 25% of installation and equip. costs of constructing a renewable energy equip. facility. Credit for donating funds to a nonprofit organization to enable nonprofit to acquire renewable energy property equal to taxpayer's share of credit nonprofit could claim under credit for investing in renewable energy property.

(30) Credit for renewable resource energy systems (sun, wind, geothermal and biomass sources).

(31) *Haw.* —Special sales tax rate allowed on sale to utility for resale of nonfossil fuel generated electricity. Exempts waste-electric generating facility sale-leaseback (specified amts.) by Haw. subdiv. owning-construction pre-5-1-88. Income tax credit allowed for specified part of cost of energy conservation devices put in service pre-7-1-2003.

(32) *Haw.* —Exempt if alternative energy improvement installed pre-1993.

(33) *Md.*—Exempts wood, and refuse-derived fuel for heating.

(34) *Mich.* —Solar, wind, or water energy conversion device property exemption applies if installed pre-1984.

(35) Residential energy credit for renewable energy source expenditures (federal IRC §44C expenditures, earth shelter dwelling unit, biomass conversion, solar energy systems); corps. can't claim credit.

(36) *Minn.; Miss.; Mo.* —Residential heating fuels (oil, wood, steam, propane, gas, electricity).

(37) *N.Y.* —Exemption for certain alternative fuel vehicles.

(38) *S.D.* —Credit for renewable energy resource system producing ethyl alocohol for use as fuel.

(39) Deduction for conversion to wood as primary home heating source.

(40) *Colo.* —Electricity, coal, wood, gas, fueloil, or coke for operating residential fixtures and appliances.

(41) *Vt.*—Towns can exempt or fix valuation of alternative energy devices.

(42) *N.Y.* —Credit is allowed for certain costs for incorporating certain property into a green building.

(43) Cities and towns empowered to exempt solar energy and wind-powered energy systems.

(44) *N.Y.* —Exemption for value added to 1-, 2-, 3-, or 4-family homes by insulation and other energy conservation measures.

(45) *Ala.* —Exempt when otherwise taxed by motor fuels excise tax.

(46) *Fla.* —Household fuel; boiler fuel for manufacturing.

(47) Household fuels.

FOOTNOTES to chart ¶ 299 (corresponding to numbers in parentheses in the chart): **(continued)**

(48) *Utah* —Individual gets nonrefundable credit equal to 25% of the reasonable costs of each residential energy system (active solar, passive solar, biomass, direct-use geothermal, geothermal heat-pump system, wind, or hydroenergy system), including installation costs (max. $2,000) for units placed in service on or after 1-1-2007. For tax yrs. starting on or after 1-1-2007, businesses get: (a) a nonrefundable credit equal to 25% of the costs of a residential energy system (active solar, passive solar, biomass, direct-use geothermal, geothermal heat-pump system, wind, or hydroenergy system) installed, including installation costs (max. $2,000 per residential unit); and (b) a refundable credit of up to 10% of the reasonable costs of a commercial system (active solar, passive solar, biomass, geothermal electricity, direct-use geothermnal, geothermal heat-pump system, wind, hydroenergy or biomass system used to supply energy to a commercial unit or as a commercial enterprise) installed, including installation costs (max. $5,000 per commercial unit).

(49) *Ind.* —Deduction is allowed for hydroelectric power devices and geothermal energy heating or cooling devices.

(50) *Calif.* Exclusion from gross income for rebates, vouchers, other financial incentives issued by Calif. Energy Comm. or PUC or utility for expenses in buying or installing solar or thermal system; wind energy system; fuel cell generating system.

(51) *Ore.* allows credits for cost of certified energy conservation facilities, commercial lending institution's energy conservation loans made up to 1-1-2002 to heat residences, cost of connecting to geothermal heating district systems, and resident individual's 1st yr. energy yield of qualified alternative energy device. Credit is also allowed for certain percentage of cost of fueling station installed in a dwelling to run an alternative fuel vehicle.

(52) 15-yr. tax abatement is available.

(53) Home heating fuels.

(54) *Wash.* —Property used for producing wood biomass and alcohol fuel.

(55) *Mass.* —Deduction is allowed for income from sale, lease, or transfer of property or materials manufactured in Mass., related to energy conservation or alternative energy development, and subject to Mass.-approved patent.

(56) Exempts property used in making gasohol.

(57) *Ariz.* —Registered solar contractors can deduct up to $5,000 of the retail cost of each solar energy device supplied and installed.

(58) *Kan.* —Applies to systems installed pre-1986. Note (59) also applied.

(59) In addition to credit, election to amortize basis of property.

(60) Percentage of tax paid reimbursed. In Kan. applies to systems installed pre-1986. Exempt are electric generation facilities or additions to such facilities, and newly constructed independent electric generation facilities placed into service after 2000.

(61) *Mont.* —Property tax exemption for nonfossil form of energy generation. Grants income tax credit for investment in energy conservation installations; also allowed for commercial energy generated by wind power.

(62) *Ida.* —Insulation added to residence. Deduction spread over 3 yrs. for 1st $5,000 of cost of qualifying alternative energy device added to residence: 40% in 1st yr., 20% in 2nd yr., 20% in 3rd yr., 20% in 4th yr.

(63) *Wis.* —Exempts residential fuels except natural gas and electricity exempt only during Nov.-Apr.

(64) Federal IRC credits adopted.

(65) *La.*—Eff. for tax periods starting after 12-31-2007, credit is allowed for 50% of first $25,000 of cost of eligible wind energy or solar energy systems at qualified residential properties.

(66) *Calif.* —Exempts transfers or leases to or by Calif. Alternative Energy Sources and Advanced Transp. Financing Authority.

(67) *Calif.* —Solar energy systems get lower assessment under Prop. 13.

(68) *Mich.* —For single business tax (until 12-31-2007) and Mich. business tax (eff. 1-1-2008), investment tax credit allowed for tangible non-mobile personalty physically in-state used for an in-state business activity and eligible for depreciation, amortization or accelerated cost recovery under federal IRC.

(69) *N.Y.; N.D.; Wis.* —Solar and wind energy systems. 15-yr. property tax exemption in N.Y. if built pre-7-1-88 or in 1-2-91—12-31-2005. Applies also to geothermal devices in N.D.

(70) *Ky.*—Household fuels exempt; limited exemption for production fuels.

(71) *La.*—Solar energy systems attached to residential buildings or swimming pools.

(72) *S.C.* —Applies to conservation tillage equip., truck-crane, drip-trickle irrigation system for energy conservation and renewable energy production measures.

(73) Localities can grant credit.

(74) *Mich.* —Home heating fuel for residential use taxed at 4% instead of 6%.

(75) *Okla.* —Credit of 50% of amount contributed to Energy Conservation Loan Fund.

FOOTNOTES to chart ¶ 299 (corresponding to numbers in parentheses in the chart):
(continued)

(76) *Calif.*—Deduction allowed for interest paid on a loan financed thru a public utility to purchase energy efficient equipment or products for in-state residences. Deduction is in lieu of any credit for purchasing such items.
(77) *Mich.* —Credits under single business tax (until 12-31-2007) and Mich. business tax (eff. 1-1-2008) for: (1) amount taxpayer's tax liability attributed to qualified business activity under Mich. Next Energy Auth. for tax yr. exceeds taxpayer's baseline tax liability attributed to qualified business activity; (2) qualified alternative energy entity can claim credit for its qualified payroll account.
(78) *Va.*—Sales tax holiday for qualified energy-efficient products, 10-8-2008 through 10-13-2008.
(79) *Va.*—Special classification for certain energy-efficient buildings.
(80) Commercial lenders get credit for energy-related loans.
(81) Cities or towns may exempt any renewable energy system located in the city or town.
(82) 4.5% of purchase price (exclude transportation costs) of coal bought to generate steam and hot water for space heating or industrial processing.
(83) *R.I.* —Credit for cost of purchasing a qualified renewable energy system, which includes either a photovoltaic system, a solar domestic hot water system, a solar space heating system, a geothermal system, or a wind energy system.
(84) *Va.*—Exempts artificial or propane gas, firewood, coal, or home heating oil used for domestic consumption.
(85) *Minn.* —Building supplies for business incubators that use solar technology and energy-efficient appliances. Solar energy systems are exempt.
(86) *N.C.* —Special classification.
(87) *R.I.* —Gross receipts from renewable energy products are exempt from sales-use tax.
(88) *Ind.* —Blended biodiesel tax credits: (a) biodiesel production credit is $1 times gallons of biodiesel produced during tax year and used to produce blended biodiesel; (b) blended biodiesel production credit is $.02 times gallons of blended biodiesel produced at Ind. facility and blended with Ind. produced biodiesel; (c) credit for sale of blended biodiesel to end user is $.01 multiplied by the total number of gallons of blended biodiesel distributed at retail by the taxpayer in a taxable year. Ethanol production tax credit is $.125 multiplied by gallons of ethanol produced at Ind. facility.
(89) *D.C.* —Sales of residential heating oil, residential natural or artificial gas and residential electricity exempt.
(90) Credits for renewable fuel facilities: 15% of cost constructing and installing the part of the dispensing facility that is directly and exclusively used for dispensing or storing renewable fuel; and 25% of the cost of constucting and equipping the facility.
(91) *N.Y.* —25% of qualified solar energy system equipment expenditures (capped at $5,000). Credit includes equipment using solar radiation to provide heating, cooling or hot water.
(92) *Me.*—Until 12-31-2007, credit for qualified community wind power generators.
(93) *Me.*—Exemption for sales to qualified community wind power generator for use in directly and primarily in generating electricity.
(94) *Va.*—20% of sum paid by an individual as sales-use tax, up to $500 per taxable yr., in purchasing certain energy-efficient appliances and equipment for taxpayer's own use.
(95) (Reserved.)
(96) *Utah* —Exemption for certain renewable energy production facilities leased more than 7 yrs. or acquired after 6-30-2004 and before 6-30-2009 and having an economic life of 5 or more yrs.
(97) *Vt.*—Exemption for hot water heating systems that convert solar energy into thermal energy used to heat water.
(98) *Iowa* —Following credits allowed against corporate income and financial institution franchise taxes: (a) wind production credit for each kilowatt-hour of qualified electricity that owner sells during first 10 yrs. from date qualified facility was originally placed in service; and (b) renewable energy credit for a purchaser or producer of renewable energy whose facility has been approved by the Iowa utilities bd.
(99) *S.C.* —25% of costs of installing a solar energy heating or cooling system or a solar energy system for the generation of electricity in a facility in the state and owned by the taxpayer; limited to lesser of $3,500 or 50% of tax liability.
(100) *Conn.* —Exemptions are provided for home weatherization products, compact fluorescent light bulbs, solar energy electricity generating systems, passive or active solar water or space heating systems, geothermal resource systems and ice storage systems.
(101) *Ky.* —Tax refund for manufacturing machinery or equipment that reduces energy consumption by 15%.
(102) *Ky.* —Companies that invest in renewable energy facilities that use solar, wind or other alternative energy sources may qualify for recoupment of up to 100% of sales and incentives.
(103) *Tex.* —Sales of specified Energy Star qualified products are exempt 5-24-2008 through 5-26-2008.

CALENDARS

¶300 Overview of calendars and abbreviations used. ¶ 305 through ¶ 380 list report, payment, and other pertinent tax dates (1) requiring positive action on the part of the taxpayer, or (2) alerting taxpayers to impending action that will affect or determine their tax status. Those paragraphs show the subject of the levy or the entity taxed. For income taxes, fiscal year returns and payment are generally due in months corresponding to calendar year return dates shown.

Calendars, at ¶ 305 through ¶ 360, for each of the 12 months, list the annual, semi-annual, quarterly, and other non-monthly dates that concern a taxpayer throughout the year. **Recurring monthly dates,** those that come up every month, are listed separately in the special calendar at ¶ 380.

The final date for action is the one usually given where an act can be performed over a period of time. No cognizance is taken of Sundays and holidays, because in such cases the taxpayer's time is generally extended to the next business day.

Unemployment insurance dates are listed at ¶ 272.

Abbreviations: In the calendar entries, state and local officials and other terms are designated by these abbreviations:

ABC	=	Alcoholic Beverage Commission
Acctg.	=	Accounting
Accts.	=	Accounts
Admin. or Admn.	=	Administration
Admr.	=	Administrator
Agri.	=	Agriculture
Al. Bev.	=	Alcoholic Beverages
Assmt.	=	Assessment
Assn.	=	Association
Assr.	=	Assessor
Appl.	=	Appeal
ATB	=	Appellate Tax Board
Atty. Gen.	=	Attorney General
Bd.	=	Board
BEQ	=	Board of Equalization
BTA	=	Board of Tax Appeals
Bur.	=	Bureau
Cal.	=	Calendar
Clk.	=	Clerk
Co.	=	Company
Coll.	=	Collector
Comptr.	=	Comptroller
Comm. or Comn.	=	Commission
Commr. or Comr.	=	Commissioner
Conserv.	=	Conservation
Co-ops	=	Cooperatives
Corp.	=	Corporation
Cos.	=	Companies
Ct.	=	Court
Cty.	=	County
Dept.	=	Department
Dev.	=	Development
Dir.	=	Director
Dist.	=	District
Div.	=	Division
Dom.	=	Domestic
Econ.	=	Economic
Equal.	=	Equalization
Equip.	=	Equipment
Estim.	=	Estimated
Fin.	=	Finance
Fisc.	=	Fiscal
FTB	=	Franchise Tax Board
Franch.	=	Franchise
Gen.	=	General
Info	=	Information
Ins.	=	Insurance
Lic.	=	License; Licensing
LLC	=	Limited liability company
LLP	=	Limited liability partnership
Machy	=	Machinery
Merch.	=	Merchants
Mfrs.	=	Manufacturers
MV	=	Motor Vehicle
Mo.	=	Month
O&G	=	Oil and Gas
Org.	=	Organization
Pbgh.	=	Pittsburgh
Phila.	=	Philadelphia
Prop.	=	Property
PSC	=	Public Service Commission or Commissioner
Pub.	=	Public
PUC	=	Public Utility Commission or Commissioner
Pyt.	=	Payment
Qtr.	=	Quarter
RR	=	Railroad
Recr.	=	Receiver
Reg.	=	Regulation
Rev.	=	Revenue; Revenues
Ry.	=	Railway
SBE	=	State Board of Equalization
Sch.	=	School
Secy., Sec'y, or Sec'y.	=	Secretary
Serv.	=	Services

St.	=	State
STC	=	State Tax Commission
Suprvsr.	=	Supervisor
Supt.	=	Superintendent
TAB	=	Tax Appeal Board
Tax.	=	Taxation
Tel. or Tele.	=	Telegraph or telephone
Transp.	=	Transportation
Treas.	=	Treasurer; Treasury
Val.	=	Valuation
Wgts.	=	Weights
Yr.	=	Year

¶305 JANUARY CALENDAR

For RECURRING MONTHLY dates, see ¶ 380.
For UNEMPLOYMENT INSURANCE report dates, see ¶ 272.

Martin Luther King's Birthday: All States follow Fed law in observing Martin Luther King Jr. Day on the 3rd Monday in January.

ALABAMA 1	Property—Levy on personalty for nonpayment begins after this date.
1	Property—Taxes become delinquent
1	Specified utilities—Report, pay license tax to Dept. Rev.
1	Dry cleaning fee—Quarterly report, payment due to Dept. Rev.
15	Income—Individual estimate and/or installment to Dept. Rev.
3rd Mon.	Property—Return on Assr.'s demand between Jan. 1 and this date
20	Sales-use-rental—Quarterly return, payment if liability averages less than $200 per month during past calendar yr.
20	Sales-use-rental—Annual return, payment if sales tax due for past cal. yr. not more than $10
30	Forest products—Manufacturers, exporters—report, pay to Dept. Rev.
30	Lodgings—Report, pay annually to Dept. Rev.
31	Income—Quarterly withholding report, pay to Dept. Rev.; wage & tax statements to employees
31	Fuel-use—Motor carriers file quarterly report, pay to Dept. Rev.
ALASKA 1	Property—Commonly chosen assessment date
1	Corporations—Biennial report, pay to Dept. Commerce and Econ. Dev.
15	Property—Oil and gas businesses file business property statement with Rev. Dept.
15	Property—File homestead exemption claim with clerk or Cty. Assr.
31	Business license—Biennial renewal, initial to Commr. Rev.
31	Corporations—Biennial report, payment (last day without penalty)
ARIZONA 1	Property—Property assessed as of this date; liens attach
10	Utilities—File estimated revenue statement with Corp. Comm. if gross operating revenue over $250,000.
15	Personal income—Report, pay final estimated tax installment to Dept. Rev. if income is $75,000 or more
20	Sales-use—Quarterly or annual report, pay Dept. Rev. if authorized
25	Motor carriers—Report, pay motor carrier tax to Director of Transportation
31	Withholding—Quarterly return, pay Dept. Rev.; wage & tax statement.
ARKANSAS 1	Property—Assessment date (not stock of merchants or mfrs.)
1st Mon.	Property—Lien attaches
15	Personal income—Farmers file estimated return and pay tax to Dept. Fin. & Admn. if 2/3 of gross income is from farming
20	Gross receipts—sales—Quarterly report, pay to Dept. Fin. & Admn. if monthly tax is not over $100
25	Liquefied gas—Interstate users quarterly report and payment to Dept. Fin. & Admin.
31	Withholding—Employer's statement to employee
31	Motor fuel—Interstate users quarterly report and payment to Dept. Fin. & Admin.
31	Distillate special fuels—Interstate user's quarterly report and payment to Dept. Fin. & Admn.
CALIFORNIA 1	Property—Taxes are a lien on property
1	Property—Assessment date generally
15	Carriers—Quarterly report, also (not RRs and vessel operators) gross operating revenue fee to PUC
15	Income—Estimate and/or installment to FTB
31	Withholding—Quarterly report, pay to Employment Dev. Dept.
31	Sales-use—Report, pay (or balance after prepayment) to SBE
31	Withholding—Annual reconciliation return delinquent if not filed by this date

31 Use fuel—Quarterly report, pay to SBE
31 Timber yield—Timber owners report-pay yield tax to SBE
31 Personal income—Information statement must be given to recipients of $600 or more

COLORADO 1 Sales—Biennial license renewal from Exec. Dir.
1 Property—Assessment and lien day.
15 Personal income—Quarterly estimate to Dept. Rev.
15 Utilities—Quarterly maintenance fee to Dept. Rev.
15 Severance (molybdenum ore)—Report, pay quarterly installment to Dept. Rev.
20 Sales-use—Annual report, payment to Dept. Rev. if average tax liability is $15 or less per month
20 Sales-use—Quarterly report, pay to Dept. Rev. if average tax liability is under $300 per month
31 Withholding—Quarterly report, pay to Dept. Rev. if under $7,000 withheld in a year; information report to employee

CONNECTICUT 15 Personal income—File, pay quarterly estimated tax and estimated composite payments to Tax Commr.
31 Sales-use—Quarterly report, pay to Tax Commr.
31 Sales-use—Annual return (by permission, sales not over $1000), pay to Tax Commr.
31 Use—Annual individual return, pay to Tax Commr.
31 Motor carrier road—Quarterly report, pay to Tax Commr.
31 Oil—Refiners and distributors quarterly report, pay added tax to Tax Commr.
31 Carriers—Apply for identification stamps and cab cards to PUC
31 Utilities—Gross earnings quarterly report and payment to Commr. Rev. Serv.
31 Personal income—Send employees Fed. form W-2 showing tax withheld
31 Petroleum importers—Over $100,000 worth of deliveries, report, pay quarterly to Commr. Rev. Serv.

DELAWARE 1 RRs—Quarterly fee to Div. Fin.
1 Licenses—Mfrs., contractors, wholesalers, food processors, feed dealers, restaurant and farm machinery retailers renew license
15 Personal income—Estimate, pay to Dept. Fin.
15 Wilmington earned income—Quarterly payment to Dept. Fin.
30 Motor carriers fuel purchase—Carriers file and pay Dept. Public Safety
31 Leasing use & lessors' license—Quarterly report, pay to Dept. Fin.
31 Use (tangible personalty leases)—Lessor must report, pay to Dept. Fin.
31 Withholding—Annual report, pay to Div. Rev. (if allowed)
31 Withholding—Statements to employees
31 Withholding—Quarterly return, pay to Dept. Rev. when withholding for lookback 12-month period not over $3,600
31 Wilmington earned income—Quarterly report to Dept. Fin.

DISTRICT OF COLUMBIA 1 Property—Assessment date for realty
15 Personal income—Estimated return and/or installment to Office of Tax and Revenue
15 Income—Final return, pay Office of Tax and Revenue in lieu of Jan. 15 declaration and estimated installment
20 Sales-use—Annual return, payment if monthly tax under $50
20 Withholding—Annual return, pay to Office of Tax and Revenue (annual filers)
30 Sales-use taxes—Report and pay tax on amounts not reported in monthly returns to Office of Tax and Revenue (30 days after close of vendor's tax year)
31 Withholding—Wage statements to employees
31 Withholding—Annual reconciliation to Office of Tax and Revenue

FLORIDA 1 Corporate income—Estimate and/or installment to Dept. Rev.
1 Property—Assessment date
1 Property—Lien attaches

1 Diesel fuel and motor fuel use tax—Motor carriers report, pay to Dept. of Highway Safety and Motor Vehicles
1 Severance tax—Quarterly estimated payment to Dept. Rev.
31 Property—Pay Cty. Coll. for 2% discount
GEORGIA 1 Property—Assessment date for state and county taxes
2 Property—MV dealers file inventory returns
15 Personal income—Farmers' and fishermen's return, pay to Commr. Rev. if no estimated tax paid
15 Income—Estimated and/or installment to Commr. Rev.
20 Sales-use—If tax under $200 (max.) for six consecutive mos., quarterly report, pay to Commr. Rev.
20 Public service corporations—Pay PSC fee to Commr. Rev.
31 Withholding—Quarterly report, annual reconciliation, receipts to Commr. Rev.
31 Withholding—Statements to employees
31 Income—Final return, pay to Commr. Rev. if no estimated returns filed
31 Property—DeKalb Cty. apply for homestead exemption to Cty. Tax Recr.
31 Motor carriers—Quarterly motor fuel tax report, pay to Commr. Rev.
HAWAII 1 Property—Assessment and lien date for upcoming 7-1—6-30 fiscal year
15 Withholding—Quarterly payment by permittees if annual liability $5,000 or less
15 Property—Realty report (if required) to district Assr.
15 Glass container importers—Report, pay advance disposal fee to Dept. Health
20 Personal income—Pay fourth quarter estimated tax to Dept. Tax
20 Corporation income—Pay ¼ of estimated tax to Dept. Tax
31 Withholding—Employers give employees annual wage and withholding statements
31 General excise (sales) and use—Report, pay last quarter if annual tax not over $4,000
31 MV registration—State and county weight tax due
IDAHO 1 Property—Assessment and lien day
25 Oil & Gas production—Quarterly report, pay to Oil & Gas Comm.
30 Income—Wage & tax statements to employees
31 Withholding—Quarterly report, pay Tax Comm. if quarterly tax under $600
ILLINOIS 1 Property—Realty assessment date; lien attaches
1 Property—Owners of airports apply to chief county assessment officer for special assessment
1 RRs—All in-state property, except noncarrier realty, is assessed by Dept. Rev.
10 Utilities—Quarterly payment of gross revenue tax to Commerce Comm. (plus annual return)
10 MVs—Semiannual mileage weight report, pay Sec'y State
15 Personal income—Estimate and/or installment to Dept. Rev.
20 Motor fuel—Distributors producing/blending less than 10,000 proof gallons file annual report
20 Sales-use—Annual return, pay to Dept. Rev. if average monthly tax under $50
20 Sales-use—Quarterly return, pay to Dept. Rev. if average monthly tax under $200
30 Electric suppliers—Report, pay gross revenue tax to Commerce Comm.
31 Utilities (telecommunications excise tax)—File quarterly return if authorized or annual return and pay gross revenue tax to Commerce Comm. if total tax under $400
31 Property—File verified application for registered land or conservation rights valuation with chief county assmt. officer
31 Special fuel—Motor fuel use tax licensees make quarterly report, pay to Dept. Rev.
31 Motor carriers—Report miles traveled and gallons of fuel used

31	Withholding—Quarterly return, pay to Dept. Rev.
31	Withholding—Annual wage statements to employees
31	Property—File certificate supporting exemption with chief county assmt. officer
31	Property—Record owner or owner of beneficial interest in property with certificate of rehabilitation files affidavit with chief county assmt. officer
31	Property—Owners of open space land apply to chief county assessment officer for special assessment; claim open-space realty or lose right to do so
31	Hotel operators—If monthly tax $200 (max.), report, pay quarterly to Dept. Rev.; annual return if monthly tax $50 (max.)
31	Utilities (gross receipts tax on electricity and gas)—Quarterly report, pay to Dept. Rev. if authorized and monthly tax isn't over $100
31	Utilities (gross receipts tax on electricity and gas)—Annual return, pay to Dept. Rev. if authorized and average monthly tax isn't over $20
31	Property—Last day to apply to chief county assessment officer for alternate valuation of model home
INDIANA 1	Utilities—Quarterly public utility fee to PSC
15	Property—Mobile homes assessment date
15	Adjusted gross income—Report, pay 4th estimated installment
30	Adjusted gross income—Annual return, pay Dept. Rev. in lieu of estimate
30	Adjusted gross income—Withholding statement incl. CAGIT-CEDIT-COIT to employee
31	Adjusted gross income—Corps. report, pay quarter if estimate exceeds gross income tax by $1000
31	Sales-use—Quarterly report, pay to Dept. Rev. if average monthly tax is $75 or less
31	Sales-use—Semiannual report, pay to Dept. Rev. if average monthly tax isn't over $25
31	Sales-use—Annual return, pay to Dept. Rev. if average monthly tax is $10 or less
31	Adjusted gross income—Quarterly withholding to Dept. Rev. if $75 (max) average monthly in previous calendar year
31	Adjusted gross income—Semi-annual withholding if average monthly tax in previous yr. is not over $25
31	Motor carrier fuel tax—Quarterly report, pay to Dept. Rev.
31	Financial institutions—Quarterly estimated tax report, pay to Dept. Rev. if annual tax over $1,000
IOWA 1	Property—Assessment day
1	Railroads—Plats of new lines to Cty. Treas.
31	Personal income—Quarterly estimate to Dept. Rev.
31	Income—Information return to Dept. Rev.
31	Sales-use—Quarterly report, pay to Dept. Rev.
31	Withholding—Quarterly return, pay to Dept. Rev.; wage & tax statement
31	Foreign corps. (old law)—Annual report, pay fee to avoid forfeiture
31	Pipeline cos.—Annual inspection fee to Commerce Comm.
31	Domestic corp. (old law) report, fee—Avoid fee by dissolving-filing publication proof with Sec'y State
31	Special Fuel—Distributors quarterly report, pay to Dept. Rev.
KANSAS 1	Property—Assessment date
1	Property—Mobile home park owner/operator submits list of manufactured homes to Cty. Clerk or Appraiser
15	Personal income—Estimate, pay to Dir. Tax.
15	Utilities—MV carriers register vehicles with Corp. Comm.
15	Income—Farmers and fishermen file-pay estimates, if no final return by 3-1
25	Sales-use—Quarterly report (if calendar year tax is over $80 but under $3,200); annual report ($80 or less), pay to Dir. Rev.
25	Tire tax—Report, pay annually if annual tax under $80, or for qtr. if annual tax $80–$1,600.

25 Withholding — Quarterly report-pay to Dir. Tax if tax $200–$1200 per year
25 Withholding — Annual report-pay to Dir. Rev. if tax $200 or less for calendar year
31 Interstate motor fuel use — quarterly report, pay to Div. Tax.
31 Property — Banks report capital, income, etc. to Assr.
KENTUCKY 1 Property — Assessment date
1 Property (2nd class cities) — BEQ hears appeals not later than this date
1 Property — Distillery bonded warehouse report to Dept. of Rev. and Cty. Ct. Clerk
1 Property — Bank or trust co. report on common trust funds to Prop. Val. Admn.
1 Property — Tax on distilled spirits in bonded warehouse or federal premises is delinquent if not paid 9–15
15 Personal income — Estimate, pay tax to Dept. of Rev.
31 Income — Quarterly withholding, report-pay, if withholding for any quarter is less than $900 reconciliation statement to Dept. of Rev.; statements to employee
31 Property — S&L Assn. report to Dept. of Rev.
31 Gasoline — Users quarterly report and pay to Dept of Rev.
31 Motor carrier fuel use — Quarter report, pay to Dept. of Rev.
31 Withholding — Employer furnishes employee with annual statement.
31 Louisville license — Employer's info and quarterly return, pay Commrs. Sinking Fund
31 Paducah payroll — Employee's return to City Treas.; employer's info and quarterly return, pay City Treas.
31 Lexington license — Employer's information and quarterly return, pay City Treas.
31 Covington license — Employer's report, pay to Lic. Inspector
LOUISIANA 1 Property — Assessment date
1 Licenses — Annual occupational license tax due
15 Income — Farmers or individuals estimate, pay tax to Sec'y Rev.
25 Special fuel — Interstate users report, pay to Sec'y Rev.
30 Utilities — Report, pay to Sec'y Rev.
31 Natural gas lines — Report, pay franchise tax to Sec'y Rev.
31 Withholding — Quarterly and annual returns, pay to Sec'y Rev.
31 Withholding — Employer's annual report, pay to Sec'y Rev.; statement to employees.
MAINE 15 Personal income — Pay quarterly estimated to Rev. Services
15 Sales-use — Quarterly, semi-annual, annual returns, payments to Rev. Services
31 Withholding — Quarterly report, pay to Rev. Services
MARYLAND 1 Property — General assessment date (triennial)
15 Personal income — Farmers, fishermen, estimate, pay tax unless final return-pay by 3-1
15 Personal income — Final estimate and pay to Comptr.
21 Sales-use — Small vendors report, pay quarterly to Retail Sales Tax Div.
31 Personal income — Final report, pay to Comptr. if no estimate filed
31 Withholding — Quarterly report, pay to Comptr.
31 Income — Employee withholding wage statement to employees
MASSACHUSETTS 1 Property — Assessment date; lien attaches to realty
15 Personal income — Estimated tax installment to Commr. Rev.
20 Sales-use — Quarterly report, pay to Commr. Rev. if tax is over $100 but under $1200 for calendar year; annual report-pay if tax is $100 or less for calendar year if allowed
30 Imported fuels tax — Carriers report, pay Commr. Rev. for prior calendar quarter
30 Transporters of hazardous waste — Report, pay Dept. of Environmental Protection
31 Withholding — Quarterly (or monthly) return, payment for period ended Dec. 31
31 Personal income — Withholding return, payment for calendar yr. ended Dec. 31 (max. withheld $100)

31	Personal income—Employer must give employees statement of tax withheld
31	Pipeline cos.—Return to State Tax Commr.
MICHIGAN 1	Canal, harbor cos.—Report to Sec'y State
1st Mon.	River improvement cos.—Report to Sec'y State
1st Mon.	Water and water power companies—Report to Sec'y State
1st Mon.	Power companies—Report to Sec'y State
2d Mon.	Street Railways—Report to Sec'y State
9	In 4th class cities, pay county, city and school taxes to city treas.
9	Property—Pay 4th class city taxes (if one tax roll, all taxes due; if two tax rolls, county and school taxes due)
10	Telegraph cos.—Report to Sec'y State and Cty. Clerk
15	Personal income—Report, pay 4th quarter estimate
15	Personal income tax—Farmers and fishermen make tentative annual return/payment to Dept. Treas. if elected
15	Single Business Tax—Farmers and fishermen make tentative annual return/payment to Dept. Treas. if elected
15	Single business tax—Optional quarterly 1% estimate/payment for previous quarter to Dept. Treas.
20	Withholding—Quarterly report, pay to Dept. Treas.
20	Motor carrier fuel—Quarterly report, pay to Dept. Treas.
20	Motor fuel exporters—Quarterly report, pay to Dept. Treas.
20	Motor fuel vendors—Quarterly report, pay to Dept. Treas.
20	Motor fuel vendors—Annual report to Dept. Treas.
20	Retail diesel fuel dealers—Quarterly report, pay to Dept. Treas.
20	Motor fuel tank wagon operator-importers—Quarterly report, pay to Dept. Treas.
20	Motor fuel transporters—Quarterly report to Dept. Treas.
20	Motor fuel—Quarterly LP gas report, pay to Dept. Treas.
31	Boundary river improvement cos.—Report to Cty. Clerk
31	Single business tax—Estimate and quarterly payment
31	Withholding—Employers' statement of wages furnished to employees
MINNESOTA 1	Airlines cos.—Pay tax to Commr. Rev.
2	Property—Assessment and lien date
15	Personal income—Estimate, pay to Commr. Rev.
15	Income—Farmers file, pay estimated tax, instead of final return by 3-1
15	Aviation—Aircraft mfrs. report to Commr. Trans.
20	Sales-use—Quarterly report, pay to Commr. Rev.
20	Liquor gross receipts—Quarterly report, pay to Commr. Rev.
31	Income—Employee withholding wage statement and/or information return
31	Withholding—Quarterly return, pay to Commr. Rev.
31	Motor carriers—Report, pay quarterly road tax to Dept. Rev.
MISSISSIPPI 1	Property—Assessment and lien date
15	Personal income—Individuals/farmers estimate, pay to Commr. Income Tax
15	Withholding—Quarterly report, pay to Commr. if given permission
15	Timber—Quarterly (if qualified) report, pay to Tax. Commr.
20	Sales-use—Quarterly report, pay to Tax Commr., if allowed
30	Oil severance—Quarterly report to Tax Commr.
31	Fuel use—Interstate permittees quarterly report, pay to Tax Comm.
31	Withholding—Annual statement to employees, copy to Tax Commr.; annual reconciliation report to Tax Commr.
MISSOURI 1	Gasoline—Statement electing tax base to Dir. Rev.
1	Property—Ownership and valuation date
1	Merchants, manufacturers—Inventory listing date (state and Kansas City)
1	Merchants, manufacturers (State, Cty., School)—Payment due if business commenced after 1st Mon. in Jan.
1	Property—Real and tangible property taxes become delinquent
2	Property (Kansas City)—BEQ meets
2	Property—Merchants, manufacturers (Kansas City)—BEQ meets

1st Mon. Merchants, manufacturers (St. Louis City)—Tax based on highest value of machy and equip. between this date and 1st Mon. in Apr.
15 Personal income—Estimate, pay Dir. Rev.
15 Utilities—Assessment for expenses of PSC; quarterly installment
25 Earnings (Kansas City)—Employer's quarterly withholding report, pay Fin. Dir.
30 Gasoline—Interstate special fuel users report, pay to Dir. Rev.
30 Minerals—Mine inspection fee, report, pay Dir. Rev.
31 Sales-use—Quarterly or annual report, pay to Dir. Rev.
31 Withholding—Quarterly return and annual reconciliation
31 Income—1–15 estimate (individuals, farmers) avoided by final return.
31 St. Louis earnings—Quarterly withholding report, pay to Coll. Rev.
31 Motor fuels—Pay special fuel use decal fee to Dir. Rev.
31 Gasoline—Report, pay fuel inspection fee (annual basis) to Dir. Agric.
31 St. Louis City payroll expense tax—Report, pay qtrly. tax to Coll. Rev.

MONTANA 1 Petroleum products—Renew license with State Sealer of Wgts. & Measures
1 Property—Assessment
15 Personal income—Pay 4th quarterly estimated tax to Dept. Rev. (15th day of month fol. tax year)
30 Minerals—Micaceous mines operators quarterly report to Dept. Rev.
30 Minerals—Coal severance tax—Coal mine operators and coal dealers, quarterly report, pay to Dept. Rev.
30 Lodgings—Owner or operator of facility pay quarterly lodgings tax to Dept. Rev.
30 Utilities—Motor carriers pay annual fee to PSC
30 Minerals—Cement and gypsum producers and dealers quarterly report to Dept. Rev.
30 Utilities—Electrical supply producers quarterly report, pay license tax to Dept. Rev.
31 Personal income—Employers give annual withholding statement to employees
31 Withholding—Quarterly return, pay to Commr. Rev.
31 Special fuel—Users' quarterly or annual report, pay to Dept. Rev.
31 Minerals—Qtrly. report of new or interim production of petroleum or other mineral or crude oil to Dept. Rev.
31 Property—File refund claim with Bd. Cty. Commrs.

NEBRASKA 1 Property—Assessment day; lien attaches
1 Property—Homestead exemption eligibility found as of this date
1 Agricultural use—Special assmt. eligibility determined
1 Property—Realty assessment roll prepared
1 Property—Realty taxes for previous year due to Cty. Treas.
1 Property—Personalty listed and assessed
1 Property—Exempt organizations file affidavit that ownership and use of exempt property hasn't changed
1 Intrastate motor carriers—Permit fee to State Public Service. Comm.
15 Personal income—Estimate, pay final installment to Dept. Rev.
15 Personal income—Farmers, ranchers, fishermen pay estimated tax to Dept. Rev.
15 Property—Annual report to Cty. Assr. by owner, lessee or manager of cabin trailer or mobile home parks
25 Sales-use—State and city 2003 annual and quarterly return, pay to Dept. Rev.
25 Tire fee—Quarterly return, pay to Dept. Rev.
31 Withholding—Quarterly report, pay to Dept. Rev.
31 Property—Last day to renew mobile home park permit
31 Agricultural excise taxes and fees (potato, wheat, soybean, corn, dry bean, grain, sorghum)—First purchasers or shippers pay to appropriate board in Dept. of Agriculture

31 Motor vehicle and diesel fuel interstate truckers—Report, pay tax to Dept. Rev.

NEVADA 1 Utilities—Pay 3rd quarter of assessment to Public Utility Comm.
1 Property—Inspect completed tax roll
1st Mon. Property—Pay 3rd quarter installment to Cty. Treas.
15 Property—Last day to file with Cty. BEQ appeals
31 Special fuels—Dealers or users report, pay Dept. MVs
31 Sales-use—Quarterly return, pay to Dept. Tax.
31 Sales-use—Quarterly short-term passenger car lessor return, payment due to Dept. Tax.

NEW HAMPSHIRE 15 Refined petroleum products—Quarterly report, pay to Dept. Rev. Admn.
15 Refined petroleum products—Estimate, pay one-third tax to Dept. Rev. Admn.
15 Utilities—Retailers file quarterly return, pay communications services tax to Dept. Rev. Admn.
15 Income—Individuals quarterly return due
31 Road toll—Fuel users (not motor fuel) report, pay for 4th quarter to Dir. of MV Div.

NEW JERSEY 1 Corporation business—Lien attaches
1 Property—Depreciated value and improvements assessment date
1 RRs—Property assessments date; lien attaches
1 Property—Lien attaches to realty
9 Property—File claim for depreciated value assessment.
15 Personal income (gross income tax)—Pay 4th quarter estimate to Div. Tax; pay full tax if first estimate (including farmers or $100 taxpayers)
15 Withholding—Employers quarterly report, pay to Div. Tax if aggregate withheld is under $500 per month of calendar quarter
15 Al. bev.—Mfrs., distributors, etc., report, pay to Div. Tax for Nov. and Dec.
20 Sales-use—Quarterly report, pay to Dir. Tax, return must be received by this date
20 Sales-use—Direct payment permittees report, pay to Div. Tax., return must be received by this date
20 Public community water system—Owners or operators report, pay to Dir. Tax.
25 Petroleum products—Refiners and distributors quarterly report, pay to Dir. Tax, return must be received by this date
25 Cable TV “franchise revenue”—Cable TV cos. file with chief financial officer of each municipality and pay tax
25 Major hazardous waste facilities—Owners, operators report, pay to Chief fiscal officer of locality
31 Fuels use—Quarterly report, payment to Dir. M.V.
31 Withholding (gross income)—Quarterly report, pay to Div. Tax. (withholding $200 monthly)

NEW MEXICO 1 Property—Assessment date; lien attaches
20 Inspection and supervision fee—Utilities and carriers doing in-state business, pay full or quarter tax to Corp. Comm.
25 Special fuels supplier tax—Users' quarterly report, payment to Tax. and Rev. Dept.
25 Special fuels supplier tax—Users' annual report, payment to Tax. and Rev. Dept., if elected
25 MVs—Quarterly report, pay weight distance tax to Motor Transp. Div.
25 MVs—Pay to Motor Transp. Div. weight distance tax if annual payment elected
31 Withholding—Employers furnish copy of annual withholding statement to employees

NEW YORK 1 Property (NYC)—Pay quarter to City Coll. in borough
1 Property—Valuation date for property assessed as of a March 1 taxable status date
1 Property (NYC)—Third quarter or second half installment due
1 Property—3rd quarterly installment due if assessment not over $40,000

5 Property (NYC)—Taxable status date in N.Y. City; last day to file for certain exemptions
14 NYC property tax—Tentative assessment roll published
15 NYC unincorporated business—Report, pay quarter estimate to Commr.Rev.
15 E-911 surcharge—Return and payment due
15 Personal Income (also NYC)—Pay 4th quarter estimate to Dept. Tax. & Fin.; estimate and full tax if farmer, fisherman or under $50 taxpayer or initial estimate
25 NYC utility tax—Semi-annual return and payment due
27 Gasoline—Diesel truckers (not retail vendor or bulk user) annual return to Dept. Tax. & Fin. if all purchases retail
31 Highway use—Annual return, pay, and quarterly report, pay to Misc. Tax Bur.
31 Fuel use—Quarterly report, pay to Misc. Tax Bur.
31 Property—Realty taxes due, pay Cty. Treas.
31 Cigarette—Dealers' licenses expire
31 LLC/LLP—Filing fee for calendar year filers due

NORTH CAROLINA 1 Property—Assessment and lien date
1 Property—Mobile home park operators' report to cty. assr.
1 Property—Marina owner reports to cty. assr.
1 Property—Rental of airplane storage space report to cty. assr.
6 Property—Last day to pay without penalty
15 Personal income—Final estimated installment to Sec'y Rev.
15 Personal income—Farmers and fishermen make only declaration and payment of estimated tax
15 Property—Persons having custody of tangible personalty of others report to Cty. Assr. last day to file without penalty
31 Sales-use—Report, pay quarterly tax to Sec'y. Rev.
31 Withholding—Employers furnish employees wage statements
31 Withholding—Quarterly report, pay Sec'y Rev.
31 Severance—Report, pay quarterly forest products tax to Sec'y Rev.
31 Motor carriers—Report, pay road use tax to Sec'y. Rev.
31 Alternative fuels—Bulk-end users file information return with Sec'y. Rev.
31 Motor fuels—Distributors apply to Sec'y Rev. for quarterly refund
31 Public utilities—Quarterly franchise tax report, pay to Sec'y Rev.
31 Newsprint publisher tax—Annual report, pay to Sec'y Rev.

NORTH DAKOTA 1 Property—Realty lien attaches
15 Income—Final installment of estimated tax to Tax Commr.
15 Corporate income—Pay quarterly estimate to Tax Commr.
31 Sales-use—Quarterly report, pay Tax Commr.
31 Withholding—Annual report to Tax Commr.; wage and tax statements to employees
31 Withholding—Quarterly return and payment to Tax Commr.
31 Motor fuels—Importers for use of gasoline and special fuels report, pay to Tax Commr.

OHIO 1 Property—Assessment and lien date
15 Personal income—Quarterly estimate and/or pay State Treas.
23 Sales-use—Vendor-seller's report, pay to State Treas.
23 Sales-use—Direct permit holders report, pay to State Treas.
23 Sales-use—Semi-annual return, pay State Treas.: counties—Adams, Allen, Ashland, Ashtabula, Athens, Auglaize, Belmont, Brown, Butler, Carroll, Champaign, Clark, Clermont, Clinton, Columbiana, Coshocton, Crawford, Montgomery
23 Consumer use tax—Pay to State Treas.
30 Property—Apply to county auditor for reduced valuation of property injured or destroyed during preceding quarter
31 Withholding—Quarterly report, pay to Tax Commr.
31 Corporate income—Estimate, pay State Treas. unless final return-payment made
31 Withholding—Annual reconciliation to Tax Commr. annual statements to employees
31 Cigarette—Dealers semiannual report, pay State Treas.

31 Highway use tax—Quarterly report, pay to State Treas.

OKLAHOMA 1 Property—General assessment date

15 Income—Corporations, individuals report, pay quarterly estimated tax to Tax Comm.

20 Withholding—Quarterly report-pay to Tax Comm. if tax under $500 per quarter

20 Sales-use—Semiannual report, payment by group three vendors and taxpayers owing $50 or less for any one mo.

30 Property—Textile mfrs. report to cty. assr., pay to cty. treas.

30 Mine operators—Report, pay to Dept. of Mines

31 Withholding—Annual statement to employees and recipients with payments of winnings.

31 Withholding—Report and pay on withholdings from nonresident aliens or foreign corps.; report to payees

31 Motor fuel importers use—Quarterly report, pay Tax Commr.

OREGON 15 Personal income—Pay 4th estimated payment to Dept. Rev. (15th day of 9th month after due date)

20 Use fuel—Report, pay quarterly if monthly under $100 to Div. MV (Dept. Trans.)

30 Employers give copies of withholding return to employees

31 Personal income—Report, pay last quarter withholding to Dir. Rev.

31 Forest products harvests—Annual report pay Dept. Rev.

31 Timber (Eastern & Western Ore.) severance—Annual report, pay to Dir. Rev.

31 Forest products harvest tax—Quarterly estim. report, pay to Dept. Rev.

31 Timber severance taxes (East and West Ore.)—Quarterly estim. report, pay to Dept. Rev.

PENNSYLVANIA 1 RRs—Coal and coke report to Dept. Rev.

1 Property (dists., optional tax sale procedure)—Realty claims filed 6-30 become absolute unless paid or compromised

1 Realty (unseated land in 7th and 8th class Cty)—Interest added to unpaid taxes for year

1 Mercantile license (Pbgh.)—Annual license from City Treas.

15 Personal income—Pay quarterly estimated tax payment to Dept. Rev.

15 Phila. City estimated net profits—Fourth quarter installment report, payment due to Phila. Dept. Rev.

15 Pbgh. City and Sch. Dist. net profits—Fourth quarter report, pay estimated net profits.

20 Sales tax—Quarterly report-pay to Dept. Rev.

20 Sales tax—Annual return (if required), pay to Dept. Rev.

31 Philadelphia wage tax—Employer's quarterly withholding return, pay to Phila. Dept. Rev.

31 Philadelphia wage tax—Employer's annual information return to Phila Dept. Rev. and reconciliation of tax withheld

31 Phila. Sch. Dist. income from property tax—Fiduciaries file information with Phila. Dept. Rev.

31 Pbgh. City & Sch. Dist. earned income—Employer's quarterly withholding; employees return, pay Treas.

31 Pbgh. City & Sch. Dist. earned income—Employees report, pay Treas. tax on earnings not subject to withholding

31 Motor carrier—Quarterly report, pay road tax to Dept. Rev.

31 Withholding—Report, pay last quarter to Dept. Rev.

31 Personal income—Employer's annual reconciliation and report of withheld taxes to Dept. Rev.

RHODE ISLAND 15 Intangibles tax—Banks (including national banks or credit unions) report to Tax Admr.

15 Personal income—Pay last estimated installment, or in full to Tax Admr.

20 Sales—Flea market return to Tax Div. (if tax liability exceeds $120)

30 Property—Last day to apply to assr. for classification as farm, forest or open space for special assmt.

31 Sales-use—Quarterly report, pay to Tax Admr.

31 Withholding—Quarterly report-payment if withholding less than $50 monthly, annual reconciliation to Tax Admr.; statements to employees
31 Motor carrier—Quarterly report, pay to Tax Admr.
SOUTH CAROLINA 1 Motor carriers—Register with, pay PSC
15 Personal income—Pay 4th quarter of estimate to Dept. Rev.
20 Sales-use—Quarterly report, pay Dept. Rev.
20 Property—3% penalty applied for nonpayment
20 Property—Apply to county assessor for special assessment for agricultural realty or homestead
31 Motor carriers—Quarterly report, pay road tax to Dept. Rev.
SOUTH DAKOTA 1 Property—Valuation date
1 Property—Airline flight property tax due
15 Income—Banks and financial orgs. quarterly estimate report-pay to Dept. Rev. and Reg.
30 Energy mineral severance—Report, pay quarterly to Dept. Rev. and Reg.
31 Precious metals severance—File estimate, pay ¼ of estimated tax to Dept. Rev. and Reg.
31 Motor fuel—LPG users file semi-annual report to Dept. Rev. and Reg.
31 Motor fuel—Highway contractors report, pay to Dept. Rev. and Reg.
31 Motor fuel—Carriers permanently licensed as interstate fuel users report, pay to Dept. Rev. and Reg.
TENNESSEE 1 Property—Assessment and lien date
10 Property—Loan cos., investment cos., and cemetery cos. pay tax on stock of shareholders
15 Corporate income—Estimated tax to Commr. Rev.
25 Liquefied gas—Dealer permittees report, pay tax to Commr. Rev.
30 Sales and use—Aviation fuel dealers report, pay tax to Commr. Rev.
31 Highway user fuel—Quarterly report, pay tax to Commr. Rev.
TEXAS 1 Contract carriers—Intangibles assessment
1 Property—Assessment date
20 Sales-use—Quarterly report-pay to Comptr.
25 Gasoline—Motor fuel transporters, interstate truckers report, pay Comptr.
25 Diesel fuel—Motor fuel transporters, interstate truckers, dyed diesel fuel bonded users report, pay Comptr.
25 Liquefied gas—Licensed dealers and licensed interstate truckers report, pay Comptr.
31 Utilities—Last day to file gross receipts quarterly report with, pay Comptr.
31 Hotel occupancy—Quarterly report, pay to Comptr.
31 Property—Fully due, if not paid in Nov., to Cty. Assr.
31 Sulphur producers—Quarterly report to, pay Comptr.
UTAH 1 Property—Assessment day
1 Property—Realty and personalty tax liens attach to realty
1 Property—Apply for "agricultural use" assessment to avoid late fee
1 Mines—Property taxes a lien on mines and mining claims
15 Property—Pay delinquent realty taxes to avoid interest
31 County transient room—Quarterly report, pay to Tax Comm.
31 Sales-use (Cty., municipal)—Quarterly report, pay to Tax Comm.
31 Sales-use—Quarterly return, pay Tax Comm.
31 Withholding—Quarterly reports, pay to Tax Comm.
31 Tobacco products (not cigarettes)—Report, pay quarterly to Tax Comm.
31 Minerals—Pay quarterly withholdings from gross proceeds of uranium or vanadium mines and from mineral production to Tax Comm.
31 Gross receipts—Corporations not paying franchise/income tax and electrical corps. report, pay semiannually to State Tax Comm.

VERMONT	**15**	Personal income—Pay quarterly estimate to Commr. Taxes
	15	Property—File objections to assmt. with town clerk
	25	Bank franchise—Pay Commr. Taxes for last quarter
	25	Meals and rooms—Quarterly return, pay to Commr. Taxes if past yr. tax $500 or less
	25	Withholding—Quarterly report, pay to Commr. Taxes if tax $2,500 or less for quarter
	25	Sales-use—Quarterly return, pay Commr. Taxes if tax more than $500 but less than $2,500 for past yr.
	25	Sales-use—Annual return, pay Commr. Taxes if tax $500 or less for past yr.
	25	Telephone companies—Report, pay qtrly. alt. gross operating revenue tax to Tax Commr.
	30	Withholding—Statements to employees
VIRGINIA	**1**	Property—Assessment date; lien attaches
	1	Corporation registration—Capital stock assessed for fee
	1	Property—Status of taxpayer and value of property determined
	15	Income—Estimated return, to city or county Commr. Rev.; pay city or Cty. Treas.
	15	Income—Farmers file estimate with city or Cty. Commr. Rev.; pay local Treas.
	15	Contractors' use tax—Contractors bringing machinery into Va. report to and pay Tax. Commr.
	15	Hog tax—Pay Treas. any taxes collected between 7-1 and 12-31
	15	Passenger carriers—Pay quarterly road tax to State Treas.
	20	Sales-use—Quarterly report, pay to Tax Commr.
	30	Forest products—Registration fee to Dept. Tax.
	31	Forest products—Limited producers annual (others quarterly) report, pay State Tax Dept.
	31	Withholding—Report, pay to Dept. Tax quarterly if liability sum under $100
	31	Motor carriers—Quarterly report, pay State Treas. on in-state fuel use
WASHINGTON	**1**	Property—Assessment and lien date
	15	Auto transportation cos.—Quarterly report, pay to Utilities & Transp. Comm.
	25	Special fuels—Report, pay to Dept. MV (quarterly, semiannual or annual filers)
	31	Timber harvest—Quarterly payment of excise tax to Dept. Rev.
	31	B & O tax—Report, pay to Dept. Rev. if reporting annually or quarterly
	31	Sales-use—Report, pay to Dept. Rev. if reporting annually or quarterly
	31	Utilities—Report, pay to Dept. Rev. if reporting annually or quarterly
WEST VIRGINIA	**1**	Alcohol—Renew license with ABC Commr.
	15	Personal income—Estimated return and/or pay Tax Commr.
	20	Sales-use—Quarterly return, pay to Tax Commr.
	20	Utilities—Pay special license fee to PSC
	25	Motor fuels—Motor carriers road tax, quarterly report-pay to Tax Commr.
	31	Sales—Annual return to Tax Commr.; quarterly return if tax not over $250 in any month; monthly return for Dec.
	31	Gross sales (B & O):—Annual report, quarterly payment to Tax Commr.
	31	Withholding—Annual or quarterly report, pay to Tax Commr.
	31	Coal severance—Report, pay min. tax to Tax Commr. quarterly if monthly tax under $1,000
	31	Telecommunications—Annual return, pay tax to Tax Commr. (end of month after tax year); quarterly estimated tax if $1,000 or less per month)
	31	Sales—Motor fuel, quarterly report-pay to Tax Commr.
WISCONSIN	**1**	Property—Assessment day shares lien attaches
	1	Property (Mfg.)—Last day for Dept. Rev. to assess
	10	Property—File statement of saw logs or timber in transit with assessor

15 Personal income—Estimate return, pay quarterly to Dept. Rev.
15 Personal Income—Estimate by farmers or fishers (if no final return by 3-1) to Dept. Rev.
31 Withholding—Report, deposit quarterly to designated bank.
31 Sales-use—Report, deposit for quarter to Dept. Rev.
31 Withholding—Annual report to to employees with copy to Dept. Rev.
31 Property—Pay first half realty tax to local Treas.
31 Property—Serve excessive valuation claim on taxation district clerk
31 Withholding—Employers furnish W-2 to employees with copy to Dept. Rev.
31 Personal income—File information returns with Dept. Rev.
31 Acreage tax—Pay to taxation district treasurer
31 Occupation taxes—Operators of grain elevators or warehouses, iron ore concentrate docks, coal docks, crude oil refinery, and mink farms pay taxation district treasurer

WYOMING 1 Property—Taxable property listed, valued, and assessed
10 Tobacco products—Consumers report, pay tax to Dept. Rev. for past quarter
20 Tobacco products—Wholesalers report, pay to Dept. Rev. for past quarter
31 Sales—Non-nexus filers, annual report, pay to Dept. Rev. if tax under $150 during any month.
31 Sales—Quarterly filers report, pay to Dept. Rev. if tax under $150 during any month
31 Property—Last day for car companies to pay delinquent tax and interest to avoid collection by distress and sale
31 Gasoline, diesel fuel—IFTA-licensed carriers report, payment to Dept. Transportation.

¶310 FEBRUARY CALENDAR

For RECURRING MONTHLY dates, see ¶ 380.
For UNEMPLOYMENT INSURANCE report dates, see ¶ 272.

Washington's Birthday: All States follow Fed law in observing Washington's Birthday on 3rd Monday in February.

ALABAMA 1	Transportation, transmission, other utilities—Pay quarterly fee to PUC
Last Mon.	Property—Assessor completes assessment
Last day	Income—Annual withholding reconciliation with copies of W-2s
ARIZONA 1	Gasoline—MV fuel distributors file license application and fee with Vehicle Supt.
28	Income—Information return to Dept. Rev.
28	Oil and gas well cos.—Report to Dept. Rev.
ARKANSAS 28	Income tax—Employers file annual reconciliation with Dept. Fin. & Admin.
CALIFORNIA 1	Oil-gas producer—Assmts. of $500 or more; delinquent 2nd half, added penalty on 1st half
15	Property—Exemption affidavits to county assr.
24	Sales-use—Prepay SBE, if so ordered
28	Income—Information returns to FTB
COLORADO 28	Withholding—Annual reconciliation statement to Dept. Rev.
Last	Property—First half taxes to Cty. Treas.
CONNECTICUT 28	Withholding—Annual reconciliation report and information return to Commr. Rev. Services
DELAWARE 1	Property—Report land use change to Assr. (year of change)
28	Withholding—Annual reconciliation to Div. Rev.
DISTRICT OF COLUMBIA 28	Income—Information returns to Office of Tax and Revenue if paying to residents interest or dividends of at least $10 or other income of $600 or more
FLORIDA 1	Corporate income—Application to Dept. of Rev. for renewable energy production credit due
Last	Property—Pay Cty. Tax Coll. for 1% discount
GEORGIA 28	Withholding—Annual report to Commr. Rev. if quitting business; wage statements
HAWAII 20	Property—Pay 2d half realty tax
28	Income—Information return by persons making payments of $600 or more to Dept. Tax
IDAHO Last day	Withholding—Annual reconciliation and summary to Tax Comm.
Last day	Income tax—Information return to Tax Commr.
ILLINOIS 1	Surplus line producers—Report, pay semiannual tax to Dir. Ins.
15	Utilities—File amended return showing actual gross revenues with Commerce Comm.
28	Withholding—Annual reconciliation to Dept. Rev.
INDIANA 28	Adjusted gross income—File withholding return and informations with Dept. Rev.
Last	Aircraft pays annual registration fees and license excise taxes.
Last	Withholding—Annual information return to Dept. Rev.
IOWA 1	Property—War veteran's assns., religious, charitable, and literary societies and educational institutions file exemption claim
1	Property—Application for pollution control equipment exemption due
1	Property—owners of improved industrial property apply to assr. for partial exemption
15	Property—Supplemental return on Assr.'s demand
28	Income—Information return
Last day	Income—Withholding agents file year-end summary reports
KANSAS Last day	Withholding—Annual reconciliation and wage-tax statements
KENTUCKY 1	Property—Trust or title insurance cos. information returns to Dept. Rev.
1st Mon.	Property (3rd class cities)—Board of supervisors meets
15	Corporations—List of stock and bondholders to Dept. Rev.
15	Property—Insurance cos. report to Dept. Rev.
LOUISIANA 1	Chain stores—Report, pay local Collector
15	Property—State and national banks report to local Assr. and Tax Commr.

First business day after 27	Withholding—Annual return to Sec'y. Rev.
MAINE 1	Property—Commercial forestry excise returns to Rev. Services
1st Mon.	Property—Pay local Coll. to avoid sale of realty
15	Income—Employer provides wage and information statement to employee
28	Income—Information returns and employers' annual wage reconciliation to Rev. Services
MARYLAND 28	Withholding—Annual reconciliation to Comptr.; employee wage and tax statements with copies to Comptr.
MASSACHUSETTS 28	Personal income—Annual reconciliation and periodic withholding returns
MICHIGAN 1	Property—Owner of personalty leased on long-term basis file statement with county assr.
1st Mon.	Telegraph cos.—Pay annual stock tax to state treas.
14	Property—Last day to pay county tax without penalty
20	Property—Statement of personalty to Detroit Assr.
20	Property—Statement of personalty to local assessor or supervisor
25	Motor fuel—Annual report, pay of terminal operators or suppliers operating Mich. terminals to Dept. Treas.
28	Withholding—Annual reconciliation and transmittal of wage and tax statements report to Div. Rev.
MINNESOTA 1	Property—File exemption statement with dist. assr.
1	Unmined taconite and iron sulfides—Producers file reports
5	Sales-use—Annual report, pay to Commr. Rev.
5	Liquor gross receipts—Annual report, pay to Commr. Rev.
15	Property—Business lessor files list of personalty in lessors' possession with Commr. Rev.
15	Property—File exemption claim for pollution control property
15	Severance—Iron ore (not taconite) producers, final report to Commr. Rev.
28	Income—Annual reconciliation return and employee statement copies to Commr. Rev.
28	Income—Promoters who hired nonresident entertainers file annual reconciliation and information return statements with Commr. Rev.
MISSISSIPPI 1	Property—Pay all or first half to Tax Coll.
1	Utilities—Pay STC in-lieu tax on nuclear generating plants
MISSOURI 15	Cigarettes—Apply for wholesaler's annual license from Dir. Rev.
28	Income—Information returns to Dir. Rev.
28	Property (First class counties)—Return of personalty to Assr.
28	Utilities—Motor carriers' annual license fee, pay to Dir. Rev.
28	MVs—Pay Dir. Rev. annual reg. fee on commercial MV
MONTANA 1	Property—Assessment date for nonexempt livestock.
Last	Withholding—Annual summary to Dept. Rev.; withholding statement to employee.
Last	Minerals—Producers pay quarterly tax on new production or interim production to Cty. Treas.
NEBRASKA 1	Property—Annual report to Cty. Assr. by owner, lessee or manager of land or hangar on which aircraft is parked as of 1-1
15	Withholding—Last day to give W-2 to employees
NEVADA 16	Mine operators and royalty recipients—Annual report due to Dept. Tax.
NEW JERSEY 1	Property—Pay 1st quarter of tax to Tax. Coll.
1	Property—Local collectors mail income report forms to last year's grantees of homestead deductions for elderly and disabled
1	Sewage and water corporations—Report gross receipts
2	Domestic security fee—Quarterly return
15	Personal income (gross income tax)—Final return-payment (instead of 1–15 estimate)
15	Withholding (gross income tax)—Annual reconciliation due Div. Tax.; statement to employees
15	Personal income (gross income tax)—Information return due Div. Tax.
NEW MEXICO Last	Utilities—Quarterly inspection and supervision fee to PSC (last day)
Last	Property—Annual report due

Last	Withholding—Annual return to Dept. Tax. & Rev.
Last	Property—File for veteran and head of family exemptions with county assr.
NEW YORK 15	Withholding—Statement to employees
15	NYC gen. corp. tax and banking corp. tax—Return and payment due in lieu of Dec. 15 compliance
15	NYC unincorporated business tax—Return and payment due in lieu of Jan. 15 compliance
15	Property (NYC)—Coops and condos file abatement application
15	Property transfer (NYC)—Coops file information return; return and payments can be made by certain taxpayers
25	Property (NYC)—Last day for Class 1 property owners to file request for assessment review
28	Withholding—Report, pay to Tax Commr. for last calendar qtr. if qtrly. withholding under $700.
28	Withholding—Information return and reconciliation to Tax Commr.
NORTH CAROLINA 15	Motor fuels—Terminal operators file annual return for compensating tax with Sec'y. Rev.
15	Public utility regulatory fee—Pay to Utilities Comm.
NORTH DAKOTA 1	Property—Assmt. date
15	Property—Fully pay realty tax to Cty. Treas. for 5% discount
15	RRs—Annual statement of corporate name, principal place of business and officers to cty. auditors
28	Income—Information returns to Tax Commr.
OHIO 1	Sales-use—Vendor's license, pay Cty. Treas. (Tax Commr. if for transient or service vendor's license)
14	Severance—Quarterly report, pay to Tax Commr. (check to State Treas.)
15	Natural gas excise—Quarterly return, pay to Tax Commr.
20	Natural gas dist (MCF)—Quarterly return, pay to Tax Commr.
23	Sales-use—Semiannual return, pay State Treas.; counties—Cuyahoga, Darke, Defiance, Delaware
28	Withholding—File wage and tax statements with Tax Commr.
OKLAHOMA 27	Income—Information return to Tax Comm.
Last	Insurance—Annual report due to Insurance Commr.
OREGON 1	Utilities—Property tax statement to Dept. Rev.
1	Property—Nonprofit mutual or cooperative water associations file annual statement for continuance of exemption
1	Public utilities—Rural telephone exchanges, cooperatives and mutual electric distribution lines—Gross earnings report, pay to Dept. Rev.
14	Oil and gas gross production tax—4th quarterly report, pay to Dept. Rev.
14	Property—Pay 2nd installment to Cty. Assr.
28	Withholding—Annual report to Dept. Rev.
28	Information returns to Dept. Rev.
28	Motor carrier tax—Annual report or 4th quarterly report if gross weight not over 30,000 lbs. to PUC
PENNSYLVANIA 10	Property—(Pbgh & 2nd class cities) 2% discount expires
15	Property (Phila.)—Residents personalty return to Cty. Assrs.
15	Private bankers—Gross receipts tax annual return, pay to Dept. Rev.
20	Sales—Semiannual report, pay to Dept. Rev.
28	Property (Phila)—1% discount expires
RHODE ISLAND 1	Property—Owners of ships engaged in foreign commerce make statement of net profits and pay tax to Town Treas.
1	Sales—Renew vendor/seller permit with Tax Admr.
15	Personal income—Final return, pay to Tax Admr. (instead of 1–15 estimate)
15	Sales—Auto rental surcharge report to Tax Admr.
28	Income—Information returns to Tax Admr.
SOUTH CAROLINA 2	Property—Last day before 1st 7% penalty added for unpaid taxes
28	Withholding—Quarterly and annual reconciliation reports, pay to Dept. Rev.

SOUTH DAKOTA 1	Property tax—mobile homes—Owner lists mobile home with Cty. Dir. Equal.
TENNESSEE 15	Mining—Annual production report to Dept. Labor, Div. Mines
TEXAS 15	Sales—Prepayment to Comptr. for discount
20	Natural gas pipeline cos.—Quarterly report to RR Comm, pay Comptr.
UTAH 14	Oil and gas conservation fee—Report, pay to State Tax Comm.
28	Withholding—Employers file annual reconciliation with State Tax Comm.; issue W-2's to employees
Last day	Property—Apply for agricultural use assmt., pay late filing fee
VERMONT 15	Utilities—Transportation cos. appraisal appeal time expires
28	Withholding—Final return and annual reconciliation, pay Commr. Taxes
VIRGINIA 1	Property—Apartment house owners file names, etc., of tenants (if 4 or more) as of Jan. 1 with Cty. or City Commr. Rev.
5	Property—5% penalty new building assessed after Sept. 1—substantially completed and fit for use by Nov. 1 of completion year
WEST VIRGINIA 1	Property—Cty. court hears assessment complaints, reviews and equalizes assessments
15	Income—Final return and full payment of estimated tax to Tax Commr. in lieu of 1-15 declaration and payment
15	Withholding—Employers issue information statements to employees
28	Withholding—Employers file annual reconciliation return with Dept. of Tax and Revenue
WISCONSIN 1	Crude oil refiners—Annual report to local Assr.
1	Coal dock operators—Annual report to local Assr.
1	Iron ore concentrates dock—Annual report to local Assr.
1	Grain storage tax—Report to local Assr.
1	Property—Full realty tax delinquent if 1st installment not paid by 1-31
WYOMING 25	Mining, oil, and gas cos.—Report, pay severance tax to Dept. Rev. if last yr.'s tax under $30,000

¶315 MARCH CALENDAR

For RECURRING MONTHLY dates, see ¶ 380.
For UNEMPLOYMENT INSURANCE report dates, see ¶ 272.

ALABAMA	**1**	Freight line and equipment cos.—Report, payment to Dept. Rev.
	1	RRs—Mileage report to Dept. Rev.
	1	Transportation, transmission, and other utilities—report taxable property to Dept. Rev.
	15	Corporation income—Report, pay tax to Dept. Rev.
	15	Income—Information return to Dept. Rev.
	15	Franchise—Members of financial institution group report, pay business privilege tax to Dept. Rev.
	31	Gasoline—Farm-use refund to Dept. Rev.
ALASKA	**1**	Salmon enhancement tax—Buyers file annual report with Rev. Dept.
	1	Salmon marketing tax—Buyers file annual report with Rev. Dept.
	15	Corporation income—Final payment of tax for preceding calendar year to Dept. of Rev.
	31	Fishery business tax—Report, pay to Dept. of Rev.
	31	Fishery resource landing tax—Owners file annual report and pay Rev. Dept.
	31	Oil and gas production tax—Report, pay tax owed after installment payments to Dept. Rev.
ARIZONA	**1**	Property—Pay 2nd half taxes on realty and personalty secured by realty
	1	Property—Exemption must be claimed by this date
	15	Corporation Income—S corps file annual return, pay tax to Dept. Rev.
ARKANSAS	**1**	Utilities (not motor carriers)—Property tax report to PSC Tax Div.
	15	Income—Farmers' final return-payment instead of estimate
	31	Franchise—Corporations not receiving franchise tax return forms must file written request to Sec'y of State
	31	Carriers—Gross revenue report to Transp. Comm.
	31	Motor carriers—Property tax report to Transp. Comm.
CALIFORNIA	**1**	Property—Report separate ownership of land and improvements before this date
	15	Oil and gas producers—Report to Dept. Conserv.
	15	Corporate income—Report, pay tax to Franch. Tax Bd.
	16	Property—Airport owner or operator lists aircraft owners with Cty. Assr.
	24	Sales-use—Prepay SBE, if so ordered
COLORADO	**1**	Oil & gas conservation—Quarterly report, pay to Oil and Gas Conservation Comm.
	15	Income—Annual withholding reconciliation to Dept. Rev.
CONNECTICUT	**1**	Insurance companies—Annual return, payment of net direct premiums tax to Commr. Rev. Services
	15	Corporation business income—Report, pay 1st estimated tax installment to Commr. Rev. Services
	15	Insurance companies—Net direct premiums estimated tax report, payment (30%) to Commr. Revenue Services
	31	Licenses—Report and delivery of property presumed abandoned due to Treas.
DELAWARE	**1**	Franchise—Domestic corps report, pay to Secretary of State, file tentative return if estimated tax over $5000
	1	Franchise—Domestic corporations file annual report and pay rest of prior year's tax to Sec'y State; petition Sec'y State for refund or reduction of taxes, penalties, or interest for past year
	1	Escheat (abandoned property)—Holders, except banks and insurance companies, file report with state escheator
	1	Financial institutions—Banks and trust cos. pay annual tax; when annual liability is estimated to exceed $10,000, pay 20% of estimated tax and file tentative return
	1	Property (Kent Cty)—Quarterly supplemental assessment
	1	Property (New Castle Cty)—Last date for assmt.
	1	Property (Wilmington)—Assessment date

15 Financial institutions—Building and loan associations report, pay to Bank Commr. (75 days after fiscal year end)
15 Property (Wilmington)—Valuation appeals to Cty. Assmt. Bd.
15 Property (New Castle Cty)—Valuation appeals to Cty. Assmt. Bd.
31 Utilities—Report, pay regulatory assessment to PSC

DISTRICT OF COLUMBIA 1 Property tax—Owners of specified federally assisted housing file income and expense statement
15 Franchise tax—Corporations and financial institutions report, pay to Office of Tax and Revenue (15th of 3d mo.)
31 Property tax—Pay 1st half realty tax (and in lieu payments on PILOT parcels) to Office of Tax and Revenue
31 Property—Pay supplemental assessment of realty that became effective 10-1
31 Property—Pay 1/2 of Business Improvement District Taxes

FLORIDA 1 Property—Apply to Cty. Assr. for homestead exemption and exemption for leasehold interest in government property
1 Property—Report due for farm classification
1 Insurance—Report, pay marine and fire insurance tax
1 Property—Last day to apply to appraiser for reduction in assessed value on construction for older relatives
1 Property—Application for property tax exemptions must be filed with county appraiser
15 Insurance—Final tax return and payment due
31 Property—Last day to pay previous year's tax before delinquency
31 Property—Pay ¼ of estimated tax plus ½ of adjustment for actual liability (if prepayment elected)
31 Utilities—Water and waste water cos. regulatory assessment fee due
31 Fuel—Claim for refund of tax on undyed diesel fuel used by noncommercial vessels

GEORGIA 1 Utilities—Annual special franchise, property tax return to Commr. Rev.
1 Personal income—Final return for farmers and fishermen
15 Corporation franchise—Report, pay to Commr. Rev.
15 Corporation income—Return, pay in full to Dept. Rev.

HAWAII 31 General excise (sales) and use—Exempt organizations file for exemption with Dir. Tax.
31 Domestic corps.—Annual report to Dir. Commerce & Consumer Affairs

IDAHO 15 Property—File property declaration with assr.

ILLINOIS 1 Property—Pay (last day) accelerated 1st installment realty tax (no interest) in Cook Cty.; other counties with accelerated method
1 Insurance cos.—Report to Dept. Ins.
15 Utilities (invested capital tax)—Message, electric, gas and water cos. file annual report, pay balance to Dept. Rev. (also pay 1st quarter estimate)
15 Corporation income—Annual return and payment to Dept. Rev. (15th of 3rd month after end of fiscal year) (incl. replacement tax)
31 Surplus line producers and fire insurers—File report with Dir. Ins. on taxable fire insurance and pay fire marshall tax

INDIANA 1 Adjusted Gross income—Annual withholding information return to Dept. Rev.
1 Property—Assessment day (except mobile homes); lien attaches
1 Utilities (not RR car cos.)—Annual property report to State Bd. Tax Commrs.
1 Adjusted gross income—Individuals with ⅔ or more gross income from farming or fishing file return (in lieu of estimated tax due 1-15)
31 Property—Realty reassmt. petitions filed with Dept. of Local Government Finance (not in general election yrs. or when periodic reassmt. is made)

IOWA 1 Loan and investment cos.—File annual business statement with Dist. Assr. of Rev. Div.
1 Telephone and telegraph cos.—File maps of changes with Cty. auditor

1 Grain handlers—Report filed with Assr.
1 Property—Realty, mobile homeowners, grain handlers, loan and investment agencies, credit unions, pipeline companies, telegraph and telephone companies, railway companies, express companies, and electric transmission lines pay 2nd half to city treeas.
1 Express cos.—Property tax report to Dept. Rev.
1 Property—File application for historic property exemption with cty.
2 Underground petroleum storage—Report, pay balance of fees if granted extension for filing quarterly report (30 days after Jan. 31)
31 Gambling—Manufacturers, distributors of gambling machines and gambling implements apply for license, pay fee with STC

KANSAS 1 Property—File exemption claims with Cty. Assr.
1 RR car leasing cos.—Report to Dir. Tax.
1 Property—Cty. appraiser must notify taxpayers of classification or appraisal of realty by this date
15 Property—File personal property statement with Cty. Assr.
15 Property—Last day to file statement of assessment for oil and gas properties to Cty. Assr.

KENTUCKY 1 Private toll bridges and ferries— Report to Dept. Highways
1 Property—List with property Valuation Admr. between 1-1 and this date
1 Property—File for farm valuation
1 Property—Broker's-dealer's stock and bondholders report to Dept. Rev.
1 Property—Pledgee's report to Property Valuation Admr.
1 Property—Nonresident report interstate watercraft to Dept. Rev.
1 Motor carriers—Pay passenger seat tax to Dept. Vehicle Reg.
1 Financial institutions—Pay tax on deposits
1st Mon. Property (5th class cities)—BEQ meets
15 Personal income—Partnership return due
30 Gasoline—Apply to Dept. Rev. for 90% refund on fuel used for farming
31 RR and express cos.—Report to R.R. Comm.
31 Utilities—Reports to Dept. Rev. and PSC (except public service corps.)

LOUISIANA 31 Utilities—Report, pay inspection fee to Sec'y Rev.

MAINE 15 Corporate income—Annual report to Rev. Services
15 Financial institutions—Franchise tax return to Rev. Services
31 Fuel Retailers—File for semiannual refund
31 Utilities—File balance sheet with PUC

MARYLAND 1 Income—Farmers, fishermen final return instead of 1-15 declaration
15 Corporation income—Report, pay to Comptr.
15 Property—Report distilled spirits inventory to State Dept. Assmt. & Tax.
15 Utilities—Gross receipts franchise tax report, pay to State Dept. Assmt. & Tax.

MASSACHUSETTS 1 Property—Report charitable property to Assr.
1 Property—Farm excise annual report to local Assr.
1 Telephone, telegraph cos.—Property report to Commr. Rev.
15 Annual report—Corporations file with Sec'y State
15 Banks.—Income return to Commr. Rev.
15 Corporate franchise tax—cemetery, crematory, canal and safe deposit companies file with Commr.
15 Corporate excise—File declaration, pay quarterly estimate to Commr. Rev.
15 Corporate excise—excise tax on vessels—report and pay tax to Commr.
15 Fire, marine and other insurance cos.—Excise report to, pay Commr. Rev.
15 Utilities—Net income tax report, pay Commr. Rev.
15 Life insurance cos—Excise report pay Commr. Rev.

MICHIGAN 1	Single Business—Farmers, fishermen and seafarers may elect to file/pay instead of estimated tax
1	Personal income—Farmers and fisherman may elect to file/pay instead of estimated tax
1	Single business—Insurers make annual return and payment to Dept. Treas.
Tues. following 1st Mon.	Property—Assessment rolls reviewed by local Bd. Review
2nd Mon.	Property—Appeal assmt, to local Bd. Review
15	RRs—Property tax report (receipts over $1 million) to STC.
31	RRs—Property tax report (receipts not over $1 million) to STC.
31	Sleeping car cos—Report to State Bd. Assrs.
MINNESOTA 1	Cooperative utility—Pay Commr. Rev.
1	Iron ore (non-taconite)—Pay to Commr. Rev.
15	Corporation income—Report, pay Commr. Rev.
15	Corporation income—Pay estimate to Commr. Rev.
15	Gasoline—Farmers who use fuel on which tax has not been paid report and pay for past yr.
31	Property—RR cos. report to Commr. Rev.
31	Property—Electric light, power, gas and water cos. file report with Commr. Rev.
MISSISSIPPI 1	Personal income—Farmers filing regular return by this date need not file estimated return
15	Corporation income—Report, pay full tax to Tax Commr.
15	Income—Information return to Tax Commr.
15	Franchise—Corporations report, pay to Tax Comm.
MISSOURI 1	Income—Farmers' return instead of 1–15 estimate
31	Property (St. Louis)—Report personalty to Assr.
31	Utilities—Statement of gross operating revenue for preceding year
MONTANA 1	Property—Possessors or beneficial users of tax-exempt property (energy producers) report to Dept. Rev.
1	Petroleum license tax—Petroleum or liquified petroleum dealers pay license tax to Dept. Commerce
15	Utilities—Report to PSC if accounts closed 12–31
31	Minerals—Report mine's net proceeds to Dept. Rev.
31	Minerals—Metalliferous mines license tax annual payment to Dept. Rev.
31	Minerals—Resource indemnity trust payment due Dept. Rev.
31	Minerals—Oil and gas producers report, pay tax to Dept. Rev. (60 days after quarter end)
31	Property—Airline cos. annual flight property report to Dept. Rev.
31	Utilities—Regulated companies quarterly report to PSC and Dept. Rev., pay fees to Dept. Rev. (90 days after quarter ends)
NEBRASKA 1	Personal income—Last date for farmers to file return, in lieu of estimated tax payments, to Dept. Rev.
1	Withholding—Last day for employers to give statement of wages to Dept. Rev.
1	Intrastate motor carrier—Annual fees become delinquent
1	Car line cos.—First-half tax on railroad cars delinquent if unpaid on this date
1	Air carriers—First-half tax on property is delinquent if unpaid on this date
1	Corporate occupation—Annual report and fee, pay Sec'y. State
15	Corporate income—Report, pay Dept. Rev.
15	Financial institutions—Report, pay franchise tax to Dept. Rev.
15	Withholding—Annual reconciliation returns due
NEVADA 1	Loan associations—Report to Commr. of Financial Institutions
1	Minerals—Extractors file annual estimate of minerals tax on net proceeds with Dept. Tax.
1st Mon.	Property—Pay 4th quarter installment to Cty. Treas.
1st Mon.	Utilities—Franchise report to Cty. Assr.
10	Property—Last day to appeal to State Bd. Equal.
31	Foreign corporations—Publish and file report with Cty Assr.
NEW HAMPSHIRE 1	Property—Senior citizens apply to selectmen or accessors for residence realty exemption
1	Property—File solar energy exemption claim

15 Franchise—Utilities report, pay tax on gross receipts for past calendar year to Dept. Rev. Admin.

15 Business profits—Corporations and others filing US corporate returns file final return, pay Dept. Rev. Admn.; also file declaration and pay ¼ of estimated tax

15 Business enterprise—Annual report, pay to Dept. Rev. Admin. if required of file Fed corporation tax return

31 Gasoline—Retailers apply for refund for losses due to evaporation of motor fuel

NEW JERSEY 1 Property—Seniors and disableds file income statements for homestead deduction with collector

1 Property—Cty. tax administrator prepares equalization table

1 Personal income (gross income tax)—Employer's annual reconciliation

15 Litter tax—Report, pay to Div. Tax.

15 Casino—Licensees report, pay annual tax to Casino Control Comm.

15 Alcoholic beverage—Mfrs., distributors, etc. file, pay to Div. Tax.

31 Cigarettes—Licenses expire

31 Motor fuels—Renew licenses with Dir. Tax.

31 Professional corporations—Annual report to Sec'y State

NEW MEXICO 1 RRs—Report, pay gross earnings tax withheld from car cos.

15 Corporate franchise—Annual report, pay to Tax & Rev. Dept.

15 Corporate income—Annual report, pay to Tax & Rev. Dept.

15 Corporations—Biannual report, pay to Corp. Comm.

31 Copper production ad valorem tax—Copper mineral property owners file annual report of value with Tax. and Rev. Dept.

NEW YORK 1 Insurance cos.—Foreign and alien insurers return and payment due

1 Property—Taxable status date

1 Property (NYC)—Deadline for applications to correct valuation of class 2, 3, and 4 property

1 Personal income—Farmers-fishermen report, pay instead of 1–15 estimate

1 NYC Foreign and alien insurers—Return and payment of tax

15 Utilities—Franchise tax—Report, pay to Tax Commr.; oil cos. report, pay added tax on gross receipts to Tax Commr.

15 Business corporations—Franchise tax (calendar year), report (annual), pay Tax Comm. balance in full; pay 1st estimated installment

15 Property—Nassau Cty. nonresidents demand board of Assr.'s notice

15 Insurance corporations—Franchise tax—Report, pay annual State Tax Commr.

15 Banking corporations including national banks—Franchise tax (calendar year)—Annual report, pay balance to Tax Commr.; pay 25% as 1st quarter estimated tax

15 NYC business corporations—Report, pay annual corporation tax to Dept. Fin.

15 NYC banks, financials—Report, pay annual business return to Dept. Fin.

15 Franchise—Transportation, transmission, and agricultural cooperatives—Report, pay to Tax Commr.

15 Utilities—Report, pay excess dividends tax to Tax Commr.

15 Utilities—Gross income tax report, payment to Tax Commr.

15 Utilities—Transportation, transmission, water works, gas, electric or steam heating, lighting and power cos. and cos. furnishing utility services, report pay to Tax Commr.

15 S corporations—File state election (§660) to avoid tax on corporate level (due any time in prior year or in 75 days of elected tax year)

15 NYC Property tax—Deadline for applications to correct valuations for class 1 properties; deadline for senior citizen exemption application

20 NYC commercial rent or occupancy—Quarterly return, payment due to Dept. Fin.

20	NYC hotel occupancy—Quarterly return, payment due to Dept. Fin.
20	Sales-use (state, local)—Quarter (or annual, if authorized) report, pay to Dept. Tax. & Fin.
NORTH CAROLINA 1	Freight lines—Report, pay Sec'y. Rev.
1	Income—Farmers and fishermen report, pay to Sec'y. Rev.
31	Property—Public service cos. report to Dept. Rev.
NORTH DAKOTA 1	Property—1st installment delinquency due
OHIO 1	Utilities—Report (property tax) to Tax Commr.
1	Utilities subject to regular public utility excise tax—If prior year's tax $1,000 or more, report to Tax Commr., pay State Treas. ⅓ tax due.
1	Personal income—Farmers, fishermen final report-pay in full, in lieu of estimated tax
1	Motor fuel tax—Last day for retailers to file semiannual refund claim
Before 1st Mon.	Property—Original agricultural-use application to Cty. auditor
Before 2d Mon.	Property—Intangible dealers report to Tax Commr.
23	Sales-use—Vendors in Group C counties file semiannual return with State Treas.
30	Corporate franchise (income)—File S corporation notice of election with Tax Commr.
31	Corporate franchise (income)—Last day to report to Tax Commr. and pay to State Treas.
31	Corporate franchise—Pay estimated tax to State Treas.
31	Foreign corporations—Report to Sec'y State
31	Property—File assessment complaint with cty. auditor
31	Corporate franchise (income)—In absence of waiver, REITs, RICs, REMICs file report with Tax Commr. to maintain tax exempt status.
OKLAHOMA 1	Utilities—Rural cooperatives report to Tax Comm., copy to county treasurer.
1	Insurance—Captive insurance cos. pay tax to Dept. of Insurance
1	Insurance—Prepaid dental plan org. must file report and pay tax through Insurance Commr. to State Treasurer
15	Property—Applications for exemptions for new or expanded manufacturing concerns are due
15	Property—Application for intangible property exemption must be filed
15	Corporate income—Report, pay to Tax Comm.
15	Property—Homestead exemption application to Cty. Assr.
15	Property—Report personal and intangible property to Cty. Assr.
OREGON 1	Use fuel—Small vehicle owners report, pay use fuel tax to Dept. Transp.
1	Property—Nonprofits file low income housing exemption application with assr.
15	Utilities (specified)—Property tax report to Dept. Rev.
PENNSYLVANIA 1	Personal income—Farmers with two third (min.) such income, report, pay final return instead of 1–15 declaration
15	Public utilities—File annual report, pay balance if any; report and pay tentative tax for current yr.
15	Corporate net income—Report, pay 1st quarterly installment of estimated tax (15th of 3rd month of current yr.)
15	Capital stock and franchise—Report, pay 1st quarterly installment of estimated tax
15	Mutual thrifts—Report, pay 1st quarterly installment of estimated tax
15	Banks (with capital stock)—Annual report, pay bank shares tax to Dept. Rev.
15	Trust and title insurance—Report, pay shares tax to Dept. Rev.
31	Property (Pbgh. & 2nd class cities)—Pay realty tax in full or 1st quarter installment to Treas.
RHODE ISLAND 1	Utilities—Gross earnings report, pay to Tax Admr.
1	Corporation—Annual report with filing fee to Sec'y. State
15	Estimated tax—Corp., utility, bank or ins. cos., or oil cos. report, pay to Tax Admr.

15 Bank excise—report, pay to Tax Admr. (15th of 3rd month)
15 Franchise—Domestic corporations report to Tax Admr. (Pay 15 days after assmt.)
15 Property—File property acct. with Assr. if notified
15 Property—Mfrs. report inventory stored outside city where plant located
15 Business corporation—Return, pay to Tax Admn. (15th of 3rd month)

SOUTH CAROLINA 1 Personalty—File return
15 Corporations—Annual report to Sec'y State and Dept. Rev., fee to Sec'y State
15 Corporate income—Report, pay to Dept. Rev.
15 Corporate income—File estimate, pay 1st quarter
15 Corporate franchise—Report, license fee to Dept. Rev.
15 Corporate license—Report and pay to Dept. Rev.
15 Income—Information returns to Dept. Rev.
17 Property—Last day before second added penalty (5%) added

SOUTH DAKOTA 31 Banks and financial institutions—File annual return, pay income tax (90 days after end of tax year)

TENNESSEE 1 Property—Elderly or disabled apply for annual realty tax deferral
30 Fuel tax—Claim refund for fuel for ancillary engines

UTAH 1 Property—Statement for mines and mining claims due Tax Comm.
1 Property—Owners of charitable, educational, or religious property, cemeteries, and farm equip. and machy file use affidavits
1 Public utilities and multi-county pipe-line, power, canal, irrigation or telephone companies—Annual property tax report to Tax Comm.
1 Oil and gas, mining severance taxes—Taxpayers whose total taxes for past cal. year were $3,000 or more pay quarterly installment to Tax Comm.
1 Property—Tax Comm. must decide all appeals of County BEQ decisions on realty assmts. or exemptions by this date
15 Property—Redeem realty held by county under preliminary sale occurring in January or any prior 4 yrs.
31 Property—Report, pay agricultural fee to Commr. Agriculture

VERMONT 15 Corporate income—Report, pay to Commr. Taxes
15 Corporations—Annual report to Sec'y State (2½mos. after fiscal year)
25 Telephone cos.—Report, pay qtrly. installment of net value tax on personalty to Tax Commr.
31 Utilities—Property inventory to Div. of Property Valuation

VIRGINIA 1 Motor carriers—Report rolling stock and instate and out-of-state mileage for year ending 12–31 to State Corp. Comm.
1 Personal income—Final report or pay instead of 1–15 declaration
1 Property—Banks report deposits in branches as of start of tax year to local Commr. Rev.
14 Corporation registration—Fee assmt. made and notice given by this date

WASHINGTON 15 Utilities (specified)—Annual operating property report to Dept. Rev.
31 Property—File initial application for exemption with Dept. Rev. (renew each yr.)

WEST VIRGINIA 1 Property—2½% discount if 2nd half paid to Cty. Sheriff
15 Corporate income—Annual report, pay to Tax Commr.
15 Franchise—Annual report, pay to Tax Commr.
15 Utilities—Carriers gross and net income—Report, pay full or 1st half to Tax Commr.

WISCONSIN 1 Telephone cos.—Gross receipts report to Dept. Rev.
1 Income—Farmers or fishers final return, pay in full (to avoid estimated return)
1 Property—File personalty return with local Assr.
1 Property—File annual manufacturing property report with local Assr.
1 Light, heat & power cos.—File annual report with Dept. Rev.

15 Electrical cooperatives—Gross receipts report to Dept. Rev.
15 Corporate income—Declaration of estimated tax or installment to Dept. Rev. (installment to Dept. Rev.
15 Corporate income—Annual return, pay all or balance of tax to Dept. Rev.
15 Corporate income—Information return to Dept. Rev.
15 Property—Report exempt property used in trade or business to taxation district clerk
15 Corporate income—Information returns of stock transfers and payments of rents and royalties to individuals due
31 Property—File property tax exemption report on even-numbered years

WYOMING 1 Property—2nd half of realty tax becomes due
1 Property—Last day to file statement of personalty holdings with county assessor
31 MVs—Last day to register and pay Cty. Treas. or Dept. of Transportation annual fee for commercial MVs

¶320 APRIL CALENDAR

For RECURRING MONTHLY dates, see ¶ 380.
For UNEMPLOYMENT INSURANCE report dates, see ¶ 272.

ALABAMA 1	Specified utilities—Report, pay ¼ license tax to Dept. Rev.
1	Dry cleaning fee—Quarterly report, payment due to Dept. Rev.
1	Dry cleaning registration fee—Wholesale distributors annual payment (delinquent on Apr. 20)
15	Financial institutions—Excise tax return, payment to Dept. Rev.
15	Corporate income—Declaration, quarterly estimated tax to Dept. Rev.
15	Personal income—Annual return, estimate or installment to Dept. Rev.
15	Income—Fiduciaries report, pay (calendar yr.) to Dept. Rev.
15	Income—Partnership return due
20	Dry cleaning registration fee—Wholesale distributors annual payment
20	Sales-use-rental—Quarterly return, payment if liability averages less than $200 per month for past calendar yr.
30	Forest products—manufacturers, exporters—Report, pay to Dept. Rev.
30	Income—Quarterly withholding report, payment to Dept. Rev.
30	Motor carriers fuel use—Quarterly report, pay to Dept. Rev.
ALASKA 15	Corporation income—Annual return to Dept. of Rev.; report, pay 1st estimated tax installment
30	Mines—Report, pay license tax to Dept. of Rev.
30	Mines—Apply to Dept. of Rev. for renewal of license
ARIZONA 1	Tel. & tel., RRs cos., air commerce cos., private car cos.—Report to Dept. Rev.
1	Property—File flight property information with Dept. Rev.
15	Corporate income—Annual return, pay tax to Dept. Rev.
15	Corporate income—Pay 1st estimated tax installment to Dept. Rev.
15	Personal income—Annual return, pay tax to Dept. Rev.
15	Personal income—Report, pay 1st estimated tax to Dept. Rev.
15	Income—Request extension for filing claim for credit for property tax or rent
20	Sales-use—Quarterly report, payment to Dept. Rev. (if authorized)
30	Withholding—Quarterly report-pay to Dept. Rev., and statement to employees
ARKANSAS 1	R&Rs and private car cos.—Car mileage report to PSC Tax Div.
10	Property—Report to Cty. Assr. (intangibles are exempt)
15	Income—Calendar year taxpayer's return and payment due to Dept. Fin. and Admin.
20	Gross receipt—sales—Quarterly report, pay Dir. Fin. & Admn. if monthly tax not over $100
3rd Mon.	Property—Pay yr. ad valorem tax to Cty. Coll.
Last Day	Motor fuels—Interstate user's quarterly report and payment to Dept. Fin. & Admn.
Last Day	Liquefied gas—Users report, pay to Dept. Fin. & Admn.
CALIFORNIA 10	Property—Pay county collector 2nd ½ realty tax
15	Carriers—Quarterly report, fee and (for all but railroads and vessel operators) gross operating revenue fee to PUC
15	Corporate income—Estimate, pay to Franchise Tax Bd.
15	Personal income—Estimate, pay to Franchise Tax Bd.
15	Personal income—Report, pay tax to Franchise Tax Bd.
30	Withholding—Quarterly report, pay to Employment Dev. Dept.
30	Private car—Report to SBE
30	Sales-use—Quarterly Report, pay to SBE
30	Use fuel—Quarterly report, pay to SBE
30	Timber yield—Timber owners report, pay tax to SBE
COLORADO 1	Sales—File biotechnology refund claim with Dept. Rev.
15	Property—File personalty report with Cty. assr.
15	Income—Annual return, full payment to Dir. Rev.
15	Corporate income—Estimated return or installment to Dir. Rev.

15 Severance—Quarterly molybdenum tax report, pay to Dept. Rev.
15 Severance—Annual report, pay to Dept. Rev. (15th of 4th mo. after tax year close).
15 Personal income—Estimate, pay to Dept. Rev. if expected tax over $1000
15 Utilities—Quarterly payment to Dept. Rev.
15 Use—Nonbusiness consumers, report, pay Dir. Rev. if tax not paid to retailer
15 Property—Oil and gas leaseholders and owners, producing mine owners and operators report to Assr.
20 Sales—Report, pay quarterly to Dept. Rev.
30 Severance—Producers' annual report to Dept. Rev. (copy to Dept. of Local Affairs)
30 Withholding—Quarterly report, pay to Dept. Rev.
30 Property—Full payment to Cty. Treas.

CONNECTICUT 1 Corporation business (income)—Annual report, pay to Commr. Rev. Services
1 CATV or satellite cos.—Gross earnings tax report, pay to Commr. Rev. Services
1 Corporation business tax—Tentative return and request for time extension due to Commr. Rev. Serv.
15 Corporate income—Business entity tax returns and payment due to Commr. Rev.
15 Use—Annual personal use tax return, payment to Commr. Rev. Serv.
15 Personal income—Return, pay to Tax Commr.
15 Personal income—File, pay quarterly estimated tax and composite payments to Tax Commr.
15 Withholding—Employers NY residents info report to Commr. Rev. Services (or filing with N.Y. Inc. Tax Bur. allowed)
30 Sales-use—Quarterly report, pay to Commr. Rev. Services
30 Petroleum importers—Over $100,000 worth of deliveries during preceding quarter report, pay quarterly to Commr. Rev. Serv.
30 Motor carrier road tax—Quarterly return, pay to Commr. Rev. Services
30 Utilities—Quarterly report, pay gross earnings tax to Commr. Rev. Services
30 Oil Cos. gross earnings tax—Quarterly return, payment to Commr. Rev. Services.

DELAWARE 1 Corporate income—Tentative return, half estimated; for current year to Dept. Fin.
1 Corporate income—Final return, pay balance for preceding year to Dept. Fin.
1 Franchise—Tax unpaid by this date is collectible by suit
1 Property—Kent Cty. Bd. hears valuation appeals
1 Property (New Castle Cty.)—Quarterly assmt.
1 RR companies—Quarterly fee to Dept. Fin.
2 Property—Mobile home park operators report names and addresses of persons with mobile homes on land
15 Wilmington net profits—Quarterly payment to City Dept. Fin.
30 Personal income—Estimate and quarterly payment to Dept. Fin.
30 Leasing use & lessors' license—Quarterly report, pay to Dept. Fin.
30 Withholding—Quarterly return, pay to Div. Rev. if withholding for lookback period not over $3,600
30 Motor carriers' fuel purchase—Report, pay to Dept. Pub. Safety
30 Personal income—Report, pay annual return to Dept. Fin.
30 Wilmington earned income—Quarterly report to City Dept. Fin.

DISTRICT OF COLUMBIA 1 Property—Last day to file income-expense form with Office of Tax and Revenue
1 Property—Last day to seek administrative review of supplemental assessment made between July 1 and December 31.
1 Property—Last day to seek administrative review of assessed value or classification of realty.
1 Property—Exempt organizations report exempt property use to Office of Tax and Revenue.

15 2-yr. report—Corporations, domestic and foreign, file, pay report fee to Department of Consumer and Regulatory Affairs, Corporation Division, every 2d yr.
15 Income—Individuals, estates, trusts, and unincorporated business report, pay to Office of Tax and Revenue (15th of 4th mo.)
15 Income-franchise tax—Declaration and/or payment of estimated tax to Office of Tax and Revenue

FLORIDA 1 Corporate income; Bank tax—Annual return, pay to Dept. Rev., including emergency excise tax (1st day of 4th mo. after end of tax year or 15th day after due date for related Fed return)
1 Corporate income—Claimant of enterprise zone property tax credit must file notice with appraiser of county where the business property is located
1 Property—Personal property annual return, previous year's tax to Cty Assr.
1 Diesel fuel use—Motor carriers report, pay to Dept. of Highway Safety and Motor Vehicles
1 Severance—Report, pay to Dept. Rev.
1 Property—Requests for separate assessments for minerals and subsurface rights and real property are due
1 Everglades agricultural privilege tax—Tax due
1 Property—Returns for reduced assessment for pollution control facilities are due
1 Property—Railroad co. information returns are due
15 Generation-skipping transfer tax—Last day to file return for taxable distribution
15 Insurance—Estimated taxes are due
30 Escheat—Holders report abandoned property to Dept. of Banking and Finance

GEORGIA 1 Corporation—Annual report to Sec'y State
1 Property—Return to Cty. tax receiver
1 Property—Dealer pays tax on sold MVs to county tax collector
15 Corporate income—Estimated return, pay quarter tax to Commr. Rev. (15th of 4th month)
15 Personal income—Return and payment of full unpaid tax to Commr. Rev.
15 Personal income—Estimated return and/or installment to Commr. Rev.
20 Sales-use—Report, pay quarter to Commr. Rev.
30 Motor carriers—Quarterly motor fuel tax report, pay to Commr. Rev.
30 Withholding—Quarterly report, pay to Commr. Rev.

HAWAII 1 MV—Registration, state county tax payable
9 Property—Appeal assessment to review bd. or tax appeal court
15 Withholding—Quarterly report, pay to Dept. Tax. if permitted and annual tax $5,000 or less
15 Glass container importers—Report, pay advance disposal fee to Dept. Health
20 General excise (sales) and use—Annual return, pay Dept. Tax.
20 Income—Corporations and individuals file annual return, pay tax to Dept. Tax
20 Personal and corporation income.—File declaration of estimated tax, pay first quarter to Dept. Tax
20 Utilities—Report, pay all or 1st quarter installment to Dept. Tax
20 Franchise—Financial institutions report, pay installment to Dept. Tax.
30 General excise (sales) and use—Report, pay 1st quarter if permitted and annual tax is under $4,000 to Dept. Tax.

IDAHO 1 Utilities (specified)—Report to PUC
1 RRs—Maintenance tax report to PUC
15 Income—Annual return, pay to Tax Comm.
15 Income—Corporations estimate and pay installment to Tax Comm.
15 Severance—Productive mines report, pay to Tax Comm.
15 Mining cos.—Pay license tax to Tax Comm. (15th day of 4th mo.)
15 Utilities (specified)—Annual report to PUC

15 Property—Claim exemption for homestead reduction with Cty. Assr.
25 Oil, gas production—Return, pay quarter to Oil and Gas Comm.
25 Motor carriers—Quarterly report, pay gross mileage fee to Dept. Trans.
30 Withholding—Quarterly report, pay to Tax Comm. if quarterly under $600
30 RR, and utilities (specified)—Report to Tax Comm.
30 Electrical co-ops—Report to Tax Comm.
30 Mining cos.—Report to Assr. in Cty. where mine located

ILLINOIS 10 Utilities—Quarterly payment gross revenue tax to Commerce Comm.
15 Income—Individuals, partnerships and fiduciaries annual report, pay to Dept. Rev.
15 Income—Corporations and individuals pay estimated tax to Dept. Rev.
15 Insurance cos.—Quarterly payment of estimated privilege tax unless annual tax under $5,000
15 Special fuel—Bulk users annual report to Dept. Rev.
20 Sales-use—Quarterly report, pay Dept. Rev. if average monthly tax not over $200
30 Special fuel—Motor fuel use tax licensees make quarterly report, pay to Dept. Rev.
30 Hotel operators' occupation—Quarterly report, pay Dept. Rev.
30 Withholding—Quarterly report, pay to Dept. Rev.
30 Motor carriers—Report miles traveled and gallons of fuel used
30 Escheats—Last day for business assns., utilities, and life ins. cos. to file annual report with Dir. Fin. Institutions
30 Utilities (gross receipts tax on gas)—Quarterly report, pay to Dept. Rev. if authorized and monthly tax is not over $100
30 Utilities (telecommunications excise tax)—Quarterly report, pay to Dept. Rev.

INDIANA 1 Utilities—Pay quarterly public utility fee to PSC
15 Utility receipts—Annual return, pay to Dept. Rev.
15 Adjusted gross income—Annual return pay (15th day of 4th mo.) Dept. Rev.
15 Personal income—Annual report, pay to Dept. Rev.
15 Personal income—Estimated return, pay to Dept. Rev.
15 Gasoline—File refund claim for gasoline used by local transit system or by person for agricultural or industrial purposes
15 Financial institutions—Annual report, pay to Dept. Rev.
15 Corporations—File business activity report with Dept. Rev.
20 Utility receipts—Quarterly estimated return, pay to Dept. Rev. (if estimated annual liablity exceeds $1,000)
30 Adjusted gross income—Corporations estimate tax, pay quarter to Dept. Rev. if estimated tax exceeds gross income tax by $1,000 for tax year
30 Carriers' road tax—Report, pay quarter to Dept. Rev.
30 Adjusted gross income—Report, pay quarter withholding to Dept. Rev. if average monthly withholding isn't over $75 for previous year
30 Capital improvement—Report, pay quarter installment to Dept. Rev.
30 Sales-use—Quarterly report, pay to Dept. Rev. if average monthly tax is $75 or less
30 Financial institutions—Quarterly estimated pay to Dept. Rev.

IOWA 1 Pipeline cos.—Property tax report to Dir. Rev.
1 Corporations—File annual report with, pay Sec'y State
1 RRs—Property tax reports to Dept. Rev. & Fin.
1 Property tax—2d installment of delinquent tax due
15 Property—Realty owners must be notified of adjustment in assessment
30 Income—Pay quarterly estimate to Dept. Rev.
30 Income—Annual return, pay to Dept. Rev.
30 Income—Employers file quarterly withholding report, pay to Dept. Rev.

30 Sales-use—Quarterly report, pay to Dept. Rev.
30 Special fuel—Distributors report, pay to Dept. Rev.
30 Special fuels—Distributors file quarterly report with Dept. Rev.
30 Underground petroleum storage—Pay 90% of quarterly estimated charges to Dept. Rev. if granted extension
30 Underground petroleum storage—Quarterly return, pay to Dept. Rev.

KANSAS 15 Property—Last day to appeal realty assessment to Cty. Appraiser
15 Income—Estimate, pay to Dir. Tax.
15 Income—Corporations and individuals file annual return, pay to Dir. Tax.
15 Franchise—Corporations, limited partnerships, co-ops, business trusts report, pay to Sec'y State
15 Property—Intangibles return to Dir. Tax.
15 Bank tax—Financial institutions make estimated privilege tax declaration, payment to Dir. Tax.
15 Bank tax—Financial institutions file annual return, pay privilege tax to Dir. Tax.
15 Sales-use—Last day to claim refund of tax on food for past yr. from Dept. Rev.
25 Sales-use—Small taxpayers (tax over $80 but under $3,200) quarterly report, pay to Dir. Tax.
25 Tire tax—Report, pay for qtr. if annual tax $80–$1,600
25 Withholding—Quarterly report, pay to Dir. Tax. if tax over $200 but under $1200
30 Interstate motor fuel use—Quarterly report, pay to Dir. Tax.

KENTUCKY 15 Corporate income, limited liability entity tax—Annual return, pay to Dept. Rev.
15 Personal income—Annual return, pay to Dept. Rev. report, pay estimated tax
15 Use tax—Individual use tax returns, payment due to Dept. Rev.
15 Lexington license—Employee's annual return, pay to City Treas.
15 Louisville license—Employee's annual return, pay to Commrs.' Sinking Fund
15 Motor fuel—Taxable user's report, pay to Dept. Rev.
15 Motor fuel use tax—City and suburban bus quarterly refund application to Dept. Rev.
15 Lexington license—Employer's quarterly report, pay to City Treas.
15 Louisville license—Employer's quarterly report, pay City Sec'y-Treas.
15 Paducah payroll—Employer's quarterly report, pay to City Treas.
15 Property (Louisville)—Payment to Recr. Taxes; 3% discount expires
15 Property (2d class cities)—Discount expires
30 Income—Employer's quarterly withholding report, pay to Dept. Rev.

LOUISIANA 1 Property—Return to parish assessor (except Orleans)
1 Public service cos.—Report to Tax Commr.
15 Corporation income—Annual return-payment and estimated tax installment to Dept. Rev.
15 Personal income—Estimated tax installment to Dept. Rev.
15 Franchise—Report, pay to Dept. Rev.
25 Special fuel—Interstate users report, pay to Sec'y Rev.
30 Utilities (except electric cos.)—Report to Dept. Rev.
30 Natural gas lines—Report, pay franchise tax to Dept. Rev.
30 Withholding—Quarterly report, pay to Dept. Rev.
30 Escheats—Last day for insurance cos. to file annual report with Dept. Rev.

MAINE 1 Property—Assessment date; lien attaches
1 Property—Machinery and other personalty inshipped after this date and pre-12-31 taxable where first used
1 Property—Initial application for veteran exemption
1 Property—Last day to file claim for property tax deferral with municipal assr.
15 Gross receipts—RR and railway cos. report to Rev. Services

15 Personal income—Annual return and pay to Rev. Services
15 Income—Estimate declaration and 1st installment due
15 Sales-use—Quarterly returns, payment to Rev. Services
30 Withholding—Quarterly report, pay to Rev. Services

MARYLAND 15 Personal income—Report to Comptr.
15 Corporate income—Estimate, pay 25% to Comptr.
15 Personal income—Estimated return and/or installment to Comptr.
15 Property—Personalty report to Dept. Assmts. & Tax.
15 Utilities franchise—File declaration of estimated tax if over $1,000 and pay 25% of tax
21 Sales-use—Small vendors report, pay quarter tax to Retail Sales Tax Div.
30 Withholding—Quarterly report, pay to Comptr.
30 Escheats—Last day for insurance cos. to file annual report with State Comptr.

MASSACHUSETTS 1 Excise on ships—Report to town assr.
15 Personal income—Annual report, pay to Commr. Rev.
15 Personal income—Estimate return and installment to Commr. Rev.
15 Personal income—Partnerships' information return to Commr. Rev.
15 Gasoline—Farmers file with Tax Comm. for refund
15 Sales-use—Vendors report accounts worthless during past year; claim refund of taxes paid
15 Alcoholic beverages—Report, pay to Commr. Rev.
20 Sales-use—Quarterly report, pay to Commr. Rev. if tax over $100 but under $1,200 for calendar year
30 Transporters of hazardous waste—Report and payment to Dept. of Environmental Quality Engineering
30 Imported fuel—Carriers report, pay to Commr. Rev.
30 Withholding—Quarterly return, pay to Commr. Rev. for calendar quarter ending Mar. 31
30 Forest lands and products—Report to local assessor

MICHIGAN 1 Gas pipelines—Report to PSC
15 Personal income—Report, pay Dept. Treas. (15th day of 4th mo. after tax year)
15 Personal income—Estimate, pay quarter to Dept. Treas.
15 Personal income—Farmers, fishermen make final report-pay if tentative report-pay was made
15 Single business—Farmers, fishermen make final report-pay if tentative report-pay was made
15 Mich. business tax—Estimate, pay quarter to Dept. Treas.
20 Withholding—Quarterly report, pay to Dept. Treas.
20 Motor carrier fuel—Quarterly report, pay to Dept. Treas.
20 Motor fuel exporters—Quarterly report, pay to Dept. Treas.
20 Motor fuel vendors—Quarterly report, pay to Dept. Treas.
20 Retail diesel fuel vendors—Quarterly report, pay to Dept. Treas.
20 Motor fuel tank wagon operator-importers—Quarterly report, pay to Dept. Treas.
20 Motor fuel transporters—Quarterly report, pay to Dept. Treas.
20 Motor fuel—Quarterly LP gas report, pay to Dept. Treas.
30 Single business tax—Report, pay to Dept. Treas. (last day of 4th mo. except insurers; see Mar. 1)

MINNESOTA 1 Minerals—Occupation tax—Exploration data report to Commr. Rev.
15 Personal income—Report to Commr. Rev.
15 Personal income—Estimated return and/or installment to Commr. Rev.
15 Income—Foreign corporations obtaining business in the state must file notice of business activities report with Dept. Rev.
15 Income—Nonresident entertainers file form with Commr. Rev.
15 Property—Report of timber cut on auxiliary forests to Dir. Lands and Forestry
15 Aviation—Aircraft mfrs. report to Commr. Transp.
15 Use—File annual return if annual taxable purchases under $18,500 and not required to hold sales tax permit.

20	Sales-use—Quarterly report, pay to Commr. Rev.
20	Liquor gross receipts—Quarterly report, pay to Commr. Rev.
30	Property—Appeal to district court or tax court
30	Withholding—Quarterly report, pay tax not deposited to Commr. Rev.
30	Motor carriers—Report, pay quarterly road tax to Dept. Rev.
30	Gasoline—File aviation gasoline refund claim with Commr. Rev.
MISSISSIPPI 1	Property—Returns to tax assessor
1	Property—Application to assessor for homestead exemption
1	Property—Freight line and equipment cos. report to Tax Comm.
1	Property—Banks file statement of net worth with Cty. assr.
1	Utilities—Gross revenue statement to Tax Comm.
1	Railroad regulation tax—File statement of track miles to Public Service Comm.
1st Mon.	Utilities—Property tax report to Tax Comm.
15	Corporate income—File declaration of estimated tax, pay to Tax Comm.
15	Withholding—Quarterly report, pay Tax Comm.
15	Personal income—Report, pay to Tax Comm.
15	Personal income—Estimate-pay to Tax Comm.
15	Timber—Quarterly report, pay to Tax Commr. if tax $10 or less for month
20	Sales-use—Quarterly report, pay to Tax Commr.
30	Fuel use—Interstate permittees report, pay to Tax Comm.
30	Oil severance—Quarterly report to Tax Comm.
MISSOURI 1	Express cos.—Report, pay to Dir. Rev.
14	Sales-use—Apply for credit or refund for tax on nondomestic utilities used for domestic purposes
15	Sales-use—Report, pay to Dir. Rev. on utilities bought for domestic use, used for nondomestic purposes
15	Banks, trust cos., credit institutions, credit unions, S&L assns., farmers coop. credit assns.—Report, pay to Dir. Rev.
15	Income—Report, pay to Dir. Rev.
15	Earnings (Kansas City)—Annual report, pay to Finance Dir. (105 days from close of fiscal year)
15	Earnings (St. Louis)—Annual report, pay to Collector (105 days from close of fiscal year)
15	Income—Estimate, pay first quarter to Dir. Rev.
15	Utilities—Intrastate common-contract carrier financial statement to Div. of Transp.
15	Utilities—Assessment for expenses of PSC; 4th installment
15	Utilities—RR, street RR, freight liner, bridge and public utiity, tel. and tel. cos. statement to State Tax Comm. and to Cty. Clerks
15	Franchise (incl annual registration fee)—Report, pay to Sec'y State
15	Corporations—Annual registration report to Sec'y State; registration fee to Dir. Rev.
25	Kansas City earnings—Employer's quarterly withholding return, pay Fin. Dir.
29	Gasoline—Interstate special fuel users report, pay to Dir. Rev.
30	Utilities—Local agent's of express cos. reports, pays to Dir. Rev. if company hasn't
30	Income—Quarterly withholding report, pay to Dir. Rev.
30	St. Louis earnings—Employer's quarterly withholding return, pay to Coll. Rev.
30	Sales—Report, pay to Dir. Rev.
30	Use—Quarterly report, pay Dir. Rev.
30	Payroll expense tax (St. Louis)—Employer's quarterly report, pay to Coll. Rev.
MONTANA 1	Utilities—Motor carriers file annual report to PSC
15	Initial—Corporations, annual report, pay fees to Sec'y State
15	Corporation income—Estimate, pay Dept. Rev.
15	Utilities—RR annual report to Dept. Rev.
15	Personal income—Estimate, pay quarter to Dept. Rev.
15	Personal income—Report, pay to Dept. Rev.
15	Income—Information returns to Dept. Rev.

15 Corporations (domestic, foreign)—Annual report to Sec'y State (copy to Cty. clerk).
30 Sales—Owner or operator of facility report, pay quarterly lodgings tax to Dept. Rev.
30 Coal dealers, retail—License fees plus quarterly license payment to Dept. Rev.
30 Coal mine operators and dealers—Quarterly report, pay to Dept. Rev.
30 Micaceous mineral mines—Quarterly report, pay Dept. Rev.
30 Electrical energy producers—Quarterly report, pay to Dept. Rev.
30 Cement and gypsum producers and dealers—Quarterly report to Dept. Rev.
30 Withholding—Quarterly report, pay to Dept. Rev.
30 Special fuel—Users' quarterly report, pay to Dept. Rev.

NEBRASKA 1 Property (counties with pop. over 100,000)—First-half gen. realty tax delinquent.
1 Property—File application for mobile home exemption with Cty. Assr.
1 Utilities—Car line cos. and railroads annual report of railroad cars operating in state to Tax Commr.
15 RRs—Annual return of operating property to Dept. Rev.
15 Personal income—Return, pay remaining tax in full to Dept. Rev.
15 Personal income—Last day to file, pay estimated tax installment if over $300
15 Partnerships—File return to Dept. Rev.
15 Trusts and estates—Report, pay to Dept. Rev.
15 Corporation income—Report, pay estimated tax installment
16 Corporate occupation—Corporations dissolved for failure to report-pay occupation tax
20 Diesel fuel—Quarterly return, pay to Dept. Rev. for users of untaxed fuel
25 Sales-use—First quarter return, pay to Dept. Rev.
25 Tire fee—First quarter return, pay to Dept. Rev.
30 Common carriers (no report to Fed agency)—Annual report to Tax Comm.
30 Withholding—Quarterly report, pay to Tax Commr.
30 Escheats—Last day for Insurance Cos. to file annual report with State Treas.
30 Property—Last day to file homestead application exemption with county assessor
30 Agricultural excise taxes and fees—First purchasers or shippers report, pay to appropriate board in Dept. Agriculture
30 Motor vehicle and diesel fuel—Interstate truckers report, pay tax to Dept. Rev.

NEVADA 1 Utilities—Pay 4th quarterly assessment to PUC
30 Property—Last day to file for senior homeowner's refund with Cty. assr.
30 Special fuels—Dealers, users report, pay to Dept. of MVs
30 Sales-use—Quarterly report, pay to Dept. Tax.
30 Sales-use—Short-term passenger car lessor return, payment due to Dept. Tax.

NEW HAMPSHIRE 1 Domestic corporations—Report, pay annual fee (incl filing fee) to Sec'y State
1 Foreign corporations—Annual report, pay fee to Sec'y State
1 Property—Assrs. or selectmen announce hearings
1 Property—Assmt. date
1 Resident tax—Payable in town or residence
1 Forest tax—Timber owners report intended cutting operations
1 Railroad, express, and car cos.—Pay annual tax
1 Utilities—Property assessment date; lien attaches
15 Business profits tax—Individuals and others not filing Fed corporate returns file annual (final report, pay to Dept. Rev. Admn.; also file declaration of estimated tax, pay to Dept of Rev. Admn.
15 Business profits—Annual return, pay to Dept. of Rev. Admn. by business orgs not filing Fed corp. tax returns

15 Business enterprise—Annual report, pay to Dept. Rev. Admin. if not required to file Fed corporation tax return
15 Income—Individuals file annual return, pay tax to Dept. Rev. Admn.
15 Income—Individuals report, pay quarterly estimated tax
15 Business profits—Pay estimated tax to Dept. Rev. Admn.
15 Property—Reports to assessors or selectmen.
15 Property—"Seniors" apply to selectmen or Assr. for permanent residence exemption
15 Property—File for permanent classification of open space land with conservation restrictions as restricted land.
15 Property—Report of local Assr. or selectmen, unless prevented by accident, etc.
15 Property—File for alternative energy exemption with Assr. or selectmen
15 Property Nonprofit org. annual list of exempt property to Dept. Rev. Admn.
15 Forest tax—Timber yield tax report due
15 RRs and communication cos.—Report, pay quarterly estimated tax to Dept. Rev. Admn.
15 Refined petroleum products—Report, pay quarterly tax to Dept. Rev. Admn.
15 Refined petroleum products—Estimated tax, pay third to Dept. Rev. Admn.
15 Utilities—Quarterly payment to Dept. Rev. Admn.
15 Utilities—Retailers must file quarterly return, pay communications services tax to Dept. Rev. Admn.
30 Special fuel use—Quarterly report, pay road toll to MV Dir., pay Dept. Rev. Admn.
30 Road toll—Users of fuel (other than motor fuel) pay for quarter ended March 31
30 Escheat—Report money owing under life insurance policies to State Treas.

NEW JERSEY 1 RRs—Franchise report to Dir. tax.
1 Property—Local collectors send notices of disallowance to claimants of homestead deduction for elderly and disabled
1 Property—Last day to appeal to cty. bd.
15 Corporate business (franchise)—File annual return, pay Div. Tax
15 Corporation business (franchise)—Pay 2nd installment to Div. Tax
15 Foreign corporation (unqualified)—Business activities report due Div. Tax.
15 Personal income (gross)—Residents & nonresidents report, pay to Div. Tax.
15 Personal (gross) income—Quarterly withholding report, pay to Div. Tax.
15 Personal (gross) income—Partnerships file information returns
15 Personal income (gross income tax)—Estimate and installment due Div. Tax.
20 Sales-use—Permittees direct report, pay to Div. Tax.
20 Sales-use—Quarterly return, pay to Dir. Tax.
20 Public community water system—Owners or operators file with and pay Div. Tax.
25 Petroleum products—Refiners and distributors quarterly report, pay to Dir. Tax
30 Fuel use—Quarterly report, pay to Dir. MV
30 Unemployment comp.—Employer report-pay Labor Dept.
30 Domestic security fee—Quarterly return to Div. Tax

NEW MEXICO 1 Special fuels supplier tax—Eligible users electing to pay on annual basis must file election with Tax. and Rev. Dept.
1 MVs—Qualified owners file statement with Tax. and Rev. Dept. to pay weight distance tax on annual basis
10 Property—Pay 2nd (last) installment to Cty. Treas.
15 Corporation income—Pay quarterly estimated tax to Tax. & Rev. Dept.
15 Individual income—Report, pay full tax to Tax. & Rev. Dept.

20 Utilities—Quarterly inspection and supervision fee to State Corp. Comm.

25 Special fuels supplier tax—Users' quarterly report, payment to Tax. and Rev. Dept.

25 MVs—Pay to Motor Transp. Div. weight distance tax for previous calendar quarter.

30 Escheats—Last day for Insurance Cos. to file annual report with Tax. & Rev. Dept.

NEW YORK 1 NYC Property tax—4th quarterly installment due on class 1 and 2 property assessed at $80,000 or less, class 3 and 4 at not more than $40,000

1 NYC property—ICIP certificate of continuing use application due

15 Personal income—Annual return, estimated tax, pay to N.Y. Income Tax Bur.

15 NYC income—Individuals report, pay estimate to N.Y. Income Tax Bur.

15 NYC unincorporated business—File annual return; report, pay estimate to Commr. Fin.

30 Highway use—Quarterly report and payment due

30 Fuel use—Quarterly report and payment due

30 Withholding—Quarterly report, pay to Tax Commr.

NORTH CAROLINA 15 Personal income—Individuals, estates, and trusts return, pay to Sec'y Rev.

15 Personal income—Estimated return or installment to Sec'y Rev.

15 Corporate income—Estimated return and installment

15 Corporate income—Annual return, pay Sec'y. Rev. (15th of 4th month)

15 Corporate franchise—Report, pay Sec'y. Rev. (15th of 4th month)

15 Sales-use—Last day for nonprofit organizations to file with Sec'y Rev. for refund for 2nd 6 months of calendar yr.

30 Sales-use—Quarterly report, pay tax to Sec'y. Rev.

30 Public utilities—Quarterly franchise tax report, pay to Sec'y. Rev.

30 Severance—Report, pay quarterly forest products tax to Sec'y Rev.

30 Withholding—Report, pay quarterly to Sec'y Rev.

30 Motor carriers—Report, pay road use tax to Sec'y. Rev.

30 Alternative fuels—Bulk-end users file information return with Sec'y. Rev.

30 Motor fuels—Distributors file with Sec'y. Rev. for quaterly refund

30 Utilities—Annual utilities report to Utilities Comm.

NORTH DAKOTA 1 Cooperative electrical generating plants—Report gross receipts to Tax Commr.

2d Mon. Property—Meeting date for city bds. equal.

15 Corporate income—Pay quarterly estimated tax to Tax Commr.

15 Income—Return, pay to Tax Commr.

15 Personal income—Pay quarterly estimated tax to Tax Commr.

15 Income—Information returns to Tax Commr.

30 Withholding—Employers' quarterly withholding report, pay to Tax Commr.

30 Sales-use—Quarterly return, pay to Tax Commr.

30 Motor fuels—Gasoline and special fuels—importer's for use report, quarter pay to Tax Commr.

OHIO Before 1st Mon. Property—File application for current agricultural use valuation with cty. auditor

15 Personal income—Estimate and 1st quarter to Dept. Tax. (payable to Treas.)

15 Personal income—Annual return (pay State Treas.) to Tax Commr.

20 Property—Consolidated return discontinuance notice to Tax Commr.

23 Sales-use—Vendors in Group D counties file semiannual return, pay to State Treas.

23 Sales and use—Direct payment permit holders file return, pay State Treas.

23 Consumer use—Pay State Treas.

30 Withholding—Quarterly report, pay quarterly to Dept. Tax. (pay to Treas.)
30 Property—Personalty report to Cty. Auditor, if inter-county corporation to Tax Commr.; pay half to Cty. Treas. if single county (with supp. to Cty., if needed)
30 Property—personalty report to County Auditor (single co. corp. pay 1st half)
30 Property—personalty file intercounty report with Tax Commr.
30 Property—Apply to county auditor for reduced valuation of property injured or destroyed during preceding quarter
30 Highway use—Quarterly return, pay State Treas.; information return to Tax Commr.

OKLAHOMA 1 Property—Cty. Bd. Equal. hears assmt. complaints in counties with valuation under $1 billion
1 Utilities, freight line cos., and RRs—Report gross earnings to Tax Comm.
1 Insurance—File surplus line brokers verified statement with Ins. Commr.
15 Insurance—Estimated tax due for insurance cos. with tax of $1,000 or more in previous yr.
15 Corporation and personal income—Report, pay to Tax Comm.
15 Income—Estimate pay to Tax Commr. if over $500 for tax year
15 Property—Personalty listed or added penalty imposed
15 Income—Report and pay estimated tax (if amount not over $100, with annual return; if over $100, all or ¼; to Tax Comm.) (15th of 4th month after fiscal year)
15 Property—RR and public service corporations make return of property lists to Tax Commr.
20 Withholding—Employers quarterly report, pay quarter to Tax Comm. if tax under $500 per quarter
30 Escheats—Last day for Insurance Cos. to file annual report with State Tax Comm.
30 Coal mines—Operators Quarterly report, pay to Tax Comm.
30 Motor fuel importers use—Quarterly report, pay tax to Tax Comm.
30 Property—Textile manufacturers report to cty. Assr., pay to cty. treas.
30 Income—Small business capital cos. annual report to Tax Commr.

OREGON 1 Motor carriers—Report to PUC
1 Property—Veterans' and for fall-out shelters, file for exemption with Cty. Assr.
1 Utilities, RRs, and other carriers—Report to PUC
1 Property—Farm land, apply for special assessment to Cty. Assr.
1 Property—Owners of pollution controls file for exemption with Cty. Assr.
1 Property—Western Ore. forest lands apply to Cty. Assr. for valuation as forest land.
1 Property—Literary, charitable, religious, etc., orgs. file exemption claim with Assr.
1 Property—Claim exemption for RR property put to alternate public transportation use
15 Corporate income and excise—Report, pay to Dept. Rev; estimate and installment also due
15 Excise and income—Corporations report, pay quarterly estimate to Dept. Rev.; file annual return
15 Partnerships—Information returns to Dept. Rev.
15 Personal income—Report, pay ¼; estimated tax to Dept. Rev.
15 Property—File homestead deferral claim with Cty. Assr.
15 Property—File rental assistance claim with Dept. Rev.
20 Use fuel—Quarterly (substitute for monthly) report, pay to Dept. MV
30 Withholding—Quarterly report, pay to Dept. Rev.
30 Escheats—Last day for Insurance Cos. to file annual report with Div. State lands
30 Forest products harvest tax—Quarterly estim. report, pay to Dept. Rev.

30 Timber severance taxes (East and West Ore.)—Quarterly estim. report, pay to Dept. Rev.

PENNSYLVANIA 15 Escheats—Report property to Dept. Rev.

15 Capital stock, franchise, loans—Annual return, pay to Dept. Rev.

15 Corporate income—Annual return and payment (95% of tax if paying in installments) to Dept. Rev.; S corps. file returns

15 Corporate loans—Annual report, pay tax to Dept. Rev.

15 Personal income—Annual return, pay to Dept. Rev.; estimated, pay quarter to Dept. Rev. if 4-1 requirements met

15 Pbgh. City mercantile license—Report, pay to Treas.

15 Pbgh. Sch. Dist. mercantile license—Report, pay to Coll.

15 Public utility realty tax (PURTA)—Tentative tax, pay in full to Dept. Rev.

15 Mutual thrift institutions (nonstock)—Annual report, pay balance to Dept. Rev.

15 Philadelphia Sch. Dist. income from property—Report, pay to Phila. Dept. Rev.

15 Phila. City net profits—Annual combined return (with 1st estimated net profits tax installment), pay Phila. Dept. Rev.

15 Phila. wage tax—Employees' annual information report to Dept. Rev. of unwithheld pay

15 Pittsburgh City and Sch. Dist. earned income—File annual declaration, pay first ¼; estimate to Treas.

15 Pbgh. business privilege—Annual return, pay to City Treas.

15 Phila. realty non-utilization—Report, pay to Phila. Dept. Rev.

15 Phila. business privilege—Report, pay to Phila. Dept. Rev.

20 Sales—Quarterly return, pay to Dept. Rev.

30 Pbgh. City and Sch. Dist. earned income—Employee's quarterly return, payment to Treas. on nonwithheld compensation

30 Pbgh. City and Sch. Dist. earned income—Employer's quarterly withholding return, pay to School Treas.

30 Pbgh. City & Sch Dist. occupational priv.—Report, pay withholding on employees working before 3-31

30 Personal income—Withholding report, pay for 1st quarter to Dept. Rev. if under $300 quarterly

30 Phila. wage tax—Employer's report, pay to Phila. Dept. Rev. on withheld pay

30 Phila. wage tax—Employee's quarterly report, pay to Phila. Dept. Rev. on unwithheld pay

30 Property (Pbgh., 2nd class cities)—Pay 2nd quarter installment to City Treas.

30 Motor carrier—Quarterly report, pay road tax to Dept. Rev.

RHODE ISLAND 15 Personal income—Individuals, estates and trusts file annual return and make payment to Tax Admr.

15 Personal income—Estimate and first quarterly installment to Tax Admr.

15 Personal income—Partnership information return (Form RI-1065)

30 Withholding—Pay quarterly return if withholding less than $50 monthly

30 Motor carrier—Quarterly report, pay to Tax Admr.

30 Sales and use—Quarterly report and payment to Tax Admr. (if liability averages less than $200 per month for 6 mos)

SOUTH CAROLINA 15 Income—Estimated tax (1st installment) of individual, fiduciary to Dept. Rev.

15 Income—Individual, fiduciary annual report, pay to Dept. Rev.

15 Property—Airline, private cars returns due

20 Sales—Quarterly report, pay to Dept. Rev.

20 Use—Quarterly return, pay to Dept. Rev.

20 Motor carriers—Quarterly return, payment of road tax to Dept. Rev.

30 Withholding—Quarterly report, pay to Dept. Rev.

30 Property—Mfrs.' realty and personalty, fishermen's and commercial boat-owners' returns; merchants' and pawnbrokers' stock statements to Dept. Rev.

30 Property—Return due to cty. auditor

SOUTH DAKOTA	**15**	Income—Banks and financial orgs. quarterly estimate report-pay to Dept. Rev. and Reg.
	15	Utilities—Property report to Dept. Rev. and Reg.
	15	Rural electric cos.—Report gross receipts to Dept. Rev. and Reg.
	15	Pipe line cos.—Annual report and statement of property to Dept. Rev. and Reg.
	15	Telephone cos.—Gross receipts report and statement of property to Dept. Rev. and Reg.
	30	Energy mineral severance—Quarterly report, pay to Dept. Rev. and Reg.
	30	Precious metals severance—File estimate, pay ¼ of estimated tax to Dept. Rev. and Reg.
	30	Motor fuel—Carriers permanently licensed as interstate fuel users report, pay to Dept. Rev. and Reg.
TENNESSEE	**15**	Corporate excise (income)—Report, pay tax to Dept. Rev.
	15	Corporate franchise—Report, pay to Dept. Rev.
	15	Personal income—Corporations, information to Dept. Rev. on dividends paid
	15	Corporate excise (income)—Estimate, pay to Dept. Rev.
	15	Personal income—Report and pay to Commr. Rev.
	25	Gasoline—Report-pay liquefied gas used in vehicles on instate roads to Dept. Rev.
	30	Highway user fuel—sales-use—aviation fuel dealers—Report to Commr. Rev.
	30	Sales and use—Aviation fuel dealers report to Commr. Rev.
TEXAS	**15**	Property tax—File rendition statements and property reports with chief appraiser
	20	Sales—Quarterly report, pay to Comptr. if liability under $500 monthly or $1500 quarterly
	25	Gasoline—Motor fuel transporters, interstate truckers report, pay to Comptr.
	25	Diesel fuel—Motor fuel transporters, interstate truckers, dyed diesel fuel bonded users report, pay to Comptr.
	25	Liquefied gas—Licensed dealers and licensed interstate truckers report, pay to Comptr.
	30	Sulphur producers—Gross production tax quarterly report, pay Comptr.
	30	Interstate motor carrier—Report, pay sales-use tax to Comptr.
	30	Utilities—gross receipts—Last day for quarterly report, pay to Comptr.
	30	Hotel occupancy—Quarterly report, pay to Comptr.
UTAH	**1**	Property—County BEQ must notify property owner who failed to file affidavit of intent to revoke exemption
	15	Corporate income-franchise—Return and full tax to State Tax Comm.
	15	Income—Corporations pay estimated tax to State Tax Comm.
	15	Public utilities—Gross intrastate operating revenue report to Tax Comm.
	15	Personal income—Return and tax to State Tax Comm.
	15	Last day to claim refund for agricultural nonhighway use fuel purchased in prior calendar year
	30	Sales-use—Quarterly return, pay Tax Comm.
	30	County, municipal sales-use tax, quarterly return, pay Tax Comm.
	30	County transient room tax, quarterly return, pay Tax Comm.
	30	Withholding—Report, pay Tax Comm.
	30	Tobacco products (not cigarettes)—Quarterly return-payment to Tax Comm.
	30	Quarterly withholding from gross proceeds of uranium or vanadium mines to Tax Comm.
	30	Quarterly withholding tax on mineral production to Tax Comm.
	30	Property—Holders of unclaimed property report to state treasurer
VERMONT	**1**	Property—Assessment date
	1	Property—Notice of personalty lien filed
	15	Personal income—Report, pay to Commr. Taxes
	15	Income—File declaration of estimted tax and pay 1st quarterly installment

15 Property—File homestead declaration, homestead tax adjustment claim, with Commr. of Taxes
15 Utilities—Gross operating revenue tax payment to State Treas.
15 Utilities—Transportation companies report, pay half to Commr. Taxes
20 Property—Report to Town Listers
25 Bank franchise—Pay Commr. Taxes for last quarter
25 Withholding—Quarterly report, pay to Commr. Taxes
25 Sales-use—Quarterly report, pay to Commr. Taxes
25 Meals and rooms—Quarterly report, pay to Commr. Taxes if past yr. tax $500 or less
25 Telephone companies—Report, pay qtrly. alt. gross operating revenue tax to Tax Commr.
30 Property—Report abandoned property to State Treas.

VIRGINIA 1 Corporation registration—Annual report, fee to Corp. Comm.
15 Income—Report, pay to Tax Dept.
15 Passenger carriers—Pay quarterly road tax to State Treas.
15 Corporate income—Estimate, pay installment Dept. Tax. if tax over $1000
15 Contractors' use tax—Contractors bringing machinery into Va. report to and pay Tax Commr.
15 Rolling stock—RR and freight car cos. report to Dept. Tax.
15 Utilities—Estimate to Corp. Comm., pay State Treas. if gross receipts tax over $500
20 Sales-use—Quarterly report, pay to Tax Commr.
30 Withholding—Quarterly report, and pay (if monthly tax under $100) to State Tax Commr.
30 Forest products—Quarterly report, pay to Tax Dept.
30 Escheats—Last day for Insurance Cos. to file annual report with State Treas.
30 Motor carriers—Quarterly road tax report, pay to State Treas.

WASHINGTON 1 RRs cos.—Car mileage report to Dept. Rev.
1 Specified utilities—Report, pay to Utilities and Transp. Comm.
15 Auto transportation cos.—Quarterly report, pay to Utilities and Transp. Comm.
25 Special fuels—Report, pay to Dept. MV (quarterly filers)
30 Property—Last day to pay Cty. Treas. 1st half tax, (all if under $30)
30 Property—Listing of personalty must be filed with Assr.
30 Property—Unprocessed timber and specified farm and fish products in storage or in transit must be shipped out-of-state of this date to be exempt
30 Property—Application for current use classification of farm and agricultural lands deemed approved if not acted on by Assr.
30 B&O tax—Quarterly report, pay to Dept. Rev.
30 Sales-use—Quarterly report, pay to Dept. Rev.
30 Utilities—Quarterly report, pay to Dept. Rev.
30 Timber excise—Quarterly report, pay to Dept. Rev.

WEST VIRGINIA 1 Property—2nd installment delinquent; personalty may be distrained
15 Corporate income—Estimate, pay installment to Tax Dept.
15 Personal income—Estimated return and/or installment to Tax Commr.
15 Personal income—Report, pay (15th of 4th month after tax year) to Tax Commr.
15 Franchise—Estimate and quarterly tax payment to Tax Commr.
20 Sales-use—Quarterly return, pay to Tax Commr.
25 Motor fuel—Motor carriers road tax quarterly report, pay to Tax Commr.
30 Gross sales (B & O)—Estimated quarterly return, pay to Tax Commr.
30 Withholding—Quarterly report, pay to Tax Commr.
30 Escheats—Last day for Insurance Cos. to file annual report with State Treas.
30 Coal severance—Report, pay min. tax to Tax Commr. quarterly

30 Telecommunications—Quarterly estimated tax if $1,000 or less per month
30 Sales—Quarterly motor fuel report, pay to Tax Commr.
WISCONSIN 1 Property—Last day to file manufacturing property report, if extension obtained
1st Monday Property—Assr. completes assessments on this day (except 1st & 2nd class cities)
15 Income—Partnership return to Dept. Rev.
15 Personal income—Estimated return and installment to Dept. Rev.
15 Personal income—Annual return, pay any balance to Dept. Rev.
15 Personal income—Information return to Dept. Rev.
15 Utilities—RR's sleeping car, & express cos. file annual report to Dept. Rev.
15 Car line cos.—File annual gross earnings statement from non-Wisconsin RRs to Dept. Rev.
15 Railroads—Report rentals to Dept. Rev.
15 Car line cos.—Pay gross earnings tax installment, on full tax if under $2,000, to Dept. Rev.
30 Sales-use—Report, pay for quarter to Dept. Rev.
30 Withholding—Report, deposit quarterly amount in designated bank
WYOMING 1 Pipeline cos., electric utilities, telephone & telegraph cos. & other public utilities—Info statement to Dept. Rev.
1 Water cos.—Report to cty. assr. reservoir water impounded or stored in-state for use out-of-state
1 Utilities—Pay one-half uniform assessment fee
10 Tobacco products—Consumers report, pay tax to Dept. Rev. for past quarter
20 Tobacco products—Wholesalers report, pay to Dept. Rev. for past quarter
30 Sales-use—Quarterly report, pay to Dept. Rev. if tax under $150 during any month
30 Gasoline, diesel fuel—IFTA-licensed carriers report, payment to Dept. Transportation

¶325 MAY CALENDAR

For RECURRING MONTHLY dates, see ¶ 380.
For UNEMPLOYMENT INSURANCE report dates, see ¶ 272.

Memorial Day: The following state—Vt. (shown below by asterisk (*))—*doesn't* follow Fed law in observing Memorial Day on last Monday in May. Vt. celebrates it on May 30.

ALABAMA 1	Transportation, transmission, other utilities—Pay quarterly fee to PUC.
ALASKA 15	Property—Apply for farm use assessment to Assr.
ARIZONA 1	Property—Pay Cty. Treas. 2nd half tax on realty and personalty secured by realty (last day without penalty)
10	Utilities—File statement of revenues from preceding calendar year with Corp. Comm.
15	Corporate income—Exempt organizations file information return with Dept. Rev.
31	Corporate income—Corporations exempt from filing annual report give disclosure certificate to Corp. Comm.
ARKANSAS 1	Corporate franchise—Report, pay to Sec'y State
CALIFORNIA 15	Corporate income—Exempt corporations' return to FTB
24	Sales-use—Prepay SBE if so ordered
Last Fri.	Property—Statement to Cty. Assr. unless earlier date, not pre-4-1
31	Property—State-assessed; last day for notice of assessed value of unitary property
COLORADO 15	Utilities—Maintenance fee report
26	Property—Protest of realty valuation must be mailed (postmarked) to assr.
CONNECTICUT 15	Property—File tax relief application for elderly or disabled
31	Utilities—Public service companies operating report due to Dept. of Public Utility Control
DELAWARE 1	Telephonic business—Wire, transmitter tax computed as of date
1	Financial institutions—Banks pay Bank Commr.
1	Property (Sussex Cty.)—Quarterly supplemental assmt.; pay realty and capitation taxes
1	Escheat (abandoned property)—Life insurance cos. report to Div. Rev.
1st Mon.	Steam, gas, electric cos.—Gross receipts report to Dept. Fin.
15	Property (Dover)—Assmt. posted by this date
DISTRICT OF COLUMBIA 15	Exempt organizations—Unrelated business income return (15th of 5th month)
FLORIDA 1	Income—Partnerships make annual information report to Dept. Rev.
1	Corporation report—Corporations file annual report and pay fees to Sec'y. of State
1	Initial—LLCs file annual report with Dept. of State
1	Severance—Report, pay quarterly estimate to Dept. Rev.
GEORGIA 1	Escheats—Last day for insurance cos. to file annual report with Commr. Rev.
IDAHO 15	RR maintenance—Pay one-half fee to PUC
15	Motor carriers—Pay PUC second half maintenance fee
ILLINOIS 15	Income—Organizations exempt under IRC §501(c) report to, pay Dept. Rev.
31	Property—Titleholder or owner of beneficial interest files affidavit with chief county assmt. officer about ownership or use of property receiving senior citizen's homestead exemption, if required
INDIANA 1	RR car cos.—Report to State Bd. Tax Commrs.
1	Utilities—File annual gross revenue report with Comm.
10	Property—File homestead tax credit claim with Cty. Auditor; application for property exemption also due (exceptions)
10	Property—Pay 1st half tax to Cty. & City Treas.
15	Property—Report personalty to township Assr.
IOWA 1	Electric transmission lines—Report to Dir. Rev.
1	Telephone, telegraph cos.—Report to Dir. Rev.
1	Utilities—Nonprofit utilities report to Dir. Rev.
1	Utilities (specified)—Report to Dir. Rev.
5	Property—File assessment protest with local Bd. Review

20	Property—Disaster areas, last day to file assmt. protest with bd. review
30	Underground petroleum storage—Report, pay balance of fees if granted extension for quarterly report
31	Property—Bd. Review adjourns; appeals to Dist. Ct. made in 20 days of this date
KANSAS 1	Property—Cty. Appraiser must notify personal property owners of classification or appraisal by this date
15	Property—Last day to complain about classification or appraisal of personalty
20	Property—Last day for Cty. Appraiser to issue final determination as to realty
KENTUCKY 1st Mon.	Property—Assmt. roll open for inspection
1st Mon.	Property (4th class cities)—Bd. Supervisors meets
31	Property (2nd class cities)—2% discount expires
LOUISIANA 15	Personal income—Annual return, pay to Sec'y Rev.
MAINE 1	Property—Inventory in unorganized township to Rev. Services
MASSACHUSETTS 1	Forest product and forest land taxes—Report to local assessor
1	Property—Pay semiannual and quarterly taxes to local assessor
15	Marine insurers' underwriting profits return to Commr.
15	Property—Commr. values telephone and telegraph cos.
MICHIGAN 15	Corporations—Annual report, pay to Dept. Commerce
15	Foreign corporations—Report increased authorized capital stock, pay fee
3rd Mon.	Utilities—State Board of Assessors hears valuation complaint
4th Mon.	Property—State Bd. Equal. hears Cty. appeals
MINNESOTA 1	Property—Application to Assr. for deferment of taxes and assmt. under Agricultural Property Tax Law
1	Mining cos.—File return
15	Property—Apply to court for permission to continue appeal without payment of realty tax (notify county auditor and county attorney)
15	Income—Exempt orgs. report, pay on taxable income to Dept. Rev.
15	Property—Pay tax by this date or before 21 days after postmark date of statement
15	Property—Pay first half of tax due (rest by Oct. 15)
16	Property—Apply to court for permission to continue appeal without payment
31	Property—Pay auxiliary forest and yield taxes to Cty. Treas.
MISSISSIPPI 1	Property—Pay ¼ of tax to tax coll. with interest per month from Feb. 1 if locality allows
1	RRs—Car mileage report to Tax Commr.
MISSOURI 1	Property—Airline cos. statement to Tax Comm.
1	Alcoholic beverage—Renewal license with Supervisor of Liquor Control
1	Bingo tax—Annual report to Dir. Rev.
1st Mon.	Merchants (except St. Louis)—Report to Assr.
2nd Mon.	Property—(St. Louis)—File with assr. assmt. appeal to Bd. Equal.
3rd Mon.	Property (St. Louis)—BEQ hears complaints, equalizes assmt.
31	Express cos.—Daily penalties attach for failure to report or pay tax
MONTANA 15	Corporate license—income—Report pay to Dept. Rev.
30	Utilities—Tel. cos. qtrly. report, pay gross income tax to Dept. Rev. (60 days after end of qtr.)
31	Minerals—Pay net or gross proceeds tax (not coal) and royalties tax to Cty. Treas.
31	Minerals—Crude petroleum and natural gas producers report, pay qtrly. taxes to State Treas.; duplicate report to Bd. Oil & Gas Conservation
NEBRASKA 1	Property—File personal property return with Cty. Assr.
1	Property—First-half realty tax for counties with population of 100,000 or less is delinquent
NEVADA 10	Minerals tax on net proceeds—Pay tax to Dept. Tax.
15	Property—Last day to appeal protested assmt. to State Bd. Equal.

15	Utilities--Annual report to PSC
NEW HAMPSHIRE 1	Small business corporations—Annual information report to Dept. Rev. Admn.
31	Property—Last day to file return
31	Property—Charitable orgs. (not religious and educational) file statement of finances with Board Tax and Land Appeals
NEW JERSEY 1	Property—Pay 2d quarter to Tax Coll.
1	Property—Last day for elderly and disabled homeowners to file income statements for homestead deduction, if extension granted
1	Sewage and water corps.—Pay ½ of excise tax
5	Utilities (Water, and sewage cos.)—Last day for Dir. Div. Tax to certify gross receipts tax and franchise tax to state Treas. (15 days from certification to pay 1st 35%)
15	Al. bev.—Mfrs., distbtrs., etc. report, pay Div. Tax. for March and April
NEW MEXICO 10	Property—Copper production ad valorem tax installment due, pay Tax. & Rev. Dept.
31	Utilities (specified)—Pay quarterly inspection and supervision fee to PSC
NEW YORK 1	Property—Taxable status date for various counties
15	Exempt orgs. (unrelated business income)—Report, pay to Commr.
15	Property—Nonresidents of cities or towns in Westchester County demand notice of assmt. (in Nassau County, must be mailed between May 1 and May 5)
28	Property (NYC)—Final assmt. roll published
4th Tues.	Property—First day for hearing assmt. complaints (hearing for nonresidents and corps. with property in more than one city or town must meet no later than 21 days afterward)
NORTH CAROLINA 15	Corporation income—Tax-exempt orgs. report, pay tax on unrelated business income to Sec'y Rev.
15	Public utility regulatory fee—Pay to Utilities Comm.
NORTH DAKOTA 1	Telecommunications—Report to Tax Commr. and Cty. Auditors
1	Rural Electric Co-ops—Gross receipts return to Tax Commr.; Cty. line mileage reports to Cty. auditors
1	Property—RRs report to Tax Commr.
1	Property—Airlines, aircraft, and airports—Last day to pay tax
15	Foreign corps.—Annual report, pay filing fee to Sec'y State
OHIO 10	Property—If personalty not paid with return due 4–30; pay half
15	Severance—Quarterly report, pay to Treas.
15	Natural gas excise—Quarterly return, pay to Tax Commr.
20	Natural gas dist. (MCF)—Quarterly return, pay to Tax Commr.
23	Sales-use—Vendors in Group E counties file semi-annual return, pay to State Treas.
31	Franchise (income)—If granted extension pay third estimate or full payment
OKLAHOMA 31	Property Unmanufactured farm product assmt. date
OREGON 2nd Mon.	Property—Cty. BEQ meets
15	Oil & Gas gross production—Quarterly report, pay to Dept. Rev.
15	Property—Pay 3rd installment of tax to Coll.
15	Property—Taxes delinquent if installment not paid
PENNSYLVANIA 1	Property—6% interest added to unpaid realty tax for past year except unseated land in 7th & 8th class counties
31	Personal property (Phila.)—Last day to pay without penalty
SOUTH CAROLINA 15	Corporate income—Annual report of exempt orgs. to Tax Comm.
SOUTH DAKOTA 1	Property—RR reports and leasehold site reports to Dept. Rev. and Reg.
3d Fri	Property—Last day to appeal decision of cty. BEQ to Office of Hearing Examiners
TENNESSEE 20	Property—Institutions claiming exemption for 1st time file claim with State BEQ
TEXAS 1	Property—Exemption application
15	Franchise tax—Report, pay Comptr. Pub. Accts.
15	Sales-use—Prepayment for discount to Comptr. Pub. Accts.

20	Natural gas pipeline cos.—Quarterly report to RR Comm, pay Comptr.
UTAH 15	Oil and gas conservation fee—Report, pay to Tax Comm.
31	Alcoholic beverages—Renew private club liquor license
***VERMONT 20**	Property—Listers hear complaints on appraisals
VIRGINIA 1	Personal income—Report, pay to Cty. or City Treas.
1	Personal income—Estimate to Cty. or City Commr. Rev., pay quarterly tax to Cty. or City Treas.
1	Property—Pay tangible and intangible personalty tax to Cty. or City Commr. Rev. and Treas.
1	Litter control—Specified businesses file Form 200 and pay tax to Dept. Tax.
WASHINGTON 1	Private car cos.—Report property to Dept. Rev.
31	Property—Present proof to Cty. Assr. that specified fish and farm products in storage or in transit were shipped out-of-state by 4–30
WEST VIRGINIA 1	Utilities—Deliver to Tax Commr. annual property tax report to Bd. Pub. Works
15	Income; franchise—Exempt entities file unrelated business income returns with Tax Commr.
WISCONSIN 1	Utilities (specified)—Annual report to Dept. Rev.; license fee assessment date
10	Utilities—Pay 1st installment of property tax to Dept. Rev.
10	Utilities (specified)—Pay 1st installment of license fees to Dept. Rev.
3rd Monday	Property (1st class cities)—File objections to property valuation
WYOMING 1	RRs and rail car cos.—Report to Dept. Rev.
10	Property—2nd half of realty tax becomes payable
4th Mon.	Property—File homestead and veteran exemption claims with cty. assr.

¶330 JUNE CALENDAR

For RECURRING MONTHLY dates, see ¶ 380.
For UNEMPLOYMENT INSURANCE report dates, see ¶ 272.

ALABAMA.	**15**	Corporate income—Quarterly estimated tax report-pay to Dept. Rev.
	15	Personal income—Estimate and/or installment to Dept. Rev.
ALASKA	**15**	Corporation income—Report pay 2nd estimated tax installment to Dept. Rev.
	30	Oil & gas—Property tax payment due
ARIZONA	**15**	Corporate income—Report, pay 2nd estimated tax installment to Dept. Rev.
	15	Personal income—Report, pay 2nd estimated tax installment to Dept. Rev.
	15	Property—Dept. Rev. notifies owners of preliminary values of centrally assessed property
ARKANSAS	**15**	Income—Pay 2nd estimated tax installment to Dept. Fin. & Admn.
	3rd. Mon.	Property—Pay ¼ ad valorem tax to Cty. Coll.
	30	Pipeline cos.—Pay pipeline safety fee to PSC
CALIFORNIA	**8**	Property—Collector publishes delinquent list
	15	Corporate income—Estimate, pay 2nd installment to Franch. Tax Bd.
	15	Personal income—Estimate and/or installment to Franch. Tax Bd.
	20	Property—State-assessed property; assessee has to at least this date to file declaration of intent to petition for reassessment of unitary property
	23	Sales-use—Prepay SBE if so ordered
COLORADO	**1**	Oil and gas conservation—Quarterly report, pay to Oil and Gas Conservation Comm.
	1	Property—Protest of realty valuation must be received by assr. if personally delivered.
	15	Income—Estimate and/or installment to Dept. Rev.
	15	Property—Pay last half realty, personalty taxes to Cty. Treas.
	29	Property—Protest of personalty valuation must be mailed (postmarked) to assr.
CONNECTICUT	**15**	Corporation business income—Report, pay 2d estimated tax installment to Commr. Rev. Services
	15	Personal income—Declare, pay quarterly estimated tax and composite payments to Commr. Rev. Services
	15	Income—Unrelated business income tax return to Commr. Rev. Services
	15	Insurance companies—Net direct premiums estimated tax report, payment (60%) to Commr. Rev. Services
	30	Utilities—Public service cos. pay installment of assessment for Dept. of Public Utility expenses
DELAWARE	**1**	Franchise—Pay 1st tentative tax installment
	1	Tel. & Tel.—Report wire mileage, transmitters to State Treas.
	1	Property (Kent Cty.)—First quarterly supplemental assmt.
	1	Financial institutions—Banks and trust cos. pay Bank Commr.
	1	Escheat (abandoned property)—Holders except banks and insurance cos. deliver abandoned property to State Escheator (90 days after filing report).
	1st Mon.	Utilities—Steam, gas and electric cos. temporary licenses expire
	15	Personal income—Estimated return, installment to Div. Rev.
	15	Corporate income—Tentative return, installment to Div. Rev.
	15	Utilities—Tel. & tel. cos. pay tax on telephonic business
	25	Gasoline—Distributors with avg. monthly sales of ½ million or more gals. pay 75% of tax on June sales and file statement of estimated taxes with Dept. Public Safety
	30	Foreign corporations—Annual report to Sec'y State
DISTRICT OF COLUMBIA	**15**	Franchise—Declare and/or pay estimated tax to Office of Tax and Revenue
	15	Personal income—Estimated tax installment or declaration

16	LLC—File two-year report, pay registration fee to Business Regulation Administration, Corporation Div. of Dept. of Consumer and Regulatory Affairs
FLORIDA 1	Property—Dept. Rev. must submit county railroad property assessments to county appraisers
1	Insurance—Annual insurer's license tax due
15	Insurance—Estimated tax installment due
30	Property tax—Pay ¼ of estimated tax (if prepayment elected).
GEORGIA 15	Corporate income—Estimate and/or pay Commr. Rev. (15th day of 6th mo)
15	Personal income—Estimated tax report, payment to Commr. Rev.
HAWAII 20	Property—Cty. council sets rates for next tax year
20	Personal and corporation income—Pay 2nd quarter of estimate to Dept. Tax
20	Financial institutions—Pay 2nd installment franchise tax to Dept. Tax
20	Public service cos.—Pay 2nd quarter gross receipts tax to Dept. Tax.
30	Corporations—Foreign corporation file annual report with, pay license fee to Dir. Commerce & Consumer Affairs
30	Property—Last day to file disaster claim
IDAHO 1st Mon.	Property—Taxpayer assessment notices must be delivered or mailed
15	Income—Corporations estimate and/or installment to Tax Comm.
20	Property—Pay Tax Coll. 2nd half realty or personalty tax; last day for exemption claimants to appeal to city BEQ
20	Forest products—Report, pay yield tax to Cty. Treas.
20	Property—File claim for hardship exemption with Cty. BEQ
4th Mon.	Property—Cty. BEQ hears assessment complaints
4th Mon.	Property—Last day for realty and personalty to be assessed
ILLINOIS 1	Property (Except Cook Cty).—Pay half realty tax to Coll. in counties not accelerating payment (3-1) dates
1	Railroads—File statement of realty or changes to original statement with Dept. Rev.
15	Income—Individuals and corporations pay estimated tax to Dept. Rev.
15	Insurance cos.—Quarterly estimate unless annual tax under $5,000.
15	Gas and water cos. (invested capital tax)—Quarterly estimated payment to Dept. Rev.
15	Electric cos. (taxes on invested capital & distribution of electricity)—Quarterly estimated payment to Dept. Rev.
INDIANA 1	Utilities—Last day for property assessment
1st Mon.	Property—Cty. Bd. Rev. starts meetings for Cty. with 350,000 or less pop.
15	Personal income—Estimate or pay tax to Dept. Rev.
20	Utility receipts—Quarterly estimated return, pay to Dept. Rev. (if estimated annual liability exceeds $1,000)
IOWA 1	Property—Elderly, disabled, low income, mobile homeowners file claim for credit for property taxes
3rd Mon.	Property—Realty may be sold for taxes starting this date
30	Personal income—Pay 2nd quarter estimated tax to Dept. Rev. & Fin.
KANSAS 15	Income—Estimate and/or installment to Dir. Tax.
15	Bank tax—Financial institutions make estimated privilege tax declaration, payment to Dir. Tax.
15	Franchise—Nonprofit corporations file annual report, pay to Sec'y of State
20	Property—MV carriers—Pay 2nd half tax to Dir. Property Valuation
20	Property—Pay last ½ personalty tax and last ½ of realty taxes (if paying in 2 installments) to Cty. Treas.
KENTUCKY 1	Business development corporations—Report, pay to Dept. Rev.
1	Property (2nd class cities)—Pay City Treas.
15	Income, limited liability entity tax—Individuals and corporations estimate and pay installment to Dept. Rev.

30	Corporations—Annual report and fee to Sec'y State
LOUISIANA 15	Personal Income—Estimate and/or pay to Sec'y Rev.
15	Corporate income—Pay estimated tax installment to Sec'y Rev.
30	Chain stores—Opened after this date, pay half tax
30	Utilities—Report, pay inspection fee to Sec'y Rev.
MAINE 15	RRs—Pay 1st one-third of excise tax to Rev. Services
15	Income—Estimate and/or pay to Rev. Services
MARYLAND 15	Individual and corporate income—Estimate and/or pay tax to Comptr.
15	Utilities franchise tax—File quarterly estimated tax return, pay 25% of tax
MASSACHUSETTS 1	Assn. or trust with transferable shares—Annual report to Sec'y State
1	Income—Information returns to Commr. Rev.
15	Corporate excise or personal income—Pay quarterly estimated tax to Commr. Rev.
15	Telephone and telegraph companies—Appeal assessment to ATB
30	Property—Application for forest land certification to state forester
MICHIGAN 15	Personal income—Estimate tax, pay 2nd quarter to Dept. Treas.
30	Sales—License renewal/fee to Dept. Treas.
30	Cigarettes—Licenses expire on this date
MINNESOTA 15	Income—Estimate and/or pay tax to Commr. Rev.
2 business days before 30	Sales-use—Vendors with liability of $120,000 or more during fiscal yr. ending June 30 pay 78% of estimated June liability to Commr. Rev. (see also Aug. 20)
2 business days before 30	Liquor gross receipts—Vendors with liability of $120,000 or more during fiscal yr. ending June 30 pay 78% of estimated June liability to Commr. Rev. (see also Aug. 20)
30	Gasoline distributors, etc.—Renew licenses and permits
30	Aircraft owners—Register, pay tax to Commr. Transp.
30	Property—Last day to apply for homestead exemption
MISSISSIPPI 1st Mon.	Utilities—STC assesses all property of railroads, oil or gas pipelines, electric cos. and public services cos.
15	Corporate income—Pay quarterly estimated tax to Commr. Rev.
15	Personal income—Estimate and/or pay Tax Commr.
25	Sales-use—Employers pay at least 75% of June tax liability for current or past yr. if avg. monthly liability is at least $20,000 for the past yr.
MISSOURI 1st Mon.	Property (1st class Cty.)—BEQ meets
Fri. before 3rd Mon.	Property (1st class Cty.)—File appeal with Cty. BEQ
15	Income—Estimate and or pay to Dir. Rev.
3rd Mon.	Merchants and mfrs. (1st class counties)—BEQ meets
MONTANA 15	Personal income—Pay 2nd quarter estimated tax to Dept. Rev. (15th day of 6th month of fiscal year)
15	Corporation income—Estimate, pay Dept. Rev.
30	Utilities—Quarterly statement to PSC and Dept. Rev.; pay quarterly gross earnings tax to Dept. Rev.
NEBRASKA 1	Air carriers—Report to Tax Commr.
15	Personal income—Report, pay 2nd installment of estimated tax to Dept. Rev.
15	Corporation income—Report, pay 2nd installment of estimated tax to Dept. Rev.
NEVADA 1	Property—File claim for farm or open space use with Cty. Assr.
15	Property—Last day to apply for exemption with Cty. Assr.
30	Slot machine tax—Pay annual tax to Gaming Commr.
NEW HAMPSHIRE 15	Income—Individuals pay quarterly estimate to Dept. Rev. Admn.
15	Business profits—Pay 2nd quarter estimated tax to Dept. Rev. Admn.
15	RRs—Report, pay ¼ estimated tax
15	Utilities—Report, pay ¼ estimated tax
30	Sales-use—License for each business place expires (June 30 of odd-numbered years)
NEW JERSEY 1	Property—Last day for local collector to mail notice of disallowance of claim for homestead deduction for elderly and disabled if extension for claim granted

1	Property—Last day for elderly or disabled homesteader to pay remainder of tax if claim was disallowed and no extension was granted
1	Cable TV companies file statement of revenues with Office of Cable TV
15	Personal income (gross income tax)—Estimate or pay Div. Tax.
NEW MEXICO 15	Corporation income—Pay Tax & Rev. Dept. quarterly estimated tax
NEW YORK 1	Property—Taxable status date for various counties.
1	Commercial motor vehicle tax (NYC)—Medallion taxicab owners' semi-annual payment due; non-medallion annual return and payment due
15	Franchise—Business corporations report, pay ⅓ estimate to Tax Commr.
15	Franchise—Banks, financial institutions report-pay ⅓ estimate to Tax Commr.
15	Franchise—Transportation and transmission cos. report-pay ⅓ estimate to Dept. Tax. & Fin.
15	Gross income tax—Utilities report-pay ⅓ estimate to Dept. Tax. & Fin.
15	Franchise—Water, steam, gas and electric cos. report-pay ⅓ estimate to Dept. Tax. & Fin.
15	Petroleum business tax—Petroleum businesses report-pay ⅓ estimate to Dept. Tax. & Fin.
15	NYC business income—Corporations, banks and thrift institutions report, pay ⅓ franchise estimate to Dept. Fin.
15	Personal income—Pay estimated tax installment to Dept. Tax. & Fin.
15	Franchise (transportation and transmission cos.)—File estimated tax declaration, pay to Dept. Tax. & Fin.
15	Utilities (gross earnings, income, dividends)—Estimated tax declaration and installment to Dept. Tax. & Fin.
15	NYC income—Individual estimate and installment to Commr. Fin.
15	NYC unincorporated business—Estimate and quarterly pay (exceptions) to Commr. Fin.
15	NYC bank franchise—Estimate, pay to Dept. Fin.
15	Oil cos.—Additional franchise tax—Pay ⅓ estimate to Tax Commr.
20	Lubricating oil—Report, pay Dept. Tax. Fin. for quarterly period ending last day of May
20	Nonrefillable containers—Container sale initiator reports, pay for previous quarterly period ending on the last day of May
20	NYC commercial rent tax—Report, pay to Commr. Fin.
20	NYC commercial, transportation, vehicles—Report, pay to Commr. Fin.
20	NYC hotel occupancy—Quarterly report, pay to Fin. Admr.
20	Sales-use (state-local)—Quarterly report, pay to Dept. Tax. & Fin. annual return if tax not over $250
25	NYC tax on state licensed liquor retailer—Report, pay annual tax to Dept. Fin.
25	NYC wine and liquor license tax—Annual retail return
30	Water frontage & sewer rent—Annual water frontage & sewer rent charges due
NORTH CAROLINA 15	Income—Corporations or individuals file estimate and/or pay to Sec'y Rev.
NORTH DAKOTA 1	Property—Cty. Bd. Equal. meets
15	Income—Pay 2nd installment of estimated tax
OHIO 1	Utilities—Report to Tax Commr., ⅓ tax payment to State Treas. if estimate $1,000 (min.)
1st Mon.	Property—File application for homestead exemption (elderly or disabled; manufactured home) with Cty. Auditor
15	Personal income—Estimate and/or pay installment to Tax Commr.
20	Property—Pay Cty. Treas. 2nd half realty tax
20	Utilities—Pay 2nd half of property tax to county treasurer

23	Sales-use—Vendors in Group F counties file semi-annual return with State Treas.
29	Franchise—Added penalties attach for report delinquency
29	Property—Amend or file personalty report to avoid 50% penalty
30	Utilities—Telephone and telegraph cos. report to Tax Commr.
OKLAHOMA 15	Income—Estimate and/or 2nd installment to Tax Comm.
15	Property—Cty. assessor's report due to Tax Comm.
15	Insurance—Estimated tax payments due
30	Income—File claim for low income property tax credit with Tax Comm.
30	Franchise—No-tax licenses of new corps. expire
OREGON 2nd Mon.	Utilities—Petition Dept. Rev. to reduce or re-apportion assmt.
15	Corporate income-excise—Estimate, and/or installment to Dept. Rev.
15	Personal income—Quarterly estimated payment to Dept. Rev.
PENNSYLVANIA 1	Property—Last day to apply for farm and forest land assessment
15	Pbgh. City and Sch. Dist. earned income—Report, pay 2nd installment of estimated tax to City Treas. report, pay if earning profits by 4–15
15	Personal income—Pay 2nd quarter estimate to Dept. Rev.
15	Corporate net income—Pay second installment of estimated tax to Dept. Rev.
15	Phila. City net profits—Report, pay 2nd installment to Phila. Dept. Rev.
15	Corporate stock and franchise—Report, pay 2nd installment of estimated tax to Dept. Rev.
RHODE ISLAND 15	Personal income—Estimate and/or pay to Tax Admr.
15	Business corporation—Estimate, pay balance to Tax Admr.
15	Intangibles tax—Banks (including national banks or credit unions) return, pay to Tax Admr.
SOUTH CAROLINA 15	Corporate income—Pay 2nd estimated tax installment
15	Personal income—Pay 2nd installment of estimated tax
SOUTH DAKOTA 1	Airlines—Property tax report to Dept. Rev. and Reg.
1	Utilities—Report, pay tax on intrastate gross receipts to PVC (regulatory fund)
3rd Fri.	Property—Last day to file notice appealing county BEQ action to State BEQ
TENNESSEE 15	Corporate income —Estimate, pay to Dept. Rev.
TEXAS 30	Property—Pay 2nd half to Cty. Coll.
UTAH 1	Oil and gas, mining severance taxes—Taxpayers whose total taxes for past cal. year were $3,000 or more pay quarterly installment to Tax Comm.
1	Property—Owner of property assessed by Tax Comm. or county can apply to Comm. to correct assessment
1	Oil and gas, mining severance taxes—Annual statement, tax payment to Tax Comm.
15	Income—Corporations pay estimated tax to State Tax Comm.
22	Property—Tax rate determination and adoption deadline
VERMONT 1	Property—Electric generating plant education property tax—Pay 1/2 to Commr. Taxes
15	Income—Estimated return, pay 2nd quarterly installment to Commr. Taxes
25	Telephone cos.—Report, pay qtrly. installment of net value tax on personalty to Tax Commr.
VIRGINIA 1	Financial institutions—Pay franchise tax
1	Utilities—Pay franchise, license, gross receipts or property tax to State Treas.
15	Personal income—Estimates to Cty. Commr. Rev.; pay local Treas.
15	Corporate income—2d estimated installment to Commr.
15	Pub. Service Corps.—2d estimated installment Corp. Comm., pay State Treas.
WASHINGTON 1	Property—3% penalty for late payment kicks in
30	Property—Suit for refund must be filed in Cty. Superior Court
30	Private car cos.—Last day operative property assessed by Dept. Rev.

WEST VIRGINIA 15	Corporate income—Estimate report, pay to Tax Commr.
15	Personal income—Estimate and/or pay to Tax Commr.
15	Corporate income—Carrier's tax on gross and net income—pay 2nd half to Tax Commr.
15	Franchise—Quarterly estimated tax payment to Tax Commr.
15	Property—Mine, mill, factor, etc., report industrial realty improvements in past year to assrs.
20	Sales—Accelerated payments for first 15 days of June if averaging $100,000 tax monthly for previous yr.
30	Franchise—Application and fee to State Tax Commr. for renewal of certificate that expires July 1 of each year.
30	Motor carriers—Permit application, fee to PSC
30	Motor carriers—Assessment to PSC
30	Nonintoxicating beer—Renew license with Tax Dept.
WISCONSIN 15	Corporate income—Report, pay estimated tax installment to Dept. Rev.
15	Personal income—Report, pay estimated tax installment to Dept. Rev.
15	Oil & gas severance tax—Annual report, pay to Dept. Rev.
15	Metalliferous minerals—Annual report, pay to Dept. Rev.
WYOMING 1	Mines and mining claims, pipeline cos., electric and other utilities—Dept. Rev. certifies property value
1st Mon.	Telephone & telegraph cos.—Dept. Rev. certifies property value

¶335 JULY CALENDAR

For RECURRING MONTHLY dates, see ¶ 380.
For UNEMPLOYMENT INSURANCE report dates, see ¶ 272.

ALABAMA 1	Utilities (specified)—Report, pay license tax to Dept. Rev.
1	Dry cleaning fee—Quarterly report, payment due to Dept. Rev.
20	Sales-use-rental—Quarterly return, pyt. if liability averages less than $200 per month for past calendar yr.
30	Forest products—Manufacturers and exporters report, pay ¼ to Dept. Rev.
31	Withholding—Quarterly report, pay to Dept. Rev.
31	Motor carriers—Quarterly fuel tax report, pay to Dept. Rev.
ARIZONA 20	Sales-use—Quarterly report, payment to Dept. Rev. (if authorized)
31	Withholding—Quarterly report, pay to Dept. Rev.
ARKANSAS 1	Coal mines—Report to State Mine Inspector
3rd Mon.	Property—Pay ¼ as valorem tax to Cty. Coll.
20	Gross receipts—sales—Quarterly report, pay to Dept. Fin. & Admn. if monthly tax isn't over $100
31	Motor fuel, liquefied gas, and distillate special fuels—Interstate user's quarterly report and payment to Commr. Rev.
31	Property—Corporations (except financial institutions) file tangible property valuation statements to Cty. Assr.
CALIFORNIA 1	Oil and gas producers—Pay assessments of over $10
2	Property—First day for assmt. complaints to Cty. BEQ
Before 1st Mon.	Oil and gas producers—Apply to State Controller to correct assmt.
15	Carriers—Quarterly report, fee (not RRs, vessel operators); also gross operating revenue fee to PUC
20	Property—State-assessed property: assessee has until this date to file petition for reassessment of unitary property
30	Property taxes—State assessed property; last day for notice of assessment of nonunitary property
31	Sales-use—Quarterly report, pay (or balance after prepayment) to SBE
31	Use fuel—Quarterly report, pay to SBE
31	Withholding—Report, pay quarter to Employment Dev. Dept.
31	Timber yield—Timber owners report-pay to SBE
31	Property taxes—State assessed property; last day for SBE to notify assessee of decision on petition for correction of allocated assessment
COLORADO 1	Property—Cty. BEQ hears complaints
5	Property—Protest of personalty valuation must be received by assr. if personally delivered
15	Severance—Quarterly molybdenum tax report, pay to Dept. Rev.
15	Property—Senior citizens file homestead exemption claims with assessor
15	Utilities—Pay quarterly maintenance fee to Dir. Rev.
20	Sales—Quarterly report, pay to Dept. Rev.
31	Withholding—Quarterly report, pay to Dept. Rev. if under $400 withheld in quarter
CONNECTICUT 1	Property—Pay Assr. in most towns
1	RRs—Gross earnings report, pay to Commr. Rev. Services
31	Sales-use—Quarterly report, pay to Commr. Rev. Services
31	Motor carrier road—Quarterly fuel tax report, pay to Commr. Rev. Services
31	Oil cos. gross earnings—Quarterly report-payment to Commr. Rev. Services
31	Utilities—Gross earnings quarterly report and payment to Commr. Rev. Serv.
31	Petroleum importers—Over $100,000 worth of deliveries, report, pay quarterly to Commr. Rev. Serv.
DELAWARE 1	Property—New Castle Cty., quarterly supp. assmt.; realty tax due
1	Gasoline—Renew distributor's license with Dept. Public Safety before this date
1	Gasoline—Renew retailers license with Dept. Public Safety

	1	RRs—Pay quarterly fee to Div. Rev.
	15	Wilmington earned income—Quarterly payment to Dept. Fin.
	25	Gasoline—Distributors pay final installment for gallons sold or used in June to Dept. Public Safety
	31	Withholding—Quarterly return, pay to Dept. Rev. when withholding for lookback 12-month period not over $3,600
	31	Leasing use and lessors' license—Quarterly report, pay to Dept. Fin.
	31	Motor carriers—Quarterly report, pay to Dept. Public Safety
	31	Wilmington earned income tax—Quarterly return to City Dept. Fin.
DISTRICT OF COLUMBIA	1	Property—Personalty assessment date
	31	Rolling stock—Car and railroad companies report, pay personalty tax to Office of Tax and Revenue (last day)
	31	Property—Personalty report, payment to Office of Tax and Revenue (last day)
FLORIDA	1	Corporate income, emergency excise tax and bank franchise—Estimate, pay to Dept. Rev.
	1	Severance—Pay quarterly estimate to Dept. Rev.
	1	Diesel fuel use—Annual, semi-annual, or quarterly returns due
	1	Property—Assessors must complete assessments
	1	Sales-use—Indexed tax on asphalt is adjusted
	1	General—Floating interest rate on underpayments and overpayments is adjusted
	1	Environmental taxes—Tax on commercial hazardous waste facilities is due
GEORGIA	1	Rural telephone co-ops—Pay annual license fee to Commr. Rev.
	20	Sales-use—Quarterly report, pay to Commr. Rev. if liability is $200 or under monthly for six consecutive months
	31	Motor carriers—Quarterly motor fuel tax report, pay to Comm. Rev.
	31	Withholding—Quarterly, monthly report (after quarter close), pay to Commr. Rev.
HAWAII	1	Cigarette, tobacco—Wholesalers, and dealers' license renewal
	15	Withholding—Report, pay 2nd quarter to Dept. Tax. if annual tax $5,000 or less
	31	General excise (sales) and use—Report, pay 2nd quarter to Dept. Tax. if annual tax is not over $4,000
	31	Utility inspection—Pay PUC
IDAHO	1	Electric co-ops—Pay Cty. Treas.
	1	Sales-use—Owners of amusement devices renew annual permits
	25	Oil, gas production severance—Report, pay 2nd quarter to Oil & Gas Comm.
	31	Withholding—Quarterly report, pay to Tax Comm. if quarterly tax under $600
ILLINOIS	10	Public utilities—Quarterly payment gross revenue tax to Commerce Comm.
	10	MVs—Semiannual mileage weight report, pay Sec'y State
	20	Sales-use—Quarter annual return, pay to Dept. Rev. if monthly liability is under $200
	31	Special fuels—Motor fuel use tax licensees make quarterly report, pay to Dept. Rev.
	31	Motor carriers—Report miles traveled and gallons of fuel used
	31	Occupation—Hotel operators quarterly report, pay to Dept. Rev.
	31	Withholding—Quarterly report, pay to Dept. Rev.
	31	Utilities (gross receipts tax on electricity or gas)—Quarterly report, pay to Dept. Rev. if authorized and average monthly tax not over $100
	31	Utilities (telecommunications excise tax)—Quarterly report, pay to Dept. Rev.
INDIANA	1	Commercial vessel tonnage—Report, pay property tax (including navigation companies)
	1	Utilities—Quarterly report, pay to PSC
	31	Sales-use—Semiannual report, pay to Dept. Rev. if average monthly tax isn't over $25

31 Adjusted gross income—Corporations report, pay quarterly to Dept. Rev. if estimated tax exceeds tax by over $1,000 for year
31 Adjusted gross income—Report, pay withholdings to Dept. Rev. semiannually if average monthly tax for prior year wasn't over $25
31 Adjusted gross income—Quarterly withholding report, pay to Dept. Rev. if average monthly withholding in prior year isn't over $75
31 Carriers' road tax—Report, pay 2nd quarter to Dept. Rev.
31 Financial institutions—Quarterly estimated pay to Dept. Rev.
IOWA 1 Corporations—Annual report returned for correction, refiled with Sec'y State
1 Property—Elderly and disabled file for relief
1 Property—File servicemen's exemption claim with city or Cty. Assr.
1 Property—Veteran, religious, literary or charitable orgs. file exemption claim with Cty. Aud. or Bd. Review
2d Mon. Utilities (specified)—Dir. Rev. meets, assesses and hears complaints
30 Underground petroleum storage—Pay 90% of quarterly estimated charges to Dept. Rev. & Fin. if granted extension
31 Underground petroleum storage—Quarterly return, pay to Dept. Rev. & Fin.
31 Withholding—Quarterly report, pay to Dept. Rev. & Fin.
31 Sales-use—Quarterly report, pay to Dept. Rev. & Fin.
31 Special fuel—Distributors quarterly report to Dept. Rev. & Fin.
KANSAS 1 Property—Cty. hearings of appeals of final determinations of Cty. Appraiser must be held by this date
25 Withholding—Quarterly report, pay to Dept. Rev. if tax $200–$1200 per yr.
25 Sales-use—Quarterly report, pay to Dept. Rev. if tax is over $80 but under $3,200 in any calendar year
25 Tire tax—Report, pay for qtr. if annual tax $80–$1,600
31 Interstate motor fuel use—Report, pay to Dept. Rev.
KENTUCKY 1 Property—Assmt. date in 2nd class cities
1 Cigarette license—Pay Dept. Rev.
1 Tobacco warehouse license—Pay Dept. Agriculture
1 Property—Financial institutions pay tax on capital to Dept. Rev.
20 Sales-use—Small retailers quarterly report, pay to Dept. Rev. if permitted
31 Withholding—Quarterly report, pay to Dept. Rev.
31 Covington license—Employer's quarterly report, pay to Lic. Inspector
31 Louisville license—Employer's quarterly report, pay to Commrs. of Sinking Fund
31 Paducah payroll—Employer's quarterly report, pay to City Treas.
31 Lexington license—Employer's quarterly report, pay to City Treas.
31 Motor fuel (taxable users)—Report, pay to Dept. Rev.
31 Motor fuel use tax—City and suburban bus quarterly refund application to Dept. Rev.
LOUISIANA 1 Property—Assessment list due in all parishes (except Orleans)
25 Special fuel—Interstate users report, pay to Sec'y Rev.
30 Utilities—Report to Sec'y Rev. (except electric cos.)
31 Withholding—Quarterly report, pay to Sec'y Rev.
MAINE 15 Sales-use—Quarterly, semi-annual returns to Rev. Services
31 Withholding—Quarterly report, pay to Rev. Services
MARYLAND 21 Sales-use—Small vendors report, pay 2nd quarter Retail Sales Tax Div.
31 Withholding—Quarterly report and payment.
MASSACHUSETTS 1 Property taxes due
1 Property—Assmt. date for ships and vessels
15 Pipeline cos. appeal assessment to ATB.
20 Sales-use—Quarterly report, pay to Commr. Rev.
31 Transporters of hazardous waste—report, pay Dept. of Environmental Engineering

31	Imported fuel—Carriers file quarterly report, pay Commr. Rev.
31	Withholding—Quarterly report, pay to Commr. Rev.; quarter-monthly payers report plus underpayment
MICHIGAN 1st Mon.	Boundary river improvement cos.—Pay tax on paid in capital to State Treas.
1st Mon.	Water and water power cos.—Report to Sec'y State
15	Mich. business tax—Estimate, pay quarter to Dept. Treas.
20	Withholding—Quarterly report, pay to Dept. Treas.
20	Motor carrier fuel—Quarterly report, pay to Dept. Treas.
20	Motor fuel exporters—Quarterly report, pay to Dept. Treas.
20	Motor fuel vendors—Quarterly report, pay to Dept. Treas.
20	Retail diesel fuel dealers—Quarterly report, pay to Dept. Treas.
20	Motor fuel tank-wagon operator-importers—Quarterly report, pay to Dept. Treas.
20	Motor fuel transporters—Quarterly report, pay to Dept. Treas.
20	Motor fuel—LP gas report, pay to Dept. Treas.
31	Utilities—Pay property tax or 1st ½ to Commr. Rev.
MINNESOTA 10	Aviation—Pay aircraft tax
15	Aviation—Aircraft mfrs. report to Commr. Transp.
20	Sales-use—Quarterly report, pay to Commr. Rev.
20	Liquor gross receipts—Quarterly report, pay to Commr. Rev.
31	Withholding—Quarterly report, pay to Commr. Rev.
31	Motor carriers—Quarterly report to Commr. Rev. by motor carriers subject to road tax
MISSISSIPPI 1	Property—Pay ¼ of tax to tax coll. with interest per month from Feb. 1 if locality allows
1st Mon.	Utilities—Tax Comm. hears assessment complaints
15	Timber—Quarterly report, pay to Tax Commr.
15	Withholding—Quarterly report, pay to Tax Commr.
20	Sales-use—Quarterly report, pay to Tax Commr.
30	Severance—Oil producers quarterly report to Tax Commr.
31	Fuel use—Interstate permittees quarterly report, pay to Tax Comm.
MISSOURI 1st Mon.	Merchants, mfrs. (St. Louis)—Report to Lic. Coll.
15	Utilities—Pay PSC assmt. in full or 1st installment
25	Kansas City earnings—Quarterly withholding report, pay to Fin. Dir.
30	Gasoline—Interstate special fuel users report, pay to Dir. Rev.
31	Sales-use—Quarterly report, pay Dir. Rev.
31	Income—Employers quarterly withholding report, pay to Dir. Rev
31	St. Louis earnings—Employer's quarterly withholding return, pay Coll.
31	St. Louis—Employer's quarterly report, pay to Coll. Rev.
31	St. Louis City Graduated Business License tax—Report, pay to Lic. Coll.
MONTANA 30	Coal—Strip mine operators, dealers quarterly report, pay to Dept. Rev.
30	Micaceous mineral mines—Quarterly production report, pay to Dept. Rev.
30	Minerals—Cement and gypsum producers and dealers quarterly report, pay of license tax to Dept. Rev.
30	Sales—Pay quarterly lodgings tax to Dept. Rev.
30	Utilities—Electrical producers quarterly report, payment of license tax to Dept. Rev.
31	Minerals—Quarterly report of new production of petroleum, mineral or crude oil to Dept. Rev.
31	Gasoline—Special fuel users quarterly report, pay to Dir. Rev.
NEBRASKA 1	Car line cos.—Second-half tax on railroad cars is delinquent if unpaid at this date
1	Property—2nd half personalty (except MVs) is delinquent
1	Air carriers—Second half tax on property is delinquent if unpaid on this date.
20	Diesel fuel—Quarterly return to Dept. Rev. for users of untaxed fuel
25	Sales-use—File state and city 2nd quarter return, pay to Dept. Rev.

25	Tire fee—File 2nd quarter return, pay to Dept. Rev.
31	Withholding—Quarterly report, pay to Dept. Rev.
31	Property—Personalty brought from another state or county between Dec. 1 and July 1 must be listed with Cty. assr.
31	Agricultural excise taxes and fees (potato, wheat, soybean, forn, dry bean, grain, sorghum)—First purchasers or shippers report, pay to appropriate board in Dept. Agriculture
31	Motor vehicle and diesel fuel—Interstate truckers report, pay tax to Dept. Rev.
NEVADA 1st Mon.	Utilities—Pay Cty. Franch. tax to Cty. Treas.
1	Utilities—Pay full or 1st quarter assmt. to PUC
1	Utilities—Revenue report to PSC
1	Property—Lien for taxes attaches
31	Sales-use—Quarterly return, pay Dept. Tax.
31	Sales-use—Quarterly short-term passenger car lessor return, payment due to Dept. Tax.
31	Special fuel—Dealers, users file and pay to MV Dept.
31	Property—Personal property statement due to cty. assr.
NEW HAMPSHIRE 1	RRs—Report of stock ownership to Commr. Rev. Admin.; also report of expenditures in each town for bldgs. and rights of way every five years
15	Refined petroleum products—Report, pay quarterly to Dept. Rev. Admn.
15	Utilities—Retailers must file quarterly return, payment for communications services tax for previous calendar quarter to Dept. Rev. Admn.
31	Road toll—Fuel users (not motor) quarterly report, pay to Dir. Div. MVs.
NEW JERSEY 15	Al. bev.—Mfrs., distributors, etc., report, pay to Div. Tax. for May and June
15	Personal (gross) income—Quarterly withholding report, pay to Div. Tax.
20	Sales-use—Direct payment permittees report, pay to Div. Tax.
20	Sales-use—Quarterly report, pay to Dir. Tax.
20	Public community water system—File with, pay Div. Tax.
25	Petroleum products—Refiners and distributors quarterly report, pay to Dir. Tax
31	Fuel use—Road tax quarterly report, pay to Dir. MV.
31	Domestic security fee—Quarterly return to Div. Tax
NEW MEXICO 20	Transportation, transmission cos., carriers—Quarterly inspection, supervision fee to State Corp. Comm.
25	Special fuels supplier tax—Users' quarterly report, payment to Tax. and Rev. Dept.
25	MVs—Pay to Motor Transp. Div. weight distance tax for previous calendar quarter
31	Utilities—Renew pipeline license from Corp. Comm. and pay fee
NEW YORK 1	Property—Last day to pay village taxes to village treas. without penalty
1	NYC Real property—First installment due
25	NYC utility tax—Semiannual returns and payments due
31	Highway use—Carriers report-pay for quarter
31	Fuel use—Carriers file quarterly and information returns to Tax Commr.
31	Withholding—Quarterly report, pay to Tax Commr. if qtrly.
NORTH CAROLINA 31	Sales-use—Quarterly report, pay to Sec'y Rev.
31	Withholding—Quarterly report, pay to Sec'y Rev.
31	Motor carriers—Report, pay road use tax to Sec'y. Rev.
31	Alternative fuels—Bulk-end users file information return with Sec'y. Rev.
31	Utilities—Quarterly report, pay to Sec'y Rev.
31	Motor fuels—Distributors apply to Sec'y Rev. for quarterly refund
31	Severance—Report, pay quarterly forest products tax to Sec'y Rev.
NORTH DAKOTA 31	Withholding—Quarterly report, pay to Tax Commr.

	31	Motor fuels—Importers for use of gasoline and special fuels report, pay quarterly to Tax Commr.
	31	Sales-use—Quarterly return, pay to Tax Commr.
OHIO	**1**	Utilities—File report with PUC, copy to office of Consumers Counsel
	15	Common and motor carriers—Pay PUC maintenance fee
	23	Use—Consumers report, pay to State Treas.
	23	Sales-use—Vendors in Group A counties file semi-annual report, pay to State Treas.
	23	Sales-use—Direct payment permittee report, payment to State Treas.
	23	Consumer use—Pay to State Treas.
	30	Property—Apply to county auditor for reduced valuation of property injured or destroyed during preceding quarter
	31	Withholding—Quarterly report pay to Dept. Tax (pay Treas.)
	31	Property—Manufactured home owners pay 2nd half tax to Cty. Treas.
	31	Highway use—Quarterly report, pay to State Treas.; info return to Tax Commr.
	31	Motor fuel—Dealers report inventory on hand as of July 1 rate change, pay to Tax Commr.
	31	Cigarettes—Dealer semiannual report, pay State Treas.
OKLAHOMA	**20**	Withholding—Quarterly report, pay to Tax Comm.
	20	Sales-use—Group III vendor semiannual report, and taxpayers owing $50 or less for any one month pay Tax Comm.
	30	Property—Textile mfrs. report to cty. assr., pay to cty. treas.
	30	Coal mines—Operators quarterly report, pay to Tax Comm.
	31	Motor fuel importers use—Quarterly report, pay tax to Tax Comm.
OREGON	**1**	Property—Taxes become lien
	1	Motor carriers (to 18,000 lbs)—Pay quarterly in lieu tax to PUC
	1	Forest severance—Forest lands assessed at true value
	5	Property—Board of Ratio Review convenes
	15	Property—Realty return to Cty. Assr.
	15	Property—File written petition to reduce assmt. with Bd. of Ratio Review
	20	Use fuel—Quarterly (substitute for monthly) report, pay to Dept. Transp.
	31	Forest products harvest tax—Quarterly estim. report, pay to Dept. Rev.
	31	Timber severance taxes (East and West Ore.)—Quarterly estim. report, pay to Dept. Rev.
	31	Withholding—Quarterly report, pay to Dept. Rev.
PENNSYLVANIA	**20**	Sales-use—Quarterly return-pay to Dept. Rev.
	31	Withholding (personal income)—Report, pay quarterly withholding to Dept. Rev.
	31	Motor carriers—Quarterly report, pay road tax to Dept. Rev.
	31	Phila. wage tax—Quarterly return due from employees not subject to withholding
	31	Phila. wage tax—Employer's quarterly return of withholdings due to Phila. Dept. Rev.
	31	Pbgh. City & Sch. Dist. earned income—Quarterly withholding report, pay to City Treas.
	31	Pbgh. City & Sch. Dist. earned income—Employees quarterly report, pay City Treas. on pay not covered by withholding.
	31	Pbgh. City occupational priv.—Report, pay April—June withholding to City Treas.
	31	Property (Pbgh.)—3rd quarter realty taxes to City Treas.
RHODE ISLAND	**31**	Motor carrier—Quarterly report, pay to Tax Admr.
	31	Withholding—Quarterly report, payment to Tax Admr. if withholding less than $50 monthly
	31	Sales-use—Quarterly report, pay to Tax Admr., if liability averages less than $200 per month for 6 months
SOUTH CAROLINA	**1**	Motor carriers—Pay PSC semiannual fee
	20	Sales-use—Quarterly report, pay to Dept. Rev.
	31	Motor carriers—Pay installment of road tax to Dept. Rev.

31 Withholding—Quarterly report, pay to Dept. Rev.
SOUTH DAKOTA 5 Property—Assessment date for property of airline flight cos., telephone cos., light and power, heating, water, and gas cos. owned on Feb. 1
7 Railroads—Operating property owned on Feb. 1 assessed on this date
15 Banks and financial institutions—Declare and pay quarterly estimated tax
30 Energy mineral severance—Report, pay quarter to Sec'y Rev. and Reg.
31 Precious metals severance—File estimate, pay ¼ of estimated tax to Dept. Rev. and Reg.
31 Motor fuel—Carriers permanently licensed as interstate fuel users report, pay to Dept. Rev. and Reg.
31 Motor fuel—Highway contractors report, pay to Dept. Rev. and Reg.
31 Motor fuel—LPG users file semi-annual report, pay to Dept. Rev. and Reg.
TENNESSEE 25 Gasoline—Report-pay liquefied gas used in vehicles on instate roads to Dept. Rev.
30 Sales-use—Aviation fuel dealers report, pay to Commr. Rev.
31 Highway user fuel—Motor freight carriers report in-state mileage, pay quarterly fuel tax to Commr. Rev.
TEXAS 20 Sales-use—Quarterly report, pay to Comptr.
25 Gasoline—Motor fuel transporters, interstate truckers quarterly report, pay Comptr.
25 Diesel fuel—Motor fuel transporters, interstate truckers, dyed diesel fuel bonded users quarterly report, pay Comptr.
25 Liquefied gas—Licensed dealers and licensed interstate truckers quarterly report, pay Comptr.
31 Interstate motor carrier sales-use—Quarterly report, pay Comptr.
31 Utilities (gross receipts)—Last day to quarterly file and pay without penalty
31 Hotel occupancy—Quarterly report, pay to Comptr.
31 Sulphur producers—Quarterly report to, pay Comptr. Pub. Accts.
UTAH 1 Utilities—Special regulation fee to Tax Comm.
31 Sales-use—Quarterly report, pay to State Tax Comm.
31 Withholding—Quarterly report, pay to State Tax Comm.
31 County, municipal sales-use tax, quarterly return, pay Tax Comm.
31 County transient room tax, quarterly return, pay Tax Comm.
31 Property—Pay quarterly withholding from gross proceeds of uranium or vanadium mines to Tax Comm.
31 Minerals—Pay quarterly withholding tax on mineral production to Tax Comm.
31 Tobacco products (not cigarettes)—Quarterly report, pay to Tax Comm.
31 Gross receipts—Corporations not paying franchise/income tax and electrical corps. report, pay semiannually to State Tax Comm.
VERMONT 1 Car or transportation co.—File annual return with Commr.
25 Bank franchise—Pay Commr. Taxes for last quarter
25 Withholding—Quarterly report, pay to Commr. Taxes
25 Sales-use—Quarterly report, pay to Commr. Taxes
25 Meals and rooms—Quarterly report, pay to Commr. Taxes if past yr. tax $500 or less
25 Telephone companies—Report, pay qtrly. alt. gross operating revenue tax to Tax Commr.
VIRGINIA 1 Gasoline-special fuels—Suppliers renew license
1 Property—Optional assessment date for realty and personalty in localities adopting ordinance
10 Peanuts and hogs—Semi annual payment due
15 Contractor's use tax—Contractors bringing machy into Va. report, pay to Tax Commr.
20 Sales-use—Quarterly report, pay to Tax Commr.
30 Forest products—Quarterly report, pay to Dept. Tax

31 Withholding—Quarterly and monthly report, pay to State Dept. Tax.
31 Motor carriers—Quarterly payment of tax figured on fuel used in-state
31 Special fuels—Quarterly licensed user report to MV Div.
31 Corn—Quarterly report, pay to Tax Commr.
WASHINGTON 1 Corporations—Affidavit and fee to Sec'y State (foreign)
1 Private car cos.—Dept. Rev. assesses between March 1 and this day
1st Mon. Property—Cty. BEQ meet
9 Utilities (specified)—Last day to request Dept. Rev. assmt. hearing
15 Auto transport cos.—Quarterly report, pay to Utilities & Transp. Comm.
20 Private car cos.—Request Dept. Rev. assmt. hearing
25 Special fuels—Report, pay to Dept. MV (quarterly or semiannual filers)
31 B&O tax—Quarterly report, pay to Dept. Rev.
31 Sales-use—Quarterly report, pay to Dept. Rev.
31 Utilities—Quarterly report, pay to Dept. Rev.
31 Timber excise—Quarterly report, pay to Dept. Rev.
WEST VIRGINIA 1 Corporations, S corporations, partnerships liable for business franchise, telecommunications or severance tax (except certain nonprofit insurance cos. sole-proprietorships) report to Tax Dept.
1 Property—Assessment day
1 Utilities—Pay special license fee to PSC
1 Motor carriers—Pay annual assessment to PSC
1 O & G conserv.—Pay annual tax to O & G Conserv. Comm.
10 Property—Individuals not in business furnish lists to Assrs.
20 Sales-use—Quarterly return, pay to Tax Commr.
25 Motor fuels—Motor carriers road tax quarterly report, pay to Tax Commr.
31 Telecommunications—Quarterly estimated tax if $1,000 or less per month
31 Gross (B & O) sales—Quarterly report, pay to Tax Commr.
31 Withholding—Quarterly report, pay to Tax Commr.
31 Coal severance—Report, pay min. tax to Tax Commr. quarterly
31 Motor carrier road tax—Carriers file annual reports if operate solely in-state and use only gasoline or special fuel on which taxes have been paid
31 Sales—Quarterly motor fuel return, pay to Tax Commr.
WISCONSIN 31 Sales-use—Quarterly report, pay to Dept. Rev.
31 Withholding—Report, deposit quarter amount to designated bank or as required
31 Property—Pay 2nd half realty tax
WYOMING 1st Mon. RR cos.—Dept. Rev. certifies property values
10 Tobacco products—Consumers report, pay tax to Dept. Rev. for past quarter
20 Tobacco products—Wholesalers report, pay to Dept. Rev. for past quarter
31 Sales-use—Quarterly report, pay to Dept. Rev. if tax under $150 during any month
31 Gasoline, diesel fuel—IFTA-licensed carriers report, pay to Dept. Transportation

¶340 AUGUST CALENDAR

For RECURRING MONTHLY dates, see ¶ 380.
For UNEMPLOYMENT INSURANCE report dates, see ¶ 272.

ALABAMA 1	Transportation, transmission, other utilities—Pay quarterly fee to PUC.
ARIZONA 29	Annual report—Corporations exempt from filing annual report file disclosure certificate with Corp. Comm. (in 90 days after 5-31)
31	Air cos.—Assessment of flight property by Dept. Rev.
31	RRs—Assessment of property by Dept. Rev.
31	Telecommunication cos.—Assessment of property by Dept. Rev.
31	Mining cos.—Dept. Rev. values producing mines.
ARKANSAS 3d Mon.	Property—Petition Cty. BEQ to adjust assmt.
31	Utilities—Pay Public Utility Comm. fee to PSC or Transp. Comm.
CALIFORNIA 15	Oil & gas producers—Pay State Treas. 1st half tax
20	Property—Latest date assessee of nonunitary property can file declaration of intent to petition for reassessment
24	Sales-use—Prepay SBE if so ordered
31	Property—Pay taxes on unsecured roll to Coll.
COLORADO 5	Property—Last day for BEQ to hear assessment appeals
DELAWARE 1	Property (Sussex)—Quarterly supplemental assmt.
1	Escheat (abandoned property)—Banks report unclaimed funds to Dir. Rev.
HAWAII 20	Property—Pay 1st half realty tax
ILLINOIS 1	Property—Pay balance of tax without interest in Cook Cty.; in other counties with estimated 1st installment method
1	Surplus line producer—Semiannual return and payment to Dept. Ins.
10	Property (counties with less than 150,000)—Last day to file assmt. complaint with Cty. Bd. of Review (30 days after assessment list is published)
IOWA 30	Underground petroleum storage—Report, pay balance of fees if granted extension for quarterly report
LOUISIANA 1	Property (Orleans Parish)—Assessment list due; 1st day for assessor to post assessment list
15	Property (Orleans Parish)—Last day for display of assessment list
MASSACHUSETTS 1	Boat, ship and vessel excise—Owners as on 7-1 file returns with cities, towns where vessels habitually docked
MINNESOTA 1	Aircraft mfrs.—Report to Comm. Transp. about models and prices
15	Property—Homestead tax refund claims to Commr. Rev.
20	Sales-use—Vendors paying accelerated June payment pay balance to Commr. Rev.
20	Liquor gross receipts—Vendors paying accelerated June payment pay balance to Commr. Rev.
MISSOURI 1	Other corporation taxes—Annual registration report to Sec'y State; registration fee to Dir. Rev. (if not for profit corp.) Merchants, mfrs. Cty. and St. Louis BEQs hear appeals
2nd Mon.	Property—(not Kansas City, St. Louis City and 1st class counties)—Cty. BEQs hear appeals
15	Property (1st class ctys.)—Complaint to Tax Comm. from Cty. BEQ ruling
MONTANA 31	Minerals—Mineral and oil producers pay quarterly tax on new production to Dept. Rev.
NEBRASKA 1	Property (counties with pop. over 100,000)—2nd half realty tax is delinquent.
NEVADA 1st Mon.	Property—Pay 1st quarter installment tax to Cty. Treas.
3rd Mon.	Real property and secured personal property—Pay full tax to Cty. Treas.
NEW JERSEY 1	Property—Pay 3rd quarter tax to Coll.
1	Property—File for farm assmt. with local Assr.
1	Property—Apply for certification of conservation and recreation land by Dept. Environmental Protection

15	Utilities—Pay 2nd 35% of franchise tax and/or gross receipts tax to Dir., Div. Tax.
NEW MEXICO 31	Utilities (electric, local piped gas, water and steam)—Pay quarterly inspection and supervision fee to PSC
NEW YORK 15	Personal income—Return due for taxpayers who requested extension
20	NYC Coin-operated amusement devices—Return and payment due
NORTH CAROLINA 15	Public utility regulatory fee—Pay to Utilities Comm.
NORTH DAKOTA 1	Domestic corps.—Annual report, filing fee to Sec'y State
2nd Tues.	Property—SBE meets to equalize values
OHIO 1	Utilities (not RRs)—Annual report to Tax Commr.
9	Commercial activity tax—Quarterly tax due
14	Severance—Report, pay for quarter ending June 30
15	Natural gas excise—Quarterly return, pay to State Treas.
20	Natural gas. dist. (MCF)--Quarterly return, pay to State Treas.
23	Sales-use—Vendors in Group B counties file semiannual return with State Treas.
29	Motor fuel—Last day for retailers to file semiannual refund claim
OKLAHOMA 31	Franchise—Report, pay to Tax Comm. annually
OREGON 1	Property—File proof exemption for new bldg. under construction
1	Property—File proof with assessor that shipyard materials are used in watercraft to cancel assessment
1	Property—Personal property returns to Cty. Assr.
14	Oil and gas gross production tax—2nd quarterly report, pay to Dept. Rev.
31	Motor carrier tax—2nd quarterly report if gross weight not over 30,000 lbs, pay to PUC
PENNSYLVANIA 20	Sales—Semiannual report, pay to Dept. Rev. if annual tax not over $75
RHODE ISLAND 1	Environmental—Renew litter control participation permit, pay fee to Tax Admr.
TENNESSEE 1st Mon.	Utilities—Assessment complaints can be filed within 10 days from this date
1	Utilities gross receipts tax—Pay to Commr. Rev.
TEXAS 15	Sales-use—Prepay Comptr. Pub. Accts. for prepayment discount
20	Natural gas pipeline cos.—Quarterly report to RR Comm, pay State Treas.
UTAH 14	Oil and gas conservation fee—Report, pay Tax Comm.
31	Property—Seniors file claim for homeowner's credit with county
WISCONSIN 1	Utilities—Last day for Dept. Rev. to value utility property of R&Rs, sleeping car, & express cos.
WYOMING Last work day	Senior and disabled warrant for refund—Last day to file application with Dept. Rev.

¶345 SEPTEMBER CALENDAR

For RECURRING MONTHLY dates, see ¶ 380.
For UNEMPLOYMENT INSURANCE report dates, see ¶ 272.

ALABAMA 15	Corporate income—Report, pay estimate installment to Dept. Rev.
15	Individual income—Report, pay estimate installment to Dept. Rev.
25	Hydroelectric manufacturers—Pay privilege-license tax on sales
ALASKA 15	Corporation income—Report, pay 3rd estimated tax installment to Commr. Rev.
ARIZONA 15	Corporate income—Report, pay 3rd estimated tax installment to Dept. Rev.
15	Personal income—Report, pay 3rd estimated tax installment to Det. Rev.
ARKANSAS 15	Income—Pay third estimated tax installment to Dir. Fin. Admn.
Sat. before 3rd Mon.	Property—Petition Cty. Equal. Bd. for adjustment of equalized assessment
CALIFORNIA 15	Corporate income—Farmer's co-op reports to Franch. Tax Bd.
15	Corporate income—Estimate, pay Franch. Tax Bd.
15	Personal income—Estimate, pay Franch. Tax Bd.
15	Property—File assmt. complaints with Cty. BEQ
24	Sales-use—Prepay SBE if so ordered.
COLORADO 1	Oil & gas conservation—Quarterly report, pay to Oil and Gas Conservation Comm.
15	Income—Estimate or pay to Dir. Rev.
CONNECTICUT 15	Corporation business income—Report, pay 3d estimated tax installment to Commr. Rev. Services
15	Personal income—Report, pay quarterly estimated tax and composite payments to Commr. Rev. Services
15	Insurance companies—Net direct premiums estimated tax report, payment (80%) to Commr. Rev. Services
30	Cigarettes—Distributor's license expires, apply to Commr. Rev. Services
30	Property—Appeal MV assmt. to Bds. of Tax Review
DELAWARE 1	Franchise—Pay 2nd installment of tentative tax to Dept. State and file tentative return
1	Property tax (Kent Cty.)—Quarterly supplemental assessment
1	Escheat—Life insurance co. publish notice of unclaimed funds.
1	Financial institutions—Banks and trust cos. pay Bank Commr. 20% of estimated tax if annual tax expected to exceed $10,000
15	Corporate income—Estimate, pay to Dept. Fin. 20%
15	Personal income—Estimate, pay to Div. Rev.
30	Property (counties)—last day to pay without penalty
DISTRICT OF COLUMBIA 15	Income-franchise tax—Declare, pay estimated tax to Office of Tax and Revenue
15	Property tax—Owners of specified federally assisted housing make payment in lieu of taxes
15	Property tax—Pay 2nd half of realty taxes (and in lieu payments on PILOT parcels) to Office of Tax and Revenue
15	Property—Pay supplemental assessment of realty that became effective 4-1
15	Property—Pay 1/2 of Business Improvement District taxes
30	Property tax—Last day to appeal assessed value or classification made in previous yr. to Superior Court
30	Property—Last day to file application for realty tax exemption for full tax year
FLORIDA 30	Property—Prepay 2d installment of estimated realty tax for discount
30	Sales-use—Dealers holding direct pay permits report on purchases to Dept. Rev.
GEORGIA 15	Corporate income—Estimated tax report, installment to Commr. Rev.
15	Personal income—Estimated tax report, payment to Commr. Rev.
HAWAII 1	Property—Last day to petition for nonresidential urban land to be dedicated for landscaping, open-space or public recreation

20	Personal income—Pay third installment to Dept. Tax.
20	Corporate income—¼ of estimated tax to Dept. Tax.
20	Financial institutions—Franchise tax installment to Dept. Tax.
20	Utilities—Pay 3rd installment to Dept. Tax.
IDAHO 15	Corporate income—File estimated return, pay installment
ILLINOIS 1	Property—Pay 2d half realty tax (except Cook Cty. and counties with payments in Mar. and Aug.)
2nd Mon.	Property—Bd. Review (Cook County) meets to revise assessments
10	Property (counties of 150,000 or more; not Cook)—File assessment complaint with Bd. Review or claim exemption (30 days after assessment list is published)
15	Income—Cooperatives file annual return and pay any tax due to Dept. Rev. (15th of 9th mo. after end of tax year)
15	Income—Corporations and individuals pay estimated tax to Dept. Rev
15	Insurance cos.—Quarterly estimated payment of privilege tax unless annual tax under $5,000
15	Gas and water cos. (invested capital tax)—Pay quarterly estimate to Dept. Rev.
15	Electric cos. (taxes on invested capital and distribution of electricity)—Pay quarterly estimate
INDIANA 15	Personal income—Estimate and/or pay to Dept. Rev.
20	Utility receipts—Quarterly estimated return, pay to Dept. Rev. (if estimated annual liability exceeds $1,000)
IOWA 1	Property—Pay 1st half to Cty. Treas.
30	Income—Estimate, installment to Commr. Rev.
30	Property—1st semi-annual payment is delinquent after today
KANSAS 1	Gas pipelines—Pay inspection fees to State Corp. Comm.
15	Income—Estimate and/or pay to Dir. Tax.
15	Bank tax—Financial institutions make estimated privilege tax declaration, payment to Dir. Tax
KENTUCKY 1	Personalty (2nd class cities)—List personalty with City Assr.
1	Property—Assmt. date for resident deposits, raw tobacco and money
1	Property—Report on distilled spirits in bonded warehouse and federal premises due to Dept. Rev.
15	Income, limited liability entity tax—Estimate and/or pay to Dept. Rev.
15	Property—Distillery bonded warehouses pay to local Coll.
15	Property (Louisville)—Assessment books open
21	Property—Credit unions report members savings account to Dept. Rev.
29	Property (Louisville)—Appeal to BEQ institutions report to City Assr.
30	Property (Louisville)—Report to Assr.
LOUISIANA 15	Corporate income—Pay estimated tax installment to Sec'y Rev.
15	Personal income—Individual (not farmer) estimate and/or pay to Sec'y Rev.
15	Property—Last day assessment list displayed by assr. (except in Orleans parish).
30	Utilities—Report, pay inspection fee to Sec'y Rev.
MAINE 1	Fertilizer—Annual report and payment to Rev. Services
1	MV excise—Lessors of MVs for periods under 1 yr. file report with Rev. Services to claim refunds
15	Income—Estimate, pay Rev. Services
15	Railroads—Pay ⅓ excise tax to Rev. Services
28	Fuel tax—Retailers file refund application
MARYLAND 15	Corporate and personal income—Estimate and/or pay to Comptr.
15	Utilities franchise—File quarterly estimated tax return, pay 25% of tax
30	Property (State-county-local)—pay Cty.-Local Collector
MASSACHUSETTS 15	Corporate excise—Pay estimated tax to Comr. Rev.
15	Personal income—Pay installment to Commr. Rev.
MICHIGAN 15	Personal income—Quarterly estimate/pay to Dept. Rev.

15	Property—low grade iron ore taxes—pay 4th class city taxes (if city has 2 tax rolls)
MINNESOTA 15	Income (corp. and personal)—Estimated installment to Commr. Rev.
15	Income—Co-op assns. file return and/or pay tax to Commr.
MISSISSIPPI 15	Income—Corporations and individuals pay 3rd quarter installment Commr. Tax
MISSOURI 1st Mon.	Merchants' & Mfr.'s (St. Louis)—Pay to License Coll.
15	Income—Estimate/installment to Dir. Rev.
30	Common carriers, RRs—Report to PSC
30	Property—Appeal to Tax Comm. from Bd. Eq. (except 1st class counties and St. Louis Cty.)
MONTANA 15	Personal income—Pay 3rd quarter estimated tax to Dept. Rev. (15th day of 9th month of fiscal year)
15	Corporation income—Estimate, pay Dept. Rev.
NEBRASKA 1	Property—In counties with pop. of 100,000 or less, 2d ½ realty taxes delinquent
15	Personal income—Report, pay 3rd installment of estimated tax to Dept. Rev.
15	Corporation income—Report, pay 3rd installment of estimated tax to Dept. Rev.
NEW HAMPSHIRE 9	RRs—Tax exemption determined by PUC
15	Business profits—Report-pay 3rd qtr. estimated tax to Dept. Rev. Admn.
15	Franchise—Utilities report, pay quarter estimated tax to Dept. Rev. Admn.
15	Personal income—Report-pay 3rd quarter estimated tax to Dept. Rev. Admn.
15	Railroads—Report, pay quarter estimated tax to Dept. Rev. Admin.
15	Utilities—PUC files with Comm. Rev. Admin. certificate saying street railways didn't earn specified minimum sums for year and so are exempt
NEW JERSEY 1	Sewage and water corps.—Report to Dir. Div. Tax
15	Personal income (gross income tax)—Estimate, pay Div. Tax.
15	Alcoholic bev.—mfrs., distributors etc. report, pay to Div. Tax. for July and Aug.
NEW MEXICO 15	Corporation income—Pay quarterly estimated tax to Tax. & Rev. Dept.
NEW YORK 1	NYC property—RPIE filing deadline
15	Personal income—Pay estimated tax to Dept. Tax. & Fin.
15	Banks, financial institution—Estimate, pay to Dept. Tax & Fin.
15	Franchise—Business corporations estimate/pay ⅓ estimated tax to Dept. Tax. & Fin.
15	Franchise—Water, steam, gas and electric cos., transportation, and transmission cos. file estimated tax declaration, pay ⅓ to Dept. Tax & Fin.
15	Unincorporated business tax (NYC)—Estimated tax due
15	Oil cos.—Estimated additional franchise tax declaration and installment to Dept. Tax. & Fin.
15	Utilities—Gross income tax estimate/payment to Commr.
15	NYC business corporations—Pay 2d ⅓ estimated tax—if meeting requirements after 5-31 and before 9-1, file declaration and pay ½ tax to Dept. Fin.
15	NYC personal income estimates—Report, pay to N.Y. State Dept. Tax. & Fin.
20	NYC commercial rent or occupancy tax—Quarterly return and payment due
20	NYC hotel occupancy—Quarterly return and payment due
20	Sales-use (state-local)—Quarterly report, pay to Dept. Tax. & Fin.
NORTH CAROLINA 1	Property—County and municipal taxes due and payable
1	Property—Unregistered motor vehicle tax due and payable
15	Income—Corporations and individuals estimate, payment to Sec'y Rev.
15	Mutual associations—Annual return to Sec'y State (15th day of 9th month)

NORTH DAKOTA	**15**	Income—Individuals report, pay quarterly estimate to Tax Commr.
	15	Corporate income—Pay quarterly estimate to Tax Commr.
	15	Corporate income—FSCs, DISCs, and cooperatives file annual return if made on calendar year basis (fiscal year, 15th day of 9th mo. after fiscal year ends)
OHIO	**15**	Personal Income—Pay 3rd installment of estimated tax
	20	Property—Report, pay 2nd half of personalty taxes to Cty. auditors
	20	Property—Intercounty tangible personalty returns, pay Cty. Treas.
	23	Sales-use—Vendors in Group C counties file semiannual return, pay to State Treas.
OKLAHOMA	**15**	Income—Estimate and/or installment to Tax Comm.
OREGON	**1**	Property—Apply for multiple housing exemption
	1	Property—Precertified new, modified, or installations on commercial facility, file for enterprise zone exemption with cty. assr.
	1	Property—Last day to file claim for deferral with Cty. governing body on farm use land in disaster area
	15	Excise and income tax (corporations)—3rd quarter estimated pay to Dept. Rev. (15th day of 9th month of fiscal year)
	15	Personal income—Pay quarterly estimated tax to Dept. Rev.
PENNSYLVANIA	**1**	Property (4th-8th class Cities; 2nd A and 3rd class counties)—File appeal with Bd. Assmt. and Revision of Taxes
	15	Corporate net income—Pay 3rd installment of estimated tax to Dept. Rev.
	15	Personal income—Pay 3rd installment estimated tax to Dept. Rev.
	15	Capital stock and franchise—Pay 3rd installment of estimated tax to Dept. Rev.
	15	Mutual thrifts—Pay 3rd installment of estimated tax to Dept. Rev.
	15	Phila. net profits—Report, pay 3rd quarter estimate to Phila. Dept. Rev.
	15	Pbgh. City & Sch. Dist. earned income—Pay one-third on estimated net profits from 6–16 to City Treas.
	30	Liquid fuel—Agricultural user's refund claim to Bd. Fin. & Rev.
	30	Loans—Corps. assuming obligations must give notice to persons liable for tax on same debts.
RHODE ISLAND	**15**	Personal income—Estimate, pay Tax Admr.
SOUTH CAROLINA	**15**	Corporate income—Quarterly estimated tax to Tax Comm.
	15	Personal income—Pay 3rd installment of estimated tax to Tax Comm.
SOUTH DAKOTA	**1**	Rural electric, telephone cos.—Gross receipts tax to Cty. Treas.
TENNESSEE	**27**	Fuel tax—Claim refund for fuel for ancillary engines
TEXAS	**15**	Motor carriers—Pay special fee to Comptr.
UTAH	**1**	Oil and gas, mining severance taxes—Taxpayers whose total taxes for past cal. year were $3,000 or more pay quarterly installment to Tax Comm.
	1	Property—File indigent, veteran or blind exemption applications with county
	15	Income—Corporations pay estimated tax to State Tax Commr.
VERMONT	**15**	Income—Quarterly estimate, pay to Commr. Taxes
	15	Utilities—Report to Commr. Taxes
	25	Telephone cos.—Report, pay qtrly. installment of net value tax on personalty to Tax Commr.
VIRGINIA	**15**	Corporate income—Estimate and/or pay to Dept. of Tax
	15	Personal income—Estimate and/or pay to local Commr. Rev.
	15	Utilities—Estimate and/or pay gross receipts tax (pay State Treas.)
WEST VIRGINIA	**1**	Property—Pay 1st installment to Sheriff for discount
	15	Corporate and personal income—Estimate and/or pay to Tax Commr.
	15	Franchise—Quarterly estimated tax payment to Tax Commr.
WISCONSIN	**15**	Personal income—Estimate and/or pay to Dept. Rev.
	15	Corporate income—Report, pay estimated tax installment to Dept. Rev.

15	Utilities—Last day for Dept. Rev. to value property (except R&Rs, carline & express cos.)
WYOMING 1	Property—1st half of realty tax becomes due

¶350 OCTOBER CALENDAR

For RECURRING MONTHLY dates, see ¶ 380.
For UNEMPLOYMENT INSURANCE report dates, see ¶ 272.

Columbus Day: States *not* following Fed law in observing Columbus Day on the 2nd Monday in Oct.—Alaska, Ark., Fla., Haw., Iowa, Miss., Nev., N.D. (shown below by asterisk (*)).

ALABAMA 1	Property—Assmt. day, lien attaches, tax payment due (most property)
1	Property—File application with county assessor to have property assessed at current use value (file not later than Jan. 1)
1	Business privilege licenses—Renew license with Cty. Lic. Commr. or Probate Judge (delinquent after 10-31)
1	Vehicles—Motor vehicle licenses become due (delinquent after 11-15)
1	Dry cleaning fee—Quarterly report, payment due to Dept. Rev.
1	Express cos.—Report, pay to Dept. Rev.
1	Utilities (specified)—Report, pay license tax to Dept. Rev.
14	Wholesale oil license—Annual return, payment
20	Sales-use-rental—Quarterly report, pay if liability averages less than $200 per month for past calendar yr.
30	Forest products—Mfrs., exporters report, pay to Dept. Rev.
31	Withholding—Quarterly report, pay to Dept. Rev.
31	Motor carrier's fuel tax—Quarterly report, pay to Commr. Rev.
31	Escheats—File annual report with State Treas.
ARIZONA 1	Property—Pay 1st ½ tax on realty and personalty secured by realty (last day without penalty)
20	Sales-use—Quarterly report, pay Dept. Rev. if authorized
31	Withholding—Quarterly report, pay to Dept. Rev. and statement to employees
***ARKANSAS 10**	Property—Pay ad valorem tax to Cty. Coll.; unpaid tax becomes delinquent
20	Gross receipts—sales—Quarterly report, pay to Dir. Fin. & Admn. if monthly tax isn't over $100
25	Liquefied gas—Interstate users' quarterly report and payment to Dept. Fin. & Admin.
31	Distillate special fuels—Interstate user's quarterly report and payment to Dept. Fin. & Admn.
CALIFORNIA 15	Carriers—Quarterly report, fee and gross operating revenue fee to PUC (except RRs, vessel operators)
31	Sales-use—Quarterly report, pay balance of tax to SBE
31	Use fuel—Quarterly report, pay to SBE
31	Withholding—Quarterly report, pay to Employment Development Dept.
31	Timber yield—Owners report, pay tax to SBE
COLORADO 15	Severance—Quarterly molybdenum tax report, pay to Dept. Rev.
15	Utilities—pay quarterly maintenance fee to Dept. Rev.
20	Sales—Retailer's quarterly return to Dept. Rev.
31	Withholding—Quarterly report, pay to Dept. Rev. if under $400 withheld in quarter
CONNECTICUT 1	Property—Assmt. and lien date (exceptions)
31	Sales-use—Quarterly report, pay to Commr.
31	Utilities—Gross earnings quarterly report and payment to Commr. Rev. Serv.
31	Petroleum importers—Over $100,000 worth of deliveries, report, pay quarterly to Commr. Rev. Serv.
31	Oil cos. gross earnings—Quarterly return, pay to Commr. Rev. Services
31	Motor carrier road—Quarterly report, pay to Commr. Rev. Services
DELAWARE 1	Property (New Castle Cty.)—Quarterly supplemental assmt.
1	RRs (specified)—Pay quarterly fee to Dept. Fin.
1	Motor carriers—Get I.D.-registration from Dept. Public Safety
15	Wilmington earned income—Quarterly payment to Dept. Fin.
31	Withholding—Quarterly return, pay to Dept. Rev. when withholding for lookback 12-month period not over $3,600
31	Motor carriers fuel purchase—Report, pay to Dept. Public Safety

31	Leasing use and lessors' license—Quarterly report, pay to Dept. Fin.
31	Wilmington earned income—Quarterly return to City Dept. Fin.
DISTRICT OF COLUMBIA 1	Property—Last day to seek administrative review of supplemental assessment made between January 1 and June 30
1	Property—Last day for Qualified High Technology Company to apply for abatement
***FLORIDA 1**	Corporate income—Estimate and/or pay 3rd qtr. to Dept. Rev.
1	Corporate reports—Quarterly reports due
1	Diesel fuel use—Quarterly return due
1	Diesel fuel use—Motor carriers report, pay to Dept. of Highway Safety and Motor Vehicles
1	Severance—Report, pay quarterly estimate to Dept. Rev.
1	Sales-use—Secondhand dealers must renew annual registration
15	Insurance—Estimated tax installment due
GEORGIA 20	Sales-use—Quarterly report, pay to Commr. Rev. if liability is $200 or under monthly for six consecutive months
31	Motor carriers—Quarterly motor fuel tax report, pay to Commr. Rev.
31	Withholding—Quarterly report, pay to Commr. Rev.
***HAWAII 15**	Withholding—Quarterly report, pay to Dept. Tax if annual tax $5,000 or less
31	General excise (sales) and use—Quarterly return, payment to Dept. Tax if annual tax is not over $4,000
IDAHO 25	Oil & gas severance—Report, pay 3rd quarter to O&G Tax Comm.
31	Withholding—Quarterly report, pay to Tax Comm. if quarterly tax under $600
ILLINOIS 10	Utilities—Pay quarterly gross revenue tax to Commerce Comm.
20	Sales-use—Quarterly report, pay to Dept. Rev. if monthly tax liability is under $200
31	Special fuels—Motor fuel use tax licensees make quarterly report, pay to Dept. Rev.
31	Motor carriers—Report miles traveled and gallons of fuel used
31	Withholding—Quarterly report, pay to Dept. Rev.
31	Hotel operator's occupation—Quarterly report, pay to Dept. Rev.
31	Escheats—Banking and financial orgs., insurance cos., (other than life insurance cos.), and governmental entities report abandoned property to Dir. Fin. Institutions
31	Utilities (gross receipts tax on electricity and gas)—Quarterly report, pay to Dept. Rev. if authorized and average monthly tax not over $100
31	Utilities (telecommunications excise tax)—Quarterly report, pay to Dept. Rev.
INDIANA 1	Utilities—Pay quarter to PSC
31	Adjusted gross income—Corporations report, pay quarterly to Dept. Rev. if estimated tax exceeds tax by $1,000 for year
31	Carrier road tax—Report, pay quarter to Dept. Rev.
31	Adjusted gross income—Quarterly withholding return, pay Dept. Rev. if average monthly withholding in prior years wasn't over $75
31	Sales use—Quarterly report, pay Dept. Rev. if average monthly tax is $75 or less
31	Financial institutions—Quarterly estimated tax report, pay to Dept. Rev. if tax for the year is over $1,000
***IOWA 15**	Property—Advertised notice of equalization orders is made; appeal to Bd. Review from such orders from now until Nov. 15 (odd-numbered years)
30	Underground petroleum storage—Pay 90% of quarterly estimated charges to Dept. Rev. if granted extension
31	Underground petroleum storage—Quarterly return, pay to Dept. Rev.
31	Sales-use—Quarterly report, pay Dept. Rev.
31	Withholding—Quarterly report, pay Dept. Rev.
31	Special fuels—Distributors file quarterly report with Dept. Rev.

KANSAS 15	Homestead—Disabled, unremarried widows, elderly apply to Dept. Rev.
25	Withholding—Quarterly report, pay to Dir. Tax. if tax $200–$1200
25	Sales—Quarterly report, pay to Dir. Tax. if tax over $800 but under $3,200 in any calendar year
25	Tire tax—Report, pay for qtr. if annual tax $80–$1,600
31	Interstate motor fuel use—Quarterly report, pay to Dir. Tax.
31	Property—Cty. Clerk accepts adjustment applications to this date
31	Motor fuel tax—Distributors, importers, mfrs. renew licenses
KENTUCKY 1	Property (Louisville)—BEQ meets
1	Property (2nd class cities)—Second installment to City Treas.
20	Sales-use—quarterly report, pay to Dept. Rev. Small retailers if allowed
31	Covington license—Employer's quarterly return, pay to Lic. Inspector
31	Louisville license—Employer's quarterly return, pay to Commrs. of Sinking Fund
31	Paducah payroll—Employer's quarterly return, pay to City Treas.
31	Withholding—Quarterly report, pay to Dept. Rev.
31	Motor fuel users—Report, pay to Dept. Rev.
31	Motor fuel use tax—City and suburban bus quarterly refund application to Dept. Rev.
31	Lexington license—Employer's quarterly return, pay to City Treas.
LOUISIANA 25	Special fuel—Interstate users report, pay to Sec'y Rev.
30	Utilities—Report to Sec'y Rev. (except electric cos.)
31	Natural gas lines—Report, pay franshise tax
31	Withholding—Quarterly report-pay to Sec.'y Rev.
31	Escheats—Abandoned property report due Sec'y Rev. by this date
MAINE 1	Property—Unorganized territory education and service tax due
15	Sales-use—Quarterly return, payment to Rev. Services
31	Withholding—Quarterly report, pay to Rev. Services
31	Escheats—Holders (not insurance cos.) report abandoned property to State Treas.
MARYLAND 21	Sales-use—Small vendors report, pay quarter tax to Retail Sales Tax Div.
31	Withholding—Quarterly report, pay to Comptr.
31	Abandoned property—Companies, other than life insurance companies, file annual report with Comptroller
MASSACHUSETTS 1	Property—Abatement applications (except specified widows, minors, veterans (and relatives), blind, elderly) to local Assr.
1	Forest land products and land taxes due
20	Sales-use—Quarterly report, pay to Commr. Rev.
30	Imported fuel—Carriers file quarterly report, pay to Commr. Rev.
30	Transporters of hazardous waste—Report, pay Dept. of Environmental Engineering
31	Withholding—Quarterly report, pay to Commr. Rev.
MICHIGAN 1	Nonprofit corp.—Report, fee to Dir. Commerce
15	Mich. business tax—Estimate, pay quarter to Dept. Treas.
20	Withholding—Quarterly report, pay to Dept. Treas.
20	Motor carrier fuel—Quarterly report, pay to Dept. Treas.
20	Motor fuel exporters—Quarterly report, pay to Dept. Treas.
20	Motor fuel vendors—Quarterly report, pay to Dept. Treas.
20	Retail diesel fuel dealers—Quarterly report, pay to Dept. Treas.
20	Motor fuel tank wagon operator-importers—Quarterly report, pay to Dept. Treas.
20	Motor fuel transporters—Quarterly report, pay to Dept. Treas.
20	Motor fuel—Quarterly LP gas report, pay to Dept. Treas.
MINNESOTA 1	Minerals—Iron bearing material report to Tax Comm.
1	Aviation—Dealers pay tax, register aircrafts with Commr. Trans.
1	Escheats (abandoned property)—Insurance cos. report to Commr. Commerce
10	Unmined taconite and iron sulphides—Producers file annual estimate with Commr. Rev.
15	Aviation—Aircraft mrf.'s report to Commr. of Transportation

	15	Property—Pay remaining installment
	15	Severance—Iron ore (not taconite) producers file annual estimate with Commr. Rev.
	20	Sales-use—Quarterly report, pay to Commr. Rev.
	20	Liquor gross receipts—Quarterly report, pay to Commr. Rev.
	31	Withholding—Quarterly report, pay to Commr. Rev.
	31	Motor carriers—Report, pay quarterly road tax to Dept. Rev.
***MISSISSIPPI**	**15**	Timber—Quarterly report, pay to Tax Commr.
	15	Withholding—Quarterly return, pay Tax. Commr.
	20	Sales-use—Quarterly report, pay to Tax Commr.
	30	Severance—Oil producers quarterly report to Tax Commr.
	31	Fuel use—Interstate permittees file report, pay to Tax Comm.
	31	Abandoned property—Companies holding abandoned property report to State Treasurer
MISSOURI	**15**	Utilities—Assmt. for PSC expenses; 2nd installment to State Treas.
	25	Kansas City earnings—Employer's quarterly withholding report, pay to Fin. Dir.
	30	Gasoline—Interstate special fuel users report, pay to Dir. Rev.
	30	Minerals—Pay mine inspection fee to Div. Rev.
	31	Sales-use—Report, pay to Dir. Rev.
	31	St. Louis City earnings—Employer's quarterly withholding return, pay to Coll.
	31	Withholding—Quarterly report, pay to Dir. Rev.
	31	Abandoned property—Holders (except life ins. cos.) of unclaimed property report to Dir., Dept. Cons. Affairs Reg. & Licensing
	31	Employment (St. Louis)—Employers quarterly return-payment to Coll. Rev.
MONTANA	**30**	Severance—Coal mine operators and dealers report, pay to Dept. Rev.
	30	Micaceous mineral mines—Quarterly report, pay to Dept. Rev.
	30	Gypsum producers—Quarterly report, pay license tax to Dept. Rev.
	31	Withholding—Quarterly report, pay to Dept. Rev.
NEBRASKA	**1**	Litter fee—Return, pay to Dept. Rev.
	25	Sales-use—State and city 3rd quarter returns, pay to Dept. Rev.
	25	Tire fee—3rd quarter return, pay to Dept. Rev.
	31	Income—Quarterly withholding to Dept. Rev.
	31	Agricultural excise taxes and fees (potato, wheat, soybean, corn, dry bean, grain, sorghum)—First shippers or purchasers report, pay to appropriate board in Dept. Agriculture
	31	Motor vehicle and diesel fuel—Interstate truckers report, pay tax to Dept. Rev.
***NEVADA**	**1**	Utilities—Pay 2nd quarter assmt. to PUC
	1st Mon.	Property—Pay 2nd quarter installment to Cty. Treas.
	31	Sales-use—Quarterly report, pay to Dept. Tax.
	31	Sales-use—Quarterly short-term passenger car lessor return, payment due to Dept. Tax.
	31	Special fuels—Dealers or users report, pay to Dept. MVs
***NEW HAMPSHIRE**	**1**	Property—Lien date
	15	Refined petroleum products—Quarterly report, pay to Dept. Rev. Admn.
	15	Refined petroleum products—Estimated tax for next quarter, one-third payment to Dept. Rev. Admn.
	15	Utilities—Retailers must file quarterly return, payment for communications services tax for previous calendar quarter to Dept. Rev. Admn.
	31	Road toll—Fuel users other than motor fuel, report, pay for quarter ended 9–30
	31	Escheats—Holder of unclaimed property must file report with State Treas.
NEW JERSEY	**1**	Property—Assmt. date except communication property
	1	Property—Apply for exemption for water supply and sewage disposal equipment
	15	Withholding (gross (personal) income)—Quarterly report, pay to Div. Tax.

	20	Sales-use—Quarterly report, pay to Div. Tax.
	20	Sales-use—Direct payment permittees report, pay to Div. Tax.
	20	Public community water system—Owners or operators file with, pay Dir. Div. Tax.
	25	Petroleum products—Refiners and distributors quarterly report, pay to Dir. Tax
	31	Motor fuel use—Users quarterly report, pay to Div. MVs.
	31	Domestic security fee—Quarterly return, pay Div. Tax
NEW MEXICO	**20**	Utilities—Inspection and supervision fee to Corp. Comm.
	25	Special fuels supplier tax—Users' quarterly report, payment to Tax. and Rev. Dept.
	25	MVs—Pay to Motor Transp. Div. weight distance tax for previous calendar quarter.
	30	Escheats—Holders of unclaimed property report to Tax. and Rev. Dept.
NEW YORK	**1**	NYC Property—Pay 2nd quarter tax bill; quarterly installment on class 1 and 2 property assessed at $80,000 or less, and class 3 and 4 property assessed at $40,000 or less
	15	Personal income—Return due for taxpayers who requested additional 2-month extension
	24	NYC Property—Deadline for seeking review of final tax determination
	31	Highway use—Quarterly report, pay to Dept. Tax. & Fin.
	31	Fuel use—Quarterly report, pay to Dept. Tax. & Fin.
	31	Withholding—Quarterly report, pay to Tax Commr.
NORTH CAROLINA	**15**	Sales-use—Nonprofit orgs. file refund claim with Sec'y. Rev.
	15	Sales-use—Quarterly report, pay to Sec'y. Rev.
	31	Motor fuels—Distributors apply to Sec'y Rev. for quarterly refund
	31	Motor carriers—Report, pay road use tax to Sec'y. Rev.
	31	Alternative fuels—Bulk-end users file information return with Sec'y. Rev.
	31	Primary forest products assmts.—Processors report, pay to Sec'y. Rev.
	31	Withholding—Quarterly report, pay to Sec'y Rev.
	31	Public utilities—Quarterly report, pay to Sec'y Rev.
***NORTH DAKOTA**	**15**	Property—Pay 2nd tax installment to Cty. Treas.
	31	Sales-use—Report, pay to Tax Commr.
	31	Withholding—Quarterly report, pay for nonresidents.
	31	Motor fuels—Importers for use of gasoline and special fuels report, quarter pay to Tax Commr.
OHIO	**15**	Utilities—Report, pay est. tax if $1,000 or more
	23	Sales-use—Direct payment permit holders return, pay to State Treas.
	23	Sales-use—Vendors in Group D counties file semiannual report, pay to St. Treas.
	30	Property—Apply to county auditor for reduced valuation of property injured or destroyed during preceding quarter
	31	Withholding—Quarterly report, pay to State Treas.
	31	Highway-use—Quarterly report, pay to State Treas.; information to Tax Commr.
	31	Escheats—Report abandoned property to Dir. Commerce
OKLAHOMA	**1st Mon.**	Property—Sale of tax delinquent real estate
	1	Property—Lien for realty tax attaches between grantor and grantee
	20	Withholding—Quarterly report, pay to Tax Comm. if tax under $500 per quarter
	31	Motor fuel importers use tax—Quarter report, pay to Tax Commr.
***OREGON**	**1**	Property—Last day for mortgagee to ask statements from collector
	20	Use fuel—Quarterly report, pay to MV Div.
	30	Telephone exchange access service—Report, pay quarterly to Dept. Rev.
	30	Forest products harvest tax—Quarterly estim. report, pay to Dept. Rev.

30 Timber severence taxes (East and West Ore.)—Quarterly report, pay to Dept. Rev.
31 Withholding—Quarterly report, payment to Dept. Rev.
PENNSYLVANIA 1st Mon. Property (Phila.)—Realty appeal to Bd. Revision of Taxes
20 Sales—Quarterly report, pay to Dept. Rev.
31 Withholding—Quarterly report, pay to Dept. Rev.
31 Pbgh. City & Sch. Dist. earned income—Taxpayers not subject to withholding report, pay quarterly to City Treas.
31 Pbgh. City occupational priv.—Report, pay July—Sept. withholding to City Treas.
31 Phila. wage tax—Employee's quarterly report, pay to Phila. Dept. Rev. on income not subject to withholding
31 Phila. wage tax—Employer's withholding report, pay to Phila. Dept. Rev.
31 Pittsburgh income—Employer's quarterly withholding report, pay to City Treas.
31 Pbgh. City & Sch. Dist. earned income —Report, pay withholdings to City Treas.
31 Realty (Pbgh.)—Pay 4th quarter installment to City Treas.
31 Motor carrier—Quarterly report, pay road tax to Dept. Rev.
RHODE ISLAND 1 Property—Manufacturer's report on machy, and equipment
31 Motor carrier—Quarter report, pay to Tax Admr.
31 Sales-use—Quarterly report-pay to Tax Admr. if monthly tax under $200 per month for 6 mos.
31 Withholding—Quarterly report, pay to Tax Admr. if withholding less than $50 monthly
SOUTH CAROLINA 20 Sales-use—Quarterly report, pay to Dept. Rev.
31 Motor carriers—Pay installment of road tax to Dept. Rev.
31 Withholding—Quarterly report, pay to Dept. Rev.
SOUTH DAKOTA 15 Banking and financial institutions—Report, pay quarter estim. to Dept. Rev. and Reg.
30 Energy mineral severance—Report, pay quarter to Dept. Rev. and Reg.
31 Property—Pay last half to Cty. Treas.
31 Precious metals severance—File estimate, pay ¼ of estimated tax to Dept. Rev. and Reg.
31 Property—Mobile homes—Pay last half to Cty. Treas.
31 Motor fuel—Highway contractors file quarterly report, pay Dept. Rev. and Reg.
31 Motor fuel—Carriers permanently licensed as interstate fuel users report, pay to Dept. Rev. and Reg.
31 Escheats—Last day to file annual report with State Treas. (except life insurance cos.)
TENNESSEE 1st Mon. Property—Pay to Cty. Trustee
25 Liquefied gas—Dealer permittees report, pay to Commr. Rev.
30 Sales-use tax—Aviation fuel dealers report, pay to Commr. Rev.
31 Highway user fuel—Motor freight carriers report in-state mileage, pay quarterly fuel tax to Commr. Rev.
TEXAS 20 Sales-use—Quarterly report, pay to Comptr.
20 Hotel occupancy—Quarterly report, pay Comptr.
25 Gasoline—Motor fuel transporters, interstate truckers quarterly report, pay Comptr.
25 Diesel fuel—Motor fuel transporters, interstate truckers, dyed diesel fuel bonded users quarterly report, pay Comptr.
25 Liquefied gas—Licensed dealers and licensed interstate truckers quarterly report, pay Comptr.
31 Interstate motor carrier sales-use—Quarterly report, pay Comptr.
31 Sulphur production—Quarterly report to, pay Comptr.
31 Utilities (gas, electric, light etc.)—Last day to make quarterly gross receipts tax report to and pay Comptr.
31 Hotel occupancy—Quarterly report, pay to Comptr.
31 Property—Last day for 3% prepayment discount
UTAH 1 Property—County BEQ must decide appeals of valuation or equalization by this date
31 County transient room—Quarterly report, pay St. Tax Comm.

31 Tobacco products (not cigarettes)—Quarterly report, pay to Tax Comm.
31 Uranium or vanadium mines—Pay quarterly withholdings from gross proceeds to Tax Comm.
31 Mineral production—Quarterly withholding tax to Tax Comm.
31 Sales-use—Quarterly report, pay to Tax Comm. (incl. local taxes)
31 Withholding—Quarterly report, pay to Tax Comm.

VERMONT 15 Express cos.—Pay utility tax to Commr. Taxes
15 RRs, car, and transportation cos.—Pay 1st half tax to Commr. Taxes
25 Bank Franchise—Quarterly report-payment to Commr. Taxes
25 Withholding—Quarterly report, pay to Commr. Taxes
25 Sales-use—Quarterly report, pay to Commr. Taxes
25 Meals and rooms—Quarterly report, pay to Commr. Taxes if past yr. tax $500 or less
25 Telephone cos.—Report, pay qtrly. alt. gross operating revenue tax to Tax Commr.

VIRGINIA 1 Annual registration fee—LLCs pay State Corp. Comm.
15 Contractor's use tax—Contractors bringing machy into Va. report, pay to Tax Commr.
20 Sales-use—Quarterly report, pay to Tax Commr.
30 Forest products—Quarterly report, pay to Tax Dept.
31 Withholding—Quarterly report, pay to Tax Commr. (if under $100 per month)
31 Escheats—Report (not insurance cos.) abandoned property to Dept. Rev.
31 Motor carriers—Quarterly road tax (fuel) report to Corp. Comm., pay State Treas.

WASHINGTON 15 Auto transportation cos.—Quarterly report, pay to Utilities and Transp. Comm.
25 Special fuels—Quarterly report, pay to Dept. Licensing if estimated annual tax is $251–499
31 B&O tax—Quarterly report, pay to Dept. Rev.
31 Sales-use—Quarterly report, pay to Dept. Rev.
31 Utilities—Quarterly report, pay to Dept. Rev.
31 Timber excise—Quarterly report, pay to Dept. Rev.
31 Property—Last day to pay second half to Cty. Treas.

WEST VIRGINIA 1 Property—1st half delinquent; personalty may be distrained
1 Property—Last day to file homestead exemption claim with Cty. Assr.
1 Property—Corporations and other businesses file return with Cty. Assr.
20 Sales-use—Quarterly return, pay Tax Commr.
25 Motor fuels—Motor carrier road tax quarterly report, pay to Tax Comm.
31 Business and occupation tax—Report, pay to Tax Commr.
31 Telecommunications—Pay estimated tax to Tax Commr. (quarterly if estimated tax $1,000 or less per month)
31 Withholding—Quarterly report, pay to Tax Commr.
31 Sales—Quarterly motor fuel report, pay to Tax Comm.
31 Coal severance—Report, pay min. tax to Tax Commr. quarterly

WISCONSIN 1 Utilities—Appeal state assessment to Dept. Rev.
31 Withholding—Quarterly report, deposit withholding with designated bank
31 Sales-use—Quarterly report, pay to Dept. Rev.

WYOMING 1 Utilities—Pay one-half uniform assessment fee
10 Tobacco products—Consumers report, pay tax to Dept. Rev. for past quarter
20 Tobacco products—Wholesalers report, pay to Dept. Rev. for past quarter
31 Sales-use—Quarterly report, pay to Dept. Rev. if tax under $150 during any month
31 Gasoline, diesel fuel—IFTA-licensed carriers report, pay to Dept. Transportation

¶355 NOVEMBER CALENDAR

For RECURRING MONTHLY dates, see ¶ 380.
For UNEMPLOYMENT INSURANCE report dates, see ¶ 272.

Veterans' Day: Fed law observes Veterans' Day on Nov. 11; all states follow Fed.

ALABAMA 1	Transportation, transmission, other utilities—Pay quarterly fee to PUC.
ARIZONA 1	Property—1st half on realty and realty-secured personalty delinquent
CALIFORNIA 24	Sales-use—Prepay (SBE) if so ordered
CONNECTICUT 1	Property—Report to Assr. in most districts
11	Property—Mortgagees file returns not filed by owners
DELAWARE 1	Property—Sussex Cty.—Quarterly supplemental assmt.
10	Escheats—Banks deliver abandoned property to State Escheator
FLORIDA 1	Property—Taxes due and payable to cty. coll.
30	Property—Pay Cty. Tax Coll. for discount
HAWAII 1	Escheats—Holders of abandoned property report to Dir. Fin. before this date
IDAHO 1st Mon.	Property—Transient personalty report to Cty. Assr.
15	Utilities, RRs—Pay 2nd half regulatory fee to PUC
15	Utilities—File list of consumers with PUC
4th Mon.	Property—Last day to appeal subsequent assessments
INDIANA 1	Escheats—Banks, financial institutions report annually to Atty. Gen.
10	Property—Pay 2nd half to local Treas.
IOWA 30	Underground petroleum storage—Report, pay balance of fees if granted extension for quarterly report
KANSAS 1	Property tax—Realty tax becomes lien
KENTUCKY 1	Property—2% discount expires
1	Escheats—Holders of abandoned property must file report with Dept. of Treasury
MAINE 1	Blueberry—Processors-shippers report, pay to Rev. Services
MASSACHUSETTS 1	Escheats—Report abandoned property to State Treas.
1	Forest lands and forest products—Last day to pay local collectors without penalty
1	Property—Penalty imposed if taxes not paid by this date
MICHIGAN 1	Escheats (abandoned property)—Report to State Treasurer
15	Property—4th class cities—Last day to pay taxes on city July roll, that are on Dec. tax roll for collection, without interest
30	Utilities—Property tax—Pay 2d ½ to Commr. Rev. (see July 31)
MINNESOTA 1	Escheats (abandoned property)—Report to Commr. Commerce
3	Property—File for open space assessment with Dist. Assr.
15	Property—Owners of certain agricultural homesteads apply for permission to pursue appeals without tax payment
30	Special fuel—Dealers & bulk purchasers renew permit with Commr. Rev.
MISSOURI 1	Income—Apply to Dir. Rev. for separate allocation
1	Utilities—RR and bridge & public utilities property tax due Cty. Coll.
MONTANA 30	Property—Pay 1st half to Cty. Treas.
30	Minerals—Pay net or gross proceeds tax (except on coal) and royalties tax to Cty. Treas.
30	Minerals—Oil and gas producers quarterly report to State Treas., Dept. Rev.
NEBRASKA 1	Property—Personalty tax lien attaches
NEW JERSEY 1	Property—Pay 4th quarter to Tax Coll.
1	Property—Pay tax on added or omitted property
1	Property—Exemption claim filed (due every 3 yrs.)
15	Al. bev.—Mfrs. distributors, etc., report, pay for Sept. and Oct.
15	Utilities—Pay remaining 30% of franchise tax and/or gross receipts tax to Dir. Div. Tax.
NEW MEXICO 10	Property—Pay 1st installment to Cty Treas.
30	Oil & gas production equipment—Pay tax on oil & gas production equipment to Oil & Gas Acctg. Div.
30	Utilities—Pay quarterly inspection and supervision fee to PSC
NEW YORK 1	Property—Taxable status date for supplemental assessment roll

NORTH CAROLINA 15	Public utility regulatory fee—Pay to Utilities Comm.
NORTH DAKOTA 1	Property—Apply to Bd. Cty. Commrs. for assmt. abatement
OHIO 1	Utilities—File report with PUC, copy to office of Consumer Counsel
14	Severance—Quarterly report, pay to State Treas.
15	Natural gas excise—Quarterly return, pay to State Treas.
20	Natural gas dist. (MCF)—Quarterly return, pay to State Treas.
23	Sales-use—Group E counties file semi-annual report, pay State Treas.
OKLAHOMA 1	Property—Pay Cty. Treas.
OREGON 14	Gross production—Quarterly report, pay Dept. Rev.
15	Property—Pay sheriff for discounts, 3% full payment; 2% if ⅔ paid or in 14 business days after statement is mailed by collector whichever's later.
15	Property—Farm labor camps and day care centers pay Cty. Treas. in lieu tax
20	Property—Tender estimated tax (in 15 days after 11-5) to Assr. if taxes can't be determined from tax roll
30	Motor carrier tax—3rd quarter report, pay to PUC if gross weight not over 30,000 lbs.
PENNSYLVANIA 15	Property (Pbgh.)—Triennial realty assmt. appeal to Bd. Prop. Assmt. Appls.
SOUTH CAROLINA 1	Escheats—Holders of abandoned property must report to Dept. Rev. property held as of past June 30
TEXAS 1	Abandoned property—Holders file report
15	Sales use—Prepayment to Comptr. for 1.25% discount
20	Natural gas pipeline cos.—Quarterly report to RR Comm.
30	Property—Pay half to Cty. Coll.
30	Property—Last day for 2% prepayment discount unless taxing unit adopts different payment schedule
UTAH 14	Oil and gas conservation fee—Report, pay to Tax Commr.
30	Property—Pay Cty. Treas. (Tax Comm. if property centrally assessed) to avoid delinquency
30	Alcoholic beverages—Renew manufacturing, beer wholesaling, and liquor warehousing licenses
VIRGINIA 1	Escheats—Holders (except insurance cos.) of abandoned funds or other property report to State Treas. before this date
WASHINGTON 1	Escheats—Report of abandoned property to Dept. Rev. due
WISCONSIN 1	Property—Effective date of stumpage values set by Dept. of National Resources
10	Utilities (specified)—Pay 2nd installment of license tax to Dept. Rev.
10	Utilities—Pay 2nd half of property tax to Dept. Rev.
WYOMING 10	Property (including utilities)—1st half of realty tax becomes payable

¶360 DECEMBER CALENDAR

For RECURRING MONTHLY dates, see ¶ 380.
For UNEMPLOYMENT INSURANCE report dates, see ¶ 272.

ALABAMA 15	Corporate income—Quarterly estimate report-pay to Dept. Rev.
31	Property—Report improvements or other changes to County Assr. (last day)
31	Property—Claim statutory exemption (last day)
31	Property—List of business personal property to county assessor (last day)
31	Property—Last day to appear before board of equalization to have assessment reopened after increase in valuation without notice (any time before taxes become delinquent)
ALASKA 15	Corporate income—Report, pay 4th and final estimated tax installment to Dept. Rev.
31	Al. bev.—Renew license, pay fee to Dept. Rev.
31	Initial—Renewal of corporation registered name, pay to Dept. Rev.
ARIZONA 1	Government lease excise tax—Report, pay annually to government lessor.
15	Corporate income—Report, pay 4th estimated tax installment to Dept. Rev.
15	Property—Cty. assr. finds and values property as of Jan. 1 of next year
15	Property—Last day to appeal to tax court valuation or classification of property as reviewed by assessor
31	Al. bev.—Licenses expire
ARKANSAS 15	Income—Pay 4th installment of estimated tax to Dept. Fin. & Admin.
CALIFORNIA 10	Private railroad car operator—Pay SBE
10	Property—Pay Cty. Coll. realty secured personalty tax and ½ of realty tax
15	Corporate income—Estimate and pay Franchise Tax Bd.
24	Sales-use—prepay SBE if so ordered
31	Property—Personal property statement to county assr.
COLORADO 1	Oil and gas conservation—Quarterly report, pay to Oil and Gas Conservation Comm.
15	Corporate income—Estimate and pay Dept. Rev.
CONNECTICUT 15	Corporation business income—Report, pay 4th estimated tax installment to Commr. Rev. Services
15	Insurance companies—Net direct premiums estimated tax report, payment (100%) to Commr. of Rev. Services
31	Corporate business—Lien attaches
31	Motor carriers—Apply for identification stamps to Commr. of Transp.
31	Utilities—Public service cos. pay quarterly installment of assessment for expenses of Dept. Public Utility Control
DELAWARE 1	Franchise—Pay 3rd 20% of tentative tax
1	Property (Kent Cty.)—Quarterly supplemental assmt.
15	Income—Corps. pay final 10% estimated tax to Div. Rev.
20	Escheats (abandoned property)—Life insurance cos. pay over unclaimed funds to State Escheator
31	Property—Last day for specified elderly (65 or older) to file for homestead exemption
31	Financial institutions—banks, trust cos. and national banks report to Bank Commr.
DISTRICT OF COLUMBIA 15	Franchise—Corps., financial institutions, and unincorporated businesses make declaration and/or pay estimated franchise tax to Office of Tax and Revenue
31	Car and RR cos.—Assessment date for rolling stock
31	Appeal to superior court from supplemental assessment conducted during previous calendar yr.
FLORIDA 1	Sales-use—Application for renewal of exemption for purchases by Florida high speed rail authority is due
31	Property—Prepay 25% of estimated realty tax (plus ½ of any adjustments) for discount

31	Limited partnerships—File annual report
GEORGIA 1	Public service corporations—Commr. Rev. gives notice of PSC fee due
15	Corporate income—Estimate and/or installment to Commr. Rev.
20	Property—Pay state and county taxes (2nd installment) to coll.
20	Property—Dealer pays tax on unsold motor vehicles
31	Motor carriers—Annual identification registration fee to PSC
HAWAII 20	Financial institutions—Franchise tax installment to Dept. Tax
20	Utilities—pay 4th quarter gross income tax to Dept. tax
31	Property—Last day to file for exemption with assessor
31	Utilities—pay inspection fee to PUC
IDAHO 15	Income—Corps. pay estimated tax
20	Property—Pay Cty. Assr. 1st half personalty taxes
20	Property—Pay Cty. Coll. 1st half realty tax
20	Forest products—Pay yield tax for timber severed 1-1 to 6-30
ILLINOIS 15	Corporate income—Pay estimate to Dept. Rev.
15	Insurance cos.—Quarterly estimate to Dept. Insurance unless annual tax under $5,000
15	Gas and water cos. (invested capital tax)—Pay quarterly estimated tax installment to Dept. Rev.
15	Electric cos. (taxes on invested capital and distribution of electricity)—Pay quarterly estimate to Dept. Rev.
31	Property—Last day for senior citizens and disabled persons to claim property tax relief for past calendar year
INDIANA 20	Utility receipts—Quarterly estimated return, pay to Dept. Rev. (if estimated annual liability exceeds $1,000).
IOWA 31	Corporate income—Pay estimated tax installment to Dept. Rev.
KANSAS 15	Income—Corporations report, pay estimated tax to Dir. Tax.
15	Bank tax—Financial institutions make estimated privilege tax declaration, payment to Dir. Tax.
20	Property—Pay 1st half to Cty. Treas.
20	Utilities—Motor carriers property tax payment, 1st half (in full if $50 or less) to Dir. Property Valuation
30	Franchise—Notify Sec'y State of change from calendar to fiscal year
KENTUCKY 1	Property (2nd class cities)—Assmt. lists open for inspection
1st Mon.	Property (6th class cities)—BEQ meets
15	Corporate income, limited liability entity tax—Estimate and installment to Dept. Rev.
31	Property—Pay Sheriff or Coll.
31	Motor carriers—Renew certificate with Dept. Motor Transportation
LOUISIANA 15	Corporate income—Pay estimated tax installment to Sec'y Rev.
31	Property—Realty lien attaches
31	Property (realty)—Pay sheriff (in Orleans, pay state tax collector)
31	Contractors—Contractor's license expires
31	Utilities—Report, pay inspection fee to Sec'y Rev.
MAINE 15	Corporate income—Estimate and pay to Rev. Services
15	RRs—Pay last 3rd excise to Rev. Services
31	RR—Determination of excise tax on gross receipts
31	Property—Application for credit for rent for elderly or low-income household due
MARYLAND 15	Corporate income—Estimate and pay to Comptr.
15	Utilities franchise—File quarter estimated tax return, pay 25% of tax
MASSACHUSETTS 15	Corporate excise—Pay estimate to Commr. Rev.
15	Property—Apply to local Assr. for exemption (veterans, widows, widowers, parentless minors, persons 70 or over, blind)
31	Motor vehicle excise—Last day for abatement application to local Bd. Assrs
31	Sales—Manufacturers must reapply as manufacturers if they undergo specified changes
MICHIGAN 1	Motor carriers—Apply to PSC for certificate or permit
1	Low grade iron ore—Liens attach
31	Property—Assessment date
31	Property—Realty and personalty liens attach

	31	Utilities—Property assessed as of this date
	31	Low grade iron ore—Assmt. date
	31	Motor carriers—Certificates and permits expire, apply to PSC
MINNESOTA	15	Corporate income—Pay estimated tax to Commr. Rev.
	15	Property—New homesteaders claim status with county assessor
	15	Property/income—Homestead refund claimants must have property classified by this date
MISSISSIPPI	1	Utilities—Pay annual privilege tax to Commr.
	1	Property—Banks pay tax to county tax collector
	15	Corporate income—Pay quarterly estimated tax to Commr. Rev.
MISSOURI	15	Income—Corporations estimate, pay Dir Rev.
	31	Merchants & Mfrs. (except Kansas City)—Pay local Coll. Rev.
	31	Merchants & Mfrs.—License expires
	31	Property (except Kansas City)—Pay local Coll. Rev.
	31	Property—Merchants' and mfrs.' (Kansas City) Pay personal property tax to city treas.
	31	Merchants' and mfrs.' tax (except St. Louis City)—Pay local Coll. Rev.
MONTANA	15	Corporation income—Estimate, pay Dept. Rev.
	31	Minerals—Petroleum dealers license expires
NEBRASKA	1	Property—1st half personalty (except MVs) is delinquent
	15	Corporate income—Report, pay estimated tax installment to Dept. Rev.
	31	Financial institutions—Last day to file, pay voluntary estimated tax
NEVADA	15	Property—Private car line cos. pay to Dept. Tax.
NEW HAMPSHIRE	1	Property—Pay town Coll.
	1	Property—Contractors with contracts with N.H. or locality pay appropriate taxes to collector
	15	Business profits—Pay 4th qtr. estimated tax to Dept. Rev. Admn.
	15	Utilities—RRs report-pay quarterly estimated tax
	15	Franchise—Utilities report, pay estimated tax
NEW JERSEY	1	Property—Appeal added or omitted assmts. to Cty. Bds.
	1	RRs—Tax on RR operating property payable
	31	Property—Seniors (or widows) or disabled apply for homestead deduction with local Assr.
	31	Property—Veterans claim deductions by filing with Assr.
NEW MEXICO	10	Property—Copper production ad valorem tax installment due, pay to Tax. & Rev. Dept.
	15	Corporation income—Pay quarterly estimated tax to Tax. & Rev. Dept.
NEW YORK	1	NYC commercial motor vehicle tax—Semiannual payment by medallion tax cab owners due
	15	NYC Business taxes—estimated tax installment or amended declaration due
	15	Business corporations—Pay estimated tax.
	15	Petroleum business tax—Pay estimated tax.
	15	Banks, financial institutions, insurance cos.—Pay estimated tax.
	15	Franchise (Transportation and transmission cos.)—Pay tax.
	15	Oil cos. & utilities (gross income)—Estimate and pay to Tax Commr.
	15	Franchise (water, steam, gas and electric cos.)—Pay estimated tax.
	15	NYC business income and banking—Installment of estimated taxes due; declaration or amended declaration due
	20	Sales-use (state-local)—Quarterly returns, pay to Dept. Tax. & Fin.
	20	NYC Hotel occupancy—Quarterly return and payment due
NORTH CAROLINA	15	Income—Corporate estimated tax to Sec'y Rev.
OHIO	1	Property—Personalty tax lien attaches to realty
	23	Sales-use—Vendors in Group F counties file semi-annual report, pay to St. Treas.
	30	Property—File exemption claim with Tax Commr.
	30	Property—Pay Cty. Treas. full or first half on realty or utility property
	30	Property—File complaint against exemption with Tax Commr.

31	Property—Valuation date for business tangible personalty and credits, and intangible dealers' resources
31	Utilities—Pay first half of property tax to county treasurer
OKLAHOMA 31	Property—Pay 1st ½, or full tax if not over $10, to county treasurer to avoid penalty.
31	Property—Mortgage servicers pay all accounts to county treasurer annually.
31	Property—Notice of property tax appeal to county treas. due
OREGON 15	Corporation excise and income—Pay balance of estimated tax to Dept. Rev.
31	Property—File written petition for reduced assessment with Equalization Board
PENNSYLVANIA 15	Corporate net income—Report, pay 4th quarter estimated tax payment to Dept. Rev.
15	Capital franchise and stock—Report, pay estimated tax installment to Dept. Rev.
15	Mutual thrifts—Report, pay estimated tax installment to Dept. Rev.
31	Pbgh. City and Sch. Dist. earned income— File declaration for anticipated profits after 9-15
RHODE ISLAND 31	Property—Assessment date
SOUTH CAROLINA 31	Property—Assessment and lien date
31	Property—Airline taxes due following first report
SOUTH DAKOTA 3rd Mon.	Property—Land sold for unpaid taxes
TEXAS 31	Property—Last day for 1% prepayment discount
31	Utilities—Renew business permits with Comptr.
UTAH 1	Oil and gas, mining severance taxes—Taxpayers whose total taxes for past cal. year were $3,000 or more pay quarterly installment to Tax Comm.
10	Property—File claim with cty. auditor for adjustment and rebate of tax on transitory personalty removed from Utah before Dec. 1
15	Income—Corporations pay estimated tax to State Tax Comm.
30	Property—Last day (until noon) to pay if delinquency date extended
30	Car cos. and common carriers—Last date to pay delinquent taxes with penalty before seizure and sale
31	Special fuel user—Special fuel vehicle permit expires (but is honored until Feb. 28 of next year)
31	Property—File for renter's credit with Tax Comm.
31	Property—File for homeowner's credit with Tax Comm. if claim not filed before 9-1 deadline
VERMONT 1	Property—Electric generating plant education property tax—Pay 1/2 to Commr. Tax
15	Corporations—Estimate and report, pay to Commr. of Taxes
25	Telephone cos.—Report, pay qtrly. installment of net value tax on personalty to Tax Commr.
VIRGINIA 5	Property—Pay local Treas. to avoid 5% penalty
15	Corporate income—Estimate and pay to Dept. Tax.
15	Utilities—PSC estimate and pay State Treas.; gross receipts tax to Corp. Comm.
WASHINGTON 1	Property—8% penalty for late payment kicks in
31	Property—Forest land tax application due
WEST VIRGINIA 15	Corporate income—Estimate and/or installment to Tax Commr.
15	Franchise—Quarterly estimated tax payment to Tax Commr.
WISCONSIN 15	Corporation income—Estimate/and or pay to Dept. Rev.
31	Motor carriers—Pay permit fee to Dept. Transp.
WYOMING 31	Property—Last day to pay entire tax to avoid penalty if first half is unpaid
31	Car Cos.—Last day to pay property taxes to Dept. Rev. without delinquency

RECURRING MONTHLY CALENDAR

¶380 Dates repeating monthly. Calendar below lists monthly dates. For annual, semiannual, quarterly, and non-monthly dates, see monthly calendars at ¶ 300. For unemployment insurance, ¶ 272.

FEDERAL 15—	Withholding—Report, pay for past month if tax for 12-mo. before past July 1 not over $50,000.
Each Wed. and Fri.—	Withholding—Report, pay by Wed. for past Wed.—Fri. and by Fri. for past Sat.—Tue. if tax for 12-mo. period before past July 1 is over $50,000
Next banking day—	Withholding—Pay any undeposited tax of at least $100,000
ALABAMA 10	Tobacco use—Report, pay to Dept. Rev.
15	Gasoline, lubricating oil, and other petroleum products— Carriers report shipments to Dept. Rev.
15	Gasoline and lubricating oil—Warehousemen and transfer companies report shipments to Dept. Rev.
15	Motor carriers mileage tax—Report, pay to Dept. Rev.
15	Al. Bev.—Wholesalers and manufacturers pay table wine tax to ABC and localities
15	Withholding—Pay to Dept. Rev. if tax over $1000 for either first or second month of calendar quarter
15	Oil and gas production—Report, pay to Dept. Rev.
15	Privilege tax—Producers of oil and gas report, pay to Dept. Rev.
15	Beer wholesalers—Report, pay to cty. or municipality
19	Licensed manufacturers and importers—Shipments of beer and table wine to wholesalers reported to ABC (before 20th)
20	Beer wholesalers, retail beer sellers, and private clubs—Report inventory to probate judge
20	Utility gross receipts and service use taxes—Report, pay tax to Dept. Rev. (if average monthly tax liablity $10,000 or greater during preceding calendar, make estimated payments)
20	Scrap tire environment fee—Tire dealers report, pay fee to Dept. Rev.
20	Coal production—Report, pay to Dept. Rev.
20	Gasoline—Report, pay tax to Dept. Rev. (including aircraft fuel)
20	Lodgings—Report, pay to Dept. Rev. (monthly filers)
20	Iron ore—Report, pay to Dept. Rev. (transport cos. and others receiving products report)
20	Sales-use-rental—Report, pay to Dept. Rev. (monthly filers)
20	Contractors gross receipts tax—Report, pay to Dept. Rev.
20	Petroleum products—Report, pay inspection fee to Comr. Agri. & Industries
20	Coal—Transporters, purchasers report to Commr. Rev.
20	Lubricating oil—Report, pay to Dept. Rev.
20	Motor fuel other than gasoline—Report, pay to Dept. Rev.
20	Tobacco—Wholesalers report to Dept. Rev.
Last	Malt/brewed bev.—Wholesalers, distributors report, pay to ABC
ALASKA Last	Cigarettes and tobacco—Report, pay to Dept. Rev.
Last	Al. bev.—Report, pay to Dept. Rev.
Last	Motor fuel—Report, pay to Dept. Rev.
Last	Salmon enhancement tax—Buyers report, pay for past month
Last	Oil and gas production—Installment payments, pay to Dept. Rev.
ARIZONA 20	Sales-use—Report, pay to Dept. Rev. for month after tax accrues
20	Vinous, malt, and spirituous liquors—Wholesalers' returns and payments due
20	Cigar and tobacco products other than cigarettes—Returns and payment due
20	Al. bev.—Wholesalers pay to Dept. Rev.
20	Cigarette—Distributors report, pay to Dept. Rev.
25	Carriers—Report, pay motor carrier tax to Director of Transportation
25	Motor fuel use—Users report, pay to Director of Transportation unless other reporting basis elected

25 Sales-use—Tax delinquent if envelope not post marked this date or not received on or before the last business day before the last business day of the month
27 Gasoline—Suppliers report and pay tax to Dept. of Transportation
27 Use fuel—Suppliers report and pay tax to Dept. of Transportation

ARKANSAS 1 Gross receipts—sales—Last day to pay tax due 20th of preceding month without penalty
12 Gross receipts—sales—Large retailers pay 40% of current month's tax to Dept. Fin. & Admin.
15 Tobacco—Wholesalers report, pay to Dept. Fin. & Admn.
15 Withholding—Report, pay to Dept. Fin. & Admn. if tax is $200 or more per month
15 Al. bev.—Beer & light wine distributors report, pay to Dept. Fin. & Admn.
15 Al. bev.—Wine mfrs. report to Dept. Fin. & Admn.
15 Oil-gas—Producers and purchasers report; pay fee to Dept. Fin. & Admn.
15 Oil-gas—Refineries, natural gas plants report to Dept. Fin. & Admn.
15 Oil-gas—Transporters report to Dept. Fin. & Admn.
20 Gross receipts (sales) or use—Report, pay to Dept. Fin. & Admn.; large retailers pay balance of tax
20 Severance—Purchasers of natural resources report tax withheld to Dept. Fin. & Admn.
20 Motor fuel—Nondistributors report all transactions for past month
24 Gross receipts—sales—Large retailers pay 40% of current month's tax to Dept. Fin. & Admn.
25 Motor fuel—Distributors, licensed importers, terminals, suppliers, users report, pay Dept. Fin. & Admn.
25 Special fuel (liquefied gas)—Suppliers, dealers report to Dept. Fin. & Admn.; suppliers pay
25 Severance—Producers, severers, and purchasers report, pay to Dept. Fin. & Admn.
25 Alternative fuels—Suppliers report and pay tax to Dept. Fin. Admin.

CALIFORNIA 1 Alcoholic beverages—Carriers report and pay tax to SBE
15 Alcoholic beverages—Distillers report and pay tax to SBE
15 Alcoholic beverages—Beer and wine manufacturers, wine growers, and importers, report and pay tax to SBE
25th Cigarettes & tobacco products—Distributors report, pay to SBE
Last day Motor vehicle fuel—Suppliers report, pay to SBE
Diesel fuel tax—Suppliers, persons subject to backup tax report, pay to SBE
Sales—Suppliers and wholesalers prepay taxes
Withholding—Deposit state tax (if required to deposit Fed taxes) with the Employment Development Dept. within the same number of bank days set for Fed if accumulated withheld California tax is over $500

COLORADO 3 Withholding—Report, pay in three business days after this date if at least $50,000 in one-year period withheld and unremitted by this date and federal filing required
7 Withholding—Report, pay in three banking days after this date (see entry at **3** for liability)
10 Cigarettes—Report to Dept. Rev.
11 Withholding—Report, pay in three banking days after this date (see entry at **3** for liability)
15 Withholding—Report, pay in three banking days after this date (see entry at **3** for liability); employers collecting at least $7,000 but not more than $50,000 in one-year period
15 Casinos—Taxes paid by gaming casinos due; file return by electronic data interchange
15 Severance (except molybdenum ore)—Report, pay estimated tax to Dept. Rev. for preceding month
19 Withholding—Report, pay in three banking days after this date (see entry at **3** for liability)

20 Al. bev.—Mfrs., wholesalers report (copy Sec'y State), pay to Dept. Rev.
20 Sales-use—Report, pay to Dept. Rev.
20 Tobacco products—Report to Dept. Rev.
22 Withholding—Report, pay in three banking days after this date (see entry at **3** for liability)
25 Motor carriers—Mileage tax report, pay to Dept. Rev.
25 Motor fuels—Report, pay to Dept. Rev.
25 Withholding—Report, pay in three banking days after this date (see entry at **3** for liability)
Last Withholding—Report, pay in three banking days after this date (see entry at **3** for liability)

CONNECTICUT 10 Cigarettes—Report to Commr. Rev. Services
15 Cigarettes—Machine distributors report, pay Commr. Rev. Services
25 MV fuels—Distributors report to Commr. Rev. Services
Last Sales-use—Report, pay to Commr. Rev. Services if tax $4,000 or more for 12-month ending 9–30
Last Beer and liquor—Report, pay Commr. Rev. Services
Last Admission—Report, pay Commr. Rev. Services

DELAWARE 3 Withholding—Report, pay to Div. Rev. in three working days if tax over $20,000 during lookback 12-month period (eight monthly periods are set, see entries below)
7 Withholding—Second eighth monthly period, report-pay as in entry 3
11 Withholding—Third eighth monthly period (see above)
15 Withholding—Fourth eighth monthly period (see above)
15 Withholding—Report, pay Div. Rev. monthly if between $3,600 and $20,000 withheld during lookback 12-month period or no employees in Del. then
15 Alcoholic Bev.—Importers report to ABC
15 Malt beverage—Brewers, wholesalers, retailers report, pay to Commr. Rev.
15 Hotels-motels—Report, pay Dept. Fin.
19 Withholding—Fifth eighth monthly period (see above)
20 Licenses (mercantile)—Contractors, wholesalers, farm machy, retailers, feed & grain dealers, food proc., mfrs, and merchants report, pay to Dept. Fin. if monthly taxable gross receipts over $50,000
20 Utilities—Distributors of electricity, gas, Tel. & Tel. and cable TV report, pay Dept. Fin.
20 Sales use—Occupational, service tax payments due if aggregate gross receipts for past month $30,000 or more
22 Withholding—Sixth eighth monthly period (see above)
25 Withholding—Seventh eighth monthly period (see above)
25 Special city—Wilmington earned income tax withholding return and tax to City Dept. Fin if monthly withholding over $50
25 Gasoline—Distributors report, pay to Div. Motor Fuel
25 Al. bev.—Report, pay to Div. Rev.
25 Gasoline—Carriers report to Dept. Public Safety
Last Withholding—Eighth monthly period (see above)

DISTRICT OF COLUMBIA 10 Al. bev.—Common carriers report, pay to Office of Tax and Revenue
15 Al. bev.—Licensed manufacturers, wholesalers and retailers report, pay to Office of Tax and Revenue
15 Beer tax—Licensed manufacturers, wholesalers, retailers and brew pubs report, pay to Office of Tax and Revenue
20 Sales-use—Report, pay to Office of Tax and Revenue
20 Al. bev.—Licensed mfrs. report amounts manufactured to ABC Bd.
20 Utilities—Tele. cos. and non-public utility selling artificial gas to end-user, report, pay gross receipts tax to Office of Tax and Revenue
20 Electric cos.—Report, pay on kilowatt hours to Office of Tax and Revenue
20 Gas cos.—Report, pay tax on therms of natural gas delivered to end users to Office of Tax and Rev.

20 Heating oil cos.—Report, pay per-gallon tax on home heating oil delivered to end users to Office of Tax and Rev.
20 Providers of television, video, or radio service—Report, pay gross receipts tax to Office of Tax and Revenue
20 Toll and wireless telecommunication cos.—Report, pay toll telecommunication service tax to Office of Tax and Revenue
20 Income tax—Withholding report, payment to Office of Tax and Revenue
25 Motor fuel—Report, pay to Office of Tax and Revenue

FLORIDA 10 Alcoholic beverage—Report and payment of excise tax to Div. of Alcoholic Beverages and Tobacco by manufacturers and distributors; brokers, sales agents, and importers file reports with Div. of Alcoholic Beverages and Tobacco
10 Cigarette—Dealers-agents file reports with Div. Alcoholic Bev. Tobacco
15 Alcoholic beverages—Common carriers and other shippers report to Div. of Alcoholic Beverages and Tobacco; vendors must report and pay surcharge on sale of alcoholic beverages for consumption on premises
20 Motor fuel—Suppliers, importers, exporters, blenders, and wholesalers make report and payment to Dept. Rev.
20 Diesel fuel—Dealers, carriers, and terminal facilities make report and payment to Dept. Rev.
20 Sales-use—Dealers make return and payment for past month to Dept. Rev.; pay any estimated tax for current month
20 Mitigation fee on limestone and sand—Monthly fee due to Dept. Rev.
20 Gross receipts—Tax on dry cleaning due
20 Stamp—Taxpayer averaging at least five taxable transactions per month must make a return and pay for the previous month to Dept. Rev.
20 Utilities—Report, pay gross receipts tax to Dept. Rev.
20 Gross receipts—Report, pay to Dept. Rev. for utility and communications services.
25 Oil and gas production—Producers file return and production statement and pay tax to Dept. Rev.
25 Gasoline and oil inspection fee—Report and payment to Dept. Agriculture and Consumer Services
25 Gas and sulfur—Declaration plus 90% of estimated production tax to Dept. Rev. (balance of tax due by 25th of 2nd mo. after end of calendar quarter)

GEORGIA 10 Cigar, cigarette—Dealers report unstamped items to Commr. Rev.
10 Malt bev.—Wholesalers report, pay to municipality or Cty. officials
15 Withholding—Pay Commr. Rev. if over $200 monthly
15 Malt bev.—Brewers, wholesalers retailers report, pay to Commr. Rev.
20 Gasoline—Report, pay to Commr. Rev.
20 Sales-use—Report, pay to Commr. Rev.
20 Sales-use—Estimate-pay Commr. Rev. 50% of monthly estimated tax if over $2500 tax for 3 consecutive mos. (previous year)
20 Motor fuel—Distributors report, pay to Commr. Rev.

HAWAII 15 Withholding—Report, pay to Dept. Tax
Last Use-Report, pay to Dept. Tax
Last Fuel—Report, pay to Dept. Tax. (30 days from end of preceding month)
Last Gross income—Report, pay to Dept. Tax
Last Liquor excise—Report, pay to Dept. Tax.
Last Tobacco—Report, pay to Dept. Tax.

IDAHO 15 Beer, wine—Report to Tax Comm.
20 Sales-use—Report pay to Tax Comm.
20 Withholding—Report, pay to Tax Comm.
20 Withholding—Report, pay to Tax Comm., if annual tax $240,000 or more per year or avg. monthly tax $20,000 or more, for monthly period ended five days before ("split-month" period)
20 Tobacco products—Report, pay to Tax Comm.

Last Motor fuel (incl. aircraft)—Report, pay to Tax Comm.
Last Electric light & power cos.—Report, pay to Tax Comm.
ILLINOIS 3rd bank day Withholding—Quarter-monthly payment due Dept. Rev. or depositary (see entry at (7) below)
5 Cigarette—Mfrs. report, pay to Dept. Rev.
7 Sales-use—Quarter-monthly payment to Dept. Rev. if average monthly sales-use taxes $20,000 or more during preceding 4 cal. quarters (Quarter-monthly payments due from motor fuel distributors, suppliers, or resellers collecting prepaid tax from retailers if prepaid tax $20,000 or more during preceding 2 cal. quarters)(see (15), (22), and (last) below)
7 Withholding—Quarter-monthly payment due Dept. Rev. by 3rd bank day after this date if unpaid withholding $1,000 or more
7 Utilities (gross receipts tax on gas; telecommunications & electricity excise tax)—Quarter-monthly payment if average monthly tax $10,000 or more during past cal. year, excluding months of highest and lowest liability
15 Sales-use—2nd quarter-monthly pre-payment of tax due to Dept. Rev.
15 Tobacco products—Distributors (not mfrs.) report to Dept. Rev.
15 Alcoholic Liquors (Beer, wine etc)—Mfrs., importing distributors report, pay to Dept. Rev.; transporters report to Dept. Rev.
15 Electricity (excise tax), gas & telecommunications cos.—Report, pay to Dept. Rev.
15 Withholding—Pay Dept. Rev. by 15th of 2d and 3rd month of each calendar quarter if monthly tax over $500 but under $1,000 (payment for 3d month of each quarter made with quarterly return, ¶ 300)
15 Withholding—Quarter-monthly payment due by 3rd bank day after this date (see entry at (7) above)
15 Utilities—(see entry at (7) above)
20 Motor fuel—Distributors report, pay to Dept. Rev.
20 Special fuel—Suppliers report, pay to Dept. Rev.
20 Motor fuel—Persons not licensed as receiver, distributor, or supplier pay tax to Dept. Rev. on any untaxed fuel received
20 Fuel receivers—File return, pay 0.3¢ tax to Dept. Rev.
20 Sales-use—File return for preceding calendar month, pay to Dept. Rev., if required
20 Sales-use—Motor fuel resellers report, pay to Dept. Rev., if required
20 Utilities—Electric and gas utilities or cooperatives remit energy assistance charge to Dept. Rev.
20 Utilities—Electric and gas utilities or cooperatives remit renewable energy resources and coal technology development charge for past month to Dept. Rev.
22 Utilities—(see entry at (7) above)
22 Sales-use—3rd quarter-monthly pre-payment of tax due to Dept. Rev.
22 Withholding—Quarter-monthly payment due by 3rd bank day after this date (see entry at (7) above)
30 Motor fuel—Transportation cos. file report with Dept. Rev.
Last Withholding—Quarter-monthly payment (see entry at (7) above)
Last Sales-use—4th quarter-monthly payment due Dept. Rev.
Last Utilities—(see entry at (7) above)
Last Hotel operators' occupation—Report, pay for past month if average monthly tax over $200
Last Utilities (telecommunications excise tax)—File monthly return for preceding month
INDIANA 10 Gasoline—Prepaid sales tax (first filing)
10 Cigarettes—Distributors report interstate sales
15 Tobacco products tax, report-pay
15 Cigarettes—Distributors report drop shipments
15 Special fuels—Dealers report to Dept. Rev. number of alternative fuel temporary trip permits sold
15 Motor fuel use—Users, dealers report, pay to Motor Fuel Tax Div.

20 Withholding—Report, pay to Dept. Rev. if average monthly tax for prior year was over $1,000
20 Sales-use—Report, pay if average monthly tax for prior year over $1,000
20 Al. bev. (excise)—Report, pay to Dept. Rev.
20 Motor fuels—Distributors pay to Motor Fuel Tax Div.
20 Motor fuels—Carriers report instate deliveries to Motor Fuel Tax Div.
20 Gasoline—Terminal operators and qualified distributors remit prepayment received 1st—15th of previous month
25 Petroleum inspection fee—Report, pay to Oil Inspection Div. (except licensed distributors)
25 Gasoline—Prepaid sales tax (second filing)
30 Sales-use—Report, pay if average monthly tax for prior year under $1000
30 Utility services use tax—Pay, report even if no tax is due, to Dept. Rev.
30 Petroleum severance—Report, pay to Petroleum Severance Tax Div.

IOWA 10 Beer, malt liquors—Mfrs., wholesalers report, pay to Dir. Rev.
10 Beer—Class A holders report to Al. Beverages Div.
10 Sales-use—Semimonthly payment to Dept. Rev. if tax over $4000 for semimonthly period (16th to last day)
10 Withholding—Semimonthly payment due Dept. Rev. if tax over $8000 for semimonthly period (for period 16th to last day)
10 Cigarettes—Report to Dept. Rev.
15 Withholding—Report, pay to Dept. Rev. for 1st and 2nd mos. of quarter if monthly amount over $50 (3rd mo. by last day of month after quarter end)
20 Tobacco products—Report-pay tax
20 Sales-use—Pay to Dept. Rev. if sales tax over $50 but under $500 for prior month; or if over $500 but under $4000 for prior semimonthly period. Pay use tax if over $1,500 tax monthly. (See also last day)
25 Sales-use—Semimonthly payment (see entry at (10) above)
25 Withholding—Semimonthly payment (see entry at (10) above)
Last Motor fuel—Report (includes carriers) to Dept. Rev.
Last Motor fuel—Dealers and users report-pay to Dept. Rev.
Last Motor fuel—Gasohol blenders report to Dept. Rev.
Last Special fuel—Dealers and users report, pay to Dept. Rev.
Last Use—Pay to Dept. Rev. if monthly tax $1500 (except March, June, Sept., and Dec.)

KANSAS 3 Withholding—Report, pay to Dir. Tax. on withholding for 22nd through last day of previous month if calendar year tax over $100,000
10 Withholding—Report, pay to Dir. Tax. on withholding for 1st through 7th day of previous month (see entry at (3) above)
10 Withholding—Pay balance of tax for prior month (see entry at 25 below)
10 Cigarettes—Wholesalers & vending machine distributors-dealers report to Dir. Rev.
10 Al. bev.—Malt beverages and products report to Dir. Rev.
15 Withholding—Report, pay to Dir. Tax. for prior month if calendar year tax $1200–$8000
15 Al. bev.—Pay wine tax to ABC.
15 Motor fuel—Carriers report to Dir. Rev.
15 Oil & gas conservation assmt.—Producers report to Conserv. Div., operators file information Corp. Comm.
15 Al. bev.—Mfrs., wholesalers report to Dir. ABC
18 Withholding—Report, pay to Dir. Tax. on withholding for 8th through 15th day of previous month (see entry at (3) above)
20 Oil-gas-coal severance—Producers pay Dir. Rev. in 1st month after severance for oil and gas; in 2nd month after severance for coal
20 Tobacco products—Report, pay to Dir. Rev.
20 MVs—Dealers report sales—transfer to Dept. Rev.

24 Withholding—Report, pay to Dir. Tax for 16th through 21st day of month if annual amount withheld is over $100,000 per calendar yr.
25 Transient guest tax—Report, pay for past month to Dept. Rev.
25 Withholding—Report, pay to Dir. Tax. for 1st 15 days of month if calendar year tax over $8000 (for balance of mo. see entry at 10 above) but not over $10,000
25 Sales-use—Report, pay to Dir. Rev. if tax over $3,200 but not over $32,000 for calendar year; if tax $32,000 or more for calendar year, by this date report, pay for 1st 15 days of same month
25 Tire tax—Report, pay Dept. Rev. if annual tax over $1,600
25 Motor fuel—Special fuel users report, pay to Dir. Rev.
25 Motor fuel—Report, pay to Dir. Rev.
25 Motor fuel—Floor stock tax report, pay to Dir. Tax
25 Oil inspection fee—Report, pay to Dir. Rev.
25 Motor fuel (liquefied petroleum)—Report, pay to Dir. Rev.
25 Liquor enforcement—Liquor retailers report, pay to Dir. Rev.
Last Oil-gas severance—Producers report to Dir. Rev. in 1st month after severance for oil and gas; in 2nd month after severance for coal
Last Bingo—Distributors report, pay to Admr. Charitable Gaming.

KENTUCKY 15 Al. bev.—Nonretail licenses report to Dept. Rev.
15 Al. bev.—Wholesaler report, pay to Dept. Rev.
15 Withholding—Report, pay to Dept. Rev. (Dec. report is due Jan. 31)
20 Sales-use—Report, pay to Dept. Rev.
20 Oil transporters—Report, pay to Dept. Rev.
20 Cigarette stamp—Wholesalers report to Dept. Rev.
20 Coal severance—Report, pay to Dept. Rev.
20 Alcohol—Excise and gross receipts reports and payments
20 Oil production tax—Report-pay tax
20 Licenses—Tire retailers report, pay fee to Dept. Rev. if sale made in previous mo.
25 Sales-use—Large taxpayers (over $10,000) return and payment to Dept. Rev.
25 Gasoline—Dealers, transporters, refiners, importers report, pay to Dept. Rev.
25 Motor fuel (liquefied petroleum gas)—Dealers report, pay to Dept. Rev.
25 Special fuel—Dealers report, pay to Dept. Rev.
Last Gasoline, special fuels & liquefied petroleum—Report, pay to Dept. Rev. if 95% (min.) paid by 25th
Last Motor fuel (aircraft)—Refund application to Dept. Rev. Cabinet

LOUISIANA 10 Al. bev.—Importers report, pay to Sec'y Rev.
10 Severance (oysters)—Report, pay to Dept. Wildife & Fisheries
10 Shrimp excise—Report, pay to Dept. Wildife & Fisheries
15 Al. bev. (more than 6%)—Mfrs., wholesalers report, pay to Sec'y Rev.
15 Al. bev.—Carriers report to Sec'y Rev.
15 Severance (mussels)—Report, pay to Dept. Wildlife & Fisheries
15 Gasoline—Carriers report to Sec'y Rev.
15 Withholding—Semimonthly report, pay to Sec'y Rev. if monthly tax $2,000 or more
15 Property—MV and marine dealers report, pay tax on inventory to tax collector or sheriff
15 Severance (mussels)—Report, pay to Dept. of Wildlife & Fisheries
20 Gasoline—Report to Sec'y Rev.
20 Soft drinks—Report to Sec'y Rev.
20 Sales-use—Report, pay to Sec'y Rev.; in New Orleans, to Dir. Fin.
20 Cigars, cigarettes, tobacco—Dealers report to Sec'y Rev.
20 Al. bev. (not more than 6% alcohol)—Wholesalers report, pay Sec'y Rev.
20 Gasoline—Dealers report, pay to Sec'y Rev.
20 Gasoline—Mfrs., importers, tractor fuel or distillate report, pay to Sec'y Rev.
20 Gasoline—Wholesalers or jobbers delivery, if no tax paid, report to Sec'y Rev.

20	Public utility license tax report and payment due
25	Underground motor fuel storage tank fee—Report, pay to Sec'y Environmental Quality
Last	Withholding—(see entry at (15) above for semimonthly report-pay)
Last	Withholding—Monthly report, pay to Sec'y Rev. if monthly tax $500—$1,999.
Last	Severance tax—Natural resources severance tax report and payment due
MAINE 10	Alcohol-Low-alcohol spirits—Manufacturers breweries, and wineries report, pay excise taxes to State Liquor Comm.
10	Malt bev.—Mfrs., foreign wholesalers report to Liquor Comn.
15	Sales-use—Report, pay to Rev. Services
21	Withholding—Report, pay to Rev. Services
21	Motor fuels—Distributors, dealers report, pay to Rev. Services
24	Sales-use—Pay estimated tax to Rev. Services
Semiweekly	Withholding—Pay Rev. Services by Wed. for wages paid Wed.–Fri. of previous week; by following Fri. for Sat.–Tues. payments
Last	Potato—Shippers report, pay to State Tax Assr.
Last	Tobacco products tax report and payment due
Last	Quahog—Report, pay to State Tax Assr.
MARYLAND 3rd business day	Withholding—Report to Comptr. by 3rd business day after payroll period if required to withhold $15,000 or more for past yr.
10	Admission—Report, pay to Comptr.
10	Al. bev.—Mfrs. and wholesalers report, pay to Comptr.
15	Withholding—Report, pay to Comptr. if $700 per quarter
21	Sales and use—Report, pay to Comptr.
21	Cigarettes—Wholesalers report to Comptr.
25	Al. bev.—Passenger carriers pay Comptr.
Last	Motor fuel—Report, pay to Comptr.
MASSACHUSETTS 3rd business day	Withholding—Pay Commr. Rev. or depositary (for quarter-monthly period) if expecting tax $25,000 for year and unpaid withholding $500 or more
7	Withholding—Quarter-monthly payment due Commr. Rev. by 3rd business day after 7th (see entry for "3rd business day" for liability)
15	Withholding—Report, pay to Commr. Rev. or depositary for previous month if expecting tax over $1,200 but under $25,000 for year (except 4-30, 7-31, 10-31 and 1-31 for Mar., June, Sept. and Dec.)
15	Withholding—Quarter-monthly payment due Commr. Rev. by 3rd business day after 15th (see entry for "3rd business day" for liability)
20	Local aircraft fuel—Report, pay to Commr. Rev.
20	Al. bev. excise—Report, pay to Commr. Rev.
20	Cigarettes—Stampers report, pay to Commr. Rev.
20	Sales-use—Report, pay to Commr. Rev. if tax over $1200 but under $25,000 per year
20	Meals—Report, pay to Commr. if estimated tax under $25,000
20	Room occupancy—Report, pay to Commr. Rev. if tax under $25,000 per year
20	Motor Fuels—Report, pay to Commr. Rev.
Last	Withholding—Quarter-monthly payment due Commr. Rev. by 3rd business day after this date (see entry for "3rd business day" for liability)
MICHIGAN 10	Sales-use—Remit prepayments on gasoline for 16th of previous mo. to end of previous mo. to Dept. Treas.
20	Sales-use—Report, pay to Dept. Treas.
20	Withholding—Report, pay to Dept. Treas.
20	Withholding—Employers, flow-through entities, casinos, or racetracks must provide Dept. Treas. with copy of exemption certificates with over 9 exemptions or exempt status claimed
20	Aviation fuel—Report, pay to Dept. Treas.
20	Cigarette—Report, pay to Div. Rev.
20	Liquefied petroleum—Report, pay to Dept. Treas.
20	Diesel fuel—Report, pay to Dept. Treas.

20 Motor, recreational vehicle and marine fuel—Report, pay to Dept. Treas.
25 Oil production fee—Carriers' report to Dept. Rev.
25 Severance—Oil & Gas cos. report, pay to Div. Rev.
25 Sales-use—Remit prepayments on gasoline for 1st of mo. to 15th of mo. to Dept. Treas.

MINNESOTA 18 Cigarettes and tobacco products—Report, pay to Dept. Rev.
18 Wine and liquor—Report, pay to Commr. Rev.
20 Sales-use—Report, pay to Dept. Rev. (accelerated payment for June for retailers with $120,000 in prior yr. See June and August calendars.)
20 Liquor gross receipts—Report, pay to Commr. Rev. (accelerated payment for June for retailers with $120,000 in prior yr. See June and August calendars.)
23 Gasoline and special fuel—Dealers, distributors & users report, pay to Dept. Rev.
23 Petroleum inspection—Report, pay to Dept. Rev.

MISSISSIPPI 15 Withholding—Report, pay to STC if tax $300 per month
15 Withholding—Transient and seasonal employers report, pay
15 Alcohol—Wholesaler-distributor report-pay tax on beer and light wine received in prior month
15 Cigarettes—Wholesaler-distributor report-pay tax on tobacco products other than cigarettes received in prior month
15 Timber—Report, pay to STC
20 Gasoline—Common carriers report deliveries to STC
20 Gasoline—Distributors, refiners and processors report, pay to Tax Comm.
20 Lubricating oil—Report, pay to STC
20 Liquefied compressed gas—Distributors, refiners and processors report, pay to STC
20 Special fuel—Distributors, refiners, processors, and carriers report to STC.
20 Sales-use—Report, pay to STC
20 Salesmen—Report, pay to STC
20 Salt severance—Report, pay to STC
20 User tax—Natural gas, locomotive fuel and compressed gas users report, pay to STC for previous mo.
25 Oil severance—Report, pay to STC
25 Gas severance—Report, pay to STC

MISSOURI 5 Alcoholic beverages—Nonintoxicating beverage permittee report to Supvr Liquor Control
7 Sales—Quarter-monthly report, payment to Dir. Rev. 3rd banking day after this date if monthly tax $15,000 or more (see entries at 15, 22 and last)
7 Income—Withholding quarter-monthly report, payment to Dir. Rev. 3rd banking day after this date if monthly tax $9000 or more (see entries at 15, 22 and last below)
15 Income—Withholding quarter-monthly payment (see (7) above)
15 Alcoholic beverages—Report of sales to Supervisor of Liquor Control
15 Sales—Quarter-monthly payment (see (7) above)
15 Bingo—Pay Dir. Rev. prior month's taxes
15 Cigarette—Wholesalers buying stamps on deferred payment basis report to Dir. Rev.
20 Sales-use taxes—Report, pay to Dir. Rev. for preceding month if tax over $250 for 1st or 2nd calendar mo.
20 Cigarettes—Wholesalers, common carriers report to Dir. Rev.
22 Income—Withholding quarter-monthly payment (see (7) above)
22 Sales—Quarter-monthly payment (see (7) above)
Last Withholding—Quarter-monthly payment (see (7) above)
Last Special fuel use—Report, pay to Dir. Rev.
Last Sales—Quarter-monthly payment (see (7) above)
Last Gasoline—Distributors, transporters, terminals of motor fuel report to Dir. Rev.
Last Surface coal mining assmt. fee—Pay to Land Reclamation Comm.
Last Gasoline—Distributors of motor fuel pay tax to Dir. Rev.

Last Gasoline—Licensees, dealers, users of special fuel report, pay Dir. Rev.
Last Gasoline—Report, pay fuel inspection fee to Dir. Agriculture
Last Gasoline—Aviation fuel distributor forwards copy of invoices to Dept. Rev. for aviation fuel delivered for previous mo.
Last Income—Report-pay withholding for 3rd month of calendar quarter in following month

MONTANA 15 Al. Bev.—Report, pay to Dept. Rev.
25 Gasoline—Distributors report, pay to Dept. Rev.
25 Gasoline—Gasohol producers file tax incentive claim with Dept. for gasohol produced in past month
Last Special fuel—Dealers report, pay to Dept.

NEBRASKA 10 Cigarette—Distributors report to Tax Commr.
15 Withholding—Report, pay to Tax Commr. if tax over $500 for either 1st or 2nd month of quarter
15 Al. bev.—Mfrs. and wholesale distributors report to Liquor Control Comm.
20 Common carriers—Report fuels, oils, etc. transported in-state to Tax Commr.
25 Gasoline and aviation fuel—Report, pay to Tax Commr.
25 Diesel fuel—Suppliers, distributors, wholesalers, importers, exporters report, pay to Dept. Rev.
25 Lodging tax—Report, pay state and county tax to Dept. Rev.
25 Sales-use—Report, pay state and local taxes to Dept. Rev.
25 Tire fee—Report, pay to Dept. Rev.
25 Fertilizer fee—Report, pay to Dept. Rev.
25 Al. bev.—Mfrs., distributors report, pay excise tax to State Liquor Comm.
Last Oil-gas conservation—Pay to Dept. Rev.
Last Oil-gas severance—Report, pay to Dept. Rev.
Last Uranium severance—Report, pay to Dept. Rev.

NEVADA 15 Alcohol.—Pay excise tax to Dept. Tax for 0.5% discount
20 Al. bev.—Pay Dir. Tax without penalty
20 Tax on tobacco products other than cigarettes—Pay to Dept. of Taxation
24 Live entertainment tax report and payment due by licensed gaming establishment
25 Cigarettes—Dealers report to Dir. Tax.
Last Motor fuel—Report, pay to Dir. Tax
Last Oil inspection—Shippers, transporters, report, pay to Tax Comm.
Last Sales-use—Report, pay to Dir. Tax. if sales over $10,000 monthly
Last Oil-gas conservation—Report to Dept. of Minerals pay to State Treas.
Last Live entertainment tax report and payment due by taxpayers other than licensed gaming establishments

NEW HAMPSHIRE 10 Al. bev.—Mfrs., wholesalers report, pay to Liquor Comm.
15 Refined petroleum products—Pay estimated tax to Dept. Rev. Admin.
15 Meals & room—Report-pay to Dept. Rev. Admn.
15 Utilities—Retailers file return, pay communications services tax to Dept. Rev. Admn. for previous mo.
15 Utilities—Retailers with average monthly liability for communications services tax of over $10,000 pay 90% of estimate for current month's liability to Dept. Rev. Admn.
15 Utilities—Taxpayers file return, pay communications services tax for previous mo. to Dept. Rev. Admn. if not paid to retailers
20 Motor fuels—Mfr. of alcohol for gasohol report to Dir. MV
20 Motor fuels—Carriers transporting fuel report to Dir. MV
Last Interstate buses—Operators report operations to admr. of Interstate Bus Compact

NEW JERSEY 1 Motor fuels—Fuel carriers monthly report
10 Cigarette—Wholesale dealer's and distributor's informational and purchases reports to Div. Tax
10 Jitney—Report, pay to municipal coll.
10 Casino Control—Operators report, pay to State Treas. and to Casino Control Comm. and pay depositories chosen by Treas.

15 Withholding—Monthly payment of gross (personal) income tax withholding to Div. Tax. if $500 or more monthly; quarterly report-payment due if expected income tax withheld is less than $500; weekly EFT payment required if income tax withheld for past yr. is $20,000 or more
20 Sales-use—Report, pay to Dir. Tax. (1st and 2nd mos. of quarter) if monthly tax exceeds $500
20 Cigarette—Report, pay to Dir. Tax. by manufacturers, distributors and consumers
20 Tobacco products—Report, pay tobacco products wholesale sales and use tax to Div. Tax.
20 Solid waste—Sanitary landfill owners, operators report, pay to Div. Tax.
20 Hazardous waste—Terminal owners and operators report, pay tax to Div. Tax.
20 Motor fuel—Distributors, importers gas jobbers report, pay to Dir. Tax.
25 Petroleum products gross receipts tax—Report, pay to MV Commr.
25 Motor fuel—report and pay gross receipts tax to Dir. Tax.
30 Motor fuel—Carriers report to Dir. Tax.

NEW MEXICO 25 Oil-gas—Ad valorem tax report, pay to Tax. & Rev. Dept.
25 Oil-gas—Emergency Sch. privilege tax report, pay to Tax. & Rev. Dept.
25 Oil-gas conservation—Report, pay to Tax. & Rev. Dept.
25 Oil-gas severance—Report, pay to Tax. & Rev. Dept.
25 Motor fuel—Wholesalers file information with Tax & Rev. Dept.
25 Special fuel suppliers—Report, pay to Tax. and Rev. Dept.
25 Al. bev.—Wholesalers liquor and beer report, pay to ABC
25 Cigarette and tobacco products—Report, pay to Tax & Rev. Dept.
25 Resources—Report, pay to Tax & Rev. Dept. (after sale, transportation out-of-state or consumption, if earlier)
25 Severance—Report, pay to Tax & Rev. Dept.
25 Withholding—Report, pay to Tax & Rev. Dept.
25 Sales-use—Report, pay to Tax & Rev. Dept.
25 Gasoline, motor fuel—Distributors report, pay to Tax & Rev. Dept.
25 Leased vehicle gross receipts—Return, pay to Tax. & Rev. Dept.
25 Interstate telecommunications gross receipts—Return, pay to Tax. & Rev. Dept.
25 County and municipal gasoline—Return, pay tax to county and/or municipality; if joint election, report, pay to Tax. & Rev. Dept.
25 Special county hospital gasoline—Return, pay tax to county
25 Natural gas processors—Report, pay to Tax. & Rev. Dept.
30 Solid waste—Operators/owners of solid waste disposal facility remit fee to Tax. & Rev. Dept.

NEW YORK 15 Cigarette-tobacco—Report to Tax Commr.; pay tobacco tax
15 N.Y.C. cigarette—Report to Commr. Fin.
20 State-local sales-use—Report, pay to Tax Commr. if state-local taxable receipts in any of preceding 4 quarters $300,000 or more
20 Gasoline—Distributors report, pay to Tax Commr.
20 Petroleum business (gallonage)—Return, pay Dept. Tax. & Fin.
20 Al. bev.—Report, pay to Tax Commr.
25 N.Y.C. utilities—Report, pay to Commr. Fin.
25 Motor fuel—Distributor, importer, broker, jobber, wholesale dealer, storers or transporters information return to Tax Commr.
25 NYC E-911 surcharge—Return and payment due
Last Highway use—Report, pay to Dept. Tax. & Fin. if average over $4,000 for prior calendar yr.
Last Fuel use—Carriers report, pay to Dept. Tax. & Fin.
3rd business day after making payroll Withholding—Report, pay to Tax Commr. if qtrly. withholding at least $700 and at least $15,000 withheld in yr. before last yr. (if notified by Tax Commr.)
5th business day after making payroll Withholding—New businesses report, pay to Tax Commr. if qtrly. withholding at least $700 and under $15,000 withheld in yr. before last yr.

NORTH CAROLINA
Semiweekly Withholding—Large employers report, pay to Sec'y Rev.

3 Motor fuels—Occasional importers report, pay to Sec'y. Rev.

15 Withholding—Report, pay to Sec'y. Rev. if avg. monthly withholding $250 to $1,999 (except Dec. due Jan. 31)

20 Sales-use—Report, pay to Sec'y Rev. if tax more than $100; prepayment required if tax at least $10,000

20 Utilities—Local gas distribution cos. report, pay excise tax on piped natural gas

20 Cigarettes—Report to Sec'y Rev.

22 Gasoline & oil inspection—Report pay to Sec'y. Rev.

22 Motor fuels—Blenders, importers, suppliers, tank wagon importers report, pay to Sec'y. Rev.

22 Motor fuels—Distributors-exporters, terminal operators, transporters report, pay to Sec'y. Rev.

22 Alternative fuels—Providers report, pay to Sec'y. Rev.

NORTH DAKOTA 15 Al. bev.—Wholesalers pay State Treas.

15 Cigarettes-tobacco—Distributors report, pay to Tax Comm.

15 Gross gas production—Producers & buyers report, pay to Tax Comr. (15th of 2nd mo. following production)

25 Coal conversion plant tax report and payment due

25 Gasoline and special fuel —Dealers report, pay to Tax Commr.

25 Coal severance—Pay to Tax Comm.

25 Petroleum products inspection—Wholesale dealers of gasoline, kerosene, tractor fuel, heating oil, or diesel fuel report, pay fee to Tax Commr.

25 Gross oil extraction—Owners of oil extracted report, pay to Tax Commr.

25 Gross oil production—Buyers, producers, and refiners report, pay to Tax Commr.

Last Sales-use—Pay tax if sales for prior calendar year $333,000 or more (except by June 22 for May in each odd-numbered yr.)

OHIO 1st bank day Withholding—Report, pay if undeposited taxes over $100,000

3rd bank day Withholding—Report, pay in three business days after close of partial weekly withholding period if payments during 12-month period ending 6–30 of past yr. total at least $84,000

10 Beer and malt beverage tax—Report to State Treas.

14 or 15 Severance—If required to file monthly, pay State Treas. for month ending 45 days before

15 Withholding—Report, pay to Dept. Tax. for past calendar month if payments total over $2,000 during 12-month period ending 6–30 of past yr.

15 Cigarettes—Report, pay to Tax Commr.

18 Beer and liquor tax—Make advance payment to State Treas.

20 Kilowatt-hour excise—Distributors, self-assessing purchasers report, pay to State Treas.

23 Sales-use—Vendor's monthly report, pay to Tax Comr. (except Dec. due by Jan. 31 if reconciliation return); consumer use and direct pay returns are also due

23 Sales tax—Pay 75% of anticipated tax liability for this month to Dept. Tax.

23 Sales tax—Pay balance of tax due for past month to Dept. Tax.

30 Motor fuel—Utility cos. transporting motor fuel report to Tax Commr.

Last Motor fuel—Dealers, terminal operators, exporters report, pay to State Treas.

OKLAHOMA 10 Alcoholic beverage excise tax—Report, pay to Tax Comm.

15 Motor vehicle rental tax—Pay to Tax Comm.

15 Fuel—Consumers report, pay to Tax Comm. if tax not precollected

15 Tobacco tax—Report to Tax Commr.

20 Alcoholic beverage gross receipts tax—Report, pay to Tax Comm.

20 Withholding—Report, pay Tax Comm. if monthly withholding exceeds $500

20 Sales—Report, pay to Tax Comm.

20 Special fuels—Report, pay Tax Comm.

20 Utilities—Rural electric co-ops report, pay gross receipts tax to Tax Comm.

25	Gross production tax—Oil, gas and mineral producers and buyers report and payment to Tax Comm. due on second month after month of production
25	Motor fuel—Licensed tank wagon importers report due to Tax Comm.
27	Fuel—Suppliers, exporters, terminal operators report, pay to Tax Comm.
Last	Gaming tax—Pay taxes on game pieces and equipment to Tax Comm.
OREGON 10	Motor carriers—Electing carriers pay in lieu fees to Dept. Rev.
20	Use fuel—Report, pay MV Div.
20	Alcoholic beverage excise—Manufacturing reports, pay Liquor Comm.
20	Cigarette—Distributors, carriers report, pay to Dept. Rev.
25	Gasoline—Report, pay to MV Div.
Last	Motor carriers—Mileage report, pay privilege tax to PJC
PENNSYLVANIA 15	Withholding—Report, pay to Dept. Rev. (1-31 for Dec.) if monthly basis (semimonthly see "last" day)
15	Pittsburgh employers—Report, pay earned income tax (except Dec. due 1-30) if tax $200 (min) monthly
15	Phila. amusement—Report, pay to Phila. Dept. Rev.
15	Pbgh. parking—Report, pay to City Treas.
15	Alcohol—Manufacturers, distributors report, pay malt beverage tax to Dept. Rev.
20	Sales-use—Report-pay to Dept. Rev. for prior month if tax over $600 monthly
20	Phila. hotel room Report, pay hotel room rental & hotel room occupancy taxes to Phila. Dept. Rev.
25	Phila. Sch. Dist. business occupancy—Report, pay to Phila. Dept. Rev.
25	Phila. wage & net profits—Report, pay to Phila. Dept. Rev. if withholding over $50 but less than $250 per month (except March, June, Sept. & Dec. when report and payment due last day of month)
25	Phila. parking—Report, pay to Phila. Dept. Rev.
Next to last business day	Oil cos., liquid fuels and fuel use—Report, pay to Dept. Rev.
Last	Pittsburgh amusement—Producer report, pay to City Treas.
Last	Liquid fuel—Common carriers report, pay to Dept. Rev.
Last	Fuel use—Common carriers report, pay to Dept. Rev.
Last	Phila. wage & net profits—Report, pay to Phila. Dept. Rev. if withholding over $50 but less than $250 per month for March, June, Sept. & Dec. (see entry for (15) above)
Last	Withholding—Report, pay Dept. Rev. in 3 days after 15th and month's end if semimonthly basis
RHODE ISLAND 7	Withholding—Quarter-monthly report, pay (see entry at last day below)
10	Alcoholic beverages tax—Report to Tax Admr. by manufacturers
10	Tobacco tax—Report to Tax Admr. by distributors and dealers receiving unstamped products
15	Withholding—Quarterly-monthly report, pay (see entry at last day below)
20	Withholding tax—Report-pay preceding month's if $50–$599 to Tax Administrator—by 20th; but on last day in Apr., July Oct., and Jan. for previous month.
20	Sales and use tax—Report and payment to Tax Admr.
20	MV fuel tax—Report and payment to Tax Admr. by distributors
22	Withholding—Quarter-monthly report, pay (see entry at last day below)
Last	Withholding tax—Report pay quarterly-monthly by 3 banking days after this date and 7th, 15th and 22nd of month if withholding for any month reaches $600–$23,999 to Tax Admr.
Daily	Withholding—Report, pay to Tax Admr. if at least $24,000 withheld in a month
SOUTH CAROLINA 15	Withholding—Report, pay to Dept. Rev.
20	Power—Report, pay to Dept. Rev.
20	Cigarette, Tobacco Products—Dealers report, pay to Dept. Rev.

20 Beer and wine—Report, pay to Tax Comm.
20 Alcoholic beverage—Report, pay to Tax Comm.
20 Sales-use—Report, pay tax for prior month; estimate-pay to Tax Comm. if monthly over $25,000 for 3 consecutive mos. of previous year
22 Gasoline—Report, pay to Dept. Rev.

SOUTH DAKOTA 15 Cigarettes/tobacco—Distributors report to Dept. Rev. and Reg.
15 Tobacco products—Licensed distributors and wholesalers report, pay to Dept. Rev. and Reg.
20 Sales-use—Report, pay to Dept. Rev. and Reg. monthly if annual tax $1,000 (min.)
25 Liquor (including contractor's excise tax)—Report, pay Dept. Rev. and Reg. for 2nd preceding month
Last Sales-use (including contractor's excise tax)—Report, pay to Dept. Rev. and Reg. monthly if annual tax $1,000 (min.) and paying by electronic transfer
Last Sales-use (including contractor's excise tax)—Report, pay to Dept. Rev. and Reg. after two-month period if annual tax under $1,000
Last Motor fuel—Suppliers, importers, exporters, blenders, liquefied petroleum gas, and natural gas vendors report, pay to Dept. Rev. and Reg.
Last Motor fuel—Transporters, terminal operators, bulk plant operators report to Dept. Rev. and Reg.

TENNESSEE 1 Coal products severance tax—Return, pay Dept. Rev.
15 Minerals other than coal—Operators report, pay Dept. Rev.
20 Petroleum products—Distributors report to Commr. Rev.
20 Sales-use—Report, pay to Commr. Rev.
20 Gasoline—motor fuel—Manufacturers, refiners report on fuel imported, mfr'd or sold in state to Commr. Rev.
25 Petroleum products—Transporters report to Dept. Rev.
25 MV fuel use—Licensees report to Commr. Rev.
Last Fuel tax—Dealers or distgributors claim government unit exemption with Commr. Rev. (by last day of 2nd month after month in which exempt sale made)

TEXAS 15 Cigarettes—Distributors report to Comptr.
15 Liquor—Ale-malt brewers, importers report, pay to ABC
15 Mixed drinks—Licensees report, pay to Comptr.
15 Al. bev.—Beer importers, manufacturers report, pay to ABC
15 Sales-use—Prepayment to Comptr. for discount, if tax over $1500 monthly
20 Sales-use—Report, pay Comptr., if tax $500 or more
20 Natural gas production—Report, pay to Comptr.
20 Oil-gas well service—Report, pay to Comptr.
20 Pipeline cos.—Petroleum report to RR Comm.
20 Uranium-metals—Report, pay to General Land Office Commr.
25 Cement tax—Report, pay to Comptr.
25 Crude petroleum—Report, pay to Comptr.
25 Gasoline—Liable persons, terminal operators, and licensed distributors report, pay to Comptr.
25 Diesel fuel—Liable persons, terminal operators, and licensed distributors report, pay to Comptr.

UTAH Before last Beer—Brewers, wholesalers, distributors, report, pay to Alcoholic Beverage Comm.
Before last Beer—Carriers and wholesalers, distributors, and brewers delivering beer in the state report to Alcoholic Beverage Comm.
Last Motor and special fuel—Carriers report deliveries to St. Tax Comm.
Last Motor fuel—Distributors report and pay tax to State Tax Comm.
Last Special fuel tax—User-dealers and users report, pay State Tax Comm.
Last Sales-use—Report, pay to State Tax Comm. if state-local tax liability was $50,000 or more for past year
Last Sales-use—Pay electronically if state, local, and public transit tax was $96,000 or more for past year
Last Withholding—Report, pay to Tax Comm. if withholding $1,000 or more per month

VERMONT Wed. & Fri. Withholding—Report, pay by Wed. for tax withheld for pay days on past Wed.—Fri. and by Fri. for past Sat.—Tues. if tax over $9,000 for that qtr.

10 Al. bev.—Bottlers-wholesalers of malt and vinous beverages report, pay to Commr. Taxes

15 Tobacco products—Distributors report, pay to Commr. Taxes

15 Cigarettes—Wholesalers report to Commr. Taxes

25 Meals-rooms—Report, pay to Tax Commr. (23rd in Feb.)

25 Withholding—Report, pay to Commr. Taxes if quarterly withholding $2,501–$9,000 (except 23d in Feb.)

25 Sales-use—Report, pay to Tax Commr. (except 23d in Feb.)

25 Motor fuel—Report, pay to Dept. MV

VIRGINIA 3rd bank day Withholding—Quarter-monthly report, pay to Tax Commr. if average monthly liability $1000 (min.) and withholding during quarter-monthly period over $500

7 Withholding—Quarter-monthly report, pay to Tax Commr. by 3rd bank day after 7th (see "3rd bank day" (above) for liability)

10 Al. bev.—Beer tax report to Tax Commr.

10 Cigarettes—Wholesalers report to Dept. Tax

10 Tobacco products—Distributor's report to Dept. Tax

15 Withholding—Quarter-monthly report, pay to Tax Commr. by 3rd bank day after 15th (see "3rd bank day" (above) for liability)

20 Sales-use—Dealers and communications service providers report, pay to Tax Commr.

20 Gasoline—Nontaxable dealers, distributors report to Commr. MV

22 Withholding—Quarter-monthly report, pay to Tax Commr. by 3rd bank day after 22nd (see "3rd bank day" above for liability)

25 Withholding—Report, pay to Tax Commr. if $100 or more

Last Gasoline—Dealers report, pay to Commr. MV

Last Motor fuel—Carriers report to Commr. MV

Last Special fuels—Suppliers report, pay—user-sellers report to MV Div.

WASHINGTON 10 Motor fuel—Report certain imports to Dept. of Licensing

15 Cigarettes—Dealers with unstamped interstate goods report to Dept. Rev.

15 Fish & shellfish (excise)—Report, pay to Dept. Rev.

20 Butterfat dealers—Pay to Dairy Products Comm.

20 Sales-use—Report, pay to Dept. Rev.

20 B & O—Report, pay to Dept. Rev.

25 Special fuel—Report, pay to Dept. MV (quarterly, semiannual or annual filers)

25 Motor vehicle fuel—Distributors report, pay to Dept. MV

25 Aircraft fuel—Report, pay to Dept. MV

25 Utilities—Report, pay to Dept. Rev.

Last business day (state) Motor vehicle fuels & special fuels—Pay by electronic funds transfer before this date if tax $50,000 (min) for previous month

Last day Leasehold excise—Report, pay to Dept. Rev.

WEST VIRGINIA 10 Nonintoxicating beer—Report, pay to Tax Commr.

15 Soft drinks—Report to Tax Commr.

15 Al. bev.—Licensees report to Liquor Control Comm.

15 Cigarettes & tobacco products—Report, pay to Tax Commr.

20 Withholding—Report, pay to Commr. if monthly tax $250 (min.) (except Dec. report-pay due by Jan. 31; if withholding over $100,000 a month, pay 1st half of June by June 23)

20 Sales—Report, pay to Tax Commr. (except for Dec. tax due Jan. 31)

Last Sales—Report, pay tax on motor fuels

Last Gasoline, special fuel or motor carrier fuel—Distributors, producers, importers and retailers report, pay to Tax Commr.

Last Business and occupation (utilities)—Report, pay if monthly tax over $1000 (except for May tax due June 15)

Last Telecommunications—Pay Tax Commr. if estimated tax over $1,000 per month (except for May, due June 15)

Last Coal severance—Report, pay min. tax to Tax Commr. if monthly over $1,000 (except for May tax due June 15)

WISCONSIN 15	Withholding—If over $5000 quarterly report, pay withholding from 16th day to last day of month to Dept. Rev.
15	Al. bev.—Manufacturers, bottlers and wholesalers report, pay to Dept. Rev.
15	Cigarettes—Return to Dept. Rev.
15	Motor fuel—Pay to Dept. Rev.
20	Sales—If over $3600 quarterly tax report, pay to Dept. Rev. on written notice
20	Motor and special fuels—Report, pay Dept. Rev.
20	Motor fuel—Report, pay general aviation fuel tax to Dept. Rev.
30	Motor fuel—Carriers report to Dept. Rev.
Last	Withholding—If over $5,000 report, pay withholding from 1st to 15th day of month to Dept. Rev.
Last	Withholding—Deposit in bank (on request) if quarterly over $300
Last	Sales—If over $600 quarterly tax report, pay to Dept. Rev. if notified to pay monthly
Last	Motor fuel—Report motor fuel tax to Dept. Rev.
Last	Motor fuel—Report, pay alternative fuel tax to Dept. Rev.
Last	Property—Pay forest land severance tax (last day of next month after mailing of assessment certificate) to Dept. Natural Resources.
WYOMING 10	Gasoline—Transporters and carriers report to Dept. Transportation
20	Cigarettes—Wholesalers report to Dept. Rev.
25	Oil and gas conservation—Pay to O&G Conserv. Comm.
25	Mining, oil, and gas cos.—Report, pay severance tax to Dept. Rev. if last yr.'s tax at least $30,000
Last (business)	Gasoline—Suppliers, refiners, importers, blenders, report, pay to Dept. Transportation
Last (business)	Diesel—Dealers not licensed as distributors report to Dept. Transportation
Last (business)	Diesel—Suppliers, refiners, importers, & blenders report, pay to Dept. Transportation
Last	Diesel—Transporters and carriers report to Dept. Transportation
Last	Sales-use—Return, pay to Dept. Rev.